Mark Gertler

Mark Gertler

SARAH MACDOUGALL

JOHN MURRAY
Albemarle Street, London

First published in 2002
by John Murray (Publishers) Ltd,
50 Albemarle Street, London W1S 4BD

A catalogue record for this book is available from the British Library.

ISBN 0-7195-5799-2

Typeset in 12.25/13.5 Monotype Garamond by
Servis Filmsetting Ltd, Manchester

Printed and bound in Great Britain by
Butler and Tanner Ltd
Frome and London

To Huw

Contents

Illustrations

Colour Plates

(between pages 142 and 143)

Black-and-white Plates

(between pages 238 and 239)

The author and publishers would like to thank the following for permission to reproduce illustrations: *Colour plates* 1, 2, 6 and 12, Private Collection; 3, purchased 1953, National Gallery of Victoria, Melbourne, Australia; 4, City & County of Swansea: Glynn Vivian Art Gallery Collection; 5, New Walk Museum, Leicester City Museum Service/Bridgeman Art Library, London; 7 and 11, © Tate, London 2002; 8, Ashmolean Museum, Oxford; 9, Abbot Hall Art Gallery, Kendal, Cumbria/Bridgeman Art Library, London; 10, Bevan Collection on loan to the Tate Gallery, London. *Black-and-white plates* 4, National Portrait Gallery, London; 6, and 17, © Tate, London 2002; 7, The Whitworth Art Gallery, The University of Manchester; 9, The Potteries Museum & Art Gallery, Stoke-on-Trent; 10, Southampton City Art Gallery, Hampshire/Bridgeman Art Library, London; 12, Ashmolean Museum, Oxford; 14, Private Collection; 18, Collection of Edgar Astaire; 21, Arts Council Collection, Hayward Gallery, London; 23, Luke Gertler; 25, Bevan Collection on loan to the Tate Gallery, London. All black-and-white photographs are reproduced courtesy of Luke Gertler, with the exception of Nos. 15, 19 and 22 (Private Collection), and No. 32, courtesy of John Foster-Turner.

Preface

TODAY GERTLER'S MASTERPIECE *The Merry-Go-Round* hangs prominently at London's Tate Modern, regularly attracting large crowds. The painting has become an iconic image of the First World War, easily recognizable as an image of cultural discontent – though it is also a highly personal expression of the artist's own private disillusionment. Yet, despite the painting's frequent reproduction on postcards, posters, books, even jigsaw puzzles, to many viewers the name of the artist remains virtually unknown.

Ironically, during Gertler's lifetime the position was reversed. The painting received little serious critical attention and the canvas remained unsold, rolled up in a corner of the artist's studio until after his death. But Gertler's name was so well known that when news of his death broke in June 1939 it was splashed across the front page of many of the tabloids, as well as the obituary columns of the broadsheets. He had made his name as a child prodigy – a poor Jewish boy from an East End slum who entered the Slade School of Art as a teenager, carried off many of its prizes and left with a reputation as 'the genius of the place' and a handful of patrons and admirers already in tow. Barely two years later his work was sought after by collectors, such as Winston Churchill's secretary Edward Marsh, and one of his pictures even hung in Downing Street. He was taken up by the indefatigable society hostess Lady Ottoline Morrell, and mixed socially with many of the best-known artists, politicians and writers of his day.

To the latter Gertler's life and personality made irresistible copy; as one commentator later noted, he 'at once tempted any novelist who knew him to put him into a book'. Many of them did just that, and the portraits range from the earnest youth of *Mendel*, the *roman à clef* written by the novelist Gilbert Cannan in eight weeks in 1916 and based (in parts verbatim) on Gertler's own stories to the vain and egotistical writer Raoul Duquette of Katherine Mansfield's short story 'Je ne parle pas français' the divisive sculptor Herr Loerke of D. H. Lawrence's *Women in Love*, the dashing, Byronic painter Gombauld of Aldous Huxley's *Crome Yellow*, the self-absorbed young politician in Virginia Woolf's short story 'Solid Objects', the difficult, suicidal painter Julian at the heart of Greville Texidor's novella *These Dark Glasses* and the womanizing, much-loved 'crude young genius' Jack Flitestone in V. S. Pritchett's short story 'The Skeleton'. However, the most important portrait – in biographical, if not literary, terms – is Cannan's *Mendel*. Part fiction, part biography, it is the only story derived directly from its subject, and though Gertler later repudiated it, his widow always maintained that it stood as a better monument to the artist than any official life. The novel provides a unique account of Gertler's early years, and a fascinating commentary on a part of his life that is little documented elsewhere; as such, frequent reference is made to it in the early chapters of this biography.

Cannan's opening image of the Gertler family sets up the key elements of the artist's life: the uprootedness, the close family unit, the 'exotic' and 'outsider' labels which first attached themselves to Gertler in his childhood and which he struggled ever afterward to throw off, his constant battle against poverty, and a certain performance streak that, added to his gifts and vitality, ensured his rapid elevation to the middle and upper ranks of English society, but never his complete assimilation.

Recent literature has tended to relegate Gertler to the sidelines as Dora Carrington's petulant lover or a mere Bloomsbury satellite, a judgement that would have horrified him. Gertler's doomed love affair with Carrington was indeed central to his complex emotional life, but his uneven relationship with Bloomsbury never bloomed more than briefly. He was by nature passionate, instinctive, individual and essentially isolated, and therefore temperamentally unsuited to membership of a group that favoured reason, intellect, tolerance and co-operation, and which was formed by a cultural élite. His resistance arose partly from his ambivalence about class, and partly from his ambivalence to groups in general. He would only ever ally himself to artistic societies in order to exhibit his work, and never as a statement of common belief. Determined to follow his own path, wherever it led, he always remained true to his own conviction: 'I just want to express myself and be personal', he wrote. 'When a Bird is inspired it sings – it sings. It does not wonder if its manner of singing is different to a bird that sang a thousand years ago – it just sings.' Later, he expanded this metaphor: 'It is as natural for me to paint as it is for a bird to fly,' he explained, 'but that does not necessarily mean I must paint great works. For although it is natural for all birds to fly, some fly higher than others.'

In his later years illness, depression, financial worries and the fickleness of public taste all contributed to Gertler's loss of confidence, but at the same time there was a late flowering in his work that belies his personal difficulties. Nevertheless, his reputation remained at a low ebb for several decades after his death. Throughout his career he changed styles so radically and so often that his very eclecticism has made it difficult for art historians to reassess him. But perhaps the time has now come when his diversity and virtuosity can be seen rather as a cause for celebration than condemnation. The extraordinary achievement of *The Merry-Go-Round* surely demonstrates the best of which Gertler is capable, and indicates that he should now be recognized as one of the most significant British painters in the first half of the twentieth century. However, since this is a biography rather than a monograph, the focus remains squarely on Gertler's life rather than his art.

This book has been a long time in preparation, and I have had much help along the way from countless individuals and institutions. First, I would like to thank Luke Gertler for his unstinting enthusiasm and encouragement, and his generosity with both time and materials; Bernard Adams OBE, retired librarian of the British Council, who generously gave me full use of his own extensive Gertler archive; Sally Brown of the British Library, and Ann Wilson of the Strachey Trust, who both expressed vital early support for the project; the Society of Authors, for an Authors' Foundation Grant; and the University of Texas at Austin, for a one-month Cline-Cowles Visiting Fellowship.

I would also like to thank all of the following, who gave generously of their time in differing ways: Mary Audsley, Betty Battiscombe, Gabriele Berndt-Fann, Bryan Burrough CBE, Nancy Carline, Catharine Carrington, Emma Chambers (Curator of the College Art Collections, University College, London), Stephen Chaplin (former Slade archivist), Honor Clark, Joan Day (*née* Lowenthal), Michael Dickens, Timothy Everest, the late Nan Evans (*née* Marley), Mrs Maurice Farquharson, Diana Farr, Ernest Fedarb, Linda Fu, Margaret Gardiner, Stephen Gardiner, the late Diana Gardner, Richard Garnett, Wynne Godley, Frederick Gore, the late Ida Graves, Anna

Gruetzner-Robins, Francis Guilfoyle, Diana Gurney, Penelope Hughes-Stanton, Phyllis Kutcher Martin (*née* Landau), Wayne McKenna, Dr Tim Moreton, the late Dorothy Morland, Jeanette Paros, John Pawle, John Penry, S. P. Rosenbaum, Alan Rowlands, Miranda Seymour, Richard Shone, Ruth Silver (*née* Wayner), Stan Smith, Ursula Thompson (*née* Hooper), Barbara Wadsworth, Miss F. R. Watson (Archivist for Northern Health Services Archives), Denys Wilcox and Professor Zimmermann of the University of Neuchâtel.

I would also like to thank the following institutions for their assistance: the Alexander Turnbull Library, Wellington, New Zealand; the Anglo-Jewish Archives, Hartley Library Special Collections, at the University of Southampton; the Beinecke Rare Book and Manuscript Library, Yale University; the Ben Uri Art Gallery, London; the Bodleian Library, Oxford (particularly Stephen Tomlinson); Victoria Griffiths, Sarah Harrington and Ron Ferriroli of the Book Information Department at Book Trust, London; the Manuscripts Department at the British Library, London; the Brotherton Library, University of Leeds; the Family Records Centre, London; the Fitzwilliam Museum, Cambridge; the Harry Ransom Humanities Research Center, University of Texas at Austin (particularly Pat Fox and Barbara Smith LaBorde); the London Library; the Manchester City Art Gallery; the Metropolitan Archives, London; the Mills Memorial Library, Canada; the National Art Library at the Victoria and Albert Museum; the National Portrait Gallery Archives, London; the New York Public Library; the Public Record Office, Kew; the Regent Street Polytechnic Archive, University of Westminster, London; the Royal Academy Archive and Library; the McFarlin Library, University of Tulsa, Oklahoma; the Slade School of Art, University College, London; the Tate Gallery Archive (particularly Adrian Glew); the Theatre Museum; Toynbee Hall; the University of New Zealand; the Westminster Archives; the Whitechapel Reference Library; and the Witt Library at the Courtauld Institute of Art.

For permission to quote from unpublished sources I am grateful to the following copyright holders: Olivier Bell on behalf of Clive Bell; Lord Esher for (Dorothy) Brett; Claire Gardner for Diana Gardner; Luke Gertler for Mark Gertler and Marjorie Kostenz; the Goodman family for Ottoline Morrell; Lord Hutchinson for Mary Hutchinson; Griselda Lewis for Gilbert Cannan; Mr Anthony Mitchell-Smith for Adrian Allinson; John Foster-Turner for Margaret Geddes; The Strachey Trust for Lytton Strachey; and the Slade School of Art for permission to quote from its unpublished history. Extracts from Carrington's letters © The Estate of Dora Carrington are reproduced by permission of Francis Partridge, c/o Rogers, Coleridge & White Ltd, 20 Powis Mews, London W11 1JN.

I also wish to thank my editor, Grant McIntyre, and all at John Murray for help and advice, and my agent, Jane Turnbull. Finally, I would like to thank all my family and friends for their support throughout the many years it has taken to bring this project to fruition. Most of all, my heartfelt thanks go to my long-suffering husband, Huw Molseed, without whose patience and support in so many ways this book would never have been possible.

'Goodness only knows whether people will write about us in the future – Damn them [all]. I long to paint – only to paint – . . .'

Mark Gertler to Dorothy Brett, 29 March 1920

PART I

Child of the Ghetto

'Essentially I am a child of the ghetto.'
Mark Gertler, *Jewish Chronicle*, 9 February 1912

I

The Emigrants

> 'I suppose my roots are in England and my work lies there. One must have roots somewhere and Headquarters, don't you think?'
>
> Mark Gertler to W. J. Turner, 20 April 1924

MARK GERTLER WAS born on 9 December 1891 in London, in a slum lodging-house in Gun Street, Spitalfields, in the heart of the Jewish East End.[1] The most important influence on his early life was this tightly knit community, whose heritage he simultaneously celebrated and rejected throughout his career. Today the East End of Gertler's childhood is all but a vanished world. Although many of the streets survive, and even the houses where he grew up, nothing now remains of the 'superabundant vitality' of the Jewish community which so impressed him as a child. But there had definitely been 'something different', he later wrote in a fragment of autobiography. 'The rich dark-complexioned boys and girls seemed to move and talk with unusual intensity – as if life was fearfully important – momentous. The whole narrow street itself seemed to vibrate with a quickened pulse, and a life of its own.'[2]

The Gertler family had first arrived in London in 1886, on the wave of immigration that washed over Britain and America throughout the late nineteenth century. His parents, Louis and Kate (always known as Golda), were both natives of Przemsyl in Galicia, then part of Austria-Poland, a province comprising an uneasy mix of Germans, Poles, Ruthenians and Jews. Power lay in the hands of a privileged nobility, who crippled the mainly peasant population with taxes, resulting directly in the highest death rates and lowest life expectancy in Europe.[3]

Little is known of Louis's family background, but it is likely that he was from peasant stock, since when he first met Golda he was in military service (then compulsory for peasants), from which he only obtained a discharge by self-inflicted injuries. This may also account for the fact that Louis seems to have had no fixed trade in Galicia – only an overwhelming determination to escape the proverbial 'Galician misery' and establish a better life for his wife and children. Golda's family, the Berenbaums, appears to have been more prosperous than the Gertlers, and looked down on Louis as an inferior match. Golda may also have been better educated, for she apparently spoke fluent German, as well as Polish and Yiddish. However, when in 1880, at the age of sixteen, she agreed to marry Louis, Golda turned her back on her former comfortable life and embraced with courage the bare existence he had to offer her. Their first child, Deborah, was born in 1881, and the rest of their children followed in quick succession: Harry in 1882, Sophie in 1883 and Jacob, or Jack, in 1886.[4]

By the mid-nineteenth century London's Jewish population had risen to 20,000, and between 1870 and 1914 more than 120,000 Jewish people would pass through London, some staying only briefly before going on to America. Those who remained joined the settlements in and around Whitechapel established by the earlier immigrants, and *Landsleit* (families from the same town or village) formed their own self-contained Yiddish-speaking communities, with their own *shteibels* (small house-based synagogues) and workshops (also usually house-based), where they worked in 'sweated' trades such as tailoring, jewellery or furniture making. Louis eventually found work as a furrier, a trade that could be started with relatively little skill, making cheap capes and dyed rabbit skins in imitation of more expensive furs and tolerating the unhealthy odours from the furs, dyes and feathers.

Domestic conditions were cramped. Roy Porter in his *Social History of London* noted that during this period 'the East End had the worst slums, the worst overcrowding, [and] the worst death rates.' It was no coincidence, therefore, that 'it also housed London's immigrants.'[5] At the Gun Street lodging-house the six members of the Gertler family and their 'lodger' Mechlowich (a laster, or shoe repairer, from Poland) occupied two rooms. An eighty-year-old London-born shoemaker and widower named John Wise lived in a single room next door; the Breslaw family of four and their Irish 'domestic' shared another room, and the Mezzier family of five had a further three rooms; finally, the Cohen family, who numbered seven, squeezed into the remaining two.[6] Altogether twenty-five people were crammed into nine rooms and when Mark – or Max, as he was named by his family – arrived, he was the twenty-sixth.

The furriery industry was one of the most over-manned, and there was severe competition for work. It was also a seasonal occupation, and during a lapse in the trade boom in 1892 there was a corresponding rise in unemployment.[7] Less than a year after Max's birth the Gertlers left London and returned to Galicia, their fares paid by the Jewish Board of Guardians, and with 'only me, as it were,' Gertler later wrote, 'to show for it'.[8]

Back in Przemsyl conditions had not improved and the prodigal family was not received 'exactly with enthusiasm by their relations'[9] who clubbed together to buy them a small inn on the outskirts of the city. Briefly, Louis became one of the 220,000 Jewish innkeepers in the province.[10] The inn was badly situated between two rival establishments, and attracted few customers – mostly soldiers, already drunk, usually broke and unwilling or unable to pay for the drinks they ordered. There were almost nightly scenes of violence. On one occasion as the soldiers pounded on the door demanding entry, Louis barricaded his terrified family in for protection, before escaping out of a window to fetch help. Max, however, was a general favourite with the soldiers and Golda was often forced to fetch him from his cradle to appease them. Despite their habitual indigence, the soldiers managed to kit him out in a miniature officer's uniform, complete with the correct number of stars attached to the collar, after which they spent many hours teaching him to return the proper salute.

Eventually Louis was forced to concede the failure of the inn and, arriving home one evening, admitted to his incredulous wife that he had swapped the inn for a pile of old boots. The boots were succeeded by a sack of buttons and for days Louis, accompanied by his two eldest sons, stood shyly in the market, hoarsely articulating the trader's cry: 'Buttons, buttons'. But, Max later learned, during the many hours they stood there only one customer approached, and even she was unable to find the buttons she wanted. Finally, Louis disappeared to America one night with only a clean shirt tucked under his arm, leaving Golda 'with no means and five children' to provide for.[11] He left instructions for his wife and children to follow on as soon as he was settled, but it was nearly four years before they were reunited.

After Louis's departure there was no further help from their relatives. Golda's widowed father had recently remarried, and the new Mrs

Berenbaum was not interested in the misfortunes of her stepdaughter. Golda worked in a variety of badly paid jobs, sometimes accepting left-over food in lieu of wages. Providing food for the children was her overriding concern, and when obtained it had to be strictly rationed. Even Harry, who could not have been much more than ten and was now working full-time in a factory, could not be allowed to take more than his share, and on at least one occasion Golda was forced to hide the remaining food when she saw him approaching the house. All the children became adept at stealing vegetables from fields and market barrows.[12]

Max remembered almost nothing of his early years in Galicia, except occasionally being taken by his siblings to hear the military bands. A sensitive and imaginative child, he enjoyed the music, but his sense of anticipation was such that at the very moment the conductor raised his arms to begin he could hardly prevent himself letting out a terrifying yell. To frighten him into order, his brothers and sisters invented 'a sort of phantom figure or bogey' which they called Mickey-coo, who exerted such a powerful effect on his imagination that even the smallest trifle became an object of the greatest significance if it was presented as an award from Mickey-Coo.

Max received no schooling in Przemsyl, but according to family legend he showed a precocious talent for drawing when, at the age of three, he drew a watch and chain in a letter to his absent father, telling his astounded family, 'I want Father to send me this!'[13] Two years later, in 1896, Louis at last wrote to say he had 'prospects' in Britain, having apparently learned 'some new process in furriery' in America, which he hoped to exploit in London.[14] Finally, he sent for his family to join him.

The journey to Britain lasted several weeks, mostly in bad weather.[15] Herded together in cattle boats, the passengers travelled steerage, packed into the ship's hold – pitch dark and without any ventilation, except that provided by the hatchway. Many suffered from sickness, disease and hunger. 'All of us slept overcrowded in bunks, stretched side by side over the whole length of the ship. We lived in hot, stuffy, filthy conditions . . . [and] ate salt herring out of barrels', recalled Rose Robins, another immigrant making the same journey, some fifteen years later.[16] Golda, who was in constant fear of imminent shipwreck, could only be consoled by another passenger, a fellow Jew, 'who used to comfort her by pointing to the lamp and saying, "How can you be frightened, Mrs Gertler, when the lamp hangs so straight?"'[17] Max, entirely unconcerned, would flit among them like 'a gay sprite', dressed in his Hungarian coat of deep orange-coloured leather, decorated with gold and scarlet braid, vermilion tam-o'-shanter and top boots up to the knee, breaking into dance at the first note of any song or music.[18] His performances so charmed the other passengers that they threw scraps of food, even money. Without Max, Golda later declared, the family could not have survived.

When the ship finally steamed into the broad estuary of the Thames, the passengers lined the deck. Some, who had booked passages to America, waited for the Statue of Liberty to materialize out of the mist, but to the small boy, swaying on the wooden boards of the gangplank, England seemed to rise up and advance to greet him.[19] His first impression was of 'land – England . . . moving towards me, not I to it', and he took this as a formal gesture of welcome.[20] His true history commenced, he later wrote, from the moment he set foot in England, when instinctively he recognized London, not Przemsyl, as his natural home. His earlier memories had relied on family stories, but as soon as he arrived in London, his own memory was vitalized, 'the sequence of each event . . . vivid and the essentials connected and alive'. It was the beginning of a lifelong love affair with London, such that eventually Gertler could 'almost imagine life more easily without the people I have known than [the city's] own embodiment and peculiarity'.[21]

2

The Immigrants

'London is my life.'

Mark Gertler to S. S. Koteliansky, 19 August 1916

'In one . . . yard . . . there was a Jewish boy taking his Hebrew lesson from an aged Rabbi. As usual, the Rabbi was doing both the teaching and the learning, whilst the boy was thinking vacantly of his "pals" outside. How like my youth! Only instead of "pals" I thought of *art*.'

Mark Gertler to Carrington, 6 May 1912

EVERY WEEK UP to a dozen crowded steamers arrived from Eastern Europe via the Thames alone; others sailed on to Glasgow, Grimsby and Harwich. Landing was a scene of great confusion, with women screaming and men shouting, and Max noticed apprehensive families – like his own – all 'grasping rebellious packages'.[1] Golda anxiously scanned the crowds for Louis. At length a voice emerged from the throng, shouting: 'Golda! Golda! Here I am . . . Leib will be late . . . come, where are you all? Sacha – Harrish – Max – come – Golda!'[2] And they recognized their 'kinsman' Louis Weinig, a lifelong friend from Przemysl, who took them on to Liverpool Street Station, where they were to meet Louis. There this 'little knot of strange-looking people in brilliant clothes' attracted attention, and passers-by, thinking them gypsies, threw coins (a strikingly picturesque moment later chosen by Gertler's friend Gilbert Cannan to open his novel *Mendel*, based on the artist's life).

When Louis finally appeared, 'a wave of emotion' swept over his family, and only Max remained unmoved, fixing his attention instead on a throbbing vein in Harry's neck, which was strained by the enormous bundle of bedding he shouldered. Gertler's own relationship with his father never fully recovered from their early separation. Later he conceded that his father was 'in his way an extraordinary man', and certainly he grew to love him, but Louis was never more than a shadowy presence in his son's paintings, always enclosed, even eclipsed, by Golda. In Przemysl it had been Golda who held the family together, and certainly for Max it was she who defined it. At the emotional reunion that engulfed the rest of the family, and from which he felt excluded, Max probably realized for the first time that he now had a rival for his mother's affections.

Later the family trooped through Whitechapel, passing on the corner of Commercial Road the brightly lit up façade of Gardiners department store, known simultaneously as 'the Harrods of the East End' and 'the gateway to the East End's Jewish ghetto'.[3] Transfixed, Max asked Golda, 'Mother, does the king live here?' and she replied, that in London nearly everybody had such large and brightly lit houses. Though their previous experience of London had been one of hardship and rejection, the Gertlers were unwavering in their optimism for their new life and adopted home.

On that first night, and for several weeks afterwards, Louis Weinig housed the whole Gertler family, alongside his own, in two rooms in a drab Shoreditch tenement. Weinig, his tubercular wife and their children occupied one room; the Gertlers occupied the other (despite her illness, Mrs Weinig 'was compelled to crawl about and do the housework, bring up the children and even help others who were as poor as herself, when she was obviously feverish and hardly able to stand'). Such short-term 'doubling-up' was common among the poor, and tuberculosis, often brought on by slum conditions and overcrowding, was so common as to pass almost without comment. The Gertlers were not in the least surprised that Mrs Weinig would 'often be seized with a fit of coughing which generally ended in haemorrhage', only that she always remained 'cheerful and sweet-tempered' throughout.[4]

The Gertlers slept on the floor, on the bedding they had brought from Przemysl, and covered themselves with sacks to keep warm. Waking one night to find himself lying on the floor next to his mother, Max consciously suffered what he later identified as his first fit of depression. Sitting up, he looked over the sleeping bodies of the rest of his family, and the sight 'somehow filled my heart with overwhelming sadness'. Although he was not yet six years old, he wept silently so as not to awaken his mother. Looking back some forty years later, he thought it 'curious that I should have felt it like that, for it was not as if I were accustomed to more luxurious circumstances. Yet as I sat there in the quiet of the night I was filled with a sort of pathos and feeling of gloom which remains as vivid today as it was then, and I have always remembered it.'[5]

Despite their circumstances the Weinigs were good company. Louis Weinig was a great storyteller, and from these stories he would always

> somehow emerge triumphant – having had the last word – or won the fight . . . When he told one of his stories he was quite frankly the hero and mostly a very glowing hero. Nobody was critical, because modesty was not the fashion and most people used conversation chiefly to boost themselves. The difference between him and the others was that he was funny.

Max observed that Weinig's style was 'the important element, not the matter, so one could hear him often without getting bored'.[6] In adulthood all three Gertler brothers would become consummate performers: Harry at dancing, Jack at boxing and piano-playing and Max as a celebrated mimic and raconteur. In an obituary his friend the poet Sylvia Lynd recalled that his stories were 'those of a man of genius whose experience passed through the whole scale of living', yet, unlike Louis Weinig, during the seventeen years of their acquaintance, she never once heard Gertler repeat himself.[7]

Louis Gertler's hopes for establishing a furrier's business had not worked out, and after his family's arrival his first job was sanding down walking sticks for a modest 12*s.* 6*d.* a week – well below the estimated poverty line of £1 10*s.*[8] Nevertheless, a short time later the family was able to move into lodgings of its own, a single room at 2 Sion Square (or 'Zion' Square, as Gertler called it in his memoirs), an area consisting of fewer than a dozen slum houses, largely occupied by poor Jewish artisans. All trace of Sion Square has now disappeared, and even in the 1890s it was so insignificant that it often went unnamed on contemporary maps.[9] Squeezed between the apex of Commercial Road and Whitechapel Road, it was barely a mile from Gun Street, where Max had been born only five years earlier.

The Gertlers' landlord, Mr Levy[10] (who proved very understanding over the rent), had his own workshop on site, a sweatshop where four or five children huddled over machines worked an incredible number of hours at a stretch, cooped up in that dirty, airless little room'. His son Moisha was one of Gertler's earliest friends; the two boys spent much of their time playing in and around the workshop at the feet of the treadling machinists. Levy himself was a bootmaker and the yard resounded to the noises of hammers and rattling looms, shouting children, hawkers and labourers, a microcosm of the Jewish life of the district. The Gertlers rented one room with 'some kind of detached corner' which served as a kitchen for Golda. The family remained here for the next three years.

Almost immediately after the move the Gertlers decided to send Max to the local Jewish school, or *chaida*, at a cost of between 6*d.* and 1*s.* 6*d.* a week. Here he wrote his first Hebrew alphabet (lovingly preserved by Golda) and learned 'how to be a good Jew'. In this period there were over 200 *chaidarim* in the East End. The class consisted of one room with a long narrow table, around which sat the children. The rabbi sat at the head and read stories from the Old Testament in Hebrew, translating them into Yiddish 'in a rapid, hardly intelligible monotone', which the children repeated, using imitative noises for the words they had failed to catch. Occasionally the rabbi would reprimand the children, in order to make sure they were paying attention, selecting a boy at random to punish.

Max, a favoured pupil, not only escaped punishment but was also frequently selected to sit on the rabbi's knee while he took the lesson. This he described as 'a doubtful pleasure' since the rabbi's long, pointed beard used to tickle him 'intolerably', and he was far more interested in the fish – fried 'the *Jewish* way' – which the rabbi's wife, or rabbitzin, served to the rabbi in front of the children, its exotic smell pervading the whole classroom. Max, who had a small appetite and had always refused to eat fried fish, subsequently surprised Golda by demanding the same dish at home, and devouring it with an unusually hearty appetite. The easy life of *chaida* came to an abrupt end, however, when Golda received a visit from the local schools inspector who informed her – Mrs Levy translating Golda's very 'embryonic' English – that her youngest child was long overdue to attend the local board school.[11]

By the time they arrived in Britain childhood was effectively over for the other children, but Max, the youngest by five years, had always been his 'mother's darling', and even his brothers and sisters always referred to him as the 'babe'.[12] The first Monday of school both mother and son awoke 'much too early – nervous and flustered – to prepare for [the] fearful event'. Washed, brushed and dressed in a sailor suit, Max set out with his mother on the ten minute walk to the local school in Settles Street, where they found a queue of mothers ready to enrol their children.[13] Golda, who hardly ever set foot out of

Sion Square, reacted with maternal protectiveness, gathering Max up in her arms, though it was a hot day and the strain of holding him caused 'beads of sweat [to] gather like pearls on her forehead and temples, then join and trickle down her cheeks in thin glistening streams'. A woman addressed them, asking, 'Why do you carry such a big boy in your arms, Missis, ain't he old enough to stand?' and Max felt ashamed and tried to wriggle down, but Golda simply tightened her grip, 'not deigning even to answer the woman'. When they reached their turn in the queue they sensed the antagonism of the inspector, who ordered Golda to set the child down immediately – 'He is not a babe!' – and asked for his Christian name. Golda was at a loss until a voice from the crowd shouted 'Mux'. '"Mux!" said the man, "Never heard such a name – no such name in this country – we'll call him Mark Gertler," and nodding to a woman near by and pointing his pen at me he said, "Next!"' And so Mark Gertler he became.[14]

The anglicization of his name was the first step on the ladder of Mark's difficult assimilation into the English community, but from the start he was aware of subtle differences between the community he regarded as home and the new world in which he suddenly found himself.[15] Desolate at being separated from his mother, he 'glanced at the children nearest me, as if to discover whether I dare give way to the tears that were choking me, but realised instantly that here was a new situation – that here in this atmosphere one must try not to cry and I succeeded in controlling my emotions – perhaps for the first time in my short life'.[16] Much later he would observe of his mother that, 'everything to [her], with her primitive and unsophisticated nature, is a great event . . . through which she has to live passionately'.[17] School was the first place in which he learned that such a response was not always acceptable.

At home Mark's family quickly learned to identify itself with the Jewish community, 'a tiny alien enclave utterly cut off from the encircling population by religious observance, prejudice and, during these first years, by the barrier of language'.[18] London's Jewish quarter had its own shops, baths, a hospital (in Stepney Green) and its own newspapers. Both written and spoken, the language was Yiddish. Mark continued to speak Yiddish to Golda for the rest of his life, and only began to learn English when he started school, where his friendship with a Christian boy was quickly discouraged by his family. Although his parents were later naturalized, this was simply to throw off the label 'enemy aliens' in the First World War, and though Harry and Jack's own naturalization (in 1913) may have been an attempt to become better assimilated, by and large they remained content to stay in 'Jewish' London and to follow the trade established by their father. Mark, through his ambition, would consciously estrange himself from this heritage but never fully succeed in acquiring another. It has even been suggested that his marriage to a middle-class English woman was an extension of his continuing attempts at assimilation.

Despite the poverty and overcrowding, on Fridays – the eve of Sabbath – the Jewish community sprang to life, with the cobbled streets and dark alleys ablaze as candles were set in the front windows of the crowded tenements. The orthodox bathed on Fridays at Schveik's Russian Vapour Baths in Brick Lane, and after the evening service at the synagogue Kiddush wine would be drunk and bread broken, and fathers blessed their children. Outside Jewish homes the ornamental container (the *mezuzah*) always hung, containing a parchment on which were written the first two sections of Deuteronomy, known as the *Shema*.[19] In the evening of the Sabbath, the religious observances over, friends and family gathered together.

Mark, who by his own account had developed into a 'very nervous, highly strung, and emotional child, somewhat undersized, thin and pale', found his excitable nature intensified by these continual late nights. He later recalled that as a child he would hardly ever be put to bed before the rest of the family: midnight during the week, and much later at weekends, when the gatherings went on into the small hours. Golda, though a devoted mother, seemed unaware of the detrimental effect on Mark's health, and when he started at Settles Street School, he soon began to buckle under the strain. Afterwards he always remembered 'that awful mixture of exhaustion and despair I felt every morning when I had to make myself get up in time for school, for I was very conscientious and terrified of losing a mark, and every morning the strain made me weep and cry as I dressed, "It is late already, I shall be late." '[20]

Almost three years after the Gertler family's arrival in Britain, the matchmakers arranged a match for Mark's striking older sister, Deby, to a Russo-Polish cabinetmaker named Abraham Attleson, a 28-year-old bachelor and son of a dealer called Lazarus Attleson. They married in style in the Great Synagogue in St James on 20 June 1889, but only months later Attleson was declared bankrupt.[21] This must have seemed a disaster at the time, but it was common enough in the East End, and his fortunes seem to have quickly recovered.

Louis's fortunes took a little longer. On Deby's marriage certificate he described himself as a 'traveller', or travelling salesman, and it was another five years before he opened his own furrier's workshop. In 1900 Louis moved his family moved into 8 Bacon Street, a dark, narrow house, now demolished, just off Brick Lane, where the limits of the Jewish community were conclusively defined by the Great Eastern Railway which edged along its perimeter, the rumbling of the trains mixing with the hammering and screeching from the surrounding sawmills and sweatshops.

Mark began at his new school in Deal Street in March 1900 and remained there for the next six years. Racial tension had led to a policy of virtual segregation at the schools and Deal Street catered predominantly for Jewish pupils, who spoke Yiddish in the playground but English in class. The headmaster was quoted as saying that at Deal Street, 'Jewish boys soon bec[a]me Anglicised and ceased to be foreigners.'[22] The school itself, which still stands, was a classic Victorian board school, housing infants on the ground floor, older boys on the first floor and girls on the second floor. On each floor there was a hall and seven classrooms with up to sixty pupils in each, seated in rows on long fixed forms which rose in a tier on the steps of a construction called a 'gallery'. There they learned the basic steps of literacy and numeracy through chanting and repetition, and with frequent use of a 'spit-rubbed slate and a shrieking pencil'.[23]

Since the 1880s drawing instruction had been included in the curriculum as a vocational skill for boys, who had previously learned needlework with the girls. Contemporary photographs show that at some schools the lessons were quite advanced, with pupils copying specially purchased models and plaster casts, but at Deal Street School there was no proper art master, very few props and the drawing lessons were generally regarded by most pupils as of little value. Still, Mark, who was 'brimming over with vague youthful desires', later recalled that he was 'never content till I was given pencil and paper and allowed to draw'.[24] Though 'utterly ignorant of everything connected with art', he admitted to a journalist in 1912, he had 'longed to draw and paint, right from the very beginning'.[25]

Stimulated by the crude colours of an advertisement for beef extract and some still lifes by a pavement artist (a story related in all known accounts of his childhood),[26] Mark soon began to chalk his own still lifes on the pavement outside his home and was encouraged by his family, who supplied him with materials. When he was nine,

Louis gave Mark his first set of paints – watercolours – and the resulting picture, *The Sailor's Return*, still hung in the family kitchen over ten years later, when a picture of his was first hung in the Tate Gallery.

Looking back, Gertler admitted that as a child 'it was probably vanity that made me do these things', yet simultaneously he felt a deeper motivation, the stirring of 'the crude artist spirit . . . strong [with]in me'.[27] During playtime at school he began to avoid games and felt a 'keen delight' in chalking pictures on the blackboard. To his fellow pupils his drawing skill was 'extraordinary', and he was voted 'the most popular boy in the form', probably on the strength of it.[28] His schoolmaster 'prophesied great things' for him, and Henrietta Adler, the daughter of the chief rabbi, who carried out social work in the local schools, called his drawings 'brilliant'.[29]

In 1903 Jack was arrested with several of his friends on a charge of 'behaving in a disorderly manner, and using obscene language in Hyde Park', and Louis was forced to pay a fine of 40*s*. Jack's behaviour may simply have been youthful high spirits, but his East End address made a difference when dealing with the police (as Mark would also later find out when indulging in a little 'horseplay' of his own). Mark later claimed that 'for a timid, sensitive child, allowed to run wild in the streets', he ran 'great risk of never evolving as an artist', but he also recognized that it was the sheer vitality of the East End that first inspired him.[30] He had a strong visual memory, and absorbed everything, replaying it later in a series of Jewish portraits that made his reputation as a painter. One particular scene inside the local Machzike Hadas synagogue, where the old men sat resplendent in their prayer shawls and side curls, he found 'picturesque in the extreme'.[31] Outside he was equally entranced by the brilliant colours of the meat, fish, vegetables and fruit sold by the costers, which he sometimes persuaded Golda to buy simply in order for him to paint.

The family moved house several times during his childhood, but always within the Jewish quarter. Perhaps it was this which drew Mark into an ever deeper identification with the London which had already stirred his imagination. He adored the local Yiddish theatre and the music-halls, and later used both to extend his own repertoire. In the 1930s he told a friend that as a small child he remembered heading the queue for the 'gods' at the local theatre on Saturday afternoons, when the Sabbath officially ended. When the doors opened, he would be thrust forward by the crowd, swept up the rickety wooden stairs and deposited in the front row of the gallery, where, clutching at his orange or a bag of nuts, he could lean forward and enjoy the glamour of the performance.[32]

The repertoire was similar to that of the music-halls, which had spread all over London in the mid-nineteenth century and become the chief Saturday night entertainment among the working class. Typically costing between sixpence and a shilling (though seats in the gallery could be had for a penny), the music-halls attracted a 'sometimes critical, frequently vulgar and always robust' audience. The programme included singers (often 'in character'), sketches, circus acts, conjurors, dancers, illusionists, acrobats, quick-change artists and strong men, and audience participation remained the key to its popularity, which continued up until the First World War, when the introduction of cinema brought about its decline. Perhaps nearer in spirit to the music-hall than the English theatre, Mark always considered the Yiddish theatre far more 'vital' than the English.

In 1905 the Gertlers moved to 56 Leman Street, where Louis finally set up his own furrier's business.[33] By this time his youngest son was already obsessed with painting, and at mealtimes had sometimes to be forcibly separated from his paints. During this period Mark and his schoolfriend Cyril Ross would spend several hours a day drawing and painting on the kitchen floor in the dim gaslight, occasionally forced to stop to allow the steam to clear as Golda washed clothes in a cement copper in the corner. Mark sketched simple objects, such as vegetables, pots and pans, with apparent ease and confidence, and Ross marvelled at his drawing, which seemed 'so accurate, clean and perfect; it was correct from the very start'.[34] Even after he had acquired a studio of his own, Mark often returned to his mother's kitchen to paint, looking back on these times as 'my finer moments . . . [when] I painted my earliest pictures, simple and loveable little still lifes which expressed so directly my life, simple and clear as it was then'.[35]

Still, these pleasures were an end in themselves, and Mark had no idea that they could become a way of life, until one day he discovered by accident the autobiography of the Victorian artist W. P. Frith in a local bookshop. He returned to the shop repeatedly over the next few weeks until he had finished reading it, by which time he had determined that he too would become an artist. Once this decision, which frankly baffled his family, had been taken, Mark never wavered. 'As far back as I can remember,' he wrote to the curator of the Manchester Art Gallery in 1924, 'I always wanted passionately to be an artist.'[36] This sense of vocation – or, as his friend Dorothy Brett put it, 'complete and utter devotion to his art' – was one of the qualities that most impressed Gertler's contemporaries. And in 1929, at a point of crisis in both his life and career, Gertler would confess to his diary that, his work had always been 'my faith – my purpose'.[37] He would pursue it throughout his life with all the zeal of an evangelist.

3

Mendel

'I have, underneath all, a certain undying impetus to paint and paint. It is inexplicable, yet the most living thing about me. At bottom I know that the most satisfactory thing in life is work – to work regardless of achievement or failure.'

Mark Gertler to Carrington, June 1915

WHEN MARK LEFT school at the statutory minimum age of fourteen in January 1906, Louis was keen to start him as an apprentice in a timber firm. He foresaw either that there would not be enough work for all three of his sons in the family business or that the youngest would not fit in there. However, Mark held tight to his ambition of becoming an artist, and his determination proved unshakeable in the face of all opposition. Although his family were very proud of his talent, such a profession was virtually unknown among their community and class, and none of them had any idea how to proceed. Eventually a family friend, a Scottish fur traveller, recommended the Regent Street Polytechnic, and even managed to secure Mark an interview with the headmaster, G. Percival Gaskell. On the appointed day the pair arrived so early that they had to wait outside until the cleaners agreed to let them in.[1] Gaskell, Mark recalled, 'was kindness itself, but very damping as to the monetary feasibility of an artist's career'. However, the unnamed fur traveller impressed Gaskell with 'a sudden inspired gesture of faith' in Mark's ability, and this 'carried the day'.[2] Though at fourteen Mark was barely old enough to attend classes, Gaskell agreed to admit him.[3]

In the nineteenth century all art education in London, with the exception of the Royal Academy and the Slade School of Art at

University College, was taught outside the universities.[4] The RA, following the principles of its founder, Joshua Reynolds, had always observed 'a strict delineation between the fine artist and the craftsman', as much to preserve a social distinction as an aesthetic one.[5] The government established a school of design in 1836, and opened up a network of technical schools, many associated with the polytechnics, which offered a wide range of classes from elementary drawing to fine art and design. In the national art competitions of 1905–8 the Regent Street Polytechnic could boast of having obtained 'higher and more numerous awards than any other London School of Art'.[6]

The Polytechnic, originally 'a Young Men's Christian Institute for artisans and apprentices' and now the University of Westminster, owed its foundation to Quintin Hogg,[7] the 'greatest of the Institute Philanthropists'.[8] Born in 1845 and educated at Eton, Hogg eschewed the traditional family path to Oxford and entered trade, where his rapid financial success enabled him to devote a large part of his life and fortune to the education of the working classes. He began with an impromptu reading lesson to two crossing-sweepers at the Adelphi arches, and progressed to founding a ragged school (1864), a boys' home (1868), evening classes (1871) and finally an evening institute in Long Acre (1878). In 1881 Hogg moved to the Regent Street site, where his aim was to 'provide both technical education and facilities for leisure for the poorer classes in central London'.[9] Within a year there were nearly 100 classes and 5,000 enrolments, and the Regent Street Polytechnic proved so successful that it subsequently became the model for all similar establishments across London.[10]

Although the following fifteen years saw an explosion of progression and talent, in which Gertler was to play a part, at the time of his entry to the Polytechnic the Edwardian art scene was characterized by a 'sleepy complacency'. The Royal Academy, still the dominant institution, continued to hark back to Victorian classicism, and even the New English Art Club, which had been established to challenge the Academy and promote progressive British Art, was seen as 'little more than a nursery to the older institution'.[11]

At the Polytechnic, however, the Academy was still revered. Students were encouraged to work for any of the teaching certificates awarded by the South Kensington School and for admission to the RA schools. Many of the staff were practising artists themselves, and some exhibited at the Academy, but the Polytechnic was first and foremost a vocational institution, with a strong emphasis on developing skills for business.[12] Several of Gertler's tutors had attended the Polytechnic for their own art training, and clearly it was regarded as suitable for turning out well-qualified instructors. On the whole, the system upheld the distinction that the fine arts were for gentlemen and design for the working class.

For Gertler, previously unaware of the existence of even the public art galleries, entrance to the Polytechnic, and the wider world of art, was the realization of a dream. For him every day became 'romantic, though he suffered tortures of shyness and used to bolt like a rabbit through the doors of the Polytechnic, rush upstairs to his easel, and never raise his eyes from it except to gaze at the objects placed before him'.[13]

Probably guided by Gaskell, he began elementary classes in drawing in light and shade, drawing wooden models, and design.[14] Up to ten staff, with wide-ranging skills, supervised the elementary classes and provided general assistance',[15] among them the landscape and figure painter Harry Watson, who oversaw the still life classes, and Harry George Theaker, a painter, designer and potter, who later succeeded Gaskell as head, and who tutored Gertler in design. Gertler always retained great respect for craftsmen, but never distinguished himself in this type of practical art. He failed the 1907 summer exam, and subsequently abandoned design altogether.[16] He had only one ambition, and that, as he constantly reminded his friends in later years, was to paint.

And it was still life painting, an advanced subject, that quickly became his main interest. Several of Gertler's pictures survive from this period and reveal an early mastery of oils and a skilful portrayal of still life objects. Among them is a tiny *Still Life with Apples* of 1907, almost identical in composition to a Fantin-Latour still life that Gertler may have seen in the National Gallery.[17] This was probably Gertler's first oil painting; he always refused to part with it, and it was found in his studio after his death.[18] Formal and academic, these paintings nevertheless show a quietly impressive technique, remarkable in such a young student, and although Gertler achieved only second-class certificates in drawing and painting in his first year exams,[19] at least four of these student compositions eventually ended up in major public collections.[20]

At first only his youth, and perhaps his determination, set Gertler apart. In appearance he had the look of a shy young animal, 'rather small for his age and . . . almost absurdly beautiful, with his curly hair, round Austrian head, and amusing pricked ears'.[21] But he was still the thin, nervous child of his school-days, and before he could begin to learn he had to overcome his shyness, which manifested itself in his awkward manner and his serious application. 'He worked in a frenzy, convinced that it was his business to translate the object on to the canvas. When he had done he felt that the object had no further existence.'[22] He knew that if he failed he would be forced into an apprenticeship like his brothers, and already Louis was beginning to find the fees 'insuperable'.[23]

Gertler's greatest influence at the Poly was the head, Gaskell, who clearly singled him out for special attention, taking him on his first visit to the National Gallery and opening up a world of imagination and stimulation that would sustain him throughout his student years. 'What more does one want', Gertler would write in 1910, 'but a room, materials, and the National Gallery?'[24] Gaskell was a Royal College of Art graduate who had also studied in Paris and Italy. At the Poly he lectured enthusiastically on the history of art, offering a reduced fee to encourage both staff and students (though even this is likely to have been out of Gertler's reach).[25] That autumn, when he began a course of twelve lectures on German, Dutch and Flemish painters, Gertler benefited from Gaskell's one-to-one tuition, and the school of Dutch realism and its later followers, especially the eighteenth-century still life painter Jean-Siméon Chardin, the subject of one of Gaskell's lectures in 1907–8, made a deep impression on him.

After this, Gertler later told a friend, he began to 'haunt' the National Gallery, intently studying the pictures until 'Chardin, Velasquez, and the Dutchmen, first shaped his realism'.[26] Drawn to the simple kitchen scenes of pots, vegetables, meat and fruit (those objects he had been copying with such concentration since his school-days) and their underlying endorsement of domestic values, Gertler immediately began work himself along 'the lines of strictest academic realism, of the old Dutch still-life schools'.[27] Their influence is reflected in compositions such as *Still Life with Bottle of Benedictine* (1908), which, in its simplicity and truth to form, relates closely to a *Study of a Still Life* by a follower of Chardin in the National Gallery, although the use of impasto suggests he had also been looking at Rembrandt.[28]

Away from the Poly, Gertler began to explore London and re-enacted what he saw for his mother, Golda, who remained rooted in Spital Square and marvelled at his stories, as at those of a traveller newly returned from foreign lands. He learned to mimic 'the strange people he saw, the mincing ladies and the lordly shopwalkers, the tittering girls and the men working in the streets', and so reproduced 'the whirl, the glitter, the roar, the splendour of London' with its inherent contradictions and vitality.[29] Yet his observations remained those of a spectator rather than a participant; he was still only an outsider looking in.

Mark appears to have formed no friendships at the Poly, probably feeling excluded by his youth.[30] In Gilbert Cannan's novel Gertler's *alter ego* Mendel is distinguished from his fellow pupils as an 'infant prodigy' and his work is much admired by Mr Sivwright (Gaskell) and his fellow students, 'the young women and old ladies who attended the class'. 'Prodigy' does not quite fit the facts here.[31] Nevertheless, it is certainly true that most of Gertler's fellow students followed the more traditional path of the Poly, and became teachers and illustrators, and none of them achieved anything like his own dizzying ascent to fame.[32] By the time he left the Poly the label of 'child prodigy' had stuck fast; he later found it a bitter legacy.

The Poly was the first overtly Christian institution with which Gertler came into contact, and it was here that he first confronted anti-Semitism. In an incident recorded by Cannan, Mendel's teacher Mr Sivwright passes him off as a Pole. When Mendel protests, his objections are emphatically swept aside by his teacher, who explains that, 'the Jews don't stand for anything but money', and 'there's no swing about being a Jew'.[33] Mendel suffers an intense, blind anger at these insults, and Sivwright is subsequently revealed as 'a shoddy failure of a man'. There is no way of authenticating the incident, but it has the ring of truth, and Gertler does not appear to have kept up any contact with Gaskell after he left the Poly. Certainly, he grew up with a lasting sense of grievance at being made to feel a 'foreigner in England', and though he remained defiantly attached to his Jewish background, his talent would increasingly propel him into the orbit of Christian society.

From *Mendel* it can also be inferred that Gertler at least flirted with the idea of Christianity in this period, although Mendel himself is perhaps less influenced by the Polytechnic than by his friendship with Edward Tufnell, a 'good young man' who hears of his talent and seeks him out, and later introduces him to the New Testament. His parents are horrified, but Mendel finds Christianity wanting: though 'charming in its results, its spirit was ultimately unsatisfying to him who had been bred on stronger fare.'[34] Tufnell's real-life counterpart was Thomas Edward Harvey, a Quaker and Oxford postgraduate who had also studied in Berlin and Paris and who acted as an assistant in the British Museum for four years before, in 1906, becoming warden at Toynbee Hall, the university settlement in the Whitechapel Road, near Gertler's home.

Toynbee Hall was the result of the pioneering social work movement spearheaded by Samuel Barnett in the East End of London in the 1870s. It opened in 1884, and was named after the social philosopher and economist Arnold Toynbee, who promised in his lectures to working men in the East End to devote his life to their service. Although the idea that those studying poverty and unemployment should live among the poorer classes was not new, at Toynbee Hall the students lived together 'in a fellowship like that of a college'.[35] It was the first settlement of its kind in the world and the model for many others. In the East End it was soon followed by the opening of the Whitechapel Library and the Whitechapel Art Gallery in 1901.

Toynbee organized a wide range of activities, ranging from lectures and outings to an art club. However, it is not clear exactly what Gertler did there since his name does not appear in any of the records for this period.[36] In *Mendel*, Tufnell encourages the boy to attend poetry lectures and French classes, and though Mendel understands practically nothing, he is grateful for the opportunity to escape from his home in the evenings. He also likes and admires Tufnell, partly because of his courtesy towards Mendel's mother, whom he treats 'exactly as he would have treated an elderly duchess'.

More importantly, Harvey listened to and encouraged Gertler as he outlined his dreams and ambitions, and when the financial situation at home became acute, it was probably Harvey who advised him to apply for help to Sir Isidore Spielmann at the Jewish Board of Guardians. Spielmann pronounced Mark's work 'promising', and referred him to the Jewish Education Aid Society (where he was also on the board), but the application was ill timed, since most of the Society's members were away for the summer. Gertler was asked to 'let the matter stand over until the middle of September', and advised to 'profitably employ' himself during the interval visiting the London galleries 'with a view to studying the masterpieces of portrait painting that some of them contain'.[37] However, no mention of Gertler is to be found in the Society's minutes until he renewed his application the following year. In the interim he was forced in December to take up the apprenticeship he feared at Clayton & Bell, stained-glass makers, in Regent Street, and so conveniently situated next door to the Polytechnic that it is likely that Harvey exerted his influence on Gertler's behalf to keep him as near as possible to his place of study.[38]

The partnership of J. R. Clayton and Alfred Bell had been formed in 1855 while both men were working in the architectural practice of Gilbert Scott. There they also encountered the architects G. F. Bodley and G. E. Street, who were later to give them important commissions. By the end of the decade Clayton & Bell had become one of the most successful stained-glass studios in the country, employing up to 300 people, and reputedly able to produce 'a window a day, and two on Sunday'.[39]

The firm employed artists, designers and draughtsmen, paid according to the complexity of their task: those who did figure work were the most highly paid, then painters of backgrounds and grisaille, then those who did draperies and folds, texts and inscriptions, down to the many apprentices and colourmen. Gertler started work as an apprentice in December 1907. Louis could not afford the usual premium, but the company generously offered Mark a six-month trial at the rate of 5*s.* a week, with the expectation of rising to 7*s.* 6*d.* if he progressed 'satisfactorily'.[40] His job, which he hated, was to produce charcoal cherubim traced from a larger cartoon. Cannan reproduces this experience in *Mendel*, where the images include the Virgin Mary, Saint John the Baptist and 'other figures of whom [Mender] has never heard'. None the less, he understands that these figures are 'worthy of respect', and is shocked by the workmen's harmless banter: '"Billy, chuck us down another Mary", or "Jack, heave up that there J. C . . ."'[41] Mark does not seem to have minded producing Christian imagery, but he was 'tortured' by the necessity of drawing 'without impulse or delight', and could not 'put pencil to paper without a thrill of eagerness and desire, which was immediately baffled when his pencil had to follow out the conventional lines of the stained-glass windows'.[42]

Gertler seldom spoke about the stained-glass factory in later life, but he confessed to a friend in 1912 that the experience had nearly broken his heart, and to an interviewer in 1932 that he had 'longed to be free of its restrictions and to get forward with my own real work'.[43] The factory atmosphere may have been good-humoured, but it could not nurture the talent of a young artist, and, as Noel Carrington has pointed out, Mark quickly found the work 'as frustrating as Dickens had found the blacking factory'.[44] The poet–painter Isaac Rosenberg, a fellow 'Whitechapel boy' who was apprenticed to a process engraver, expressed similar feelings of torment in his letters: 'It is horrible', he wrote, 'to think that all these hours, when my days are full of vigour and my hands and soul craving for self-expression, I am bound, chained to this fiendish mangling-machine, without hope and almost desire of deliverance.'[45] Gertler never accepted that a real artist should endure poverty.

For the next eight months Gertler became one of the evening class students at the Polytechnic, attending classes between 7 and 9.30 p.m., after a full day's work. None the less, his choice of classes – drawing from the plaster cast (with the hope of progressing to life drawing) and painting still life in oils – although made before he was forced into his apprenticeship, show that his determination to become a professional painter remained unshaken. And the fact that Gertler failed cast drawing in the 1908 exams suggests that he was again concentrating almost exclusively on painting. He was awarded a second class in his painting examination, but his work may have been out of sympathy with the examiners, for when he entered his *Still Life with Melon*[46] in the national art competition for the Board of Education, he was awarded a bronze medal.[47] It was the first of the many prizes that distinguished his early career, and was also the sort of proof of his ability with which he might impress the Jewish Education Aid Society, and so he renewed his application in July 1908.

The JEAS had been established in 1896, and was still only in its tenth year when Gertler made his first application. Fortunately, by then it had widened its scope from the original aim of helping promising Jewish junior pupils go onto secondary education, 'in the direction of helping all promising students needing assistance'. A consultative committee of experts in literature and academic studies, art, music, and science now presided over individual cases.[48] The main art consultant was Solomon J. Solomon, still only the second Jewish painter to be appointed a Royal Academician (1906), and an enormously influential figure, particularly in Jewish circles. Yet despite his vast experience, Solomon was unable to come to a decision about Gertler's application,[49] and instead referred him to another prominent Jewish artist, William Rothenstein, who immediately invited the young hopeful to visit his Hampstead home.

Rothenstein's substantial house was in Oak Hill Park, at the top of the Frognal area of Hampstead. On this, as on future trips, Jack helped Mark to carry his paintings and slipped away silently when the door was answered by Rothenstein's seven-year-old son John, who discovered 'a shortish, handsome boy with apricot-coloured skin and a dense mop of dark brown hair so stiff that it stood on end', hesitating on the doorstep.[50] Even to a seven-year-old boy class distinctions were very obvious, and John immediately 'took him for a barrow boy', until in his 'sullen, nervous manner' Gertler told him he had been sent to see his father.

The only version Gertler left of the meeting is that which appears in Cannan's *Mendel*, but which he later repudiated. In this account the Froitzheims (William Rothenstein and his wife, Alice), note that Mendel 'responds to beauty like a flower to the sun' and, quickly convinced of his promise, decide that he must attend the 'Detmold' (the Slade School of Art).[51] Mendel, however, though he reveres Froitzheim as an artist, distrusts him as a man. In an extraordinary phrase, which perhaps reveals his own deep-seated prejudice, Cannan wrote that, 'it takes a Jew to catch a Jew, and Mendel scented in Mr. Froitzheim the Jew turned Englishman and prosperous gentleman'. Not surprisingly, when Rothenstein read this description over a decade later, he was horrified.

Rothenstein wrote generously to Golda and Louis, telling them that their son had 'gifts of a high order', that a good artist was 'a very noble man' and that it was 'worth while giving up many things which men consider very important, for others which we think still more so'.[52] There can be no doubt that this letter had a formative influence on Louis's decision to allow Gertler to abandon his apprenticeship and to train as a painter.

A tiny vital figure, with dark, round head and eyes, accentuated by his round spectacles, and punctuated by a pair of inquisitive eyebrows, Rothenstein was a generous man, with a clear eye for talent, and in many ways an ideal first mentor for a young painter. From his student days in Paris, when he had been an early friend of Whistler's and mixed with many of the leading French artists of the day (including Degas, Pissarro and Toulouse-Lautrec), Rothenstein seemed always to be in the thick of it. He was a co-founder of the Carfax Gallery in London, which opened in the 1890s with Oscar Wilde's friend Robert Ross as director and Sickert's brother Robert as manager, while Rothenstein took up what became his habitual role as advisor.

He had provided the sculptor Jacob Epstein, among others, with vital early financial support, by introducing him to the JEAS.[53] Some, usually those who had most benefited from his help, found

Rothenstein more than a little sanctimonious, but the Gertlers were deeply impressed by his faith in their son. On a later visit to their home Rothenstein was astonished to find his letter framed and hung on the wall of Golda's kitchen; after Gertler's death it was found carefully preserved among his belongings.[54]

Rothenstein recommended that Gertler begin by studying three days a week at his old school, the Slade, then the most celebrated art school in London, and the other three days a week under Rothenstein himself. Although it was highly unusual for apprentices to be removed at such short notice, perhaps the fact that the current proprietor, John Clement Bell, had himself been at the Slade made him sympathetic, for the firm agreed to release Gertler immediately. Ernest Lesser, the secretary of the JEAS, was appointed his case guardian, and wrote to tell Gertler his application had been approved and his fees would be paid. Gertler was told to present himself at the Slade in less than a week's time.

PART II

Whitechapel Boy

'That remarkable group of talented East-end painters and writers known as "the Whitechapel Boys . . ."'
Ian Parsons, *The Collected Works of Isaac Rosenberg*

4

The Slade

'My World is a World of Beauty and Joy, marred only by one thing, "Progress", and if at any time I am encouraged on that point, my world becomes perfect: all is bliss.'
Mark Gertler to William Rothenstein, 1909

GERTLER PUT HIS first signature on the Slade register on 13 October 1908, a week after term began, and on a day when his fellow students included Gwen Darwin (later Raverat), who became a distinguished printmaker, and Maxwell Lightfoot, an older student who later befriended him. For the first time Gertler was among fellow students with the same purpose as himself, in an institution where it was expected that masterpieces would be not the exception but the norm.

The school had been established in 1871 with an endowment from the late collector and connoisseur of the arts Felix Slade,[1] and conceived as part of the college quadrangle at the University of London in Gower Street, its 'inscrutable' edifice rising up from a 'curving asphalt path which flow[ed] like a grey stream between the bright green lawns'.[2] In his inaugural lecture of 1871 the first Slade professor, Sir Edward Poynter, had conceded that, apart from Burlington House (the Royal Academy), there had previously been 'no school of any importance in London for the study of high art' – an omission he intended to remedy. Though Poynter insisted that the new school could never compete with the Royal Academy (where he himself succeeded as president in 1876), the Slade had rapidly challenged this assertion. Its students soon learned to despise the Academy's stuffy, old-fashioned practices, and the quality of both staff and pupils ensured that it soon eclipsed the older school's reputation.

Principal among Poynter's reforms was the popular decision to shorten the obligatory period of work in the Antique Room before admission to the life class. Instead of copying plaster models for long periods, students were to draw direct from the living model and to be encouraged to use their 'intelligence freely . . . to achieve style', as in many French schools.[3] These simple precepts, which revolutionized the teaching of art in Britain, were still being upheld when Gertler joined the Slade in 1908. All the teachers were practising artists, the teaching was progressive and, in contrast to the 'elaborately stippled drawing from the antique' required by the Royal College of Art, there was no examination for admission. New students were obliged to seek an interview and display their drawings to either Professor Frederick Brown or the assistant Slade professor Henry Tonks.[4]

To his friends and supporters Tonks was 'a man unspoilt, uncontaminated by others or by anything', whose 'fierce insistence on his wishes, defence of his privacy, and expression of his strong dislikes only added to his integrity.[5] To his foes he was a rude and even a cruel man, whose appearance underlined the effect: tall, lean, aquiline, lined about the forehead, mouth and jaws, and with small, hooded piercing eyes. He could be summed up, as his short Dutch name suggested, as uncompromising and terse. Yet his knowledge of anatomy and commanding presence enabled him to become the best teacher of figure drawing in England and the dominating personality at the Slade. Paul Nash's striking description of his 'hooded stare and sardonic mouth, [as] he hung in the air above me, like a tall question mark, backwards and bent over from the neck, a question mark, moreover, of a derisive, rather than an inquisitive order,' perhaps best captures the terror of the uninitiated student.[6] 'Tonks was the Slade and the Slade was Tonks', a contemporary observed, and no student ever forgot it.[7]

Tonks had begun his career as a surgeon and demonstrator of anatomy at the London hospital, attending art classes part-time at the South Kensington schools under Frederick Brown. When, in 1877, Brown moved to the Westminster School of Art, both Tonks and the young Aubrey Beardsley went with him. In spite of a gruff, bearded exterior, behind his spectacles Brown's 'critical eye' was outstandingly sharp. He immediately recognized Tonks's qualities, and his first action at the Slade was to appoint him assistant. His second appointment, of Philip Wilson Steer as painting master, was equally brave.[8] Trained in Paris under Bouguereau and Cabanel, Steer's progressive painting methods demonstrated an understanding of Monet and

Pissarro, but had been much criticized by the British press. Yet in spite of their youth (Tonks and Steer were both in their early thirties and Brown himself was only forty-two when appointed) together these three men formed a triumvirate that would dominate the British art school scene for the next quarter of a century.

Flung into the Slade, like a 'leggy colt in a new field', Gertler's first steps were tentative.[9] He began his training in the Antique Room copying casts of late Greek, Greco-Roman and Italian Renaissance sculpture under the supervision of Walter Russell,[10] armed with 'Michelet' paper (very popular in pre-war Britain, it was slightly ribbed, and made with linen rags), sticks of charcoal and chunks of bread for rubbing out. Though considered extremely boring by the students, copying had the consolation of admitting both sexes, but the 'serious atmosphere of work that permeated the building' discouraged any contact between them.[11] Only in the late afternoon (between 4 and 5 o'clock) would the chosen students be admitted to the Life Room, where sitting astride the low drawing stools known as 'donkeys', they made rapid sketches from the life model.

Segregation was strictly enforced and the women's Life Room was situated away from the men's, on the lower floor. For many students their first sight of the nude model, amid the stuffy heat and tobacco fug of the Life Room, was as alarming as the prospect of producing an accurate study under the 'raking, surgical eye' of Tonks. Though the model took the same pose every day for a fortnight from 10 a.m. to 3.45 p.m., beginners were only admitted for the final hour, when short 'action' poses were struck, with a chorus of voices crying out 'Change!' every five minutes, leaving the uninitiated still sharpening their fragile vine charcoal.[12] Stanley Spencer, a fellow student who always missed these sessions in order to catch his train home to Cookham in time for tea, developed a lasting disapproval of rapid sketching as a result. But Gertler, as he wrote earnestly to Rothenstein, thought it 'excellent practice'.[13]

Gertler's first lesson with Tonks seems to have been disastrous. Stimulated yet enervated by the serious atmosphere, he attacked his drawing with sheer force of will, 'wield[ing] his pencil like a chisel' and subduing his paper like 'a block of stone out of which he was to carve the likeness of the model'.[14] Taken aback when his proudly displayed drawing only elicited the response: 'Is that the best you can do?', he was outraged and humiliated when his humble nod earned the rejoinder 'Then why do it?', and he heard the class titter.[15] Gertler had yet to learn that this was Tonks's classic put-down, a courage test for new students, many of whom he reduced to tears.

Yet Tonks's precise instruction awakened in Gertler a lifelong fascination with the mystery of the human (particularly the female) form. Tonks maintained that by mastering the directions of the bones the student mastered the direction of a contour, and he encouraged pupils to keep their drawings 'open' until they were 'tolerably sure where the contour had to go'. The word 'outline' was banned. Instead, using light strokes of charcoal or pencil, he would fill in the sharp angles of the basic skeleton with egg-like shapes rounding the limbs, later adding shading in the form of light longitudinal slashes to 'set up' the drawing. Tonks's surgical training lay at the root of his precision, and he later confessed that he had no idea what the figure looked like to anyone unacquainted with anatomy.[16] Cannan's description of Mendel's early days at 'the Detmold' are a clue to Gertler's early feelings of exclusion: 'He went there every day, and never spoke to a soul, because he realized that his speech was different from that of the others, and he would not open his mouth until he could speak without betraying himself. He listened carefully to their pronunciation and intonation, and practised to himself in bed and as he walked through the streets.'

Paul Nash, who started at the Slade the year after Gertler, compared it to 'a typical English Public School seen in a nightmare', and it was still difficult and unusual for gifted working-class students to join the school,[17] particularly the Jewish working class, since so few qualified for the JEAS's valuable assistance.[18] It was nevertheless not impossible. Three fellow 'Whitechapel boys'[19] – David Bomberg, Isaac Rosenberg and Mark Wayner (whom Gertler knew and occasionally met up with at the Whitechapel Library and Art Gallery) – later followed him to the Slade, their training also supported by the JEAS.[20] Moreover, Professor Brown was so keen to assist poor gifted students, that it was rumoured that he paid Bomberg's fees himself.[21] Nevertheless, when Gertler entered the Slade in 1908 at the age of seventeen, he was the first working-class Jewish student of his generation to do so.[22]

Originally it had been intended that Gertler should divide his time between Rothenstein's studio and the Slade, spending half of the week in each. Only three weeks into this arrangement, however, Rothenstein advised the JEAS that Gertler should be registered at the Slade full-time, and the necessary £21 was immediately approved. The

JEAS's readiness to vote another £11, only weeks after the original sum had been agreed and advanced, and to allow Gertler 8*d.* a day for his fares and a further 1*s.* 6*d.* a week for materials was surely proof of their great faith in his abilities.[23] In November they voted him a further £5 for expenses, and throughout his Slade years they treated Gertler with unrivalled generosity.[24]

Though his first term seems to have been lonely and confusing, Gertler applied himself with typical assiduity. Few of his drawings survive from his first year at the Slade, but a fine early self-portrait (dated 1909) shows how quickly he began to absorb Tonks's lessons, and he was rewarded at the end of the first term when the drawing master actually praised one of his drawings. The self-portrait, as the critic Quentin Bell has observed, is 'precise and yet free, intelligent but nevertheless a little sentimental. In short, it is all that a Slade drawing should be.'[25] And Gertler was also praised by the JEAS, who noted his 'great enthusiasm and earnestness' in their annual report.[26]

Away from the Slade life continued much as before. The family had moved in February 1908 to 14 Spital Square, a Georgian terrace, where Louis at last made a permanent home for his family and his business. He remained here for the rest of his life, and the business itself remained registered at this address until 1930. Meanwhile, Gertler continued to paint in Golda's kitchen, and her quiet pleasure in his success and the peace he found painting at her side brought them closer than ever. Nevertheless, he also kept up local friendships, and one of his paintings, *Still Life and Fish* (dated 1909), is teasingly enscribed '*Fresh Herrings and a Loaf*, painted by my friend Swingler, who lives at 3 Fulham Park Gardens' (though nothing further is known of Swingler).[27] At the Whitechapel Library and Art Gallery Gertler continued to mix with Bomberg, Rosenberg and Wayner, but his main companions during his first year were the two youngest children of the Berlinsky family, whose father, Solomon, had a military outfitter's next door.[28]

David Berlinsky (who later changed his name to Burleigh) was about Gertler's age and a keen amateur photographer. When Gertler finished a painting, the two of them would climb out of a back window on to the roof and David would photograph Mark with his paintings (in some cases preserving the only known version for posterity). David's younger sister May, who was fourteen in 1909, became Gertler's first sweetheart, and sat many times for her portrait. Gertler later compared her picturesque qualities to those of the girl in the

Rembrandt picture at Dulwich Picture Gallery (*Girl at the Window*, 1645) and perhaps May's 'paintability' was her main attraction.

In *Mendel* she appears as Sara, a small, plump, dark-complexioned girl with a beautiful face 'the colour of rich old ivory', which conforms to the known pictures of May Berlinsky. Cannan's description captures Sara's sensuality, with her eyes 'black and golden from a ruddy tinge in her eyelashes', her lips 'full and pouting' and the 'long blue-black hair' which she is always tossing back over her shoulder.[29] Cannan suggests that their relationship is physical (though it is not clear whether it is consummated), but Sara's main attraction for Mendel is as a sitter. He draws her obsessively, pouring into his work

> a strong cool passion altogether new to him, a joy so magnificent that he would forget her altogether. He was tyrannical, and kept her so still that she would almost weep from fatigue and boredom. But he was not satisfied until he had drawn every line of her, and had translated her from the world of the body to the world of vision and the spirit . . . Certain parts of her body – her little budding breasts and her round arms – especially delighted him, and he drew them over and over again. Her head he drew twenty times, and he found a shop in the West End where he could sell every one.[30]

It is unclear how the real affair ended, but in *Mendel* the couple are discovered by Golda and Sara is banished, though Mendel, who has drawn her to the point of exhaustion, is by then content to forget her.

In his second term Gertler was allowed to progress to painting as well as drawing, and on the strength of this was granted a further £10 from the JEAS to cover the extra expense.[31] The painting master was Philip Wilson Steer, whose sleepy benevolence provided a contrast to the intolerance of Tonks. Steer's large, silent, somnolent figure exuded 'inarticulate wisdom', though many an anxious student, eagerly awaiting the master's criticism, turned round to find he had actually given way to sleep. 'Like his agreeable social life', one of his supporters maintained, it was simply that 'teaching was conducted with the least possible exertion'.[32] To the students, the rarity of Steer's comments only increased their value, and they were enormously impressed by his 'massive integrity'.[33] Even those advised merely to 'muddle along' considered this valuable advice, since it encouraged them not to follow a technique slavishly but to work through problems for themselves.

Left alone with a student, the painting master became much more communicative. Though he made no active criticism of the student's work, David Sassoon, a student whose promise as a landscape painter had secured him a rare interview, recalled how Steer told him instead 'about things he himself had observed, particularly with regard to shadows, how they changed colour with distance and how and at what distance from eye local colour would be seen through them, and nearer still local detail'.[34] As a result, when Sassoon studied his own picture he could see 'where my own observation had begun and where it had ended and could see it as if it had been painted by someone else . . . Steer drew from my mind things I had not known were in it, and I have never learnt so much in so short a time with so little effort.'[35] Although Gertler left the Slade with a reputation as a draughtsman to equal that of Augustus John (the star pupil of a former generation), it was as a painter that he eventually excelled, and Sassoon's explanation of Steer's teaching methods goes some way towards explaining this since Gertler also believed that every artist must find his or her own way in painting.

Gertler worked feverishly at the Slade, attempting to find his own way by incorporating the many influences contending within him. From Rothenstein he learned to carry a pencil and sketchbook everywhere and to 'care very much for beautiful things',[36] and under Tonks he learned to draw with 'a bold, sharp decisive use of line'. In still life painting, however, he remained under the influence of Chardin and continued to revere simple, domestic objects, which he reflected in studies such as *Still Life and Fish* (1909) and *Onions* (1909). 'Painted with the master-touch of a Chardin,' he asserted in 1912, 'even the commonplace onion does not lack beauty.'[37] But he had still to make the transition from pure realism to a more expressive style, and Marjorie Lilly, a fellow Slade student, recalled how one of Gertler's early still lifes of fish, which he had entered for a Slade sketch club competition, was dismissed by Professor Brown as 'too realistic'. 'I can almost smell them – faugh!' he exclaimed, a criticism that surprised the other students as they had been impressed by Gertler's realism. 'No doubt the Professor had his reasons for disliking them', Lilly added, 'but poor Gertler took his rebuffs very much to heart; . . . and to win a prize in the summer competition meant a great deal to him.' She recalled Gertler standing by the door 'in anguish' as his still life was condemned.[38]

Under Steer, however, Gertler began to master the naturalistic style of portrait painting that later made his name, using members of his family, usually Golda, as models. A profile, *The Artist's Mother*, showing a fluid handling of oils, is dated 1908, before his lessons with Steer began, but was soon followed by a head and shoulders (1909), which highlights his mother's finely modelled hands. However, it was his still life *Onions* that brought Gertler to the attention of a final-year student, John Fothergill, who was so keen that Gertler submit the picture to the New English Art Club that he made a frame for it himself. Awed at the suggestion, Mark asked Rothenstein's advice, and only submitted the picture with his approval; and though the NEAC rejected it, it was subsequently purchased in August by the JEAS's secretary for the princely sum of £1.

Fothergill was a friend of Rothenstein's and co-founder with him of the Carfax Gallery, St James'. Older than the other students, he was admired by them as 'an exquisite in dark blue velvet suiting, pale-yellow silk shirt and stock, with a silver pin as large as an egg, and patent court shoes with silver buckles', and his almond-shaped eyes, lightly curled beard and generally romantic looks had been much admired by Oscar Wilde. He had already edited a book on the Slade and later became an archaeologist and finally innkeeper of the Spread Eagle at Thame. It was perhaps characteristic of Gertler's need to impress that, in his early months at the Slade, his first friendship should be with an older man.

The summer term brought him a period of unprecedented success. Even before the annual examinations began in June Gertler was awarded one of the two Slade art scholarships worth £35 for two years, after one of the regulations governing the competition had been specially relaxed in his favour.[39] Although he had been 'passed as eligible by Brown in early May, both he and Rothenstein had been worried that 'the school question' might prove a difficulty.[40] (Candidates were supposed to produce 'satisfactory evidence of having studied with credit in some Public School or approved place of Education'.[41]) But Stanley Spencer, who had failed a general knowledge examination completely, recalled that he was awarded a scholarship anyway, 'by the skin of [his] teeth', which he called 'a kind of cheating'.[42]

Gertler's parents were almost overwhelmed by another generous letter from Rothenstein, congratulating them on Mark's success. 'You may be quite sure that he has deserved it', Rothenstein wrote, 'and that his beginning is an indication of the path which he is to follow. Everyone who meets him feels that he is one day going to express the beauty he feels so deeply.'[43] Three years later Gertler told a journalist that once he had gained the scholarship he had given the JEAS little further trouble. In fact, the financial backing of the JEAS remained vital throughout his Slade years, even though (as Lesser pointed out) 'the finances of the society . . . gain[ed] little by Gertler's recent success'. Now he was painting he needed more expensive materials, and he had also received an offer from 'Mr St John Joiner [*sic*] . . . to coach him for a month during a holiday in the country'. The committee responded with a further grant of £20.

Term ended in early July 1909, and in August Mark set off to Berkshire on his sketching holiday, under the supervision of the landscape painter Harry St John Joyner, an active exhibitor at the Royal Society of British Artists and one of Gertler's former tutors at the Regent Street Poly. No doubt this holiday was on the recommendation of William Rothenstein, who took Gertler for bracing walks on Hampstead Heath and always advised him 'to live as much with nature as possible. Painting is done in the studio', he maintained, 'but inspiration comes from outside, and you must get away into the fields whenever you get a chance [and] spend as much of your time as you can in the open air.'[44] Gertler sent weekly letters to Rothenstein, dutifully reporting that he was enjoying the holiday 'immensely', but it was his first trip from home and he missed his family dreadfully, and admitted he would be very glad 'to see all their dear faces again'. And they too, he told Rothenstein, were 'longing for me to come home'.[45]

It was on this holiday that Gertler established the punishing routine that he was to follow more or less for the rest of his life. From 10 a.m. to 1 p.m. he painted in the fields and woods; from 2 p.m. to 4 p.m. he drew; and from 5 p.m. to 8.30 p.m. he continued painting.[46] If it rained, he told Rothenstein, he painted stables and other interiors. Gertler felt the opportunity to learn to paint landscape, 'would be of great use to me in my other works'.[47] Initially Goyson (Joyner's assistant) set him to painting the surrounding farm, but he quickly progressed to painting meadows and was astonished to see fish swimming in water for the first time. He told Rothenstein that he found the stream-covered landscape 'beautiful beyond words'.[48] At his first encounter with sheep, however 'not knowing if they were tame or savage, he ran like a hare and jumped over a hedge'.[49]

Gertler summed up his visit for Rothenstein as 'very beautiful and ideal-like,' assuring him that the 'number of canvases I shall have to bring home will be quite large'.[50] These included an early *Landscape with Trees* executed on a visit to Newbury, and the masterly *Self-Portrait with Fishing Cap*, which shows the eager and determined youth who had so impressed the JEAS.[51] Framed by a wide-brimmed fishing hat, and turned slightly side-on to the viewer, the face of the young painter looks out with with confident assurance. It was a remarkable portrait for a boy of only eighteen.[52]

5

The Quintet

> 'The Slade at that date, about 1910, was in one of its periodical triumphal flows, when from the unknown deeps arise a few gifted ones. And now, upon the crest of the wave, were riding nearly half a dozen – Stanley Spencer, Mark Gertler, William Roberts, Edward Wadsworth, Charles Nevinson . . .'
>
> Paul Nash, *Outline*

When he returned to the Slade in the autumn term of 1909, Gertler immediately began to make friends. The award of the scholarship satisfied his craving for acknowledgment and he no longer had to try so hard to impress. If the staff had begun to regard him as a star pupil – he was rumoured to have created 'an excitement comparable to that associated with the names of Orpen and John'[1] – among his fellow students Gertler began to gain a reputation as 'the genius of the place'.[2] Though C. R. W. Nevinson 'managed to bear up' when advised by Tonks to abandon his art career, he admitted that, 'had Gertler . . . told me seriously that I was wasting my time, I should have been heartbroken'.[3]

Every morning students would register in the signing-in book in the hall, which was divided, like the Life Room, by gender – 'women on the left page and men on the right'.[4] Nevinson, who had arrived in the second term of Gertler's first year, signed in with a flamboyance that soon made him the acknowledged ringleader, or 'first violin', of 'a quintet . . . inseparable in work and play'.[5] Edward Wadsworth fell in as second violin, Gertler and Adrian Allinson as viola and cello, and David Sassoon was 'occasionally audible in the background in the part of the double bass'.[6] Allinson would later write in his (unpublished) autobiography that 'some unconscious element of attraction'[7] had drawn them all together, but since female students outnumbered men by four to one most days the quintet may well have represented almost half the male contingent. Dressed in black jerseys, scarlet mufflers and black caps, they behaved 'abominably' with evident relish, and were known 'in correct Kensington circles', Nevinson claimed, as 'the Slade Coster gang'.[8]

It was undoubtedly this group that Gertler had in mind when he wrote to Rothenstein of his 'nice friends among the Upper Class . . . so much nicer than the rough "East Ends" ' he was used to.[9] Most of his former schoolfriends, he noted, were now selling newspapers outside the Mansion House. Nevinson, though only a couple of years older, was greatly Gertler's senior in sophistication. He was the son of liberal, intellectual parents: his father was a famous journalist, who fought emphatically for social reform and was an officer of an East End cadet corps, and his mother was 'a shingled, sandalled progressive' who taught French to the working classes at Toynbee Hall. Brought up among the 'precious aesthetes of Kensington', Nevinson professed to despise snobbery.[10] As a child he had accompanied his parents so often along the docks, the lower river and Whitechapel High Street that they had become as familiar to him as the local heath at Hampstead, and consequently he retained 'no English fear of the poor or the uneducated'.[11] The East End was not for him, as it was for the other students, '*terra incognita*'.[12]

Though he dressed like an 'old hand' at the Slade, in a 'bewaisted coat' with peacock blue accessories and a 'slight growth of whiskers *à la Rapin*' about the ears,[13] Nevinson's defiant exterior hid a shy, even morbid, sensitivity. His temperament, strikingly similar to Gertler's own, swung between 'easy bursts of laughter (usually at his own witticisms) and deep depression',[14] from which, however, he could be lifted by the comradeship of the quintet, especially Gertler.

Edward Wadsworth's appearance was the complete antithesis of Nevinson's; his 'angular sloping forehead [and] blue chin reced[ing] into a long neck with a prominent Adam's apple' which Allinson never tired of caricaturing.[15] Like Nevinson's, Wadsworth's background was privileged, though his was more austere. Born in Cleckheaton, Yorkshire, he was brought up by his father after the early death of his mother, and had learned engineering before deciding to study art. He developed a reputation as 'a ladykiller', and was involved in 'various high-spirited student escapades' with the other members of the quintet.[16] But having recently spent a year at the Knirr Art School in Munich, he was the most mature personality among them, and his deep-set eyes glinted with intelligence and humour.

Adrian Allinson, who joined the Slade later than the others in 1910, had originally, like Tonks, studied medicine. His privileged background secured him a place at the Slade, but the skill in drawing and ready sense of humour that made him such a successful caricaturist quickly overcame any initial timidity on that account.[17] He was tall, elegant and willowy, but pictured himself as 'the buffoon of the party' joking, tap-dancing and caricaturing his way through student life.[18]

David Sassoon, the second of the five sons of the Anglo-Indian banker Joseph Sassoon (and distantly related to the poet Siegfried), was a shy student who pursued a quiet path through the Slade for three years before becoming 'auditor' to the 'noisy fiddling' of his companions. Eventually he disappeared from the quintet altogether, squeezed out by a far more forceful personality. Nevertheless, he proved a generous friend to Gertler, and later gave him his first evening suit. Gertler described him to Rothenstein as 'a chap that does you a kindness *without fuss* from his heart'.[19]

Among such stimulating company Gertler's natural exuberance was suddenly released. He entertained his circle with his imitations and was delighted to discover that Nevinson had also formed the 'music-hall habit'. Soon the East End's Bedford and Middlesex music-halls became the 'Mecca' of the gang,[20] and while the others may have been attracted to a scene painted so intensively by Walter Sickert, with its 'full-blooded, god-blessed vulgarity',[21] Gertler was drawn, as he had been since childhood, to the theatre of everyday life. From this experience, and from watching the performances of his old kinsman Louis Weinig, he had learned early on to harness his own 'exceptional powers of mimicry and burlesque', and it was the contrast between this earthy humour and his 'sweetly pretty' looks that delighted his friends.[22] The silent observations of his first year now paid off, and Paul Nash recalled Gertler's imitation Oxford accent as 'one of the best of his clever repertoire'.[23]

Anti-Semitism was not entirely absent from the Slade.[24] One fellow student, Darsie Japp, later admitted that he had been 'silly enough to feel some antipathy to Gertler because he was a Jew'.[25] Later, when he heard Gertler telling stories of his background and family, particularly of his brothers, Japp listened 'with interest and admiration', but, he later wrote, 'the admiration was for Gertler's unprejudiced description' and not for his brothers.[26] Gertler, conscious that he lacked the education of his companions, remained 'acutely sensitive about his background and origins', and sometimes expressed his opinions with such 'naiveté and solemnity' that he would unintentionally reduce his friends to 'fits of laughter'.[27] (This sensitivity is echoed by Mendel, who considers himself 'the poor, isolated Yiddisher' until he strikes up a friendship with Mitchell/Nevinson. His chief ambition is that 'his wonderful work' will allow everybody to forget that he is 'a Jew, and [allow him to] move freely and easily in that wonderful England which he had begun to perceive . . . at the school'.[28]) For Gertler the acute dilemma of celebrating and rejecting his heritage had already begun.

To outsiders there was little evidence of any lingering insecurity, and Gertler was always the 'charmer' of the circle.[29] His working-class blue collar had become acceptable, even romantic, and his curly hair, which he wore first in a Florentine page-boy cut, and later cropped into short curls, made him look like 'a Jewish Botticelli'.[30] Only Sassoon recognized that Gertler 'not only looked younger than his age . . . [but] was young for his age in psychological makeup'.[31] His youth seemed only to emphasize his precocious gifts, and Gertler was once again cast in the role of brilliant younger brother.

One morning, marching into the Life Room with a sheaf of drawings under his arm, he sat down on the floor, spread his drawings out in front of him, and to his friends' astonishment deliberately tore them up one by one. Evidently, he expected the quintet to remonstrate with him, but they were more sophisticated and waited until he had destroyed all the drawings, before talking to him of 'the wisdom of, from time to time, weeding out one's work'. They suggested he bring in all the drawings he had at home and they would go through them with him to help him 'separate the grain from the chaff'.[32] Yet Gertler's grand gesture was more than an empty bid for attention, as Sassoon alone seems to have recognized. Although the symptoms of depression were already deeply woven into his personality, when he suffered 'these fits of despondency', Sassoon noted, Gertler clearly had 'need of some praise and admiration, and quite unconsciously had a way of asking for it in time to prevent the state of mind becoming more than temporary'.[33]

Yet, as Frances Spalding has pointed out, it was probably the effect of this new society which 'turned him back to his family with renewed appreciation'.[34] Away from the Slade Gertler began to consolidate the extraordinary portfolio of family portraits begun in 1908 with his first studies of Golda, who even now remained the linchpin of his existence. In the remarkable double portrait of his parents executed in this period, Louis's proud, sensitive face is highlighted while Golda remains in the background, but it is 'her hand, sharply lit and resting on the far side of her husband's shoulders, that confirms her all-embracing presence'.[35]

That Easter the quintet made a trip to Paris,[36] travelling steerage via Dieppe, a 'ghastly' journey, during which Gertler, always a delicate traveller, 'nearly died from sea-sickness, being revived only by French sailors hosing him [down] in the early dawn'.[37] Fortified against the bitter cold, with endless rum babas, the gang engaged in a hectic week of sightseeing, their 'terrific' enthusiasm carrying them to galleries, museums and *boîtes de nuit* all over Paris, but most frequently to the Primitive Room at the Louvre which 'compensated . . . for much'.[38] They were beginning to throw off their Slade training, and now despised artists such as Rubens, much favoured by Tonks.

Though they were, after all, only young men in search of excitement and gratified to be 'no example[s] for placid modern youth', as artists they were all undoubtedly 'serious' (a word on which much stress is laid in all their accounts of this period).[39] Some twenty-seven years later Nevinson still considered Gertler 'the most serious single-minded artist' he had ever come across. And the art historian Bruce Laughton later credited Gertler and Stanley Spencer with starting a new tradition at the Slade, the 'student as artist' tradition, which he described as 'almost impossible to maintain except when the students happen to be exceptionally gifted'.[40]

On a visit to the Académie Julian on Paris's left bank the quintet soon found itself at the mercy of the other students, who naturally prepared to 'rag' them.[41] Gertler, clearly the youngest, was singled out, handed pencil, paper and drawing board, and ordered to sit down and begin drawing, 'which he did as calmly and deliberately', Sasson recalled,

> as he would have done at the Slade. Ribald remarks died down as the students watched him, and then after a spell of complete silence they began to ask us who we were and where we came from. On hearing we were from the Slade School in London, they told us there was no better school of drawing anywhere, and advised us to stay out our time there and then come to Paris where they would teach us to paint.[42]

On his return from Paris in May 1910 Gertler found another appreciative audience among the JEAS committee, who wished to see for themselves the results of their investment. He was granted a further £6 10*s.* (at the rate of 5*s.* a week),[43] to take a private room to work in, since most of his painting was still carried out in Golda's kitchen in Spital Square, and became the 'proud possessor of his first studio, a sparsely furnished attic in the middle of the noisy market place in Commercial Street.[44]

Inside Gertler felt gloriously free, and 'gloat[ed]', as he told Rothenstein, 'over the quiet solitude' of it all. For once financially secure, he could afford to live 'almost spiritually, looking down with a cynical smile at all the petty little worries of mankind'. He, by contrast, was a 'superman' (under the influence of a fellow student, John Currie he had been reading Nietzsche) who could go out and 'thrill with happiness over a tree, a blade of grass, a cloud, a child, an onion, any part of nature's innocent work. Have I not the advantage?' he asked.[45] The childish glee he felt in his freedom to sing, run, put his feet on the table and do just as he pleased, was matched only by a sense of possession. He could sit at one end of the room, look uninterruptedly across to the other, and say 'Look! this is all my own.'[46] Although the tiny studio was only the first step in the difficult leave-taking of his family (which would not be fully accomplished for another five years), it was further tangible proof of his validity as an artist.

That June Gertler made his exhibition début at the 'Friday Club' at the Alpine Club Gallery, Mill Street, where his work hung alongside that of the Bloomsbury artists Duncan Grant and Vanessa Bell. His work so impressed Vanessa that she wrote to her husband, Clive: 'One young man of 17 I marked down as promising. His name is Mark Gertler and he has two rather remarkable paintings – remarkable really only considering his age but I think he must be going to be good.'[47] As Vanessa Stephen, she had established this informal 'Painters' Club' back in 1905, aiming to encourage 'new contacts and practical discussion' among members.[48] Its membership mostly consisted of students from the Royal Academy and the Slade, and had no dominant style, though it often featured 'work of a decorative nature', such as murals and large figure compositions, and the acclaimed French mural painter Puvis de Chavannes had been included in the 1910 exhibition.[49] Artists as diverse as J. D. Innes, David Bomberg, Bernard Leech, Gwen Raverat, Jessie Etchells and Nina Hamnett all exhibited there during the club's seventeen-year lifetime.

Several of Gertler's contemporaries, such as Derwent Lees, a part-time drawing teacher at the Slade,[50] and fellow students John Currie and Maxwell Lightfoot were also members and may well have introduced him.[51] All of the quintet would exhibit at the Friday Club at least once, even Nevinson (who later dismissed it as a Bloomsbury-dominated 'little clique . . . ruined by the amateurish dilettantism of Roger Fry'),[52] and after his début Gertler continued to exhibit there until the club's demise in 1922.[53] For a young art student it was an invaluable introduction to the contemporary art scene.

Gertler's work was now developing a recognizable theme. Since his first studies of his family and the local rabbis he had gradually conceived an idea for a series of Jewish portraits. Clearly impressed by Rothenstein's own Jewish work (shown as part of the Whitechapel exhibition in May 1910), he wrote telling him that 'of all the fine things of that very fine show I like your pictures best.'[54] Both artists were working in a tradition handed down from Rembrandt, as Gertler himself acknowledged, when he later described the scene inside the local synagogue as 'like one huge Rembrandt brought to life'. His own series of Jewish paintings was an attempt to capture not merely the picturesque qualities of his subjects but the essence of their everyday lives. In this, his personal experience and empathy were an incalculable advantage, and when he wrote to Lightfoot that he intended carrying out a composition of Jewish figures for the Slade summer competition, Lightfoot approved it as 'an excellent idea for you who understand the people' (hoping, he added, that Gertler would produce a 'da---d good painting').[55]

The JEAS minutes for 29 June 1910 record Gertler entering for 'rather an ambitious figure subject competition for which he require[d] Oriental draperies'. The result was *The Return of Jephtha*, a large multiple figure composition, now known only from one of David Berlinsky's rooftop photographs. However, the JEAS also reported that from now on Gertler had been advised by his professors to attend the Slade only three days a week and to 'concentrate on Jewish subjects'.[56] It seems to have been widely accepted that this was his milieu.

When he returned to the Slade in the autumn of 1910,[57] Gertler was still concentrating on family portraits: Deborah, Harry, Harry's wife, Annie, and his youngest sister, Sophie (one of his favourite models) would all sit for their portraits over the next few months. Nevertheless, Gertler's letters show that Rothenstein helped him to obtain other Jewish models, one of whom may have sat for one of Gertler's finest Jewish paintings, the highly accomplished double portrait *Talmudic*

Discussion. He probably borrowed elements of its composition from Giovanni Bellini's *Circumcision*[58] (which he later cited as one of his favourite paintings[59]) and Rembrandt's *Two Scholars Disputing*.[60]

In June the JEAS was delighted to report that Gertler had gained 'more successes than anyone else at the Slade School'.[61] Slade records show that he was awarded first prize for head painting and second prize for painting from the cast and that his scholarship was renewed for another year; but the JEAS recorded that Gertler also won first prize for drawing of the head, a prize for figure painting, a prize for head painting (shared with another student), and a prize for a special competition for painting of the head (also shared with another student).[62] The extra prizes referred to may have been those awarded to Slade students who were members of an internal sketch club, which held periodic competitions on set subjects, usually biblical. Entries were submitted anonymously to the judgement of Tonks, and the prizewinners were awarded the handsome sum of 3 guineas.[63] (This would further explain the predominance of biblical subjects in Gertler's work of this period, and why none of these works was signed or dated.)

Since the previous November the JEAS's secretary, Ernest Lesser, had been encouraged by the committee to 'use his influence' to try and sell some of Gertler's paintings on his behalf. However, this was not as altruistic as it sounds since the JEAS money was not a gift but a loan, and Gertler was expected to accept commissions throughout his student years and to use a percentage of the profits to begin his repayments. Lesser had long been impressed by Gertler, but now other members of the JEAS also began to watch him with special interest. In the summer of 1910 Lesser received a £10 cheque from the JEAS's president, Sir Edward Sassoon, 'earmarked for Gertler', and in June a further £8 was voted for fares, lunches and materials, intended to last him until the end of the year.[64] But by December Gertler's noisy Commercial Street studio had become 'unsuitable' and to facilitate his move to Primrose Hill the JEAS allowed him a further £5, and also renewed its grant of 10*s*. a week for another six months.

In November a member of the general committee (identified only as Mr C. Wertheimer) stated that he 'might be able to interest someone in this student, who would give a [further] donation earmarked for him', and Walter Samuel, another general committee member, promised Gertler two commissions, including one to paint his wife.[65] Gertler had already begun to carry out commissions among his Slade contemporaries, and Paul Nash remembered 'a delightful person called Have-a-smoke, from his ingratiating habit of offering everyone a cigarette on every occasion . . . [who] once commissioned Gertler to paint his wife, watching him the while. At every successful stroke of the brush, Have-a-smoke called out "Good stroke, Gertler, oh, good stroke!" Gertler told us he felt as if he were playing cricket.'[66]

Not all commissions proved this entertaining, however, and Gertler was extremely wary of rich patrons. According to Henry Ginsbury (one of Gertler's students at the Westminster School of Art in the 1930s), in his youth 'a social worker [presumably Henrietta Adler] who recognized his talent had arranged for Gertler to show some paintings to possible patrons.'[67]

> The first appointment was made for him with a prominent communal figure and Gertler excitedly took some paintings by bicycle to his house in Hampstead. The door was opened by a butler who sent Gertler to the tradesman's entrance from which he was led to the hall. Apparently the potential patron considered the visit as an occasion for charity rather than an exhibition of paintings; he pointed to one, held three sovereigns towards Gertler who failed to catch them in his unready hand, and left the hall leaving Gertler and the butler crawling on the floor for the coins. Gertler recalled it as the most humiliating experience in his life.[68]

He was determined not to repeat it. But his visit to Samuel's 'nice big house' only reinforced his earlier experience. He found Samuel a cold, 'touch me not' sort of person, and was 'never more socialistically inclined' than when he returned home, carrying the same two heavy loads of pictures he had set out with. Samuel had let him go, he wrote to Rothenstein in disgust, without buying one.[69] Gertler's relations with patrons, particularly rich Jewish ones, would be continually damaged by his sensitivity to their patronizing behaviour, and his volatile mix of truthfulness and quick temper. His subsequent behaviour also suggests that Gertler had already come to resent the high level of 'interference' from the JEAS. No other student, it seems, was subject to such intense interest.[70] He was beginning to learn that there would always be a high price to pay for attracting attention.

6

Foreigners in England

'. . . Were one to meet him in any capital in the world, one would think not "Here is a foreigner" but "Here is a Jew". Though he would be recognised anywhere, he would be at home nowhere except here, in the midst of his family.'

Olivia Manning, *The Great Fortune*, The Balkan Trilogy

On Saturday 5 November 1910 the press view of a show entitled 'Manet and the Post-Impressionists', organized by the painter and critic Roger Fry, opened at the Grafton Galleries, Bond Street, to a 'wild hurricane of newspaper abuse from all quarters'.[1] Dominated by Cézanne, Gauguin and Van Gogh, and drawing 25,000 visitors over the next two months, the exhibition introduced most of the British public (who had barely come to terms with Impressionism) to French Post-Impressionist painting for the first time. 'The Art-Quake of 1910', as it was later termed, had erupted.[2]

The pictures had been chosen by Fry and his friend the literary journalist Desmond MacCarthy. MacCarthy was aware when choosing the pictures that they would administer 'the most tremendous shocks',[3] and in the catalogue introduction attempted to draw the viewer's attention away from conventional ideas of representation and towards 'the emotional significance which lies in things'[4]; but this advice proved frankly baffling to many. The responses ranged from outrage to hilarity. 'The ordinary visitor', it was reported, 'collapsed with laughter at the sight of the Cézannes.' Indeed, one elderly man was seized by 'such convulsions of laughter . . . that his companion had to take him out and walk him up and down in the fresh air'.[5] The so-called 'cultured classes', Fry observed, who had previously attended his lectures on Italian art, were the most outraged. His comments, that 'all one needed to appreciate a Matisse was a certain sensibility', had, as Frances Spalding has written, 'rather terrifying democratic implications', such that Fry was even accused of anarchism.[6] A few perceptive critics, such as Frank Rutter and Hugh Blaker, defended the show, but conservatives such as C. J. Weld-Blundell of *The Times* denounced it as 'degenerate'. Detractors seized upon Van Gogh's insanity as 'a pretext for dismissing his art as the raving of a madman',[7] and the critic Robert Ross went further, announcing that all the exhibitors were 'lunatics', and mounting a mock exhibition of Post-Impressionists at the Chelsea Arts Club later the same month.[8]

Nevertheless, young artists and art lovers recognized in the pictures 'a sudden liberation and encouragement to feel for oneself which were absolutely overwhelming'.[9] It was 'impossible to think', wrote Vanessa Bell, 'that any other single exhibition can ever have had so much effect as did that on the rising generation'.[10] When the painter and critic D. S. MacColl returned to London only three months later, he found that Post-Impressionism was 'the new religion . . . the old gods being bundled without ceremony into the lumber room'.[11]

At the Slade, Paul Nash observed, 'all this had a disturbing effect'.[12] Tonks and Steer worried that the students risked contamination from the 'virus of the new art', asked them to stay away.[13] It is unlikely that Gertler heeded this advice, but it was not until the second Post-Impressionist exhibition in 1912 that the impact of the new painting became apparent in his own work. Fry's name would certainly have been familiar to Gertler. He was external lecturer on the history of art for three out of the four years that Gertler attended the Slade,[14] and also (until 1912) exhibited with the Friday Club, where, even before the opening of the first Post-Impressionist exhibition, an awareness of modern French painting was already apparent in Duncan Grant's painting, and soon afterwards in that of Fry himself and Vanessa Bell.

At the close of 1910, however, for many critics there was still only one artist who could be regarded as 'chief of the English representatives of the new movement in modern art', and that was Augustus John.[15] His new exhibition, 'Provençal Studies and Other Works', opened at the Chenil Galleries, Chelsea, in November 1910, and this Gertler almost certainly visited. John and William Orpen had been the most prominent Slade artists of their generation (the late 1890s), and it was only natural that the current students should idolize them.[16]

When Gertler was interviewed in February 1912, John was still the only 'modern' whose 'greatness' he would allow.

In *Mendel* Cannan drew a striking picture of John as the artist Calthrop, a man of genius who had made the Detmold art school famous. Regarded with awe by the quintet, Calthrop becomes, for a time, their role model in all things. If Calthrop 'dressed extravagantly', Cannan wrote, so did the gang; if he smashed furniture, they did likewise; and as he 'drank, embraced women, and sometimes painted outrageously,' the gang too did all these things.[17] Nevertheless, it was not only as an *enfant terrible* that John paved the way. By 1910 the exquisite draughtsmanship with which he had made his Slade reputation had been replaced by a more experimental style, and it was this, and not Post-Impressionism, which for Gertler and many of his Slade contemporaries represented 'democratic and revolutionary ideals of the most uncompromising kind'.[18] John had simplified his figures in a way that seemed radical, employing a brilliant palette to produce works of a 'jewelled and painterly effect', and replacing the elaborate costumes of Edwardian England with the loose, Bohemian garments which had become as distinctively 'John' as his own signature.[19] Some critics thought him 'largely influenced by the Pre-Renaissance Italian masters', while for others, writes Michael Holroyd in his biography of John, 'he was the last word in modernity'.[20] To Gertler, whose own heart remained lost to the early Italians, it was probably this Italian influence that appealed most.

Gertler's initial reaction to these new influences was to focus more distinctly on the old masters, and in 1910 the National Gallery still remained more of a draw than the Grafton. In this constantly shifting flux of change and ideas, his mother remained his inspiration. A fine painting of Golda, *The Artist's Mother in her Kitchen*, strikingly recalls Velázquez's *Kitchen Scene with Christ in the House of Martha and Mary* in its arrangement of still life objects, and Golda's solid figure echoes that of Velázquez's kitchen maid.[21] (One of Gertler's close friends later cited this painting as Gertler's favourite in the National Gallery.) At the Friday Club in February 1911 Gertler exhibited six pictures, including the highly accomplished *Talmudic Discussion, Girl with Red Hair* (probably a portrait of a Jewish neighbour, Rose Landau[22]), and four drawings, two of which sold for £5 10*s*. each.[23] The exquisite *Head of an Old Woman*, a portrait of Golda, also sold quickly to an important new patron, Professor Michael Sadler, the vice-chancellor of Leeds University.

After Harry Gertler's marriage to a local milliner, Annie Hyman, in December 1910 (her father, Gershon Hyman, was a bootmaker in Spital Square[24]), the newly weds had moved to Amhurst Road, Hackney, which left only Jack (intermittently) and Sophie (who continued to reject the matchmakers' proposed suitors) at home with Gertler and their parents. Sophie and Golda continued to be his usual models, and John's increasing influence is apparent in several studies of Sophie wearing John's trademark Bohemian clothes, scarf and earrings.

Meanwhile, the JEAS committee continued to encourage Gertler to accept commissions (10 per cent of his fees being paid back into the society to cover past and future expenses.) He had given particular 'satisfaction', they noted, with a fine patrician portrait of Henry Cardwell, the vicar of St Anne's, Soho, dashed off in January in under ten days, and boldly signed with his trademark red paint signature.[25] Chiefly, however, 1911, was characterized by Gertler's testy relations with his patrons, in particular with a prosperous Jewish family, the Wertheimers, and would culminate in his explosive rejection of their interference at the close of the year.

The Wertheimers were a powerful force on the national art scene. Samson Wertheimer had settled in Britain in 1830, and for many years ran his business as a fine art dealer from his Bond Street gallery. After his death the business was divided between his two sons, Charles and Asher, both of whom became influential art dealers in their own right. Charles specialized in French paintings by Boucher, Fragonard and Watteau, and also in painters of the British school, such as Romney, Gainsborough, Hoppner and Lawrence. He had also commissioned the young William Orpen to paint his portrait at a time when the rest of the London art world regarded this patronage as 'rash'.[26] Afterwards he engineered the hanging of this portrait in the place of honour at the Royal Academy's annual exhibition, ensuring not only the portrait's maximum impact but also Orpen's own smooth transition from respected member of the New English Art Club to Royal Academician. As Charles well realized, the status of the painter also reflected glory on his sitters.

Asher Wertheimer and his wife, Flora, conducted life on 'a lively, individual and immense scale' from their exquisitely furnished house in Connaught Place, Hyde Park, which swarmed with children, dogs and 'a continuous stream of painters, musicians and writers'.[27] Among them was the painter John Singer Sargent, whose fashionable society portraits summed up for many the ideal representation of the Edwardian aristocrat. For his sitters Sargent's signature on a portrait was the visual equivalent of an entry in *Who's Who*. 'Looking at his portraits,' the writer Osbert Sitwell later observed, 'they understood at last how rich they really were.'[28]

Asher's barrister son Conway developed a strong interest in both patronage and the arts early in his career.[29] His niece remembers him as 'a great philanthropist', who helped to rebuild the inns of court and Guy's Hospital after the Second World War, and he also donated a silver collection to Oxford's Ashmolean Museum. The painter Gilbert Spencer recalled being interviewed by Conway for a prospective mural commission for Balliol College. In 1911, however, Conway was only a member of the JEAS's general committee, and his artistic patronage seems to have been limited to Gertler, to whom he had lent some 'oriental robes' for *The Return of Jephtha* the previous year. By January 1911 Wertheimer had started to complain that Gertler was carrying out too many assignments, and the committee finally agreed that he should 'never have more than two commissions unfulfilled at the same time'. Gertler, of course, was not consulted.[30] Wertheimer also 'expressed a willingness' to make a special collection for Gertler if he would undertake not to work on commissions in the future. By this stage, it seems, he had already begun to regard Gertler as his protégé.[31]

In February 1911 Wertheimer consulted his father's friend Sargent about Gertler's progress. When Gertler informed the JEAS that he again wished to move studio, he was no doubt unpleasantly surprised to learn that Sargent had advised that he could 'very well remain' in the studio he now occupied. However, Wertheimer undertook to provide Gertler with the generous sum of between £20 and £25 for six months, and the JEAS pledged him a further 15*s.* a week. The subject of commissions was raised again, and this time the committee unanimously decided that Gertler 'was not to feel bound by his debt to the Society to take commissions'. And when, in March 1911, Nevinson's mother invited Gertler to spend a week in Paris with herself and her son, the committee immediately had a whip-round to raise the necessary £3 10*s.*[32]

Spring was a difficult time for the Gertlers: the furriery business was 'slack' almost to the point of standstill and the Nevinsons went out of their way to try and help Mark.[33] In May, when Nevinson senior arranged a visit for himself and his son to the collector Professor Sadler in Leeds, he asked if he could bring 'another artist boy as well – the Whitechapel Jew Goertler [*sic*]. He is of great promise, and is having a hard fight for it', Nevinson wrote, adding that Rothenstein thought well of him.[34] Sadler had already shown interest in Gertler's work by acquiring a drawing at the Friday Club, and whether or not the meeting actually took place, he confirmed his interest that autumn by purchasing one of Gertler's most important portraits of Golda.[35] These would always be among his most sought-after pictures, and when the American John Quinn, who had started to collect contemporary British art on the advice of Augustus John, also bought a sketch of Golda, *The Artist's Mother*, Gertler's reputation as a promising young artist was confirmed.[36]

Back at the Slade he was still winning prizes, if less spectacularly than before. A £10 prize awarded in the summer term was shared between four students, each of whom, however, netted only £2 5*s*., as Stanley Spencer, one of the recipients, noted ruefully in a letter to his brother).[37] When Gertler once again moved studio in June, the JEAS voted £5 for his moving expenses.[38] There is no record of whether Gertler entered the Slade summer competition in 1911, but in any case Maxwell Lightfoot was no longer there to advise him. A *frisson* of shock had run through the Slade in the autumn, when Lightfoot had committed suicide on the eve of his marriage, after discovering that his fiancée, an artist's model, was notorious for her promiscuity.

By October 1911 Gertler was advised by Professor Brown to 'commence to earn his own living' as an artist. His attendance was probably very limited from now on, but he did not officially leave the Slade until 1912, and retained strong links there for the next few months, particularly with Brown.[39] In November Gertler heard that (after a unanimous vote in his favour) he had been awarded a British Institute scholarship of £100 over two years, with the likelihood of further renewal. This guaranteed him a minimum income of £1 a week for at least two years – in the East End, he knew, some families were forced to survive on much less[40] – and unlike the JEAS's grants, it had no onerous conditions of repayment. While he was still celebrating this good news, he also heard that his portrait of Golda, which he had submitted to the New English Art Club under the title *Portrait of an Elderly Woman*, had been accepted. Gertler later spoke of his 'great happiness at having achieved that great distinction' barely a month before his twentieth birthday.[41]

The New English Art Club was founded in 1886, when it held its first exhibition at the Marlborough Gallery in Pall Mall, and its original aim was to promote 'progressive English painting', in direct opposition to the Royal Academy's openly hostile attitude to change.[42] Crucially, the NEAC was also run by elected juries (much in the manner of the French salons) and soon incorporated such diverse schools of painting as the Newlyn school, the Glasgow Boys and the short-lived London Impressionists (the group name under which Walter Sickert, Fred Brown and Philip Wilson Steer had exhibited in 1889). Tonks had also become a member of the NEAC in 1895, and was such an active jurist that soon the NEAC came to be seen as a natural stepping-stone for star Slade pupils.

By 1907, however, the NEAC had lost its radical edge. Some of the original members had joined the enemy camp and now exhibited at the RA or, worse still, at both venues, a sign that it was beginning to develop the same 'hardened arteries' as some of its elderly members. None the less, until overtaken by Roger Fry's Omega Workshops in 1913 and the London Group the following year, the NEAC remained a valuable platform for rising artists. And Gertler, who was delighted when his portrait of Golda was accepted, was soon quite overcome when he learned that it had been prominently displayed 'on the line' in the main room of the exhibition. It was a tribute to the painting's extraordinary power of 'psychological insight', a quality that makes it not only his finest portrait of Golda, but also one of his most outstanding works.[43]

The picture also exemplified, Quentin Bell later observed, the type of portrait that Gertler's teachers were trying to paint, though they rarely managed it 'with such a fine mixture of brilliance and sincerity'.[44] Golda's hands, in particular – large, capable and 'instinct with life', more accustomed to activity than repose – are so skilfully painted that the 'solidity and . . . character . . . implicit in their quiet tension' are among the portrait's most memorable features.[45] At the close of November Gertler learned that it had been acquired by Michael Sadler. This portrait would mark the culmination of Gertler's naturalistic style of portraiture (though not his fascination with Golda as a model) and, though he continued to be a remarkable portraitist, he rarely recaptured such an extraordinary depth of character.

In 1911 Sadler was just beginning to rise to prominence as a collector. His earliest acquisitions had reflected the taste of the 'New English circle', but Roger Fry's Post-Impressionist show in 1910 had come as a 'revelation' to him, and was followed by a period of 'frantic buying' in the autumn of 1911, such that by the time he acquired Golda's portrait in November his collection already contained several

Gauguins and at least one Cézanne.[46] Keen to acquire more, Sadler, together with his son Michael (who changed his surname to Sadleir to distinguish it from his father's) asked the new director of the Stafford Gallery, John Neville, to visit Paris to negotiate the acquisition of further Post-Impressionist pictures. The gallery had only recently moved premises from Bond Street to Mayfair, and on his return Neville used his inaugural exhibition in November 1911 to show his colours as a modernist, showcasing Sadler's new Post-Impressionist pictures. During the exhibition Sadler also asked Gertler to drop off some of his recent pictures at the Stafford, and Gertler explained rather nervously in a letter that he was 'only just beginning' to feel his way in work, and hoped soon to produce pictures that would be 'ever so far superior' to those he was sending, the most recent of which, he wrote, was *A Jew Praying*, which was 'not quite complete'.

Gertler probably began to feel irked at this stage by the continuing interference, as he saw it, of the JEAS and Conway Wertheimer. Yet, it was at this moment of triumph that Conway attempted to take control of his protégé, reporting to the committee that Sargent, whom he had again consulted, 'considered Gertler's sense of colour poor', and had recommended that he study painting in Italy for two years, at Conway's expense. Anxious not to stand in Gertler's way, the committee immediately consented to forgo the repayment of 10 per cent they would have expected from his earnings during that time.

No first-hand evidence of Gertler's response survives, but many years later his friend Beatrice Campbell gave one version in her memoirs. 'When Gertler was a boy in Whitechapel', she wrote, Wertheimer 'took him up'.

> He was to be sent to Italy to study art and great things were to be done for him. There was tremendous excitement among his people when Wertheimer's Rolls-Royce arrived with a chauffeur and a footman to take him and his painting to Wertheimer's house to be inspected. As he was putting his canvases in the back of the car, the footman leaned forward and said, 'Be careful of the paint.' Gertler replied gaily, 'It's alright, they are quite dry.' The footman said, 'the paint on the car.' Gertler later decided not to be 'taken up' or sent anywhere, a decision which distressed his family.[47]

In another version, which Gertler told to one of his students at the Westminster School of Art in the 1930s, when he visited Sargent's studio, the older painter left his guests to scrutinize Gertler's paintings 'with obvious interest before turning to say "If you want to work in my studio, you will be welcome: but I would advise you not to: any influence would not be good for you." '[48]

However, it is *Mendel* (which is, after all, based on verbatim accounts of Gertler's own experience) which provides the most likely version. Here the young artist, 'tired of being swung from one idea to another', sees the plan to send him to Italy as a 'conspiracy', and finally rebels:

> At the Polytechnic they had told him that the essential thing in a picture was 'tone', that he must remember the existence of the atmosphere between himself and the object he was painting, and that there were no bright colours in nature. At the Detmold little was said about 'tone', but he was told that the essence of a picture was drawing, 'the expression of form' . . . What next? He had a foreboding that Italy was only another name for another essence of a picture. Besides he wanted to live. Though he adored art, yet it did not contain all that was precious to him – liberty and gaiety, friendship and affection.[49]

And Mendel writes to Birnbaum telling him that he 'would not go to Italy, that he did not want any more of his commissions, and that he would not be interfered with any more'.[50] His letter is never answered, but Birnbaum's patronage, and that of his friends, is instantly withdrawn. Certainly Gertler's defiance must have been perceived as the equivalent of sticking up two fingers at the Jewish establishment. Why should a penniless Jewish art student, even one as sensitive as Gertler, be prepared to throw it all away?

First it was an exciting time for an artist to be in England, as the number of groups forming, dividing and reforming, and the emergence of independent galleries showed. London was 'a city with a future, not merely a past', in comparison with which Rome seemed a city existing only 'on its past glories'.[51] Second, Gertler was temperamentally, as he put it 'a London bird', and a reluctant traveller, who always believed, like his father, that England was the best country in the world. He had already discovered that he could be treated with cold disdain by English patrons, so what chance, he must have reasoned would he stand abroad? There is a telling incident in *Mendel* where on a visit to the Birnbaum/Wertheimer's country estate Mendel is humiliated at being lodged in a servant's bedroom and enraged by the patronizing attitude of the host and his guests. This treatment makes him feel 'utterly and crushingly foreign', as he is regarded 'with a cold interest not unmingled with horror,' and also made acutely 'conscious of bearing the marks of the place he came from, of smelling of the gutter. Against that separation', Cannan writes, 'even art was powerless.'[52] Gertler was always extremely sensitive to race and class prejudice, but he reserved his harshest criticism for the rich society English Jews, whom he later dismissed to a friend as 'patronising horrors'.[53]

The consequences of Gertler's rejection of Wertheimer were rapid. He received no further payments from the JEAS, and his name (formerly mentioned with such frequency in committee minutes) was dropped altogether until 1916, when the committee felt able to report that he was 'altogether steadier than formerly'.[54] From now on whenever Gertler heard from the JEAS it was simply to remind him of his repayments.[55]

By November, however, Gertler had already learned of his British Institute scholarship – of which only three were awarded annually in the United Kingdom[56] – and must have felt that he no longer needed Wertheimer's patronage.[57] Yet his future dealings with the prosperous English Jewish community, who had hitherto nurtured him as a young 'genius', and as one of their own, were irretrievably soured by this incident.[58]

PART III

Ardent Spirit

'Gertler was so gay, so passionate of life and living . . .
Such an ardent spirit'

Brett to Noel Carrington, 21 November 1965

7

The Importance of Being Earnest

'How *earnest* I am.'
Mark Gertler to Carrington, *c.* April 1912

GERTLER WAS IN ebullient form and the row with Wertheimer forgotten when, in February 1912, he was celebrated as a 'Triumph of Education Aid' in a full-page interview in the *Jewish Chronicle*. An accompanying 'swagger'-style photograph shows the eager young artist, page-boy curls slicked back, the jacket casually open in a display of ease and confidence. 'Artistic London', the *Chronicle* declared, had been 'electrified' by his recent achievements.[1]

Gertler's remarks were no less bold than his photograph. He declared his allegiance to the old masters, citing the greatness of Piero della Francesca's *Nativity* ('assuredly one of the finest pictures in the world'), of Giovanni Bellini's *Circumcision* (particularly for 'the music and rhythm of [its] colour') and of the work of Botticelli in general.[2] He doubted whether the old masters could ever be bettered. Their work, he maintained, had an integrity and sincerity that modern painting (with the exception of Augustus John's) lacked. Regarding Jewish painters, he did not think 'we have yet distinguished ourselves as much as we could do'.[3]

By February Gertler had already put his faith in the old masters to the test. His old friend T. E. Harvey, the former warden of Toynbee Hall and now MP for Leeds West,[4] wished to celebrate his recent marriage with a pair of commemorative portraits of his wife, Alice, and himself, and he had chosen Gertler to undertake the commission.[5] On this first visit it is likely that Gertler only finished Alice Harvey's portrait, the finer of the pair. (The looser style of Harvey's portrait indicates it was completed much later.[6]) Dressed in Quaker shawl and bonnet, against a landscape inspired by the early work of Bellini and Giorgione, Alice's clear profile is outlined with a fine, dark line which shows the lingering quattrocento influence. The portrait remains Gertler's best example of the Italianate style briefly adopted by the Slade quintet, known among its followers as Neo-Primitivism.

The origins of this style can be traced back to the quintet's first trip to Paris in Easter 1910, and their mutual enthusiasm for the Primitive room at the Louvre. By the time fellow student John Currie depicted them all in a portrait of 1912, they had become *Some Later Primitives*.[7] The Neo-Primitives derived their creed very much from Slade teaching, sharing a sincerity of purpose with the Pre-Raphaelites and of technique with the early Italians, both schools greatly admired by Tonks,[8] who is said to have told his students that to study a Michelangelo drawing should be an almost 'unbearable experience'.

'Neo-Primitive' was an imprecise label. The term 'primitive' had been commonly used since the mid-nineteenth century to describe pre-Renaissance European masters such as Cimabue and Giotto in Italy and the early Netherlandish painters. By the end of the nineteenth century, however, the label was more generally applied to the art associated with those cultures believed to be less 'advanced' than the European. Post-Impressionism contributed to this myth with Gauguin's 'primitive' pictures of Tahiti and, later, the influence of African carvings in the work of Picasso and Braque. (Indeed, in less than a year Gertler would also be reapplying the word 'primitive' in this later context to his own work.) Contemporary critics such as Sir Claude Phillips of the *Daily Telegraph* had no difficulty in identifying the Neo-Primitive style by its 'Florentine element' (also discernible in the work of fellow students Stanley Spencer and David Bomberg),[9] and when at the close of 1912 Gertler painted a portrait of a fellow student in tempera, it was immediately interpreted as 'a close study of the early Florentines'.[10]

The Neo-Primitives enjoyed only the briefest period of harmony, but each member produced at least one painting that reflects this 'later Primitive' influence before abandoning the style. Thus Gertler's *Portrait of Alice Harvey*, should be seen alongside Nevinson's *Self-Portrait* (1911), Wadsworth's *Self-Portrait Wearing a Turban* (1911), Allinson's *Portrait of Ruth* (*c.* 1911) and John Currie's group portrait *Some Later Primitives* (1912), which was carried out in the old masters' favoured medium of tempera. Yet even as Currie captured them for posterity, the group was beginning to disband, and by 1912 the label 'Neo-

Primitive' could strictly be applied only to the work of Gertler and Currie, who continued to paint together until events at the end of the year signalled a sea change in the direction of Gertler's art.

In May 1912 he travelled up to Cambridge to complete another commissioned portrait, this time of the warm and generous George Howard Darwin, son of the great naturalist Charles Darwin and Plumian professor and fellow of Trinity College.[11] Begun a few months before Darwin became seriously ill, and completed in May, the oil depicts a patrician figure, gowned and bearded, in a half-length formal portrait, reminiscent of the earlier commission of the vicar of St Anne's, Soho.[12] Darwin had been particularly struck by Gertler's striking portrait of Harry (1911), which lingered in his memory, he wrote, as 'the best of all'. Gertler obligingly painted him in similar pose, but the portrait lacks the 'swagger' of Harry's sensual good looks and, particularly in the fine modelling of the hands, is closer in style to the *Portrait of the Artist's Mother*. A certain stiffness in Darwin's pose also suggests Gertler's continuing difficulty with commissioned work.

Moreover, despite Darwin's friendly manner, the visit to Cambridge only emphasized Gertler's alienation. Nevinson was delighted when Gertler described dining among the Cambridge dons and being offered asparagus for the first time: 'Accustomed to spring onion, he started at the white end first, and the beautifully mannered don followed suit in order not to embarrass him.'[13] Gertler's sense of not belonging, of encountering another new world to which he did not know the rules, was made more acute as his train sped home past the 'slums' of Hackney and Bethnal Green. Reminded of his early life, he believed that the poverty, although striking, 'had a beautiful simplicity which was to be envied'.[14] He recognized that this simplicity was already slipping from his grasp.

The previous month Gertler had left his parents' home in Spital Square and moved round the corner to 32 Elder Street to share a Georgian terraced house with his brother Harry and his wife, Annie, who was expecting her first child.[15] The house was cramped and narrow. Harry and Annie had the two lower floors, but part of the ground floor and basement were probably shared with another family.[16] There was no bathroom or toilet, and a single sink in the basement served for both kitchen and bathroom. A wooden staircase wound up through the hall to the top floor, and here Gertler had a bedroom at the back and an attic studio at the front, each not more than five yards square, and hedged in outside by the neighbouring brick walls and chimneys.[17] Nevertheless, in winter, Gertler found, the light had a luminous quality, which filtered through his bedroom window to reveal skies of an 'indescribable grey' flecked with rose, and he spent more than one afternoon dangling his legs from the narrow sill and admiring the beautifully faded colours of the washing that hung in the yards below.[18] After the birth of baby Irene (known as Renée) in September, however, the peace was shattered by her continual 'howling', and Gertler often returned to Spital Square for his meals (and weekly bath), often staying on to paint in Golda's kitchen, where her silent presence at least seemed to restore him to the simplicity of his earlier life.

One day in April 1912 Nevinson surprised Gertler by bringing a visitor to his new studio.[19] A second-year student known simply as 'Carrington', she was already 'a conspicuous and popular figure at the Slade', admired for being 'both clever and good-looking to an unusual degree'.[20] Nevinson (though Gertler seems initially not to have realized it) was already smitten with her, and this was not the first time Gertler had noticed Carrington himself. Several months earlier she had hurried past him on a staircase on her way to a class, but after a frank physical appraisal of her long pigtail and turned-in toes, Gertler had turned away. 'No good I thought', he later told her honestly.[21] And yet, even at that first meeting, something about her had made him look back.

After his death Gertler's friend the poet Sylvia Lynd wrote that at one early meeting Carrington had by chance quoted a 'phrase of great literature', which gave Gertler, 'in a single moment, a passion both for her and for a wholly different kind of life'.[22] In 1912 the East End remained out of bounds to most of the middle classes (Nevinson excepted) but Carrington, who had spent the past two years at the Slade throwing off her middle-class shackles, was not to be intimidated; and at the Slade she was already the ringleader of a quintet of her own, a 'spirited group of women' known as the 'Wild Group'.[23]

Carrington was born in Bedford in 1893 and christened Dora, a name she always considered 'vulgar' and 'sentimental'. She was the fourth child of Samuel Carrington, a retired civil engineer from the Anglo-Indian Railway, and his wife, Charlotte, an ex-governess with formidable standards of conventional behaviour. Dora was diffident, yet rebellious; only her talent for drawing sustained her through a miserable childhood, and while she idolized her unconventional father for his 'independence and wildness', she detested her mother for having 'tamed' him. When she gained a place at the Slade in 1910, she saw a chance to escape the 'life of "convention . . . and . . . taboos" in which [she] had been raised', and set out to shed her early life like a butterfly sloughing off its chrysalis.[24]

First, she set herself a challenging course of reading, ranging from Tolstoy to Mary Wollstonecraft, books that even her well-educated brothers found daunting. It was the beginning, her brother Noel noted, 'of her long odyssey in self-education'.[25] Her old compositions 'once . . . shown around with pride, were now torn up or hidden',[26] and she bribed her father and siblings to sit patiently until she had perfected her draughtsmanship to Slade standards. In London she abandoned traditional Edwardian dress in favour of the loose, wide skirts (and later breeches) popularized by Augustus John, and cut her hair into a distinctive page-boy bob that would earn her the nicknames 'crophead' from Virginia Woolf and 'herla' (literally, 'hairless one') from Golda. Finally, in keeping with the Slade tradition, she dropped the 'middle-class' name of Dora, and for the rest of her life was known simply as 'Carrington'.

Gertler was entranced by this transformation. In place of the heavy plait, Carrington's boyish cropped hair only enhanced her feminine appeal. Beneath a heavy fringe, the colour of 'weathered straw', her china-blue eyes peeped out from a complexion as delicate as 'a white heart cherry'. Even her 'curious crooked nose', the result of a childhood accident, only added 'character' to her face, which, Gertler later told Augustus John, was like 'a beautiful flower encased in a form of gold'. She spoke in a breathy, gasping voice, which, at first, he found irritating, even insincere, but which later made it seem as though he was the special confidant of her many secrets and gave her an intriguing, inscrutable air, as if she had 'just come on one in the thick of a great mystery'.[27] Uncertain how best to approach her, he decided to send her an invitation to tea.

To Gertler's astonishment, Carrington was furious at receiving an envelope marked 'Miss D. Carrington, artist'. It was not the despised initial 'D' that had offended her, but the label 'artist' which, in her insecurity, she had thought he meant 'cynically'. Gertler hastened to explain that not knowing her Christian name 'and thinking that you might have dozens of sisters, I was afraid that my "passionate" love letter might fall into their hands – !!!'[28] In fact, this 'love letter' contained nothing more amorous than the invitation to tea, but was not typical of a correspondence in which he admitted early on, 'I could easily worship you'.[29] Only weeks after they first met he wrote that she had become 'the *only* thing outside painting worth living for'.[30] As the writer Gerald Brenan, whose later love affair with Carrington paralleled Gertler's own, tried to explain, 'Once she got under your skin, you couldn't get her out'.[31]

Despite his view that 'words cannot express love, just as words cannot express painting', Gertler's letters are full of his thoughts on both.[32] They were for him perfectly combined in Carrington's 'beautiful little person. I don't know anyone to equal you', he wrote.[33] Such passion poured from his pen that even Gertler was taken aback. 'I have never written such a letter before', he confessed, requesting her to 'tear this up at once'.[34] If Carrington failed to reply promptly he would demand, 'How is it that you have not yet answered my last letter? . . . Nothing unbalances me more than not hearing from you.'[35] On holiday in Ostend in July he implored her to 'write to me here as soon you can',[36] though he was only to be gone for a week. Frequently underlined, erratically punctuated, the words tumbling over each other in his eagerness to set them down, these early letters show how urgently Gertler wanted to communicate with her.

A prodigious letter-writer herself, Carrington best revealed in her letters the eclectic nature that so delighted her friends. 'You are like a tin of mixed biscuits,' wrote her friend Iris Tree, 'your parents were Huntley and Palmer.'[37] Intuitively, she would address herself to the exact tone of her correspondent, so that her letters could be 'alternatively cajoling, flirtatious, tender, gossipy, encouraging, affectionate, digressive, and focused'.[38] They were, Gerald Brenan famously wrote, 'like the rustling of leaves, the voices of birds, the arrangement of natural forms'.[39] They reduced Nevinson to 'an exotic condition',[40] but Gertler they inflamed. 'Yes!' he confessed to Nevinson, 'I have become the most sentimental hero in the most sentimental drama on the "Halls". I who was so cynical and caricatured those heroes. A music-hall sketch makes me – now – weep, I weep over its truth and realism' (and he even admitted to devouring 'little love scenes in penny novelettes').[41] Nevertheless, Carrington's early letters have not survived and for the first three years of their relationship only Gertler's side of their correspondence remains.

From this it is clear that Gertler did not know how to behave with Carrington. Though Nevinson claimed in his autobiography that Gertler was always 'fond of the girls and adored by them' – one of several remarks by contemporaries that suggest Gertler had something of a womanizing reputation – he almost certainly did not mean middle-class girls. Some time before this Harry and Jack had organized Gertler's sexual initiation with a prostitute, an episode that had horrified him, and in *Mendel* there are several encounters with shop girls and artists' models. Torn between sexual and 'spiritual' feelings for Carrington, Gertler was also confused by his previous experience of women (like his mother) as traditional homemakers and the independent, artistic, spirited young women he met at the Slade.

In June 1912 he tried to seize the initiative with a bold proposal of marriage. In his emphatic and absolute world there must be love or there must be a parting; there could be no room for compromise. 'Dear Carrington', he wrote, 'I have thought of ourselves, and I've come to the conclusion that I love you far too much for us to be merely friends. Therefore, unless you would agree to marry me, or in some other way be more than friends, I am afraid we must part for always.' And he set down a 'list of the advantages you would have by marrying me':

1. I am a very promising artist – one who is likely to make alot [*sic*] of money.
2. I am an intelligent companion.
3. You would not have to rely on your people.
4. I could help you in your art career.
5. You would have absolute freedom and a nice studio of your own.

How these generous proposals were to be funded was less clear. None the less, Gertler acknowledged, even as he wrote, that 'I know of course you would not agree to this'.[42]

Carrington did not agree. During her first two years at the Slade she had won the Melville Nettleship prize for figure composition and a second prize for figure painting, and in 1912 she was awarded the Slade scholarship (with William Roberts).[43] Her freedom from her family had been hard-won, and in loving Gertler Carrington would always perceive 'an innate menace' to that freedom,[44] particularly since she viewed marriage as 'a dependency that she would not submit to'.[45] Her mother, she later claimed, had tamed her fathers by putting him in a cage until he was now 'too old to chirp or sing', and she was determined not to be tamed herself. 'Yes,' she later acknowledged to Gertler, 'it is my work that comes between us . . . I at least, could not work if I saw you every day.'[46]

Paradoxically, Gertler could no longer work without her. Ever since he had got to know her, he confessed, he had thought of her 'in every stroke I did',[47] and although he was forced to retract his proposal, he now found he badly wanted her to see everything he painted: 'I keep wondering what you will think of my work,' he told her. 'I can't bear the idea of developing without you and I am developing so quickly.' So she agreed to be his 'friend' again and having, as her brother Noel noted, 'something like a genius for friendship', became his inspiration, even when they were apart for three months over the summer holidays.[48] 'Oh! I shall paint such good things before I'm done – you['ll] see', Gertler told her. 'I'm going to live such a simple life while you're away . . . [but] you mustn't expect good Pictures from me yet. It will take many years.'

'To touch her hand is bliss!' Gertler told Nevinson, 'to kiss it Heaven itself,[49] but when he learned that Nevinson had actually kissed Carrington, he was beside himself with jealousy and in July wrote to break off the friendship with his former best friend, 'my sole reason being', he explained, 'that I am in love with Carrington and I have reason to believe that you are so too. Therefore, much as I have tried to overlook it, I have come to the conclusion that rivals, and rivals in love, cannot be friends.' The friendship was off and on throughout August, but seems finally to have been over by September, leaving Nevinson naturally distressed. 'All this worry has again succeeded in enlarging my liver', he wrote to Carrington, but he assured her that she could rely on him 'always nipping my affection in the bud and mak[ing] it run nicely and pleasantly in a small and babbling brook; a Japanese tree form of affection, stunted but beautiful and nice to have about the house and no danger of ever growing'.[50] But he felt the loss of Gertler, he admitted, 'more intensely than I thought possible', particularly, as he saw himself rapidly supplanted by Gertler's growing friendship with fellow painter John Currie.

'Square, dark-haired, handsome in a Southern way', Currie was a strikingly charismatic figure, whose intensity matched, perhaps even outshone, Gertler's own.[51] Michael Sadler, calling on him at home, found Currie 'blazing with genius. All his nature . . . aflame'.[52] His manners and speech were somewhat rough, and he could be 'vigorous, outspoken and robust',[53] yet to his admirers he exuded a curious mixture of confidence and humility, and was 'simple and absorbed in his work – conscious of genius without being conceited, [and] full of himself but not egoistic . . . [his] fierce artistic integrity sweetened and made appealing by a natural and unaffected timidity'.[54] Nevertheless, Currie's presence in the quintet had been forceful enough to jostle out the gentle, acquiescent David Sassoon (who is absent from Currie's painting) and eventually drove the final wedge between Gertler and Nevinson.

Currie was some ten years Gertler's senior, and by the time he enrolled for classes at the Slade in the summer of 1910, he had already attended the Hanley School of Art, worked as a ceramic decorator under Camille Solon at Minton's potteries, and been employed as an art inspector in Dublin and as an art master for the Greater London Council. He had been born and bred in Staffordshire, but liked to talk up his Irish ancestry, drinking 'raw Irish whisky, reciting Yeats and Synge, and boasting of his future conquests'.[55] His new friends accepted this romanticized version of his roots, and Allinson called him 'an emotional Irishman, of peasant origin'.[56] But Currie also applied his liking for romance to his complex emotional life, with disastrous results. In 1907 he had married Jessie Brandon, a fellow student at Newcastle under Lyme School of Art, with whom, a year later, he had a son named Mark. Two years later, passing a dress shop in Regent Street, Currie spotted a red-haired model called Dolly Henry and asked her to come and sit for him. They soon became entangled in a stormy affair, and when his wife confronted them in 1911, Currie left her to join Dolly. By 1912 they were living openly together in a flat in St George's Square (now Chalcot Gardens, Primrose Hill), and later moved to a small house in Hampstead, where Gertler often visited them.

By July 1912 Gertler was writing to Carrington that Currie was his 'greatest friend' and had replaced Nevinson in his affections. He responded instinctively to Currie's emotionalism and spontaneity, probably finding his unpolished manners something of a relief after the baffling codes of middle-class behaviour Gertler had struggled to absorb during his time at the Slade. United by their ambition and the struggle to escape their early environments, Gertler and Currie made a good partnership, but with Dolly's constant presence they formed an uneasy threesome. This was the first in a long line of relationships that Gertler established with couples, in each of which he was strongly dependent on the man and the woman wholly devolved to a position in the background, though later in life this was sometimes reversed, usually when the woman proved particularly maternal.

This arrangement emphatically did not suit Dolly, who demanded pre-eminence in Currie's life. Gertler always disliked Dolly, whom he considered greedy and unintelligent, and his portrait of her, probably painted in the Hampstead flat and tellingly entitled *Vanity*, portrays her as a broad, plain woman. Currie himself made numerous sketches and paintings of Dolly's sly, sensual beauty, and his 1913 portrait of her as *The Witch*, perhaps best captures his turbulent feelings about her dangerous allure.[57]

That July the threesome spent a week at Ostend in order to have 'a complete rest from work'. They swam every day and were photographed in beach attire, the men larking about in loose striped bathing suits while Dolly, sleek as a seal, posed seductively in a dark costume. This was Gertler's first non-working holiday and he found it an uncomfortable experience. Time hung 'heavily and wearily' upon him, and he had no sense of purpose. At times, he wrote to Carrington, his hand literally 'itche[d] for the brush'. In the evenings they hung about the French cafés listening to the beautiful music, but the cafés reminded Gertler of Soho, and the music made him long for Carrington, without whom, he declared dramatically, 'the sun has no rays for me, the flowers no scent, all beauty flies from me and all is blackness!'[58]

Nevertheless, while the Slade remained closed for the holidays, he and Carrington were separated, though he wrote almost daily. Since she had forbidden him to write again of his love, Gertler addressed Carrington in her new capacity as a 'most intimate friend' (a term always to be treated with scepticism in Gertler's correspondence with women). She became the sounding-board for many of his ideas, and his letters, full of his enthusiasms and despondencies, closely document the progress of his work, which was often at its most inspired during the periods of his most intense love for her.

Later in July Gertler reported several 'successes' to Carrington: he had sold one of his early pictures for £35[59]; the 'Society of Portrait Painters' had asked him to put his name down for election[60]; and Professor Brown had approached him regarding his election to the NEAC. 'I am so happy!' he wrote. 'It is such things that make me think for a moment that my ambition to become a true artist may yet be realized.' And he arranged to meet Carrington the following Friday to celebrate with 'a good dinner on the strength of it'.[61] But such meetings were rare that summer, and Gertler spent many hours in the London museums and galleries, spotting his letters with enthusiastic exclamation marks. At the thought of the National Gallery 'with all its joys[:]

Michelangelo!!! Botticelli!!! Francesca!!! . . .' he wrote, 'my mouth opens itself and smiles . . . a joyous smile!'[62] And when the sculptor Jacob Epstein showed him the Egyptian art in the British Museum his inspiration 'knew no bounds'. He concluded that ancient art was 'by far, by far, by far the greatest of all art . . . We moderns are but ants in comparison.'[63] And when he thought of this his ambition 'double[d] and redouble[d]! Oh! Carrington,' he wrote, 'if I am given many years in this world, I think! I think! I shall do great things!'[64]

In July Gertler finished an oil called *The Violinist*.[65] Its tiny size and his concentration on head-and-shoulders against a plain background, suggest that he was now focusing on the jewel-like quality of Italian Renaissance portraits, and this naturally led him on to the use of tempera, that 'finest of mediums' as he called it. Over the previous five years there had been a growing interest in the revival of tempera, and even Augustus John had admitted (as early as 1908) to being 'fired with a desire to revive that art'. In August 1912 John himself passed on to Gertler 'some very useful tips on tempera',[66] along with his own recipe.[67]

By September Gertler felt ready to begin painting in tempera himself. It was a technique that severely limited his output, since he had first to complete a picture in oil and work through any difficulties before copying it into tempera, which did not allow for alterations. In the meantime he began a large composition in oil called *The Coster Family*, but ideas for new pictures were constantly bubbling to the surface, and by early September he had four paintings on hand, including the *Coster Mother and Child* (known only from a thumbnail sketch in a letter to Carrington of 2 September), which he decided to execute in tempera. He kept reproductions of frescoes by Fra Angelico (whose dedication to religion and art he also admired) on his desk to inspire him, and planned two further tempera pictures, a small study known as *Hagar*, and an *Adam and Eve*. He became so absorbed in his work that he saw nobody at all, he told Carrington, not even Currie.

Carrington seems to have shared his enthusiasm. In the winter term of 1912 Mary Sargant-Florence, a founder member of the Society of Painters in Tempera, gave demonstrations and lectures at the Slade, which contributed to the general interest in tempera revival.[68] By the following summer Carrington and a fellow Slade painter were executing frescoes on the library wall of Brownlow Hall in the Chilterns. Gertler's own interest in tempera continued well into the spring of

1913, when he even bought a special tempera palette for authenticity, but by the autumn he was already beginning to express dissatisfaction with his efforts, and most of the tempera compositions appear to have been abandoned or lost. (A portrait of Carrington begun in tempera in November was completed in gouache.[69]) 'To speak the truth, everything I have done so far is nothing, nothing', he wrote to Carrington. 'Unless I do something far, far greater soon I shall be very miserable and unhappy.' His own standards were impossibly high, and he admitted to abandoning most of his ideas – 'So critical am I'.

These letters indicate the onset of the depression which alternated with the periods of 'excessive sociability' for which Gertler became well known in the years before the First World War. During these he lived in a heightened state, forever pushing himself forward to greater accomplishments and dissatisfied with all his former achievements. He spent sleepless nights pouring out his heart in letters to Carrington, writing by the light of a candle which, he wrote, wavered like 'an excited heart', but also like 'a dying man'.[70] It was a typical image of duality.

Gertler's dissatisfaction with his own work was coupled with his increasing awareness of the fomenting activity on the contemporary art scene. At first this struck him as bewildering: 'I went out and saw more unfortunate artists', he wrote to Carrington in September. 'I looked at them talking art, Ancient art, Modern art, Impressionism, Post-Impressionism, Neo-Impressionism, Cubists, Spottists, Futurists, Cave-dwelling, Wyndham Lewis, Duncan Grant, Etchells, Roger Fry!' It was like entering the tower of Babel, and he walked home 'disgusted with them all' and glad to find Golda waiting up for him 'with a nice roll, that she knows I like, and a cup of hot coffee. Dear mother, the same mother of all my life, twenty years. You, dear mother, I thought are the only modern artist.'[71] All this would change in October, when Roger Fry's second Post-Impressionist exhibition opened at the Grafton.

Before choosing the pictures for this second show, Fry had written to his mother that he was afraid the British public had 'dozed off' since the last exhibition and were now in need of 'another electric shock'.[72] This time Fry's reputation went before him, and some 50,000 people visited the show, which ran from October to December 1912. It was then rehung and extended until the end of January 1913. In the first show Fry had introduced the 'old masters' of Post-Impressionism. This time he intended to show the contemporary development, 'not only in France, its native ground, but also in England, where it was still of very recent growth, and in Russia where, he believed, Post-Impressionism had liberated and revived an old native tradition'.[73] The English section included the work of Bloomsbury artists and Stanley Spencer, but for both press and public alike the second show was dominated by the work of Matisse and Picasso, and the effect on Gertler was overwhelming. Some twenty years later he recalled 'the entry of Cézanne, Gauguin, Matisse, etc., upon my horizon as equivalent to the impact of the scientists of this age upon a simple student of Sir Isaac Newton'.[74]

The impact is immediately discernible in his work. Its first effect was to release a strong surge of colour into his formerly low-toned palette, and *Vanity*, the study of Dolly Henry and her cousin Mary, uses a range that extends from emerald green and turquoise blue through to deep purple and flaming orange. The modelling of the figures may have been influenced by Gauguin, but the movement towards a simplification of form marks a shift away from the earlier Neo-Primitive studies and towards the daringly simplified Jewish portraits he would produce the following year.

The portrait of Carrington which Gertler began in November and completed by December marks this transition. However, the portrait itself remains something of an unhappy compromise. Gertler appears to have been aiming for the clear, flat modelling of Bellini's *Doge of Venice*, but it captures neither Carrington's animation and vivacity nor a genuine likeness. Gertler did not find her an easy sitter. 'You shouldn't jump about so much when I'm struggling with tempera',[75] he told her, and the picture lacks the quality of psychological depth he had brought to the pictures of Golda and his family. (In fact it remains so untypical of Gertler's work, that when his widow was shown the picture many years later, she refused to believe it was by him.)

Under the title *Portrait of a Girl in a Blue Jersey*, the portrait of Carrington was among the works shown by Gertler in a joint exhibition with Currie at the Chenil Gallery in December 1912. The Chenil, a converted house in Chelsea, had been opened in 1906 by John (Jack) Knewstub, brother-in-law to both William Orpen (who provided the financial backing) and William Rothenstein, each painter having married one of Knewstub's two beautiful sisters. Knewstub himself has been described as an 'artist *manqué*',[76] and he proved equally incompetent as secretary of the Chelsea Arts School and as manager of the Chenil, particularly when he muddled the two accounts. His ineptitude could be so exasperating that in 1913 Orpen tried to shoot him (he missed Knewstub and hit one of his own pictures instead), but Knewstub had a flair both for spotting talent and for advertising it.

Most of the gallery was given over to Augustus John (which guaranteed press exposure), and Gertler and Currie's Neo-Primitive studies filled the neighbouring room. The catalogue for this exhibition has not survived, so there is no record of exactly what Gertler showed, but the JEAS minutes reveal that he sold at least two paintings for a total of £110, and contemporary press reports mention the portrait of Carrington, *The Violinist* and the *Coster Woman and Child*.[77] *The Star* called Gertler and Currie 'the men of the future', and Gertler's drawings, he told Carrington, went 'like hot buns'. He sold seven in the first few days, including one to the sculptor Eric Gill. Gertler remained involved with the Chenil for the next two years, but it was Currie who was seen as the leader and to whom, six months later, Knewstub offered a solo show.

8

In the Clothes of a Gentleman

'With this outfit I can look aristocracy in the face.'
Mark Gertler to Carrington, *c.* 1912

DESPITE HIS SUCCESS, Gertler continued to experience acute feelings of isolation, as he tried to explain in a particularly poignant letter to Carrington:

> Yes, my isolation is extraordinary. I am alone, alone in the whole of this world! Yes, if only like my brothers I was an ordinary workman, as I should have been. But no! I must desire, desire. How I pay for those desires! Oh! God! Do I deserve to be so tormented? By my own ambitions I am cut off from my own family and class and by them I have been raised to be equal to a class I hate! They do not understand me, nor I them. So I am an outcast. As I look at my desk I laugh, for there are dozens of notices of me in the daily papers, a lot of them praising my talents. Oh! yes I am quite well known, and yet alone.[1]

The following year this tension produced his most articulate portrayal of the Jewish community at the very moment that he began to distance himself from it. This series of portraits not only made his name as a painter but also brought him into the orbit of his most radical contemporaries, though he continued to feel a marked ambivalence towards the society into which his fame and talent launched him. The tension was further heightened by the continuing difficulties of his relationship with Carrington.

Towards the close of December 1912 Gertler and Carrington began to plan a joint trip to Paris, code-named 'P' in their letters, and Gertler sent Carrington the 10*s.* fare expressly for her to come to London to discuss it. Instead she began to put forward excuses for postponing the trip. First, she pleaded that her family would miss her; then, when Gertler urged her to be more independent, she began to move the departure date imperceptibly forward, until at last he impatiently demanded, 'I thought we were to start on the 2nd. Why are you making it so late?' Finally she was forced to admit that she had no intention of going at all. Her biographer suggests that while she enjoyed dreaming about and planning the trip with Gertler, she realized that going alone with him to Paris would have made a sexual relationship between them, for which she was not at all ready, 'almost inevitable'.[2] Instead, by way of compensation, she sent Gertler a handmade shirt which was good enough to earn Golda's praise and which he wore proudly, although the sleeves proved a little short. This pattern of promises, prevarication and propitiation would become a familiar feature of their relationship over the next five years.

Carrington's refusal to confront difficult situations head-on harked back to her complex relationship with her mother, whose discipline she constantly evaded by a system of complicated alibis and little white lies that became second nature. Eventually she was forced to admit that she could not tell the truth even if she wanted to. If Gertler became too possessive or demanding she would simply fail to turn up for meetings, cancel them or arrive so late he had already given her up. 'She is a very peculiar person and terribly difficult to manage', he wrote in bewilderment to Carrington's friend Brett.[3] 'It is a terrible thing to be so hopelessly in love'.[4] But when they were together Carrington and Gertler made an impressive couple. The artist Nina Hamnett asked them both to tea and felt 'rather as if I had invited a god and goddess'. Carrington appeared in one red shoe and one blue and they all discussed 'art and the future'. Afterwards Nina preserved Gertler's teacup 'intact and unwashed on the mantelpiece', where it remained 'for about a month'; she felt that it 'ought to be given to a museum'.[5]

Gertler continued to see much of the flamboyant Currie. The novelist Arnold Bennett had discovered Currie in the Potteries and helped him, and now in London Currie had been taken up by the collector Sydney Schiff, a rich connoisseur and patron of the arts, better known as the writer and translator Stephen Hudson.[6] In *Mendel* the character of Mr Tilney Tysoe – 'a fool of a patron' and an 'idealist' who delights in the Bohemianism of his young artist friends – is probably based on Schiff. Schiff bought several of Gertler's pictures over the years, but he seems to have been more interested in, and genuinely fond of,

Currie, who encouraged Gertler to act up to Schiff's expectations of Bohemian behaviour. Gertler, as he explained in a letter (March 1913) to Carrington, was only too happy to oblige:

> Saturday night Currie, Henry and myself went up to Schiff's for dinner. There were a lot of people there, also a very graceful girl, who made me dance a ballet with her. I took the part of Nijinsky. I had on a jersey and a belt. We did it so well that everybody applauded very much. They told me I looked very nice! Then we did a music hall sketch, and they roared with laughter, including the girl with whom I was acting. They thought I was very clever.[7]

At Easter, Currie, who was intending to go to Ireland, became ill with rheumatism and at the last minute could not go. Instead, he and Gertler spent many quiet, peaceful evenings comfortably closeted in his Hampstead rooms, while Dolly (in a rare mood of domestic tranquillity) prepared supper. It was probably during this period that the two men completed their widely differing portraits of one another. In Currie's portrait of Gertler we see the hungry young artist: lean, ambitious, a broad-rimmed black hat rammed over the Renaissance curls and something decidedly ruthless in the pursed and determined lips. Gertler's pencil portrait of Currie, however, is a surprisingly gentle portrayal of such a charismatic and ultimately violent character. The overall effect is almost feminine (and was for long mistakenly catalogued as a *Head of a Girl*).

Although Gertler now regarded Currie as his closest male friend, he was also beginning to sense that his 'burning eyes' could blaze with instability as well as genius, and periodically he began to try and break free. Currie's passionate relationship with Dolly teetered on the edge of violence, and sometimes made Gertler nervous and exhausted. (Nevinson later diagnosed a 'Napoleonic complex', considering Currie 'non-moral because of an over-reading of Nietzsche'.[8]) There was 'much of the playboy' about Currie,[9] but he had met his match in Dolly, whose 'flower-like loveliness masked a nature' apparently 'lascivious and possessive to the last degree', yet aroused in him such a 'fiery, consuming love' that it eventually destroyed them both.[10]

When Currie did get to Ireland later in 1913, Gertler had an opportunity to gain some distance from the close circle of their friendship, and even affect boredom with it all. 'Currie and Henry sometimes amuse me terribly', he told Carrington's friend Brett, but 'sometimes I feel I want to break that tie between us. Friendships are terribly difficult to manage and I don't think they are worth the trouble.'[11] Gertler's aims were beginning to diverge from Currie's, and he even told Brett that Currie's work was 'not very great' (though since neither Brett nor Carrington liked Currie, Gertler may have been trying to please them). He concluded that he preferred to 'stand alone. I need no great friend at all. Ties', he declared, 'are a terrible nuisance and hindrance to an artist.'[12] But this was not entirely convincing, since Gertler always had at least one significant male friendship in his life.

In the spring of 1913 Gertler alternated between periods of 'excessive sociability' and almost reclusive isolation, sometimes sealing himself up in his studio for days on end, absorbed in his work. From March to May he was preoccupied with a picture of two local Jewish figures, an elderly man and a young girl called Dora Plaskowsky, whose father had been a schoolfriend and was now the family butcher.[13] Dora remembered how Gertler had singled her out in her father's shop for her 'unusual colouring', and over the next year she went to his Elder Street studio 'two or three times a week after school to sit until the light went', receiving *2s. 6d.* for each sitting. Over this period Gertler executed several pencil drawings of her, both head-and-shoulders and three-quarter face, but she did not recall him ever using paints.

For several months Gertler worked simultaneously on separate studies of Dora and the elderly local man (an exquisite pencil study of the latter was later exhibited under the title *The Old Jew*). Suddenly, however, he wrote to Carrington, he conceived the idea of combining the two pictures. The idea of contrast had worked well in two double portraits of his parents, and now he decided on a scheme of 'just two heads together: his very old, pale and wrinkled head near that healthy, fresh, young face of my little girl. The old man will be with one hand most delicately touching the girl's face, the other will be round her shoulder.' He was 'terribly inspired with the idea' and felt sure it would be 'one of the best things I've done'.[14]

Dora, who was only eight at the time of her sittings, was not sure what to make of this strange young man. His clothes were unexceptional but his hair, still cut in a page-boy bob with a straight fringe over his forehead, was very unusual, and his deep set eyes were 'rather intense and frightening'. Sitting alone on her chair, on the raised platform at one end of the attic studio, she looked over the bare boards in the direction of his easel, but Gertler, who seemed very stern, 'never spoke to her except to give directions', and finally she grew tired of the sittings and abandoned them before the painting was finished.[15] Only once, when Gertler was not in the room, did she dare to take a peep at the painting, which at that time extended below the rabbi's knees, on which she was astonished to see herself sitting. She ran home to ask her mother how Gertler could possibly have painted the picture when she had 'never seen or met the old man'.[16]

It was probably at this juncture that Gertler temporarily abandoned the picture for a brief holiday in Brighton. From there he wrote to Carrington of the 'ravishing' sight of beautiful girls, and a brief flirtation with just such a girl who allowed him to kiss her. 'To my mind, those that justify their existence most are the beautiful girls and the great artists. A man should be a great artist, and a woman beautiful. I see nothing in between.' No doubt this annoyed Carrington, who would have preferred to be judged a great artist, but Gertler explained that to him they were 'really both the same. The artist creates beauty and the beautiful girl is beauty . . . Yes, beauty rules my whole life. I paint because I want to create beauty, I love you, because you are beautiful and so on.'[17] Even as he wrote, the contrast between the beauty of youth and the decay of old age was constantly before him, in the form of the many invalids who were promenaded along the seafront – 'horrible old emaciated women who sit upright in chariots, drawn by degraded and shabby men'. He longed to kick both them and their chariots into the sea.[18] None the less, this gave him the impetus to rework his picture of the rabbi and the young girl, and on his return in April he took it up with new energy, working so hard he was unable to concentrate on anything else.

First, he added a third head (in profile) but, finding the effect 'too ordinary', he replaced it with a full-face and then painted it out altogether. At times the picture went badly and he grew disgusted with his 'horrible incompetence'. 'Sometimes', he wrote to Carrington, 'it is really difficult to go living.'[19] Yet he recognized that he was 'still young and full of energy', and would wake up the following morning 'with renewed vigour and go for it like a warrior!' When at last he completed the picture in May, the final version was much nearer to his original vision: the girl, blooming with the vitality of untroubled youth, is set against the ashen weariness of old age, the two figures simultaneously linked and separated by the long, bony fingers of the rabbi's extended palm. In the simplification and exaggeration of the rabbi's features Gertler's work was moving in a new direction.

Both *The Rabbi and His Grandchild* and *The Old Jew* were among

Gertler's pictures at the NEAC's summer exhibition, and prompted a letter from a rich Jewish woman, who wrote that she thought there must be something wrong with his eyes 'and that I would do her a great favour if I would – at her expense – see an oculist!' he told Brett. This incident settled Gertler's 'dealings with the upper-class Jew' for good, and forced him to realize that his previous patrons found the new work, with its element of exaggeration, frankly unacceptable.

Already Gertler was desperately short of money, and in April, when Carrington wanted a copy of Voltaire's *Candide*, he stole the copy from his dentist's waiting room. By July 1913 he could no longer afford evenings out or models, and was thrown back upon the charity of his family. 'It is very uncomfortable to have to worry . . . over every penny one spends', he admitted, but he realized that as his work became 'more and more personal', it would become 'less and less understood'. Even 'the most cultured buyer', he told Brett, 'almost unconsciously looks for a bit of prettiness', but his recent pictures had been likened by the press to caricatures. 'My types, they say, are ugly.' Brett responded generously by purchasing two of his NEAC drawings for £5, and this cemented the deepening friendship between them.

To begin with, Gertler had viewed Brett as no more than a confidante and an ally in his long battle to win Carrington over. He found a release in simply discussing her, and as Brett – 'the only person I can talk about Carrington with'[20] – responded sympathetically her own personality began to swim into focus. The Hon. Dorothy Eugenie Brett, known to her family as 'Doll', was born in London in 1883, the third of the four children of the second Viscount Esher. Her father's role as unofficial adviser to both Queen Victoria and Edward VII dominated a sheltered childhood spent in the shadow of the royal family. In 1902 complications arising from an operation for acute appendicitis left her battling with increasing deafness (from 1914 onwards she was seldom without her ear-trumpet 'Toby') and she made an unsuccessful débutante. Emotionally immature, Doll developed a number of 'crushes' throughout her life. The object of one of the earliest and most intense was Margaret Brooke, the estranged wife of Rajah Brooke of Sarawak, whose son Vyner later married Dorothy's younger sister Sylvia and became the last white rajah of Sarawak.

On the strength of her watercolours Brett was reluctantly admitted to the Slade in 1910 on a six-month trial, which she easily passed, and stayed on until 1916, developing a close platonic friendship with the self-effacing Professor Brown, whom she nicknamed 'Nutty'. At the

Slade, like Carrington, Doll was 'born again' as plain 'Brett', though she too had initially to deal with class prejudice. At first Gertler regarded her as 'little more than a debutante filling her time . . . some kind of "sport" . . . freak or oddity'. Brett only became an artist, noted Carrington's brother Noel, 'through sheer persistence and was only gradually accepted by her contemporaries at the Slade who held a continuing suspicion of her background'.[21]

A natural recruit to the 'wild group', Brett also bobbed her hair and dressed in jodhpurs and bright-coloured jumpers beneath her artist's smock. Some ten years older than the other students – though she scarcely looked it, with her turned-up nose and large brown eyes, which gave her the expression of a startled hare – Brett naturally took on the role of adviser to her friends, 'acting, as the occasion demanded, as mother figure, father confessor, go-between and favourite aunt'.[22] 'She is one of the "sisters" of this life', D. H. Lawrence commented in 1915,[23] and Gertler nicknamed her the 'virgin aunt'. Throughout her life Brett would be drawn to dominant, intelligent, artistic figures and as such was always destined, as one commentator has observed, to be 'more loving than loved'.[24]

Gertler was never the object of one of Brett's crushes, but everything about him impressed her: 'the utter poverty he came out of . . . [his] amazing mind' and his 'knowledge of fine painting'. He was 'gay, high-spirited, clever', she wrote, 'a wild lovely boy, and a fine artist'. When her father was out of town, Brett made use of his permanent box at Covent Garden by inviting Carrington and Gertler, who, she noted, became 'tremendously excited' by the performances, and would afterwards dash off *La Bohème* with great fervour on the pianola at her studio in Logan Place, or perform 'wild impromptu dances'. At the opera the women's short hair drew stares, but it was Gertler, whom Brett considered almost 'amazingly beautiful in his teens', who attracted the most attention. On one occasion a strange man who had been watching them from the stalls suddenly barged in, during an interval, 'stared hard at Gertler, said "I wanted to see if he was a boy or a girl", and dashed out again'.[25]

'What fun we all had', Brett recalled, 'on very little money', eating supper in Soho, 'for one shilling and sixpence each plus wine!' or frequenting the 'very low' bars of Limehouse. To cure Carrington of her perpetual lateness, they would wait for fifteen minutes, then pin a note to the door saying which Soho restaurant they were going to. If they failed to find a table, they would move on to another, and Carrington would be forced to hunt through the all cafés until she found them. They all paid their share, Brett recalled, but 'whenever one of us had any money, we would take the others out'.[26] More often than not, of course, the bill would fall to Brett.

Throughout 1913 Gertler, Brett and Carrington formed an inseparable trio, which took precedence over his threesome with Currie and Henry, though the two groups sometimes intermingled at the Café Royal in Regent Street, Piccadilly, then 'in its heyday as an artistic and Bohemian resort'.[27] The heart of the place was the ground-floor brasserie, known as the Domino Room. The painter Walter Sickert described the Café Royal as 'a sort of natural promotion from the day-nursery of art school', and it became the stronghold of many an ex-Slade student. Both Allinson and Nevinson left paintings of the Domino Room, famously recalled by Max Beerbohm as an 'exuberant vista of gilding and crimson velvet set amongst . . . opposing mirrors and upholding caryatids, with fumes of tobacco ever rising to the painted and pagan ceiling'.[28]

The only English café of the period run along French lines, the Café Royal permitted drinkers and diners to move freely from table to table, allowing for an eclectic mix of artists and aristocrats. 'Amid the haze', recalled Adrian Allinson, 'old friendships were maintained and new ones cemented. Across its marble topped tables many an argument on aesthetics was hammered out, a wit sharpened, or an amorous adventure begun.'[29] In the pre-war years the star turn was Augustus John, who dominated the Café by 'sheer force of personality', dressed in trademark black hat and cape, and knocking back hock and seltzer, or brandy. It was a special honour to be invited to join his table, and his popularity was secured by the fact that he often paid off the bills at the end of the evening with a fistful of banknotes. For those less well-off, a fourpenny coffee could be made to last the whole evening, and the manager, Judah, usually to be found playing dominoes with a group of retired French journalists, would sometimes himself lend money to customers.

Anyone who was anyone in the arts passed through the Café at some point in this period, from Roger Fry and the 'Bloomsberries' to Wyndham Lewis and the Vorticists, the poet and 'wickedest man in the world' (his own description) Aleister Crowley, and composers Philip Heseltine (better known as Peter Warlock) and Cecil Gray, along with the philosopher T. E. Hulme and a host of glamorous, emancipated 'new' women, such as Nancy Cunard, Iris Tree, Marie

Beerbohm and Lady Diana Manners (later Duff Cooper), who wore make-up, and drank and smoked freely. Sometimes even Carrington, though she strongly disapproved of Gertler's 'dissipated' evenings, could not resist the Café's allure.

Gertler plunged into café society with such exhilaration that, together with the artist Nina Hamnett, the poet Osbert Sitwell and the writers Michael Arlen and Ronald Firbank, he was said to comprise 'the last real Café Royal generation'.[30] Nina herself became such a celebrated café figure – both in Paris, where she danced naked in Modigliani's studio, and in London, where she posed for Henri Gaudier-Brzeska's celebrated sculpture *The Dancer* – that she was unofficially crowned the 'Queen of Bohemia'. Gertler later recalled how, after drinking too much one evening, he and Nina had ended up sharing a bed together, and while they slept, other members of the party, for a joke, placed a large cod between them. When Gertler woke up in the morning and his hand touched the fish, he sprang up, shouting, 'What on earth is this?', rousing Nina, who replied, 'That's my breakfast!'[31]

Gertler's own exuberance was notable, even among such contemporaries, 'and the many who remember him before and during the First World War', wrote his friend the publisher Thomas Balston in the late 1940s, 'speak of the excitement aroused by his exuberant vitality, his exotic beauty and his artistic gifts'.[32] According to Stanley Spencer's brother Gilbert (though his memoirs are not entirely reliable), Gertler, 'perhaps emulating Augustus John', even began to dress the part of a famous artist. 'People would stand up in restaurants to see him as he came in, with his black sombrero perched on the top of his black curls.'[33]

July 1913 marked the opening of Roger Fry's Omega Workshops, an artists' co-operative that produced a wide range of articles from textiles to painted furniture, all sold anonymously, and which lasted until 1919, despite financial losses. Gertler remained sceptical of Fry and his followers for some time to come, and probably did not visit the Omega at this stage, but he did accompany Currie and Gaudier-Brzeska (a friend of Currie's and one of the exhibitors) to the sixth annual exhibition of the Allied Artists' Association at the Albert Hall. The AAA had been founded in 1908 by the critic Frank Rutter, and modelled itself on the system of the Société des Artistes Indépendants in Paris by allowing painters, sculptors, engravers and crafts workers who paid the annual subscription fee to exhibit up to five works, without first submitting them to a selecting jury. Unfortunately, the sheer quantity of exhibits became so overwhelming that no one group could make a commanding impact, and while the 1913 show included radical work by the likes of Brancusi, Kandinsky and Ossip Zadkine, 'individual visions were swamped by a mass of mediocrity'.[34]

Gertler distanced himself from the AAA; he never exhibited there and reported back to Brett in July that he disliked the show. Certainly, he preferred a more intimate showcase for his pictures, and was probably discouraged by the tendency to price the pictures low. Moreover, he and Currie had been invited to mount a second show at the Chenil Gallery the following January, again alongside Augustus John. Nevertheless, the AAA remained a valuable market-place for astute collectors, and it was here that Currie first introduced Gertler to 'a Mr Marsh', a classical scholar and key Whitehall civil servant who acted as private secretary to Winston Churchill and mixed in the same circles as Brett's father.

Today Eddie Marsh is best remembered for his five-volume anthology *Georgian Poetry*, which aimed to 'signal a reaction against the expansive sententiousness of the Victorians', and included poets as diverse as D. H. Lawrence, Robert Graves, Walter de la Mare, John Masefield, Siegfried Sassoon and Rupert Brooke (Marsh's most beloved protégé). By 1913 Marsh had also become a discriminating collector of modern British art, and a few days after their first meeting he invited Gertler to view this collection at his apartment in Raymond Buildings, Grays Inn.[35] Gertler thought Marsh 'a very nice man', but feared 'he likes *me* more than my work', and told Brett, 'he buys everybody's work except my own'.[36]

Initially, Marsh was certainly attracted by Gertler's 'Lippo Lippi cherub' looks, and wrote to Rupert Brooke that he found Gertler, 'rather beautiful . . . his mind is deep and simple, and I think he's got the *feu sacré*'.[37] As he was a latent homosexual, handsome young men had an enduring appeal for Marsh, but 'his prance,' quipped Cyril Connolly, 'was worse than his pounce', and it was, after all, the '*feu sacré*'' that made the greatest impression. Marsh considered Gertler and Currie 'two of the most interesting of *les jeunes*,' and over the next two years, it was the talks in their studios, and at Marsh's flat, which had the greatest influence on his taste. At first Marsh considered Currie the greater painter, but over the next two years he came to consider Gertler 'the greatest genius of the age'.[38]

Marsh was a tireless champion of literature and the visual arts, and provided valuable support to many aspiring poets and artists. However, in Brooke's case his Rugby and Cambridge background lent him an ease in society that Gertler found impossible to acquire, and Marsh did not find Gertler such an easy-going protégé.

By July Gertler had begun work on a new composition called *Family Group*, depicting Harry and Annie united by their child, and set against the bare floorboards of his studio. Gertler acknowledged the new spirit of this work when he wrote in a letter to Brett, 'simplification is terribly difficult in art'. The atmosphere is reminiscent of Picasso's studies of the 'blue period' half a dozen years earlier, and Gertler also used a limited palette to reflect the barrenness and poverty of his subjects' lives.[39] The juxtaposition of primary reds and blues and the contrast between the simplified forms and the exaggeration of their facial expressions both add to the picture's emotive intensity. Gertler's aim was still to produce an art that was 'genuine' rather than specifically 'modern'. ('Oh, God! I pray you', he wrote to Brett in the same year, 'keep me from all these noises, Horrible, Competitive, Struggling, Heartless Schools of Painting! Cubism, Futurism! God knows what!'[40])

Some viewers found Gertler's new style disconcerting, and when another picture, *The Jewish Family*, was displayed the following year *The Star* complained that: 'so much emphasis is placed upon certain characteristics of the sitters that representation is occasionally pushed to caricature. The seated old man in this picture is as monstrously grotesque as a gargoyle, or some of the figures in medieval woodcarvings.'[41] Nevertheless, the reviewer conceded that the overall effect stirred the imagination and sympathy. Gertler was now evolving a definite style and felt that earlier Post-Impressionist compositions such as *Vanity* had merely side-tracked him from his main objective. Although 'the earlier work was more essentially personal', Currie explained in a letter to Marsh, the present work was 'a return to the fuller expression of the earlier'.[42]

Gertler's ideas had gradually undergone a transformation, and he began to prefer the 'simple, childish expression' of the Post-Impressionists to the 'perhaps too dramatic, and sometimes theatrical expression of the early Italians'.[43] The result was a harsh new portrait, *The Artist's Mother*, in which against a spartan background, Golda's enlarged hands lie 'heavily and wearily on her lap', suggesting 'suffering and a life that has known hardship'.[44] Gertler called this portrait 'barbaric and symbolic'. Working in a fever, he completed it with unusual speed, concerned only to catch the essential 'character of the woman'. 'I know it is not new, and our revolutionists would say of it that it was academic', he wrote to Carrington. 'I don't care. Newness doesn't concern me. I just want to express myself and be personal.'[45] It is no coincidence that Gertler began to develop this 'primitive', simplified language in his art at the same time as he began to acquire greater social sophistication, chiefly through his friendship with Marsh.

When accepting an invitation to meet Marsh one Tuesday in November, Gertler signalled that he understood that evening dress – 'the clothes of a gentleman' – was required.[46] Gertler had first worn evening clothes (given to him by the kindly David Sassoon) the previous May in response to an invitation from Carrington. Deeply aware of the class difference between them – 'You are the lady and I am the East End boy', he once told her – he may have hoped that the clothes would help bridge the gap between them. 'With this outfit', he declared, he could 'look aristocracy in the face'. None the less, whenever the seemingly casual phrase 'clothes of a gentleman' recurs in Gertler's correspondence, he appears to feel that his own fragile status as a 'gentleman' is in question.

At the theatre, standing next to Marsh, who was immaculately attired and monocled, Gertler felt self-conscious. 'My face looks so dirty in comparison with those well-washed gentry', he told Brett. (He had bought a hard sponge to scrub his face clean, but it was mostly to please Carrington, who did not approve of his habit of bathing only once a week.) In general, Gertler disliked the 'over-washed . . . awful red, beetrooty, port-winey, raw-fleshed complexion of the aristocrat!', but clearly he felt an impostor in evening dress.[47] 'I felt so awkward!' he told Brett. 'Everybody in the theatre looked at me', and he was ashamed.[48]

In September Gertler had been forced to rearrange one of his meetings with Marsh, after being arrested for brawling and temporarily banned from the Café Royal. On another occasion when Marsh attempted to introduce him to his Cambridge friends, Gertler became enraged when one of them attempted to argue him down on the subject of painting, and he stormed out of the room. Afterwards, he tried to explain to Marsh the 'bridge of tremendous length between such people and myself. I don't know what it is. Perhaps its merely difference of class.' 'They talk well, argue masterly, and yet and yet there is something – something – that makes me dislike them. Some moments I hate them!'[49] He longed instead to put into his work 'that passion, that inspiration, that profundity of soul that I know I possess' and to 'triumph over those learned Cambridge youths'.[50] Throughout his life he advocated that painting should not come from the head but from the heart, a view that later brought him into conflict with the dominant Bloomsbury aesthetic.

Intrigued by Gertler's and Currie's admiration for Stanley Spencer, Marsh asked Gertler to arrange a meeting. But in the correspondence that followed, Spencer somehow implied that Gertler's work showed a lack of understanding of Cézanne, the painter whom Gertler now revered above all, and to whom he referred in a letter to Brett as 'that great, great man'.[51] Outraged, Gertler refused to having anything further to do with Spencer, whose mild reply that he had not meant to be insulting only rubbed salt into the wound. It was six months before the row was finally smoothed over, and although in their early work the two painters had much to unite them, their relationship would never really recovered.

Gertler's friendship with Marsh meanwhile continued to deepen. In September Marsh had arrived at Gertler's studio to find him at work on *The Jewish Family*, and was so impressed that he immediately asked the price, but Gertler was so overwhelmed (he later told Brett) that he asked only £35. In November 1913 Gertler learned that the British Institution scholarship, which had given him two years of security, would not be renewed, and for the first time he faced a future without loans, scholarships or guaranteed patronage. Nevertheless, he was selfless in trying to help his fellow 'Whitechapel Boys'. He introduced the poet–painter Isaac Rosenberg to Marsh at the Café Royal in November 1913, and encouraged him to buy both Rosenberg's and Bomberg's work.

In December, when Marsh took Gertler to a production of Bernard Shaw's *The Doctor's Dilemma*, he became so indignant that he wrote a long diatribe to Carrington. The affected portrayal of an artist and the reaction of the 'terrible middle-class audience laughing in an enlightened way' horrified him and made him feel like 'excit[ing] all the working classes to, one night, break into these theatres and destroy all those rich pleasure seekers!'[52] What angered him most was that the play had no connection with reality. He returned home to Spital Square to find his father sitting at the kitchen table, with his 'thin bony suffering face and his working hands, all rough and hard . . . and I thanked God that this man was my father' and that he had 'never heard that name Bernard Shaw!'[53]

Yet even as he completed the 'barbaric' portrait of his mother, he rowed violently with his father, because, 'whilst painting my mother, I forgot the dinner hour and went on painting till 2.30! Oh! he was wild – he was so hungry . . . The meat and potatoes got burned! Everybody was annoyed with me. They said I love my art more than them!'[54]

9

The Widening Circle

> 'A young man is watched by collectors to see if he is a clever student. Then he makes a sensation and sells his work. Then he is dropped for a bit and they watch out for his next move. By that time Society women are on the lookout for him and get him in tow if they can and buy a few works and keep him alive until the collectors return to him.'
>
> Brett to Lord Esher, 1915

GERTLER NOW SAW little of Currie and Henry, with whom his ties had weakened, as he was drawn closer into Carrington's circle with Brett and their friend Ruth Humphries. He was touched when all three girls bought him Christmas presents, but still feared that he was 'too rough and vulgar' for them, and he tried to sublimate his sexual feelings for Carrington into the sort of relationship he felt she wanted: 'Friendship! The Spiritual Linking Together of Two Souls!'[1]

At the start of 1914, however, Carrington was back under the watchful eye of her mother, in the small village of Hurstbourne Tarrant in the Hampshire Downs. This was her final year at the Slade, and desperate at the prospect of remaining financially dependent on her family, she spoke recklessly (if half-seriously) of becoming 'a teacher with spectacles', or of winning the Prix de Rome scholarship and escaping abroad. Gertler sympathized, knowing how stifled she felt by her mother's respectability. 'Carrington does seem to be having a hard time with her people', he agreed with Brett; 'it is merely because she is above them.'[2] Unwilling to lose her for three long years to that 'decadent city Rome', he urged Carrington to try instead for the British Institute scholarship, but admitted to Brett that if the Prix de Rome was the only way out of Carrington's 'people trouble, I don't see how I can interfere'.[3]

As she laboured on her submission for the prize throughout January, he flung himself back into painting, but after a day's work alone in the studio he became desperate for someone to 'interchange an idea with.'[4] Then suddenly, seizing on 'a funny doll belonging to my little niece', he painted it 'furiously', and included it in a still life that he exhibited in February at the Friday Club.[5] 'I am doing work now, which is real work', he explained to Carrington. 'Far better than anything I've done before and I should like you to share it with, but as long as that obsession for you sexually is there, I cannot. Remember, I've tried to fight it for three years, without success.' But Carrington remained obdurate, and their 'sex problem' – as they came to refer to it – remained an unresolved source of tension.

Meantime there was Brett. They talked for hours about art and visited the South Kensington museum together to see the tapestries, before returning to her family house in Mayfair for dinner. A sympathetic companion and a good listener, despite her increasing deafness, she bolstered his confidence, sending 'wonderful descriptions' of his painting to Carrington. Still, Gertler insisted in his letters to Carrington, that 'apart from Brett I see nobody. I hardly go out at all.'[6] But this state of affairs did not last long. Towards the close of 1913 Marsh had introduced Gertler to Gilbert Cannan, a young writer for whom the novelist Henry James had predicted a great future. Cannan had an impressive Roman nose, a thatch of yellow hair, an air of moody meditation said to put his friends in mind of Hamlet, and a rather crooked smile. The two young men warmed to one another immediately, and early in 1914 Gertler accepted an invitation to stay at Cannan's Mill Cottage in Cholesbury, Buckinghamshire. Before his visit Gertler was nervous, fearing Gilbert would turn out to be one of those 'intellectuals' he so disliked, but once comfortably installed at the Cannans' fireside, he immediately relaxed, and wrote enthusiastically to Brett, 'Gilbert Cannan is an extremely nice man and ought to do good things'.[7]

Cannan was some seven years older than Gertler. He had read law at Manchester University and Cambridge, and worked briefly as an actor before becoming a drama critic. By 1914 he had already published four novels, a collection of plays, a book on the theatre and translations of three foreign novels, as well as regularly contributing theatre reviews to the avant-garde quarterly *Rhythm*, where he formed a friendship with the magazine's writers and co-owners Katherine Mansfield and John Middleton Murry (to whom he introduced Gertler that autumn).[8] However, Cannan made enemies as well as friends, chiefly through his scathing reviews, which had so offended many of the old guard in the theatre that Bernard Shaw lampooned him as the supercilious drama critic Gilbert Gunn in *Fanny's First Play*.

In 1909 Cannan's moderate fame as a writer was almost eclipsed by his notoriety as the man who ran off with the wife of J. M. Barrie, then at the height of his fame for *Peter Pan*. While working as Barrie's secretary, Cannan had drifted into an affair with his unhappy wife, Mary. Barrie sued for divorce and Cannan was trapped into marriage with a woman seventeen years his senior, with whom, ultimately, he had little in common. He took to inviting a stream of friends to Mill Cottage to escape what he would increasingly refer to as the 'cloying security' of marriage,[9] and Gertler became one of his most frequent guests.

Seven hundred feet up in the Chilterns, Mill Cottage was the perfect country retreat. The comfortable rooms were lit up by huge fires, and bright frescoes by the Russian artist Vladimir Polunin decorated the dining room walls. Adjoining the house was Cannan's sanctuary, an extraordinary disused windmill which looked out across a common blazing with gorse. Here, he had a small private sitting room, pasted with flower patterns of Mary's own design and linked to his sunny, book-lined study by a spiral staircase, which his friend Compton Mackenzie claimed to believe eventually turned Cannan's head and drove him mad.[10]

On his first visit the Cannans encouraged Gertler to talk 'all about where I came from and all about my people'. Gilbert considered Gertler 'extremely fortunate to live in the East End among real people'[11] and greatly preferred the young painter's raw earnestness to the 'milk and water outlook of Roger Fry and his followers'. He even agreed that the Yiddish theatre was 'far more vital than the English'. They 'talked and talked' well into the night, and by the end of his stay Gertler liked Cannan so much he could 'scarcely tear myself away'.[12]

Perhaps inevitably, Cannan romanticized Gertler: 'He reminds me greatly of Heine' (whose *Memoirs* Cannan had translated) 'though stronger', he wrote to his friend Lady Ottoline Morrell, perhaps seeing Gertler, like the German poet, as a gifted Jew adrift in Christian society, torn apart by poverty and conflict, and unhappy in love.[13] Gertler was a 'genius', a 'prodigy', whose difficulties had been intensified by his own turbulent nature. As they sat night after night in the dimly lit mill, with Cannan playing Beethoven on the pianola, reading out his poetry or simply maintaining 'wise silences', Gertler's stories fired his imagination. He admired the younger man's frankness, his youthful egotism and his early struggles; even his difficult affair with Carrington seemed to mirror Cannan's own earlier unrequited passion for the sculptress Kathleen Bruce (who had rejected him to marry the explorer Robert Falcon Scott). Later, in *Mendel*, Cannan used many of Gertler's stories verbatim.

Cannan's friendship opened a new door for Gertler, just as the door on his friendship with Currie was closing. The two painters collaborated on their second and final joint exhibition at the Chenil in 1914, but now saw each other seldom. It was probably Dolly Henry who came between them. 'I think he will be done for if he doesn't get Dolly out of his head', Marsh confided to Gertler in January,[14] but the lovers seemed locked into their violent and agonizing relationship, and though they had agreed to part in February, by April they were back together. Both attended a 'painters' evening' at Marsh's flat, where Spencer, Gaudier-Brzeska and Gertler met to discuss Spencer's idea of a Georgian painters series to accompany Marsh's volumes of Georgian poets.[15]

Knewstub continued to represent both Gertler and Currie, and sold Gertler's portrait of Golda in the kitchen (as *The Housekeeper*) for £40 at the Leeds City Art Galleries that spring. Works by both painters surfaced occasionally at the Chenil over the next few years, but they never collaborated again. In his one surviving letter to Gertler, Currie hinted at an estrangement, but also made clear his enduring feelings of friendship. Currie left for Brittany in May, in a final effort to forget Dolly, and Gertler quickly closed the gap by forming a new threesome with the Cannans.

In their home Gertler became almost a third partner, just as he had in the early days of his friendship with Currie and Dolly. As the youngest and most gifted member of his family, Gertler had always been indulged and protected, and he unconsciously sought the same reassurance in his adult relationships. At the beginning of a new friendship he often displayed the child-like side of his nature, which could prove very attractive to those who offered him protection.

Both Cannans were intensely aware of Gertler's Jewishness – his 'otherness' – but while Gilbert was attracted by Gertler's exoticism and vitality, and his appealingly 'naive letter[s] of bursting happiness',[16] Mary found him merely 'egotistical and unrestrained'.[17] Gilbert was paternal, and encouraged Gertler to treat the cottage as his own and to drop in for meals or chats whenever the mood took him. To Mary, however, Gertler was a cuckoo in the nest, not least because she secretly considered him 'too much of the back street Jew to be a wholly agreeable companion' (though probably Gertler never realized this).[18]

Gertler spent his days at Cholesbury making studies from nature, marvelling at the peaceful countryside and embracing it with the rapture of a poor city-dweller seeing its beauty as if for the first time. There, he somehow felt closer to Carrington, and wrote to her of the 'vague longings' with which the countryside filled him. 'I love all the beautiful things that grow and the sunshine most passionately! I want so much to introduce all these things into the backgrounds of my pictures', he told her.[19] The result was his first major outdoor composition, *The Fruit Sorters*.

This painting, dominated by three figures holding baskets laden with fruit, marks a transition between the eloquently spartan interiors of the Jewish portraits and the vibrant landscapes to come. The figures are undoubtedly influenced by Spencer's *Apple Gatherers* (which had been in Marsh's collection since the previous December), and the frieze-like patterning is reminiscent of Duncan Grant's *Lemon Gatherers*. The colouring, however, was all Gertler's own, inspired by a rainbow he had seen on a recent visit to the home of the brothers Paul and John Nash, which had formed 'a blaze of different colours', turning some of the trees in the adjoining wood 'bright green, whilst others were purple [and] the ground was Orange Brown, with the fallen and faded leaves'.[20] The two female figures were modelled on his sister Sophie and the subject of the earlier *Violinist*, but the male model was a hired professional and came at great cost. Gertler made several vigorous pencil studies of him, but found them difficult to transfer on to canvas, and wrote despairingly to Carrington that he had spent the whole day painting the man's back. 'Of the two,' he pointed out, 'the model triumphed most, because he went away with my people's hard-earned 7*s*.'[21]

On his return Gertler threw himself back into the social life of London, attending endless concerts, parties and night-clubs, and enjoying four-course suppers at the Savoy, paid for by Brett or her sister Syv, the ranee of Sarawak. It was a source of great satisfaction to him that the waiters, dressed in plush coats and stockings, had no idea of his penury. But in the sobering light of day, as he watched his family scrape together the money to pay for his models, Gertler, like

Carrington, had to contemplate taking up a teaching position. He was interviewed at the Boys Foundation School, which he found 'all very frightening and very official and rather depressing', but failed to secure the post. Somehow, his applications or references always seemed to arrive too late. In truth, he was unwilling to take time off from his own work and was too absorbed by his own vision to wish to direct that of others. But he was forced to economize severely after his brother Jack took out £3 – his entire savings – to pay for his models and materials.

A struggle now began between what Gertler called 'the sordidness of material cares' and the 'world of imagination and infinite beauty' into which art raised him. Unable to resolve these contradictions, he wished only to express himself 'simply and beautifully in paint. I have no ambitions in life but that.' Cannan, ever sympathetic, wrote tactfully to Lady Ottoline Morrell that if she could 'persuade anyone to buy a drawing of his occasionally you would be helping him both materially and spiritually'.[22] Lady Ottoline, wife of the Liberal MP Philip Morrell and half-sister to the Duke of Portland, gathered around her an army of artists, writers, politicians and intellectuals, for whom she held a weekly salon at her home in Bedford Square. 'Conversation, talk, interchange of ideas – how good it was!' she wrote in her memoirs, 'I gave myself in reckless energy to these people.'[23] A generous patron who often championed the unconventional in the arts, she was always on the look-out for new talent and decided to visit the young painter and view his work for herself.

Ottoline was startling and somewhat eccentric in appearance. Over six feet tall, with flaming Titian hair, she had a fine 'Medusa head', Virginia Woolf noted, and a long equine face, with extraordinary 'turquoise eyes that looked like ice-chips in sunlight when she was enraged'.[24] Henry James described her as 'a gorgeous heraldic creature – a Gryphon perhaps or a Dragon Volant!' She accentuated her height with large hats, high heels and 'window-curtaining clothes', exotic creations of gorgeous coloured fabric that seemed to floated around her as she walked. Such a figure was bound to create a stir in Spitalfields.

Years later, in her memoirs, Ottoline recalled that first meeting with Gertler, 'in the mean, hot, stuffy, smelly little street' where he lived. Strangers, particularly the middle- and upper-class variety, were ill at ease in the foreign atmosphere of London's Jewish community, and even the Bohemian Nina Hamnett had been disconcerted on a visit to Gertler's to find herself in a market 'where hardly anyone spoke

English'. Ottoline was further alarmed by the contrast between her own uncomfortably large, towering figure and the tiny East End house with its creaking stairs, while Gertler, nervously awaiting her arrival in his attic studio, was astonished to see only the crest of a purple feathered hat ascending nearer and nearer, then at last the hat itself and finally Ottoline. When she finally emerged, they both felt, she recalled, as if a large and odd bird had arrived: 'Indeed, I hardly believe that I was able to stand upright . . . so tall and erect was the feather, so low was his room.'[25]

She was impressed with Gertler's work, though, and with the strength and tenacity she glimpsed behind his fragile, even feminine appearance, confiding to her diary that he was 'in reality passionate and ambitious and exceedingly observant and sensitive'.[26] She sent him daffodils and an invitation to tea – and since Ottoline was, as Cannan pointed out, like 'a good fairy godmother', he could not refuse.[27]

The following week Gertler entered Ottoline's famous dove-grey drawing room at 44 Bedford Square for the first time and was quickly manoeuvred into a tête-à-tête with his hostess. Ottoline's drawling voice and intimate manner could be intimidating, but Gertler responded with warmth to anyone who showed a genuine interest in himself or his art, and she soon coaxed him into confessing his ambivalence about 'Society'. Despite his friends among the upper class, his antagonism to their way of life lingered, and though he realized that he owed everything to his family, their own lack of cultivation often depressed him. Listening closely, Ottoline realized that Gertler's confession echoed her own sense of 'having a passport to several worlds and belonging to none',[28] and it established an understanding between them that led to a lifelong friendship.

Ottoline recognized that the very narrowness of Gertler's upbringing had fed his artistic hunger: 'Such a limited, almost walled in youth may give great intensity of vision', she wrote in her diary, and she identified this same 'intense, tangible, ruthless, hot quality' in his paintings.[29] She extended a further invitation to one of her Thursday evening 'at homes' where his work could be displayed to a larger audience, and enclosed a cheque for one of his drawings. Grateful and excited, Gertler wrote to thank her, with the youthful spontaneity that sparked off generous responses in so many of his new acquaintances:

> I shall send it to you next Thursday . . . May I suggest if you hang it that you hang it a little tilted . . . because the paint not being dry yet, it might

> otherwise shine. It is good of you to want to show it. – Then on Thursday – Mark Gertler

He added nervously, 'It looks quite well on the floor leaning against the wall – but just as you like.'[30]

Among the guests the following Thursday was the painter Walter Sickert. That evening Ottoline noticed Gertler standing by his picture, 'thin, erect and trembling internally, if not externally, at the excitement of having his work looked at and discussed by anyone like Sickert, whom he so respected'. The painting Gertler showed was probably *The Fruit Sorters*, which Sickert later commended for its 'intensity and raciness', calling it 'a masterly piece of painting'.[31] Ottoline also admired it, and in May she purchased it in her capacity as buyer for the Contemporary Arts Society.

Gertler was soon admitted to Ottoline's wide circle and, Cannan told Ottoline, acknowledged her as 'Queen of his world, a simple one in which reigning is an easy and delightful job. I should accept the position if I were you.'[32] And when Ottoline re-established her Thursday evening 'at homes' in the autumn of 1914 Gertler became one of her 'regulars'. *The Fruit Sorters* pointed his work in a new direction, but still he hesitated, drawn to the old, familiar subjects in his community, works that still found immediate buyers. His next major picture, *The Creation of Eve*, a highly original treatment of a familiar biblical subject, may have been inspired by the book of Cranach reproductions Gertler had been poring over in March, but also has echoes of Blake. It portrays God as a pot-bellied patrician, pulling a naked, doll-like Eve by her hair from the rib of a sleeping Adam, and it caused an outcry when exhibited the following year.

In May 1914 an exhibition of British art entitled 'Twentieth Century Art: A Review of Modern Movements' opened at the Whitechapel Gallery. Its aim was to show 'the progress of art' since Impressionism, and it was loosely divided into: landscapes, works of a 'decorative design', work showing the influence of Cézanne (which included Vanessa Bell, Duncan Grant and Roger Fry) and, finally, works said to have 'abandoned representation almost entirely'.[33] This last category included not only Wyndham Lewis and the artists of the Rebel Arts Centre (which had been set up in April in direct opposition to the Omega Workshops) but also a specifically 'Jewish section', curated by David Bomberg, and including several of Gertler's Jewish portraits.[34]

Gertler's scenes of Jewish life gained grudging admiration from the *Jewish Chronicle*, but many of the works were too extreme for the critics, particularly those of Bomberg himself, which one critic called 'a waste of good pigment, canvas and wall space'.[35] However, Gertler's inclusion in such a group demonstrated that he was now being numbered among the contemporary radicals.

Gertler was beginning to find himself increasingly drawn to the company of writers, and in the early summer of 1914 was introduced to D. H. Lawrence, who had recently made his name with *Sons and Lovers* (1913) and just returned from Italy with his new bride, Frieda von Richthoffen. The couple took an instinctive liking to Gertler, with Frieda pronouncing his name 'Gairrrtler' with an impressive roll of the *r*.[36]

In July Gertler set off for a holiday in Sussex (possibly arranged by Jack Knewstub, who had a cottage near by). It was his first and only holiday alone – and he seems to have enjoyed it: bathing naked on the beach and drying himself in the hot sun, or painting landscape, undisturbed, all day. He stayed with a working-class family, who aroused a strong attachment in him, and through them he felt closer to his own family: 'I see beauties in my own people which I never saw before', he wrote to Carrington. In this company he was no longer an outsider and his bitterness and cynicism dissolved. He spent his evening drinking beer with the fishermen and sailors, acknowledging, 'My place is by these sort of people. I belong to this class. I shall always be unhappy if I try to get away from this class to which I belong.'[37] Significantly, he felt no desire to paint them.

The sculptor Jacob Epstein and his entourage were staying in a cottage near by, but Gertler avoided them as much as possible. He told Brett that Epstein's presence had worried him 'to such an extent that I couldn't work the whole of the first week'.[38] Gertler's main objection seems to have been that Epstein always had 'some girl living with him, including his wife',[39] and he took a particular dislike to one of Epstein's Gauguinesque black models, who told him that she had modelled at the Slade.

Epstein's presence did not prevent Gertler from completing his first mature landscape, *The Black and White Cottage*, in which he depicted nature with a tenderness captured in his description of the pampas grass as 'a strikingly beautiful plant . . . flirt[ing] with the wind . . . like a ruffled head of hair'.[40] Much as he loved the country, however, Gertler realized that he must return to the East End, for 'there lies my work, sordid as it is'.[41] But he hoped to combine 'the beauties of the East End and the country', he told Carrington, by renting a room in a country retreat of his own, a bolt-hole where he would always be able to escape. He returned from this holiday refreshed, full of plans for the future and eager to resume painting. He was completely unprepared for the news that confronted him on his arrival: Europe was at war.

Gertler's fragile sense of harmony was shattered. 'War is indeed terrible, but how ludicrous!' he wrote to Carrington, amazed that this seemingly distant news could cause the closure of his father's workshop.[42] His brothers Harry and Jack were both naturalized, but Golda and Louis, technically classed as Austrian, were now 'enemy aliens', and Cannan predicted that they would be 'in for a stiff time'.[43] In the autumn they suffered 'agonies' when Russian soldiers marched over Galicia.

Nevertheless, Gertler wrote to Carrington with confident naïvety, 'Do not be unhappy about the war. The best way we can help is to paint.'[44] Cannan had found him a beautiful cottage to rent near by, and he planned to return to the country as soon as possible, since his heart was 'in the trees!' Even before his suitcase was packed, however, he had to concede, reluctantly, that some friends of Cannan's, 'Refugees from the war – quite Homeless – wanting somewhere to live', had a more pressing claim than his. Although he soon found another cottage, he was unable to recapture the tranquillity of his Hastings trip, especially, he explained to Brett, since his money was beginning to run out again.[45] Once more, the 'extraordinarily generous' Brett came to Gertler's assistance, offering him a subsidy of '£1 a week during [times of] distress', which he accepted, promising to 'repay every farthing', and reminding Brett that he owed her £15 already.[46]

Brett had been one of the few to learn of the war in advance. Her father, Lord Esher, was in Paris just before the conflict started, and one of her first actions when writing to him there was to ask him to use his 'influence in finding a safe niche for Gertler'. 'Gertler had better enlist in the R. A. M. C.', Esher replied. 'He will be quite safe and will have some physical exercise that will do him good. Then he will not be molested.'[47] On 7 August, amid a general mood of excitement, Lord Kitchener began a campaign to enlist 100,000 volunteers, and many of Gertler's Slade contemporaries, such as Paul Nash, joined up immediately, to be joined by Nevinson and Stanley Spencer in 1915. At the close of the month Brett wrote to ask Gertler about enlisting, but he recoiled at the suggestion, calling the fighting 'wretched[,] sordid Butchery!! . . . Only when I work', he told her, 'do I forget.'[48]

But Cannan, who planned to sit the war out himself, noted that autumn that Gertler was sometimes 'in despair, because his friends were looking askance at him because he was not in uniform',[49] so following Gilbert's example, Gertler put his name down as a constable to guard the waters in Chesham (an offer that was luckily never taken up). He felt such a loathing for the whole business of war, he told Brett, that he was determined to go away to the country 'to rot away my life until the Butchery is completed'.[50] But in the meantime, with the oppressive heat of a stifling English summer and the hysteria of war all around him, he worked on with his simple appreciations of nature. *Agapanthus* in September was immediately snapped up by Marsh and *Apples* (November), exhibited at both the NEAC winter salon and the winter Friday Club, was much admired by Carrington, who thought it one of his best pictures to date. 'The war in no way prevents me from working', he told Carrington firmly.[51] His total absorption in painting left little room for anything else.

Yet as autumn closed in Gertler's mood changed to despondency. As he explained to the ever patient Brett: 'I am clean out of money just now, and that rascal Knewstub is grumbling and practically refusing to let me have any. I went down and asked him for £10. He made a fuss; Half promised; and not sent it yet.'[52] Knewstub, pushed, finally admitted that he could not, or would not, let Gertler have any more money. Gertler finally broke with him in November, but was immediately presented with a bill for paints from Percy Young, who kept the materials shop below. Fortunately, Marsh gave him £5 to settle it.

Gertler was left with a double sense of failure: first, at letting down his family, and second, at remaining a 'burden on their perilous finances. This is after years of Labour', he told Brett. 'Here in the East End, it is considered a disgrace for a man of 22 to live on his people – I agree.' There seemed no solution in painting, since he hated doing 'Pot Boilers' and, 'even if I wanted to paint work that would sell, I wouldn't know what does sell!' he wrote to Brett.[53] He took to working back in Golda's kitchen, in the hope of recapturing his former life of simplicity.

It was there on 9 October, as he began work on a new portrait of his father, that Gertler received shocking news about John Currie.[54] After a final, violent disagreement with Dolly Henry, who had begun a relationship with another man, Currie had shot her in a fit of jealousy, then turned the gun on himself. Now fatally wounded, he lay dying in the Chelsea infirmary and Gertler, distraught, rushed to be with him. Currie's loss made an indelible impression on Gertler; he never entered into another painting partnership. From now on (with the exception of Carrington and Brett) he deliberately chose his close friends from among non-painters.

It was at Ottoline's Thursday evening 'at homes' in November 1914 that Gertler first came into significant contact with that circle of family and friends collectively known as the 'Bloomsbury group'. The seeds of Bloomsbury had been sown by a small group of Cambridge undergraduates, many of whom were 'Apostles' (a secret fraternity of intellectuals much influenced by a close reading of G. E. Moore's *Principia Ethica*), and centred around Thoby Stephen, the eldest son of the Victorian biographer Sir Leslie Stephen. After Cambridge, Thoby brought his friends back to Bloomsbury to continue their discussions, and introduced them to his sisters Vanessa and Virginia, who would not only choose their husbands – Clive Bell and Leonard Woolf – from among their number, but after Thoby's premature death in 1906 would themselves form its new centre.

The 'Bloomsberries' took Moore's belief that 'personal affections and aesthetic enjoyments include all the greatest, and by far the greatest, goods we can imagine' to heart. And this, together with 'Moore's first desideratum – a perfect respect for truth' or, as Clive Bell put it, 'a taste for discussion in pursuit of truth and a contempt for conventional ways of thinking and feeling' formed the basic tenets of the Bloomsbury creed.[55] Their taste for discussion could (and often did) descend to the level of gossip. Gertler called it a 'vicious and capricious' attitude, and it was at the heart of his later antipathy to 'the Bloomsberries'.

Bloomsbury's core membership has been much disputed, particularly by its own members, but among those who attended Ottoline's pre-war salons were the writer David Garnett, the novelist E. M. Forster, the painters Duncan Grant and Vanessa Bell, the economist Gerald Shove, the journalist and bookseller Francis Birrell, and Ottoline's favourite, the essayist and future biographer Lytton Strachey, who was greatly respected among his circle for his intelligence, learning and wit, and for his famously bawdy humour, voiced in a high falsetto peculiar to the Strachey family.

A homosexual given to falling in and out of love with unsuitable partners, Strachey's friendship with the (heterosexual) painter Henry Lamb had just broken up, and when he met Gertler, his biographer Michael Holroyd suggests, he may have been casting around for a replacement.[56] Gertler's combination of cherubic looks and 'artistic' temperament apparently made him irresistible to many homosexuals, but Strachey's own appearance held little attraction for Gertler. Tall, lanky, red-haired, bearded and bespectacled, he resembled nothing so much as an outsized spider, as he folded and refolded his long limbs into an armchair. On a later occasion when he and Gertler walked together on Hampstead Heath, Strachey's appearance invited hoots of derision from bystanders, and 'some people shouted at us – imitating a goat', Gertler told Carrington. ('This', he explained, 'was aimed at Strachey's beard.[57]) Strachey was a natural teacher and did not attempt to 'talk down' to Gertler about painting, but urged him instead to further his education by reading poetry and learning French. By the end of November he was regularly picking his way across the East End to take tea in Gertler's studio.

That autumn Gertler also rekindled his friendship with the Lawrences, who had moved to a cottage called The Triangle, near the Cannans in Cholesbury, and whom he met on his regular visits to Mill House. Recent scholarship suggests that it was probably after viewing Gertler's *Creation of Eve* (and possibly a charcoal drawing, *Abraham and the Angels*) that autumn that Lawrence completed the passage of his novel *The Rainbow*, in which a carved low relief panel, also entitled the *Creation of Eve*, 'occupies a central place in the symbolic and literal narrative dynamic' of the story.[58]

In October the Cholesbury circle of writers was completed by 'the tigers', Cannan's nickname for Katherine Mansfield and John Middleton Murry, who took Rose Cottage, some three miles across the fields. The 'tigers' had met towards the close of 1911, the year of the publication of Katherine Mansfield's first collection of short stories, *In a German Pension*, and had begun to correspond over Mansfield's contributions to the magazine *Rhythm*. The following year Murry left Oxford without taking his finals and went to live in Katherine's London flat, where the pair became lovers. They eventually married in 1918, but their relationship was always complex and stormy, and Katherine, whose health was delicate (like Lawrence she was later diagnosed as tubercular), often found Murry insufficiently supportive. Their relationship hit one of its intermittent troughs over the Christmas of 1914.

Gertler arrived in Cholesbury on 21 December, and took rooms for a fortnight in a cottage called The Gables, with a landlady called Mrs Gomm. The first few days were cold and miserable. The cottage was crammed with ornaments, samplers and antimaccassars of such intricate lace that they constantly became entangled in his hair or his brushes, and he found it impossible to paint. He consoled himself by taking tea with the Lawrences and writing to Strachey, who sent him a copy of *Hamlet* for 'holiday reading'. Soon the other guests arrived: a young Irish lawyer with literary aspirations, called Gordon Campbell, and his friend Samuel Solomonovich Koteliansky, or 'Kot', whom Lawrence had met while on a walking tour of the Lakes in August.

Kot, thought Leonard Woolf, resembled the prophet Jeremiah. 'Physically', he was 'a Jew of the Trotsky type'; his 'pelt of thick black bristly hair' grew straight up into the air and crowned a splendid head and long, pale, sensitive face.[59] He was a Russian *émigré* whose childhood had been spent in a small village in the Ukraine undergoing 'a round of religious observances, pogroms and sufferings', and he had spoken only Yiddish until the age of nine, when he rejected the Jewish faith, asked to learn Russian and attended a Russian school. Later he became a student in Kiev, where he organized a revolution against the ruling regime, but was so devastated when no one turned up (or so Katherine Mansfield liked to claim) that he began walking and continued until he reached the Tottenham Court Road (a hotbed of anarchy and insurrection in the 1890s). 'I came for three months', Kot once said, 'and I stayed for ever.'[60]

Although he later became an acclaimed translator of Russian novels for the Woolfs' Hogarth Press, Kot's first attempts to fit in with London life were as unsuccessful as his revolution. In an effort to look more like an Englishman he wore a Panama hat and white tennis shoes with his usual embroidered Russian blouse, and was astonished at the reaction of his neighbours, who became helpless with laughter whenever he appeared. (Eventually he overcame this by only going out at night.) He took a job at the Russian Law Bureau in High Holborn, which he hated but refused to leave. Nobody knew quite what he did there, but Gertler used to joke that his job was 'to black his boss's beard'.[61] Kot was 'bewitched' by Katherine after their first meeting, and subsequently became devoted to her, but he always remained critical of Murry, and seems to have encouraged a friendship between Katherine and Gertler. Kot's fierceness could be frightening, but he was not without a sense of humour and a streak of wildness which was never far below the surface and liable to raise its head in a very particular party turn: the ability to howl like a dog.

Gertler cheered up as everyone settled in, making The Triangle 'splendid with holly and mistletoe' and drinking the lethal punch concocted by Lawrence on a Primus stove in Cannan's attic. 'We cooked and boiled, roasted and baked', Frieda recalled. 'We had a gay feast.' Afterwards they danced 'on the shaky floor. Gilbert singing "I feel, I feel like an eagle in the sky" ' with uplifted head, and Kot performing soulful Hebrew songs.[62] Mary Cannan was slightly out of her depth amid this unpredictable company, but Gilbert presided in his distracted, fatherly way over them all.

Late in the evening, when everyone was very drunk, they performed a short play written by Murry, which dramatized the strained situation between himself and Katherine, and cast Gertler in the role of her lover. At the climax of the play Katherine was supposed to leave Gertler and return to Murry, but when they reached that point, she departed from the script and stayed with Gertler, kissing him with a passion realistic enough to shock the other guests. 'Katherine Mansfield and myself – both very drunk – made passionate love to each other in front of everybody!' was the version Gertler gave to Carrington, no doubt in the hope of arousing her jealousy, which he failed to do. 'No-one knew whether to take it as a joke or scandal. Fortunately the next day everybody decided to take it as a joke – the Lawrences were the last to come to this decision, as they were the most anxious to weave a real romance out of it.'[63] It had been 'the strangest and most astonishing evening . . . like a chapter out of a Dostoievsky novel',[64] Cannan reported to Ottoline next day, and Gertler told Strachey that 'all the writers of Cholesbury [felt] inspired to use it in their work'.[65]

Katherine was the first to 'weave a romance' out of the episode, in a short story entitled *Brave Love*, written in January 1915, in which her biographer Claire Tomalin has identified Gertler as a possible model for the innocent Russian sailor at the heart of the story (an 'artificial and melodramatic' failure, which Murry chose not to publish after Katherine's death).[66] Katherine later reworked some of the material to better effect in another story, *Je ne parle pas français*, which featured a composite portrait, based partly on Gertler and partly on her French lover the poet and novelist Francis Carco, as the rapaciously egotistical writer Raoul Duquette.[67]

But it was Lawrence who was moved most strongly by the charade, and who transferred the dynamic of the triangular relationship to his next novel, *Women in Love*, where in the closing stages of the novel the divisive sculptor Loerke acts as the catalyst in the deteriorating relationship between Gudrun (the character based on Katherine) and Gerald (Murry). Gertler was the model for Loerke, 'a thin, dark-skinned man with full eyes, an odd creature like a child . . . with the boyish figure and the round, full, sensitive-looking head, and the quick, full eyes, like a mouse's'. When he is first introduced, he is engaged in a particularly Gertleresque occupation, imitating a quarrel between an old Cologne woman and a railway guard. His voice is 'mature, sardonic', with 'the flexibility of essential energy, and of a mocking, penetrating understanding . . . He must be an artist', the narrator concludes, 'nobody else could have such fine adjustment and singleness'. But Loerke is also something of a sinister figure, described in slightly grotesque similes as 'like a troll, quick, detached', and elsewhere as like a rabbit, a bat, and a rat, and it is probably here that the comparison ends; for Loerke is used as a mouthpiece for Lawrence's ideas on art, which were often at odds with Gertler's own. None the less, Lawrence's powerful personality and forthright views not only affected Gertler's attitude to the war but also found a reflection in his 1916 masterpiece *The Merry-Go-Round.*

PART IV

The Unfortunate Possessor of a Very Peculiar Temperament

'I am the unfortunate possessor of a very curious temperament believe me.'

Mark Gertler to Edward Marsh, 17 August 1914

10

Rare Times

'Rare times these, aren't they?'
Mark Gertler to Brett [October 1915]

EXHILARATED BUT EXHAUSTED after his dissipated Christmas, Gertler decided to 'lie low for a bit in order to recover'.[1] After the incident with Katherine and some inconclusive flirting at a London party with former Slade student Iris Tree, he told Strachey that he had 'had enough of woman [sic] and love for a bit'.[2] This moratorium included even Carrington, to whom he wrote to 'tell her plainly that our friendship was over. She didn't seem to understand why I was silent', he told Brett but inevitably he resumed the correspondence within days.[3]

More definite was Gertler's decision to break with the East End and his family. In January 1915 he put all his energy into the search for a perfect studio, and in February he finally settled in Hampstead in a conscious attempt to shrug off his earlier identity. 'There, I shall be free and detached – shall belong to no parents', he explained to Carrington (who surely understood about families). 'I shall be neither Jew nor Christian and shall belong to no class. I shall be just myself and be able to work out things according to my own tastes.'[4] To Strachey he admitted that he felt 'both sad and immensely relieved at having to leave the East End and my parents. But the feeling of relief is greater than the feeling of sadness.'[5] It was to be 'Chapter one of the second book' of his life, and like the first move from his parents' home in 1912, it would not only signal, but precipitate, a further radical change in his art.[6]

The move was only made possible by the support of Brett and Eddie Marsh. In an agreement that had come into force on 1

December Marsh arranged to pay Gertler a £5 monthly subsidy and to secure the rent on his studio in return for first refusal on his paintings.[7] Gertler was delighted, not only by the money but also by the 'generous and friendly feelings' behind the offer, and he at once determined to do 'such good work' that Marsh would feel he was truly worthy of his help.[8]

Brett's assistance was largely practical. Throughout January, as Gertler scoured Hampstead for a studio – a 'terribly depressing occupation' – she resolutely tagged along behind him, 'her little startled face . . . quite white with exhaustion', and her deafness preventing her from hearing anything the estate agents said.[9] And when he finally found 'Penn Studio', situated 'practically on the Heath' at 13a Rudall Crescent, it was Brett who helped him to move in, dusting his books and doing many other things, he told Carrington, that he should not have thought of doing for himself. Penn Studio was to be Gertler's sanctuary for the next seventeen years. Accounts by his contemporaries suggest that it was quite small and shabby, even depressing, but to Gertler it was a paradise. Lying on his back, looking up through the skylight in the studio roof, he glimpsed 'the bellies and chests of the birds' and watched the 'bare black branches of trees against the sky'.[10]

In the interim, while he was still searching, Gertler stayed at Raymond Buildings with Marsh for much of January, and was given his own bedroom and latchkey so that he might come and go as he pleased. Here, he told Carrington, he had 'never been so comfortable before in my life'.[11] He awoke to Eddie announcing that his morning bath was ready, before helping him into a 'PURPLE SILK DRESSING GOWN!' in which to take breakfast, served by Marsh's faithful retainer Mrs Elgy. Carrington teased him about 'living the life of the idle rich at Eddie's', asking if Marsh admired his legs from beneath the purple silk dressing gown at breakfast and predicting that when next she saw him he would be 'surrounded by the Lady Ottoline and nobility (and Winston, if the war is over) lounging in a silk dressing gown and you will despise me, or reject me for my humble attire and because I have no title'.[12] Gertler assured her that Eddie preferred the figures of Jim Barnes and Rupert Brooke, whose legs were 'as pink and plump as yours! I cut a very sorry figure after those people. However, Eddie is very kind to me in spite of my figure.'[13] Nevertheless, the experience gave him a lasting appetite for luxury. Searching for studios, he pointed out to Strachey, had taught him that money was 'the most important thing in life . . . I loathe poverty.

Besides it doesn't suit me', he concluded, for he had already developed, 'such aristocratic tastes'.[14]

The period of lying low also proved short-lived, and Gertler began to enjoy 'very exciting times here in London just now'. There were regular parties at Brett's studio on Tuesdays, which 'half dead' from searching for a studio, he found 'a relief and almost necessary'.[15] As well as his frequent weekending at Cholesbury, Gertler also attended Ottoline's 'Thursdays' in Bedford Square, to which he brought along Brett and another Slade student, Barbara Bagenal. The girls came in fancy dress and were 'a great success', and the meeting initiated an affectionate friendship between Brett and Ottoline. By February, however, Ottoline's parties were beginning to echo the violent spirit of the times. On the 'wildest of all possible nights!' Gertler told Carrington, he had managed to smash one guest's glasses, kick Miss Strachey until her foot bled, and make a 'Belgian girl's arm black and blue!!!'[16] Afterwards Ottoline temporarily suspended the Thursdays.

There was a hint of desperation about Gertler's constant partying, a consolation for and escape from the frustrating stalemate in his relationship with Carrington, and throughout the early months of 1915 he made an effort to preserve a distance between them. His letters described his 'large and varying train of . . . girlfriends': the love scenes with Katherine Mansfield, the parties at Brett's and Brett herself, who, he told Carrington, had 'simply grown a part of me'. Then there was Barbara Hiles, 'a good and affectionate girl', who re-covered his cushions when he moved into the studio, and even agreed to 'sit nude to Brett and me!' and the audacious beauty Iris Tree, whom he admitted to liking 'very much's (and with whom he retained a friendly, flirtatious relationship well into the 1920s). He also flirted with a 'little German girl'[17] whom Carrington had recently drawn nude, and with whom he had danced at one of Brett's parties, telling Carrington that she had 'a lovely little figure to clasp'.[18] Finally, he succeeded in fanning a tiny flame of regret. 'We have shared so much, nearly everything for so long that now I miss not having you here with me', she told him. 'You spoilt me by loving me so much, and so often.'[19] However, just as Gertler was beginning to feel 'how good it is to meet people after one's work . . . so stimulating,' and concluding 'one mustn't begin being a hermit too soon',[20] Carrington was settling into an isolated country existence at her parents' house in Hampshire, and though she missed her London friends, she found she could always 'run up a hill to get happy again'.[21]

Despite his talk of independence, Gertler had not fully cut the apron strings, and when the parties proved too much and he came down with a cold, he locked up his studio and returned to the East End to be nursed by his mother. Now 'fed up with Lady Ottoline and her parties and dancing', he longed simply to get back to his studio and to work. When he did return a few days later, he abandoned his original idea of renting a separate room to sleep in and decided to live full-time at the studio to save money.[22] However, his general air of helplessness soon attracted help in the form of his 'marvellous landlady', the first in a succession of doting females who mothered him and who soon found herself lighting his fire, making his bed, carrying out his cleaning, and cooking his meals 'all for two shillings a week!'[23] After this he declared himself 'as comfortable as a Duke!'[24]

All the same, it was a further squeeze on his precarious finances, and by February Gertler found he could no longer afford to employ professional models, despite Marsh's subsidy. However, he remained buoyant, after selling all three of his exhibits at the NEAC's winter show: his *Black and White Cottage* went to Lady Hamilton for £12, his drawing of *The Old Jew* to Marsh and *Apples* – which he thought 'about the best things I've done'[25] – to a high court judge, though he told Carrington it had hurt him to part with them. The studio light was excellent, and he resumed work on a portrait of Brett, which had previously been put aside, as she was 'so very difficult to do'. At the NEAC spring show it sold immediately to Brett's admirer Professor Brown for £20, despite press criticism of his 'horrible distortion' of her features.[26]

The war remained a remote but undeniable presence. One evening at the cinema Gertler watched in horrified fascination as a newsreel showed French troops in action, 'long rows of black spots running along the snow and then some [other] "spots" dropping down dead or wounded'.[27] In February he ran into Nevinson, dressed in uniform and just back from Dunkirk, where he had been working as a nurse in the Friends Ambulance Unit's St Pierre Hospital. 'Told me in five minutes all about it', Gertler reported to Carrington, 'and you can imagine how ghastly it sounded in "Nevinsonian" language'.[28]

But Gertler's thoughts remained bound up in his work and in Carrington, and just before Easter he persuaded her to join him for a few days at Cannan's cottage in Cholesbury. Here she seemed 'somehow so much more sympathetic than usual' that Gertler was now convinced he loved her more than ever. 'Your friendship', he told her, 'is the best thing in my life.'[29] Carrington, too, felt they had made progress, and afterwards responded to his 'husbandly' behaviour with a 'wifely' letter. 'I never valued you as much as yesterday', she told him. 'You were splendid! The way you helped me into my train and gave me lunch . . . It was the best time we ever spent there. It makes me awfully happy dear, when you love me. Do not think it ever vexes me now. I value it too much. You are such a good comrade.'[30]

But Gertler wanted more than comradeship, and inevitably all 'the old feelings' returned. 'I mean again I want all of you or nothing. I want you to love me. To love me properly or not at all.'[31] He wanted her body as well as her mind and had been 'insincere' or 'hysterical', he told her, when he had pretended otherwise. Anxious to prove that his desire was 'not low, but beautiful', he tried to convince her that as 'painting expresse[d] art', so physical contact expressed love, and he asked her to write 'frankly and plainly' in return, explaining exactly why she did not want such contact.

Carrington responded furiously on 16 April, cutting out fragments of Gertler's previous 'hysterical or insincere' letters and pasting them at the top of her own.[32] She reminded him that it was only four months since he had told her not to mention their 'sex trouble', and had declared himself 'heartily sick of it'. This time she wrote frankly and plainly, as he had asked her to. 'I cannot love you as you want me to. You must know one could not do, what you ask, sexual intercourse, unless one does love a man's body. I have never felt any desire for that in my life . . . I do love you but not in the way you want. Once, you made love to me in your studio . . . many years ago now. One thing, I can never forget, it made me inside feel ashamed unclean. Can I help it? I wish to God I could.' He had once offered to sacrifice his 'very life' if she asked it of him, she pointed out, whereas, she was asking only for 'something less'.[33] Of course he capitulated. 'Thank God it is over and we are friends again', he wrote. 'I only try and leave you because you cannot give me as much of you as I want. But now I have definitely proved that though what you give me is little in comparison to what I desire, yet that little I must have. I cannot live or paint without it.'[34]

As usual he took refuge in his other relationships, in particular his friendship with Lytton Strachey, who was a frequent guest for tea at the studio. They took long tramps together over the heath, and Gertler pronounced him 'splendid to talk to'.[35] In February Gertler had enjoyed a weekend at Strachey's cottage The Lacket in Wiltshire, where the writer was at work on *Eminent Victorians*. For the train journey home he lent Gertler Dostoyevsky's *The Possessed*, which sparked off Gertler's lifelong love for Russian literature (which was only then becoming known in Britain through the translations of Constance Garnett and Koteliansky). Afterwards Strachey continued to ply Gertler with poetry, and even sent some of his own poems with the flatteringly conspiratorial instruction: 'Please don't show any of them to other people.'[36]

However, Strachey may have been hinting at his homosexuality, for when Gertler wrote that he had been reading Virgil's *Pastorals*, the older man asked mischievously, 'Isn't there one that describes a nice young shepherd in love with another nice young shepherd boy, who, however, will have nothing to say to him? If I remember right, that one is never to be found in the School Editions!' And he closed his letter with a teasing verse:

> Why do this world's delights so quickly fall?
> Why is this life so gloomy and so glum?
> – Because, however loud a cock may call,
> He can't be sure the hen he wants will come.
>
> Yours L. S.[37]

Around May these hints seem finally to have got through, and in his next letter to Strachey Gertler recounted in some detail a recent sexual encounter with a woman (though it is not clear whether this was real or invented).[38] His teatime diary suddenly became inexplicably full, and one day in June when Strachey called at the studio, Gertler only 'peeped through the hole in the door and didn't let him in!'[39] Their friendship began to cool. Gertler still liked Strachey, he later explained to Carrington, but 'you can't think how uncomfortable it is for a man to feel he is attracting another man that way . . . to any decent man to attract another physically is revolting!'[40] The two men continued to correspond irregularly, but Gertler usually made sure they no longer enjoyed teatimes alone.

There was never any risk of this kind of difficulty with Marsh, but after the devastating loss of Rupert Brooke (who had died from blood poisoning on the island of Skiros in April 1915) Marsh kept a special eye on Gertler. When he became run down in May, Eddie sent him to Churchill's doctor, settled regular bills for him at the oculist's, and generally alleviated the 'deleterious effects' of what Gertler called 'excessive tea and smoke'.[41] And in May Marsh carried off Gertler's *Daffodils*, the second painting claimed under their new arrangement (the first was *Agapanthus*), which he considered 'the most lovely picture that I ever saw'. 'Two bunches of daffodils against a blue background – it's a real inspiration I think', Marsh wrote to a friend, 'and convinces me of his genius more than anything he has done – and it's wonderfully painted.'[42] It may have been some consolation for the current disappointments in Marsh's own career when, following the failed Allied landings at Gallipoli that spring, Churchill was replaced by Balfour as First Lord of the Admiralty. Where Churchill went, Marsh followed, and they found themselves banished 'like Adam and Eve from the Garden of Eden', Gertler wrote, to the Chancellorship of the Duchy of Lancaster.[43] 'Never was I so feverishly interested in a political move', Gertler admitted frankly to Strachey, 'simply because it was the only one that stood any chance of directly affecting me.'[44] He loyally offered Marsh the chance to withdraw his subsidy, but was greatly relieved when Marsh refused.

It was just as well, since by June Gertler already owed £8 to his family. Later the same month he learned to his indignation that the NEAC had refused his *Creation of Eve* for the summer exhibition, because the figure of Eve was considered 'indecent'. 'I was absolutely amazed and very vexed because I had hopes of selling it there, and any extra money would have been very useful just now', he told Strachey.[45] It put a further strain of his relationship with his parents, who were under pressure as 'enemy aliens', and felt obliged to take up Polish citizenship. All summer long they watched helplessly as their old neighbours – 'no more Austrian in spirit than hotentot!' – were repatriated to their homelands. They both became ill, and Louis accused his youngest son of indifference and neglect.[46]

These experiences, and the Zeppelin raids (which began on the last day of May), forced Gertler to begin facing up to the reality of the war. Although Marsh remained unaware of it, Gertler's unease infected their relationship, and by July, Gertler confided to Carrington, he was beginning to feel depressed every time they met. 'I expect I shall be dragged into this wretched war, before it's all over', he wrote, 'but I shall keep out of it as long as I possibly can . . . How I shall hate it if it spoils my life and prevents me from carrying on my work. How hateful it would be to lose one's life, or even be maimed for life, through a purpose in which one has no sort of belief.'[47]

This bitterness also invaded his relationship with Carrington, and he was bewildered by her behaviour. 'How dreadfully disappointing and inconsiderate you are very often', he told her. 'You are a sort of person with whom one never gets beyond a certain point of intimacy, or if one for a moment oversteps the boundary line, one finds that you have immediately rushed back, leaving one alone gaping.'[48] He found her 'in some ways amazingly inhuman' and concluded that satisfaction from life could come only from his work. To prove this, he broke off all contact for three months.

He holed himself up at Cholesbury as much as possible that summer, renting Baldwin's Farm Cottage from a neighbour of the Cannans, and escaping there whenever he could. He invited no one to visit him – though Gilbert and Mary were on hand – for he had gone there to work. It was also a cost-cutting device, for in the country he could live on £1 a week, and did not have to rely so heavily on Marsh. He began work on a new portrait, *Gilbert Cannan at his Mill*, a strangely prophetic study that seems to hint at the troubled writer's future breakdown, as he stands flanked by his two enormous dogs, almost overwhelmed by the 'upright converging gothic forms' of the trees and the mill. Sir John Rothenstein in *Modern English Painters* later observed, 'it is the skill with which the highly original composition has been worked out and the intense energy with which every small feature has been painted, and not the subject itself, to which the picture's impressiveness is due.'[49] After Gertler's death Rothenstein came across a photograph of the Mill among Gertler's papers, from which the picture had been closely observed, but it bore 'the same relation to the painting', he wrote, 'as a score does to a finished symphony'.

Gertler's small cottage made a difficult studio, but Mary came to the rescue by suggesting he use Gilbert's old motor shed instead. However, at this point Gertler received a commission from his old friend T. E. Harvey to paint his cousin Professor Sadler. It meant spending part of August in Leeds, but it also came with a £50 fee, so Gertler wrote to accept. On arrival he found himself in difficulties almost at once. Sadler could spare no time from his post as vice-chancellor, and Gertler was forced to work around him in his office at the university, where, as part of his war work, Sadler was often consulted by officers. It was almost impossible to concentrate in the hubbub, and Gertler did not find Sadler interesting as a sitter. He also resented having to take time off from his own work, and in his letters to Marsh complained that commissioned portrait painting was 'a dreadful occupation . . . Never again will I accept a portrait unless the sitter interests or inspires me . . . I would rather starve.'[50] Nevertheless, he grew fond of Sadler, who was kindly and tried hard to make him comfortable, so that Gertler determined not to leave until he had achieved at least 'an honest likeness of the man', and made as good a picture of it as he could.[51] Clearly, he no longer considered the two concepts as necessarily related.

In the evenings Gertler began to work on a small oil study of swing boats on Hampstead Heath, inspired by a fair he had seen at Easter. Since the spring he had been rising early to go out on the heath, which he found a constant source of inspiration. 'I got wonderful ideas here on Bank Holiday', he had written to Carrington back in May. 'Multitudes of people. Bright feathers, swinging in and out of the clouds in coloured boats, coloured ropes, a blaze of whirling colours'.[52] Ideas, as he tried to explain to Marsh, constantly welled up inside him with an almost physical force. 'These ideas are so mysterious and wonderful that when they come over me – they come in waves.'[53] Sometimes he literally trembled with excitement and could hardly stand. 'I only want to arrange my life', he told Marsh, in order to 'give birth one after the other to the pictures which are fighting in me to come out'.[54]

Marsh was all sympathy, believing Gertler to have been 'born a great painter, and if that is true', he wrote, 'it will have been a proud thing in my life to have been able to help you . . . Fertility', he counselled, 'if it doesn't water down intensity, is a fine promising thing in a young artist.' He advised Gertler to take heart from the examples of other great artists, quoting a letter from Keats to his friend the painter Benjamin Haydon: 'I am glad you say every man of great views is at times as tormented as I am.'[55]

In June 1915 the Morrells moved into their new country estate, comprising a manor house, two farmsteads and a handful of cottages, in the tiny village of Garsington, five miles outside Oxford.[56] The first trickle of visitors arrived to celebrate Ottoline's birthday, but the number soon swelled to a flood, and by the end of the war Garsington had become so famous that there is scarcely a memoir of the period in which it is not mentioned. The Morrells were to live there for almost fourteen years, during which time Ottoline would transform the house and surrounding gardens into 'a habitable work of art'.[57] 'The first view of the house', one of her guests recorded, 'was always a shock of delight.'[58] A pretty grey-stoned Tudor manor house, edged by yew hedges, it offered commanding views over the Oxfordshire countryside from the back lawn. Ottoline left the exterior of the house untouched, and kept the interior of the upper house fairly plain and comfortable, but the lower rooms she transformed into something approaching splendour. The hall was painted a pearly grey with streaks of pink to resemble a sunset, and the windows edged with lemon-yellow curtains. In the main sitting room, known as the Red Room, the panelled walls were painted a Venetian red and each panel was outlined with a thin gold line (many of them completed by the guests). In the evenings, after dinner, the company would sit here and read aloud to one another, or perhaps perform strange Hungarian dances on the lawn, as Philip pounded out music on the pianola. At dinner they gathered round the 'long dark oak polished table, with candles shaded with little red paper hoods', the guests making 'brilliant conversation', occasionally 'punctuated with Clive Bell's shrill gusts of laughter' or Bertie Russell's 'high cackle', as Gertler performed 'one of his flawless imitations'.[59] 'I can so well visualise it', he later wrote fondly to Ottoline from France in 1922, 'the lawn, the pond, the meals, the red room[,] the general atmosphere, and how I miss it!'[60]

After his first visit in September Gertler became one of Ottoline's most regular guests. By 1920 he admitted that Garsington had become 'a sort of home to me now', and Ottoline's daughter Julian confirmed that he was always treated as 'a son of the house'.[61] You are so one of us – one of the family',[62] Ottoline would write, 'Come to your home at G[arsington] whenever you like'.[63] He felt a special affinity for the Italianate gardens, especially the main lawn behind the house with its cypresses, and the brooding ilex tree, which overhung a rectangular pond edged with statues, where they bathed on summer afternoons. He recorded his love affair with the house and gardens in a series of paintings that spanned the many years of hospitality he enjoyed there and was broken-hearted when the Morrells eventually sold Garsington in 1928.[64]

Amid all the fun and laughter, however, much serious talk went on at Garsington, and by 1916 it had become the most 'notorious' refuge for pacifists in the country.[65] Here 'pacifism was not only respectable, but the orthodox religion'[66] and throughout the war Garsington would swarm with the groups of conscientious objectors sent to carry out work of 'national importance' on the farm. The Morrells own pacifism had been well publicized, since Philip, as Liberal MP for the constituency of Burnley, had made a speech against Britain's involvement in the war in the House of Commons in August 1914, and was one of thirty liberal MPs who insisted on including a clause of exemption for pacifists when the Military Service Act was passed in January 1916.

Moreover, since 1911 Ottoline had been involved in a love affair with the philosopher Bertrand Russell, who, on his return from lecturing in the United States at the outbreak of war, became the leading member of the 'No Conscription Fellowship', and lectured publicly against the war. A 'puckish figure', with his sharp nose, wide mouth and 'shock of springy hair', he bubbled over with outrageous, sometimes iconoclastic ideas, and usually dominated the Garsington dinner table by sheer force of intellect.[67] (Brett and her ear-trumpet 'Toby' often retreated into silence out of sheer terror.) At Garsington, Russell's views had great authority. Gilbert Cannan, for instance, was delighted when Russell praised his recently published novel *Windmills*, and told Ottoline, 'I would rather have his commendation than anyone's'.[68]

Another of Ottoline's frequent guests in the autumn of 1915 was D. H. Lawrence. It was a particularly gloomy period for Lawrence, whose novel *The Rainbow* had been published to damning notices in September, with reviewers expressing outrage at its lesbian love scenes and the anti-military views expressed by the heroine, Ursula Brangwyn. (The fact that his wife, Frieda, was German only fuelled the hostility and, although Lawrence was declared medically unfit for service, the couple were persecuted throughout the war as suspected German agents.) By November Lawrence's publisher Methuen had been fined 10 guineas and ordered to withdraw the book, and Lawrence's view of England as 'a collapsing civilization' was confirmed by the reported burning of the remaining copies of *The Rainbow* by the public hangman outside the Royal Exchange in December.[69]

The next year was a nightmare for Lawrence, and his humiliating treatment rapidly coloured the conception of his next novel, *Women in Love*. Though he began it as a life-affirming celebration of his joy in marriage, it soon became a vehicle for the disintegration of civilization that he observed all around him, and his apocalyptic vision of the war. Even his early enjoyment of Garsington as 'a retreat where we come and knit ourselves together'[70] became polluted by what he called the 'mental and wearying'[71] attitude of his fellow guests. (Some of them found their personal characteristics grafted onto the fictional characters of *Women in Love*.[72])

In the meantime the vehemence of Lawrence's views easily overwhelmed the rather vague pacifism of his friends. Towards the end of

September Gertler wrote ominously to Marsh, 'Mrs Lawrence tells me she has written to you about your attitude towards the war. She seemed quite upset',[73] and Cannan, who had at the start of the conflict merely considered that 'active service would [not] be a particularly valuable experience for an artist', came to believe, after talking to Lawrence, that it was 'the duty of all artists to hate this war and do nothing which will help it in any way'.[74] These were almost exactly the words that Gertler used in a letter to Marsh in October, when he wrote to break off their friendship and Marsh's subsidy (and they also curiously duplicated the words with which he had broken with Nevinson over Carrington some three years earlier). 'I have come to the conclusion,' he wrote, 'that we two are too fundamentally different to continue to be friends. Since the war', he explained:

> You have gone in one direction and I in another. All the time I have been stifling my feelings. Firstly because of your kindness to me and secondly I did not want to hurt you. I am I believe what you call a 'Passivist'. I don't know exactly what that means, but I just hate this war and should really loathe to help in it.[75]

He acknowledged, however, Marsh's extraordinary kindness in the past, and promised that 'if ever I earn any money by painting I shall return you what I owe you' (though these noble sentiments were somewhat marred by his request for Mrs Elgy to send on his pyjamas and slippers, which he had left behind).[76] To Marsh, still struggling to come to terms with the loss of Rupert Brooke, Gertler's letter was an unexpected blow, and must have seemed callously naïve, but Gertler's surrender of financial security was also an act of great bravery. He was undoubtedly influenced, however, by the Garsington circle: 'I am so glad you kicked off from Eddie Marsh', Ottoline later told him.[77]

Even as he voiced his pacifism, Gertler began to be caught up in the casualties of war: Carrington's brother Noel, who had been injured fighting, was now at home on convalescent leave and Katherine Mansfield's beloved brother Leslie was reported killed – 'blown to bits' – in early October. Katherine was inconsolable. One evening later the same month, as Gertler boarded a London bus, he saw the sky light up in front of him as a Zeppelin streaked across it, shots bursting all around 'like huge stars'. Rushing to the tube for shelter, he looked back 'like Lot, and was like him nearly petrified into a block of salt!'[78] Mostly, he tried to turn these experiences into stories to entertain his friends. Frieda Lawrence long remembered one when 'he panicked and kept running up and down the stairs of a strange house'; but the raids were a sobering experience all the same.

By November, having relinquished Marsh's subsidy, Gertler now had to face the terrifying possibility that he might lose his studio. 'In about two months unless something happens', he confessed to Carrington, 'I shall be penniless!'[79] He had some hopes of raising money through the conductor Thomas Beecham, who he believed had 'practically engaged' him to paint the scenery for his next opera production. There seemed some justification for this optimism when Beecham, accompanied by the society hostess Lady Cunard (who was living openly with him in London), visited Gertler at the studio shortly before he left for a weekend at Garsington, and purchased one of his powerful Jewish studies, *Rabbi and Rabbitzin*, for £10 on the spot. The following day Gertler sold a *Study of Heads* (a preparatory piece for his 1916 painting the *Merry-Go-Round*) to the poet John Drinkwater for £5.

Gertler arrived at Garsington on 21 November in a whirl. Too excited and restless to work, he spent most of the day in the nursery playing with Ottoline's daughter Julian and her cousin Lalage, and in the evening joined in the dancing and acting with relish. There were 'extraordinary things', he told Carrington, going on in his mind.[80] Although the NEAC had refused all his work for the winter salon (with the exception of *Abraham and the Angels*), three of his pictures had been accepted by the London Group and were shortly to be exhibited at the Goupil Gallery.

The London Group had emerged in 1913 from an alliance between the Camden Town Group artists (who held their final exhibition at the Carfax Gallery in December 1912) and various smaller groups who had formerly exhibited with the AAA organized by Frank Rutter. The name, first coined by Jacob Epstein, reflected the group's aim to 'offer hospitality to all manner of artistic expression provided it has the quality of sincere personal conviction'. Here, it was proclaimed, 'Cubism meets Impressionism, Futurism and Sickertism join hands and are not ashamed.'[81] Nevertheless, anxious to avoid the mistakes of the AAA (where unlimited membership had swollen the ranks to such an extent that Rutter needed a bicycle to supervise the hangings), the London Group formulated strict rules governing election to its membership.[82] Each adverse vote, it was decreed, should cancel out each favourable one and 'to secure election a member must finally obtain the votes of at least half'.[83] These rigorous procedures (later slightly relaxed) would effectively bar many well-known artists – William

Rothenstein and Paul Nash among them – during the early membership elections. Gertler, too, failed to poll enough votes at his first two attempts, and was finally voted a member only in the spring of 1915.

The London Group's first two exhibitions have been described as 'milestones in the development of modern British art'.[84] But at the third show, in November 1915, almost half the members, including some of the most radical – Wyndham Lewis, William Roberts, David Bomberg and Edward Wadsworth – were involved with the war effort and did not take part. Nevinson, whose brutal pictures of warfare had dominated the spring show, was on this occasion the sole representative of Cubism, and 'purged . . . of several of its most violent components' the exhibition was only a pale shadow of its predecessors.[85] After attending the private view, Gertler wrote to Carrington in disgust:

> What a rubbishy show! All the pictures except my own, were composed of washed out purples and greens, and they matched so well that it seemed almost as if the artists all collaborated in order to create harmony . . . In reality it means simply that they all paint alike and equally badly![86]

Against this background his own pictures had a tremendous impact, and though his study of *Swing Boats* on Hampstead Heath (now known only by photograph) received little attention, both *The Fruit Stall* and *The Creation of Eve* made him, for different reasons, the most talked about artist in the exhibition.

The Fruit Stall, a large picture of two costers and 'triangles of bright coloured fruit' (now sadly lost), was widely praised.[87] Frank Rutter, writing for the *Sunday Times*, thought the picture ground-breaking, and Wadsworth sent Gertler a card to tell him how much he admired it. Unexpected letters of support came from Duncan Grant and Clive Bell, who told Gertler that both he and Roger Fry had been 'very much impressed'. 'I don't know', he wrote, 'when I saw an English picture that seemed to me so much the real thing.'[88]

But it was *The Creation of Eve* that created 'uproar' among the public and sent the critics 'quite mad' with rage. 'God knows what they are wild about', Gertler wrote to Carrington, in genuine bewilderment.[89] He was astonished to find that 'some people in a rage [had] stuck a label on the belly of my poor little "Eve" with "Made in Germany" written on it!'[90] The painting was dismissed by the *Daily Telegraph* (21 November 1915) as 'a deliberate piece of eccentricity', declared 'unpleasantly sensationalist' by *The Observer*, damned by the *Pall Mall*

Gazette as 'merely a piece of impertinence, with a seasoning of blasphemy' and called 'hunnishly indecent' by the *Morning Post*, a criticism that links Gertler's work to that 'sinister foreign subversion of British culture' suspected to be behind all experimental art.

Patriotic fever had been mounting since the sinking of the *Lusitania* in May 1915, and by the autumn 'atrocity rumours' were being used to blacken the enemy. Conservative critics such as Sir Claude Phillips of the *Daily Telegraph*, who had previously admired Gertler's Italianate drawings, headed the campaign against radical art. 'Less than ever', Phillips fulminated, 'do we feel inclined to look on with equanimity at these pranks in the domain of art, by which in piping times of peace it was possible to be mildly interested, or at any rate amused.'[91] Even *The Observer* claimed to believe that Gertler's paintings had been merely intended to 'shock, to offend, to arouse discussion'.[92] Gertler's German-sounding name was also likely to raise all sorts of questions, especially when it was known that he mixed with 'pro-German' pacifists at Garsington.[93] Only Walter Sickert in the *Burlington Magazine* saw fit to defend *Eve* publicly, pouring scorn on the NEAC's unimaginative decision to reject the painting:

> Here is Mr. Gertler, legitimate and sturdy child of the Slade school . . . left like a foundling in a copy of *The Times* on Mr. Marchant's doorstep. Has the old New English reached the critical age when she is no longer able to suckle her own offspring? For Mr. Gertler has passed master painter and no jury of painters has the right, it seems to me, to reject him.[94]

Initially, however, the press furore seemed to do Gertler 'more good than harm', and several offers followed for both *Eve* and *The Fruit Stall*. Lady Cunard declared he was 'the talk of London', and motored him all over the city to take tea with the lords, ladies and baronesses who asked to meet him. 'And would you believe it,' he wrote to Carrington, 'all these people pretend that they like my pictures.' Knowing that this was a game to them, and that the fame was transitory, he expected it to last 'quite four days'; but he also recognized that this might well be long enough for him to 'get some money out of these titled wretches, so that I can go on quietly again for a while and paint what I want to'.[95] (And Carrington agreed, sales were 'most important when one has to do with these idle rich'.[96])

Lady Cunard never did buy any of Gertler's pictures. She was, he told Marsh, 'so vague and has too much money herself to understand real poverty'.[97] Thomas Beecham's purchases were limited to *Rabbi and Rabbitzin*, and the much talked about commission for scenery was eventually awarded to Gertler's old Slade friend Adrian Allinson. However, Lady Hamilton, who had purchased *The Black and White Cottage* (1914) back in February, now gave it as a wedding present to Violet Asquith, the daughter of the prime minister, on her marriage to Maurice Bonham-Carter. The picture was taken to Downing Street, where it was exhibited among the other presents, and apparently 'much admired'. After this, Gertler wrote to Carrington, 'my people conclude that I am the bosom friend of the Premier and that before long the Queen will kiss me on both cheeks and say, "How do you do Mr Gertler?" '[98] And indeed, only a few months later Gertler's name made its first appearance in *Who's Who.*

'Your letters of course excite me terribly', Carrington wrote on hearing of his success. 'I am still always excited about motor cars and duchesses!!!'[99] But their paths were already beginning to diverge. Gertler appreciated the countryside but loved London, while Carrington, despite the restrictions of life with her parents, adored living in the country, revelling in 'the great space between one and the hills opposite, after the houses in Gower Street which press against my very nose, on every side'.[100] By the autumn she was living part of the time in Hove, Sussex, giving painting lessons to the son of the Baron de Forest, and in December she accepted an invitation from Clive and Vanessa Bell to spend three days at Asheham House in the Sussex Downs (the home of Virginia and Leonard Woolf, temporarily borrowed by the Bells). These three days changed her life.

Apart from Barbara Hiles, Carrington's fellow guests were all members of the Bloomsbury set. 'God knows why they asked me!!' she wrote to Gertler immediately after her return, but she had found herself 'much happier than expected'.[101] Four miles from the nearest town of Lewes, and surrounded by hills on all sides, she was in her element. Exhilarated by the countryside, she rose early to take long walks over the Downs by herself, 'like a small moth compelled to draw near to [the sun], blinking in its brilliant light', and returned to the house to find the others still in bed.[102] There were no servants and the domestic arrangements were unconventional: Carrington and Vanessa shared the cooking, and they all kept warm by drinking strong rum punch in the evenings. At first she listened wide-eyed to the Bloomsbury gossip, shocked to discover, 'what traitors all these people are! They ridicule Ottoline! . . . I think it's beastly of them to enjoy Ottoline's kindnesses and then laugh at her', she told Gertler.[103]

He was astonished to hear that she had stayed with 'the Clive Bells and that crew', and resentful that she seemed to 'shun London as if it was Hell and . . . I was the Devil!' His desire to see her was 'about a thousand times greater than all theirs put together . . . You are quite free to act as you feel you want to', he wrote, 'only you ought not to tell me that you care for me. You do not care for anybody as yet. What keeps the fire burning between us is my love for you.'[104] Characteristically, Carrington had not told him the whole truth about her weekend. Probably attracted by her boyish appearance, Lytton Strachey (whom Carrington described to Gertler as 'rather curious'), had kissed her while they were out walking on the Downs. Not reassured by Barbara's insistence that he was homosexual, a word she had to have explained to her, Carrington crept into his room next morning with a pair of scissors to cut off Strachey's beard in revenge. Instead, according to legend, as she leant over him, he opened his eyes, and she fell instantly, irretrievably, in love.

Carrington spent the next sixteen months trying to come to terms with these feelings, but at first they were too astonishing to admit, even to herself. Writing to Gertler, she insisted, 'I do not love you physically, that you know, but I care for you far more than I do for anyone else.'[105] From now on, however, her letters to Gertler, like her emotions, would be veiled, 'like woodcuts, limited in their technique, and [with] certain elements, [such] as colour . . . never . . . able to be shown'.[106]

11

Articulate Extremities

'I must say, I have for you, in your work, reverence, the reverence for the great articulate extremity of art.'
D. H. Lawrence to Mark Gertler, 9 October 1916

As THE NEW year lengthened into February and Gertler heard nothing from Lady Cunard confirming her offer for *Eve*, he began to grow alarmed. The threat of losing the studio revived, and his pacifist resolve began to weaken, 'I feel almost sorry that I gave up Eddie Marsh!' he confessed to Kot, 'for after all his money was such a help. And isn't it . . . worth undergoing any trouble and humiliation to be enabled to paint? To paint and paint is what I want.'[1] Ironically, it was Lawrence who now urged him towards reconciliation. Forbidden to leave Britain after the suppression of *The Rainbow*, the Lawrences (storing many of their possessions in Gertler's bathtub) had moved at the end of 1915 to the 'bare, forgotten . . . pre-Christian' countryside of Cornwall. From there, broke and gloomy, Lawrence wrote to Gertler on 10 February that he saw 'no prospect of the war's ever ending, and not a ghost of a hope that people will ever want sincere work from any artist', and advised him to 'make your peace with Eddie'.[2]

The day before his letter the Military Service Act had introduced conscription for unmarried men between the ages of eighteen and forty-one.[3] Gertler duly presented himself 'trembling in every limb' at the local tribunal and recruiting office, only to be refused (to his delight) on account of his parentage. 'What luck!' he told Brett, 'now I am free to go on with my work. Perhaps some day "My Country" will thank God for my Austrian [*sic*] parentage which enabled me to sit quiet and paint.'[4]

He spent most of the next year at Cholesbury, completing Cannan's portrait and working on a further painting which he described to Strachey in May as 'a large and very unsaleable picture of Merry-Go-Rounds'.[5] Occasionally, he was forced to put this aside in order to paint 'small saleable things', such as daffodils, but his heart, Gertler confessed, was 'in my Merry-Go-Rounds'.[6] *The Merry-Go-Round* is Gertler's most famous and most powerful painting. Over six feet high and roughly four feet wide, it brings the viewer up short in front of a carousel which has been frozen in motion, the mouths of its riders opened in a long, unending scream. Strident oranges, yellows, reds and blues heighten the painting's dominant atmosphere of terror and violence, and it was immediately recognized by Gertler's circle as a satire on militarism.

The original composition had been inspired by the bank holiday fair on Hampstead Heath the previous spring, and Gertler had continued to work on studies for the painting ever since. But by 1916, with the general atmosphere permeated by 'war fear', the fair had become a symbol for something far more sinister.[7] The survival of two careful drawings shows how the original conception was gradually crafted into the final image, and the figures of the riders pushed deeper into caricature.

As Gertler worked on the painting throughout 1916 the prospect of military service occupied all his friends. Lytton Strachey, though clearly unfit for military service, was originally refused exemption, and attended a farcical meeting of the Hampstead tribunal in March, at which, when asked by the committee what he would do if he saw a German trying to rape his sister, he gave the famously ambiguous reply 'I should try and come between them.'[8] He was subsequently rejected by the medical board as unfit for service of any kind. Even Kot, who was still a Russian citizen, believed that he might be called up and considered offering himself as a farm labourer at Garsington – an occupation that was to become increasingly popular among conscientious objectors, who began to move there in the summer of 1916 and stayed until the end of the war. Over the summer Bertrand Russell only narrowly escaped prison after publicly claiming authorship of a leaflet published by the No Conscription Fellowship. (In the end he was fined £100 and stripped of his Trinity lectureship.) And Gilbert Cannan, despite military exemption, carried on an acrimonious correspondence about pacifism with Eddie Marsh over the summer, writing tactlessly that Gertler had been 'doing fine stuff lately', and that war was 'certainly creating a real artistic activity – if only there could be official recognition of it'.[9]

Gertler had partially mended the breach with Marsh in April 1916, when, according to Marsh's biographer Christopher Hassall, he had reappeared at Raymond Buildings 'destitute' once again and the subsidy was temporarily restored.[10] In return, Marsh acquired a drawing and Gertler's interior of *Penn Studio* (1915) – Lawrence called it, 'Eddie . . . rak[ing] in his debts'.[11] Even after this Gertler's outstanding bill with Marsh stood at £39, and was probably never settled. However, the £5 subsidy Gertler received in April was also to be his last.

Marsh seems to have done Gertler one further service in April 1916, when it finally became clear that Lady Cunard was not going to purchase *Eve*. Lady Ridley had offered £30 for it at the close of the Goupil show, but since she had been recently widowed, Gertler considered it too delicate a time to approach her, and asked Marsh to intercede.[12] Probably Marsh did use his influence, for the picture was subsequently purchased by Lady Ridley's brother-in-law Jasper Ridley. 'You ask whether I find enough admirers to live on', Gertler wrote to William Rothenstein in April, 'well I have a few people who believe in me, but they are not buyers so that I always have difficulty about money. However at the last moment I always seem to sell a little picture which keeps the "wolf from the door".'[13]

During the many months it took to complete *The Merry-Go-Round* Gertler refused to show the canvas to anyone, including Vanessa Bell, who called at his studio in March. (Afterwards she told Ottoline that Gertler had been 'very amusing and intelligent. I liked him, and he's so much interested in his painting he can hardly talk of anything else, which I rather like. I think he must have been through an unattractive state of fearful self-consciousness and now he has more self confidence and is much nicer.'[14]) As Gertler completed the picture his view of the war darkened further. 'Lately', he wrote to Carrington in May, 'the whole horror of the War has come freshly upon me.'[15] He was worried by rumours that men were now being stopped on the London streets and asked to explain why they were not in uniform. 'Without my work', he explained, 'life would be a living Hell and especially under military authority. Yet I can hardly expect to escape.'[16]

The Merry-Go-Round was not simply a vision of cultural disintegration, however, but also a highly personal expression of Gertler's discontent at his circular relationship with Carrington, which he would characterize later that summer as having 'neither beginning nor end'. It was then entering one of its most difficult phases.

Since her fateful meeting with Strachey the previous December Carrington had become more elusive than ever. 'I will come on Friday . . . almost for certain', runs a typical letter in January 1916. 'Why not quite for certain you say. Because . . . like a Greek Philosopher you ought to be prepared to not expect me. And then you suffer no disappointment!'[17] But Gertler could not be philosophical over their relationship, and found her behaviour deeply frustrating. Lawrence advised him to give himself up in love instead of trying to dominate Carrington. 'One must learn to relinquish oneself', he wrote. 'Not to bother about oneself, but to love the other person. You hold too closely to yourself, for her to be free to love you.'[18] It was perceptive advice, but of course Gertler did not take it. He still believed that their difficulties could be resolved, and they both knew that he would always be disappointed if and when Carrington failed to turn up. Besides, he had already made up his mind at the close of 1915 never to leave her again and to devote himself 'entirely' to her,[19] a devotion that Carrington found profoundly intimidating.

When in town, however, she generally spent Monday evenings with him and, although they often quarrelled, she remained an inspiring companion. Gertler called their conversation one such Monday evening, 'a revelation . . . you can't think how much you helped me last night', he told her. 'If only you would talk more often to me like that how thankful I should be. You must try more to help me out of myself, out of my petty mean vulgar little self.'[20] But he also recognized that they would never reach 'that state of spiritual friendship' they both desired because their paths to achieving it were so different. 'Your way . . . is by leaving out sex. My way is through sex. Apparently we neither of us can change our ways, because they are ingrained in our natures. Therefore there will always be strife between us and I shall always suffer.'[21]

In fact, Carrington was seldom in London during the first half of 1917, having become, along with Brett (who had developed one of her violent crushes on Ottoline), pretty much a 'permanence' at Garsington. There she saw a good deal of Strachey, who found himself with a new pupil to instruct. Ottoline later recalled how during this period Carrington would frequently retire to a secluded corner with a volume of Donne's poems in her hand. Then 'after perhaps an hour or two she would take back her book or sit at

[Strachey's] feet gazing up at him in adoration, while he instructed her in English literature . . . Lytton always enjoyed teaching the young and Carrington was a fascinating and flattering pupil.'[22] Ottoline felt, she wrote, that she was watching 'Act I of a long play, played out on other stages'.

Initially, the secrecy of their relationship was part of the attraction for Carrington. She was at her most open, child-like and captivating with Strachey, sprinkling her letters with drawings, idiosyncratic spellings and stories that made him laugh out loud at the Garsington breakfast table. Alternately flattered and alarmed by her adoration, he found her increasingly intriguing, and in time Carrington's influence would noticeably soften him. Virginia Woolf later observed that when they were together, Strachey was 'very amusing, charming, benignant, & like a father to C. She kisses him & waits on him & gets good advice & some sort of protection'.[23] Carrington had unexpectedly found not only a father figure but also the mentor she had long been seeking. He became 'chère [*sic*] grand-père', or sometimes 'Uncle', and she was 'votre Bébé'. But with Gertler both her language and behaviour were increasingly constrained. 'You are too possessive', she wrote in a rare moment of truthfulness in April, 'and I too free. That is why we could never live together.'[24] She wrote him long letters, then tore them up, finding it difficult to set down 'what I really meant'.[25] But by late April she was advising a temporary separation, since 'it nearly sends me mad with grief, at seeing you so miserable'.[26] Gertler agreed, unaware of her 'incredible internal excitement' at seeing Strachey in the interval.[27]

By May he was once more sunk in depression, 'feeling all over again the isolation of my spirit'. He could not 'make people understand me or my work', he complained to Carrington, 'neither can I understand them.' And the problem was aggravated by their own difficulties. 'What is the good of having this depth of feeling', he asked, 'if no one wants or understands it! I paint pictures that seem to me wonderful but no one understands them; I love with a wonderful love but no wants my love.' He signed this letter 'Your very critical and unhappy friend.'[28]

These feelings were exacerbated by an incident at Cholesbury that June, when Carrington one day casually kissed Cannan in his bedroom. It meant nothing to her, but by this time Cannan was also infatuated with her. He called her 'Daisy' in his letters, transformed her into Morrison in *Mendel* (which had been written in two months that spring) and eventually dedicated the novel to Carrington when it was published in the autumn. When Cannan told Gertler of the kiss he was shattered. 'I do not think we can go further. I believe we are too fundamentally different to become lovers', he wrote to Carrington. 'You alone have tormented me for five years, and now after all that time I find you unsatisfactory. Please leave me, I cannot bear any more.'[29]

This would have been an ideal point for Carrington to close this torturous chapter of their history, but while she could not commit to him, neither could she let him go. Instead, her answer asked him to picture 'many islands of adventures which one must swim across to . . . But', she assured him, 'one will always return to the mainland. You are that mainland to me.' She would have 'mental and physical adventures perhaps, perhaps none', she wrote. 'Do you never feel the excitement of this big world and ships, and many people?' she asked, and yet promised, ' I will not fail you.'[30]

Baffled, Gertler turned to Kot for support. Since the Cholesbury Christmas their relationship had deepened, and though he could be difficult and quarrelsome, Kot was also passionately loyal. He was 'a refugee', wrote one of his friends, 'who himself provided refuge for his coterie of friends'[31]; a person 'one could trust so implicitly, whose truth was . . . undivided',[32] and he exerted a remarkable influence over Gertler. 'Your friendship', he insisted, 'is simply invaluable.'[33] And Kot did not let him down. 'You know what great value I attribute to your work though I am a profane. This is only because I know you and believe in you', he replied.[34] Together back in London they visited their own circle of friends. On Sundays they went to Gordon and Beatrice Campbells', and soon became their most welcomed visitors (the Campbells' cook called them 'them Roosshians'). Gertler was the chief performer, dancing, telling stories or doing his imitations, but sometimes Kot joined in and they performed together as 'Beattie and Babs', a pair of sisters from a famous music-hall comedy act. In this company, warmed by appreciation, Gertler showed only his fun-loving side; his laughter, Beatrice recalled, 'was a glorious thing'.[35]

Gertler and Kot also became friendly with the barrister St John (Jack) Hutchinson and his charming wife, Mary, a cousin and confidante of Lytton Strachey's, and Clive Bell's mistress for more than a decade. Through the Hutchinsons Gertler also met the francophile barrister and collector Montague Shearman, known to his friends as Monty. 'People sometimes think that if one gets to know and like a person one is hypnotized into liking his art that way',

Shearman wrote to Gertler in the summer of 1916; 'I am not like that.'[36] Throughout 1916 the two men met frequently at the Hutchinsons' River House in Hammersmith, where Shearman was deeply moved by Gertler's still life *The Dutch Doll* (1915), though he later considered it slight in comparison with his 'big work'. In June he bought his first Gertler, the portrait of *Gilbert Cannan at his Mill*, and although it was followed by more than a dozen subsequent purchases, he remained 'terrifically worked up at having got it'.[37]

By the late summer Shearman found himself constantly dreaming of Gertler's pictures, though he found it 'almost impossible' in the artist's presence to explain how deeply they thrilled him. He tried to explain that he was 'a very very stand-offish and reticent person', but reticence was not the only reason: he was also homosexual, and becoming increasingly attracted to Gertler. Gertler in turn grew very fond of Monty. He was broad-minded, tolerant, learned and extremely generous; he motored Gertler (and sometimes Carrington) about in his car and provided excellent *foie gras* picnics on the rides home from Eleanor House (the Hutchinsons' Sussex home in Wittering). But he was also an undeniably useful patron, and if Gertler noticed Shearman's feelings, he did not comment on them. Perhaps he was less naïve after the earlier experience with Strachey, and he eventually learned to become quite tolerant of this sort of attention, providing he wasn't expected to 'do anything' in return.

Gertler arrived at Garsington on his first official summer visit in late July 1916. (With the exception of 1922, when he was abroad, it was a visit he would repeat annually for almost the next decade.) He was disappointed to find that Katherine Mansfield, who had arranged to meet him there after arguing with Murry, had already left and rejoined Murry in Cornwall.[38] Gertler was nervous and miserable, 'not so much because of the Lady Ottoline and the household', he told Kot, 'but because of more intimate reasons': specifically, his relationship with Carrington. 'If only the torment would end. It is like some terrible disease and incurable. We both put our heads together and try and end it, but we can't. It goes on in spite of us both being tired and worn out.'[39]

Both Carrington and Strachey were already at Garsington, and the ensuing drama, set among a 'surging mesh of pugs, peacocks, pianolas, and humans . . . the inhabitants of Circe's cave' (as Strachey described it), seemed perilously poised between tragedy and farce.[40] Strachey reported in his letters that Carrington was '*aux abois* with Gertler for ever at her, day in, day out', while Gertler himself seemed to be playing a double role, at one moment 'carolling a rag-time in union with her Ladyship' and the next 'gnashing his teeth in the background' as Carrington flew off in the opposite direction. Strachey sympathized with them both, recognizing that Carrington still admired Gertler (as he did himself) and sympathizing with him over the 'perpetual virginity question' (unless, he mused, in a letter to Mary Hutchinson, Carrington was 'the most horrible liar'[41]). But by 30 July Gertler had had enough, and suddenly decided to return to London. At his departure, Carrington wrote to Strachey (who had by then left Garsington himself), 'complicated feelings' immediately welled up inside her.[42]

After this summer Gertler's and Carrington's friendships began to polarize. Carrington drew closer to Strachey, and away from her old friends, and Gertler began to develop a more meaningful relationship with Ottoline, relishing, even after he had returned to the stifling streets of London, 'the good taste of Garsington in my mouth'. He was grateful to her for 'putting up with my troublesome self for a whole fortnight' and assured her that 'our last walk and talk meant a great deal to me'.[43] Ottoline offered him advice on his relationship with Carrington, whom she and Philip had both tried to influence – Ottoline by marching her round the 'aparagrass' bed, Carrington complained to Strachey, and Philip by walking her round the pond – each lecturing her on her disappointing virginity. After this had no effect, Ottoline likened Carrington to 'some strange wild beast – greedy of life and of tasting all the different "worms" that she can find without giving herself to any mate. Sometimes I wonder', she wrote to Gertler, 'if she will ever find a mate that fulfils all she desires.'[44] This marked a decided cooling in the friendship between Ottoline and Carrington.

In August Gertler's money situation was somewhat relieved by Shearman's acquisition of one of his early Garsington landscapes (*The Pond, Garsington*). Monty admired 'the great skill and dexterity of the design and the depth of soul most of all. You will understand I am speaking as a novice', he wrote modestly, 'with no great knowledge except what comes from looking at pictures (mostly old masters) steadily for about 12 years. Best luck at Wittering', he added. 'Protect me from the shafts of ridicule. I am a sensitive plant.'[45]

It was at Wittering that Gertler and Carrington were reunited in early August. Here over the next week Gertler enjoyed 'one of the best holidays I've ever had',[46] walking in golden-yellow cornfields, and swimming in the sea – 'looking very absurd, in a bathing dress' as he learned to swim with water wings.[47] 'Wonderful times', Carrington called them afterwards, and Gertler agreed. 'Yes, we had fine moments at Wittering. Thank you very much for them.'[48] This time it was Strachey's turn to feel a little jealous. 'Are you in the Jew's arms at the present moment?' he asked Carrington.[49]

A week later Carrington left Wittering, and set off to join Strachey, Barbara Hiles and her fiancée, Nick Bagenal (who was recuperating from a war wound), for a fortnight's holiday in Wales. Strachey was supposed to act as chaperone, but instead invited Carrington along to make up a foursome, and though she had hesitated, she finally made up her mind to go when her mother expressly forbade it. The weather was cold and rainy, and Strachey was unwell. He sat in the cottage reading Donne and Shakespeare aloud; Carrington listened and painted his portrait. It was probably the happiest holiday of her life. Free from Gertler's constant pressure, she grew even closer to Strachey (who had already admitted to David Garnett that he thought he had fallen in love with her), and wrote to tell Gertler how happy she was, though not of course the reason for it. He encouraged her to stay and enjoy herself 'as I am always with you in spirit – I never leave you for a moment. I am always talking to you and I have never loved you more and felt more thankful to you or more happy.'[50] He had no conception of the depth of her relationship with Strachey. How could he, when Carrington was writing to him that 'all other relationships besides [their] own seemed dull and lifeless'?[51] Yet how could she tell him when he wrote that his happiness was 'solely due to our wonderful friendship. Nothing else matters, everything else is subsidiary to it and [I] could not exist without it.'[52]

It was a period of intense emotional excitement for both of them. 'I live in a constant state of over-excitement – so much do my work and conceptions thrill me'.[53] Gertler wrote, and he bombarded his friends with wild, excited letters throughout August. 'Heavens! How full I am', he wrote to Mary Hutchinson. 'I want to do so much, so much. But I must take care, I must go slowly, I must learn to have patience and control or I shall destroy myself.'[54] Mentally, he seemed to be entering a period of manic energy. To Carrington he confided that he was 'terribly, terribly rich in spirit . . . I live in a world of wonder from morning to night! Every now and then a vision of a huge and wonderfully coloured piece of sculpture comes before me. It dazzles me and makes my blood run cold . . . I must stop. I can't write any more – I am full to bursting point.'[55]

Carrington channelled her feelings for Strachey into literature, and her letters reflect her growing love of the poetry to which he had introduced her. In May Carrington recommended Keats, but Gertler was reading Dostoyevsky and had 'no use for Keats in my present mood'. In August Carrington was entranced by the love poetry of John Donne, but still Gertler ploughed on with Dostoyevsky. 'I can read nothing after him', he told Carrington. 'He is my Shakespeare. I worship him.'[56] In September Carrington (with seemingly no sense of irony) praised the poetry of Andrew Marvell, whose most famous poem, 'To his Coy Mistress', exactly mirrored Gertler's own situation. One phrase in particular, 'That long-preserved virginity', might well have provided the refrain for his own poem about his relationship with Carrington, which he scribbled into a black leather notebook in August:

> If my love were not impassioned,
> Or could with will be moderate,
> I could bask, in pleasant friendship's
> Lukewarm sun, contentedly;
> But Love's Beauty once perceived,
> Mere friendship can no longer satiate:
> So when I saw your love's immensity,
> Iron-coffined by Virginity,
> Pain turned my love into Hate.[57]

Wisely, he refused to show it to Carrington.[58] Though he knew that his poetry was unoriginal, Gertler found writing it 'so exciting and relieving', he told Kot. 'What does it matter after all if I do it badly as long as I express a little of what I feel?'[59] The enormous range of ideas he experienced throughout 1916, covering poetry, philosophy, play-writing, music and sculpture, were all merely expressions of the intense 'creative ferment' in which he was enveloped for much of the year. Highly exalted states alternated with moments of utter despair, and it has been suggested that he was in the grip of manic depression. However, it is more likely that his mood swings were indicative of the incipient tuberculosis, as yet undiagnosed, that shadowed his later life.

In mid-August Gertler left Wittering with Gilbert Cannan (who had come to fill Carrington's place for the second week), and they returned together to Cholesbury. Here Gertler felt 'boringly but comfortably at home . . . The same feeling one has when one goes to stay with one's people', he told Carrington. The uneventfulness of

Cholesbury life provided a restful backdrop for his 'terrific' ideas, and he refused all other invitations, staying on until September and continuing to relieve his bursting feelings in scraps of writing.[60]

He missed Carrington and agonized over their relationship. If she was adrift on a river of islands and adventures, then his love would create 'a bridge from my heart to yours, over which I can occasionally travel into you and over which I long constantly to travel? Don't you see this? You must see this or I shall be miserable', he insisted. He celebrated the idea of the couple, of them as a couple, in a symbiotic relationship: 'My strength will feed you. It is the most nourishing food for you. You are a terribly strong person yourself and I need your support. I am weak, helpless without your strength. My strength, if severed from yours, turns into weakness . . . Let us frankly combine', he urged her. 'We can make a splendid unit.'[61] He was unaware that at Whitsun she had already written to Strachey, 'do not you hate united pairs?'[62] To Gertler, however, she replied that they could never be more than 'twin souls, always two', which he was forced to agree was 'only too true and . . . one of the greatest sorrows of my life'.[63]

Absorbed by his own problems, Gertler completely failed to detect Gilbert Cannan's deteriorating mental state, though even he had noticed the widening cracks in the Cannans' marriage. Throughout 1916 Gilbert had been troubled by overwork, his violent antipathy to the war and his disintegrating relationship with his wife, Mary. He had renewed his earlier friendship with the sculptor Kathleen Scott (now widowed), and began to write her love poems; but he transferred his sexual desire to Mary's maid, who discovered in August that she was pregnant. Before joining Gertler at the Hutchinsons, Cannan had withdrawn alone to Stratford for a week. He told his friends nothing of his domestic situation, but they had already begun to notice that something was wrong. 'He seems to me to wear about 3 feet of armour, which one cannot pierce through', Brett remarked in August.[64]

When he arrived at Wittering, Cannan's friends, hoping to lift him from his now habitual apathy, had pressed him to tell them about his background. But he spoke throughout in such a dull, dreary voice that they found the experience depressing, and Gertler came away with the impression that 'nothing ever really stirred [him], nothing ever made a real impression', and that Cannan had never been either 'impressed or excited' about anything in his life.[65] In fact, as his biographer Diana Farr explains, Cannan was actually experiencing 'an early neurological malfunction bordering on schizophrenia', a condition that seems prefigured in Gertler's haunting portrait of him at the Mill, though it was some months yet before Gertler learned the truth about Cannan's illness.[66]

Towards the end of August Carrington's letters mysteriously broke off. After the holiday in Wales she and Strachey had confounded the Bloomsbury gossips by disappearing together for a few days in Bath, where they attempted a sexual relationship. Though ultimately unsuccessful, the experience cemented their feelings for one another, and they apparently made some sort of commitment to find a country cottage together, where 'Strachey could finish writing his book, and where Carrington could paint and be free of her parents' restrictions', after their return.[67] Gertler, fearing he had offended Carrington, was 'miserable with apprehension' at her silence, and begged her to reply soon.[68] And Carrington did soon reply, but only with the vaguest of explanations. 'As it seems really impossible for you to tell me more of what you feel', Gertler decided, 'I will trouble you no further about it.'[69]

As he neared the end of his stay at Cholesbury, Gertler longed to return to London, which always drew him 'as if by a magnetic power. In London is my true life', he told Kot.[70] The tall, silent walls of his studio welcomed him back, he felt, to another new chapter of his life, but in the meantime his 'sculptural conceptions' had thrown him 'into chaos' and banished painting to the background.

On 31 August Gertler dined with Kot and Katherine Mansfield at the Eiffel Tower Restaurant before moving on to the Café Royal and securing a table next to 'a long thin white Woman with an immensely high bush of crimson hair' and two young Indians, who were all discussing literature intently.[71] Gertler's party took an instant dislike to them, and later grew incensed when they began to criticize Lawrence's poetry, reading aloud from a copy of his latest book, *Amores*. 'We could stand it no longer', Gertler confessed afterwards to Mary Hutchinson, 'something had to be done.' It was Katherine, of course, who did it:

> Suddenly she leant towards them and with a sweet imploring look, she asked to see the book[.] They gave it her with [an] even sweeter smile. But imagine their utter amazement when Kath got up, book in hand, beckoning us to follow, which we did, and walked quite quietly and calmly out of the Cafe!! Their amazement was so great that they could only let out some

> unintelligible sounds to try and stop us or have us stopped, but although everybody stared no one attempted to waylay us. So to our delight we got clean away with the Book. It was the best possible revenge.[72]

Once outside, they had 'simply trembled with excitement'. Katherine, Gertler thought, was really a 'most extraordinary woman'.[73] When Lawrence, who was still in Cornwall, heard about the incident from Kot, it only confirmed his suspicions that London, especially the Café Royal, was now 'a centre of blasphemous living'. The episode went straight into *Women in Love*, where it was transformed into the chapter known as 'Gudrun at the Pompadour'.

Back in Penn Studio Gertler's ideas for sculpture began to take on a more definite shape. In early September, working from preparatory drawings, he fashioned a small plasticine model of a single acrobat.[74] 'So far it goes well', he wrote to Carrington, 'although the technical difficulties are most worrisome . . . I must have patience and expect many failures at first. But it is all most wonderful and is opening up a new world with immense possibilities, but I must have patience, and control my excitement.'[75] In late September he consulted the sculptor Mary Randolph Craig, who showed him some of her work in progress, sent him clay and a box for the modelling of larger-sized figures, and introduced him to a carver who advised on the selection of tools. By late November Gertler had already completed the second stage, the clay models, or maquettes, but instead of moving straight on to the carving he temporarily laid *The Acrobats* aside and began work on a carving of *The Merry-Go-Round.* 'If it goes well', he wrote to Carrington, 'it will be a beautiful thing, but it is a greater job than I thought and will take a long time.'[76] However, *The Merry-Go-Round* carving has not survived and appears to have been either lost or abandoned at some point over the winter.

Meanwhile, on 9 October, as he was completing his manuscript of *Women in Love*, Lawrence received a photograph of the completed painting of *The Merry-Go-Round.* Deeply stirred, he immediately wrote Gertler a long and perceptive letter, calling it 'the best modern picture I have seen: I think it is great, and true. But it is horrible and terrifying.' He was not sure, he wrote, that he would not be too frightened to come and look at the original, for 'in this combination of blaze, and violent mechanised rotation and complex involution, and ghastly, utterly mindless human intensity of sensational extremity', he felt Gertler had made 'a real and ultimate revelation. I think this picture is your arrival.'[77] (And he afterwards changed the frieze carved by Loerke in *Women in Love* from a scene of wolves and peasants to one of a fair.[78]) His letter meant a great deal to Gertler, particularly perhaps because Lawrence suggested that the painting should be bought for the nation; it was almost the only expression of wholehearted support that Gertler received for *The Merry-Go-Round* in his lifetime.

Lawrence's interest triggered an exchange of letters between the two men over Gertler's experiments with sculpture, of which only Lawrence's letters have survived. In them he wondered aloud whether sculpture was not 'going too far – over the edge of endurance into a form of incoherent, less poignant shouting'.[79] In December he told Gertler that 'looking in a dictionary the other day' he had read the explanation: '"sculpture: the lowest of the arts" – that surprised me very much – but I think perhaps it is true'.[80] (This view is reflected in his evaluation of Loerke's character in the novel.)

Meanwhile, Gertler's friends became increasingly concerned to protect him from the critical onslaught that they felt would follow any public exhibition of *The Merry-Go-Round*. 'Oh Lord, oh Lord, Have Mercy upon us', Strachey had written to Ottoline earlier in the year after viewing it in Gertler's studio. 'I admired it of course but as for liking it one might as well think of liking a machine gun.' St John Hutchinson, who had already befriended and legally represented several conscientious objectors, was worried that *The Merry-Go-Round* would cause a stir and thereby raise public questions about Gertler's own pacifist status. 'It will, of course, raise a tremendous outcry', he predicted. 'The old, the wise, the professional critic will go mad with anger and righteous indignation – and what strikes me is that these symptoms may drive them to write all sorts of rubbish about German art and German artists in their papers and may raise the question acutely and publicly as to your position.'[81] He advised Gertler that it might not be 'quite wise' to exhibit the picture at the Goupil Gallery and suggested a private showing at Monty Shearman's Adelphi rooms instead. It is not clear whether this went ahead, but despite a place on the hanging committee at the London Group in 1916, Gertler did not exhibit either *The Merry-Go-Round* or anything else at the winter show that year.

Shearman's *pied-à-terre* at the Adelphi, fitted out with gramophone, cocktail cabinet and pianola (the last installed at 'enormous expense' and probably for the benefit of Gertler, who had a weakness for the instrument), made an ideal venue for parties. And when in September Gertler's two pictures *The Mill* and *The Pond, Garsington* were hung, the room became, Shearman wrote, 'a paradise'.[82] In an arrangement remarkably similar to Gertler's previous understanding with Eddie Marsh, he provided Gertler with a key and permission to use it whenever he wished.

In October Shearman made Gertler an even more generous offer. 'Money', he pointed out, was 'a horrible thing' and he wanted Gertler to feel that he could 'always have what you want from me if you like'. He made it clear, however, that it was to be only as an arrangement 'between friends and there must be no feeling of patronage or obligation or whatever'. He did not want to be 'another Eddie Marsh or Conway [Wertheimer]' and stipulated that if he wanted a picture 'I would buy it outright'. But he expressed himself willing 'at any time' to guarantee Gertler's studio 'or any other thing you like', convinced he would 'not ask for more than was necessary and I hope you would not mind accepting it if it is necessary. If it isn't, so much the better, but if it is I can easily afford a bit and I think it would help your work if you felt more comfortable.'[83] Gertler gladly accepted the key to the room, but it is not clear to what extent he took advantage of the offer of money. Although Shearman did not openly admit his growing affection for Gertler for some months, if he had been aware of it Gertler might well have felt uncomfortable at accepting the older man's money.

When Gilbert Cannan's novel *Mendel* was finally published in November 1916, it was common knowledge among Gertler's circle that he was the book's protagonist. 'Gilbert is not writing, but has written a book . . . about a young man who, I believe, is supposed to resemble me, but I don't know', he replied to Strachey's inquiry about the rumours in May.[84] This was slightly disingenuous. Here was Gertler's history laid out from childhood to early career, with a full account of his often less than flattering opinions of his early patrons, his difficult affair with Carrington and the unhappy fate of Currie and Dolly Henry. Not only was Gertler himself immediately recognizable, but so too were many of his friends and contemporaries.

'It is, as Gertler says,' Lawrence wrote to Kot, 'journalism: statement, without creation . . . very sickening. If Gilbert had taken Gertler's story and re-created it into art, good. But to set down all these statements is a vulgarising of life itself.'[85] Carrington was predictably furious: 'Everywhere this confounded gossip and servant-like curiosity. It's ugly, and so damned vulgar', she complained.[86] And there is no doubt that Gertler was also embarrassed by the book. Lawrence reported to a friend in December that Gertler was 'very sick about it: serve him right'.[87] Cannan had mixed fact so inextricably with fiction that it was impossible to separate them, and Lawrence's remarks may well have been prompted by the knowledge that he was popularly supposed to be the model for Logan. Only Shearman was 'deeply moved' by the novel, and even he had mixed feelings: he told Gertler it was 'fascinating because it is about yourself', but 'disgusting' because of 'the vulgarity of revealing the hidden things and sanctity of friendship and love to the world in this way'.[88] Although the storm soon blew over, the book was to haunt Gertler. Even in the 1920s he sometimes found his reviews headed 'Mendel', and was occasionally approached by strangers with the inevitable question, 'Are you Mendel?' According to his widow, the book also cost him more than one friendship.

By far the most damaging portrait was that of William Rothenstein, who had helped Gertler at such a critical early juncture and in return, it seemed, been parodied as Froitzheim. Although it was nearly two years before Rothenstein read the book himself, when he did so he was 'deeply hurt that anyone could find it in his heart to turn the pleasure of helping a beginner into [such] an ugly legend', and protested that his portrayal was 'as unjust as it is ignoble'.[89] Rothenstein's letter was a shock and Gertler apologized at once, claiming to have 'suffered a great deal from that wretched book', and explaining that he had once been:

> foolish enough to tell [Cannan] a great deal about myself. Some years later, he asked me if I would mind him writing a novel with a person something like myself in it. Of course I consented and soon this awful distorted affair came out. I have never, I assure you, ceased to blush over it.[90]

Rothenstein accepted this apology 'unreservedly', but their earlier friendship was effectively destroyed, and when Rothenstein's son John came to write his chapter on Gertler in *Modern English Painters*, he drew attention to the incident and to Gertler's 'lack of self-control' – a characteristic that he believed allowed the artist 'to sacrifice even considerations of prudence for the satisfaction of the moment'.[91]

In 1916, however, Gertler did not allow any embarrassment over the novel to destroy his friendship with Cannan, who was in any case, in urgent need of support. Soon after publication he fled his complicated home life to settle briefly in shabby rooms in west London, where he remained on the verge of a breakdown for some months.

His emotional confusion increased when he was introduced to a nineteen-year-old South African art student called Gwen Wilson, with whom he fell desperately in love. A few weeks later Mary persuaded him to return briefly to Mill House to work on a nearby farm (in accordance with the ruling of a local tribunal), but increasingly Cannan retreated into his own private fantasy world. In January 1917 he broke down altogether and was temporarily confined to a nursing home. When Gertler visited him there, Cannan communicated by drawing circular shapes and vortexes, like the suns and stars of Van Gogh's later landscapes.[92]

Carrington had spent much of the autumn cycling over the countryside in furtherance of the planned country house-sharing scheme with Strachey, but it had as yet come to nothing. Brett, however, had been planning her own 'ark' in London since the summer, and had rented John Maynard Keynes's furnished house in Gower Street. Katherine Mansfield and John Middleton Murry took the first floor, Brett the second and Carrington the attic, but both painters were soon dismayed to find that Katherine waylaid all the male visitors, and nobody got further than the first floor. The ark ended in a shambles several months later.

Now that Carrington was in London, Gertler initially saw more of her. He told her in early November, 'our love has been and is nothing less than a classic'. He was so happy that when Carrington finally consented to a physical relationship, he claimed to have lost all interest in sex except as 'a natural physical necessity'. Now that she had consented, it no longer mattered when the sexual relationship began, 'tomorrow or next year – or never!' he wrote, a response that suggests that the symbolic commitment of her surrender was just as important as the physical relationship itself.[93] Given Carrington's anger over the publication of *Mendel*, it seems extraordinary that she should have chosen this time finally to capitulate, and that the consummation should have taken place at Cannan's 'castle' in Cholesbury, which Gertler borrowed for a week in early December. Her motives were, as ever, complex.

For some months (since her trip to Bath with Strachey, in fact) Carrington had been hinting at possible surrender. 'If I find many more poems by Donne urging me to forsake my virginity I may fall by next Spring when the Sun is hot once more', she had written to Gertler in September. 'I think he is a man of such rare wisdom. That I take his words very seriously . . . But I ought not to write this to you. As

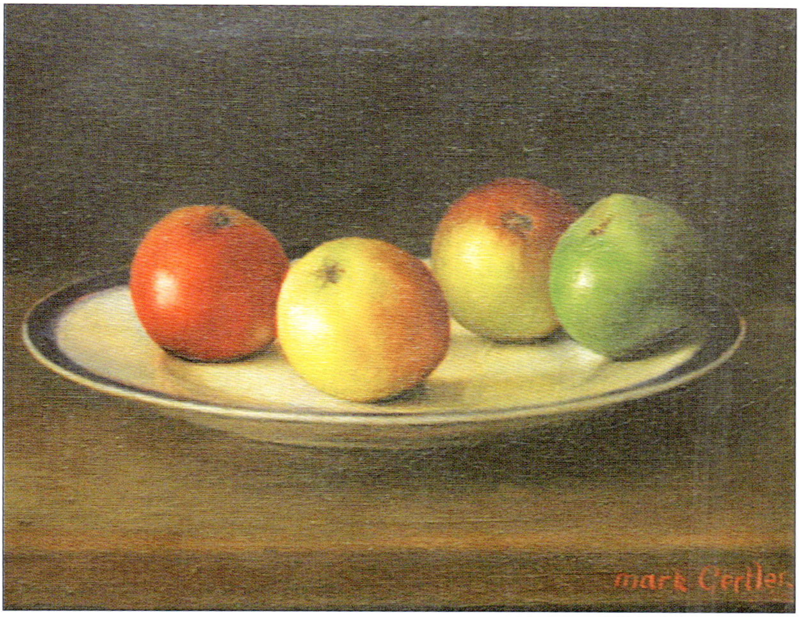

1. *Still Life with Apples*, 1907, oil on canvas, 9 x 11 in/23 x 27·5 cm. This was probably the first still life Gertler painted. He refused to part with it and it was found in his studio after his death

2. *Talmudic Discussion* (also known as *Jews Arguing*), 1911, oil on canvas, 30 x 36 in/76·2 x 92·5 cm. One of Gertler's most accomplished Jewish portraits

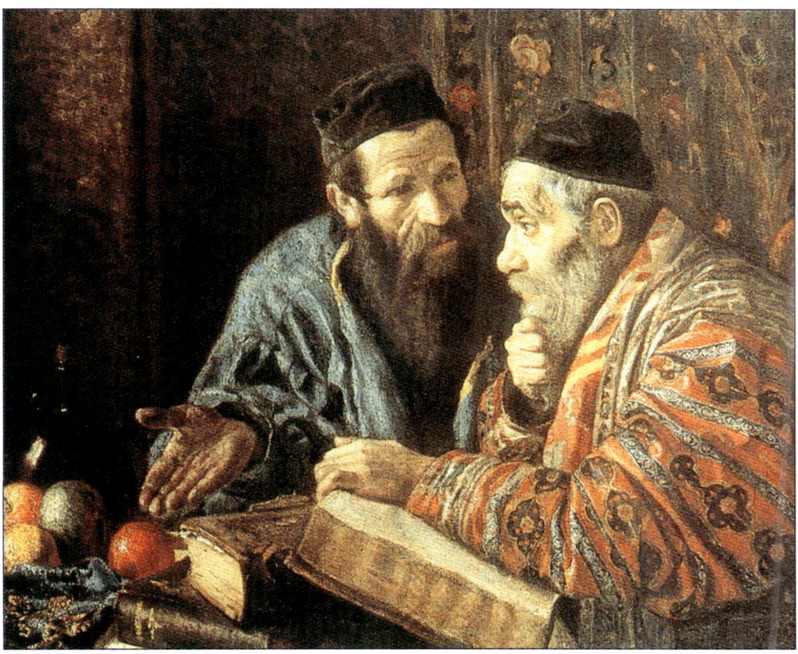

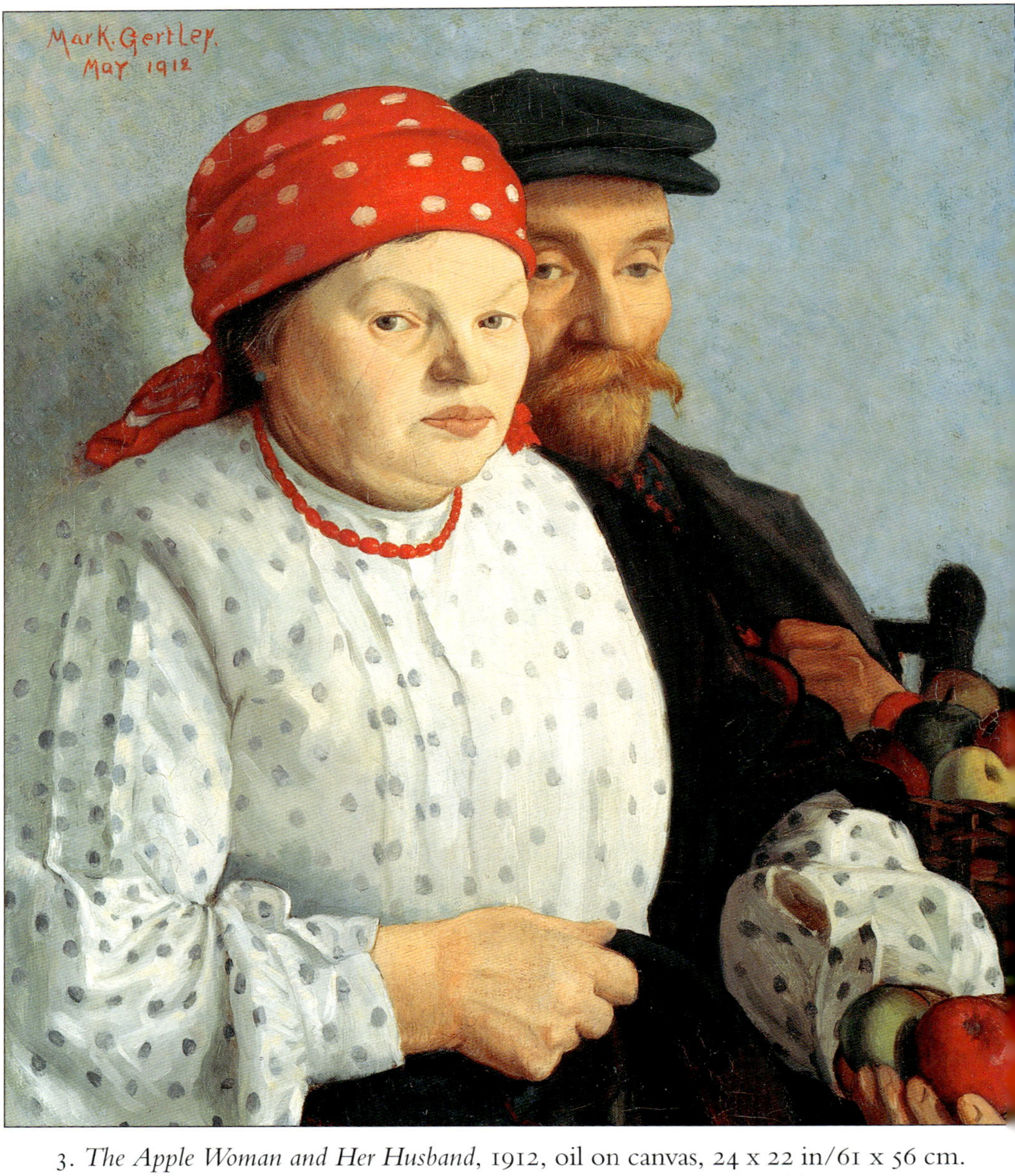

3. *The Apple Woman and Her Husband*, 1912, oil on canvas, 24 x 22 in/61 x 56 cm. Gertler's finest portrait of his parents, Louis and Golda

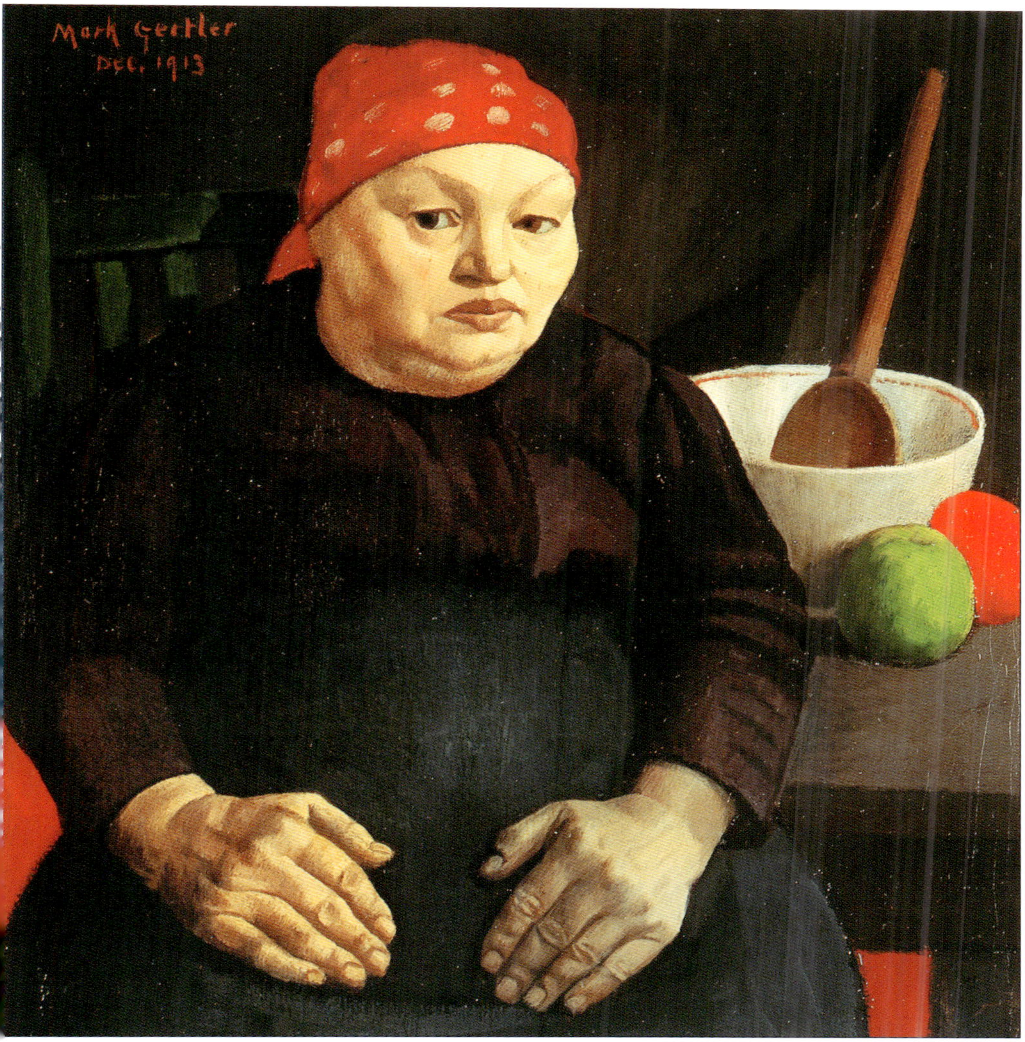

4. *The Artist's Mother*, 1913, oil on canvas, 18 x 17 in/45 x 42·5 cm. A harsher portrait of Golda, showing the influence of Post-Impressionism. Gertler called it 'Barbaric and symbolic'

5. *The Fruit Sorters*, 1914, oil on canvas, 30 x 25 in/75 x 62·5 cm. Gertler's first major outdoor composition, marking a transition between his eloquently spartan Jewish portraits and the vibrant landscapes to follow

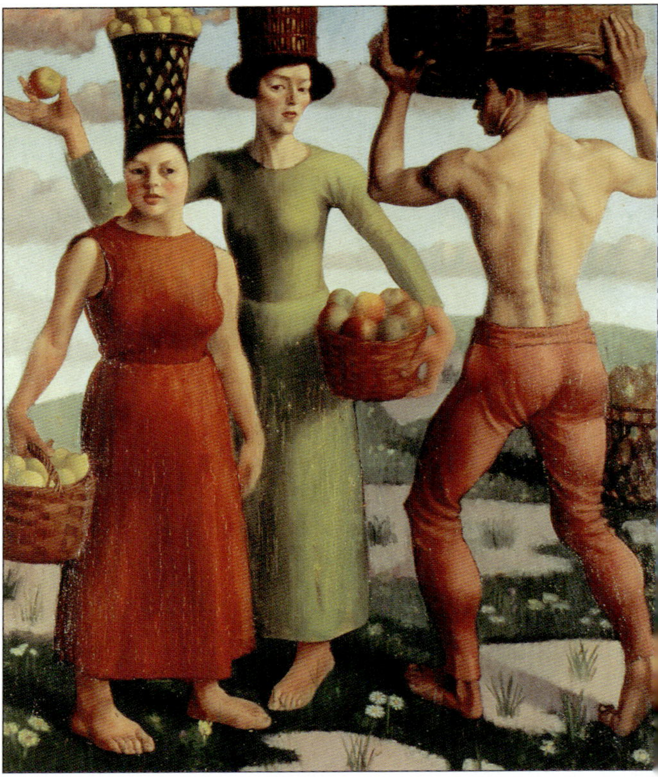

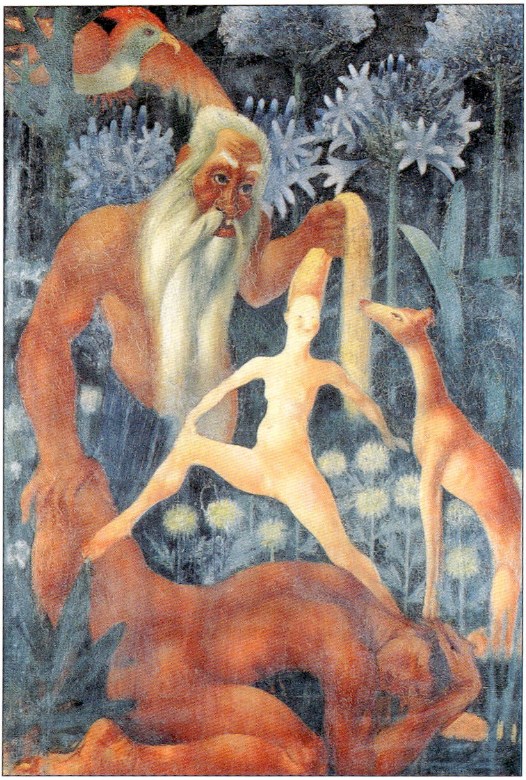

6. *The Creation of Eve*, 1914, oil on canvas, 29·5 x 23·6 in/75 x 60 cm. This picture created 'uproar' when exhibited at the London Group in 1915. The critic went 'quite wild with rage', Gertler became 'the talk of London' and someone attached a label with 'made in Germany' scrawled across it to the figure of Eve

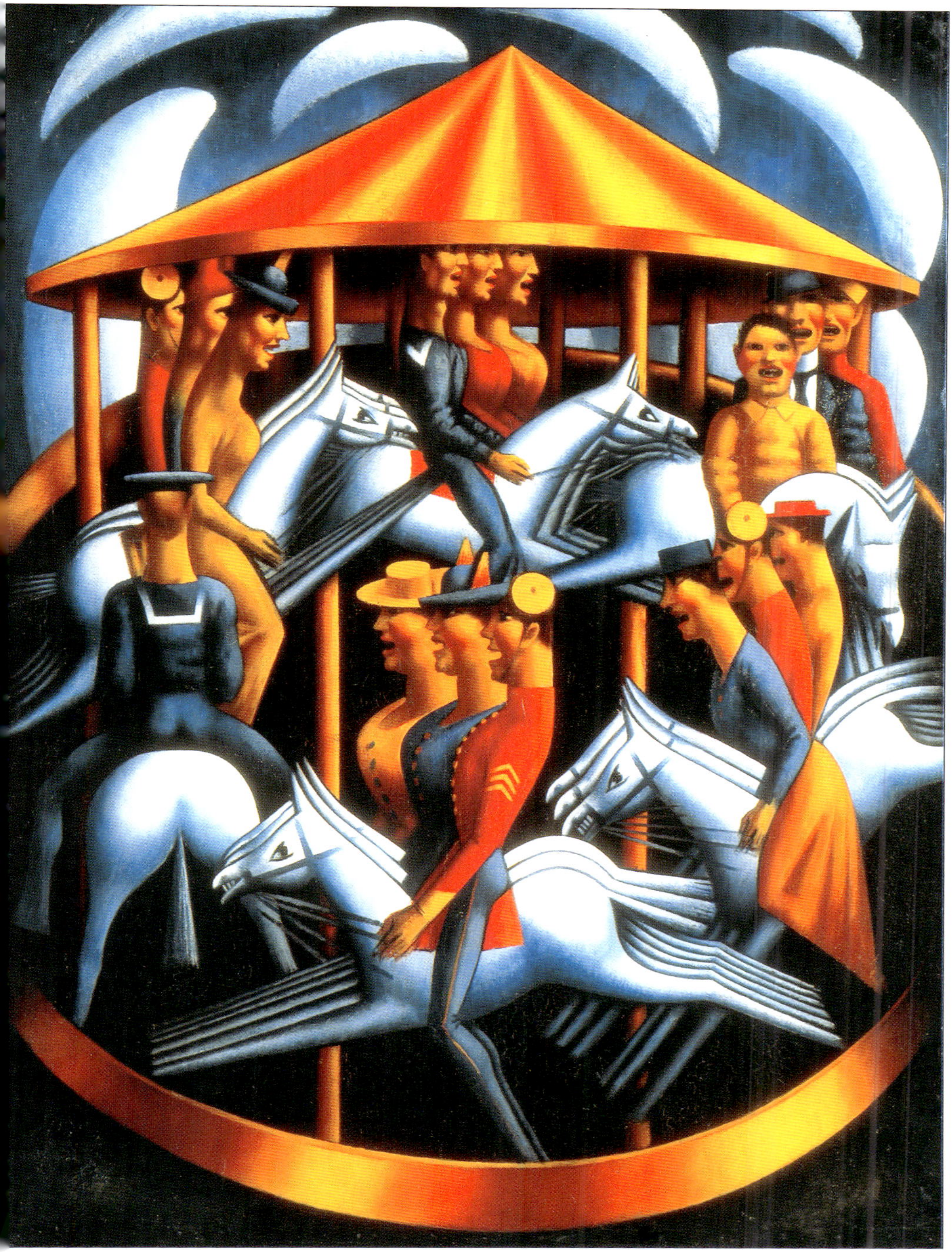

7. *The Merry-Go-Round*, 1916, 76 x 56 in/189.2 x 142.2 cm. A powerful Modernist expression of anti-war sentiment and a profound expression of personal discontent. The painting was never sold during Gertler's lifetime and lay rolled up in a corner of the studio until after his death

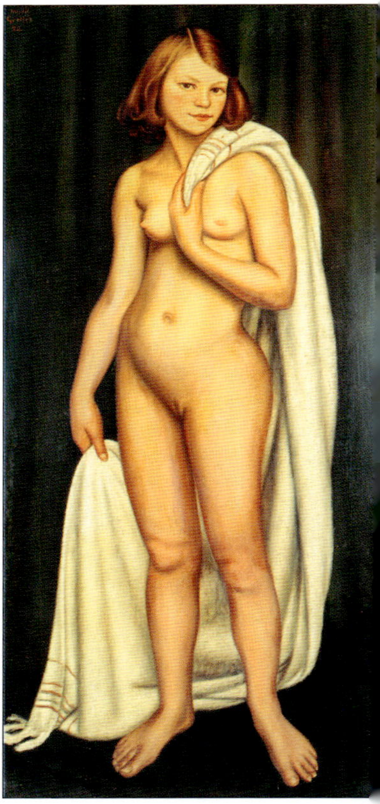

8. *Young Girlhood II*, 1925, oil on canvas, 53 x 25 in/135 x 64 cm. The second in a series of portraits of the same model, Alice Edwards, in which Gertler aimed to capture 'all the charm of young girlhood'

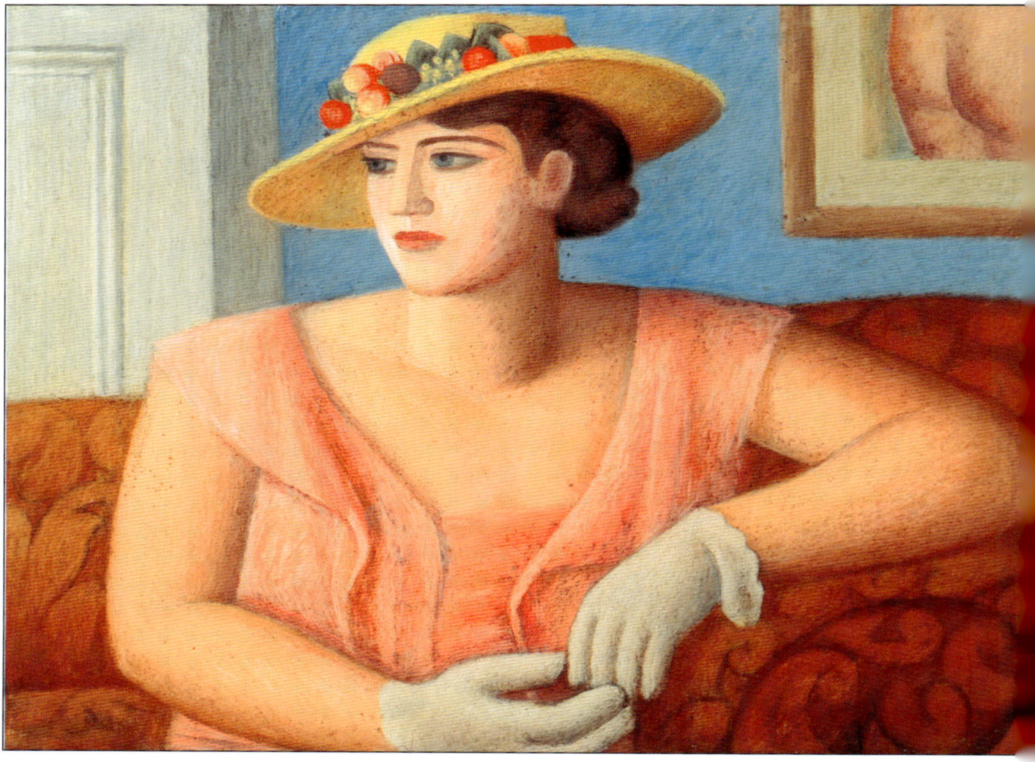

9. *Marjorie Gertler*, 1933, pastel on brown paper, 26⅞ x 34⅞ in/66 x 88 cm. Gertler's only known portrait of his wife, Marjorie

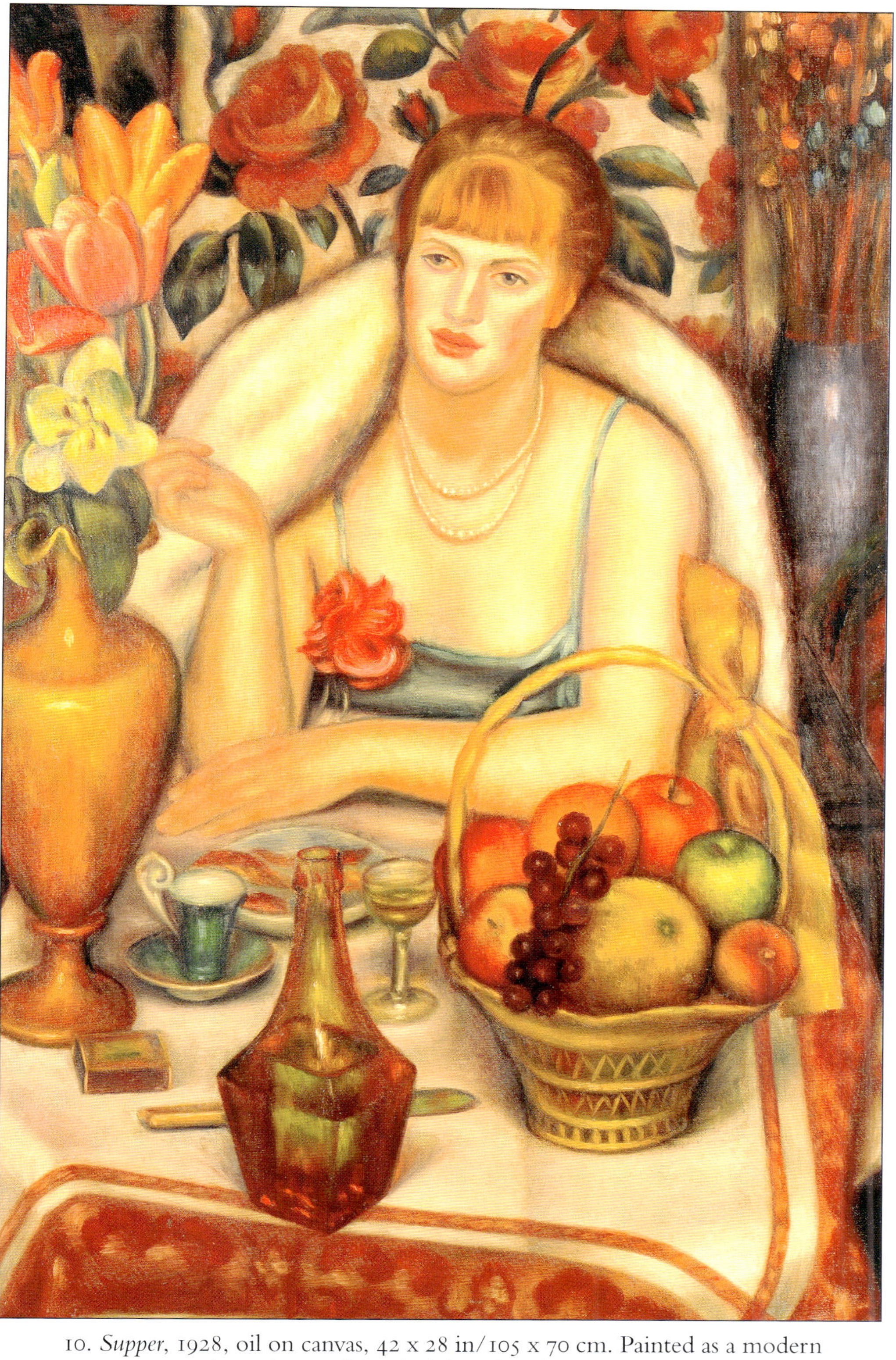

10. *Supper*, 1928, oil on canvas, 42 x 28 in/105 x 70 cm. Painted as a modern cornucopia, and one of Gertler's best female portraits of the 1920s

11. *The Mandolinist*, 1934, oil on canvas, 30 x 22 in/76·2 x 55·9 cm. Executed direct from the model in 57 one-hour sittings

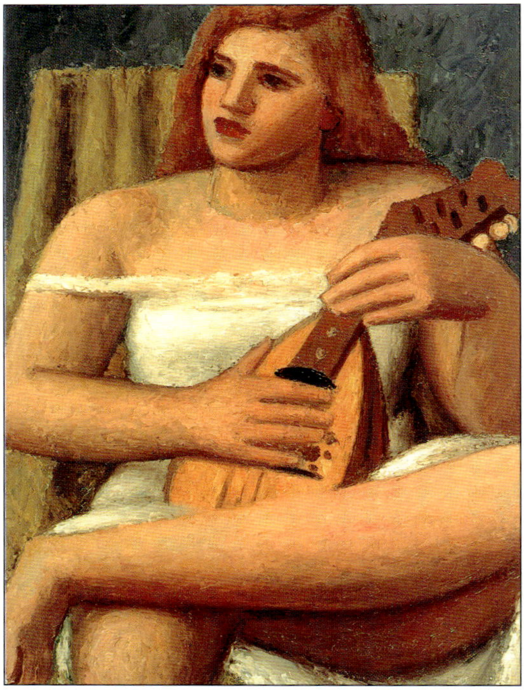

12. *The Spanish Fan*, 1938, oil, 42 x 48 in/106·6 x 121·9 cm. One of Gertler's most accomplished late still lifes and the only one of his paintings to be exhibited in Paris during his lifetime

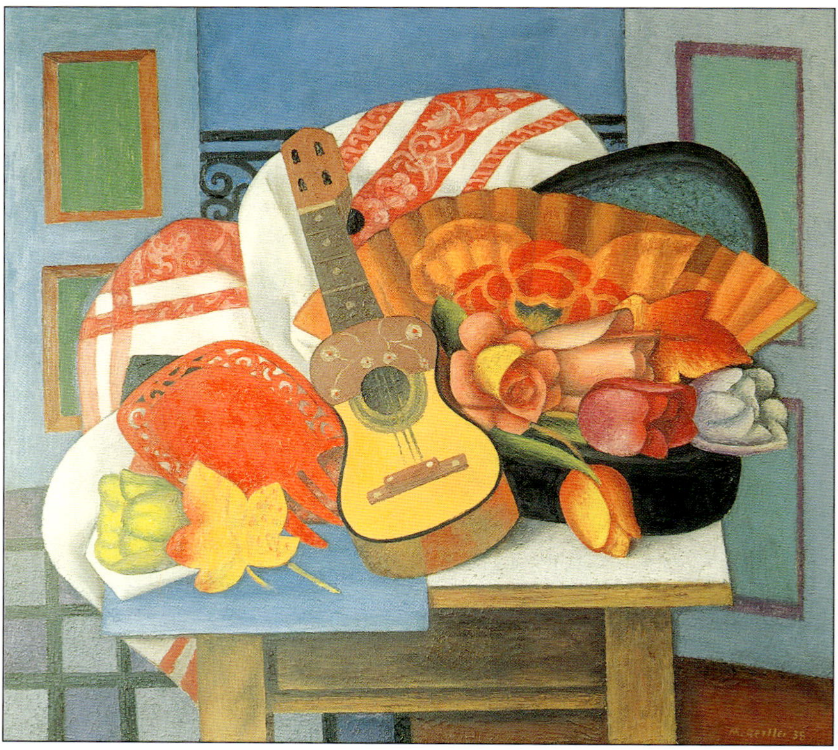

my moods varey [*sic*] like a sky of clouds!'[94] The consummation took place on 16 November (Gertler later admitted that he had marked the date in his diary), and afterwards Carrington wrote to him teasingly that sexual experience was 'certainly . . . a necessity if one wants to understand the best poets'.[95] But it is more likely to have been some sort of consolation prize to Gertler for her growing attachment to Strachey, though it may also have been a signal to Strachey that Carrington would not become in any way dependent on him. Carrington clearly did not enjoy sex with Gertler, which in her letters she referred to as 'sugar' in his coffee, and she immediately rationed him to 'three lumps a month'.

Gertler was soon bristling with indignation at this treatment. She would not call lovemaking vulgar and arrange for it to happen only three times a month, he told her, if she really loved him. In his case the lovemaking had only increased his passion, and his anger burst forth in an angry torrent in late December. He was tortured by her beauty, her constant delays, the endless postponements and rescheduling of their meetings. 'Don't believe those "advanced" fools who tell you that love is free. It is not – it is a bondage, a beautiful bondage', he wrote in desperation, using exactly the words most likely to strike fear into Carrington's heart. He had begun to hate her, he wrote, for three reasons: '1. Because you can't love passionately; 2. Because of your advanced ideas; 3. I hate you because I love you and am therefore in the power of your cruel, advanced and unpassionate self!'[96]

Gertler had been so sure for so long that if only Carrington would commit to a sexual relationship the problems between them would dissolve, but now he found to his dismay that he saw even less of her than formerly. Her behaviour, like the language in her letters, was alternately conciliatory and elusive, and their meetings were more than ever hedged about by ifs and maybes. 'Meet me here on Tuesday evening at 7.30', she would write, 'unless I wire to the contrary and make any other arrangement.' Or 'I will come next Wednesday evening . . . if I am back by then.' Gertler felt the ground constantly shift beneath his feet, and as fast as he removed one obstacle from their relationship Carrington presented him with another. He did not know that the real obstacle was Strachey.

Carrington spent Christmas Day 1916 at Garsington with Strachey, joining in the charades and parties, but somehow she did not enjoy herself. She was probably feeling guilty, and her letters to Gertler read awkwardly. In contrast to the charming and spontaneous pet names she used in her letters to Strachey, her language with Gertler is hesitant and placatory. 'Darling' is too fond, 'dear' too distant, and she settles finally on 'dearling'. 'Dearling I do want you to come back again', she wrote afterwards. 'We will have such good times, and I will be so much better to you, "a good attitude" as Kot would say . . . I wish I could love you even more but I think I shall.'[97] But Gertler had already fled to Shearman's cottage in the wild, windswept seascape of Dorset, where the two men took long walks over the cliffs in the rain. In his notebook Gertler scribbled two uncompleted plays: *The Confession*, in which an incarcerated criminal confesses his crime – the murder of the woman he loves – and the fragment of an untitled drama in which three men are locked into a cycle of murder, guilt and terror.[98] Both provided relief for his gathering feelings of violence and frustration. Once again the year ended on a note of irresolution, with Gertler and Carrington again apart, with different friends, in different locations, and an ever widening gap between them.

12

Fugitive Things

'I have been haunted by the idea (based on things that you have said sometimes) that you thought friendships were fugitive things. To me they are eternal once they passed a certain stage and ours has passed it.'

Montague Shearman to Mark Gertler, *c.* 1917

THROUGHOUT JANUARY 1917 Gertler was completely absorbed by his carving of *The Acrobats*. The difficulties in obtaining the right wood nearly drove him mad, but at last he found it, took it to an East End sawmill to have 'all the unnecessary chunks' cut off, and proudly dragged the carcass back to his studio.[1] The difficulty then, he told Carrington, was 'how to create a subtle thing out of a large rough square piece of wood', but he immediately fell to, carving the thick four-inch plank until his muscles ached with fatigue and he felt sick and giddy at the end of a day's work. Gradually, the carving began to emerge, but still he could not be certain he would succeed. If he failed, he admitted, he would be 'a defeated man'.[2]

'People . . . think my sculpture only a phase, which they would be glad to see the end of!' he complained to Dick Carline. 'You can't think how this irritates me! "Why doesn't he paint?" they say! They will not understand that it is a natural and necessary development and that it is real pleasure that makes me do it.'[3] But he also realized that, as a result, he was likely to find himself even more isolated in his sculpture than in his painting.

Meanwhile, the carving progressed with only one mishap, when he sawed off the piece that was to form the hands. This was easily remedied, however, and as he went on it became clear that completion was no longer Gertler's main motive. 'Whether I carry it through or not, it is terribly exciting to do – I have never been more excited about anything!' he could not help exclaiming.[4] The finished carving shows two intertwined acrobats, the standing figure supporting the suspended one and the pair joined at a series of focal points, giving the illusion of perfect balance. Completed by April 1917, it was boldly painted in blue and yellow, and exhibited in the London Group's spring show, where it gained little serious attention: one critic called it 'quaint' and another dismissed it as 'an entertaining and amusing toy'.[5] Although Gertler's original drawing for the piece dates back to 1915, he was possibly influenced by Henri Gaudier-Brzeska (killed in action in June 1915), who had explored the motif of two wrestlers locked in combat and used this design for several pieces that sold through the Omega Workshops.[6]

Ultimately, Gertler's involvement with sculpture, though intense, was brief, and limited to one piece. The experiments came to an end simply because he could not arouse the interest of buyers – even Shearman, who bought one of the preliminary drawings, was not interested in purchasing the sculpture – and he could not afford to go on with it. Time was a significant factor. Epstein later wrote that Gertler had once told him 'how he had started a piece of sculpture and after four or five days strenuous work, the piece was still unfinished and he gave it up. He argued that in the time he gave to one piece of sculpture he might have made several paintings.'[7] However, Gertler continued to have ideas for new sculptures well into 1917, and despite the crippling cost (£22), eventually had *The Acrobats* cast in bronze at a Battersea foundry in July, at which point the original carving seems either to have been lost or destroyed; neither version was ever sold during his lifetime.

The Merry-Go-Round, which was exhibited alongside *The Acrobats* at the London Group in May, also attracted little serious critical attention, though once again Gertler's was the most talked about exhibit in the show. Gertler himself likened the painting to Bach, but the *Evening News* set the tone for most of the reviews with the headline 'THE MAN WHO HAS PAINTED A NOISE!', calling the picture 'a shriek, a groan, a hoot, a blare, a tempest of wild rending'.[8] The *Pall Mall Gazette* heard trumpets, but unfortunately they were 'horribly out of tune' and made 'a piercing and offensive noise . . . the notes they utter hav[ing] nothing to do with music'. But the *Sunday Times* thought Gertler 'at his brazen best' in *The Merry-Go-Round*, with its almost audible 'clash of metallic blues and shrill orange yellows'. It called the painting 'a riot we almost hear as we enter the gallery . . . the apotheosis of the steam-organ in paint', a comment that pays tribute to the painting's frenzied energy.[9] However disappointing these reactions, critics detected none of its anti-militarism, and at least for the moment the question of Gertler's pacifism was not raised.

By the time *The Merry-Go-Round* appeared in public, Gertler had already struck upon another more sustainable source of inspiration. In January, while waiting for his wood to be prepared, he had been suddenly overcome with an idea for 'a good old-fashioned "Cézannish" bathing scene', with 'immense opportunities for drawing and colour'.[10] This painting and a further 'Bathing' composition occupied him on and off for much of the year. Gertler planned to use one of his studies of the Garsington pond as a backdrop, and told Carrington that he would 'revel in the drawing of the nudes', especially if he could persuade her to model, 'but you are so busy, aren't you?' he asked wistfully.[11] Apart from the obvious pleasure of having Carrington model nude, he was again desperately short of money.

At the end of January Carrington had gone to the country on a ten-day holiday at the Woolfs' house in Asheham with Barbara Bagenal and the Bloomsbury mathematician Saxon Sydney-Turner. To fight off the appalling cold they spent much of their time sledging, with Carrington sliding 'all the way down the Firle Beacon on Maynard's [Keynes] despatch case, [at] a terrific rate'. In the evenings they lit huge fires, ate enormous meals and listened to Sydney-Turner reading them Swinburne, or else 'talked very seriously' on topics such as the nature of good and evil, beauty and pleasure. 'Everyone agreed', Carrington wrote rather tactlessly to Gertler, 'that pleasure was certain, but argued over the good and evil and beauty.'[12]

Back in London, Gertler found troubles 'shower[ing] upon my head like Job'. He was already undergoing painful and expensive treatment for a slight stricture[13] when his family wired him to come home. On rushing back to the East End he found Louis suffering from acute bronchitis, and his family wretched and miserable. Only hours later, shortly after Gertler left him, Louis died. He was buried at East Ham on 7 February 1917, a day Gertler described as 'the worst . . . in my life'.[14] He had loved his father, but it was a love mingled with pity and a sense of alienation, which had often depressed him. At the funeral Gertler's anguish was largely reserved for Golda, who was inconsolable and wailed aloud over the coffin. The sight of her, he told Carrington, 'nearly broke my spirits forever', and he clung to her, declaring his 'passionate love . . . and kissing her with all my might', while his brothers stood by silently, broken with grief.[15] According to the Jewish custom, the burial was followed by 'sitting Shiva', seven days during which the family sat on low stools by the body all day until sunset, reciting special prayers and being visited by commiserating friends and relatives. Gertler felt he must 'keep this up to some extent', partly for his mother's sake, but also because 'I somehow want to'.[16] Carrington's letters over this black week were 'almost essential'.[17]

Nevertheless, in her presence he was increasingly 'nervous and awkward . . . and tongue-tied', afraid she would grow irritated and 'censure' him.[18] The painful stricture rendered him a 'Eunich' [sic] for the whole of the month – undoubtedly to Carrington's relief – and in truth he was aware of a growing separation. Carrington wanted a 'much broader friendship like old friends which nothing could move', but he wanted her as intensely as he always had done.

Throughout this period Gertler was deeply grateful for Shearman's friendship, and for the use of his Adelphi room, both of which he had described to Kot as 'a blessing'. Sometimes, Gertler knew, his black moods frightened Shearman, 'but he stands them and me bravely', he told Kot.[19] Indeed, to Shearman friendships were 'eternal once they have passed a certain stage and ours has passed it', he wrote.[20] Like many of Gertler's friends, he felt that Carrington was the cause of his unhappiness and that 'she alone could end it'.[21] He wished, he wrote, to become 'a sort of wife without the sex' to Gertler, 'but with as much tenderness and consideration as a mere man can give. Whatever you are in need of and can get from me you shall always have.'[22]

Throughout his adult life Gertler clung to the protective, encircling influence of older men; and there was to be no shortage of protectors. These father figures, a mix of homosexuals and heterosexuals, all achieved positions of some importance in their chosen professions: Harvey, Rothenstein, Currie, Marsh, Cannan, Kot, Shearman (and, for the final twelve years of his life, the publisher Thomas Balston). But however useful they were, Gertler could never sustain such a relationship without genuine feelings of friendship.

Gertler was always attractive to homosexual men. A friend of his wife was told that after the death of Rupert Brooke Gertler became 'the number one pin-up in Bloomsbury circles',[23] and Brett recalled how 'a very important friend' of her father's, had once 'lost his self control and made advances to Gertler, who was so scared he fled'.[24] Although he had reacted similarly to Strachey, Gertler was only embarrassed, not alarmed, when Shearman admitted, 'I know perfectly well that what I feel for you, you will only feel for a woman'.[25] What Gertler felt for Shearman in return was only 'a sort of pleasurable sense of intimate companionship that you can get from a man who can understand in some ways your point of view', and the moment of crisis in their friendship quickly passed.[26] Yet the degree of ambiguity in these friendships has led at least one commentator to conclude that Gertler was bisexual.

Gertler seems to have realized that the relationship with Carrington was at crisis point. Throughout April he was plagued with 'troublesome' thoughts that overshadowed his work. 'I am passing through terrible changes', he wrote. 'Veil after veil I keep tearing off my eyes and the disclosures are more and more terrible.'[27] He spent Easter at Cholesbury, but the fecundity of spring depressed him; even the trees seemed 'like lovers embracing' and reminded him of Carrington. She was spending the holiday at Marlow with her friend Alix Sargant-Florence (who was in love with, and would later marry, Strachey's brother James). Nevertheless, Gertler wrote to her there hoping that her friendship with Lytton was 'a happy one. I shouldn't like to think you are unhappy there.'[28]

Perhaps it was this that finally persuaded Carrington to tell him the truth about her feelings for Strachey. Before she left Marlow, Carrington wrote to both men arranging to meet them (separately) the following Monday, and telling Gertler something of her true state of mind. The night before their meeting Carrington dreamt of her brother Teddy, missing since the previous autumn and now presumed dead; as she had closed her fingers 'into his hard fat cheeks . . . kissing and hugging [him] till I nearly crushed him to atoms', she awoke alone and miserable, remembering her appointment with Gertler.[29] He telephoned her beforehand, not angrily, as she had feared, but horribly calm, and they arranged to meet at Penn Studio. There they talked of his pictures until finally he asked her what she intended to do about her feelings for Strachey. His calmness amazed her, she later wrote in her diary, 'and his complete unselfishness and generosity', and at this she only became 'more and more wretched and wept'. Although Strachey's cool temperament was part of his attraction, looking back over her many years with Gertler, Carrington found them 'warm because of his intense love'. Leaving him was like 'leaving the warm sun in the fields and going into a dark and cold wood surrounded by trees which were strangers'.[30]

> Then suddenly he saw it also: the end of all this closeness, the final goodbye, the separation of two brothers with a life between them, and he broke down and sobbed, and then it was agony. For he wanted to die and I thought how much this love mattered to him, and yet in spite [of] its greatness I could not keep it, and must leave.

'His loneliness', she wrote, 'was awful.' After leaving the studio they went to a local Swiss café, where they drank tea and she lied to Gertler and told him that she would not live with Strachey, and that he did not return her love. 'That', she thought, 'made it easier a little', but though Gertler begged to remain friends and still to see her, 'we both knew', she wrote sadly in her diary, 'it could not be so and it was separation'. Typically, however, they arranged to meet one final time the following evening.

Carrington went on to her meeting with Strachey, and found herself forced to join him at afternoon tea with Alix and her mother before she could get him alone. Afterwards they went out to dinner, talking all the time of other things, and only when they returned did Strachey finally ask about the meeting with Gertler. When Carrington admitted that she had told Gertler she was in love with Strachey, he seemed surprised. 'But aren't you being rather Romantic?' he asked, 'and are you certain?' 'There's nothing Romantic about it', Carrington replied (and indeed the obstacles, as she struggled to make herself indispensible to Strachey and to hold her own among the terrifying 'Bloomsberries', must have seemed formidable). Strachey was also worried that Gertler would be angry, but Carrington dismissed this. 'I'm so old and diseased', Strachey protested. 'I wish I was more able.'[31]

Their brief physical relationship had been unsuccessful, and over the years each would look elsewhere for their sexual partners; but Strachey aroused in Carrington an overwhelming and absolute devotion, of which her closest experience to date had been Gertler's own devotion to her. Strachey's own feelings at this stage are less clear. Although he cared for Carrington deeply, he remained unconvinced that their relationship would work, and was careful to offer her no false hopes. Still, she found some relief in being able finally to talk of her feelings, though they both agreed to keep them secret for the time being.

The next evening Carrington went to meet Gertler at the Eiffel Tower Restaurant, as planned, and when she told him Strachey's reaction, he 'laughed curiously', disgusted when she told him that Strachey did not care for her. 'To think that after all these years in 3 months you should love a man like Strachey twice your age . . . and emaciated and old', he told her.[32] In the silence which followed they drank their coffee awkwardly. Afterwards Carrington waited outside while Gertler settled the bill, then she walked sadly back to Gower Street, feeling, she confided to her journal, 'as if my nose had been cut away'. It had all ended 'about as crooked as it could be'.[33]

But of course it did not end there. That evening Carrington wrote tenderly to Gertler, thanking him for 'treating it as you have. And for your very great love in the past few years I thank you. I shall never forget it.'[34] And Gertler, despite his misgivings about Strachey, absolved her of all blame, writing, 'we have done well to part at last'. It was 'the end of that long and terrible struggle'.[35] He planned to begin right away to build this future life 'brick by brick'; his work would be the 'basis'. He also hoped that Carrington would find herself 'soon on her feet and with a better knowledge of your mind and feelings'.[36]

However, a letter from Clive Bell to Mary Hutchinson tells a different story and suggests that Gertler had by now determined to kill himself, and was only 'persuaded' by his friends (as Bell wrote with evident amusement), 'to put it off over the weekend. They tell me that Carrington has definitely given him his *congée*, and that he sees her in future at his own peril; but I should be surprised to hear that she really meant to let slip a *beau tellement en vue*.'[37] This was the generally held view in Bloomsbury. Even David Garnett, who greatly admired Carrington, felt that she 'found it impossible ever to be "off with the old love". For the old love always became more precious to her after the arrival of the new.'[38] By now the whole business was an open secret and Strachey, though flattered by Carrington's attention, was also (again according to Clive Bell) 'something worried about Gertler. He feels it would be awkward if Gertler were really to do himself in, but of course he won't.'[39] This fear, coupled with a desire to put Bloomsbury off the scent, may have been behind Strachey's comments to Bell at Whitsun, that Carrington had merely 'a sapphistical passion for him – the sort school-girls have for their mistresses', and that he was 'not in the least' in love with her.[40] Either way, Strachey was not yet ready openly to acknowledge his own feelings for Carrington, and that surely made the remnants of her relationship with Gertler all the more precious.

However, Carrington also seems to have genuinely feared that Gertler might attempt suicide, for though about to set out on a brief holiday with Strachey in south Hampshire, she arranged for Gertler to spend a weekend with Alix, and wrote to him there, promising that she would be with him 'a great deal' that summer at Wittering. Almost seamlessly they slipped back into the old relationship. The familiar metaphors crept back into Carrington's letters, and she now wrote that there was 'miles of land' in front of them to explore.[41] Gertler agreed, insisting he had taken his 'right place in relation to you'.[42] He was 'being reborn', but his vision for the future was bleak: 'one must be sooner or later absolutely self-contained. This is what I am struggling for. Dependence on people – on love – brings disaster. As yet I am dependent on you, therefore incomplete. Gradually, I shall grow more and more into myself, till at last I shall be free!'[43]

In practice, Gertler and Carrington picked up this 'new friendship' exactly where they had left off the old, except perhaps they met more regularly than before. Carrington came to the studio to read Gertler *King Lear*, and they resumed sexual relations, which led to a pregnancy scare in May that Carrington believed Gertler had brought about deliberately to ensnare her. Gertler continued to be bitter about Strachey and sent Carrington a cartoon of himself giving way to her 'new lover', with a crude drawing of Strachey with a limp penis. The situation was complicated by Shearman's feelings for Gertler, a parallel to which Carrington drew attention when she received the cartoon. 'I know that what you say is comic about Lytton', she replied. 'But no more comic than your lack of response to Monty.'[44] The point taken, Gertler ceased sending her the caricatures, but bitter fragments of reproach lay unposted in his studio.

By the late spring Gertler was already expressing his admiration for Cézanne in the large and ambitious painting *Bathers*, which he identified as 'a real step forward' in his work. A chance meeting with Roger Fry at the Omega Workshops in April 1917 led to further Cézanne-inspired pictures.[45] Fry told Gertler that he was mounting a show of copies, or 'translations', of past pictures by contemporary artists, and asked Gertler to contribute. 'As I very much liked the idea and always wanted to do something of the sort', Gertler wrote to Carrington, 'I have started a small copy of a Cézanne – whether I shall finish it in time for the show I don't know, as I cannot hurry.'[46]

Fry saw these copies as translations rather than replicas. 'Each generation', he maintained, 'almost each decade, has to remake its old Masters. If we did not go on revaluing and remaking them they would not be merely old, but dead.'[47] The Bloomsbury artists had long recognized the value of such an exercise: Vanessa Bell believed that copying allowed an artist to understand a picture 'in a way one can't otherwise', and in the summer of 1916 had felt nearly as free in her copying as in her own painting. Duncan Grant explained that his copies were not exact copies but 'interpretations', while Fry himself believed that this this type of study made him see with 'enlightened eyes'.[48]

Gertler too had long believed in the value of studying past masters, and he was clearly excited by the opportunities such an exercise afforded. Thereafter he sometimes used past masters as vehicles for new pictures, a technique that particularly with regard to Cézanne and later, Picasso, would lead to charges of plagiarism in later years.[49] It was in his admiration for Cézanne that Gertler drew closest to the Bloomsbury painters, and this led to allegations that he had lost his way along 'a devious path through Bloomsbury and Paris'.[50] But it is important to remember that for Gertler these enthusiasms were merely experiments to be worked through. To write off these paintings as mere imitations would be to underestimate both Gertler's motives and his achievements.

His contribution to the exhibition (delivered late) was an elaborate *Still Life* of fruit against a crumpled cloth, which has been described by the critic Richard Shone as a 'Yiddish Cézanne', and must have looked strikingly modern amid the other copies of Italian old masters. Fry himself contributed eight paintings, Vanessa Bell five, Duncan Grant four; there were also three by Fry's wife, Helen, and one by Dolores Courtney. Walter Sickert and Nina Hamnett failed to deliver, and the show was boycotted by the critics, most of whom were still suspicious of Fry. In the first week only ten people came, and by the end only two pictures (both by Duncan Grant) were sold – to Maynard Keynes, who only bought them out of a sense of loyalty. Fry himself called the exhibition a 'fiasco'.

None the less, it was the start of a connection between Gertler and Fry that was at its most intense over the next eighteen months, but which lasted until Fry's death in 1934. Fry was the only 'Bloomsberry' with whom Gertler sustained a meaningful dialogue, one that also remained unaffected by his more turbulent relationships with other members. From now on Gertler placed great value on his opinion and was greatly encouraged by Fry's 'appreciation and understanding of my work . . . especially my statue, which so few people can make anything of'.[51] He also continued to draw inspiration from Cézanne, and in September, when Clive Bell inspected the four canvases that Gertler had recently completed at Garsington, he pronounced them all 'under the influence of Cézanne'.[52]

In July 1917 Gertler was among the artists Fry selected as representative of 'The New Movement in Art' for an exhibition that opened in Birmingham, and that summer he was also approached by Vanessa Bell to produce a woodcut for the Woolfs' Hogarth Press. Carrington had already been commissioned to illustrate the first publication, *Two Stories*, and Vanessa wanted the next to be a book of artists' woodcuts, to which she asked Gertler, Fry, Duncan Grant, Edward Wolfe and the French painter Simon Bussy to contribute. Gertler produced a *Harlequinade*, but the project was called off in September, after aesthetic differences between Vanessa and Leonard Woolf. A year later Fry published *Woodcuts by Various Artists* himself, under the Omega Workshops imprint.

Gertler's relationship with Bloomsbury as a whole remained uneasy and was not improved by his close proximity to Clive Bell at Garsington over the summer. Probably Bell (wealthy, privileged and Cambridge-educated) more than anyone represented the aspects of Bloomsbury that Gertler most disliked – though their love of Cézanne might have been expected to bring them together. But Bell championed the intellectual spirit of art, exemplified by his book *Art* (1914), which coined the term 'significant form', while Gertler opposed all forms of art that came from the 'head and not the heart'. As author of the controversial anti-war pamphlet of 1915 *Peace at Once*, Bell had been one of the earliest recruits to the Garsington farm, and would also be the last to leave. In the intervening three years he and Gertler would frequently be thrust together.

Their sexual competitiveness was observed with some distaste by Brett's sister the ranee of Sarawak, who joined them at Garsington in August. In a letter to her father she complained:

> at breakfast with your bacon and eggs you get a minute and detailed account of life *à la* Oscar Wilde – by dinner time the tales become more lurid. Eleanor Glynn's *Three Weeks* would pale before one day in the life of Mark Gertler or Clive Bell.[53]

Each believed the other to be untrustworthy, and each had a reputation as a gossip, so it is hard to establish the truth. But Bell firmly believed that on one of his absences from Garsington (probably in the summer of 1916) Gertler and Carrington had steamed open one of his unposted letters and read the contents aloud to the assembled company.

Although Bell wrote to Mary Hutchinson in September that Gertler's work was 'very interesting and superbly conscientious: I don't think there is anyone in England but Duncan [Grant] who can do better', he was unwilling to champion Gertler in print. 'Roger [Fry] has written asking me to write an illustrated article about Gertler's pictures which I may do someday, perhaps,' he continued. 'He has also asked me to write about contemporary British art, and this I shall do at once.'[54]

It was during this period that Gertler had his first glimpse of Renoir, whose influence would tinge his work in the coming decade. Renoir's striking *Parapluies* was among the Hugh Lane collection of paintings on loan to the National Gallery in 1917, which Gertler would almost certainly have seen. This painting was probably the impetus for Brett's *Umbrellas – A Conversation Piece on Garsington Lawn*, an enormous painting, over six feet by six, which she worked on throughout that summer, shutting herself up in the 'monastery' and allowing only selected visitors to see it. Apart from Brett herself, it depicted Ottoline, Strachey, Aldous Huxley, Ottoline's daughter Julian – fresh from a dip in the pond – and two isolated groups: one consisted of Katherine Mansfield and John Middleton Murry enclosed by their parasols; the other, 'almost lost under his own sunshade', was Gertler.[55]

This lonely figure contrasts with the exuberant figure of Ottoline's photograph album: dancing on the lawn at Garsington, playing charades with Brett and Aldous Huxley, returning from a picnic with friends or thumping out tunes for the village fête on a pianola. Outside his own close circle he was still regarded as the ardent spirit of his youth. Aldous Huxley's portrait of Gertler as the Byronic painter Gombauld in *Crome Yellow* undoubtedly derives from the summer of 1917.

A dashing lover and a talented painter, Gombauld is viewed through the envious eyes of the ineffectual young 'hero' Denis as a figure who in the 1930s

> might have figured in a steel engraving as a type of Homo Sapiens – an honour which at that time commonly fell to Lord Byron. Indeed, with more hair and less collar, Gombauld would have been completely Byronic – more than Byronic, even, for Gombauld was of Provençal descent, a

> black-haired young corsair of thirty, with flashing teeth and luminous dark eyes.[56]

Denis, a poet, envies Gombauld 'his looks, his vitality, his easy confidence of manner'. Gombauld is equally passionate about art and sex, and expounds an earthy philosophy: 'Lots of life: that's what we want. I like pullulation; everything ought to increase and multiply as hard as it can.' He denounces sterility as 'odious, unnatural, a sin against life', while Mary Bracegirdle (Carrington) looks on with 'the indignation of a convinced birth-controller'. Like Gertler, Gombauld is continually 'pursuing something new, if only he could catch it'. This becomes almost a catch-phrase in the novel, much like Gertler's repeated (though genuine) conviction that each new picture was 'the best thing I've done', and prevents us from taking Gombauld too seriously.

Gertler, presented with a signed edition of the novel, was not offended, but Carrington was sickened at the portrayal of Mary Bracegirdle and her 'complexes', and later advised the writer Gerald Brenan not to read it. Ottoline was also caricatured as Lady Priscilla Wimbush, and was so affronted when the novel was published in 1921 that she suspended all contact with the Huxleys for six years. Unfortunately for Ottoline, it was to be only one of the many books in which she was cruelly caricatured by those who had most enjoyed her hospitality. She was a loyal and beneficent friend, but as age and illness attacked her, her appearance would become increasingly artificial, even bizarre, and seems to have led many to doubt her sincerity. That summer the manuscript of Lawrence's *Women in Love* was passed around London 'like an Elizabethan sonnet sequence'.[57] Ottoline, however, had already heard enough of it the previous autumn to recognize herself as the model for Hermione Roddice and had broken off her friendship with the Lawrences.

Mostly that summer Gertler worked on still lifes. In his imagination the ideas once more took shape fully formed as 'marvellous pictures . . . huge and world-moving', but in practice he could 'bring nothing to a finish'.[58] A paralysis hung over him: his head ached, his eyes ached and he feared his friends would be bored by his repetition, 'painting the same thing over and over again . . . all exercise – study, experimenting, wonderful internally, but no external results'. Like Gombauld, he was obsessed. He told Carrington he would paint 'thousands' of still lifes, and she pronounced this 'splendid'. 'What does it matter if nothing but exercises are produced for years if at fifty you produce work like Cézanne or Goya?'[59]

Throughout September Gertler remained as happy at Garsington as 'I, with my peculiar temperament, can be'.[60] During the day he worked, or talked about work to the 'invaluable' Brett, who assisted him with 'domestic details': washing his hair and scrubbing his back in the bath. He enjoyed the evening meal *en famille*, followed by pianola playing or reading, and only the lack of a studio prevented him staying on still longer. Philip Morrell had offered to convert one of his beautiful barns, and Ottoline was making plans to set him up in a little cottage in the village for which he would pay 'a peppercorn rent'. For the first time he experienced a sort of 'horror' at returning to London.

When he did so, Gertler struggled on with the canvas of *Bathers*, determined to 'get something new and better into this picture than I have got before into my work'.[61] That summer he had assured Kot that even 'my present failures are far more interesting than my past finished pictures'.[62] His struggles were intensified by his continuing difficulty in accepting Carrington's relationship with Strachey. By September her 'passion for LS' was estranging him more and more; poisoning his feelings and belief in her, and making him feel that she had been 'unnecessarily cruel to me in the past'. He found it difficult to forgive her.[63] It was her turn to beg to resume their contact. She was jealous that both Shearman and Brett washed his hair for him now, 'because I longed so often to look after you tenderly, to make you feel how good it was to be cared for, and like a nightmare I never could move hand or foot'. But she was 'humbled' now, she wrote from the farmhouse in Cornwall where she was staying with Strachey, and sure they could finally be friends.[64]

It was two weeks before Gertler replied, and when he did it was to tell her that he did not find 'the prospect of returning to you as at all enticing. I don't see why the future should be any better than the past, and the past visualised in perspective is pretty ghastly.'[65] He called her attitude to him 'most unhuman, and brutal, your selfishness appals me . . . You have sown seeds of bitterness inside me, by your brutality. I have to spend all my time now undoing what you have done to me.' What she had done, of course, was to have had the 'bad taste to fall in love with that half-dead man'. But when Carrington wrote to ask him 'not to think of me vilely and try and forgive me', he did so, anxious that she should understand that 'my detachment was necessary to me, and my bitterness quite natural to me with my temperament under the circumstances'. He signed the letter: 'Ever your friend . . .'[66]

That autumn the Zeppelin raids on London were relentless, and Gertler spent most nights 'huddle[d] in some basement or other listening to the almost continuous shriek and boombing [*sic*] of Guns'. The tube was 'crambed [*sic*] full of poor panic stricken people' taking shelter, and London seemed 'almost continuously under fire'.[67] The peaceful interlude at Garsington seemed just a dream. By December the air raids were so frequent that he no longer bothered to leave his bed for the shelter, but he was concerned for Golda, who was terrified as the Zeppelins targeted the East End, and shuttled back and forth across London waiting for the all-clear.

Since Louis's death only Jack and Golda were left in Spital Square. After a while Jack took a flat in the West End, where he spent much of his time, and Golda moved uneasily between her children. Gertler continued to see his family regularly, and his affection for his mother remained unchanged, but he now felt most at home at Garsington. 'Come to your home at G[arsington] whenever you like', Ottoline would write fondly.[68] And soon Gertler was telling Brett, 'how comforting it feels to have a sort of family and home [there] now'.[69] Determined not to let the dream fade away, he returned as often as possible (despite Kot's complaints about his 'new Garsington manners' and Frieda Lawrence's fear that he had lost his former 'impudence'[70]). Lawrence claimed that he had been spoiled by his association with Ottoline. 'Tell Gertler not to hop about at Lady So & So's too much, they take the guts out of him', he wrote to Kot.[71] But Gertler felt his relationship with Ottoline continued to deepen after each long stay at Garsington, and when he left missed her 'big "mountain-like" company'.[72]

In October the raids disturbed Roger Fry's rehang of 'The New Movement in Art' exhibition (now transferred from Birmingham to Heal's Mansard Gallery), confining everyone to the basement for an hour. But Fry was pleased with the result, and called the 'whole effect very discreet and yet gay and lively'. 'Except for Gertler', he added in a letter to Vanessa Bell, 'we are fearfully tasteful', and he was proud of the way in which he'd got over the 'difficulty' of hanging Gertler.[73]

Frances Spalding has identified a 'certain parochialism' in Fry's selection for this exhibition.[74] Certainly all the artists chosen were either friendly with Fry, influenced by Cézanne, or both, and Clive Bell rightly criticized the omission of work by Spencer, Lewis, Bomberg,

Roberts, Matisse and Picasso. His criticism of Gertler was particularly sharp. He concentrated on *Gilbert Cannan at the Mill*, one of Gertler's finest works of the war period:

> What he has to express is not, it must be confessed, of the highest quality, because his reactions are limited and rather undistinguished. He has only two or three notes, and they are neither rich nor rare. For an artist he is unimaginative, and often in their blank simplicity his conceptions are all but commonplace . . . Though a first-rate craftsman who paints admirably, he lacks sensibility.[75]

None the less, Bell included Gertler in the half-dozen 'young or youngish Englishmen of talent . . . on whom a discerning critic [sh]ould keep a hopeful eye – Mr Duncan Grant, Mr Lewis, Mr Stanley Spencer, Mr Gertler, Mr Roberts, Mr Bomberg, Mrs Bell, and Mr Epstein'.[76]

Later that month Gertler spent a weekend with Fry at his Guildford home, Durbins. His fellow guest was Nina Hamnett (then Fry's mistress), and the three enjoyed 'endless talks on art'. Fry was impressed to find Gertler 'really passionately an artist – a most rare and refreshing thing', and told Vanessa that he 'went wild over my photos and reproductions'. Afterwards Fry visited Penn Studio, where he found that Gertler was 'becoming almost a colourist', which he called 'a vast improvement'.[77]

Gertler submitted work to the Omega Workshops in November, and on the 10th Virginia Woolf wrote in her diary she was much 'impressed by the Gertlers'.[78] She was not alone: in the first few days Gertler sold three of his Garsington studies (at £25 each), and this success restored his good humour. He even made an effort to be friendly with Strachey, whom he invited him round for a drink on his birthday. Strachey was apprehensive but went, and reported back to Carrington that he still found Gertler 'very attractive', and would have liked 'to be friends with him; but the worst of it is that I can't feel any faith in him. He found Gertler's 'way of going on', presumably about Carrington, 'so silly'.

Both of them kept from Gertler the news that a consortium of Bloomsbury friends, headed by Oliver Strachey, had agreed to share the rent on a cottage for Lytton, and had signed the lease on Tidmarsh Mill, near Pangbourne.[79] Lytton would nominally act as caretaker, Carrington as housekeeper, and the financiers would be welcome visitors any time. From then until late December Carrington would be absorbed in making the mill habitable. She and Strachey moved in in time for Christmas, and made it their home for the next seven years. However, in a letter to Gertler she emphatically denied any such plan, offering instead the ingenious explanation that Oliver Strachey was merely storing her furniture at Tidmarsh.

Gertler spent Christmas at Garsington, and wrote to Kot on Boxing Day of his fears that Carrington would not forgive him for his last letter (which had inevitably been insulting about Strachey). 'I sometimes think', he admitted, 'that my real life will not commence before my passion for C. ends.'[80] But, as with the war, there seemed no prospect of any ending.

13

A Complex Being

> 'I am a complex being; there are many bad sides to my nature; but my real flame always burns brightly, and no wind or hurricane, ever can extinguish it.'
>
> Mark Gertler to Carrington, 20 February 1918

Gertler returned to London in time to join Shearman and the Hutchinsons to see in the new year, 1918, at Gilbert's new London flat (shared with his girlfriend Gwen). Despite his embarrassment over *Mendel*, Gertler had not deserted Cannan, but the warmth of the old attachment could not be recaptured, and Gertler detected an alarming change in Gilbert's personality. The old, gentle, dreamy Gilbert had been superseded by a far more boastful and less likeable character, and by July 1918 Gertler was ready to agree with Kot that Gilbert was 'after all just a blown-out eggshell'.[1]

At the start of 1918, however, Gertler did not seem to have any doubts; indeed he felt honoured to be one of the select few invited for dinner before the party. It was served in a plush, oak-panelled dining room, the tinkling keys of a hired pianist faintly audible in the background, the champagne flowing and the atmosphere relaxed. But after dinner other guests came trooping in, 'mostly men – conscientious objectors and Revolutionaries of all sorts, mostly unknown to me', Gertler wrote the next day to Ottoline, 'and mostly ugly, feeble and serious'.[2] He responded by downing tumbler after tumbler of neat brandy, becoming drunk, flirtatious and finally aggressive. Those people who came 'to see *Mendel* in the flesh', he admitted afterwards, certainly had 'their money's worth', and ashamed at the recollection, he now resolved to stay off drink.[3] Barely a week later this resolution had dissolved, and he spent most of January leading 'a fast life' in London.

It was a reckless kind of gaiety. His relationship with Carrington reached a new low in mid-January, when she concluded there was no point in their meeting again. 'I am tired with it all now', she told him. 'And I can't see the use of dragging on – so I wd rather not see you . . . would rather you did not write letters to me either, because they only make me feel uncomfortable – since I cannot answer them.'[4] Gertler plunged into despondency, and admitted to Ottoline that he saw 'everything in the Blackest possible light, especially the War, which I don't think will ever end! I don't think we shall survive it.'[5]

Painting remained the only 'bright light' in Gertler's life. Sometimes in the evening, however, his head whirled 'over the problem of it all, so much, that I feel, I shall go mad', he confessed to Ottoline. 'Only every now and then, do I see a brilliant light in the dim distance – for a moment – and these moments keep me going.' He largely attributed his gloom not to external events but to his own changeable temperament, concluding 'I should be unhappy, probably, even under the most favourable circumstances!'[6] He consoled himself briefly with a new Garsington friend, the celebrated Portuguese cellist Guilhermina Suggia, whose striking looks were later captured in a famous portrait by Augustus John. Her manner was captivating, and was matched by her exuberant playing. When they met up again in London, she played Gertler Bach (his favourite composer), and they went dancing. However, the beauty of her playing sometimes brought Carrington acutely to mind, and Gertler 'knew this meant a letter. But you have forgotten me now, have[n't] you?' he wrote rather wistfully.[7]

He re-immersed himself in café society as if he had never been gone. Instead of the Café Royal, the in-crowd now frequented the Eiffel Tower in Fitzrovia, seduced by its late opening hours, classless atmosphere and the generosity of the Austrian proprietor, Rudolf Stulik. Like the Café Royal, the Eiffel Tower was much celebrated in the art of its patrons. Wyndham Lewis and the Vorticists had celebrated the launch of *Blast* there, and had decorated one of the upstairs dining rooms. Stulik was a canny businessman and, realizing that the Bohemian presence lent a certain glamour to the restaurant, he introduced 'a ratio of charges based upon what he estimated to be the wealth of his clients'. This resulted in 'astronomical' bills for the fashionable set and modest enough charges for the artists, writers and poets, to whom, in an emergency, Stulik had even been known to lend money from his own pocket. Gertler went there with Shearman but he also mixed with the regulars, such as the 'tall, charming, unselfish,

[and] dissolute' Marie Beerbohm, the irrepressible Nina Hamnett, and fellow painter Geoffrey Nelson. One evening, as this trio played 'consequences', they heard a large crash as a bomb dropped near by. Unperturbed, they finished their game and ordered another round of drinks before going home.[8]

Carrington chided Gertler that life was too short, for such a 'careless evening life', and 'hate[d] to hear of you at the cafés . . . because I know you are worth more, and that more intelligent people', by which she meant Bloomsbury, 'like you [and] would be friends with you'.[9] But he sought relief in the superficiality of 'company and gaiety and youth', along with a certain oblivion.[10] 'What does it matter what I do in the evenings?' he asked her. As Loerke would say in *Women in Love*, 'What one does in one's art, that is the breath of one's being. What one does in one's life, that is a bagatelle for the outsiders to fuss about.' His real life, the 'internal life', Gertler assured her, would always go on, 'and develop, and struggle, and strive for decent things'.[11]

This letter was also an apology for his 'dissipated' behaviour a few nights before, after a Valentine's eve party at the Hutchinsons. Slightly drunk, and extremely jealous, Gertler had attacked Strachey in the street as he left the party with Carrington. A contingent of Bloomsbury pacifists came to the rescue: Maynard Keynes diffused the situation with 'amazing aplomb', the classicist John Sheppard led Carrington away and Harry Norton, the mathematician, assisted Strachey's 'trembling form from the field'.[12] 'Anything more cinematographic', Strachey wrote the next day, 'could scarcely be imagined.' 'Please forgive me', Gertler wrote to Carrington the next morning, but Carrington blamed herself for 'a neglect of my duties to you, and lack of foresight on my part', and claimed to have 'forgotten it all this morning'.[13] That evening Gertler also apologized to Strachey, who was dining at the Eiffel Tower with David Garnett, and the circle of painful apologies was complete. Yet Strachey's gracious dismissal of the incident as 'nothing at all' was perhaps, Garnett noted, as painful to Gertler as the agonies that had led to the assault.

'Really, until that relationship [with Carrington] has in some way worked itself out', he wrote to Kot, 'I am a lost, wretched creature. My Real life will only commence, when it is over. But when? When? Over and over again, I feel that I shall not survive it!'[14] Finally, Gertler learned the awful truth. 'I know that you live with Lytton', he wrote.[15] Weary of his contradictory letters, alternately reconciliatory then antagonistic, Carrington asked him not to write any more. 'We think so very differently about relative values of everything now', she pointed out.[16] Tired of London and tired of life, Gertler fled to the arms of his 'family' at Garsington.

But the war he could not escape so easily. The post followed him down, and he was finally served with the long-dreaded call-up papers for the army. He rushed back to London and was told to present himself at the Colours regiment on Monday 4th March. Immediately his friends leapt into action: Jack Hutchinson and Monty Shearman advised him to fill in an appeal form, objecting on the grounds of Austrian parentage, and Jack practised an impassioned speech before the tribunal on Mary at breakfast, which almost reduced her to tears. 'I have a conscientious objection to fighting', Gertler explained.[17] 'What I should like most', he told Ottoline, 'is to . . . get onto Philip's farm, where I could also paint.'[18]

Among his friends and acquaintances there seemed to be a complicit understanding that Gertler could not possibly be drafted. 'It would be absurd for you to do anything but paint!' Mary Hutchinson told him, 'and something must be done!'[19] When Gertler bumped into Desmond MacCarthy on the tube, he was full of sympathy and promised to try and help. Meanwhile, the painter Dick Carline, who had himself been serving in the army since 1916, did his best to console Gertler 'in such a simple kind way' that he was almost moved to tears. Even Iris Tree, who had heard the news from Ottoline, wrote from Cuba to sympathize. Most importantly, Carrington wrote at once, asking forgiveness for her last letter and promising to come up at a moment's notice if 'something horrible' happened.

Gertler was called to the local tribunal a few days later, and told that his claim for exemption would be laid aside pending a medical examination; an appointment had been arranged for the following week. He vaguely hoped, he told Carrington, that he might be able 'to work my stricture', but did not rate his chances of escaping active service highly. 'Otherwise', he told her, 'there is, I am afraid, nothing much the matter with me'.[20] In the meantime he painted furiously, determined to keep going until the last moment – 'like a captain on a sinking ship!'[21] To his great surprise, however, a few days after his medical Gertler learned that he had been rejected by the board as 'medically unfit'[22] – it is not clear on exactly what grounds – and that, like so many of his acquaintances, he had been assigned to work on the Morrells' farm. He was now 'as free as one can be during this war'. But the feeling of elation was short-lived; bewildered and unsettled, he fled once more to Garsington, where he was welcomed by Brett and Ottoline.

In February 1918 the Morrells suggested partitioning off part of Brett's Garsington studio – one of the outbuildings known as 'the Monastery' – to accommodate Gertler. 'I think . . . that Brett and myself would not be in each other's way', he told Kot. 'She is so nice and easy to get on with, in fact her quiet help and nearness, would be an advantage.'[23] As the two of them had grown further apart from Carrington, so they had grown closer to each other. Brett could not understand Carrington's love for Strachey, whom she never liked, and instinctively sided with Gertler. By March he was telling her that 'in your queer way, you have always been and are still such a help and a comfort. Carrington, with all my love for her, has not been able to help me a hundredth part as much.'[24] He also appreciated Brett's honesty, including her forthright opinions on his painting: 'I was . . . pleased with the frank way in which you "warn" me against Cézanne', he told her in May.[25]

Following his escape from service, Gertler learned almost immediately that he might be offered a commission as an Official War Artist. Initially, his response was guarded, but he agreed that 'if I could be of use, I should gladly sacrifice a certain amount of my time'.[26] He was discouraged by his enduring dislike of commissions, the need to abandon his own work and the necessity of spending the summer in London, but he was sorely tempted by the fee, which he learned in April was a generous £300, which, he admitted to Ottoline, 'would just save me'.[27] For some months he had been borrowing money from his brothers, and by April he owed them £50.

In the meantime he began work on a large self-portrait, an ambitious composition seen in a convex mirror with 'many reflections behind', the elaborate still life in front of him contrasting with the bare lightbulb and floorboards of the studio behind, and the two scenes linked by the intent figure of the artist at work. Gertler often painted self-portraits at significant moments in his personal life, usually at a time of financial crisis when there was little money available for other models.

The spring proved even gloomier than the winter; it rained constantly and London was blanketed in cloud, though this at least halted the air raids. Gertler shut himself up in Penn Studio and painted for days on end, as solitary as a castaway on a desert island. Towards the end of April he made several sales, including a flower piece for £30 to Monty's mother, Lady Shearman – one of his most faithful supporters – and a still life to Osbert Sitwell for £40, but he still owed his brothers money.

His war commission was confirmed in May by Alfred Yockney, secretary to the Official War Artists' scheme in Britain.[28] The scheme, which had been established in 1916, was run by a committee which advised the Ministry of Information on suitable appointments: William Rothenstein was among those commissioned in 1917, and later in 1918 Dick Carline at twenty-two became the youngest of the commissioned war artists. It was these appointments from the younger ranks of British artists – among them Nevinson, Paul Nash, William Roberts and Dick Carline's brother Sydney – that finally ignited Gertler's latent enthusiasm for the project.

Once he learned that 'only young and modern painters have been chosen! Not a single RA!' Gertler decided to accept 'on principle, because . . . I look upon this as something very significant, I mean, that a more or less official committee, representing the Government should do this! And so strong is it, that they are actually withdrawing people like [Stanley] Spencer and 'Bobby' [William Roberts] from the Front . . .!'[29] In his heart Gertler placed the value of British contemporary painting beyond the dominance of France.

> There is a good time coming for Art yet in England, no it shan't always be French, French, French. What will Clive Bell jaw and write about then?!! This Idea – I mean this War Memorial Committee has somehow excited me very much! Because I see so much, that is significant in it. I am ambitious about having a really good school of Painting in this country . . . Yes, about Painting I am Patriotic![30]

In practice, this meant signing on with the committee for an initial six months, and painting at least one picture on a given subject. Gertler's was 'Air Raid Night in the Tube', a subject for which he was well qualified, but when he was invited to the Ministry of Information to discuss the project, he learned that he was first expected to carry out a preparatory sketch for their approval. 'Apparently they do not give one the free hand I thought', he now wrote to Ottoline in dismay.[31] Even the size of the canvas ('about 10 feet') had already been stipulated. These restraints played on Gertler's fears about a lack of control to such a degree that they quickly withered his initial enthusiasm, and by June he was claiming to Ottoline that the whole thing bored him frightfully.[32]

When Mary Hutchinson questioned him about it in July, he replied, 'to tell you why, would take too long, I should have to explain all the peculiarity of Psychology'.[33] But the result was a near-disastrous state of artistic impotency, during which the idea of the commission, the alliance, the great resurgence of English painting, simply ebbed away and even the committee's original letter was left unanswered. Eventually the commission was cancelled, and *The Merry-Go-Round* remained Gertler's only memorial to the First World War.[34]

Gertler's behaviour suggests that he was again suffering fits of severe depression, possibly brought on by the final loss of Carrington in February. Although they had resumed their relationship after the breach, clearly Carrington now considered their personal lives irreconcilable and her recent friendly overtures had been in response to the threat of his call-up.[35] Once this was over her attention flagged, and there was an eight-month gap in their correspondence.

Gertler's vertiginous mood swings were probably also linked to the onset of the tuberculosis that struck him down less than two years later, and shadowed him for the rest of his life. In May 1918 he was diagnosed as having a weak chest and ordered to drink plenty of milk. Neither he nor his doctor associated his listlessness and unpredictable moods with TB, and Gertler put them down to his 'very peculiar temperament'. 'By nature', he told Ottoline, 'I suffer from moods of great depression, anger, reactions, and a thousand other horrible things, and these prevent me from showing my friendly and good self to people who matter to me.'[36] But Garsington always acted like 'a tonic' on his nervous system, and from each visit he took away the feeling that he and Ottoline had become 'a little nearer to each other'.[37]

In London he continued to burn the candle at both ends, painting all day and socializing in the evenings. By the end of June he was exhausted, and went to Garsington until mid-August to recover. Though officially a farm worker, his labouring was sporadic. 'I have been working on a hay rick', he told Mary Hutchinson in July, but it was necessary to clarify 'I do not mean painting'. He had just 'suddenly taken to . . . [labouring] and enjoyed it!! It was fine.'[38] None the less, he was often depressed, mostly because of his 'very experimental state of mind about my work', and though he recognized this as 'quite a healthy state', he could not help being worried. 'The last few days I've had to stop altogether, and when I don't paint', he confessed, 'I am quite undone.'[39]

In the same letter Gertler described a recent evening he had spent with Leonard and Virginia Woolf.[40] As Clive Bell's mistress, Mary had an uneasy relationship with both Vanessa and Virginia, and on her own recent visit to the Woolfs had experienced 'that strange sensation which I always get when I open a Turgeniev novel':

> All our characters were veiled and behind our temperate words no doors opened: or perhaps opened for a second and then shut so quickly one was not sure . . . Again you see it was [a] little like being in a novel . . . that is my impression. An excellent first chapter.[41]

Naturally she was keen to hear Gertler's version. 'I would have written sooner', he explained, 'but as a matter of fact, there was nothing much to write about.' He had expected Virginia to be 'rather mad, sharp, bitter, curious and effected' [*sic*], but instead found her 'quiet and pleasant and very natural'. He had liked both her and Leonard, and the evening had passed quietly and pleasantly.

Gertler had first bumped into Virginia at a concert with Carrington some years earlier, but they had not exchanged words. This second meeting probably came about through Kot, now liberated from the Russian Law Bureau and earning his living as a translator of Russian literature. He later worked on several translations for the Woolfs' Hogarth Press.

For Gertler 'the largest part of the conversation' that evening was about 'Jews, Judaism, the relation of Jews to other people, their differences, their faults, and virtues, evolution, etc. etc. You see', he explained to Mary, 'we were, with the exception of Virginia, all three Jews.'[42] However, Virginia claimed that Gertler, after admiring Vanessa's pictures, had 'talked mostly about his views of art'. She didn't like him much but concluded, 'I suppose he is what they call "powerful".'[43] In her diary she was more explicit, describing him as:

> a plump, white young man, got up for the occasion very sprucely in sponge bag trousers. His face is a little tight and pinched; but the word he would wish one to use of him is evidently 'powerful' . . . His mind certainly has a powerful spring to it. He is also evidently an immense egoist. He means by sheer willpower to conquer art. But bating this sort of aggression he was well worth talking to. L[eonard] noticed his amazing quickness. He would soon have told us the story of his life. I felt about him, as about some women, that unnatural repressions have forced him into unnatural assertions.[44]

When the Woolfs made their first visit to Garsington in July 1918, Brett took Virginia to the Monastery and showed her the still life

Gertler was working on, his 'solid "unrelenting" teapot'. The picture was generally admired. Carrington called it it 'immensely good' when she saw it at the Omega in November, and told Strachey it was 'much the best in the show'.[45] Even Clive Bell thought it 'the best thing – with the possible exception of the *Fruit Stall* he has yet done'. What particularly impressed him was the 'very complete and compelling . . . design' and 'the placing of the teapot', which Bell considered 'touched with genius. I think', he concluded, 'fine placing is the most thrilling in art – and its sheer gift it's [*sic*] not to be learnt.'[46] Virginia subsequently viewed Gertler's character along the same unrelenting lines. 'He is a resolute young man', she concluded,

> and if good pictures can be made by willing them to be good, he may do wonders. No base motive could have its way with him; and for this reason I haven't great faith in him. It's too moral and intellectual an affair; or perhaps the natural gift is not abundant enough to cover his conscience and willpower. He says straight out what he thinks, sits very upright; everything tight curled, tense, muscular about him; his art an agony often, as he told me.

Gertler had reached some conclusions about his objectives, which he had tried to articulate to Virginia. 'At last he understands', she wrote in her diary, 'that he wishes to paint form in the brightest colours.' Form, she felt, obsessed him:

> He sees a lamp as an imminent dominant overwhelming mass of matter. Ever since he was a child the solidity and the shapes of objects have tortured him. I advised him for art's sake, to keep sane; to grasp, and not exaggerate, and put sheets of glass between him and his matter. This, so he said, is now his private wish.[47]

Shortly after this Virginia wrote a short story, *Solid Objects*, in which the central character abandons a successful parliamentary career because of his obsession with objects of china and glass. Woolf's biographer Hermione Lee considers that these meetings with Gertler, as well as her own 'current, covetous fascination with glass and decorative objects, bore on this story'.[48]

Although some members of Bloomsbury had been less welcome at Garsington since January 1918, when Gertler had finally revealed the extent of their 'bitchery' to Ottoline, there was no escaping its influence at Garsington that summer. In May, Strachey's *Eminent*

Victorians had been published to immediate acclaim, and by July it was already in its third printing. All the Garsington guests, from the ex-prime minister Asquith to the Bishop of Oxford, had read it and it was the topic on everyone's lips. Now the 'darling' of society, Strachey was taken up by many of the same duchesses who had delighted in motoring Gertler around town back in 1915. By the end of July Gertler could not stand the incessant talk about Strachey, 'his duchesses and his book. If this subject had continued much longer', he admitted to Mary Hutchinson, 'I should have gone off my head.'[49]

So when the socialite-painter Patrick Dallas whirled chaotically into Garsington, displaying a complete lack of 'independence . . . or direction of his own', Gertler found him something of a relief.[50] He soothed Dallas and put him on the train to Oxford, but two days later received an urgent telephone message: 'Come at once Dallas very ill'. He rushed to Oxford, only to find Dallas 'perfectly well and gay' and ready to stand Gertler a good lunch.

By July Gertler was painting again and experimenting in watercolour, a medium in which he produced very few finished pictures. Clive Bell, who saw one of Gertler's Garsington watercolours, was sufficiently impressed to ask the price 'in a roundabout way', but on learning it was £15 told Mary Hutchinson he preferred 'a Duncan at two guineas – or a painting by Marchand at twenty'.[51] This suggests that the Bloomsbury painters priced their pictures considerably lower. However, Gertler's slow pace of working and experimental style, which he could not be sure would interest buyers, meant that he probably could not afford to lower his prices. 'Colours alone are ruinous!' he told Brett in December, and he was still surviving on money loaned by his brothers. Instead, forced to paint 'saleable things . . . and so straighten myself financially', he abandoned watercolour.

At Garsington, Gertler now shared the Monastery comfortably with Brett, despite occasional squabbles. 'I wish you were not deaf – my dear Brett', he told her, 'and learnt the art of arguing without feeling quarrelsome! You would be perfect then! However, underneath we all really love you and you know it.'[52] Brett protested that she didn't feel quarrelsome, only misunderstood; her deafness allowed her no control over her voice and she never knew if she was whispering or shouting, 'which may give the impression of being angry when I am not in the least', she explained. 'So many of the arguments are on subjects I have no real view about – I simply take a different one to promote the argument – I love the arguments only I am not a lukewarm person – I get excited and enthusiastic.'[53]

She was apparently not enthusiastic enough for Ottoline, who confided to her journal, 'I give and give to Brett, all my ideas about life and literature and religion and she gives me nothing'.[54] Increasingly irritated by Brett's 'clinging devotion', and worried at her growing dependency, in August Ottoline 'had it out with [her]' about staying on at Garsington for ever, though she afterwards relented. Brett returned a few months later but never regained her former place in Ottoline's affections, and that winter began to look for a house of her own in London.

Gertler, however, felt at ease with Brett. In December he teased her that they should go abroad 'and have one last fling before we are dodering [*sic*] and shaky in second childhood! We might even throw discretion to the winds and go in a more interesting condition than mere brother and sister!!!'[55] But at heart he knew that the success of their friendship lay in the fact that they were not in love with each other, and could therefore rub along comfortably side by side.

That August the Lawrences were back in London. Although Gertler thought Lawrence 'remarkable' – I like and respect him', he found Frieda 'intolerable – tactless, vulgar and personal', and together they had 'a depressing effect' owing to a 'kind of bitter intolerance of the whole world. Perhaps the whole world and everybody in it is bad, but even then – what good is it to spend hours cursing and cursing?' he asked Ottoline. He felt 'besmeared' and damaged by Lawrence's continual 'and largely exaggerated denunciations', and was glad to escape to Swanage for a holiday with Shearman.[56] There conditions were cramped, but the landscape more than made up for it: the sea, 'an intense blue with hot green trees silhouetted against it. The crude greens of the . . . earth, the ultramarine of the sea and the sunlit whites of the cliff . . . clear cut and solid, like coloured sculpture', inspired him with ideas for future landscapes.

The following week Gertler began his now annual holiday with the Hutchinsons at West Wittering. It was here that he first became inspired by Jack's collection of china ornaments, a subject he painted often in the following decade, and he was touched when the Hutchinsons presented him with a china horse on departure. Back in London he found that the Murrys had become Hampstead neighbours after moving into an ugly red brick house in East Heath Road, which Katherine immediately nicknamed 'The Elephant'. Gertler was astounded to receive a letter from Murry, reminding him that he had once promised Murry a picture, 'and that was all!' he told Kot.

On the weekend of 22 September Gertler set off on a pre-arranged visit to the Woolfs at Asheham, only to find himself the sole guest. 'Now Gertler is here talking about Gertler', Leonard wrote, with humorous exasperation to Strachey.[57] Virginia recorded in her diary that they had talked 'about Gertler to Gertler for some 30 hours. It is like putting a microscope to your eye', she wrote. 'One molehill is wonderfully clear; the surrounding world ceases to exist. But he is a forcible young man; if limited, able & respectable within those limits; as hard as a cricket ball; & as tightly rounded & stuffed in at the edges.'[58] He was, both Woolfs agreed with one tongue, a supreme 'egoist'.

Despite this, the visit passed off quietly enough, and it was not in fact Gertler's 'egoism' that brought this tentative friendship to a close. A few weeks later rumours reached Mary Hutchinson (apparently passed on from Gertler via Virginia) that Vanessa found her boring, and Mary burst into tears in the Café Royal. Both parties denied the rumours, and though Virginia did not think Gertler 'in the least malicious or even inquisitive, but entirely absorbed in himself and his own relations as usual', she objected to being 'made the victim of this infernal spy system', concluding 'it's quite plain that it's hopeless for us to try and know each other's friends, and in future I shall try and steer clear of Gertler, Shearman, Mary, Jack, Clive and all the rest of that set.'[59] By November, however, Virginia apparently believed that he had 'made mischief'.[60] The following year, when they met at Garsington, Gertler told Kot that she received him 'rather coldly', which he put down to gossip by Clive.[61] And in 1920, when Virginia heard another version of the episode, and learned that Gertler 'wished to clear himself', she could not 'face a meeting' with him, and the connection was allowed to lapse for a further two years.[62]

The highlight of the 1918–19 season was the return of Diaghilev's ballet company to the London Coliseum. Ottoline, who already knew Diaghilev, now presented her entourage to the famous impresario: Gertler, Brett, Aldous Huxley and her daughter Julian all had 'a great evening of it', Huxley wrote afterwards to his future sister-in-law Juliette Baillot. André Gide was there, he wrote, resembling a 'baboon with the voice, manners and education of Bloomsbury in French',[63] while Brett noticed Diaghilev, 'like a great white fat pig trying to woo Gertler'.[64] This did not deter Gertler from attending future performances with Ottoline, Siegfried Sassoon, Roger Fry, the Sitwells and John Sheppard. This time he was introduced to Léonide Massine, the principal male dancer, and to Lydia Lopokova, the female lead, who later married Maynard Keynes and who had previously partnered Nijinsky. In fact, Gertler was seen so often with the ballet company that season that Paul Nash wrote to ask him for an introduction to Lopokova.

Gertler found the ballet company irresistible material for his own repertoire, and re-enacted the post-performance scenes in Lopokova's dressing room at the Campbells' 'Sundays'. Beatrice recalled how he went out of the room and returned 'as Lady Ottoline Morrell, then as one of the Stracheys or Sitwells or Maynard Keynes or some other, making himself fat or tall, short or thin, while we all laughed helplessly'. Kot, with a distinctive snort 'like a small continuous cough', would laugh so uncontrollably that he had to remove his pince-nez to wipe away his tears'.[65] The ballet inspired a new composition – 'a sort of ballet' of his own – and finding himself absorbed and working with a 'fluency, unusual for me', Gertler put off a weekend with the Hutchinsons, unwilling to break the spell. A further ballet, a circus picture and *Boxers* followed, reflecting his continuing interest in interacting human forms.

His money worries continued. 'I suffer no end from the lack of a permanent income', he told Brett.

> It is not the fear of starving or anything as simple as that, that haunts me. It is the general principle. I long to be free and independent for my living, both from people and my work . . . To have to think of selling pictures, all the time and to tolerate silly people coming up here to see them, is awful. It creeps into all one's moods and spoils everything.'[66]

He does not seem to have called on Shearman, possibly out of embarrassment at the older man's affection for him, which was about to be severely tested.

One evening, after dining together, Gertler, Kot and the Campbells decided to make use of Shearman's Adelphi room. They opened the door to find it immaculately arranged for a party.

> There were flowers everywhere and every sort of delicacy – sandwiches and cakes, bottles of wine, decanters and liqueurs, even a large bottle of eau-de-Cologne. We guessed that Shearman was at the ballet with a party, and would be bringing them back, probably Lopokova, Diaghilev and half

> the company, after the show. For some extraordinary reason which has never been explained, Kot and Gertler seemed to go raving mad. It was really Kot who started it. They dashed at the bottles and the liqueurs, drinking everything and eating all the sandwiches, holding them madly in both hands. They threw the flowers and cushions all over the place and Kot took a painted wooden tray made by Roger Fry at the Omega Workshop and smashed it down with both hands over Gertler's head. I can still see Gertler's startled, delighted expression. The wooden rim of the tray hung round his shoulders like a collar, as he leaped about over the furniture shaking the eau-de-Cologne everywhere. Kot was fiercely serious, Gertler was hysterical with laughter and exaltation at taking a part in something so outrageous.[67]

Beatrice, horrified, implored them to stop but Kot only became more excited and rushing at the pianola 'played it absolutely fortissimo and terribly fast'. Suddenly there was a furious knocking at the door, and they opened it to find a neighbour shaking with rage and threatening to call the police. They left as swiftly as they had arrived, leaving the room in chaos and going on to gatecrash their second party of the evening at Gilbert and Gwen's studio flat. Kot, however, would not go in, and sat instead in the courtyard with his broken glasses in his hands, muttering in despair. Gertler, Beatrice noted, was completely sober. Kot had, uncharacteristically, done the drinking for all of them, and they had great difficulty in seeing him home, since he clung to all the railings and lamp-posts moaning. When at last they got him home, they pushed him through the door and there he collapsed. 'As we walked away in silence', Beatrice recalled, Gertler said, 'That Kot should be drunk! It is as if the bottom had fallen out of everything, as if everything had come to an end.'

Beatrice later remarked that at the time none of Kot's friends realized how concerned he was about the aftermath of the Russian Revolution, and the sufferings of the family he had left behind. Kot also had an instinctive hatred of ostentation, while Gertler constantly richocheted between a craving for and a rejection of his own 'aristocratic tastes'. Clearly, both men found some sort of release in the violence, and perhaps Gertler was also driven, as he had been with all his previous patrons, to test the limits of their patience. If so, he may have been disappointed in Shearman's reaction, for he simply wrote Gertler a polite note asking him to return the key, and they remained friends, though not at the same level of intimacy as before.

Peace arrived as suddenly as the war had done. Gertler did not meet

Carrington again until 11 November 1918, Armistice Day, when peace was declared, as Carrington put it, 'with a capital P' and huge crowds gathered spontaneously to celebrate in London. An impromptu party broke out at Shearman's, and an enormous crowd of people squeezed into the small rooms. Among them were Gertler, Strachey and Carrington, between whom the declaration of national peace had signalled an uneasy truce. Carrington visited Gertler a few days later in his studio, and found him so 'charming and interesting' that they even managed four 'delightful' days together in the country in December.

Afterwards Gertler missed her 'perhaps more than usual. I think that is because we got on so much more harmoniously than ever before and without the trouble and pains we used to suffer'. The relationship entered a new mature phase which he thought made it 'worth all the struggles . . . How wonderful it is to know, as I know now, that one can develop in one's relationships as much as in one's work!'[68] And Carrington assured him that when she heard 'what good things Roger and Borenius say about your work I swell out with pride!'[69] She thought him also 'so progressed as a character'.[70]

From this time on, however, they lived their lives separately, Carrington with Strachey in the country, first at Tidmarsh and later at Ham Spray, Gertler in his beloved London. His terrible fits of depression began again in December, possibly after the resumption of their relationship. He sent her a pen drawing she had admired, and was delighted to hear she was engrossed in her own work – 'that alone creates a bond between us', he told her, sending his 'best wishes in the coming year, to you, your work and our friendship'.[71]

Gertler spent Christmas at Garsington, and returned to London in the New Year, lunching with Desmond MacCarthy, before they went together to Prince Antoine Bibesco's to view his two Cézannes. Gertler was so agitated beforehand that Desmond, 'normally a most peaceful and quiet personage', became infected, and the pictures were inevitably something of a disappointment. Gertler confided to Carrington his fear that 'I may miss something in the originals that I get from the reproductions!'[72] The pictures nevertheless had an unsettling effect on his work, and he found himself 'starting from the A. B. C. again. Right from the beginning as though I had never painted before.'[73]

PART IV

Good Times Coming

'I have a feeling that we are going to have good painting, after the war – there are good times coming if only we can hold out.'

Mark Gertler to Lady Ottoline Morrell, April 1918

14

A Permanent Trace

'One seems to work at the expense of one's body and there is no other way, apparently, of doing it. At any rate I can't find an easy way of working. However it is worth the sacrifice.'

Mark Gertler to William Rothenstein, 4 April 1916

THE ART HISTORIAN Charles Harrison has written of a 'hiatus' in the British art scene in the immediate aftermath of the First World War.[1] After all the destruction the Vorticists' celebration of the machine age rang hollow. Many of its followers had been killed, and in the public mind the innovative art of the pre-war era was now firmly linked to the 'anarchy and anxiety of [the] political and social upheaval of those years'.[2] In art, as in life, the new era was marked by a period of 'recuperation . . . a slow, cautious process of reappraisal', and this was reflected in Gertler's state of mind.[3] He felt 'a slow sort of depression set in, even a boredom, an apathy', a mood that persisted for much of the first half of the year.[4]

Bloomsbury, owing to its pacifism, had remained largely untouched by war and, quick to fill the void left by Vorticism, began to establish its dominance on the British art scene, beginning with the infiltration of the London Group. After the early death of its president, Harold Gilman, in February 1919, many of the group's most revolutionary members, such as Frederick Etchells, Wyndham Lewis and William Roberts, immediately resigned.[5] Roger Fry, already a member, was soon joined by Vanessa Bell and Duncan Grant, and though Fry later refused the post of president, Bernard Adeney, who was elected instead, was a great supporter of his.

Gertler's attitude to Bloomsbury remained ambivalent, although

Clive Bell named him and Duncan Grant as 'not only the best of the younger men, but, with Mr. Sickert, the best painters in England' in *The Athenaeum* in April.[6] Gertler continued to exhibit with the London Group throughout the 1920s and occasionally served with Fry on the hanging committee, but never became one of Bloomsbury's inner circle. When, in May 1920, Wyndham Lewis (and Ezra Pound) led the anti-Fry rebellion, severing themselves from the 'Bloomsbuggers' to form the short-lived Group X, Gertler took a lively interest.[7] 'The more they knock each other about the better', he wrote to Ottoline in March 1920, 'but I hope and think that Clive will get the "knock-out" blow in the end.'[8]

However, with the publication of Fry's collection of essays *Vision and Design* in 1920, and Bell's *Since Cézanne* (1922) and *Civilization* (1928), Bloomsbury's influence spread far beyond the London Group, reaching both dealers and collectors, and causing resentment among the majority of English artists.[9] Those who met at 47 Downshire Hill in Hampstead (the home of the Carline family of painters) were soon joined by younger artists united by a common creed, described by Dick Carline as 'antagonism to academic officialdom . . . [and] some scepticism regarding movements like "Futurism" or Clive Bell's "Significant Form".'[10] Although Gertler occasionally attended these meetings, it was not until the mid-1920s, when he became more fully integrated into Hampstead society, that they began to have more resonance for him. Gradually during this period his work became softer and more fluid, a characteristic shared by much post-war English art. By the summer of 1919 Gertler's optimism had returned, his palette lightened and he turned towards Paris for his inspiration. Yet his French influences were not those popularized by Bloomsbury.

In early January 1919 Carrington's much loved father had died. Forced to return to her family home for the funeral arrangements, she had been desperately miserable. 'Coming into contact with one's family is always most distressing', Gertler agreed, 'even if one loves them as I do . . . I think it is simply because one has become so very different, and yet, somehow, one can't help feeling that there is after all some ghastly link . . . and so one feels it would have been better either not to have changed from them at all, or having changed, the link should automatically have broken itself.'[11]

Carrington, however, only felt irritated by these persisting links. The renewed contact with her family increased her antipathy towards her mother, and she endured it, she wrote to David Garnett 'by behaving like a Strachey and reducing the poor woman! I see Strachism is a fascinating occupation.'[12] Despite the success of their shared life at Tidmarsh, Carrington genuinely feared that if she had not met Strachey before his success there would have been no place in his life for her. She reacted, as Virginia Woolf had noticed the previous June, by taking over 'the Strachey valuation of people & art', and a new note of 'Strachism' coloured her descriptions of her old friends.[13] Although she professed herself touched and grateful for Gertler's support over her father's death, a somewhat more critical picture emerged in her letters to Lytton.

In February 1919 she described a dinner at the Eiffel Tower Restaurant with Gertler and Brett:

> Brett just as vague and deaf. Mark very depressed and talking of himself the whole time. I gather Monty has now given him up and taken (what Mark resents more than the loss of Monty's heart) the key of the [Adelphi] rooms . . . I suppose, to give to some other catamite . . . Mark of course was full of gossip but all with himself as the hero. But one always sees Mark in spite of his version – as he was really appeared [*sic*] to the other people![14]

The following day Carrington attended a party in Chelsea, which she described as:

> the saddest of little collections. None of our old friends, and a silence of the dead reigned most of the time. Ottoline looking terribly ill, tired and without any energy obviously for trying to make people enjoy themselves. The company? Brett, Gabri[e]lle [Julian Morrell's French governess], two Sullivans, Maria Huxley with a drab Italian young lady, Marco Murray, two Sickerts, Iris, her Husband and a dreadfull [*sic*] American young man, Ottoline's new Lover, Esmond, who I thought rather vulgar and affected. The Silent Sitwells, Arnold Bennet [*sic*] and Massingham. C'est tout. I didn't stay long. It was really so depressing. Mark trying to be gay, and putting his foot into every direction. Really I've seldom been so bored. Mark took me back here in a taxi which was a good end to a bad evening.[15]

But there were many who saw Gertler differently, including the painter Geoffrey Nelson, who, she told Strachey 'is now an imitation of Mark in everything he says'.[16] (When Nelson turned his hand to writing, she found it was 'all about painting and the ballet and Mark and Ottoline.'[17])

That August, when Carrington and her brother Noel spent a

weekend at Garsington, 'Mark related to Noel, I suppose one of the few people who haven't heard it', Carrington told Strachey, 'the entire history of his life, which, strangely, delighted Noel, who was very impressed by him.'[18] Some forty years later, on the death of his brother-in-law Ralph Partridge, Noel was handed the bulk of Gertler's early letters to Carrington; they struck him as 'the story of a strange and unhappy genius', and he edited an authoritative edition of Gertler's letters.[19]

In February Gertler admitted to Carrington, that despite selling a recent nude to 'an old man called Taylor', he remained 'very much in debt' to his brothers.[20] Ottoline remained a staunch ally, despite discovering in April that losses from the farm had virtually 'ruined' her. Regretfully, she sold her famous pearl necklace (which had once belonged to Marie-Antoinette), but could not bring herself to tell Gertler or Brett, who now made modest contributions to the Garsington housekeeping, that these did not begin to cover the cost of feeding and housing them.[21]

For Gertler the sale of the nude had also initiated a new friendship. Walter Taylor was a landscape painter, collector and founder member of the London Group. In the 1920s he regularly accompanied Gertler to Garsington, where E. M. Forster noticed them in 1922. 'There is also an old gentleman here', he wrote to his mother, 'named Mr. Taylor, who never speaks and when he does inaudibly – a friend and patron of Goertler's [*sic*], who frisks around him with exhortations of "Pipe up Walter, they can't hear you" which Mr. Taylor seems to like.'[22] An old and intimate friend of Walter Sickert's, who affectionately called him 'my Taylor', he was generally known as 'old Taylor', and was in fact some thirty years older than Gertler. With his red face, white beard and immaculate attire, there was indeed something of the nineteenth century about him. He had the 'leisurely gait, and . . . a little of the air of a seaside dandy', Sitwell observed.[23] And 'only England', remarked another friend, 'could have produced him.'[24] Taylor's private life had been struck by tragedy early on, when his young wife had died on their honeymoon, but he never spoke of her, and was, to all appearances, a comfortable, hospitable bachelor, who also proved one of Gertler's most loyal supporters.

Sometimes Gertler still harboured hopelessly romantic fantasies about resuming a relationship with Carrington, but gradually he appeared to be reconciling himself to her loss.[25] By mid-1919 he had begun a relationship with a former art student called Valentine, who had been at the Slade with Carrington and was now living in Hampstead with her husband, the literary critic Bonamy Dobrée. Essentially creative, Valentine was variously a painter, collage-maker and ceramic painter. She had a gift for interior design, published a novel, poetry and short stories, and later contributed to *The Listener*. Everything she did, Gertler once remarked, had 'a touch of genius', and she dazzled many of the men and women who came within her radius.[26] She was dark-haired, creamy-skinned and voluptuous, and her beauty was exactly of the type that appealed to Gertler. She agreed to sit for him and by the middle of June he had already completed a large portrait of her, which, along with a recent still life, he told Carrington, 'proved the reality of certain ideas I have recently discovered'.[27]

Valentine herself was clearly an inspiration.[28] After painting a second, smaller, portrait of her Gertler found that 'things went with a flow and consistency quite unusual for me', and that summer at Garsington he completed a larger number of pictures than usual, including three studies of the pigeon house.[29] (These disappointed him but delighted Ottoline's thirteen-year-old daughter Julian, who declared herself 'so dreadfully tired of pictures of the pond, or the pond and the island, or the pond and the ilex tree.'[30]) As the art historian Andrew Causey has observed, 'in a decade that favoured landscape, Gertler largely ignored it',[31] but Garsington was the exception. By now it was his 'second home', and he painted it as obsessively as he had painted the East End. He was particularly inspired by the austere beauty of the garden and the 'fatal pond', where he had nearly drowned one afternoon but was saved by Nelson. ('With regard to your mishap,' Kot wrote afterwards, 'the Jewish saying is appropriate: Frighten me, Lord, but do not punish me.'[32]) Many of these landscapes served as backdrops for later pictures, but they often have a quiet, brooding quality that hints at a growing detachment in Gertler's personality and which later characterized his still lifes in the 1920s.

Francomania flooded London in the summer of 1919, with the return of Diaghilev's ballet company, and with designs by Derain for *La boutique fantasque* and Picasso for *Le tricorne*. Both men were in London for much of the summer, and clearly there was some jostling to offer them hospitality. Ottoline, who already knew Diaghilev, planned to organize a 'Picasso party' in late May, but this failed to come off. Catching a glimpse of Picasso at the ballet, Gertler told Ottoline that he resembled nothing so much as 'a little fat waiter . . . So far I like Derain much better.'[33] The ballet season he enjoyed less than before, claiming to breathe only 'poison in the air when our 'intellectual' and 'great' men [he meant Bloomsbury] meet in a bunch – this is a feeling I've always had and can never get over – perhaps it is my own fault – but there it is.'[34]

'I am not really anxious for Picasso to see my work as yet', he explained. First, 'without knowing the whole string of my development and just seeing one or two things in my studio – I am sure he couldn't make much of it.'[35] Second, he felt disinclined to 'enter into the "competition" – I mean to seize him by main force from Clive Bell and Roger Fry. They have pocketed him, so for the time being, I am content to leave him in their pockets.'[36] Yet he was smarting over their failure to introduce him to the French painters. It seemed the cosy coterie had once again closed its ranks. 'If Roger and Clive were really as interested in my work as they make out', he pointed out to Ottoline, 'they would have mentioned me to Picasso and Derain or brought them here.'[37] What his apprehension and defensiveness suggest is that he was unwilling to be examined and found wanting. Perhaps perplexed by this response, when Ottoline eventually did invite Picasso, his wife, Olga, Massine and Diaghilev for lunch at Garsington in late July, Aldous and Maria Huxley were the only other guests.

The other major summer event was an exhibition of modern French art, mounted by Osbert and Sacheverell Sitwell, which opened at Heal's Mansard Gallery on 1 August.[38] Ottoline, who was already in London, attended the private view, and wired her Garsington guests to join her for the exhibition and the ballet. Gertler jumped at the chance – not to see the ballet, he explained to Kot, but because he was tempted by the French pictures, which included work by Picasso, Matisse, Derain, Dufy and Modigliani. In the event he dismissed them as 'all very nice and fine and clever, but Exquise! And oh c'est formidable! They all make me feel as if I were on the stage.'[39]

At Garsington that summer the guests included André Gide 'and a supposed nephew . . . a boy of eighteen', and Simon Bussy, whom Gertler liked very much, even though he was married to Strachey's sister Dorothy. At night they walked around the pond by moonlight melodramatically reciting Verlaine's poetry, until Gertler began to 'hate the sound of French more and more. Why will they say everything is Magnifique! Horrible! Terrible!' It made him want to paint as differently from the French as possible. He rejected all things French with the words traditionally used to a *shatchan* (matchmaker) to reject a proposed Jewish bride, 'Very nice, very fine, but not for me.'[40] None the less, the new vibrancy of his palette that summer caught the mood of contemporary French painting, and even Carrington, on a now rare visit to Garsington noted the new 'charming and delicate colour' in his work.[41]

Throughout the summer Gertler buzzed with ideas for new pictures, but deliberately suppressed them, storing them up like summer fruits to be enjoyed in the contemplative quiet of his Hampstead studio that autumn. June was cold and rainy, and he and Nelson lit a fire in the studio and sat gloomily warming their hands. 'Don't be nervous', he wrote reassuringly to Brett, 'we are not using your canvas – we are treating everything with the utmost delicacy and care, as if it were all made of precious stones and glass! Observing, also', he wrote without irony, 'all your notices "Beware of Fire" etc.'[42] But Brett's own life at Garsington, which had 'stretched itself out to last three years', was in any case now coming to an end.[43] After Ottoline's ultimatum she had begun in earnest to prepare her Hampstead house, in which she had offered Gertler a room (rent-free) on his return.

Gertler arrived in September, luggage-laden and with Nelson in tow. Brett had spent months preparing the house in Thurlow Road. 'The colours will be beautiful', she had written to her father in April, 'my studio lemon colour – the little bedroom pink – the billiard room cream – the basement passage blue – the kitchen sea-green – or duck's egg – the bedroom lemon yellow – the bathroom pink' (though the decorators, she added, were 'getting slightly confused'[44]). Before long, however, much of the exotic colour scheme was eclipsed by a thin veneer of green, when Gertler's basement 'apartment' turned out to be damp. Almost at once he felt weak, and Brett obligingly moved him upstairs to 'a huge long room with variations in oak all over the place', which they nicknamed the 'state apartment'.[45] It was too large to be cosy, but he appreciated its 'ugliness', and there was enough room to partition off a small sitting room. These rooms were his London home for the next three years.

Meanwhile, the relationship between Brett and Ottoline continued to decline, partly because of their mutual attraction to Garsington's resident cheesemaker, the Canadian poet 'Toronto' Prewett. Ottoline's affection was purely platonic, and she was horrified when Prewett made a pass at her, but perhaps even more annoyed when Brett afterwards claimed to be receiving passionate love letters from Prewett by every post. In September Brett's stock fell to an all-time low when, having reluctantly agreed to look after Julian for a week while Ottoline visited relatives in Ireland, she sent reams of complaints to Ottoline about her 'wretched child'.

By contrast, Gertler and Brett now got along 'admirably . . . like a real old "Darby and Joan"!',[46] and he appreciated the security of having a more permanent home. That autumn he developed a genuine 'love for the "homestead" and its friendly fire', and even passed up a party at the Hutchinsons for a night of comfortable domesticity with Brett. 'Imagine Brett and myself sitting by a very cosy fire, divided by a small round table, on which we play "bezeek" [*sic*] only stopping every now and then to drink tea and crack nuts, or talk over "old times"! When we were young and gay, Passionate and Romantic! Even the ink', he wrote, 'turns green at the thought.'[47] He even began occasionally to host his own 'Wednesdays'.

That September, with money still a problem, Gertler again discussed the idea of teaching with Ottoline, who contacted her brother Lord Henry Bentinck about finding him a pupil. Gertler immediately hurried to retract, explaining he felt it 'quite impossible to teach any one anything about painting. I should like to take a few lessons myself!' he told her. 'But really – I'm serious – it would only be dishonest of me to pretend to teach – there is nothing to teach believe me – there are millions of ways of painting and everybody must find there [*sic*] own.'[48]

Working steadily and loath to interrupt his routine, he did not return to Garsington for another month. And it was now that he drew upon the ideas he had stored up from the summer, explaining to Carrington that he had hit upon a new method of 'evolv[ing] a sort of charcoal drawing which is so explanatory to me that I can paint almost the whole picture afterwards from it'. He used this method in a further *Bathing* composition, and then in *The Horse in an Orchard* (or *Petrushka*), in which he rekindled the blaze of a summer orchard, bringing his cold Hampstead studio alive with light and colour. By December he was telling Carrington, that 'that little "horse" that you saw at Garsington – was the first step to a new "ladder" which seems to me an important one and likely to last[,] perhaps even the beginning to my final path. And these two, (1) *Bathers*, (2) *Petrushka*, seem to be important evidence of the fact.'[49]

Gertler kept back these two pictures for Carrington to see, but inevitably she failed to turn up, and he wrote to her (without bitterness) of her 'elusive and capricious' behaviour. 'You suddenly don't turn up at a critical moment and all is severed in one fell swoop!'[50] The truth was that Carrington was preoccupied by a new relationship with a young man called Ralph Partridge, who had been at Oxford with her brother Noel, and was equally busy demonstrating to Strachey his centrality in her life. She never fully relinquished Gertler, however, whom she valued as an artist and by whom she felt 'more improved by . . . than anyone', she told Noel.[51] By contrast, Gertler still felt for her the same reverence as for 'a real work of art, or as one feels at a moment of some emotional or religious conception'.[52]

One person who did view Gertler's pictures was John Middleton Murry, who wrote to Katherine Mansfield (now his wife) that Gertler was making 'real progress', commenting on 'a certain loveliness of colour' in his recent work. Katherine, who had been diagnosed with tuberculosis in May 1918 (the month of her marriage), was then staying in Ospedaletti on the Italian Riviera for her health, and Murry told her they must buy one of Gertler's pictures for their new house when she returned. 'I know the real thing when I see it', he wrote, 'and his work has begun to be the real thing.'[53]

In the autumn of 1919 Gertler grew closer to Valentine Dobrée, whose husband, Bonamy, was away at Cambridge, leaving her alone for six months of the year.[54] They spent many cosy evenings in the studio, toasting teacakes or cooking scrambled-egg suppers, and by the winter their relationship seems to have intensified. After Christmas at Garsington, Gertler hurried back to Hampstead to spend the whole of the next week with her, though he was sometimes obliged to share her with Bonamy. On the Tuesday he and Valentine spent the evening at Penn Studio, and Gertler's comment to Carrington – 'I won't go into details about that!'[55] – suggests that they had become lovers. Although the exact nature of their relationship is never entirely clear, Gertler's letters contain many implicit references to an intimate friendship, and the following December when the Dobrées left Hampstead to live in the Pyrenees, he was 'positively furious' that Valentine 'should have voluntarily broken such a friendship as ours by going so many miles away'.[56] Whether or not they had a physical relationship, Gertler was certainly 'in love' with her to some extent for at least the next three years.

All through Christmas Gertler had been longing to get back to his studio to put the finishing touches to *Footballers*, based on a photograph he had seen in a newspaper. Yet when he arrived it all went wrong and 'now it's done for – five weeks solid work gone'. It made him feel depressed, 'unhinged' and like 'swinging a knapsack across my shoulders travelling off into the world – anywhere'.[57] Yet he remained fascinated by entertainments and planned two further such pictures, one of a tightrope walker and the other of a circus scene of two people on horseback; he also returned to the haunts of his youth, and gave up an engagement with Ottoline to attend 'an acrobatic turn' at Bedford Music Hall.[58]

In March 1920 Gertler made his first trip to Paris as a mature painter, accompanied by the Dobrées. He wanted to see many of the collections of contemporary picture owners and dealers, such as Alphonse Khan, Pellerin and Bernheim, and 'Mr Dobree' he explained to Ottoline, knew 'many influential people in Paris'. (He also planned to 'look up Picasso and get him to help me', but no more was heard of this plan once he arrived.[59]) He intended to stay 'just as long as I feel it necessary for the furthering of my work', and had enough money to last a month.[60] It was a trip that had a lasting effect on his art.

The journey was pleasant and the party put up at a hotel in the Place du Panthéon. They began their assault immediately by viewing some remarkable paintings by Velázquez, and on another day 'five or six very good Cézanne, lots of Degas – Renoir and all the impressionists[:] Monet, Manet, Pissarro, etc. Most exciting!'[61] Of the picture collections, Bernheim Jeune's was 'the finest . . . I've seen here or anywhere in my life . . . You have no idea what it meant to me!', including three Cézannes, some beautiful early Matisses and Bonnards. The Pellerin collection was remarkable for a splendid Cézanne and Pissarro – 'the best of the impressionists' – and it confirmed Gertler's mounting admiration for Renoir. 'Cézanne is the direct outcome of the impressionists – only at his best – he is better than they are and beats them – at their own game! . . . firmer – sturdier – more constructed – more monumental – and far better in the actual surface of the paint.' Cézanne, he decided, was 'a beautiful technician – I don't know anyone who's actual paint is better to look at . . . His paint alone makes one's mouth water like a beautifully ripe peach! But Renoir has all these qualities too.'[62] And it was Renoir finally who made the greatest impact.[63]

On their first night out the party dined in a little restaurant in Montparnasse, uncannily similar to 'our own dingy little holes in Soho', Gertler noted.[64] Afterwards they visited the famous Café Rotonde, which Gertler recognized as 'the equivalent of the Café Royal'.[65] It was full of artists distinguished only by a remarkable variety of beards: 'long beards, short beards, pointed beards, velvet caps, anything odd you can imagine – all artists!'[66] 'My God – what types!' he wrote to Ottoline.[67] They ran into everybody. Nelson came 'blinking in' on their first evening, quite at home in his *de rigueur* little black cap. He knew 'everybody and everything' in Paris, and whisked them off to 'amusing' parties'[68] – 'mostly foreigners', Gertler noted, and mainly Jewish, 'they talk Yiddish to me!' he wrote to Brett in surprise.[69] After three weeks (which seemed 'like years – there's so much to tell'[70]) they had encountered most of the usual crowd: St John Hutchinson, Iris Tree (now married to the decorator Curtis Moffat), Epstein, Nina Hamnett, Roger Fry, Duncan Grant, Vanessa Bell, Evan Morgan and those beautiful, decadent members of the 'fast set' Marie Beerbohm and Nancy Cunard. 'Of course I've been out with them', he wrote to Ottoline, 'Expensive meals – Beautiful women – wine – music –parties!!!'[71]

Sometimes, however, the endless round of people, talk and parties fell flat, and even the *Folies Bergère* seemed 'rather disgusting and silly' (perhaps partly because Valentine was being kept safe 'from any Parisian onslaughts', presumably including his own). His hand often 'itched' for the brush and he longed 'to paint – only to paint', although seeing the pictures he had for years admired only in reproductions was an 'extraordinary sensation . . . There is nothing that takes one's breath away like those giants', he confessed to Carrington.[72]

Contemporary French painting ranged from the 'horribly bad' to the 'quite good', but somehow Gertler did not believe he had seen 'the real thing'. He met Derain 'once or twice . . . a nice man', he told Ottoline, but he considered much of his work 'inferior – rather 'tricky'.[73] He liked best a young artist called Ortiz de Zarate, a former friend of Modigliani, whom he was quite sorry to leave. It was Ortiz's simplicity and honesty that appealed – he was without the 'tricks' that so many of the others indulged in. He even asked Gertler to sit to him, but there was not enough time. (Gertler's looks were quite a hit, and he received so many compliments; 'I've found it at times, quite embarrassing', he told Ottoline.) However, he was glad to return to London and his painting in mid-April. 'You see', he explained, 'to me, work is a constitutional necessity, without it everything loses its value or true proportion and nothing can make up for it.'[74] And although the trip had left him £40 in debt, he recognized it had been an 'extremely profitable experience'.[75]

The immediate effect of the visit was that Gertler now decided to paint 'only from nature'. He began work on a still life, *The Red Jug*, in

April 1920, but was soon 'panting to paint people'. He engaged a nude model, and also began work on a final Matisse-inspired portrait of Valentine. The nude went 'thrillingly' until the model became anaemic and was sent to the country to recuperate, so he went on with Valentine's portrait until she too became ill, and that was also abandoned. Frustrated, he engaged a third model, 'an old hag of forty-five', whom he hoped 'by leaving out the wrinkles and the crumpled skin' to turn into 'a fascinating plump woman of thirty'.[76] Yet even she was booked up and unable to come again for days. 'Painting in the way I am doing now', he complained, 'one is simply almost completely in the hands of one's sitter and this is an awful thought. Yet I can't paint any other way just now, as it is just that which is my Idea.'

That month Gertler spat blood for the first time, one of the classic signs of pulmonary tuberculosis. He spent a 'wretched unforgettable' period waiting for test results, but it is not clear what diagnosis he received at this stage, for it was not until October that he used the term tuberculosis in discussing his illness.[77] But perhaps the clearest evidence of his health during this period is the self-portrait he began in May while there was no one to sit for him. Uncompromising and direct, it is heavily shadowed by the signs of incipient illness.

In the meantime Gertler began to formulate ideas on his Paris trip. He ran into Murry in May, and explained to him 'my way of understanding these great men [Renoir and Cézanne] and how terribly misled one has been all along by the wizards' and intellectuals' interpretations of them. I mean Roger Fry and Co.' Murry, impressed, offered Gertler a chance to write an article for *The Athenaeum*, but when he refused, decided to 'crib it all' and write about it himself. Furious, Gertler vowed, 'I shall never again talk to writers! . . . I neither want nor believe in "enlightening the world" on the subject of art . . . Besides, these are my own private feelings and probably only good for me.'[78]

Gertler told Ottoline that he had turned down a solo show in Paris, since the dealers expected him to cover his own expenses. But he now signed a contract for a one-man show in March with William Marchant of the Goupil Gallery. Marchant advanced him a monthly income of £35, to be recouped (as they both hoped) by sales when the show opened. With a new goal in sight, Gertler threw himself into work and completed seven pictures between May and July 1920, including his self-portrait, two nudes, a flower piece, a portrait of a pretty young neighbour, an interior (*The Mantelpiece*) and *The Bokhara*

Coat, his portrait of Valentine. This perhaps marked the conclusion of their affair, but they remained close friends for the rest of his life. In July Gertler told Carrington he was having 'troubles of a . . . romantic nature' (presumably concerning Valentine), and his health was uncertain. He suffered 'Garsington headaches' and mood swings, and felt altogether 'about a hundred years old'.[79] Carrington found his letters 'mystifyingly gloomy',[80] but he reassured her that he was not 'hopelessly . . . unhappy . . . merely depressed by contact with doctors and disease'.[81]

He completed several pictures at Garsington in July, including a still life of a geranium standing on a windowsill, seen from the inside looking out, very much in the French tradition. In August he spent a very happy fortnight with the Hutchinsons at Wittering, lingering on to complete a portrait of Jack. For once he did not relish the return to London, and suggested to Mary that 'London is [all] played out for us. It is only good up to a certain age. We get nervous, malicious and ill there; we're at our worst . . . There's no composure no sense of interval.' The Hutchinsons motored him the 112 miles back to Garsington. Afterwards Gertler's bottom 'ached like the devil', and, more worryingly, he again spat blood.[82]

At Garsington he tried to live quietly, taking up a still life and beginning a portrait of Julian, a constant struggle as she would only sit 'an hour a day and groans with boredom'[83] so that unable to get a likeness, he declared her 'almost too good-looking to paint'.[84] Among the other visitors he developed a profound dislike of the poet W. B. Yeats, who talked continually of spiritualism and clairvoyance; Gertler much preferred Siegfried Sassoon, who was 'always in an unsettled state, nervous, and altogether chaotic'.[85] He persuaded Ottoline to defer a visit from Carrington, because of the 'numbers of different and difficult people' already coming and going, but in reality because her 'whirlwind' visits always left him unsettled.

As September drew to a close he made plans for returning to Hampstead, where because of his weak chest Brett had now installed a stove in his room. Brett and the Hannays, who lived upstairs, had been arguing, and concerned that he might become homeless, he advised her from the safe distance of Garsington to 'stick it out and win it over them'.[86] But Brett had other problems. Her deepening friendship with Murry and Katherine Mansfield was complicated by a tentative affair between herself and Murry, which although not consummated until much later, was perceived as threatening by

Katherine. To Brett's friends it appeared distinctly comic. Carrington reported back to Strachey that Brett found 'her sexual outlet playing . . . tennis balls with Murry, instead of [playing with] Murry's balls'.[87] On his return Gertler found Brett 'distant and deaf . . . lonely and reduced. I am sorry for her and yet unable to help. She is dried and shrivelled in some way', he told Ottoline.[88] He missed the charm of Garsington life, and told her that in London the fight seemed 'more serious and bloody'. They were prophetic words. Soon afterwards the blood-spitting turned to haemorrhage and Gertler collapsed. Tuberculosis was finally diagnosed.

It seems extraordinary that Gertler's illness should have escaped diagnosis for so long. Pulmonary tuberculosis was still the most prevalent form of the disease, and until the 1950s was fatal in 80 per cent cases over a period of between five and fifteen years. The earliest symptoms included lassitude, poor appetite, loss of weight, pallor, and night sweats, accompanied by a persistent cough, blood in the sputum, pains in the chest and/or fever, sleeplessness and finally haemorrhage by mouth – all of which Gertler had experienced. There was still no cure in this period, and patients were advised to winter abroad or, as in Gertler's case, to enter a sanatorium, where the therapeutic regimes largely consisted of rest, fresh air and a milk diet. Initially, his health remained too uncertain to fix a date.

As he lay recuperating after his collapse, such 'an eternal stream' of family and friends made their way to Thurlow Road to visit him that Brett felt quite deserted once he was packed off to the sanatorium and the stream dried up.[89] Chief among them, according to Carrington, were Gertler's 'fat Jewish relations', who exasperated him by arriving in droves from Kilburn and the East End every afternoon to 'lament by his sofa'.[90] Kot also came faithfully every day, and even Gertler's dealer Marchant visited and (perhaps in case of a relapse) carried off a large amount of work for the forthcoming show. Carrington also came, escorted by the handsome, healthy Ralph Partridge, who bored Gertler with his 'heavy Bloomsbury' talk (he had begun in October to work for the Hogarth Press) or sat silently smoking his pipe and reading the newspaper. 'What life he had they've already succeeded in extracting', Gertler grumbled to Ottoline, but '*au fond*', he admitted, he found his new rival almost impossible to dislike.[91] 'I take it Partridge is in love with you', he remarked coolly to Carrington. 'How much of it do you return, I wonder. I think, if I were a woman, he is the sort of man I'd love – he is so good-looking and such a figure!'[92]

But he preferred Ottoline's visits with the 'beautiful and bright' Julian, who, he claimed, did him far more good than all the others put together.

Slowly, Gertler began to revive and resume some of his old habits, walking on the Heath in the afternoons and enjoying the 'intellectual and detached' beauty of autumn. One day he visited the National Gallery and lunched with Kot and Kot's landlords, the Farbmans; he dined on another with Aldous and Maria Huxley, on a third with one of his sisters and on a fourth with Walter Taylor. He was packing everything in before 12 November, when he was due to leave for Banchory sanatorium in Scotland.

Two nights before he left, Brett (now thirty-nine, but still looking 'the youngest of all the ladies present') held a birthday party at her studio, at which, Carrington told Strachey, 'the number of people who were at daggers drawn was considerable'. She reported that the previous night, though 'dreadfully white and worn', Gertler had seemed his old self, 'completely cheerful and very amusing, [and] talking the entire time', but the party passed more quietly, 'because of not getting [him] excited'.[93]

The company included Ottoline ('a drab from the start, bleary and blotched, and tottering to her foundations'), Shearman, Jack Hutchinson, the Aldous Huxleys, Boris Anrep, Walter Taylor, Valentine, the Hannays, Iris Tree, Curtis Moffat, Vanessa Bell ('in one of her Oscar Wilde velveteen tube-like dresses') and Duncan Grant. Gertler himself was 'a comical little figure, in a white and pale lavender Blaszer [*sic*], which Gilbert once gave him, and little check trousers. Like an undergraduate in a Shaftesbury Avenue Revue'.[94] But the white, strained face had told a truer story than the comical undergraduate and two days later Gertler departed for Banchory, where he spent the next six months.

15

Exile

'All [normal life] ceases on the 12th November for that day I go into exile – the Sanatorium.'
Mark Gertler to Ottoline Morrell, *c.* October 1920

THE WHOLE OF Gertler's family and Kot, the only representative of 'our world', he told Mary Hutchinson, turned up at King's Cross to wave him off.[1] The train was stuffy (a common complaint among TB sufferers) and he could not work out how to open the window until morning, but there was, after all, 'something romantic' about the sleeper.[2] At Aberdeen he was dismayed to see his luggage arriving on one platform just as his train steamed out of the other, but he was reassured that it would be sent on. From Banchory station he was taken by car to the sanatorium. There, overcome by a sudden shyness, he was disconcerted when the young maids giggled at him but was immediately taken in hand by the formidable matron ('all the nurses . . . are hideously ugly – that's unfortunate', he noted[3]). He was given a hearty breakfast and put to bed, where he remained for several agonizingly boring days.

Situated at the foot of the Grampian mountains, a few miles from the North Sea coast, and about ten miles south of Aberdeen, Nordrach-on-Dee (usually referred to simply as 'Banchory') was an enormous purpose-built sanatorium, constructed from local granite and German timber, nestling among Scottish pine forests. It was modelled on the famous Nordrach sanatorium in the Black Forest at Baden, where Dr Otto Walther had first pioneered the open-air treatment of tuberculosis in 1888, and it first opened its doors on Christmas Eve 1900. Originally it housed only thirty-six patients, but by 1914 this number had risen to seventy-five and included the writer

Somerset Maugham, who wrote a short story, 'The Sanatorium', based on his experience there. In 1920 the sanatorium was still considered a model of its kind, and the intake had reached an all-time high of eighty-six.[4]

However, it was not for the poor. Rooms cost between £7 and £10 a week and Gertler estimated his own costs at roughly £45 a month, so he was probably once again subsidized by his family. He had continued to receive 'subs' from Harry up to September, and quite possibly from Taylor, who contributed to all of Gertler's subsequent stays in sanatoria, and often paid for him on trips abroad.

The 'Nordrach treatment' was based on the belief that it was 'essential for patients to spend the whole of their time in pure air'.[5] All the bedrooms faced south and were heated by steam pipes, and the patients were kept in 'icy coldness . . . all night, in any weather, we sleep with our two windows, as large as doors, wide open',[6] Gertler reported to Brett, while their beds were warmed by improbably large hot water bottles and plenty of blankets. Gertler found the first two weeks unbearable. 'Have you ever sweated from Boredom?' he asked Mary Hutchinson,[7] but he felt himself gradually 'sink into it' by degrees until at last, a month later, he had become 'almost completely resigned'.[8]

Once allowed up, Gertler quickly mastered the routine. Punctually at 8 o'clock every morning he took his own temperature before the nurse came in to take his pulse. Afterwards he breakfasted in his room at 8.30, when the doctor made his rounds, writing out his orders for the day on each patient's chart. About 10 o'clock he rose, shaved, washed and set off on the recommended walk about 11, then returned for the 'rest hour' between 12 and 1. Lunch in his room was followed by a walk in the afternoon, sitting out on the veranda until tea and a return to bed until six, when he had to take his temperature again. At 7 supper was brought in and the period until bedtime (9 o'clock) was usually filled by writing letters.

Although roughly half the patients were confined to bed, many of the 'ambulents' looked healthy, even plump. 'I never knew there were fat consumptives in the world', Gertler wrote to Kot in surprise.[9] The cure encouraged patients to 'fill out' and Gertler, who was considered far too thin on his arrival, found the endless round of meals left him feeling constantly sick. 'Eating such a lot is torture to me', he told Kot, and catching sight of himself in the mirror a few weeks later he was alarmed: his face appeared swollen and coarse, and his neck had grown fat. 'It rather depresses me also', he wrote, 'to think that human beings, even sensitive ones like me, can be fattened like pigs!'[10] He began a savage self-portrait as 'a memorandum of when I was fat', using a thick impasto to coarsen and flatten his features.[11] He was comforted when a fellow patient assured him that, though the other patients seemed complacent, they all longed, like him, to get away. They had also developed a fine sense of irony. During a film show one evening, when the hero of the drama was reading a note, it was magnified on the screen for the benefit of the audience. 'It ran something like this, he told Kot, "It is no use our staying here. There is no hope for any of us, nothing to look forward to. We may as well give up." ' The sanatorium audience received this with a 'roar of laughter'.[12]

Gertler's health quickly improved and he was allowed to walk up to four miles every morning and join in the 'cure without', which consisted of golf in the afternoons. He and his partner quickly became known as the sanatorium's worst players. He was not forbidden to work but was frustrated by the view of the doctors that painting was just a 'hobby'. The November days were so short that the light for painting was gone by 3.30, and Gertler determined to steal an hour's work from his exercise period between two and three each day. It was the first time he had touched his paints in three months, an experience he likened to a much beloved friend seen 'only occasionally and then only among other people – always in a bustle – and suddenly, one day, you and your beloved are shipwrecked on a deserted Island: Just you two.'[13]

His windows offered outstanding views, and he marvelled to Carrington at the varied colours of the surrounding mountains:

> Sometimes they seem painted with those old master browns, golds and varying russets; at other times they suddenly become gay and assume Matisse blues and purples. Looking at them I sometimes suffer from a rather fascinating form of optical illusion. Suddenly they all turn into painting! I mean that instead of solid earth and stone, over which men can walk, it appears to me only as a picture, an oil painting done by some super genius! When this happens to me the illusion is so strong that I simply cannot – for some time – turn back again and see the scene in front of me as real space and solid earth – just as one suddenly imagines that the train one happens to be travelling in is going the wrong way.[14]

Nevertheless, he largely limited his palette to the gloomy greens of his Garsington landscapes, which give the sanatorium paintings a claustrophic quality.

At the end of November Gertler began a painting of the view from his bedroom window, but quickly grew agitated and hot and 'chucked it in disgust and despair'. The following day produced better results, however. He had some opposition from the doctors because of his need to stand, and a special stool was obtained for him. When he went back to the landscape, he thought it so dull he would 'challenge even a Goya to make anything of it!' but really the subject hardly mattered, only the practice and sensation of painting again.[15] As soon as it was completed, he immediately began to paint the same view all over again, and most of the Banchory landscapes are subtle variations on the same sliver of landscape, which framed myriad possibilities for the artist.

Gertler also longed to paint one of the sanatorium's pretty servant girls. Her sturdy, healthy appearance – 'enormously plump – exactly like a fat and rosy doll' – delighted him, and she crept into all his letters. 'You felt if you laid her flat her eyes would automatically close', he told Mary Hutchinson.[16] To Kot he wrote that she had 'all the beauty of an apple with the additional charm of being human . . . What could be more desirable!'[17] (Kot hastily wrote back, advising him to seek the matron's permission.) When, 'after much manoeuvring', he finally persuaded the girl to sit for him, he found her 'really wonderful to paint – a typical rustic type – sturdy as an ox, and cheeks like vermilion straight from the tube!' Though he confined himself to painting a small head of her, he really wished 'to take her away with me and paint her for a year without stopping – and How I should like to do her nude!'[18] It was the 'Renoir-like' quality of her appearance that appealed to him most.

As news of his profession spread among his fellow patients Gertler particularly dreaded being asked to show photographs of his work. As he explained to Brett, 'though they look so realistic to us – they obviously look very queer to them and I find myself excusing certain "faults" and explaining and helping – alas poor me.'[19] By January the other patients had become 'jocularly sarcastic' and a drawing of a cat appeared on the hall notice-board, with the signature 'M. Gertler RA.' Later, discovering reviews of his show in the papers, his fellow patients insisted on coming to view his work, three at a time, every day.

Gertler became fond of one young medical student of twenty-two who did pen-and-ink sketches, but was put in a difficult position when asked to 'tell him what is wrong – what could I say?' he asked Brett, 'since it was all wrong! All he cares for is to "get the likeness" I tried to explain that there were other things that mattered perhaps, just as much, but he looked vaguely at me, and yet he is intelligent.' He found that 'all the ideas, and great names we care for so much and almost live for, are unknown here.' Despite these interruptions Gertler settled into a routine not unlike his old one and by April was able to inform Kot that if he finished all the work in hand he would have nine pictures to take away with him. 'As long as I work', he explained to Kot, 'I feel somehow, that I am really "functioning" to use one of your words.'[20]

What he missed most was the 'exchange of ideas', and in his letters to Brett he always enjoyed an argument (usually over Cézanne). To his surprise, one of these exchanges blew up into a major row, with Brett taking his comments as personal criticism. She was feeling sensitive at Gertler's reaction to her efforts to educate one of his nieces, which he regarded as interference. Brett was affronted, and Gertler had to reassure her of his affection, 'I swear about the tie between us, and that nothing could destroy it.'[21]

Medical examinations at Banchory took place every six weeks, and after the second Gertler was diagnosed with only very slight TB. May was fixed as the time for his departure, although he had practically determined to leave in March and to continue the regime at home. By January he was working every afternoon, and at almost the same rate as before his illness. He had adjusted to the dullness of the sanatorium, but never quite lost the feeling that there were 'good and exciting things somewhere round the corner'. He was glad to 'push out' the old year' with its worries and illnesses and events, he wrote to Kot, 'let us say "of the heart"', of which he somehow could not speak.[22] But he meant Valentine. The Dobrées had sold their house in Hampstead and were moving to France. 'Yes, "how broken up every thing is",' he wrote to Valentine,

> and your going away chops up the last fragment. Why must you go and break up a friendship like ours! . . . I don't want to be tragic or blame you, but in plain words – I love your company – your conversation – your personality – your tastes – your talents – I should have loved to feel that you were waiting for me at Hampstead, to continue our evenings as before – you have no idea how encouraging and cheering a look-out that would have been for me – to wait for – after this! But now you are going away and once friends begin to place distances between them – well.[23]

The sanatorium proved a curious place to spend Christmas. Many of the men smuggled in drinks, became 'indecently drunk' and spent several days recovering in bed. But Gertler, taking his place at the New Year's Eve party in a Pierrot costume, and sipping champagne, found it not 'altogether unamusing', especially since several of the young ladies, he observed in a letter to Carrington, were rather pretty. In early January, for the first time, Gertler suddenly felt 'more than well . . . I want to run and jump!' he wrote eagerly to Kot. Then, floored by an unexpected cold, he lost all the weight he had gained since his arrival and, confined to bed once more, nearly lost heart completely, vowing that the moment he was allowed up he 'would run away or take poison!' It soon passed, however, and only days later he could write to Carrington that his work was now 'in full flow'. Yet there is a heavy, motionless quality to many of the pictures he painted at Banchory, an echo perhaps of the feeling of suspended time peculiar to the sanatorium. One critic later suggested they should more properly be termed 'still life', since they introduced the viewer to a 'frozen and lifeless world'.[24]

Gertler's first solo exhibition opened at the Goupil Gallery, Regent Street, in February.[25] It was a small show, comprising only seventeen paintings, mainly still lifes and portraits, and nearly all from the previous year. The reviews were mixed, but largely positive. By far the longest was by Roger Fry in the *New Statesman*, drawing attention to Gertler's determination, his 'intense, almost fanatical devotion' and a certain quality of 'egoism'. Though Gertler was grateful to Fry for a 'nice and congratulatory' letter and his serious analysis, he was frustrated by Fry's 'harping too much as to the future, instead of dealing with that already achieved', and couldn't help feeling that 'my work is really not for him, that he and I are too fundamentally different for my work ever to really appeal to him or his kind', he wrote to Carrington.[26]

Carrington considered the show made up of 'very good work, not in the least advanced, merely very careful landscapes and still lives',[27] but only two pictures sold at the private view, and one of these was to 'our poor friends the Hannays', who lived above Brett's rooms in Thurlow Road. 'Everybody seems particularly hard up just now when for the first time in my life I happen to have a one-man show!' he reported to Kot in dismay.[28] 'A little less appreciation and a few more sales', he told Brett, would have suited him far better.[29] And to Jack Hutchinson he admitted that it was now the marketability of his paintings that mattered most. 'If they sell well it'll mean that I have a market for my present work, and that would [be] a good thing if I am to spend my time languishing in Expensive Sanatoriums.'[30] Sales amounted to only £139 11*s*., scarcely enough, as he pointed out, for three months' sanatorium fees.[31] Nevertheless, Marchant was sufficiently impressed to offer Gertler another show and continue his monthly advance.

Gertler assured an anxious Carrington that he was going through his cure 'with the patience of an ox, and I'm sure that in the future . . . I shall bore people with the excessive care I intend to take care of myself'.[32] Indeed, shortly before his release in April, when Brett wrote that she had given his bed to Toronto Prewett, who was suffering from flu, Gertler became distinctly alarmed at the possibility of Prewett 'puffing germs' into his eiderdown,[33] for in remission from TB even flu could prove fatal. Gertler was allowed to leave in May only on condition he did not stay in London, so he arranged to return for only two or three weeks before going on to Garsington for the rest of the summer, aware that with the 'capricious' nature of his disease he would have to stick 'almost exactly' to the sanatorium regime, a sacrifice he now considered worthwhile. He likened himself elsewhere to 'a man who comes out of a dark room into brilliant sunlight, . . . [who] can open his eyes only by degrees'.[34]

Gertler had stayed on at Banchory until May in order to complete a large landscape he had begun in March and could not bear to leave unfinished.[35] It is the finest of his Banchory landscapes and one of the finest of his paintings of this period, and he donated it to the sanatorium in gratitude for his 'cure'. In a letter to Brett, Gertler referred to 'the novelty of its shape . . . a long narrow upright 4 feet high'.[36] It radiates with the claustrophobic intensity of the TB sufferer, which is rarely apparent in Gertler's letters. As he prepared to leave, Gertler learned that a young boy of eighteen, expecting to leave at the same time, had died unexpectedly. It was a reminder of his own fragility.

Although the love affair with Carrington was over (at least for her), a 'communion of spirit' remained, and even when they rarely saw each other and their communication was scarce they executed many similar works, sometimes in ignorance of what the other was painting. In this period they shared a passion for Renoir.[37] When Gertler painted his portrait of the *Scotch Girl*, he wrote to Carrington (then working on a portrait of her own apple-cheeked maid Annie Stiles), wondering 'which is the most Renoir-like, your girl or mine?' [38] And Carrington's later portraits of *Olive Slater* (1925) and *Annie in a Pinny* (*c.* 1925) contain echoes of Gertler's *Servant Girl* (1923). Despite her emotional affiliation with Bloomsbury, Carrington's work was always closer to Gertler's own.

Carrington's tentative invitation for Gertler to recuperate at Tidmarsh in the spring was wisely refused (Tidmarsh was, in any case, notoriously damp). 'I would not think of plumping my troublesome and invalided self upon you', he replied, rejecting the idea that he needed a wife to look after him. 'No thank you, I don't want . . . a good wife nor a good mistress!!! Get me rather a £1,000 a year, and all would be well . . . I like women to be my friends and equals, or superiors as the case may be, not half mistress and half slave. I hate that state of affairs.'[39]

Meanwhile, Carrington's own marriage to Ralph Partridge was moving nearer. Life at Tidmarsh involved, as Quentin Bell has put it, a 'nearly incomprehensible trinity' composed of 'three persons who were all more or less in love with each other but in rather a different way'.[40] Carrington remained devoted to Strachey and, though aware that their life together was 'limited', was anxious to preserve it at any cost. She was fond of Partridge, willing to sleep with him and unwilling to lose him, but nevertheless perpetuated in their affair the same pattern of evasion, prevarication and capitulation that she had displayed in her relationship with Gertler. Partridge became obsessed by Carrington and wished to marry her, but he was also fond of Strachey and accepted his place in Carrington's affections. Strachey was by now in love with Partridge, though he retained his paternal affection for Carrington, as well as his practical dependence upon her.

Something in Partridge's behaviour must have rekindled Carrington's memories of Gertler, for she suddenly wrote unexpectedly recalling their early love. 'I confess that your recalling of memories saddened me rather', he replied:

> It might have been so much better – I loved you so . . . I wonder if you ever realised how much I loved you! . . . How terrible it was when you turned to L S . . . However that moment you mention was good – for once you were amiable, and you actually let me kiss the rain off your face. You even went so far as to point out a particular drop and asked me to catch it quick, which I lost no time in doing – and how good it tasted![41]

He still thought of her, he admitted, 'when I paint'.[42] And when at last in May Gertler was released from the sanatorium, he was keen to meet her again. 'How good it is to get letters from you', he wrote, 'but how much better still to see you in the flesh! . . . To me . . . you become more beautiful every time I see you. I don't mean by this just externally, but the "tout ensemble".'[43] Knowing something of her situation, he advised her:

> Whatever you do, don't tie yourself irrevocably to one man. A person like you should never belong to anyone . . . You are too good for that – you belong to the world. God knows I love you enough and I should like to own you. But I have learnt to curb my desires and, not even to expect to possess all the parts of a person like you.[44]

But Carrington had already agreed to marry Partridge in order to keep together the Tidmarsh *ménage à trois*, though she first sent Strachey a moving valediction to her love:

> All these years I have known all along that my life with you was limited. I could never hope for it to become permanent. After all Lytton, you are the only person who I have ever had an all absorbing passion for. I shall never have another . . . I had one of the most self abasing loves that a person can have . . . These years of Tidmarsh when we were quite alone will always be the happiest I ever spent . . . You never knew, or never will know the very big and devastating love I had for you. How I adored every hair, every curl on your beard. How I devoured you whilst you read to me at night. How I loved the smell of your face in the sponge . . . Say you will remember it, that it wasn't all lost and that you'll forgive me for this out burst [*sic*], and always be my friend . . . Once you said to me, that Wednesday afternoon in the sitting room, you loved me as a friend. Could you tell it to me again?[45]

On 21 May she married Partridge.

That day signalled the beginning of the end of Gertler's passion for her, as Beatrice Campbell later recalled:

> We talked of love and falling in love. [Mark] said that, for him, ten years was about the length of time that being in love could last. He said that it was ten years to the day from the time he had fallen in love with Carrington in the Slade to the time when he heard that she was going to marry someone else. He was so shattered that he felt that nothing but a revolver could end his pain. He went out to buy one, but found it was Saturday afternoon and all the shops were shut.[46]

Beatrice was impressed that 'he could laugh at his sufferings' and the ludicrousness of his situation. The affair had indeed the air of a great tragicomedy.

Initially, Gertler had written generously to Ottoline that Partridge was 'one of those born husbands – Devoted – kind – unselfish – no woman can resist the love of such a person – and I don't wonder – they do make good husbands'. He saw it as inevitable that Carrington should marry somebody and Partridge was 'as good a choice as any' – so long as it wasn't Strachey – 'I could never bear that relationship', he admitted.[47] Carrington invited Gertler to spend a day with them at Tidmarsh, and he told Kot, 'I may do so perhaps'. But he could not go through with it, and received Carrington's attempts to change his mind with some bitterness, telling her it was 'rather hard for me to believe that you are going to miss so much my company, when you choose to have it only for about two half-hours a year for the last three years! In any case I would not consider your feelings in the matter, since you never in any one instance in all the long years I have known you considered [mine].'[48] Carrington tried to reassure him that her marriage would change nothing. 'To you', she wrote, 'I shall ever be Carrington, and to myself.'[49] By Christmas she had lured him back into a correspondence, and he promised to 'try my best to get into a state of mind that may allow of our meeting again, since you seem to want to see me so much'.[50]

On his return to London in May, Gertler was dismayed to find that a craze for tennis had infected all his friends, and Brett's garden had been turned into a tennis court, full of wiry people playing 'as if their very lives depended upon it'. He sat watching from the balcony in amazement as they played themselves 'to the bone',[51] but despite his apparent detachment he was panicking and suffering terrible nightmares which betrayed his many anxieties: his health, his family, his financial situation, the loss of Carrington, and the critical reception of his work. He dreamt that he accidentally shot his brother Harry, 'and the first thing that struck me was that my chief source of maintenance was gone'. In another dream he had a haemorrhage and lost all his teeth; and in a third he quarrelled with his sister for criticizing his work.

Suddenly he became terrified of being alone. Garsington seemed to provide the solution. 'One gets people without any trouble', he told Kot.[52] Yet the company could be unsettling – particularly Ottoline's daughter Julian, who was now fifteen, full of fun and physically mature. She wished to be 'gay and playful the whole time', and he found it 'very difficult to treat her as a child, because she is as full grown and has precisely the same effect, as a very attractive young lady of 25; I see no difference whatsoever', he told Kot, advocating that Julian should wear a placard with 'Please remember I'm only 15!' written on it. The situation cannot have been helped when, because of the heat, he decided to sleep out on the roof (a standard Garsington practice), and Ottoline and Julian climbed out to join him. It was something of a relief when Julian finally went off to stay with her cousins.

He found it difficult to get back to work and complained that the sun burnt his neck or dazzled him or made him dizzy, and with a sketching umbrella the effect was too dark for painting. But when the grey weather returned, he felt his 'good old self again'. There was the usual long procession of summer visitors: first Walter Taylor accompanied by a friend, then Simon Bussy and his family, the writer Molly MacCarthy and the sculptor Eric Gill, with his sister. Siegfried Sassoon was staying near by in the village, but Gertler and Toronto Prewett were the only 'permanences' that summer. By September Gertler was ready to flee Garsington. He dreaded the parting but longed to be away, even as he knew that he would return 'over and over again'. It was, after all, his 'second home' and, like the first, aroused feelings of ambivalence. He was also attempting to flee his future, of which he now had 'a sort of horror'. To Kot he admitted, 'It all seems utterly black – so desolate. There isn't a single point I can look forward to.'[53]

That autumn first Gertler, then Mary Hutchinson and finally Ottoline all succumbed to low spirits ('going about – like a sort of influenza'[54]). He advised Ottoline to return to Garsington. 'It is extraordinary how good it is very often to return to one's own corner – I find it so.' Soon he was able to reassure Ottoline that he was 'no longer depressed – more repressed – In a state of mental convalescence – that calm state . . . after a serious illness – neither happy nor unhappy'. Once settled back in his studio, he began work on a second portrait of Kot, and his head was again full of plans for 'complicated and intriguing compositions'. Nevertheless, he continued to live quietly, carrying out 'all, or nearly all' the sanatorium regime, determined, above all, to keep his health.[55]

By November he was once again 'wholly absorbed' in his work, mostly nude studies, 'the painting of which is interesting me more than anything else just now – I hope to paint a lot of them', he wrote to Valentine, 'not just single ones – but groups. But they take such a long time to do, that so far I have only completed one small one.' It was also another expense: models cost 10*s*. a day, and he had spent a good deal doing up his studio in October. By January he was over £1,000 in debt, a staggering amount which also suggests that any sanatorium 'subs' were probably loaned rather than given. All his hopes were pinned on the financial success of his next show.

That autumn he had a new model: Maria Huxley's sister Suzanne, a nineteen-year-old blonde of angelic beauty. 'A nice good girl', he called her, and ' so good to paint – like a Bellini'. But Suzanne had been warned by her sister Maria: "Méfie toi car il embrasse les filles derrière les portes', and her sittings took place not at the studio but at Thurlow Road, probably so that Brett could act as chaperone. Suzanne found Brett rather disconcerting, as she listened to them intently through her great ear-trumpet 'Toby', but Gertler she found 'charming' – 'tout beau comme il était, pareil à un personnage de Carpaccio'.[56]

He quickly completed two portraits of Suzanne, but found himself rather 'hustled' over them, as she was due to return to Belgium. Still, there was time between sittings to walk on the heath and lie on the grass, discussing life and love, while Suzanne waited for her 'young man', whom Gertler described as 'a sort of Belgian Pardridge [*sic*] – a policeman of a fellow'. Gertler talked to her of Chekhov, of Garsington (advising her not to go there as Julian's companion) and of Carrington, with whom, Suzanne believed, he was still 'head over heels' in love. But to Ottoline, Gertler wrote that 'apart from my work, my life is as dull as ditch-water – Positively nothing happens – no affairs – nothing.'

Meanwhile Brett began her weekly 'Thursdays' for a group of friends, mostly male. It was the only group that Gertler was ever fully part of, and to which he deliberately chose to belong. 'We met, drank tea[,] eat biscuits, the men talked [and] I tried to listen as best as I could with "Toby". Those meetings were a lot of fun', Brett recalled, 'but were mostly invented to give those men a chance to get together and talk. NO WOMEN were allowed, except by the vote of everyone. Iris Tree was allowed, at intervals, and of course we were forced to have Frieda when Lawrence came.' Brett herself was only allowed to preside, she alleged, because first, she provided the venue and second, she was too deaf to intervene.[57] Three years later, when she left Britain, Gertler took over the meetings and continued to host the 'Thursdays' right up until his death.[58]

At one early meeting in December 1921 Virginia Woolf observed the company critically from her discreet post behind the black anthracite stove. 'Brett's salon', she wrote afterwards in her diary, 'is a group without teeth or claws.'[59] A year later, however, she reported to Vanessa that she and Leonard had been elected to 'that horrid muling puling society which meets on Thursdays – Murry, Sydney [Waterlow], Brett, Gertler, and Koteliansky'; and she implied that 'the absurd creatures' had modelled themselves on the Cambridge 'Apostles', possibly because Thursday evenings had also been the appointed time for the original Bloomsbury 'at homes', and also because of the idea of selection. 'First you are looked at; then voted for', she noted. 'Sydney's wife was blackballed. So it is a very great compliment.'[60]

Many of Gertler's engagements now took place on prescribed days: on Sundays he had a 'standing engagement' to dine with Walter Taylor; one night a week was given over entirely to Kot, and on Wednesdays he sometimes attended another salon at the house of Kot's friend Ridgway. That autumn he feared any change of his rare tranquil mood, and preferred to remain in Hampstead, 'hugging my rare bit of contentment hard – clucking over it and sitting on it, like a hen on its egg'.[61] He even passed up Christmas at Garsington, telling Ottoline that Kot was going to be alone and that he and Brett had invited him to come to them. 'I hope . . . you will not consider it unfriendly on my part not to come', he added.[62]

He was philosophical about Clive Bell's criticism of his recent work as 'sincere but uninteresting'; 'he may be right for all I know', Gertler commented. 'It doesn't matter much to me whether he is or not – since it is the process that I live by, and that I find all absorbing – At the same time I have the satisfaction of knowing that I am doing my best.'[63] Besides, not everyone agreed with Bell. Three of Gertler's paintings were selected by Fry, Sims and Tonks for the Grosvenor Gallery's 'Nameless' winter exhibition, and he exhibited three more at the Goupil Gallery's winter salon.

Towards the close of the year Taylor, who was planning a three-week trip to the Riviera in the new year, invited Gertler to come along. Although he dreaded the travelling, Taylor's comfortable income guaranteed a comfortable voyage, and Valentine, now living in the Pyrenees, also promised to come and visit him. By December his work had once again become 'troublesome', and deciding the rest would do him good, Gertler finally made up his mind and accepted the invitation.

16

New Departures

> 'One would guess that he was on the verge of a new departure.'
>
> Roger Fry, *New Statesman*, 18 February 1922

GERTLER AND TAYLOR set off for the French Riviera after Christmas, and after a poor journey arrived in the village of Villefranche-sur-Mer, which Gertler found so charming that, faithful to the sanatorium's fresh air regime, he astonished the concierge by immediately throwing the hotel windows open wide. Inspired by the wonderful quality of light, he longed to begin painting, but felt that three weeks was hardly long enough to begin. So he rested and continued to worry about Valentine, from whom he had heard nothing.

Gertler's next surviving letter is not until May 1922, so it is impossible to know with any certainty whether or not Valentine did arrive in Villefranche in January to meet him, as promised. By late January she and Bonamy were in Orgiva in southern Spain, where they had arranged to meet the writer Gerald Brenan, who lived in the nearby village of Yegen, on the southern slopes of the Sierra Nevada. Carrington, who had formed a brief but passionate attachment to Valentine before she left for France in December 1920, had urged Brenan to visit the Dobrées in Larrau the previous September. 'She is much more talented beautiful, & charming than your Doric [one of Carrington's pet names]', she wrote, and indeed Valentine combined all the qualities Carrington most admired in other women: beauty, independence and unconventionality:

> She has given so much out of herself to the world, lived so fiercely. It is splendid. Then I admire the ways she has no preconceived conception of

> how a woman, & an artist should live. She is as worldly as she feels worldly. She is business like, & generous, gay, & very melacholly [*sic*], unprincipalled [*sic*], & yet virtuous, & does not think it wrong to bake good cakes, & trim a hat with ribbons, & yet paints 5 hrs a day, & will not be interrupted for all the men in the world.[1]

During his visit to Larrau, Brenan, who was Ralph Partridge's best friend and had also fallen in love with Carrington, had confided his secret to Valentine. According to Brenan's biographer Jonathan Gathorne-Hardy, Valentine tried to seduce Brenan on the return visit in January 1922 but, interested only in Carrington, he refused her.[2] Brenan arranged a further Larrau holiday for himself and the Tidmarsh ménage in April 1922, when, it was agreed, Valentine would 'distract' Patridge so that Brenan could steal some time alone with Carrington. This was the basis of the so-called 'plot', which when uncovered would lead to 'the great row' in Bloomsbury and bring Carrington's marriage to the verge of break-up as well as causing a three-year hiatus in her relationship with Gertler.

In April, when the Bloomsbury contingent made their way to Larrau, 'a vertigo of ever-intensifying complications' was set in motion.[3] First, Partridge apparently took a dislike to Valentine, and they quarrelled incessantly, seldom leaving Carrington and Brenan alone. On a day trip to Pau without Partridge the car ran out of oil, and Valentine, Brenan and Carrington were forced to put up at a hotel. The would-be lovers arranged to spend the night together, but Brenan's fear of impotence kept him away until morning, when he appeared in Carrington's room to explain himself, and Valentine, coming in at this moment, naturally assumed they had spent the night together. When they returned to Larrau, she and Patridge appeared to fall 'inexplicably' in love, and shortly afterwards both Brenan and Valentine followed their new partners back to Britain. Patridge, though unaware of the relationship between Carrington and Brenan, continued to see Valentine in London, and Brenan, taking advantage of his absence, now began a sexual affair with Carrington at Pangbourne.[4] Gertler's friendship with Valentine would implicate him in the affair, but it is impossible to know how much he was really involved. None of Valentine's letters is available to tell her side of the story, and it is possible, as David Garnett suggested, that it suited both Carrington and Brenan to turn her into something of a scapegoat.[5]

Gertler arrived back in Britain in time for his second solo exhibition in February 1922 with at least one completed picture under his arm. *Boats by a Jetty, Concarneau* is reminiscent, in both subject and treatment, of Fauve pictures of boats at ports and jetties, many of them also painted on the Mediterranean coast of France.[6] 'Mark Gertler: A New Series of Paintings', which included much of the Banchory work, the portraits of Kot and Suzanne Nys, and several of his studies of china ornaments, opened to enthusiastic reviews in February: the *Burlington* ranked him as 'one of the three or four best young painters in England',[7] and Amelia Defries of *Drawing & Design* recommended that at least one of his works should be bought for the nation. Roger Fry expressed a 'profound respect' for Gertler's work, and, 'in a country where art is generally taken so lightly, . . . [an] intense gratitude, that there is at least one artist who refuses ever to trifle with his talent'.[8] Even Strachey considered buying *The Hunter*, a painting Carrington had admired and directed his attention towards, though she dissuaded him. 'I didn't know Mark's pictures were so dear. No don't buy one unless you like them. He might do something more lively this year. £40 is too much to spend unless one really likes a picture very much.'[9]

Nineteen twenty-two was something of an *annus mirabilis* for Gertler. There was scarcely a month in which his work was not on show, with his one-man exhibition in February, salons at the Goupil and the London Group, the final Friday Club show and a 'Modern British Art' show at the Whitechapel. It was also the first time that he was represented at the prestigious Venice Biennale.[10] Frank Brangwyn's original selection for this exhibition, which had not included Gertler, was considered so 'injurious to [the reputation of] British art' by the packers that they appealed to the critic P. G. Konody to save it from being a complete fiasco. Among the artists Konody picked to add 'a note of distinction' were Gertler, Sickert, Augustus John, William Nicholson and John Nash, further proof of Gertler's status on the British art scene.

Brett spent much of April organizing her move from Thurlow Road to 6 Pond Street, Hampstead. She had argued with her father over her allowance and her 'lodgers' – Gertler and occasionally Murry's brother Richard, whom she continued to subsidize – but she nevertheless arranged for the new house to be freshly painted, plastered and connected to gas, electricity and telephone, before moving in. According to her biographer Sean Hignett, Brett had allowed

Gertler to lodge at Thurlow Road 'without expense, funding him from time to time, making his bed and heating his water and fetching and carrying constantly'.[10] Even Katherine Mansfield, who was herself not averse to using her friends and later remarked that Brett had been 'born a slave and no slave could be cured of that',[12] professed herself shocked to hear of Gertler's behaviour and urged Kot to tackle him about it. But by May Gertler was again safely lodged in Brett's spare room, drinking endless pints of milk in an effort to raise his weight, which had once again sunk 'to a rather poor level', as he anxiously contemplated his 'perilous plunge into the Pyrenees'.[13] In late May Brett herself disappeared to Paris, where she had arranged to meet Murry and Katherine.

Since her marriage the previous May, Gertler had tried to avoid meeting Carrington, though she had continued to try and coax him back into a friendship. 'No sooner did Carrington return from you', he wrote to Valentine in late May,

> than she came in with Brett to the restaurant to see me. I see now it is foolish of me to strain away from her, what does it matter – I am really so detached now – If she wants to see me, let her – I shall make no objection . . . She says it is so important for her [to] talk to me about painting, etc. She came to see me the next day and was quite pleasant. I tell you this so that you should know the situation – I think it will be so much easier – if [?] we can all be friends – she spoke well of you and your place and said she had an excellent time.[14]

'He [Gertler] has been to Paris lately and told me about the latest developments of Derain, Picasso and Matisse', Carrington wrote to Brenan. 'I shall see Gertler often now because I find these discussions on technique and methods so important to one. One gets things straighter simply by arguing with opposition, things which have been confusing one's own ideas for months.'[15] She was probably also aroused by Gertler's apparent indifference, just as she was later by Brenan's.

It was Valentine who, in early June, finally revealed Carrington's and Brenan's affair to Partridge. The results were explosive. Partridge, furious, declared that he would have to kill Brenan, but apparently first rushed round to see Gertler to ask about his own sexual involvement with Carrington. Partridge did not kill Brenan, but after a terrible row forbade him to see Carrington again. Brenan returned miserably to Spain, and Carrington was once more faced with the possibility of the break-up of her life with Strachey and Partridge.

In mid-June Valentine left for Paris, and Gertler's letters suggest he also left around this date, though whether they were still lovers is not certain. His letters to Kot from the sanatorium had suggested that, by the end of 1921, the affair with Valentine was already a thing of the past. Yet, according to Michael Holroyd, when 'Bonamy Dobrée finally lost patience and summoned his wife back to Larrau [she] went, taking a new lover, Mark Gertler'. Holroyd claims Gertler had 'always hated Ralph' and may have felt there was some retributive justice in supplanting him'.[16] However, since Gertler had already been Valentine's lover before Partridge's marriage to Carrington, there would have been little retribution in this. Moreover, Gertler's trip had clearly been planned for some time, and the arrangements were well in hand in early May, over a month before 'the great row' took place. And in his earlier letter to Valentine in May Gertler made it clear that he favoured a general reconciliation.

In Paris, Gertler felt well and carefree, and wrote home that he was enjoying the food, the cafés and the art. Significantly, he made no mention of Valentine, though from the dates of letters to Partridge she was there at the same time.[17] Gertler's main companions in Paris were Brett (who had already been there for several weeks and seemed very at home, 'strut[ing] about with her toes well out... as if she had never lived anywhere else the whole of her life'[18]) and the ubiquitous Nelson, who had shown Gertler round on his last Paris trip. This time they visited a brothel. 'I'd never been to one before',[19] he explained to Ottoline:

> It was extraordinary – Rather . . . low class . . . for work people, soldiers and sailors. A long darkish room, a blind elderly man playing the piano. About six or eight girls with only chemises on[,] either sitting on men's knees or (as there were only about five men in the place) knitting or playing patience. As soon as we came in, two girls put aside their patience and knitting came over to us. One of the girls, a very fat one, just flipped away her chemise and bared her backside to another girl (who was sitting idle) in a good-natured jocular manner and the idle girl slapped it in the same spirit. They were very nice[,] good-natured[,] gay and quite wholesome-looking. One girl had been 'upstairs' with different men five times during the hour that we were there! Whenever a man succumbs to the embraces of his temptress[,] he just pays 2 francs at the counter and walks 'upstairs' with her, there he pays something more– another 10 or 15 francs I believe.

The girls seemed 'such kind, good-hearted creatures – they were all so nice to the Blind old pianist. I loved them all', and he cried a little on the way home, he admitted. He had wanted to take Brett, as it would have been 'good for her', but 'good' women, he was told, were not allowed in. These were hardly the actions of a man engaged in a passionate new love affair.[20]

Gertler revelled in 'running about [Paris] seeing pictures', and was 'especially interested in Picasso's latest development', he wrote to Ottoline. Post-war Paris had seen a great interest in classical revival, and Picasso had caught the general mood in the rounded figures of his neo-classical women. These fleshy female forms inspired Gertler, and paintings such as *Adolescence* and *Pomona* may well have been influenced by his stay in Paris.[21]

Gertler finally reached the Basses-Pyrénées in July, presumably travelling with Valentine. There he found stimulus of a different sort in the 'huge, jagged' landscape of Larrau, 'all up and down', with its deep valleys and mountains, rushing streams and beech forests, and the village itself, seemingly arranged to a haphazard plan – 'all shapeless and anyhow'.[22] He also admired the habitual courtesy of the villagers. 'Whenever they see you they raise their hats most politely and say, "Bonjour Monsieur"[.] If they see you again three minutes later, they do it all over again just as if you had not met for five years.'[23] Only at weddings and funerals, did they become 'savage'. 'Then they shriek and yell and make the most fearful noises for over 24 hours', he told Ottoline.

Gertler quickly established a routine: sleeping, breakfasting and lunching at the inn opposite the Dobrées and dining and working in their house, where the atmosphere was 'peaceful, and nice, no difficulties'.[24] He worked all day – there was 'nothing else to do' – and scarcely varied his usual Hampstead routine, even his evening walk before bedtime. 'We [all] live our lives very separately, hardly any conversation even, but we do not get on each others nerves, which is the great thing', he wrote. It was a description of a peaceful, ordered existence, with no hint of an impassioned affair with Valentine. And he missed England, particularly Garsington. 'I think a great deal of you all at Garsington', he wrote to Ottoline, 'and how I miss it! . . . How I love England!'[25] Clearly, he regarded his time abroad as an enforced separation, brought about chiefly for the sake of his health.

During his two-month stay at Larrau Gertler worked at a prodigious rate, completing two portraits, two still lifes and one landscape by early August, and he eventually left with at least nine oils and a number of drawings. He was struck by the golden faces, black hair and strong, sunburnt legs of the locals, and was particularly taken with one eleven-year-old boy. A preliminary sketch was quickly followed by an oil (on wood) painting of the boy's head, his porcelain skin and huge liquid eyes reminiscent of a Renoir. The same boy probably modelled for the *Basque Shepherd*, while the olive-skinned, slant-eyed, raven-haired innkeeper's daughter was captured in *The Blue Dress* and the *Basque Shepherdess*.

That winter, when *The Blue Dress* was shown at the Goupil, the painting mesmerized Marchant's clients and Baroness Forest pointed at it, saying, 'I want to be painted like that!' 'Fearfully excited' at the prospect of a lucrative commission, he later told Ottoline, and already 'picturing Rolls Royces by the dozen', Gertler was summoned by Marchant and, though suffering one of his 'blinding headaches', promised to paint the Baroness, 'exactly like the beauty from the Pyrenees'. But, he reported in dismay, 'she is about 50, looks 70, and [has] no face whatsoever!' The commission, which realized only £30, quickly attracted 'all those good old criticisms I used to know and hate so much in my Portrait Painting days' and the Baroness complained that she looked 'cross'. This settled the matter for Gertler; 'never more', he wrote, would he accept commissions, 'unless they are willing to pay'.[26]

However, the success of these pictures ushered in a new period of appreciation for Gertler. 'I certainly seem popular all of a sudden', he remarked in surprise to Ottoline in December, and playfully signed the letter, 'yours with love, Mendel Gertler, RA'.[27] Yet the intensity of the Larrau work was not recaptured, and the visit would never be repeated. Only London, as ever, could provide 'just the right amount of seclusion that is so necessary to me', and the necessary stimulation.[28]

When Gertler reached London on the last day of August 1922, he found that his former room at Pond Street was no longer available. Brett informed him that she needed the room for a week, though 'for what reason she cannot as yet tell me she says', he wrote to Ottoline.[29] Gertler suspected the reason to be Murry, but in fact Brett needed the room for Katherine. Gravely ill with the tuberculosis that would shortly kill her, Katherine had returned briefly from a sanatorium in Switzerland, and asked Brett to put her up. It was Katherine who asked that her visit should be kept secret and, though it would have been easier if Brett had explained this to Gertler, she agreed to guard Katherine's privacy.

Indignant at finding himself homeless without an explanation, Gertler spent the week staying with Taylor in his large old house in

Oxford Square, off the Bayswater Road. The week soon lengthened to a month, and Ottoline, who was spending a few days in London, joined them there. This was exactly the kind of arrangement that Gertler enjoyed most: days spent working in his studio, and evenings with friends on hand to meet and chat over a good dinner. 'It ought to have gone on forever and ever – alas –', he wrote to Ottoline on her return.[30]

Although Katherine left London in mid-September for Paris, Gertler never did return to Brett's. He told Mary Hutchinson airily that there were 'many reasons . . . all very dull', but did not elucidate.[31] However, a comment by Walter Taylor in a letter to Ottoline suggests that tension had been building in the Pond Street household for sometime. Brett had not told Taylor she was going to 'fire Gertler, but she said she intended putting up his rent as she could not afford to have him', Taylor wrote. The gossip soon spread to Bloomsbury, and in December Virginia wrote to Vanessa that Brett's father, Lord Esher, had expressly forbidden Brett to live with Gertler, 'not that they ever lived, save in the sense of sharing the same saucepan. So [now] he lodges 2 doors off.'[32] Brett herself later suggested Gertler's health was the reason. 'It was', she said, 'thought better for him to have a studio he could live in . . . this was much easier for him, and his landlady cooked for him,' but this was disingenuous.[33]

As for Gertler, he clearly considered that Brett had thrown him out without ceremony, and he never quite forgave her. He was profoundly disturbed by any uprooting, and the fact that he had always looked on Brett as a sister must have made it seem a double betrayal. In fact the ties had been slackening for some time, partly perhaps because of Brett's deepening intimacy with Murry, the details of which she had unwisely confided to Kot, who blithely passed them on. A virgin at forty, until Murry pressed her into a physical relationship, Brett's behaviour appeared rather ridiculous to many of her old friends, and Aldous Huxley later satirized the couple in his novel *Point Counter Point*.

Gertler stayed with Taylor until the end of September, when Valentine found him new lodgings. He continued to see Brett regularly, and made a special effort to attend her 'Thursdays'. After all, he asked Ottoline, what was the good of 'carrying on a feud'? But this was the beginning of the end of his friendship with Brett, which steadily deteriorated until she finally left Britain for good in 1924.

Gertler's new Pond Street lodgings – a ground-floor room with French windows opening onto a geranium-filled garden – were only accessible by a steep staircase, which besides smelling of food was kept pitch black by the parsimonious landlady, Mrs Pritchard, in order to save a penny a week on gas. Breakfast was served by Mrs Pritchard herself, a 'tall, languid, mottle-faced, scrambled-egg complexioned woman with an American accent', who, Gertler observed, used the word 'artistic' a good deal and was 'moth-eaten and desperately poor'.[34] Her husband was an 'elderly, large and somewhat fluffy-looking gentleman' – a cross between Dr Johnson and Asquith – who haunted the passageway, staring at Gertler 'with the utmost suspicion, as if he had never seen me before in his life, and as if I was the most savage burglar and bravado who might at any moment cut his throat!' But on the whole, he saw very little of the Pritchards and was content with what he called his 'state of complete independence of living' (by which he meant all the comforts of domesticity with none of the ties).[35] He ate out daily at a local restaurant, where Brett often dropped in to keep him company, and kept up a standing arrangement to dine with Taylor on Sundays.

Although Gertler was welcomed at Garsington just as frequently as before, his settled existence as 'artist in residence' was turned upside down by the coming of Ottoline's nephew Morven, who was then up at Oxford. The 'Bloomsberries' were seldom at Garsington after the war, but 'together with a group of Etonian contemporaries', writes Ottoline's biographer Miranda Seymour, Morven 'heralded the manor house's post-Bloomsbury renaissance . . . Visiting Garsington became part of the experience of being at Oxford, to be endured and, with luck, enjoyed: the undergraduates came in their scores.'[36] The older guests did not always appreciate the newcomers. E. M. Forster, making his first visit to Garsington in May 1922, counted at least thirty guests at tea and suspected there were many more. Forster, who had made the trip deliberately to meet the irascible Wyndham Lewis, noted that both he and Lewis were expected to 'perform' but had escaped just in time, much to Ottoline's annoyance.

Gertler clearly felt out of his depth among the hordes of students, and struck Forster as merely 'a little East End Jew, very amusing and clever . . . exactly like a street boy who makes faces at the people in carriages and imitates their gestures. He and W[yndham] L[ewis] were frightened of, and frightened, the high-born undergraduates, who motored out, gasping and undulating from Oxford.'[37] That Christmas, when Gertler presented Ottoline with some home-made cigarettes, he was only half-joking when he suggested that, 'if you or Philip won't smoke them then they can be of use to the fifty undergraduates who will no doubt come to tea on Sunday, one to each and you will stop all their mouths for at least ten minutes'.[38]

Often Gertler retreated into books. Julian Morrell later recalled him reading 'before dinner for 2 hours in the drawing room, with great concentration, in a roomful of people'.[39] When not reading his favourite Russian authors, he enjoyed biographies of 'great men', whom he infinitely preferred in print to life. After reading Francis Darwin's biography of his father, Charles Darwin, Gertler drew an analogy between the 'intuition and genius' that governed the discoveries of both artists and scientists. 'The process in fact is exactly the same', he told Ottoline excitedly, 'only the result is different – artists and scientists both start with a sort of vague idea or inspiration – they then set about proving it each in their own way'.[40]

Valentine remained a central figure in Gertler's emotional life. She was a popular guest at Pond Street gatherings, known and accepted by Gertler's circle, and even invited to Garsington. It is not clear whether they continued as lovers, though Carrington for one appeared to believe so. After the Larrau fiasco she had written to Strachey that she believed Valentine would have liked to keep Partridge as a lover, whom she could see 'at intervals in the year . . . Rather as she keeps Gertler'.[41]

Occasionally that winter Gertler suffered 'blinding headaches', and in December, probably on his doctor's advice, he began to keep a meticulous journal,[42] recording weekly changes of weight, diet, mood, sexual activity and any incipient signs of illness.[43] After a weekend at Garsington in November he was briefly unwell. Ottoline, concerned, recommended Bulgarian sour milk and sent an address where he might obtain it, but he hastened to assure her he was better and that only his weight continued low. The journal shows that he now drank a daily average of 1½ pints of milk, often supplemented by cream and Bass beer. In mid-December a slight cough produced sputum flecked with blood, and during his ten-day visit to Garsington over Christmas he gave in and began to take the sour milk as well.

The new year at Garsington was somewhat hectic. In a letter to the poet Walter Turner, Gertler numbered among the guests: 'the Asquiths, Miss Blake, the richest heiress in the world, or the "Shy Bride", Mrs. Rose, a young woman who owns a husband with £50, 000 a year, a dozen or two of young lords, a smart but elderly woman who cannot open her mouth without making an epigram, and whose name is Mrs. Lindsay, . . .Toronto [Prewett], who mooches about like a faded

Hamlet, and . . . Siegfried [Sassoon] . . . or the "Captain" as we call him. I can never look at him without wanting to slap my calves with an imaginary whip in "A hunting we will go" style!'[44] His London life, he told Turner, was by comparison, 'like that of a monk', and he returned to Hampstead once more, suffering debilitating headaches and feeling 'more dead than alive'.[45]

PART VI

A Critical Age

'I believe my age to be a critical one – I feel from now to forty to be, as it were, my last chance – the last chance to justify my existence – to really learn how to live and to achieve something. If I don't do it by the next 10 years I am done for.'

Mark Gertler to Ottoline Morrell, 7 May 1924

17

A Consistent and Inevitable Self

> Talent alone is very rarely enough – it is this formulating of oneself which is . . . the most important and difficult part – piecing one's capacities and perceptions together into one architectural whole – and so creating at last a consistent and inevitable *self*.
>
> Mark Gertler to Brett, 11 March 1921

GERTLER'S HEALTH REMAINED uncertain for much of the winter and early spring of 1922–3, and the news in January that Katherine Mansfield had died in Fontainebleau from a tubercular haemorrhage can only have increased his anxiety. He suffered frequent headaches, and a cough and his stricture troubled him intermittently. By March he was resting in the mornings and taking more exercise on Hampstead Heath, and by late spring he had developed the routine that he would scarcely vary for the rest of his life: working for a couple of hours in the morning, then walking for an hour on the Heath before lunch. Afterwards he would paint until half-past four and then receive friends for tea at the studio. Visitors calling during painting hours were refused entry, but he spent cosy evenings with close friends, which he came to prefer to the 'excessive sociability' of his youth.

In February Gertler's third annual show opened at the Goupil, with much of the work reflecting his trip to France the previous summer. Critics commented on his increased use of colour, and linked this to a broadening of his vision, which, wrote Anthony Bertram in *The Spectator*, had 'steadily grown more original and more important'. Gertler was among 'the front rank of living painters and need not fear comparison with the dead'.[1] Gertler was dismissive of this review, which he called a 'crack up' in a letter to Ottoline. What offended him most was the coupling of his name with that of Augustus John. 'I feel almost like Whistler who said "why drag in Velazquez".'[2]

Anxious to finish the work he had in hand before his annual trip to the French Riviera with Taylor in the spring, Gertler passed up Ottoline's frequent invitations to Garsington. One of his models was still at school and could only sit at weekends (chaperoned by Valentine, who was briefly back in England). This was Alice Edwards, a young girl from the East End who, like the rest of her family, went on to become a professional model and often sat at the Slade during the 1920s. For Gertler, Alice epitomized 'all the charm of young girlhood', and over the next five years he set out to try and capture something of this tantalizing essence in a series of portraits that charts her passage through girlhood to young womanhood.[3]

All of these pictures were well received and sold quickly. Yet today it is difficult not to have reservations about the first, *Young Girlhood*. A pre-pubescent nude, with beads around her neck and arms folded, Alice has an expression of defensiveness and vulnerability that makes the viewer feel invasive, and which makes her appear naked rather than nude. Only two years later, in *Young Girlhood II*, Alice is more assured and, with one arm loose and the other draping a towel behind her, seems far more at ease with her own sexuality.

Gertler and Taylor left London for the Riviera in late spring. They stopped off at Nice, which Gertler recorded in an impressionistic townscape unique in his oeuvre. Taylor was frequently ill, and they had to shorten their itinerary, but they managed to cross the border into Italy, where Gertler made several studies of Italian peasants, all of which have since disappeared.[4] In Florence, Gertler was particularly impressed at the Uffizi by the Titian nudes and Michelangelo's *David*.[5] In a little-known essay, 'A Note on Michel Angelo', which was published in Murry's recently launched periodical *The Adelphi* in July 1923, Gertler clearly restated his admiration for the old masters, and drew particular attention to what he called Michelangelo's 'miraculous capacity':

> Michel Angelo was the greatest of them all. None before, and none after, has achieved such harmony of plastic form and spiritual significance, to the point at which the one is the other, and the mere idea of separating them seems fantastic.[6]

In a second essay, 'The Architectural Element in Painting', published in the next edition of *The Adelphi*, Gertler also laid out the thinking that lay behind all his later works. 'A picture,' he explained,

> before it can have a real existence, . . . must be built up as firmly and solidly as a well-built house, and, like a well-built house, give the impression that it will stand for all time. Basically, a painting is made up of coloured masses, and it is with these that the artist builds, each one of them being as it were a brick forming part of the final edifice. To my mind, the Idea is never expressed with true pictorial force unless it is inevitably and completely interlaced with the architectural structure.
>
> In a picture, an idea or sentiment, without this structure, is like a real window set in a cardboard house. And I am bound to add, structure without vision is like a house with only the foundation laid.[7]

By the time he returned to Britain at the end of April 1923 Gertler's health and weight had largely stabilized, although the headaches persisted, and in late June he recorded a bout of depression. In August he took Julian Morrell (now a lively young lady of seventeen) to Brighton for a weekend of dancing. It is not clear how this came about, but it was certainly with Ottoline's knowledge and approval. Julian had just finished school at the Roehampton convent (which she had hated) and was bored by the prospect of another summer at Garsington. 'Julian longed to dance', Gertler explained in a letter to Valentine, 'and dragged us to the "Metropole"[,] a beastly vulgar hotel filled with Jews and Americans of the very worst type'.[8] They also bumped into Gertler's brother Jack, who was staying there with a 'smart chap' and two 'girls', and the two parties became mixed up. Later, Gertler took Julian to dinner at the home of his dealer William Marchant, where she flirted with Marchant's two young sons, and afterwards Taylor's adopted daughter also joined the party. 'Julian adored it', Gertler wrote afterwards. 'I hated and loathed it', and he described the weekend as a bad dream:

> something between a cinema film depicting 'Smart Life' (because we were all constantly getting into evening dress) and a scene out of the 'Possessed'. I was absolutely overcome with the horror and Vulgarity of that 'Metropole' place.

He retired to Garsington to try and recover his 'harmony'. After nearly a fortnight of quiet his nerves resettled, and the mood of despair temporarily receded. Perhaps a small accident put things into perspective. One afternoon, while he and Ottoline were out for a drive, her carriage suddenly overturned, trapping them both beneath it. Gertler just stepped 'nimbly out' but for one nightmarish moment he thought Ottoline had been crushed, until miraculously she emerged an instant later with only a wounded arm.

In late August Gertler learned from Kot that Frieda Lawrence was due back in London on a visit to her children. 'What a pity it is Frieda and not Lawrence that is coming!' he wrote to Kot. 'I feel that I ought to hurry back to assist you in the entertaining of Frieda but I am afraid that my work may keep me here another week.' On his return to Hampstead, Gertler discovered, to his dismay, that Brett had engaged a bedsit for Frieda on the top floor of his own lodgings. Neither he nor Brett (who had finally consummated her relationship with Murry that April) had realized that Frieda might also have been having an affair with Murry, who visited her several times during her stay at Pond Street. Gertler was not entirely unsympathetic to Frieda, but by 1923 he had begun to find her 'very uncomfortable to be with and also somewhat of a bore. She is worse than she might be because she apes Lawrence and his ideas coming out of her large German body sound silly and vulgar.' Kot violently disliked Frieda, whom he considered 'more fit to be Lawrence's servant than his wife', and his views had undoubtedly coloured Gertler's own.

In the event Gertler saw very little of Frieda, but he did see something of Murry, who was one of his earliest dinner guests when Gertler moved into his new lodgings in Worsley Road. Gertler's landlady, Mrs Bruce, had formerly worked as a housekeeper in a stately home, and proved not only an excellent cook but also the most maternal of all his landladies. 'Never', Beatrice Campbell later remarked, 'was a lodger more assiduously cared for' than he. Mrs Bruce's legendary cooking was appreciated by many of Gertler's guests, but the dinner with Murry had been most memorable for the amount of champagne and brandy the two men had consumed. After dinner they had 'discussed "old times" in a semi tearful and semi hilarious way',[9] and ended up in a box at the Alhambra, where they shared a further bottle of brandy. The following day Gertler was so hung-over that he was unable to make some delicate alterations to his painting *The Coster Woman*, which he had promised to carry out for Walter Turner, who was buying the picture.

It was Siegfried Sassoon who had introduced Turner and his wife, Delphine, to Gertler some two years earlier at Garsington, and by 1923 the Turners had become important members of Gertler's circle. An Australian by birth, Turner had travelled to London in 1907, where he had contributed satirical sketches to *The New Age* and music criticism to the *New Statesman* until his inclusion in Eddie Marsh's *Georgian Poetry* (1916–17) had gained him the admiration of W. B. Yeats and later an introduction to Garsington.

Gertler became very fond of Turner, but felt that he often promoted argumentative 'discussions of a rather superfluous nature, in the midst of which one finds oneself very excited but entirely at a loss to know what was the point'.[10] At one of Taylor's dinner parties in October Siegfried Sassoon, the Turners, the Morrells, the (Walter) de la Mares and Gertler had all been discussing Murry, whose public declarations of his grief at Katherine's death, in *The Adelphi*, had been greeted with embarrassment and general distaste. Walter de la Mare had defended Murry, and Siegfried Sassoon, who disagreed, had found himself 'talking very loud, getting excited and accusing Murry of "exploiting his emotions for journalistic purposes". I went there for a pleasant evening', Sassoon wrote afterwards,

> and it seems a horrible one when I look back on it – Gertler also shouted, and so did Philip Morrell. Walter Taylor (blinking through his glasses like the sheep in *Alice in Wonderland*) only spoke once during the meal. Gertler was saying that he 'blushed all over when he remembered the things he used to say when he was younger.' Taylor turned his mild spectacled face, and said, in his low-pitched voice, 'Do you ever blush about the things you say now?'[11]

Gertler valued Turner as one of the few close friends with whom he could discuss painting. 'I am so glad that you have got the picture', Gertler wrote when Turner purchased *The Coster Woman* in September. 'The fact that you like it is most encouraging to me. I should feel much happier if the people I see and like[,] my friends in fact, would take a greater interest in my work and appreciate it more. But so many of them happen to be writers and intellectual in another way, and really they take very little interest in not only my work but painting generally. The result is that I often feel, as an artist, very isolated.'[12] Yet Gertler himself had deliberately chosen his close friends from among non-artists since the death of John Currie back in 1914.

The Coster Woman is one of Gertler's finest portraits of the early 1920s. The mellow handling of the skin tones and the subject's rich, warm colouring are clearly influenced by Renoir, but Gertler's technique in this period owes as much to the old masters. When the following year the Manchester Art Gallery purchased his second major study of Alice Edwards (*Seated Girl with a Basket*, also known as *After*

Bathing), Gertler explained, 'I wanted my picture to be finished and realized in every respect, so that the result should be monumental like the old masters and the combination of figure and landscape appear inevitable.'[13] These ideas would concern him for much of the next two years and resurfaced in his next major composition, *The Coster Family on Hampstead Heath*.[14]

Gertler spent much of the winter of 1923 working on this challenging life-size group portrait, which attempts to unite the themes of landscape, portraiture and still life. Four figures are seen picknicking on the heath, their picnic arranged in front of them like so many still lifes and a distant view of Hampstead behind. Gertler made numerous studies for the painting throughout the previous year, but in December 1923 wrote despairingly to Valentine of his need to link the figures 'in some inevitable way'.[15] The models for the three female figures had all posed for earlier single studies: Alice Edwards for *After Bathing*; the girl with the plait for *The Servant Girl* (1923), and the striking figure of the coster mother herself for the earlier portrait *The Coster Woman*. Monumental, impressive and certainly Gertler's most ambitious picture of the decade, *The Coster Family on Hampstead Heath* never quite achieves the 'inevitable' link, or connection, that Gertler intended, possibly because, as with *The Rabbi and His Grandchild* of 1913, it seems unlikely that all the models were actually together at any one time. The family appear posed as if for a formal portrait photograph, and it is tempting to read their failure either to connect or separate satisfactorily as a reflection of Gertler's failure either to strengthen or break the persistent link with his own family. However, the picture did bring a late sense of closure to Gertler's earlier East End portraits, and 1924 was not only the last year in which he painted a major group portrait but also the last time he painted specifically Jewish East End figures.

One day in December 1923 Frieda Lawrence burst into Gertler's studio shouting, 'Prepare yourself – Lorenzo's coming!'[16] This was a rallying call for Lawrence's friends, who gathered at the Café Royal for a farewell dinner, which has come to be known in Lawrence mythology as 'the Last Supper'. The Café Royal was a most unlikely venue for Lawrence, who had parodied it as the Café Pompadour in *Women in Love*, where he drew attention to its 'atmosphere of petty vice . . . petty jealousy and petty art'. The other guests were Kot, Brett, Murry, Mary Cannan (now separated from Gilbert), Catherine Carswell (who later wrote a memoir of Lawrence) and her husband, Donald, all of whom were the chosen disciples for 'Rananim' (the name taken from one of

Kot's Hebrew songs), the ideal community that Lawrence hoped to establish in New Mexico. At dinner Lawrence became uncharacteristically drunk and asked each guest in turn to accompany him there. Out of embarrassment they all accepted, with the exception of Mary Cannan, who famously replied, 'No, I like you, Lawrence, but not so much as all that and I think you are asking what no human being has a right to ask from another'.[17] In reality, most of them had no intention of going.

In the end only Brett accompanied the Lawrences to New Mexico, although she did not know them well at this stage, and had only accepted because, according to her biographer, Murry had accepted and she wanted to be with him, and being deaf she had missed most of what was going on. Murry, however, was rapidly supplanted in Brett's affections by Lawrence himself, who seemed 'like a God' to her, and who was to be the object of her last and most enduring crush. Brett and the Lawrences confidently expected Murry to join them, but he wired two months later to say that he had remarried and settled down in Britain.

Gertler dubbed the trio 'the Mexican troupe' and began to look forward to their departure, avoiding Brett's 'Thursdays', where, since Lawrence's arrival, he found both Murry and Brett 'more impossible than ever', and even Lawrence himself was depressing. 'His vain struggle against things – Hatreds – Crazes – they get on my nerves – God help me from geniuses if that's what they are like!'[18] And Gertler's relationship with Brett had deteriorated to the point where he could not wait to be rid of her – 'What matters it where Brett bites her nails?' he wrote irritably. 'How glad I shall be when they have gone! These last maniacal weeks have depressed me and given me a prolonged bilious attack.' He felt only relief – 'so that's over'[19] – when Brett, Frieda and Lawrence finally sailed for New York on the *Acquitania* on 2 March, on the first leg of their journey to the New World.

Surprisingly, Murry himself remained for a time an intimate of Gertler's circle, and regularly attended the Thursdays even after his remarriage until November, when Gertler wrote to Ottoline, apparently with great relief that, after a final rupture at *The Adelphi*, where he had been employed as business manager, Kot had 'broken with Murry forever'.[20] In the same year Gilbert Cannan was admitted to The Priory, a private sanatorium in Roehampton for the mentally ill, and the old Cholesbury circle was destroyed.

Throughout the 1920s Garsington remained Gertler's personal

'rananim', and he identified it (with more than a hint of Lawrencian parody) as 'a sort [of] bright twinkling star in the distant heaven, above the fog and storm and stress, something to look up to and forward to'. But, secure in the knowledge and affections of this 'second family', Gertler could afford to leave it at regular intervals and return with Taylor to the French Riviera, where they lived cheaply and comfortably' – 'a sort of provincial social life' – among the expatriate artists' colony.[21] For Gertler the chief attraction of this life was that, like the East End, Hampstead, Garsington and even the sanatorium, it was self-contained. There were numerous cafés, where they could become tipsy every lunchtime, dances, a cinema and Nelson's colour shop, which sold artists' materials and survived chiefly through Taylor, who loyally bought a few things each day in order to keep it going. They spent one evening at the inevitable brothel, watching an 'indecent cinema'. 'How insipid, how uninteresting they made vice seem', he wrote to Kot.

Gertler's own frankly sensual nature was now largely expressed in his work and he watched the affairs of his friends in St Tropez with some amusement. Nelson, who had been deserted by his wife for a young American boy of eighteen (with whom she lived in a cottage near by), responded by dressing like a character from *La vie bohème* and falling violently in love with a young American Jewish girl of sixteen. But Gertler was more attracted by the romance of their setting and particularly taken with the views from Mrs Nelson's cottage. 'There is months of work for an artist from the windows alone', he told Ottoline. 'Vast stretches of warm coloured landscape . . . sea of the deepest blue and beyond that . . . the Alps!' A lemon tree shimmering on the veranda at the back of the house, heavy with enormous green-yellow fruit, disturbed him with its beauty. 'Somehow', he wrote, 'my heart ached – one's life seemed all wrongly planned besides such splendour.'[22]

Gertler and Taylor left St Tropez in late April for Paris, where Gertler was frankly perplexed by Picasso's latest show and preferred the 'happy gay decorative colours of Dufy!' or the 'bright spontaneous colour' of Matisse. The highlight of his trip was a visit to the Jewish dealer Durand-Ruel, who specialized in the Impressionists. Yet somehow the collection proved disappointing. There were too many Monets and Pissarros for Gertler's taste, and though Renoir was 'exquisite – delicious', this was 'also his fault . . . He is really too "tasty" . . . too refined for us', he wrote to Valentine. 'We must have something more brutal today.'[23] Even Cézanne had become 'far too precious', and as a result of this trip, he told Valentine, his ideas on painting were 'somewhat changed – no big pictures, no romance – just chunks of nature'. He spoke increasingly of the importance of design. 'It's design that matters not subject[,] in fact 'the less subject the better.'

Back in London, Gertler's annual show opened at the Goupil in May 1924, centred on *The Coster Family on Hampstead Heath*, along with eighteen drawings. Marchant, however, had inadvertently scheduled the opening for the same day as the Royal Academy's summer exhibition, and to Gertler's dismay initially he received no press notices. The exhibition looked to be, he wrote to Valentine in early May, 'a complete failure'.[24] His delicate financial position was made worse by the collapse of the family fur business, and Gertler's anxiety about money began to manifest itself in physical symptoms resembling those of a panic attack. He suffered bouts of giddiness well into May, until the situation was 'somewhat saved' by the sale of *After Bathing* to the Manchester City Art Gallery for £150, after which his health immediately improved. However, the large oil of *The Coster Family*, priced at 500 guineas, remained unsold, and only four drawings had been sold by the time the Goupil exhibition closed.

The family business recovered rather better. Gertler's brothers came to an agreement with their creditors which allowed them to continue, albeit in a 'much reduced manner', and they also managed a short time later to reinstate Gertler's £5 weekly stipend. He survived by drawing money from a post office account he had kept secret from his family and most of his friends, but the threat of bankruptcy made him determined to save as much as possible in future. 'The sacrifices', he told Valentine, 'will be worth it for the sake of my work.'

In September he thought yet again about teaching part-time, and approached his former mentor William Rothenstein, now Principal of the Royal College of Art. But Rothenstein told him there was nothing available and recommended him to try the London County Council schools. Perhaps he had not fully forgiven Gertler for his treatment in *Mendel*. By October Gertler was desperate and advertising for pupils, but did not receive a single reply. Fortunately, at the Goupil winter salon in November, where he showed four paintings and three drawings, he made just enough sales 'to keep Marchant happy' and the all-important monthly stipend coming in. Once again the idea of taking pupils was cast aside with relief.[25]

In July 1924 Gertler again found himself featuring in fiction. 'In spite of those rascals, the Sitwells, coming up to me so friendly the other day', he complained to Kot, 'they have written a book with a malicious description of me in it! I am so glad I was cold to them.'[26] The book was Osbert Sitwell's *Triple Fugue*, a collection of short stories containing detailed caricatures of both Eddie Marsh (as Mattie Dean) and Ottoline (as Lady Septugesima Goodley) in the title story. Sitwell was dismissive of Marsh, whom he considered 'a fool about poetry', and his description of Dean with his eyebrows 'tilt[ing] up like the eaves of a Japanese temple' was instantly identifiable.[27]

Gertler was also instantly recognizable as the (unnamed) 'real Whitechapeller', who causes great 'flutterings' among the 'nucleus of young genius' with which Mattie Dean surrounds himself. He is '*such* an extraordinary-*looking* man,' and has led 'such an interesting life!' He brings a 'whiff . . . of the East End', which makes the refined guests think 'of the French and Russian revolutions', and gives them a vicarious feeling of 'pleasurable excitement'.[28] It may seem extraordinary that Gertler should have taken such exception to this superficial stuff, but what upset him was not only that it implied he had been taken up merely for his looks and personality, but also that it clearly labelled him a 'child of the ghetto', something he thought he had long ago laid to rest.[29]

Though by the 1920s Gertler appeared to have found his own comfortable niche in society, the painter Marjorie Lilly, who had known him at the Slade, recalled in her memoir *Sickert: The Painter & His Circle* that Gertler could be 'difficult, excitable and moody, with a bristling inferiority complex . . . Many people of Gertler's own generation found him exhausting. Few were aware of the tragedy of his life, they saw him as a privileged boy whose early promise had received ample recognition.' Above all, she believed, he was obsessed with the fear that 'his talent was not powerful enough to stay the course. There were ominous signs that already he was repeating himself, that he had nothing more to say.'[30] At Garsington that summer, if there were too many guests for his comfort, he would simply 'skip off – disappear. Ottoline knows it now and does not mind', he told Kot.[31] But it left new guests with the impression of the 'difficult' personality glimpsed by Marjorie Lilly. Among old friends however, the gentler, charming Gertler was uppermost. At the tenth birthday party of Edward Wadsworth's daughter Barbara he was the children's favourite guest. Barbara later wrote that 'of all the visitors to Church Street the most popular with the Wadsworth children was Gertler.' He was 'an adult who laughed with them and fascinated them with the gentleness of his voice'.[32]

Two further events in 1924 show that Gertler had not entirely left the issue of his roots behind. First, in a final portrait of his mother he expressed 'the more brutal' vision that he had found missing in Renoir during his stay in Paris. Unlike the seductive females of much of Gertler's 1920s' work – about whom the *Times* critic could quip, 'if Mr Gertler is not careful someone will be saying that his pictures are pretty' – *The Artist's Mother* easily achieves the monumental quality Gertler had been seeking in *The Coster Family*. Critics were unanimous in their praise of it, and Gertler himself recognized its value. He was so anxious to keep it for himself that he put a price tag on it of £200, the highest sum he ever earned for any picture.

The second event can perhaps be described as Gertler's final attempt at reconciliation with his Jewish identity. After his return from France he had found himself increasingly drawn into a relationship with a young Jewish girl called Phyllis Wilkinson, who lived in Kilburn and was distantly related to his family.[33] For a time he allowed himself to daydream of living 'self-contained' with a loving young wife in St Tropez. The climate in southern France was good for his health, he could live there cheaply and he had some knowledge of the community, but to make the transition possible he needed a companion. He had once told friends that if he married at all it would only be to please his mother and then he must marry a Jewish girl.[34] Little is known about Phyllis, who was not one of his regular circle, but she was, he told Valentine, 'a nice kind-hearted decent girl and that's a great deal'.[35] She was, in other words, an ideal wife and as such must surely have met with Golda's approval. Gertler proposed to Phyllis in early October and was accepted, but they appear to have kept the news secret until after Christmas, when Phyllis's father gave his immediate consent.[36] At Garsington, Gertler told Kot, the news broke 'like a thunderbolt', and his family were also 'excited and pleased'.[37] He immediately arranged to rent Mrs Nelson's cottage in St Tropez for a three-month honeymoon in the new year.

Gertler, however, immediately began to worry obsessively about money, the engagement soon disintegrated into a 'time of crisis' and Phyllis retired to the seaside to recover. Perhaps money was not the real issue, for when writing to Valentine to seek her blessing, Gertler revealed the strength of his residual feelings for her. 'Nothing in this world', he told her, 'will make me love and respect you less, my dearest friend, than I've done since we first met. So I hope you will feel as I do that our friendship is just as before. In fact I need your friendship just as much as ever. I can hardly imagine existing without it.'[38]

Shortly after this Gertler broke off the engagement, admitting to Ottoline that he did not really love Phyllis enough. She seems to have taken the news magnanimously and remained a minor part of his life for the next year, until she eventually married a lawyer and moved to Palestine. When Gertler did marry in 1930, Phyllis generously sent £10 through Ottoline for the couple to choose a wedding present.

The obsession with money seems to have been tied up with Gertler's general fears about marriage, for once it was all over he was able to admit to Kot that he had 'ceased to worry about money now . . . I am even ashamed to think that I gave it serious thought'.[39] Curiously, however, the episode seemed to bring him some sort of reconciliation, and once back in Hampstead he settled comfortably into his bachelor existence once more, ministered to by his faithful housekeeper, Mrs Bruce. Later, he told a friend, he looked back on these times as the happiest in his life.

18

A Life without Compromise

> 'I feel now more than ever, that there is only one kind of life worth while, and that it a life devoted without compromise to some good work or cause, and to me this is represented by painting.'
>
> Mark Gertler to Valentine Dobrée, 12 February 1925

AT THE END of January 1925 Gertler set off alone for the south of France. He spent the first month staying with Taylor at the Hôtel Sube in St Tropez, and returned at intervals to the cottage where he had planned to live with Phyllis, but which he now used as a studio, painting several fine mellow landscapes of the view from the window. He admired the golden-skinned girls of St Tropez, and was soon flirting with the young pâtisserie assistant, but clearly, as he explained to Valentine, he still needed a *femme inspiratrice*. 'There must be some one special to express one's ideas to', he wrote, 'and I do not know any other woman more sympathetic and clever and gifted than you[,] and whose companionship I desire more than yours.'[1]

In late February Gertler and Taylor left St Tropez for Paris, where they hung around for a fortnight to see a retrospective Impressionists' exhibition at the Salon des Indépendants, and in the hope that Valentine might join them. But neither materialized and eventually the two men returned to London. Here Marchant reported that he had sold the portrait of Golda (*The Artist's Mother*) for the stipulated £200, and there was renewed interest in Gertler's work from fashionable society: Lady Cunard wished him to decorate the dining room walls of her new house, although that project seems to have been abandoned. None the less, Gertler's letters show that as an artistic centre he was beginning briefly to favour Paris over London, and that the hope of establishing a new school of British painting had completely evaporated. Only in Paris, he told Ottoline, were

> pictures being done . . . that are really worth looking at and interesting to study – Whereas . . . an artist working in England is do[ing] so under such great disadvantages that I am beginning to think the situation quite hopeless. There is something altogether too antipathetic between the spirit of England and real painting.[2]

But though Gertler continued to make regular trips to Paris, he made no plans to settle there or to show his work, and only exhibited one painting there during his lifetime. He would never again seriously contemplate living outside England. 'As for a country to live in', he had written to Ottoline, 'give me England always England.'[3] He even joked to Ottoline that he might be 'the one chosen to save [British art) . . . The sort of Painter Messiah of England!! And a Jew too!'[4]

In letters to Valentine he restated his absolute commitment to his art and his desire to live a life 'without compromise'.[5] Yet his social life continued to dissipate his good intentions, and he did not produce any really innovative work for the rest of the decade.

Gertler spent late July and early August with Taylor at John Fothergill's famous inn The Spread Eagle in Thame, and late August on the south coast with the Turners and some new friends, the Greek scholar and poet John Mavrogordato and his wife, Christine. They became regular holiday companions and he visited them many times over the coming years, but insisted on coming as a 'PG' (paying guest), since his dietary requirements were now so particular that he was uncomfortable at accepting more than a weekend's hospitality without contributing to expenses.[6]

At Thame, Gertler basked in the sunshine reading Amy Lowell's life of Keats, beginning several pictures of the gardens and studiously avoiding a flirtation with a fellow guest, 'an enormously fat and romantic-looking woman, with two very large, high and separated bosoms', nicknamed 'the Duchess'.[7] But at a champagne party hosted by the Mavrogordatos he became 'very tipsey [*sic*] in the old style' and confessed to kissing 'several ladies on the stairs'. The next morning he was hung-over and 'a little ashamed of myself – and so ended my "season"', he told Kot.[8]

One weekend Ottoline arrived, bringing Asquith and a party of other Garsington guests. Then, when Gertler moved to the then fashionable seaside resort of Frinton-on-Sea in Essex in late August,

Ottoline also found some mutual friends in the area and arranged to meet him there. 'I do believe that if I were to go with Amundsen to the North for a holiday', he wrote to Kot with mild exasperation, 'Ottoline would be sure to know someone in the next hut and come there!'[9] At Frinton he became absorbed in painting flower pieces and completed a portrait of Mavrogordato, but longed to return to his studio and 'dip deeply' into his work again. 'The Fit is strongly upon me', he told Kot but, having 'practically promised' to spend the first fortnight of September at Garsington, he did not like to disappoint Ottoline.

He never did reach Garsington, for, after his return from Frinton, Gertler recorded in his notebook a sudden re-occurrence of haemorrhaging, which his London specialist diagnosed as a 'return of the Trouble'.[10] Gertler noted: 'Bleeding – once at night – 5 times (about ½ egg cupful each time) next day – after that a few clots – much headache rhuematism [*sic*] pains at night',[11] and for most of the next week he spat blood daily. By mid-September the attack had receded and he told Ottoline, there was 'hardly any blood now – only a few little clots at long intervals'.[12] Worse than the blood clots were the excruciating and debilitating headaches. Holed up in his rooms and forbidden to paint, his principal mood was one of boredom and disappointment.

His friends, as ever, gathered round: Taylor and the Turners visited regularly, Ottoline wrote every few days and Kot was there so often that friends believed he had finally left Acacia Road and moved in.[13] Valentine, who heard of his collapse from Mrs Bruce, was so agitated that she was all for setting out immediately for England and had to be persuaded that he was not dying. Gertler's doctors recommended an immediate return to the sanatorium, and on 10 September Harry drove him to Mundesley on the Norfolk coast. Since Mundesley was then 'the only sanatorium in England designed for the rich who did not want to travel or were advised against it', and the most expensive in England,[14] Gertler probably received financial help from his family, and Walter Taylor and the Morrells later both donated £30 towards his expenses. He remained at Mundesley for the rest of the year, but kept the news from Golda, who was simply told that he was staying at Garsington for an indefinite period. '[How] I wish it were true!' he could not help writing to Ottoline.[15]

Mundesley housed only thirty-seven patients, each of whom paid between 8 guineas (for a shared room) and 12½ guineas (for a single room with private bath) per week. The grounds spanned fifty acres and included the only private sanatorium golf course in England. The Mundesley regime (like that at Banchory) eschewed drugs and advocated a carefully supervised combination of rest, gentle exercise, varied diet and 'above all, a tranquil and cheerful environment'.[16] In contrast to the drastic and disastrous treatments Katherine Mansfield had endured abroad, Gertler could hardly have found himself a more comfortable sanatorium.

The early reports from the specialist were good: the old wound had reopened but there was no active trouble and it was after all 'a very little affair altogether', he told Kot.[17] Nevertheless, wracked by headaches and rheumatism, his mood was gloomy. He was forbidden to paint but made mental notes of paintable views for future reference, and leafed through a book of Matisse drawings lent to him by Mavrogordato. When a few days later the X-rays confirmed the initial diagnosis, and his stay was fixed at two months, his mood and headaches lifted and he began to plan his future. By mid-September he was already classified as an 'advanced' patient and allowed to work for an hour a day. He sent off for a large canvas to begin painting.

However, when the X-rays later detected a weak spot on his lung, Gertler poured out his despair in a letter to Ottoline:

> This attack has shaken my confidence – the horrors of this desease [*sic*] will always be hanging over me like a thunderous cloud – continually clipping the wings of my spirit, my impulses and aspirations – How many times am I doomed to return to these dismal cemetery-like sanatoriums – and what sort of life can mine be anyhow – always having to take care and to lead a monastic life so contrary to my nature – for by nature I am impulsive, active – excitable – amorous – I love loving women – I love seeing people and talking!'[18]

This second breakdown in his health 'stunned' Gertler. He realized he would have to 'think myself out afresh and readjust myself accordingly'. He no longer looked forward to his future with 'much conviction . . .[or] pleasure – I feel, that I shall always be apprehensive – always fear that I am about to break out again'.[19] This apprehension was the most significant legacy of his second breakdown and led to a tightening of his strict self-regulations on sociability. Increasingly, his work and health would be his first priority.

As before, he missed the conversation of his circle and letters became 'like a hand-shake across the void'.[20] He was 'so surprised and excited' to receive one from Carrington that he could hardly eat his breakfast, and continued 'to tremble slightly half the morning!'[21] 'You do, and always will, mean something special to me', he wrote back, admitting that at times he had had 'a positive craving' to see her. He asked her to write and 'tell me [all] about yourself – every detail will interest me'.[22] But though Carrington claimed to feel 'perfectly friendly' towards him, she did not 'really want to see, or write to you again' since she knew it was 'really impracticable and incompatible with my present life'.[23]

Less than a month before his departure Gertler was summoned to the bedside of a fellow patient, a painter called Francis Unwin, who was dying and asked Gertler to witness his will. Gertler had not seen him for some days and the change was dramatic: '[I] knew he was done for', he wrote afterwards to Kot, and the event brought on a profound 'fit of glooms'.[24] For the remainder of his stay Gertler now referred to the sanatorium as 'a hateful prison'.[25]

Meanwhile in November the first monograph of Gertler's pictures was published, the first volume in the Fleuron series British Artists of Today. The book featured some of his finest recent work: the *Self-Portrait* (1920), *Young Girlhood*, *The Coster Woman*, *The Artist's Mother* (1924) and several studies of Garsington. In his preface the series editor Hubert Wellington stated that 'although he still holds Cézanne and Renoir to be the greatest of modern painters, Gertler has become convinced that for his own personal salvation he must start afresh to paint what he sees and what he loves in Nature . . . The sureness of purpose and solid achievement of Gertler's recent work', wrote Wellington, 'are rare in painting to-day and certainly justify his convictions.'

In December Gertler made an important sale at the Chenil Gallery, Chelsea, of the draped nude *Gipsy at her Toilet* to Gwen Herbert, whose husband, A. P. Herbert, a regular contributor to *Punch*, was later elected to Parliament as an Independent National candidate. The Herberts' friendship gave him entry into yet another circle, centred on their riverside house in Chiswick, and Gertler became a familiar figure in their L-shaped drawing room. 'On Boat race day, drinking mulled claret, you met everybody', writes the biographer of the writer Stephen Potter. Fellow guests included Sir John Squire (editor of *The Mercury*), the Aldous Huxleys, the columnist Robert Lynd and his wife, Sylvia, H. G. Wells, Arnold Bennett, Rose Macaulay, Charles Laughton, Elsa Lanchester and Gertler's old friends Edward Wadsworth and C. R. W. Nevinson.

Yet Gertler did not see himself as truly part of any group, with the notable exception of the 'Thursdays', the first appointment he arranged after his release from the sanatorium. Even in his absence Gertler had liked to hear of the meetings taking place in his rooms.[26] On his release Gertler began to take more assiduous care than ever of his health, 'but', he admitted to Ottoline, 'I am paying a great price for it . . . and I believe my friends are finding me a bit more tedious than before on account of it'.[27] He looked forward to 'entrenching myself in London life – just work and a few people'. And at a time when he was no longer able to chase spontaneous excitement, the prominence of the 'Thursdays' was partly to ensure that these 'few people' would be regularly and readily available.

In March Gertler was expected at Garsington, but he developed a cold and high temperature at the last minute and could not go. In a letter to Ottoline he sent his love to all, but especially to Julian, whom, he wrote, he was 'positively craving to see again'.[28] This letter may have set alarm bells ringing in Ottoline's mind, for Julian's recent behaviour, which alternated between tearful and quarrelsome, had already led her mother to conclude that she must be in love. When Julian 'reacted violently' to the news that Gertler was coming to Garsington for Easter, Ottoline wrote to question him about the true nature of his feelings for her daughter. He replied that 'my feelings towards Julian have been the same ever since she was about 12':

> . . . an affection not unmixed with admiration even – but in its nature – altogether brotherly – as you yourself term it – feelings other than these such as being in love with her (which is different to loving) or having any sort of expectation with regards to her – I have never for a moment entertained – and even if such feelings would ever have cropped up in me – I should have nipped them in the bud, knowing as I do, how very inappropriate and entirely out of place – such feelings would be, in the particular setting that we are placed.[29]

It is a tribute to the strength of his relationship with Ottoline that she accepted this explanation completely, and their friendship continued as before. But was Gertler being entirely honest about his feelings for Julian? He had always been openly fond of her, and when Julian was fourteen he had written to Mary Hutchinson of 'certain delicious fruits, which I crave for, with all my being and which are sometimes there – growing – in front of my nose – Ripe and pluckable perhaps – who knows – But I do not pluck them – and this – not through lack of

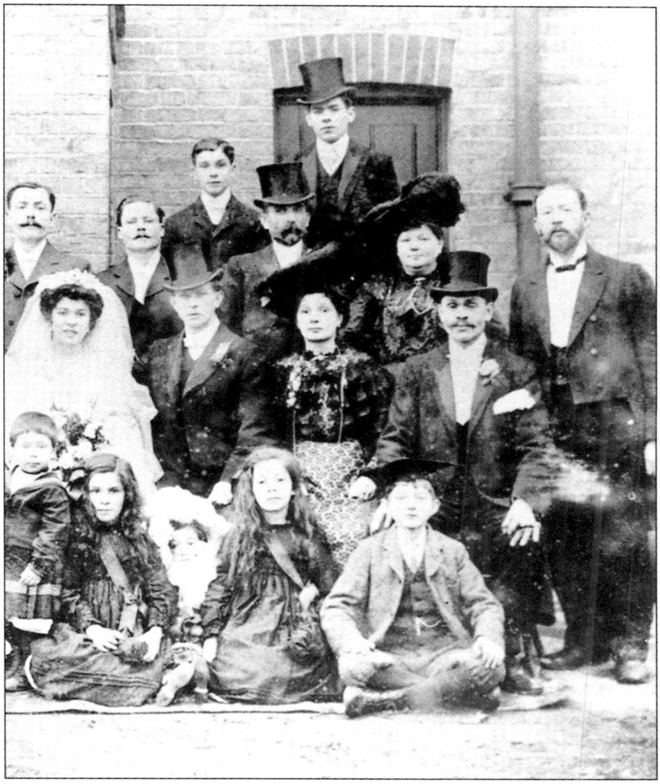

1. Family wedding photograph with Mark (*front row*) aged about 13, Deby and Abraham (*seated, right*), and Louis and Golda behind them

2. Mark Gertler aged 15 with palette and brushes, *c.* 1906–7

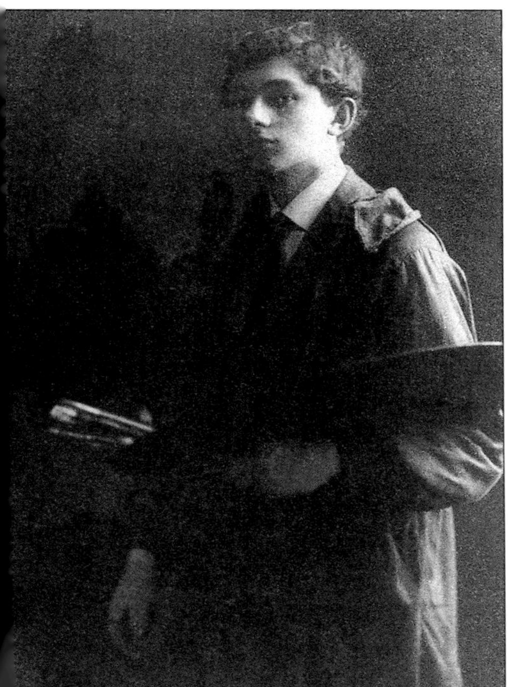

3. Mark Gertler aged 18, with his brother Jack

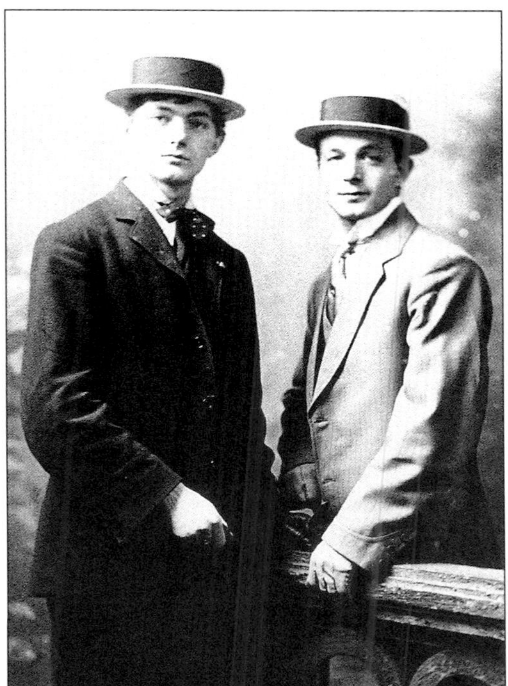

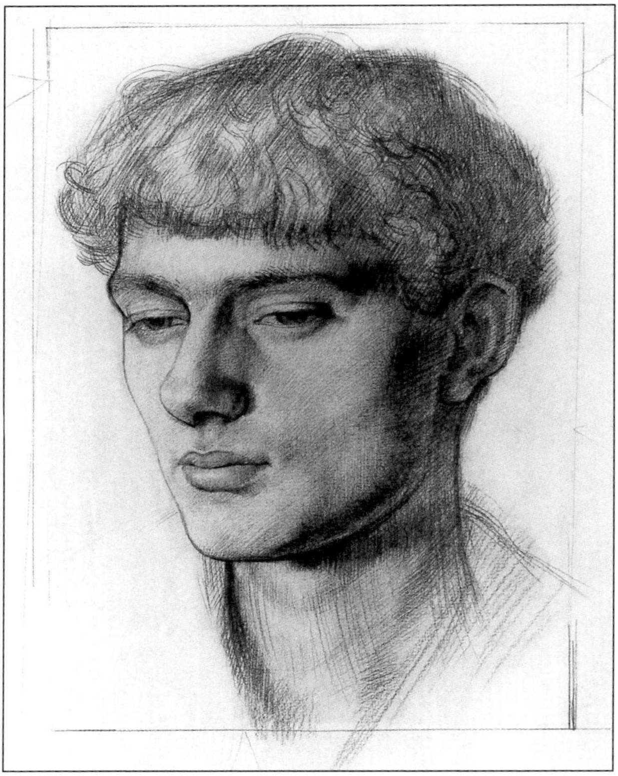

4. *Self-Portrait*, *c.*1909–11, soft pencil, 11½ x 8 in/41·9 x 31·8 cm. Catalogued as a self-portrait, this is a good likeness of Gertler finely executed in the Slade manner, but perhaps by one of his Slade contemporaries, possibly Carrington

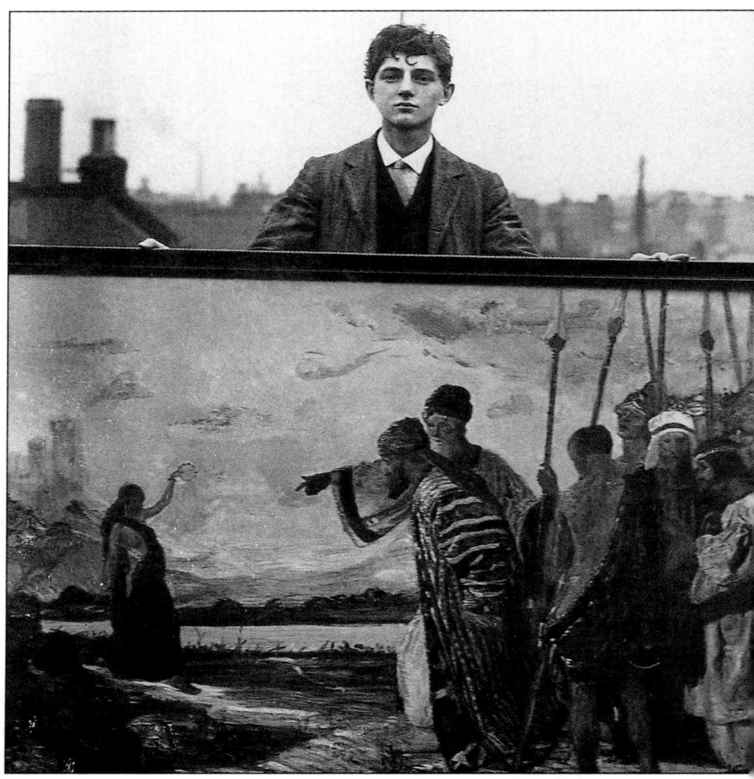

5. Mark Gertler standing on the roof at Spital Square with *The Return of Jephtha*, painted for the Slade summer competition of 1910. The photograph was taken by his neighbour David Burleigh, whose sister May was Gertler's first sweetheart

6. *The Artist's Mother*, 1911, oil on canvas, 26 x 22 in/66 x 55·9 cm. Prominently displayed at the New English Art Club in 1911, where it gained unanimous praise from the critics, this remains one of Gertler's best-loved paintings

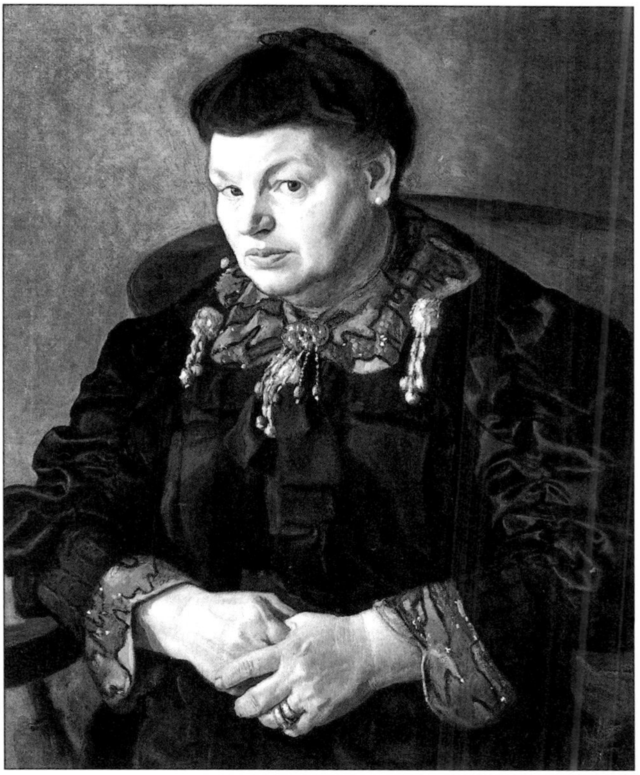

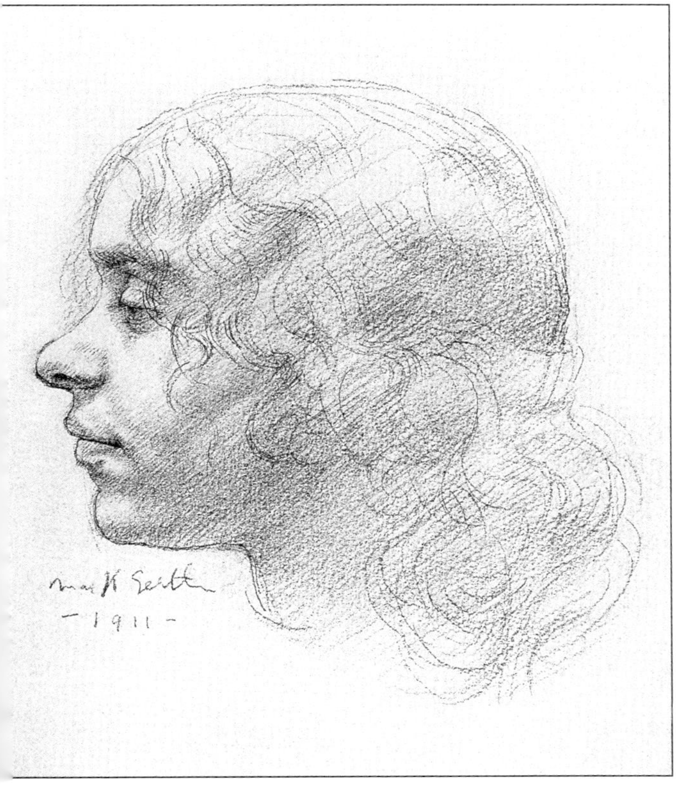

7. *Study of a Girl's Head*, 1911, pencil, 16½ x 11 in/42 x 27·7 cm. An exquisite early study which demonstrates the fine draughtsmanship for which Gertler gained a reputation at the Slade

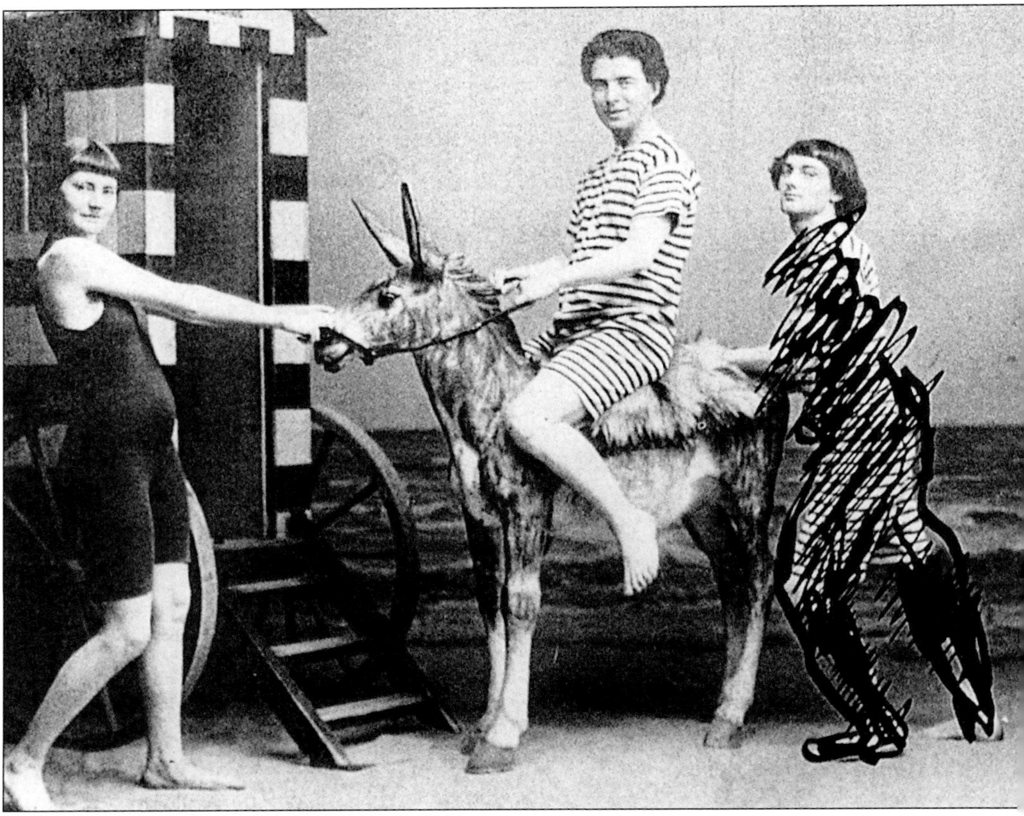

8. Dolly Henry, John Currie and Mark Gertler, photographed on holiday in Ostend in 1912. Gertler later scribbled over the photograph because he felt his figure was far too thin

9. *Some Later Primitives*, 1912, tempera on canvas, 46·2 x 127·6 cm. A portrait of the shortlived 'Neo-Primitives', captured just as the group was about to dissolve, showing (*left to right*): John Currie, Mark Gertler, C. R.W. Nevinson, Edward Wadsworth, Adrian Allinson and Madame Tisceron, the proprietor of the Soho café Le Petit Savoyard

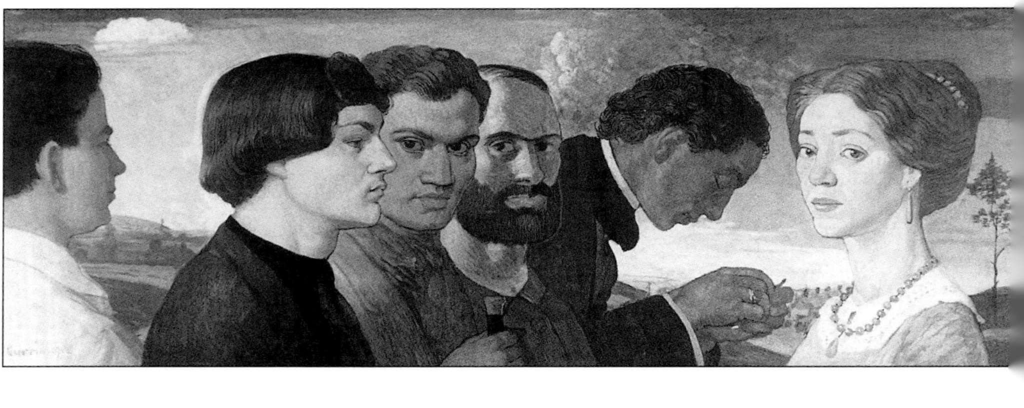

10. *The Rabbi and His Grandchild*, 1913, oil on canvas, 20 x 18 in/50·8 x 45·9 cm. A striking portrait of youth and old age, all the more remarkable in view of the fact that the two models never met

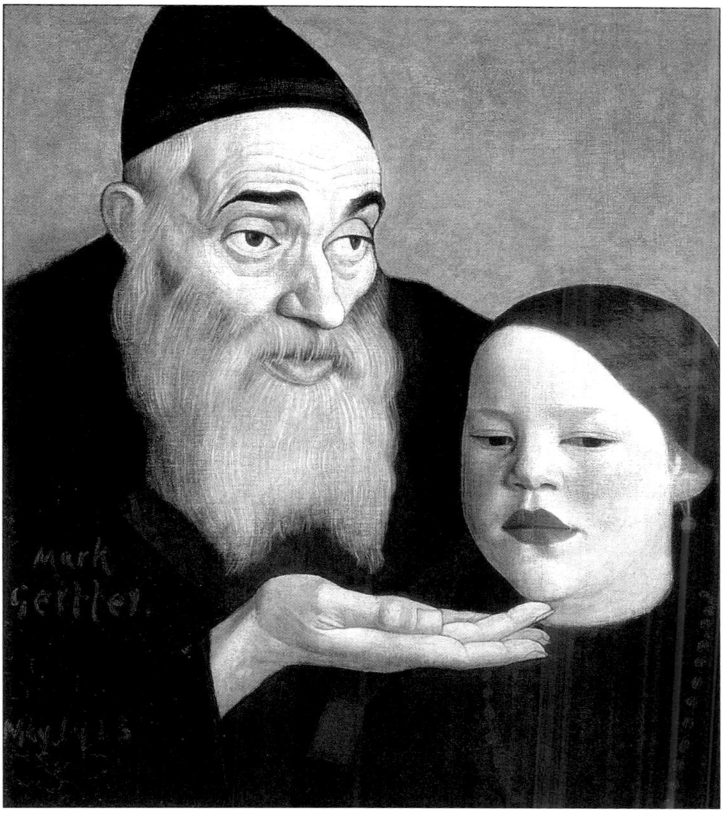

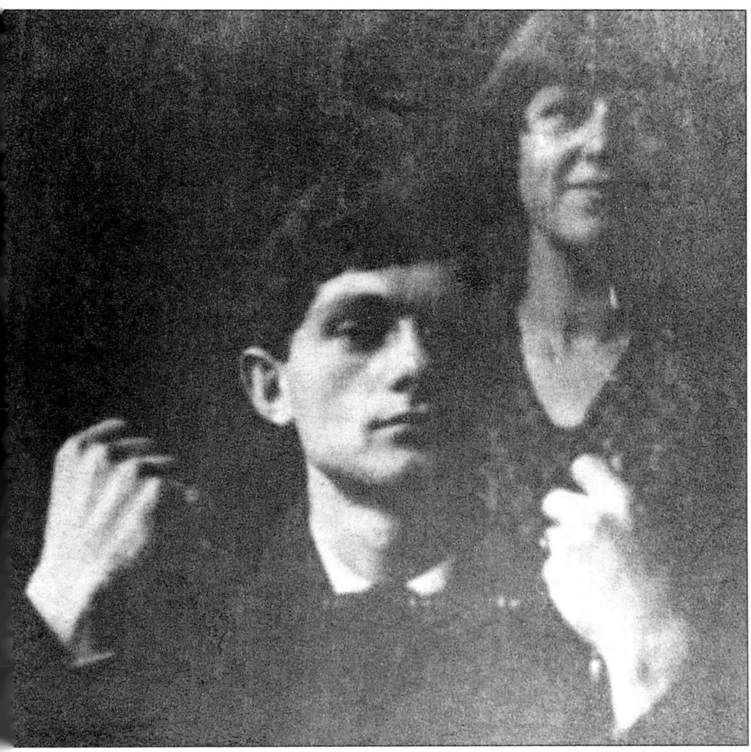

11. Mark Gertler and Carrington, *c.* 1914

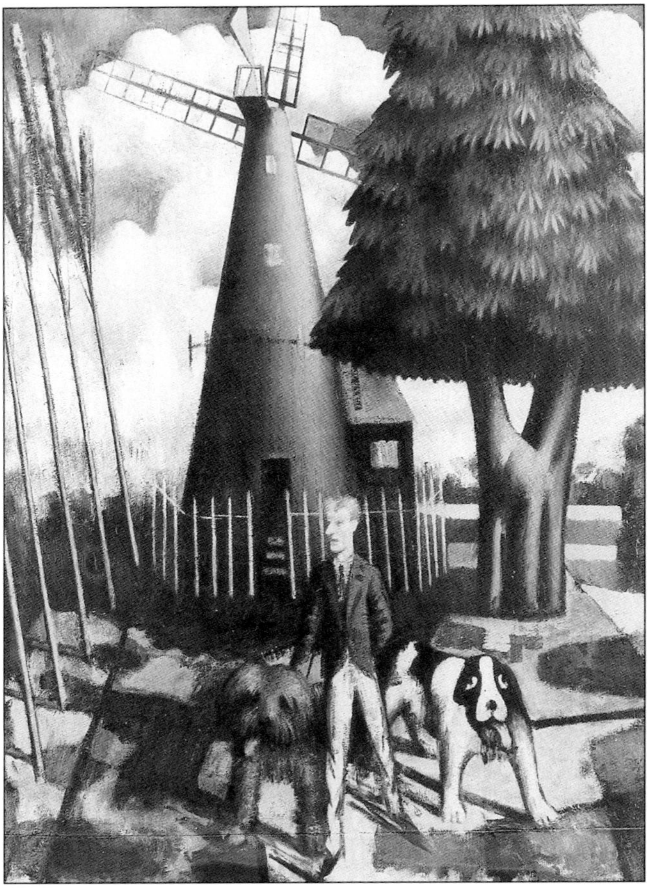

12. *Gilbert Cannan at His Mill*, 1916, oil on canvas, 40 x 28 in/99 x 71 cm. A strangely prophetic study which seems to hint at the troubled writer's future breakdown

13. Kot with Katherine Mansfield in the Campbells' garden in St John's Wood, 1916

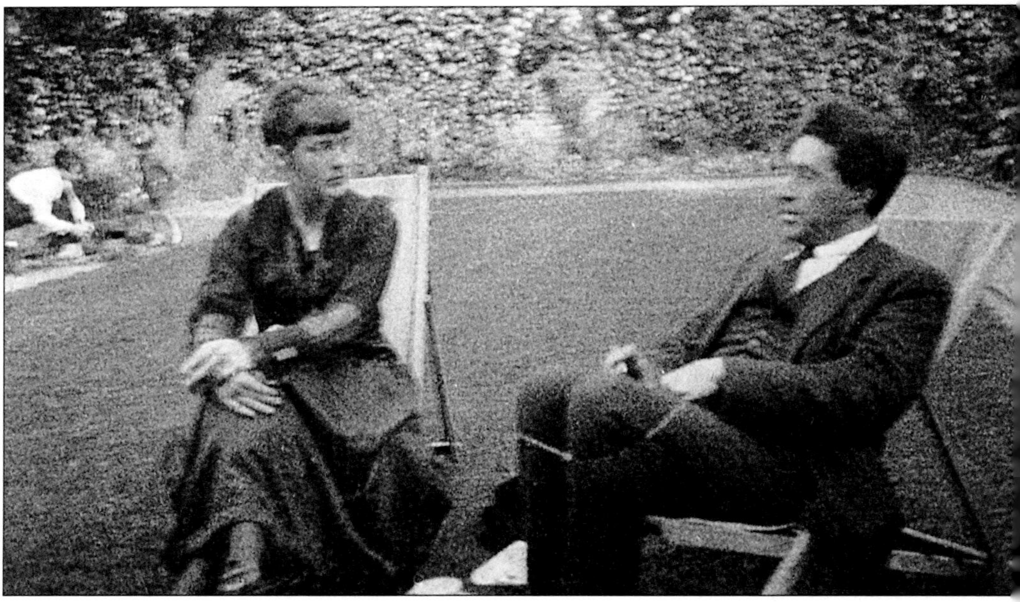

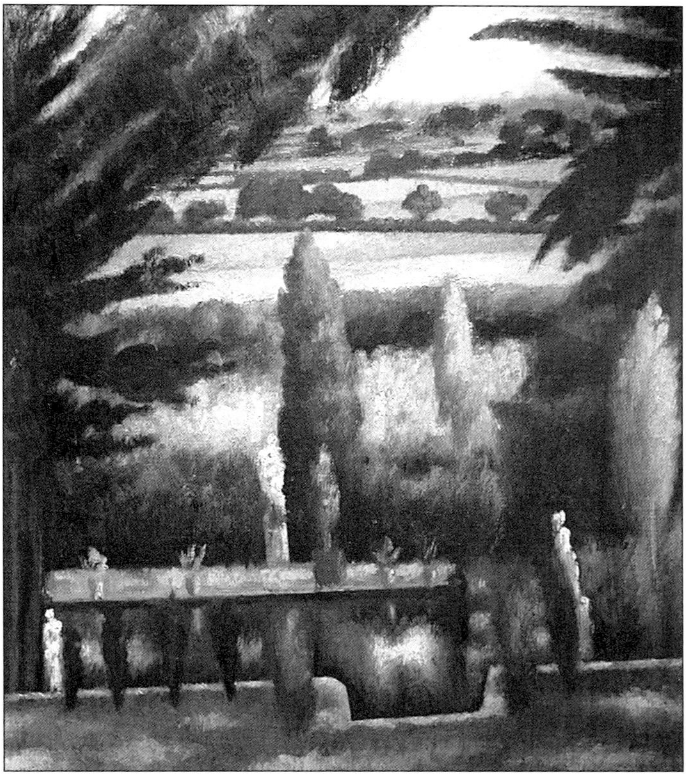

14. *The Pond, Garsington*, 1916, oil on canvas, 24 x 20 in/60 x 50cm. One of several versions of the same subject, in which Gertler captured a brooding, melancholy quality absent from most descriptions of Garsington life

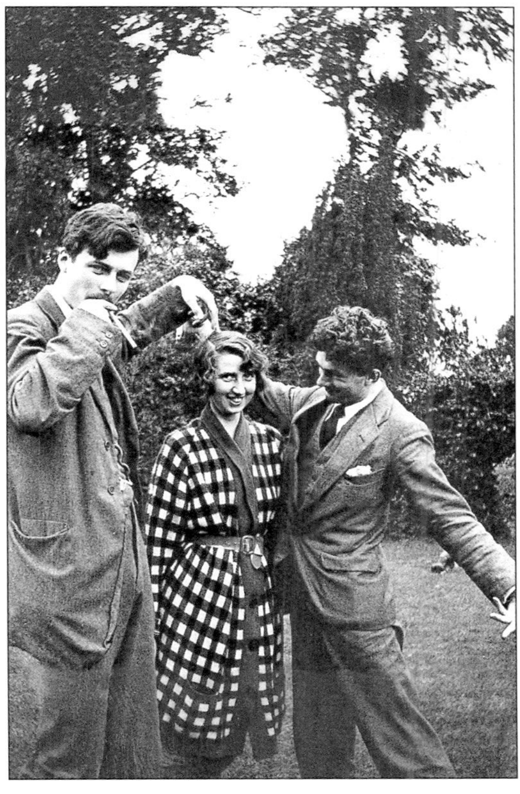

15. Aldous Huxley, Brett and Mark Gertler playing charades at Garsington, *c.* 1917

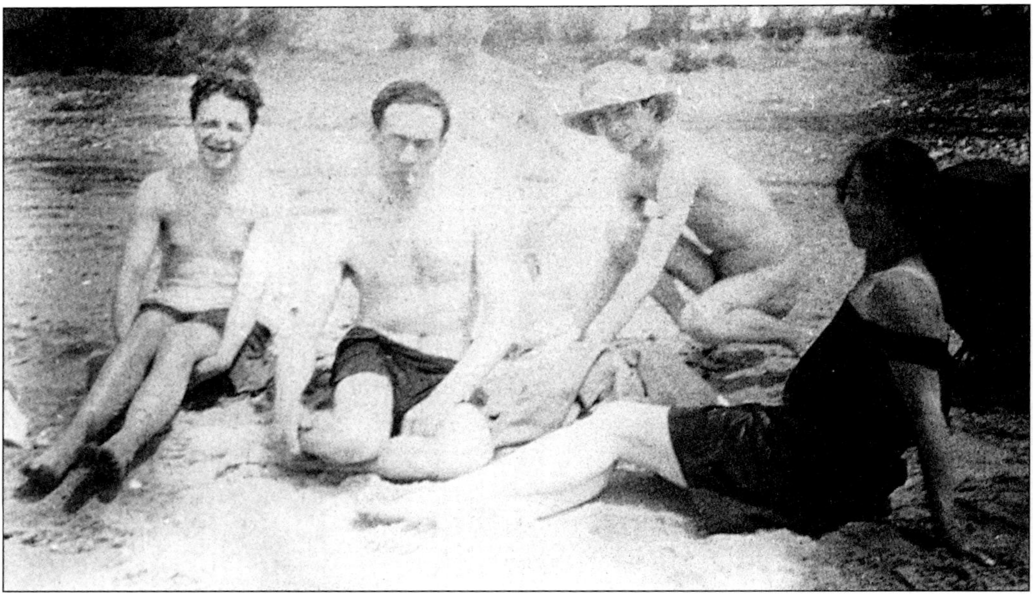

16. Monty Shearman (with cigarette), Mark Gertler and friends, *c.* 1917–18

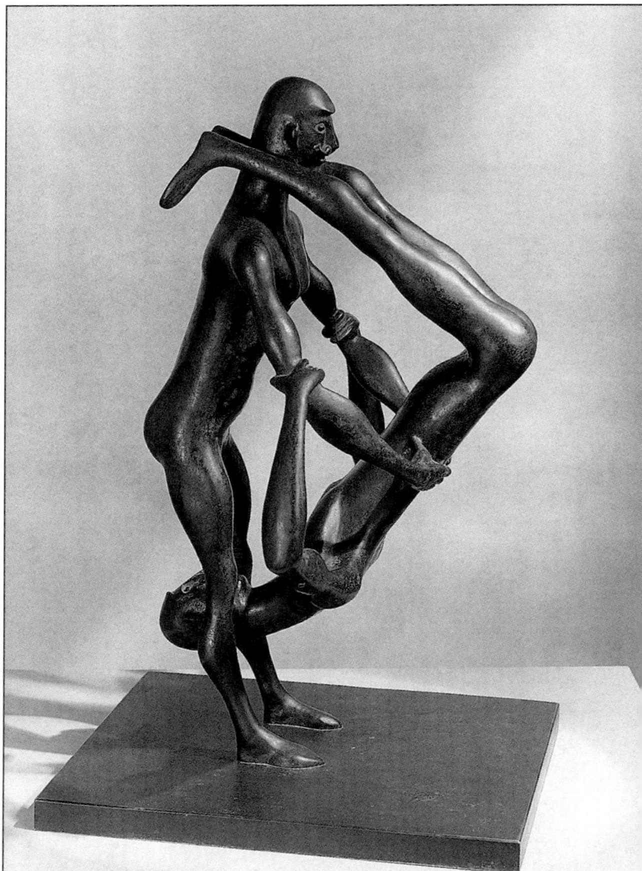

17. *The Acrobats*, 1917, bronze, 23½ x 16½ x 14¾ in/59·5 x 41·9 x 37·5 cm, including bronze base 1 in/2·5 cm high. Gertler's only surviving sculpture, which received no serious critical attention during his lifetime

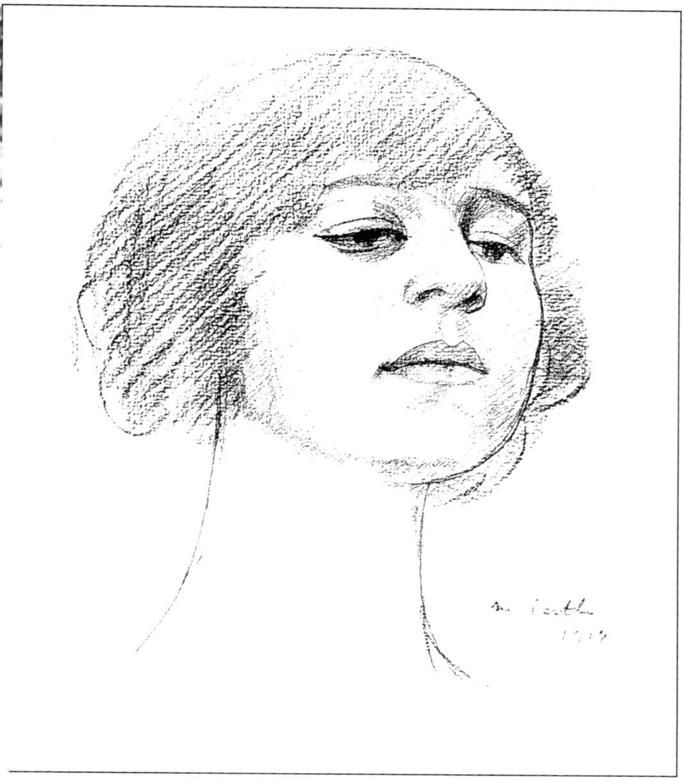

18. *Carrington*, 1917, pencil drawing, 10 x 8½ in/25·5 x 21·5 cm. This animated sketch captures something of Carrington's appeal and vivacity, while retaining an element of her irresistible 'mysteriousness'

19. (*left to right*) 'Toronto' Prewett, Julian Morrell, Juliette Huxley, Mark Gertler and Ottoline, 1918

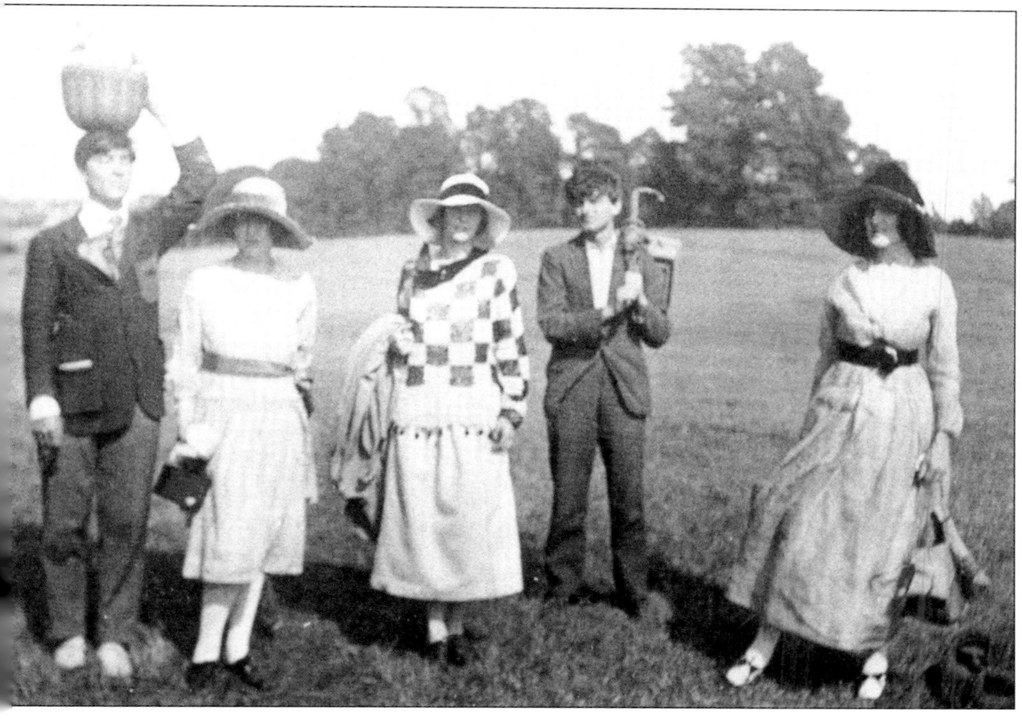

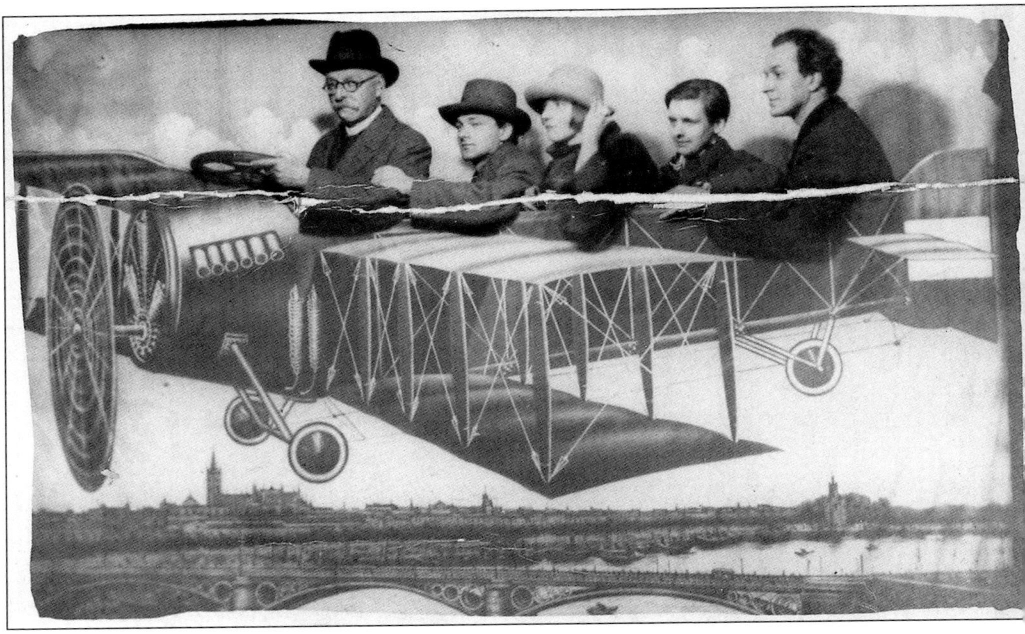

20. Walter Taylor, Mark Gertler and unidentified friends in a model aeroplane, *c.* 1920s

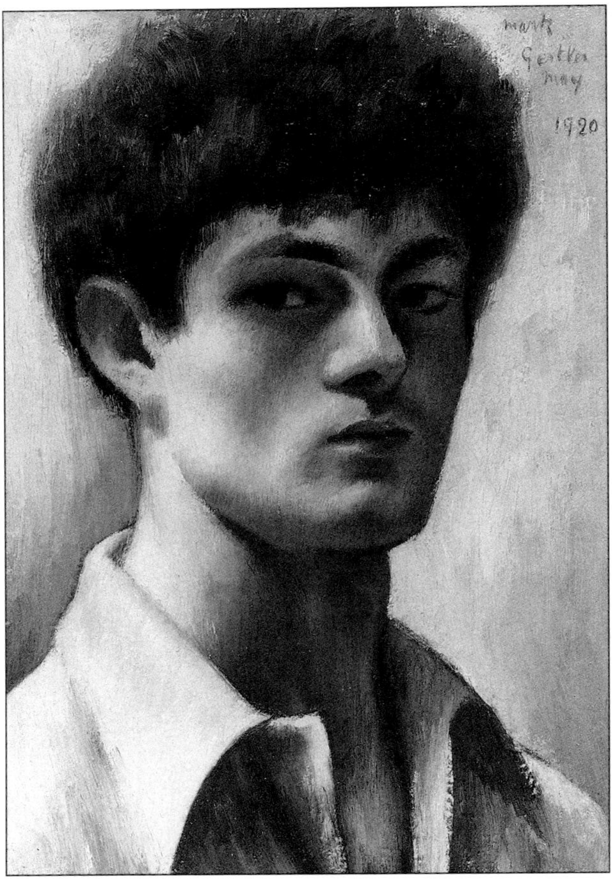

21. *Self-Portrait*, 1920, oil on canvas, 16¾ x 11¾ in/42·5 x 29·2 cm. A troubled, introspective sel portrait painted shortly before Gertler was diagnosed with tuberculosis

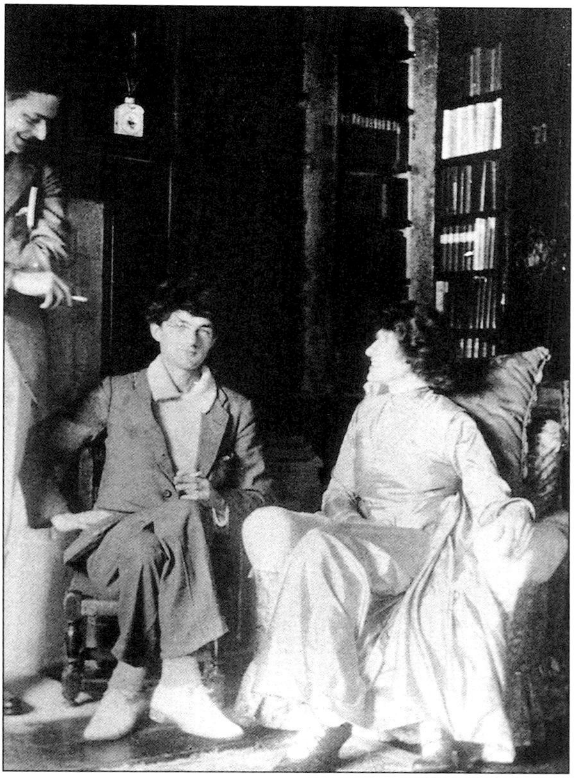

22. T. S. Eliot, Mark Gertler and Ottoline Morrell in the Red Room at Garsington, *c.* 1920s

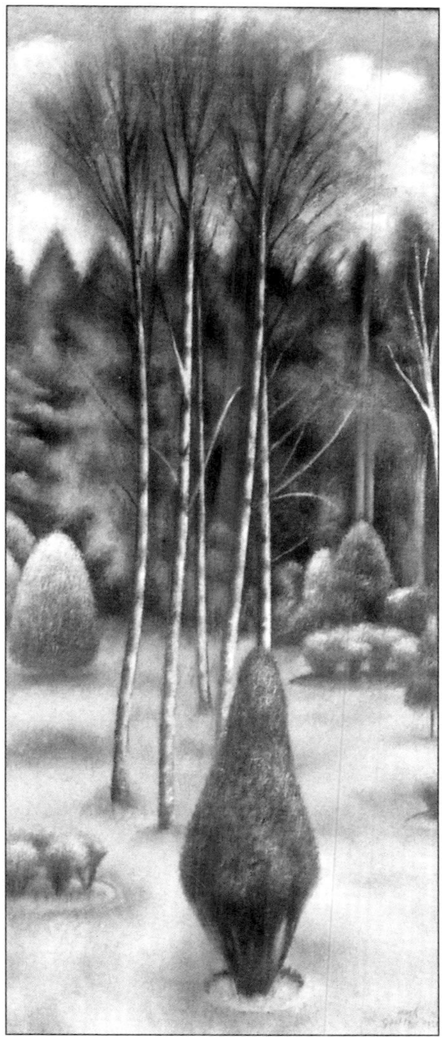

23. *Trees at Sanatorium, Scotland*, 1921, oil on canvas, 44½ x 20 in/111 x 49·5 cm. Painted from Gertler's bedroom window at Nordrach-on-Dee sanatorium, Banchory. He stayed on deliberately to complete it and donated it to the staff in gratitude for his treatment

24. Valentine Dobrée, *c.* 1920s

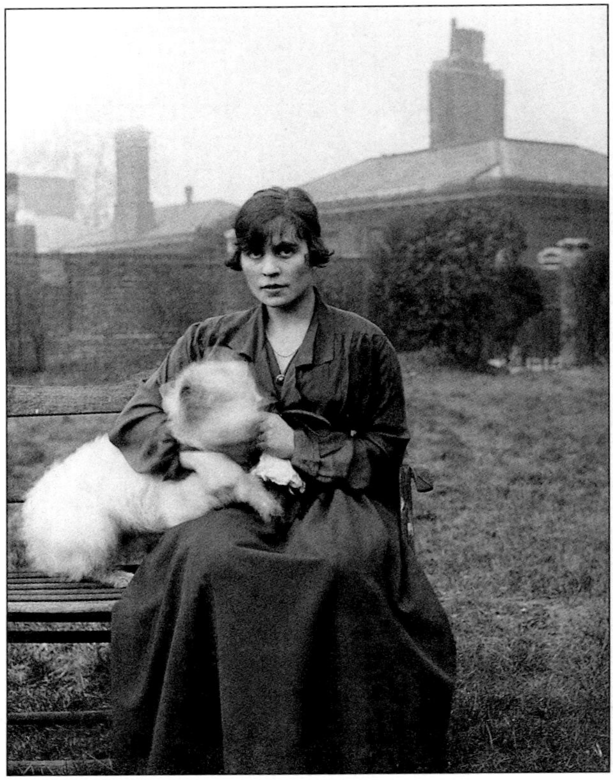

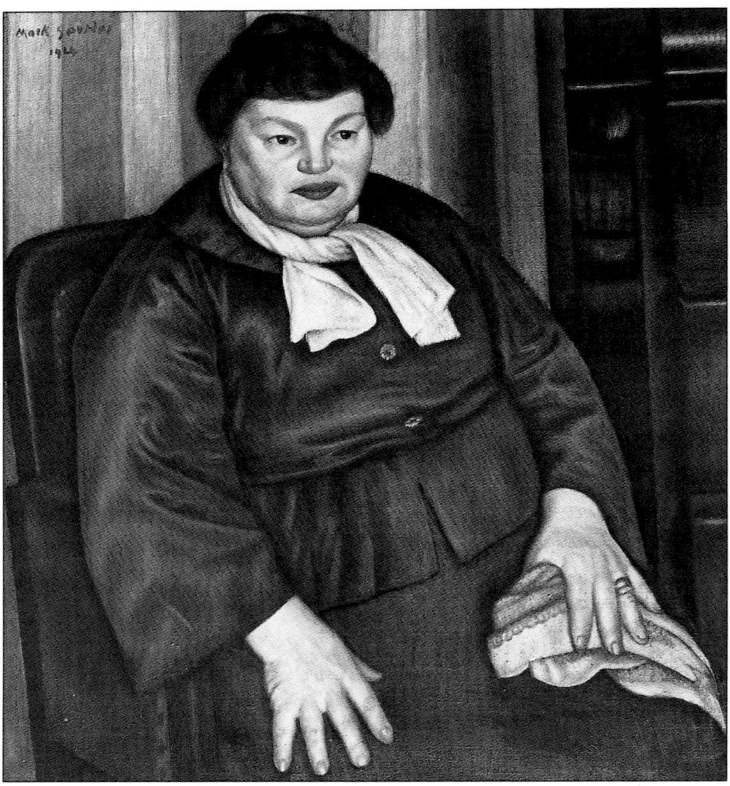

25. *The Artist's Mother*, 1924, oil on canvas, 30 x 28 in/76·5 x 71 cm. This was Gertler's final portrait of his mother and he was so anxious to keep it that he priced it at £200 – the highest sum one of his pictures earned during his lifetime

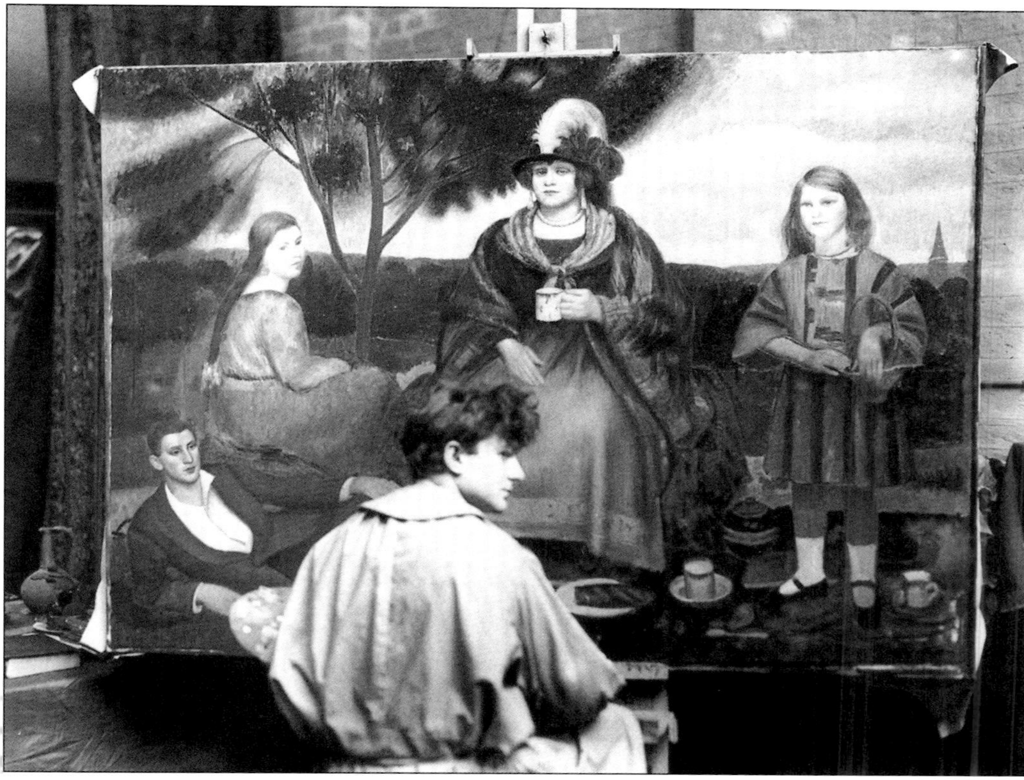

26. Gertler at work in Penn studio on *The Coster Family on Hampstead Heath*, *c.* 1924

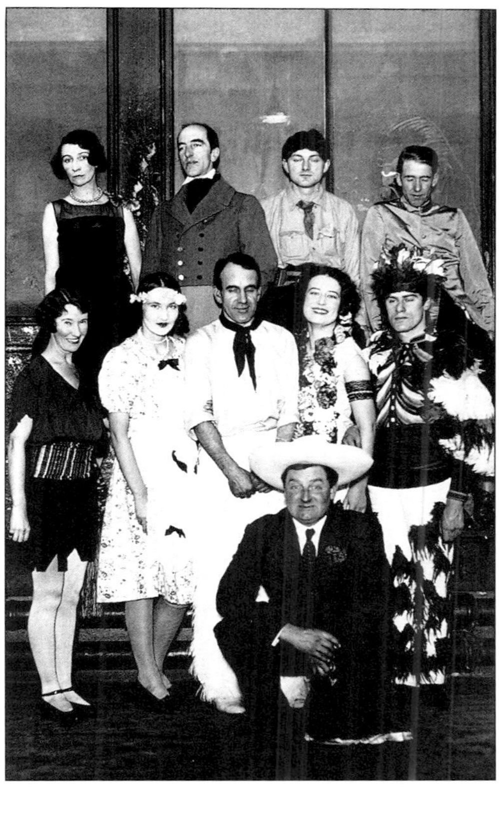

27. Fancy dress party. *Back row, left to right*: Delphine Turner, John Mavrogordato, Mark Gertler, Walter Turner; *front row*: Christine Mavrogordato, Kate Foster, Jas Wood, Marjorie, Richard Carline and unidentified figure (kneeling)

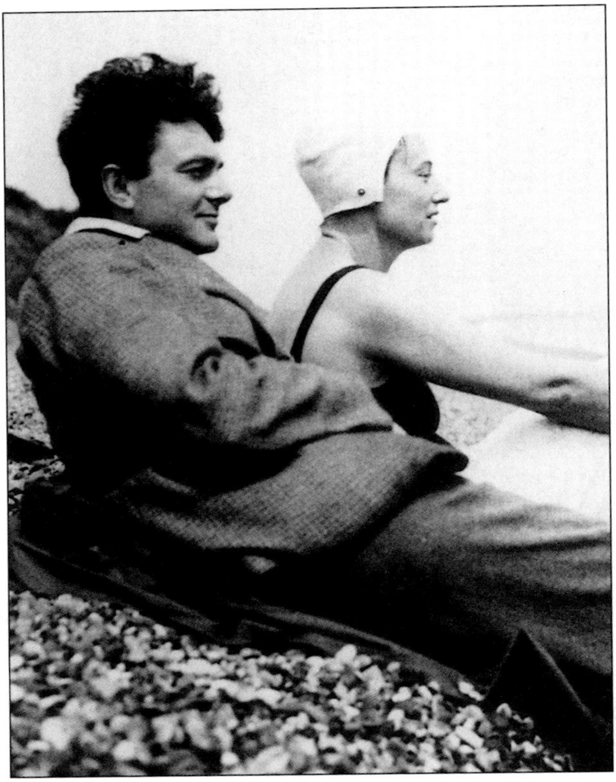

28. Mark and Marjorie on their honeymoon at Bandol, 1930

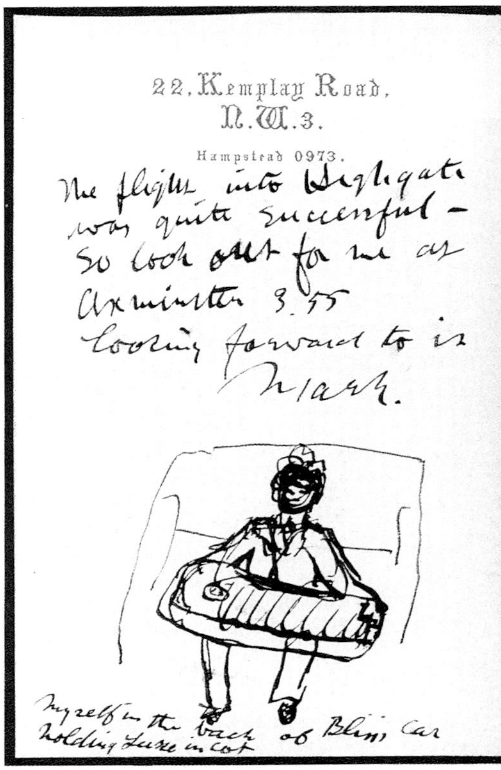

22, Kemplay Road,
N.W.3.

Hampstead 0973.

The flight into Highgate was quite successful – So look out for me at Axminster 3.55
Looking forward to it
Mark.

Myself in the back of Blin's car holding Luke in cot

29. Mark Gertler with Luke on their 'flight into Highgate', September 1932. This was the only portrait Gertler ever made of his son

30. Mark Gertler, a studio portrait taken in 1933 for the Cadbury's Chocolate Box Competition

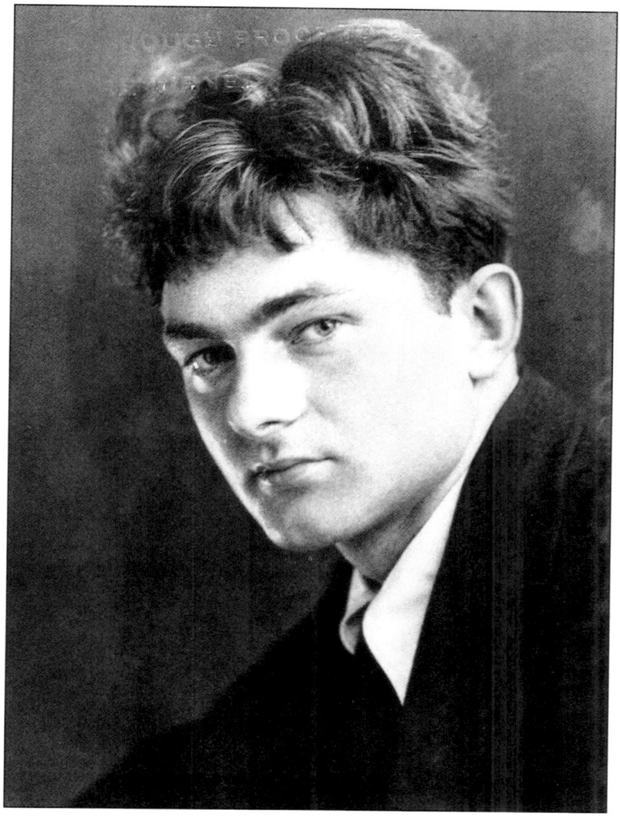

31. The Castelltersol fiesta, 1934: (*left to right*) Marjorie (seated) with Luke, Mark, Aunt Ethel, Tom Balston and Luke's nanny

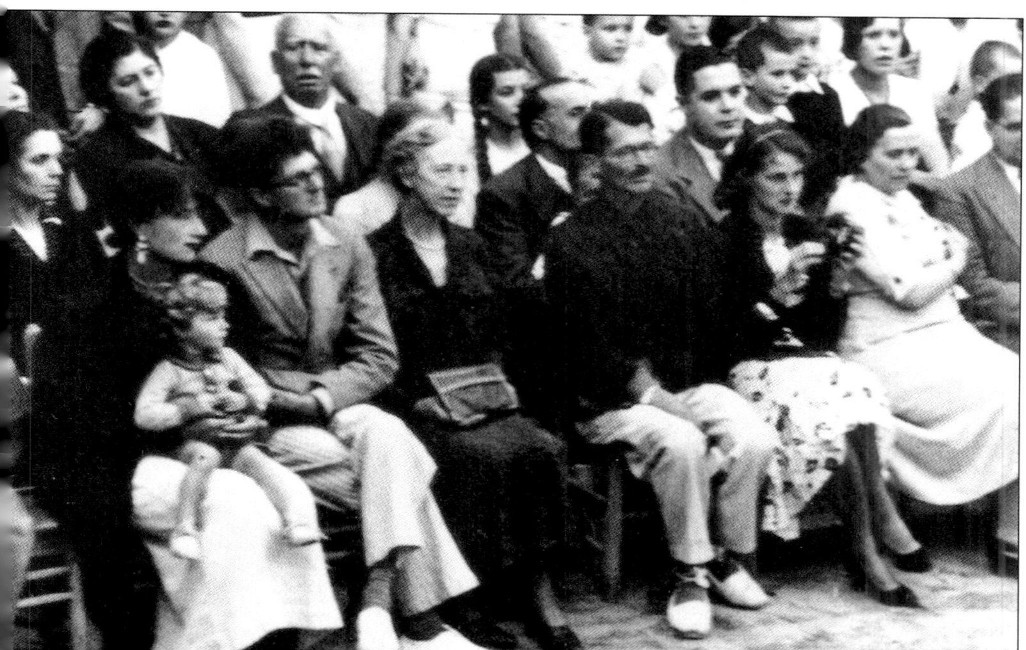

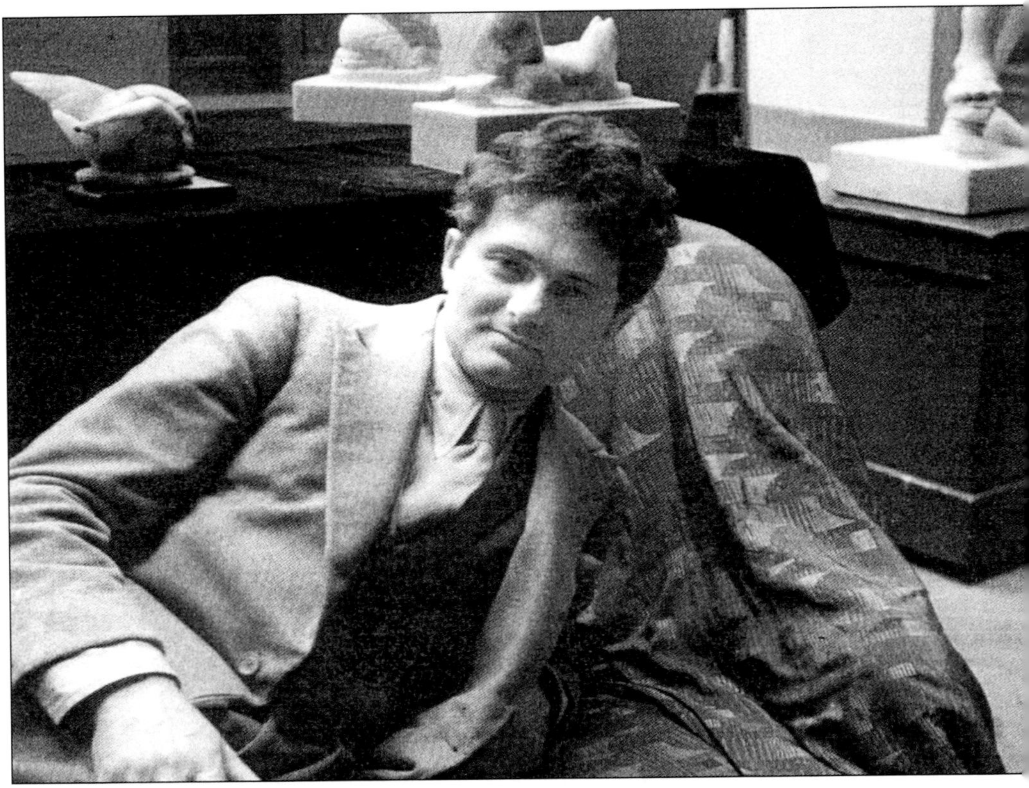

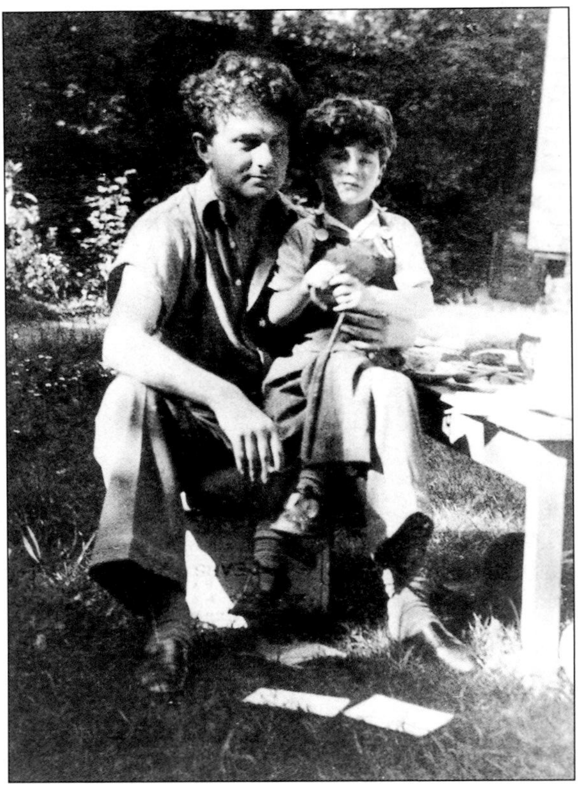

32. Mark Gertler photographed at the Westminster School of Art by one of his pupils, Margaret Geddes, in 1935. A rare, relaxed portrait of th artist in his later years

33. Mark and Luke in the garden at Grove Terrace, *c.* 1937–8

courage or through virtue, put because of a sense of suitability[.] Of course, sometimes, one has no longer the strength to calculate – then one falls upon the apple, bites it, trundles it, devours it.'[30] Some sixty years later, when Miranda Seymour was researching Ottoline's biography, Julian alleged that Gertler had once 'tried to seduce her in the Monastery studio before swearing her to secrecy. This', writes Seymour, 'makes it likely, but not certain. Julian also claimed in this interview to have been the sole object of Toronto Prewett's interest.'[31]

Gertler spent Easter at Garsington, as planned, with the Turners, Gilbert Spencer and a charming young man called Igor Vinogradoff, who turned out to be the real object of Julian's affections and proposed to her ten days after Easter. Although Julian accepted, her parents opposed the match. It was later called off and Julian married Victor Goodman instead in 1928, although she did marry Vinogradoff much later, after Goodman's death. After her marriage, Julian recalled, she saw much less of Gertler, and her own family life 'didn't interest him greatly'.[32] Although Gertler always spoke of Julian with great affection, after Ottoline's letter he had decided that it would be better for him to 'develop a sort of detachment' towards her and avoid any further misunderstandings.

In May 1926 an exhibition of Gertler's paintings and drawings, shared with John Nash and Gilbert Spencer, opened at the Leicester Galleries. Most of these predated his time at the sanatorium, but he included the *Autumn Landscape, Norfolk* and his only known *Snow Scene*, both painted at Mundesley. Unfortunately, this time the opening coincided with the General Strike, when for eight days normal business in Britain ground to a halt, which naturally squeezed out reviews by art critics in the newspapers. Gertler fell into a state of profound gloom, fearing food shortages and train cancellations, particularly to Garsington, where he was expected in mid-May. In the event the strike was short-lived, but Gertler's reaction was not untypical. Nevinson, who was in Paris at the time, later recalled that the air had been 'full of the wildest rumours of murder and sabotage', and he was told that 'the British Navy had been mobilised'. When he returned to London, on a train driven by 'over-courteous undergraduates', he found the anti-climax 'bewildering'.[33] Although Gertler once again lost out on essential press coverage and sales suffered accordingly, he made at least one propitious sale to a new buyer, named Thomas Balston, and this initiated a friendship that became of supreme importance in his final years.

After a trip to Paris in early July, Gertler arrived home to find a letter waiting from the Jewish Education Aid Society, reminding him that he had suspended repayments of his outstanding debt. He explained that he 'had been obliged to undergo further sanatorium treatment and also had suffered through his last exhibition having been held during the general strike', and was therefore 'unable to resume repayments at present, but promised to do so directly an improvement in his position permitted'.[34] It must have been a humiliating reminder of his continuing financial insecurity.

Gertler spent August in Lyme Regis with the Turners, but set off in such a hurry that he forgot his paints, and the wonderful Mrs Bruce – his 'boon' landlady – had to follow on behind, just catching up with him at the station. Though he admired Lyme, he admitted in a letter to Valentine that landscape interested him less than other subjects, and the presence of several fine books on Cézanne and Renoir contributed to a temporary painting 'paralysis'. There were moments, he admitted, when he altogether despaired.[35]

These fits of depression alternated with manic periods of activity. 'For the last month or so', he confessed to Kot, 'I have not been able to get painting out of my head – night or day – I can think of nothing else. At moments I am worn out by it.' From Lyme, Turner reported to Ottoline that Gertler was 'painting furiously under the influence of his . . . idol Renoir. We are all reading books about Renoir and the whole house is Renoir mad. Everywhere we go Mark looks out for Renoir types but there are no beauties at Lyme Regis as far as we can discover.'[36] Instead Gertler found Lyme 'a stuffy, steamy place – awful mists, heavy and liverish'. He was glad to get away. 'Holidays', he concluded, in a letter to Kot, 'never agree with me physically, [which] I believe contrary to all the laws of humanity.'[37]

Before he left, however, he arranged for his party to visit the elderly Thomas Hardy (whom Turner already knew) at his nearby Dorset home Max Gate. Hardy had long been Gertler's favourite English novelist. 'I daresay there are other writers who can perhaps write better and are cleverer and better Pchycologists [*sic*]', he told Ottoline, 'but they are not such artists as Hardy. Actually I can feel more art in Hardy than even the Russian writers whom I admire so tremendously!'[38]

But by the time of the visit on 10 August Gertler was too nervous and depressed to take much in, and simply reported that Hardy was 'very, very old. It was rather depressing – our visit. Old age terrifies me. He is charming and nice though – and fairly active still. We talked about many things, including [John Middleton] Murry, about whom they were not very enthusiastic.'[39] Afterwards the 'Mavros'(as Gertler liked to call them) drove him down to Brighton to spend a week with Taylor, where he watched his fellow guests, 'carnivorous old hags – who eat with a sort of indecent, almost sexual ferocity', with a heightened sensitivity that bordered on disgust.[40] He longed for his newly distempered Hampstead studio, but even after his return to London the very thought of painting made him sick. Yet even beneath this nausea, he recognized, 'the same old craving' persisted.[41]

19

Building Bridges

> 'Does one ever succeed in building an even stable bridge between [one]self and another I doubt it, no – that bridge – allowing such rare and magical accessibility – can only float in and out . . . for one wonderful moment . . . And the worst of it is, that the knowledge of such moments, make the intervals, by contrast, too heartrendingly prosaic, and the intervening sense of loneliness, . . . more than usually hard to bear.'
>
> Mark Gertler to Ottoline Morrell, April 1927

GERTLER HAD FORMED no lasting relationships with women since the debacle with Phyllis Wilkinson. Towards the close of 1926, however, he became entangled with two women, one of whom would dramatically affect his future. Gertler first met Marjorie Greatorex Hodgkinson at one of the Carlines' parties in 1925 – or so Dick Carline at least recalled,[1] although Marjorie later gave the date as somewhere between 1923 and 1925.[2] But the first indication of their growing friendship begins with Gertler's letters to her from Lyme in the autumn of 1926.

Slim, shy, dark-haired and striking, rather than conventionally pretty, Marjorie was then twenty-three, some eleven years younger than Gertler and rather in awe of him. Her background was solidly English middle-class. Her parents, Daisy and Edmund Hodgkinson, were farm owners. and she spent her early years in the green belt of Surrey, which left her with an enduring love of the countryside. After the early death of her mother, when Marjorie was twelve, her father sold up and moved to London, where he practised as a solicitor and took a flat in Artillery Mansions, Victoria, which Marjorie found dark and depressing. She described the rest of her childhood as 'Victorian and repressive'.[3] After three years as a boarder at Grassendale School, Southbourne, in Hampshire, she escaped, at the age of seventeen, to Paris for a year to study art. Here she shook off her younger, unhappier self and developed a deep attachment to the city, which became the backdrop to some of the most decisive events of her life.

After her return to Britain in 1921 Marjorie spent three years at the Slade under Tonks, where she naturally fell in with people who had the same ideas and interests as herself, and who shared her 'freer, airier view of life'.[4] One of her closest friends was Kate Foster, a vivacious, pretty student who lived in Hampstead with her widowed mother (a painter, who had been at the Slade with Augustus John) and her equally attractive sister Greville, an occasional art school model.

Marjorie and the Foster sisters became friendly with Gertler's old friend Dick Carline, who despite a successful exhibition with his brother Sydney in 1920 had decided to study part-time at the Slade. This brought a fresh intake of students to the gatherings at Downshire Hill, which Gertler continued to attend irregularly. By the mid-1920s these gatherings had become so popular that they were regarded by many Hampstead artists and writers as almost weekly parties. They were also the beginning of many a romance: Gertler and Marjorie, Stanley Spencer and Hilda Carline, and Noel Carrington and Catharine Alexander, another Slade student who lived locally.

In 1923, when Marjorie was twenty-one, she was granted a regular income from her father and expected to leave home when he remarried the same year. For a time she shared lodgings with Kate Foster, but as often as possible she travelled. Travel was an important expression of Marjorie's freedom, and in the early years of her friendship with Gertler her letters would arrive stamped with exotic postmarks. Gertler, however, as he freely admitted, remained 'an incorrigible Londoner'[5] and it took him at least a year to realize that he must make an effort to see more of her and make London seem 'more acceptable' if he wanted Marjorie to stick around.[6] His letters show a friendship, perhaps an attachment, but by no means an exclusive relationship. He wrote of his work, his health and his dates with other women, such as the dancer Nora Edwards (who later married the painter Bernard Meninsky), who excused herself from a dinner date because of a convenient 'fainting fit' by her mother. (John Russell Taylor in his biography of Meninsky, suggests it was Gertler's 'dangerous' reputation that put her off.[7]) But when he later desired 'a young female companion with bare arms' for a few days in Brighton he sent for Nora, he told Marjorie, and this time she dutifully came 'bare arms and all'.[8]

By October Gertler's letters had become flirtatious: 'Yes, your arms should be a comfort', he agreed, 'but not, I hope your arms alone – surely other parts are brown too – we must see them all!'[9] But on her return Marjorie proved elusive. Ringing up to find her out, apparently on repeated trips to the dentist, Gertler asked, 'what is he doing . . . carving a monument?'[10] He invited her to the studio to see his work, and they continued to meet occasionally at the Carlines. It was a warm and affectionate but, initially at least, not a serious relationship.

Meanwhile, following Marchant's death the previous December, his widow (whom Gertler found harder about business than her late husband) had continued to run the Goupil Gallery along similar lines, but on 2 November Gertler wrote to Ottoline that 'the long expected tragedy has happened – Goupil est Finitisimus!'[11] To the Mavrogordatos he explained that the gallery had 'collapsed and with [it] my finances!'[12] To Marjorie, however, he wrote spiritedly that by the end of the month he would be 'penniless and ready for the workhouse, where I hope you will come and visit me. Meanwhile let us not hearken to the rumble of the distant . . . but have tea together here on Saturday at 4.30. And what about [that] party?[13] Only to Ottoline did Gertler admit that he felt 'very gloomy'.[14]

Walter Taylor immediately offered to pay his next month's 'salary' and Ottoline, always full of helpful suggestions, came up with a plan to approach a friend of hers, the writer, philosopher and novelist Leo Myers, one of three business sponsors who had underwritten the launch of the London Artists' Association in May.[15] Largely the brainchild of Maynard Keynes, the Association offered its members a regular salary, offset by the income earned from exhibitions. All seven original members were connected to Bloomsbury, and in the coming years the shows undoubtedly did much to consolidate the reputation of the key Bloomsbury artists Duncan Grant and Vanessa Bell.[16]

Grateful as he was for Ottoline's help, Gertler told her that he considered his chances of being accepted

> extremely small – I should think I am one of the last people in the world they would include. You see in one way we are sort of enemy camps – Grant is supposed to represent one school of painting and I another . . . As you must have noticed from their last show they like unity – you could

> hardly, in fact, distinguish one artist from another – my inclusion would be rather like the entry of a Bull in a china shop.

He pointed out that he would never have approached the LAA himself, doubting if 'it would be wise of me to join them even if they wanted me', and asked Ottoline 'to explain that you did it without consulting me'.[17] Myers's reply to Ottoline was as ambivalent as Gertler's. He had, he wrote, spoken to Maynard Keynes about Gertler, and he would be 'held in mind, but I'm afraid that there is no immediate intention of taking any more artists into the Association. I will bring the matter up again when an opportunity arises.' But the opportunity never did. In any case, for Gertler Bloomsbury was now a closed chapter. 'The subject of Bloomsberries,' he wrote in a letter to Valentine in 1924, 'no longer exists for me, since I positively never see any of them.'[18]

Had his membership of the LAA been approved, Gertler could have expected a basic income of £150 out of the £400 that he calculated he needed per annum. Instead, his brothers proposed he borrow £400 a year from his bank at the rate of 5 per cent, and he thought of asking Walter Taylor to stand guarantor. 'At the end of the year', he explained to Ottoline, 'I should only have to pay the percentage – that is £20, and even if the following year I am still unable to pay them back – I would still have only to pay the percentage that is another £20.' Naïvely he assured her that he had 'studied the proposal from every point of view' and could not see 'any possibility of financial loss on the part of the signateur [*sic*]'.[19]

Alarmed, Ottoline came up with an alternative suggestion, that Gertler might show at the Claridge Gallery, run by her friend Ena Mathias. Ena was one of Asher Wertheimer's daughters and thus sister to the Conway whose interference Gertler had rejected so decisively in 1911, although she never seems to have held it against him. However, Gertler did not consider Ena's gallery prestigious enough, particularly since she could not offer him an advance payment. Nevertheless, the Mathias family did come up trumps in the end. An offer of £50 for a still life (probably *Pomegranates and Melon*) from Ena's husband, Robert, in mid-November proved 'a perfect Godsend – I was never happier over the sale of a picture', he told Ottoline. 'Now whatever happens I'm alright till Xmas.'[20]

A few days later Gertler also signed a two-year contract with Oliver Brown of the Leicester Galleries at the same percentage (33⅓) as the

Goupil, but with a lower monthly stipend of £30 (instead of £35) a month. This, combined with the Mathias sale and the fact that, rather than lose him, Mrs Bruce had reduced the fee on his rooms from £3 3*s.* to £2 10*s.*, left him in the end 'really better off than before!' so that he now considered himself, 'rather smart . . . walking straight from the Goupil to [the] Leicester in one stride . . . It is good to have friends', he told Ottoline in acknowledgment of all her efforts, 'but better still not to need them.'[21]

In December Gertler made his only recorded visit to Ham Spray, near Hungerford, where Strachey, Carrington and Partridge had moved in 1924 from Tidmarsh Mill. Despite her stated intentions, Carrington had contacted Gertler again after his release from the sanatorium, and occasionally visited his studio in Rudall Crescent. On Boxing Day she wrote to Strachey that Ottoline had telephoned to arrange a visit to Ham Spray the following Monday for tea. '"I hope Lytton won't mind-d-d . . . I'm bringing Mark . . ." DC: "I am sure he won't – as he is in Rome!!" My style of joke, but not Ottoline's I fear. So tomorrow Ottoline (and I fear Philip), Mr and Mrs Turner, and Mark come to tea. The crush will be rather severe, as we are six.'[22] No account of this meeting or of Gertler's feelings on seeing Carrington again appears to have survived. But by then, in addition to his friendship with Marjorie, he had met a pretty young actress called Lydia Sherwood, and almost immediately an understanding, 'a contact', had sprung up between them.

Gertler probably met Lydia through his old patron Sydney Schiff, who was a friend of Lydia's husband, the poet and economist Lazarus Aaranson. As their friendship developed, Gertler's health, which had been poor throughout the year, began to improve, and the various beleaguering symptoms of cold, sputum, biliousness, dry cough and headaches he had suffered in October were succeeded by days of 'generally feeling well'. The respite was short-lived, however, and by January 1927 he was again suffering 'periods of Debility [and] a sort of incipient cold', owing to general exhaustion, 'many parties' and some sort of 'sexual disturbance'.[23] It is likely that Lydia was the cause of this disturbance. In his notebook Gertler recorded: (24 January) 'Agitations with Lydia'; (5 February) 'Love [? entry difficult to read] Lydia'; and (5 March) 'Trouble with Lydia – Better now'.[24]

Lydia Sherwood was the stage name of Lily Aaronson (*née* Shavelson), a contemporary of the young Charles Laughton at RADA, where she had won much praise for her portrayal of

Desdemona and subsequently made Shakespeare's women the mainstay of her repertoire. An early photograph shows her with a Louise Brookes-style bob, but by the time she met Gertler in 1926 the sleek helmet of dark hair had given way to a nest of blonde curls. Lydia had made her stage début in July 1925 as Alice in Archibald Nettlefold's comedy *Lavender Ladies* and had scarcely been out of work since. After a successful season as Olivia in *Twelfth Night* at the 1926 Stratford upon Avon Shakespeare festival she was invited to rejoin the company the following year, but before leaving she agreed to sit to Gertler for her portrait. Working with unusual rapidity, as sometimes happened when he was absorbed by a subject, Gertler had completed by the end of March a sanguine and two oils.

In the first portrait Gertler painted Lydia wearing the embroidered dress that Noel Carrington's fiancée, Catharine Alexander, had worn the previous autumn during her sittings for *The Russian Peasant Woman*, a finely executed study of an extremely striking young woman. By contrast, his portrait of Lydia was altogether sturdier. As well as employing a bolder, more robust technique, Gertler also disguised Lydia's elegantly dressed hair with a red spotted scarf, successfully completing her transformation from sophisticated actress to vital, rosy-cheeked 'peasant'. And as soon as the portrait was completed, it was snapped up the collector Sydney Schiff. Gertler's second portrait of Lydia, wearing an orange Russian shirt and a black velvet lace-up dress from her own wardrobe, was equally successful. 'I am glad you like the 2nd portrait of Mrs. A[aronson]', he wrote to Valentine, 'I also like it and so do most people – even Taylor whose judgement I value.'[25] He was already planning a third portrait when Lydia left London in early April for Stratford.

Since meeting Lydia, Gertler had seen little of Marjorie, explaining that he had been 'exceptionally busy, chiefly because most of my sitters are not models and so they stay on to tea'.[26] But Marjorie might not have accepted this explanation, for there is a hiatus in their correspondence and Gertler's letters to her do not resume until August. In the meantime Gertler was seeing a great deal of the Huxleys: Aldous and Maria were back in London and Julian and Juliette now lived in Pond Street. Sometimes the combined Huxley clan took tea at his studio, and Gertler began to plan a portrait of Julian, though he was also engaged on an ambitious portrait of Christine Mavrogordato.

In April 1927 the Goupil Gallery turned out to have been not quite 'finitisimus', when it re-emerged and offered six of Gertler's pictures at Christie's to pay off his outstanding debt. The Leicester Gallery, which had been financing him for six months with no return on its investment to date, were understandably perturbed at the idea of a sudden influx of Gertlers on the market before he had even exhibited with them. To prevent this, Gertler was forced to buy back the pictures himself, 'for prices which should not be shameful and which should at the same time clear my debt with the Goupil',[27] using £50 which he had saved 'by careful living' and by increasing his overdraft by a further £100. Fortunately, he was able to sell two of the pictures on immediately. Ottoline bought his *Egyptian Boy* for 8 guineas and Daphne Sanger bought a flower piece for £25, which she considered 'a bargain'.

At Garsington for Easter Gertler could forget his money troubles for a while. Ottoline, who had been working for some time on her memoirs, showed him a little of her manuscript and, although he felt, like many of her other friends, that she had not 'conveyed yourself with quite the full amount of passion and emotion – which I feel is contained in your nature – not quite the depth of your hunger or the variety of temperament', he thanked her for allowing him to read an extract, which he took 'as a mark of true friendship'.[28]

Only a month later Ottoline was wounded by Walter Turner's publication of his novel *The Aesthetes*, which he described as 'a philosophical dialogue modelled on Plato', with a 'faint likeness' of Ottoline in one of the central characters, but which Ottoline saw as a caricature of the Garsington circle and never forgave.[29] Unconcerned by his own little-known portrait as the painter Fiedler – he also turned up in Turner's later novel *The Duchess of Popacatapetl* (1939) – Gertler maintained his own friendship with the Turners as before.

Towards the end of April he arranged to join Lydia at Stratford for a fortnight, and she met him at the station, he told Kot, 'with such unaffected gestures of genuine pleasure, that I shall always remember [it] with gratitude'.[30] Initially, he had asked Kot to keep the visit quiet, but soon he relaxed. 'I see no reason for secrets', he now wrote. 'Other friends of Lydia['s] have been here to see her act and many are coming later, and as people only attach scandal to where there is sexual intercourse – they can in this case set their minds at ease. My relationship with Lydia is "innocent".'[31] (He nevertheless planned to tell Valentine himself of this new 'innocent' friendship, as she would be sure to find out later, which, he admitted to Kot, 'would be less pleasant than my telling her direct.')

At first Gertler did not see as much of Lydia as he would have liked, since she spent every morning rehearsing and most evenings performing; 'every night', Gertler told Ottoline, found him 'a lonely auditor in the stalls'.[32] Gertler had never seen Lydia act before, and was so nervous at the first performance that he completely failed to recognize her. Initially scornful of the other actors with whom they mixed, he quickly settled down into theatre life, 'sinking into it by degrees'. Privately, however, he continued to feel isolated, and admitted to Ottoline that he doubted whether he could ever succeed in 'building an even stable bridge' between himself and another.[33]

He and Lydia went punting on the River Avon during the fine, cold afternoons and in the mornings, while she rehearsed, he painted. He disliked the 'Shakespearean bazaar' that was Stratford but was gradually seduced by the countryside and soon began two landscapes. One, of the 'hideous' Shakespeare memorial, was no more than an exercise, but he also sketched the young John Laurie, who played Hamlet to Lydia's Ophelia and was Gertler's fellow guest in the Arden Hotel. By the end of his stay Gertler was describing his holiday as, 'very successful . . . an interesting experience mixed with delightful moments . . . Lydia had her difficulties too but both of us became happier as time went on – and she feels, as I do, that my visit was a success and our friendship genuine.'

He returned to London on 11 May to find the Morrells moving into their new house at 10 Gower Street. The dining room, he wrote to Valentine, was 'hung with nothing but Gertlers – and not bad for a wonder'.[34] Later that month, to support Lawrence (who was in Florence and too ill to attend), he and Kot loyally attended the London opening of Lawrence's play *David*, which they clapped enthusiastically to encourage the rest of the audience (which was 'besmattered with Bloomsberries'). In a letter to Valentine he wrote that his life and work were continuing 'much as usual', but in his diary (31 May 1927) he recorded 'depression due to L[ydia]'.

By August Gertler had begun to see Marjorie again, and if his relationship with Lydia had remained 'innocent', clearly that with Marjorie had not. 'I miss you – I miss the feel of your body – How comforting it is', he wrote to her from Cornwall, where he was staying with the Mavrogordatos. This did not prevent him from writing about the 'young beauties' he glimpsed on the beach. 'One a German girl – sits sunbathing in a scanty costume – she is a dark brown all over and beautifully made – I love her ample brown thighs – delicious.'[35]

Occasionally the Mavros' cosy family life made him feel 'rather apathetic and dull. I wish I was married and had two children . . . Oh! Why did I not secure myself like everybody else – in my youth – with money and a woman', he wrote to Kot.[36] But he was only half-serious, and reassured an agitated Kot in his next letter that if he had to 'live my life over again I should live it again as I have done – and to hell with security. Only when I look at the life of a married couple – I sometimes feel peculiarly isolated and anchorless, and undoubtedly there are certain things which only a woman can supply.'[37]

Although their friends and holiday trips constantly separated them, Marjorie wrote fondly of romantic nights spent in North Africa, thinking of Gertler. They even discussed a holiday together: Gertler suggested a group trip to 'get round the "scandalous" part of it'.[38] But in the end he turned down her invitation to Paris, unable to leave his work. 'What a nuisance your going to Egypt, [and] Cypress [*sic*] in Oct. I suppose you are really going?' he asked. 'I should go in Nov. if I were you because Oct. is still nice in Hampstead.'[39]

Meanwhile Lydia returned to London to prepare for her roles as Elizabeth I in *Paul I* and Sissie in Arnold Bennett's *Mr Proback* at the Court theatre. Gertler saw her again but she had already begun to fall under the spell of the charismatic Russian theatre director Theodore Komissarjevsky, who had begun to make a name for himself by introducing Chekhov's plays and the Stanislavsky system to the English theatre. In his green notebook Gertler recorded 'Depression due to Lydia. One bad night after drink' (2 December) and on 21 December the agony of 'parting and reunion with L.' Despite the 'reunion' there is no further mention of Lydia, and she disappears from his life as suddenly as she had entered it.[40]

Gertler was also seeing Carrington again. When in London, she occasionally met him for lunch or dropped in at the studio, and he still exerted a powerful influence on her imagination. In early 1928, ten days before they were due to meet, she dreamt that she was stuck on a bus that she could not stop. Unable to leave her seat as she passed her stop, she had noticed Gertler next to her, and 'pressed six pennies into his hand. And felt sad, for some reason, that I should soon be leaving him.'[41] She woke early, feeling ill with a headache and a cough.

On Tuesday 10 January Carrington arrived punctually at the studio for 4 o'clock tea. Initially she found Gertler's manner brusque, as he greeted her with '"sit down won't you" and then "Well how are you?" I feel it's a formula, that everyone is greeted in just this manner.'[42] She found it hard to believe that ten years had gone by since she went there every Sunday evening, but they talked 'without pause till six o'clock' and she inspected Gertler's pictures; 'one very lovely like an Ingres', she noted. 'But always that lack of imagination, and vagueness, which one feels if only they had, they would be so much better.' By the end, she found him 'very charming', and almost wished she saw him more frequently. 'But I couldn't help wondering', she concluded, 'if anything about oneself interested him. His own character seems to pervade everything like a smell of oranges, and one feels that one is rather far away and behind infinitive numbers of glass windows, so one's voice is almost inaudiable [*sic*].'[43]

It was certainly true that after his disastrous early attachment to Carrington, Gertler had tried to become less emotionally dependent on other people, particularly on her. By 1928, however, with Ralph Partridge in a stable relationship with a young woman called Frances Marshall and Strachey involved with a young man called Roger Senhouse, Carrington was lonely. She longed to ask Gertler 'if he ever as he looked at the room thought of some particular evening . . . and wasn't it strange now to meet with a formal handshake', and one senses her slight pique that Gertler now seemed to have forgotten their earlier intimacy. She resolved to ask him to Ham Spray for a day when the tulips were out in early spring.[44]

With Lydia gone, Gertler's relationship with Marjorie deepened, despite her frequent absences. In February 1928 she visited Italy, then Switzerland, where she stayed with her aunt until mid-April. 'Of course I miss you too', he wrote. 'What you say is true – the moment one feels intensely about another person – there's trouble –' and yet, Gertler pointed out, 'Our relationship seems to me remarkably satisfactory – we actually "get on" so well – and are – I think – a real support to each other – But the most remarkable part, I think, is that our feelings should be growing more intense, and not stopping still or dwindling.' He became conscious, he realized, of 'a sort of blank' without her, 'then I realize its your absence'.[45]

There was clearly some religious tension, however, between them. 'I did hear something vaguely about Catholicism in connection with you' Gertler wrote,

> but did not quite know how – I must say I am relieved that you yourself aren't [an] ardent Catholic – I can't understand how any grown up person with any real intelligence can still, these days, lean on any fixed dogma for

> support. There must be some fraud or self-deception in it somewhere – [but] a religious attitude to life – purely personal – is another matter – not only understandable to me – but necessary.[46]

Although Marjorie's own views of life were essentially moderate and tolerant, she was deeply attached to her Catholic aunts, and perhaps her own views were stronger than she admitted.

Gertler was by now feeling bold and confident in his work. In 1927 he had been particularly struck by Matisse, but in the end had concluded, 'it is no use I am not Matisse – He has one thing to say and I another – I am Mark Gertler "Realist" – with light and shade . . . and all that – so I've turned again today like a Whittingdon [*sic*] – to my own kind of realism [–] Thrice Lord Mayor of Realism!'[47] When in September 1927 Marjorie wrote to ask what he thought of Surrealism, his answer was dismissive:

> I am becoming more and more suspicious of 'movements' – with intricate and startling ways of painting and writing etc. I am . . . convinced that the best methods are after all the simplest and the traditional. And at the moment they are even the newest – because to attempt to be new and unusual for its own sake is so common now – that the only possible newness and freshness left is the simple and traditional.

And he disapproved of 'the innumerable "isms" that have sprung and are apparently still springing up like mushrooms everywhere'.[48]

Gertler's subsequent experiments, 'working higher in key, brighter in colour and more fluid in the contour', exuded a luxurious sensuality that is most apparent in his two portraits of Natalie Denny, both completed in 1928. Natalie was part of the Chiswick Mall circle, where her beauty made her a general favourite, and her charm shines through Gertler's rich, exotic portraits. The first portrait, *Miss Natalie Denny in an Armchair*, was completed by the end of February: 'I believe', Gertler wrote to Marjorie, 'I like it very much.'[49] The second, *Supper*, is pervaded by an almost tangible sensuality. A small table is laid with fruit, wine and flowers, more flowers pattern the cloth behind Natalie's head, a further flower is worn as a corsage and dried flowers stand in a blue vase behind the table. The pearls around her neck and the fur slung across her shoulders highlight her bare skin, linking this modern conucopia to the symbols of abundance that surround her.

When Gertler's exhibition opened at the Leicester Galleries on 10 March 1928, with his debt to the Leicester Galleries standing at £480 (sixteen months' salary), the pictures went 'like hot cakes'. By the third day twelve paintings and five drawings, amounting to £700, had been sold, clearing his debt and ensuring him another two years' contract. Despite this, he admitted to Marjorie, he felt 'depressed – and empty' on going down to see his show for the first time, as he sometimes 'loathe [d] my own pictures beyond words!'[50]

The two works that received the most attention were the portrait of Christine Mavrogordato and Gertler's final (known) portrait of Alice Edwards, *Reclining Nude*. Together they demonstrate the best and worst of Gertler's work in this decade, for the sense of design (as Roger Fry pointed out in the *Nation & Athenaeum*) that threatens to overwhelm the portrait of Christine Mavrogordato is finely balanced in the highly sensuous *Reclining Nude*. The portrait of Christine Mavrogordato baffled the critics. W. Egerton Powell in *Apollo* found the figure 'almost two-dimensional, so flat and thin it is' and complained that 'the whole figure is out of drawing',[51] while the *Times* critic found the picture 'almost comic in its disregard of pictorial depth'.[52] Roger Fry, however, believed that the painting's defects made it 'the most ambitious work in the exhibition', and he concluded that the exhibition marked 'a great advance towards that complete realization which Mr. Gertler keeps so steadily in view'.[53]

Gertler received several good notices but was particularly grateful for Fry's and, writing to thank him, explained that 'the average review of my work depresses me not because they do not praise sufficiently my pictures but because they do not understand the Nature of my Effort, and this is just what you do – for the rest – I know I'm not painting masterpieces'.[54]

Gertler spent Easter in Brighton with Taylor and the Turners, but missed Marjorie: 'Come back soon and we will have good times in London as before', he promised.[55] However, he had still made no commitment to their relationship, as a (now rare) letter to Brett shows, 'I have nothing against marriage', he wrote, 'I approve of it, in fact, but one does not somehow come across the right woman.'[56] But Marjorie would later indicate that Gertler's difficulty in finding the 'right woman' had much to do with his enduring devotion to his mother.[57]

Marjorie could be a most irregular correspondent – something that would often cause trouble between them – and alarmed by a sudden breaking off of her letters from Rapallo, Gertler sent an anxious wire, only to find out she was bored and had not felt like writing. He contrasted his own behaviour: 'when I am away and am bored and depressed – I write all the more feverishly to friends longing for their letters or some little help to my own dreariness – you just allow yourself to sink deeper into the sloth.' Nevertheless, when Marjorie became concerned at his response, he reassured her. 'You need not fear, I shall never be seriously angry with you – we have passed that stage.'[58] After her return they were much together and became a couple. Soon they were dining every Saturday with the Turners, by autumn they had formed a 'quartet', and at Christmas they all celebrated together in Brighton.

PART VII

Shadows and Ghosts

'Individuals who have to endure their own state of war – with themselves, with things important and unimportant, even with shadows and ghosts – must not desire the state of mind that the many possess. This is the price of being.'

S. S. Koteliansky to Mark Gertler, *c.* March 1919

20

A Little Death

'It is what the mystics call a little death.'
D. H. Lawrence to Mark Gertler, 23 December 1929

IN JANUARY 1929 Gertler's mother, Golda, now in her sixties, fell and broke her hip. The injury was misdiagnosed and she was prescribed exercise, which caused such a rapid deterioration in her condition that the family were advised to expect the worst.[1] Unable to accept this, Gertler found another doctor, who corrected her treatment. However, from this time onwards she was never entirely free from pain, and her movements were slow and restricted.[2] The fine, vigorous matriach Gertler had captured in his portrait only five years earlier had dwindled into premature old age.

In April Gertler and Marjorie finally brought off their long-planned trip to Paris, which he later fondly recalled as a time when they had 'tasted many sweet-nothings' together. They spent a weekend with the Aldous Huxleys, who had recently seen D. H. Lawrence and reported his deteriorating health. 'The news of Lawrence is very depressing', Gertler told Kot. 'He seems to be ill in mind and body. The picture they gave us was gruesome and preyed on my mind all night.'[3] Gertler's own contact with Lawrence was minimal now, but they would still meet whenever the peripatetic writer was back in London, and when Lawrence himself began painting he occasionally wrote to ask Gertler's advice. Although Gertler disliked many of Lawrence's later books, he defended the author's right to create them, and was saddened when *Lady Chatterley's Lover* (privately printed in Florence in 1928) was condemned as 'pornographic'. Those copies which had not been seized by customs or police were subsequently rejected by nervous booksellers, and Kot was asked by Lawrence to collect them.

At Gertler's suggestion a number of them, discreetly wrapped in brown paper, were subsequently sold on Lawrence's behalf from beneath one of the easels in his studio.

On his return from Paris, Gertler's own health began to deteriorate. He lost weight, developed a 'slight tendency to cough' and suffered 'frightful headaches' and high temperatures. Fearing a return of 'the old trouble', he stopped work, but in his journal admitted to 'a sort of Breakdown,' which was later confirmed by his doctor, who told him that it was not his lungs, 'only over strains'. By June Gertler's weight had plummeted to nine stone, and he was prescribed rest and no work for three months. 'Of course I couldn't stop for so long', he told Tom Balston in July,[4] but at length he agreed to stop for a month and return to Mundesley sanatorium. Marjorie, who was also suffering from the strain, arranged to stay in a nearby hotel, but first she took a much needed short break. 'I hope you will come back less tired – my love', Gertler wrote affectionately. 'I am very sorry to have caused you trouble. All my love Darling, From Mark.'

At Mundesley medical opinion differed as to the cause of Gertler's breakdown, and his mood swung wildly with the prevailing diagnosis. When the head consultant, Dr Pearson, suspected that Gertler's lung might be affected, he was 'nearly annihilated altogether',[5] but when the other two doctors reported an 'all clear', his mood relaxed to merely gloomy. He missed his friends and, when he heard snatches of music on the radio, pined for evenings of dancing with the Mavrogordatos in Hampstead. 'An imprisoned invalid once more', he began to wonder how many times he would be incarcerated again before he was carried out 'feet foremost'. 'If it wasn't for Marjorie', he admitted to Kot, 'I should lose courage altogether, but she makes this place just tolerable.'[6] Sometimes, he felt, she was the only thing that kept him going.

Nevertheless, Gertler's health improved rapidly. Soon he resumed his daily walks, covering as many as seven miles a day, often accompanied by Marjorie, who returned blistered and exhausted. Although Gertler clearly benefited from her company, the sanatorium discouraged 'lady friends'. He convinced them, however, to allow Marjorie to stay on, he told Ottoline, by explaining disingenuously that 'the relationship wasn't hectic or passionate' and that they were merely 'old friends of six or seven years standing'.[7]

That summer the weather was so glorious and the Norfolk countryside so beautiful that Gertler found his convalescence at the sanatorium 'hardly different to an ordinary holiday'. In the mornings he and Marjorie generally went to the beach, and in the afternoons they walked into Mundesley to have tea. But initially Gertler discouraged his other friends from visiting him in 'a place of this sort'. 'Much better', he told Kot, 'when I'm my old self again in London.'[8] On realizing that Marjorie might benefit from company, however, he wrote again, less than a week later, recommending the beautiful countryside and excellent air. The financial burden of the sanatorium fees was eased by Taylor's generous gift of £20, and Gertler soon began to feel 'clear and ready to face life again – for the first time since I broke down – and this is important', he acknowledged, 'because my breakdown this time was entirely mental'.[9]

As he gained weight, he began to look quite 'cherubic'. 'It is a curious fact that boredom is good for me physically!' he told Ottoline. 'It acts as a sort of natural bromide – also I can only eat well when I am bored – excitement kills all appetite for me . . . as for my headaches I'm afraid they are constitutional.'[10] By now he had had to accept that illness was also constitutional with him. He told Kot that his 'wretched temperament' was a bit too much for his body, and he was appalled at the thought of always having to take care of himself, 'always to be holding oneself in – never to let oneself go – to live in a box – in fact. How can one do it?' he asked.[11] He was 'simply craving to get back to my work – Oh! to be painting again! I'm dead without work.' But this time it was absolutely forbidden.

One evening Andrew Morland, the youngest of the sanatorium doctors, invited Gertler into his rooms for coffee to meet his wife, Dorothy, a pretty, intelligent woman, several years younger than her husband, who had been educated at the Royal College of Music and was interested in the arts. Morland was 'a man's man': professional, kindly, capable and dependable – qualities on which Gertler, his temperamental opposite, would come to depend heavily. Yet it was Dorothy who immediately perceived his vulnerability, and who, when introduced to Marjorie, at once observed that she was the 'rock' that Gertler clung to.

By late August Gertler and Marjorie were both in good spirits as they began to prepare for their return to London, although their happiness was clouded by the news from Switzerland that Lilian, the elder of Marjorie's two aunts, had died unexpectedly. Marjorie dreaded the prospect of going over to comfort her surviving aunt Ethel, and Mark, still fragile and prone to setbacks, did not relish the prospect of relinquishing her. Nevertheless, he left the sanatorium on 24 August with high hopes for his health and his future. There is no proof Marjorie did go to Switzerland, but the desolate language of Gertler's diary entries suggests that he suffered acute feelings of isolation after his release. It cannot have helped that almost as soon as he arrived home he was confronted by a letter from the Jewish Education Aid Society, requesting repayment of the outstanding debt he had run up some eighteen years earlier. He had managed little work since the early summer and had exhibited nothing since the London Group in January. The most he could afford to repay was £3 a quarter, but since he wisely enclosed the first instalment with his proposal, the arrangement was accepted.[12]

In early October, despite a clean bill of health from Dr Burrell, Gertler once again plunged into terrible depression. All his old fears of inferiority and failure resurfaced, now magnified and refusing to be supressed. In an effort to reason out his desperation, he seized an old diary and using the direct, confessional, self-questioning style he had adopted in his earlier notebooks, poured out 'the greatest crisis of my life': 'The trouble is – my work', he reasoned. 'What is my value as an artist? What have I in me after all? . . . That is the point. I doubt myself, I doubt myself terribly.' He had worked 'so so hard – with my very blood – and I have lived and fed upon my work – my work was my faith – my purpose.'[13] His language is that of a believer plagued by heretical doubts, and his crisis of confidence amounted to a loss of faith. He could no longer bear to visit any house that contained his pictures. For 'at once', he wrote, 'I am flooded with misery and despair'. He felt 'inferior – inferior to all!' Carrington sent a parcel of beautifully coloured plums from her garden at Ham Spray, and Gertler took them over to his studio, hoping to be inspired. Writing to thank her, he joked that 'the alternative fates await them of being turned into a picture or jelly', but in his depressed state he was unable to paint and the fate of the fruit was undoubtedly jelly.

During this period Gertler's work was not unrepresented. He showed a still life at the London Group in October and a further eleven of his works were included in the Whitechapel Gallery's winter exhibition of contemporary art. However, all of them were borrowed from Eddie Marsh's collection and centred on the years 1907–15. Only *The Servant Girl* and *Standing Nude* were recent, and even these were at least five years old. Gertler was faced with the terrifying possibility that only old age and obscurity lay ahead. Thoughts of suicide resurfaced, and in his diary Gertler bleakly contemplated death '– over and over again'. Sometimes, he wrote, it seemed the only 'logical solution'. 'For you must know', he wrote, '– and I frankly confess it – that I cannot live without that purpose – to create real work.' He saw only two stark choices: 'Either I regain sufficient faith for my "purpose" or I die.' Again he rehearsed the old arguments: could he be contented 'just to go on', to 'shrug his shoulders' and simply do his best? He could seek another profession, but what? And then he contemplated the 'dreadful selfishness' of suicide: 'Think of my mother', he told himself, '– Marjorie – and perhaps a few others!' Simply in order to try and find a way out of this maze of despair, he began to work a little in the mornings and occasionally the depression lifted. But these were periods of remission, not of normality, and the effort of working was merely mechanical. Few paintings survive from this period, and it would be some months before he felt he was producing 'real' work again.

Beatrice Campbell had once talked with him about Kot's role as a comforter and they agreed that Kot's way of comforting was to say, 'There is no comfort, you must face it.'[14] As he faced it, Gertler struggled to find the language to describe his experience. He hoped, he wrote, 'that there will be a sort of rebirth – a new sort of adjustment – something – I don't know of what nature – but I am trying my best – to treat this dreadful period as a sort of pause – interval – giving myself time to be reborn – a kind of rest'. At last in late November he went to Leicester Square to buy a revolver to shoot himself, as he had done once before, in 1921, on hearing the news of Carrington's marriage. This time the shop was open, but as he drew near his tongue felt dry with horror and he decided that in acquiring an 'easy means' he would not be giving himself a chance. At length, feeling 'cheap and degraded', he turned away in disgust.

In early December Gertler set up the props in the studio for a new still life of pomegranates in a basket, briefly recapturing the old thrill of his own 'vision', but when he compared it to that of 'a Matisse or a Picasso', he concluded that they were 'aristocrats! moving . . . high above me', and he was a mere 'rough clumsy peasant' by comparison. Whereas previously the French masters had inspired him, now they simply paralysed him, and though he had acquired the outward trappings of 'aristocracy' – clothes, culture, friends, recognition – inside he remained a 'child of the ghetto'. A visit to his family only confirmed these feelings. Gertler felt sorry both for them and for himself.

'I feel that we are in the same boat really', he wrote in his journal, 'only I know the sort of boat it is – and they don't.'

Gertler never fully recovered from this breakdown. Although he soon regained his physical strength, he could not so easily reclaim his mental equilibrium. With each attack a little piece of the old Gertler – the impudent, eager, 'ardent spirit' of his youth – was lost, and a little more of the nervous, fussy, diffident invalid replaced it. He lost confidence like a frail invalid after a fall, and emerged depleted of the larger share of his famous vitality, which he would never regain in more than short, unsustainable bursts. In his youth he had been able to balance his feelings of loneliness and depression by 'excessive sociability' out of studio hours, but since the onset of tuberculosis this outlet was closed to him, and the only possible counter-balance seemed to be the cultivation of a certain detachment. Since detachment from painting was impossible, he increasingly distanced himself from people and from life. The legacy of his breakdown dominated his state of mind for the final decade of his life.

Meanwhile the news of D. H. Lawrence, who was still in France, was grim, and Gertler and Kot consulted Dr Morland, who agreed to travel out to Bandol in January 1930 to examine him. Lawrence, who always refused to acknowledge his own tuberculosis, agreed to see Morland but maintained that it was only his 'bronchials' that were giving him trouble. 'It's not the lungs', he insisted. However, Gertler must also have written something of his own state of mind for Lawrence sympathized with his low spirits, telling him they were

> very common with men when they pass . . . or when they draw near forty. Men seem to undergo a sort of spiritual change of life, with really painful depression and loss of energy. Even men whose physical health is quite good. So don't fret. Often an entire change of scene helps a lot. But it's a condition which often drags over several years. Then in the end, you come out with a new sort of rhythm, a new psychic rhythm, a sort of re-birth. Meanwhile it is what the mystics call a little death, & you have to put up with it.

Lawrence looked forward to Gertler's and Marjorie's planned visit to Bandol in the new year and signed his letter 'au revoir'; but in fact it was goodbye. Although Dr Morland had finally persuaded him to enter a sanatorium at Vence, Lawrence's tuberculosis was by then so far advanced that there was almost no hope of recovery.

Marjorie's constancy and support during Gertler's breakdown had both strengthened and deepened their relationship, and it had been one of the factors that had saved him from what he termed the 'logical solution': suicide. Marjorie was, above all, a 'rescuer', the term used about her most frequently by both family and friends. 'I am the sort of person who always wants to help people', she later explained to Beatrice Campbell. By 1930 Gertler had become as emotionally dependent on Marjorie as he had been on Carrington and Valentine. But Marjorie, though possessed of a 'generous and serene temper',[15] was still very young and inexperienced, and given Mark's unbroken attachment to Golda she found the mothering role a difficult one.

In any case, by 1930 Gertler had still given no serious thought to ending his comfortable bachelor existence at Worsley Road, where Mrs Bruce remained in faithful attendance. Invitations from friends were still plentiful, and he spent part of January in Charmouth, Dorset, with the Mavrogordatos, both soothed and stimulated by the warm blend of John's fine, serious intellect and Christine's vivacity. However, the news that his brothers had once again been declared bankrupt not only brought the holiday to an abrupt conclusion but also impressed on Gertler the bleak outlook of the new decade.

His health was poor throughout the winter; he was still weak and coughing up blood-flecked sputum when Marjorie set out to visit Aunt Ethel in Château d'Oex, Switzerland, in mid-February. Despite her determination to take care of Gertler, her own health also would prove more fragile than either of them had anticipated. This was the first time since his recovery that they had been apart, and although Gertler had dreaded parting from her, he was looking forward to their planned meeting a fortnight later in Paris, after which they were to travel on to the Lawrences at Bandol on the Côte d'Azur and then join Walter Taylor in St Tropez.

In the meantime Gertler staved off anxiety by keeping himself busy. He spent the first week working on a flower piece, *Bouquet of Flowers*, which fully occupied his 'studio hours', had guests to tea each afternoon and spent the evenings out in company. But he was shocked by the news on 3 March that Lawrence had died of tuberculosis in Vence. Old differences now forgotten, Gertler grieved, and Lawrence's death, he told Marjorie, 'acted as another setback' to his own fragile state. Missing Marjorie badly, he spring-cleaned the studio, destroying many of his old paintings, and having the rest of the 'rubbish' removed. 'I wish one could do likewise with parts of oneself!' he wrote to

Marjorie. 'Throw away one's inner rubbish – then one really could make a new start.'

Still further complications lay ahead when Marjorie wrote to reveal the reason for her own delicate health: she suspected she was pregnant. 'I should of course do the right thing',[16] Gertler assured her, but he had already admitted that he felt 'about as much like becoming a father as standing on my head and singing in Opera' and conjured up a depressing picture of them struggling along in a poky flat with 'a little Mark or Marjorie and a pram and perhaps my pushing it on the Heath (along side of Stanley [Spencer]).' He preferred to write of other subjects with a cheerful, almost reckless, gaiety: Eve Kirk, 'the latest success in the art world', lunch and a sunny drive with Ottoline, a visit to the dentist with the prospect of having one or two back teeth drawn – anything, in fact, but the 'harrowing prospect of becoming a father', which he hoped would not be forced upon him.

But when Gertler returned from his drive with Ottoline, he found a second letter from Marjorie confirming the news of her pregnancy. This time his reply was humourless and serious, and he described the situation as 'decidedly sordid'. His own condition, he wrote, was already so 'chaotic and disturbed, that this new disaster, seems the last straw'. As ever, he spoke 'plainly': would not a termination be the best solution? 'Providing it does you no physical harm or prevents the possibility of having children later, should we want them – I believe it is quite a simple operation and France is just the country for it . . . However should your objection to an operation be very strong I shan't press it – and promise to go through with it all, as cheerfully as I can. So my dear', he finished up, 'don't worry yourself, I only wish there was more money.' Clearly Marjorie did not have an abortion, since they subsequently made plans to get married in Paris and Marjorie later admitted to Beatrice Campbell that they had only done so because she was pregnant.[17]

On Sunday 16 March Gertler set out via the boat-train to Calais to join her in Paris, and they settled uneasily at the Hôtel d'Alsace (now famous as Oscar Wilde's last address) in the Rue des Beaux-Arts. They soon learned that to get married in Paris would take more than a fortnight – Gertler called it their 'term of imprisonment' – and they both quickly grew bored. They longed to go south and arranged to do so as soon as possible after the wedding day, which was set for 3 April. Meanwhile, they were cheered by the company of the Aldous Huxleys, who were also in Paris, trying to gather together and edit a collection of Lawrence's letters, and by the artist Matthew Smith, whom Gertler 'like[d] and admire[d] very much – we get on very well and find each others company very stimulating and exciting, we talk for hours and hours!' he wrote to Ottoline.[18]

Apart from Kot, who was kept minutely informed of their arrangements, Ottoline was one of the first to hear of the impending marriage. She agreed with them both that it was good to retain a degree of 'separateness' after marriage. 'I could not tolerate a Jack and Jill sort of a marriage', Gertler explained. Instead they would both keep their individuality as before, and even planned to return to their separate rooms in London once the honeymoon was over. Marjorie, used to what she later called 'a certain liberty of action' herself,[19] wrote to Ottoline:

> I do sincerely hope that you and any other of Mark's friends will [not] think of him as less accessible than before. It makes no difference to my mind, he is just as much an independent person, with just as much a life of his own. Please never feel that I am the inevitable accompaniment to any plans you make with him. Think of us as separate beings as we always have been.[20]

However, although he had confided in Kot, Gertler had not told Ottoline everything. Like the Mavrogordatos, she had simply been told that 'so strong is the convention [of marriage] still, that after all one has to do it in the end'.[21] Most of their other friends received the news by postcard. Carrington was, somehow, not surprised. 'It was queer', she wrote to Strachey, 'for I was lying in bed thinking of him, and Cannan days, – & thinking how quickly life changes – when Flo brought in his postcard.'[22]

The wedding took place on 3 April, conducted with the minimum ceremony by the Paris consul, and was over in less than quarter of an hour. As the couple emerged arm in arm from the consulate, they were surprised on the steps by a straggle of photographers and reporters, who wired news of 'A Romance in the Art World' back to London. A smudgy black and white snap published by the *Daily Mail* was the only official photograph of the newly weds. Gertler had left telling his family as late as possible. Jack and his wife wired their congratulations, but there was an ominous wire from Harry: 'Hold over wedding, letter following'. 'Probably my relations will continue strained and unpleasant for a long time', Gertler predicted, but the atmosphere lightened when Golda phoned to offer her blessing. Ostensibly Marjorie's family seemed more 'agreeable'.

Only her 'RC' aunt offered religious objections, wanting them to remarry in a church. Gertler considered it but was afraid that if the press found out, the shock would kill Golda. It later emerged, however, that Marjorie's father was not at all pleased at the thought of his daughter's marriage to a penniless artist. When Gertler taught at the Westminster School of Art in the 1930s, Edmund Hodgkinson strongly advised one prospective student not to go there and be taught by the man who had 'run off with his daughter'. On 4 April, the day after Gertler's 'long-lived bachelorhood' finally 'expire[d] forever!' as he wrote rather ruefully to Mavrogordato, the couple travelled south.[23]

The twelve-hour train journey was less than romantic: Gertler had a sick headache and Marjorie a cold. They arrived at Bandol to find that their preferred accommodation was full and they were forced to share a room (which they always avoided, even on honeymoon) in a small, dirty hotel. The next day, however, they moved to the Hôtel Beau Rivage, which Lawrence had recommended, where they stayed for the next three weeks. Sometimes they went sightseeing, taking the bus to Toulon, which, Gertler told Mavrogordato, 'drives like a fury and shakes the entrails out of you', and they were reunited with the Huxleys. When Mary Hutchinson turned up unexpectedly, they all went out on a picnic, and in their final week they expected Taylor and his girlfriend to join them. For newly weds they spent little time alone. A beach snap shows Marjorie sportily attired in swimming costume and cap, having clearly just taken a swim, while Gertler sits beside her, fully dressed in trousers, jacket and shirt. Even on honeymoon their identities remained firmly separate.

Gertler insisted on spending part of each day alone, walking, reading Proust, or studying the snails littering the paths, an occupation that made him feel 'soothed and happy'.[24] A walk he particularly enjoyed took him along the coast towards Lawrence's former villa Beau Soleil, which was set among fields and pine trees, with its big balcony windows looking out toward the sea. It was 'beautifully placed', he told Ottoline, 'like a fairy tale', although he could not but feel 'sad at the sight of it'.[25] He also spent part of each day painting, but his slow progress indicates that he had still not made a full recovery, and by the end of April he had produced only two landscapes in oil, and 'one rather pretty sketch of a few flowers'. To Kot he wrote that the landscapes 'might be just good enough to go into my show. But I am not certain as everything I do disgusts me.'[26]

The Gertlers planned to leave Bandol on Wednesday 30 April, but a letter to Kot on 2 May indicates that they had changed their plans unexpectedly. Marjorie had suffered a miscarriage. 'Fate has taken us entirely in hand . . . and insists on making all our plans for us', Gertler told Kot ironically. 'We are not allowed a hand in it at all.'[27] They returned to Hampstead a week later. There the Gertlers resumed their lives as 'separate beings', inhabiting their separate lodgings and spending their first summer as a married couple apart. Gertler went to the Dobrées, now living at Harleston in Norfolk in July, then on to the Mavrogordatos in Dorset in August, while Marjorie joined her former Slade friend Kate Foster at Witchampton, also in Dorset, but about fifty miles from Gertler. Here she spent her days tramping over the vast open countryside and eating hearty meals to restore her health, gratified to find she had put on seven pounds in a week. Gertler, however, suffered headaches, a cough and, for several days, a high temperature.[28] 'He invariably gets run down when he takes a holiday', Marjorie noted, 'I wish I knew why'.

In October they moved into a two-roomed flat at 22 Kemplay Road, Hampstead, where Marjorie hoped Gertler would have 'more scope for new people and a feeling of greater independence'. Soon they were employing servants to do the cooking and cleaning. This was not unusual at a time when domestic help was easily available and inexpensive, but Marjorie later revealed that Gertler also had little confidence in her practical abilities. She also believed that his devotion to Golda made any other woman seem very inadequate.

The Gertlers soon began to host regular Saturday night parties, which despite offering only 'lemon tea and talk' – Kot came well primed with beer beforehand – were so popular that many of the guests could not get in and regularly overflowed on to the staircase and hallway. On these occasions the old, vital Gertler resurfaced. His conversation, Dick Carline later recalled, 'was intensely stimulating' and he remained a 'brilliant' raconteur, sometimes teaming up with Gilbert Spencer to entertain the company.[29] Henry Moore and his wife, Irina, would later become regulars, but writers – among them A. P. Herbert, T. S. Eliot, J. B. Priestley, V. S. Pritchett and the Lynds – still outnumbered the artists.

In October Gertler's contribution to the London Group – a fine mature still life, *Violin Case and Flowers* – was singled out for praise by Herbert Furst in *Apollo*, but even this failed to inspire Gertler with confidence in his forthcoming exhibition, to be held jointly with

Ethelbert White at the Leicester Galleries in November. He recorded 'much depression over show', even before it had opened, and distributed private view cards nervously among his friends.[30] 'Perhaps you may know some rich people who might buy', he wrote hopefully to Tom. 'Times are very bad and I owe my dealers a larger sum than I ever have done before – if the show is not a financial success – I shall be absolutely stuck! So if you could help I should be ever so grateful – forgive my troubling you.'[31] Tom responded benevolently by purchasing the magnificent *Sleeping Nude*, and although Gertler remonstrated that he had not expected Tom to buy anything, he also congratulated him on acquiring 'one of the most important things I've done'.[32]

Critically, the exhibition was a success. The most widely reviewed painting was *The Sisters*, a double portrait of Gertler's two nieces Renée and Sally (Harry's eldest daughters). T. W. Earp published two highly favourable reviews, in the *New Statesman* and *The Studio*, calling the whole show 'something like the liberation of a genius'. 'Every inch of Mr Gertler's painting', he wrote, 'contributes to his picture, fortifying the composition and bringing in addition its own charm. The more gorgeously such gifts are afforded us, the better. Contemporary painting is in many cases extremely clever, but there is room for something of the old magnificence as well.'[33]

Nevertheless, only eight pictures had sold by the end of the exhibition and, though he attributed this largely to 'the slump', Gertler was left with a £300 debt to his dealers. Walter Taylor offered to settle £150, and Gertler considered trying to raise the rest among his circle, but in the event the Leicester Galleries appear to have held over the debt until his next show in 1932, and on this occasion he did not have to call upon his friends.

21

Separate Beings

'I feel very torn between the two – work and you.'
Mark Gertler to Marjorie Gertler, 1932

IN THEIR FIRST year of married life the Gertlers spent much time apart. Even their financial arrangements remained separate, and bills were split evenly down the middle, as though they were partners in business rather than life. Marjorie made her now annual trip to Aunt Ethel's in Switzerland and Mark saw in the new year, 1931, with the Mavros in Dorset, where he painted a portrait of their eldest son, Nicholas.

On a rare trip out Gertler caught sight of Frank Pick, the pioneering reformer of design and transport, who had already set new standards in advertising by commissioning prominent artists such as McKnight Kauffer to design posters for the underground and the sculptor Jacob Epstein to carve the controversial *Night & Day* figures for the London Transport building. Pick was to have a similar impact on the Empire Marketing Board, for which he commissioned Gertler to produce three posters. Gertler was supposed to be hard at work on the designs in early January, and told Kot that he felt 'quite guilty' at seeing his 'employer'.[1] By the following spring, however, he had produced three large pastels, which represent spring, summer and autumn in a dizzying combination of orange, green and purple, but lack the fluidity and control of his earlier work and were never used.

By contrast, Gertler was eager to begin a portrait of his Hampstead friend and neighbour the composer Arthur Bliss. The fact that it was not a commission allowed Gertler the freedom he desired. For some time he observed Bliss as he sat at the piano, and produced a sketch much admired by the composer and his wife. Gertler's own enthusiasm can be heard in his comment to Marjorie, that since the Blisses had been so excited by the sketch, he felt like telling them to wait until they saw 'the finished article'.[2] In the finished oil Bliss's head appears as 'a pale oval rising above the piano', with the bisecting lines of the foreground anticipating the cubist still lifes of Gertler's last years. Bliss later openly regretted that he did not own the picture 'as a permanent reminder both of the artist and of those years'.[3]

In August the Gertlers set off for a month's holiday in France, stopping first at Etaples (near Boulogne) for a short stay with some old friends of Marjorie's, the Lee Hankeys. Disorganized and delayed, the Gertlers arrived late to find their hosts in a bad humour. Indeed, throughout his stay Gertler could not quite shake off the feeling that they viewed him with suspicion. Both Hankeys were artists – Lee Hankey was an RA – but Gertler found their work frankly laughable and did his best to steer the conversation away from painting, although he respected the Hankeys for their loyalty and friendship to Marjorie.

A few days later they moved on to Paris, where they could both relax, and from there to Fontainebleau. Gertler immediately envisaged a portrait of Marjorie against a background of trees, but she had arrived feeling 'flat' and soon retired to bed.[4] He did manage to paint at least two oils, one of the statue just visible from his hotel window and one of the nearby forest with its gloomy green drapery, but neither is particularly memorable. Apart from this, Gertler kicked his heels, admired the good-looking girls from a nearby American art school, and wrote to Kot and Ottoline trying to persuade them to come out and join him.

As Marjorie's health improved, she began painting a flower piece, working, Gertler observed, 'with much passion'.[5] Although she never rated her own work highly, Marjorie, like Gertler, could never envisage a time when painting would not be an essential part of her life. She also hired a bicycle and spiritedly taught herself to ride, despite the most discouraging weather. Over the next few days, as violent rain storms raged and the forest of Fontainebleau grew 'almost tropical', they marvelled at mosses 'growing ten feet high', and mushrooms climbing trees and hanging down in 'festoons like vines', and out walking they sank up to their knees in mud.[6] Once Marjorie managed to tempt Gertler out on a 'maiden' cycle tour to Barbizon, after which he immediately retired to bed himself. Somehow, it seemed to Marjorie, they were never 'down or up together'.[7]

Soon the Gertlers could 'stick Fontainebleau no longer', and moved to a small country inn near by. Gertler settled in immediately, getting drunk in the evenings with the local peasants while the Swiss patron serenaded them with his concertina, and at the end of their stay Gertler danced for them on the table and they applauded enthusiastically. It was a rare glimpse of the old ardent spirit.

It was probably at this inn that Gertler first met Sidney Bernstein, a Jewish mogul of the entertainment industry, responsible for the 'super-cinemas' of the 1920s and then engaged on building the Phoenix Theatre in the Charing Cross Road. Generous and affluent, Bernstein's weekend parties at Cowslips, his house at Mickleham in Surrey, were famous, and attracted many of Gertler's old friends, including the Julian Huxleys and even the reclusive Kot, along with new ones such as the poet Liam O'Flaherty. When Bernstein later rented Long Barn, the Sackville-Wests' fifteenth-century house in Kent, in the 1930s, the Gertlers continued to visit him there, mixing with Sean O'Casey, Charles Laughton and even Lydia Sherwood's former husband, Laz Aaronson (later Anderson), a close friend of Bernstein's. Bernstein was an excellent host: food and wine were plentiful and meals often went on for hours. To Gertler these parties must have recalled the Garsington years, and like Ottoline, Bernstein became one of his staunchest supporters.[8]

Gertler still kept up with Ottoline, who, despite undergoing an operation on her jaw for cancer in 1928, which had left her partially disfigured, had revived (on a less grand scale) her Gower Street gatherings, and still relied on her old friend to put on a 'performance' when necessary. One of his best took place at one of her tea parties in 1931, when Gertler was drafted in to entertain his long-time idol Charlie Chaplin. The two men hit it off famously, swapping stories of their East End childhoods and even imitations: 'Gertler of a pompous colonel and Chaplin of Ascot ladies trying to catch the royal eye'.[9] Ottoline was one of the few of Gertler's old friends who took equally to Marjorie and always made her feel at ease.

After their return from Paris the Gertlers decided on 'a short separation before settling in for the Winter'. Mark arranged to spend the following week with Taylor in Hastings, and Marjorie travelled down to the south of France with a friend called Dick Cotton, before going on to the Costa Dorada to stay with Kate Foster's older sister Greville in late August. By now Greville had given up her stage career and in 1929, the year in which Gertler painted an exquisite oil of her (*Head of a Girl*), she had remarried to a Catalan called Manolo Texidor, a former international long-distance cyclist who was then establishing himself as an industrialist in Buenos Aires. Gertler never became close to Greville, but Marjorie saw her as a close friend, and this was the first of the many trips the two women would make together.

Popularized by the Catalan painter–poet Santiago Rusiñol, whose studio became the meeting place for many of the leading artists of his day, the coastal town of Sitges, just south of Barcelona, was by 1930 a fashionable watering-hole for many foreign artists and intellectuals. Greville, who lived a peripatetic existence in London, Paris, Spain and (eventually) New Zealand and Australia, was drawn to such colonies, and Marjorie, perhaps already tiring of the Hampstead élite, also loved the stimulation of such a life.

Back in Britain, as soon as Marjorie was gone, Gertler missed her. On the whole, he concluded, 'I enjoyed a holiday with you more than without. I feel all the time as if there is something missing – a sort of vacuum – the links seem so feeble – with others.' It was hardly a passionate declaration. His letters to Marjorie always seemed a little stiff and formal, and perhaps Marjorie thought so too, for he added, 'I think your confidence would be fully restored if you knew how much I miss you'.[10] A temperamental incompatability was beginning to emerge and, worse still, a conflict of interests. Already Marjorie felt that Gertler resented her time spent painting or on other decorative projects, and since his insistence on servants relieved her of responsibility for the house, she had no other occupation. What she referred to as their 'bargain',[11] was the result. On holiday they had agreed that when Marjorie returned in the winter they would try for a child.

Financially, the situation remained tight, and they survived on a constant overdraft. 'Everybody is in the same boat', Mark reassured her, but somehow money seemed to slip through their fingers. Gertler, who had become accustomed to certain little luxuries, had no desire to return to the extreme poverty of his youth, and Marjorie, though she thought they should have been able to manage (more or less) on her small private income, was inclined to be scatter-brained about money – constantly losing or lending it, or making investments that turned out badly.

Following the bankruptcy of the fur business the previous year, Gertler's brothers were no longer in a position to help him (indeed, it was now Jack who needed Gertler's help, and in the early 1930s Mark sought the backing of his rich friends to finance several of Jack's unsuccessful schemes[12]). So in October Gertler began teaching two evenings a week at the Westminster School of Art. It is not clear how this appointment came about. It may have been through the painter Bernard Meninsky, who was a friend of Gertler's and had been teaching at the Westminster since 1920, or through Gertler's residual contact with Walter Sickert, who remained a close friend of Taylor's.

The school was on the north side of Vincent Square, part of the Westminster Technical Institute, and shared the top floor with the cookery school. Like the Slade, it was staffed only by practising artists, selected on the basis of the merit of their work and not their teaching ability. It was Sickert who, between 1908 and 1918, had made the school's reputation with his brilliant evening life classes. When he retired he was succeeded by Walter Bayes, one of his own circle, who held the position of head until 1934. Bayes was a painter, illustrator and critic, as well as a founder member of the Camden Town and London groups, and was himself a former Westminster pupil. He was determined to instil in his pupils 'an almost pious regard for the mechanics of picture-making'.[13] Former students recall his emphasis was 'very much on English painting in the manner of Sickert'[14] – although he placed less importance than Sickert on drawings, and regarded them as merely 'rough scribbles' or preparations for painting – students were encouraged to apply 'ponderous and deliberate dabs of paint built up layer upon layer . . . and to restore a sober industry to the painting process'.[15] 'The aim of the Westminster School of Art', Bayes wrote in his final prospectus (1934), 'is to evolve sound methods of constructive teaching which will satisfy the legitimate demands of both older and newer schools of thought.'

Greatly respected by his students – his praise was as highly regarded as it was rarely given – Bayes was nevertheless dictatorial in manner and resented any challenge to his authority. One daring student, Margaret Geddes, who defied his ban on the use of black paint in one of her still lifes, recorded that he was at first too angry even to speak to her, and later ordered her to paint out the offending colour altogether. He often caused resentment by painting on top of a student's work, which surprisingly appears to have been standard practice. Sickert too had openly reworked his students' drawings, and teachers such as Meninsky, who made his own drawings alongside students' work, were the exception. Since Bayes was a difficult man who brooked no opposition, Gertler's relationship with him was to be profoundly antagonistic. Gertler himself was a nervous and reluctant teacher, motivated purely by money, and his early lessons were not a success. But his salary, though meagre, was essential, and he admitted to Marjorie that he would be 'much grieved' if he lost it.[15]

By the early 1930s students were flocking to Gertler's classes, however, and while some male students found his manner 'adversely critical',[17] many of his female students 'adored' him.[18] He was always a nervous and never a natural teacher; one pupil noted that 'when he sought the right word to explain some point in teaching his lips sometimes trembled a little'[19] and he invariably returned home from classes tired and tense, resentful of the time spent away from his own work. His teaching methods could be as uncompromising as Bayes's own. One colleague, Adrian Hill, believed that Gertler 'demanded complete obedience – you painted one way, his way, and if you didn't comply with the rule, you left the class.' In the event, he conceded, 'very few did.'[20] Some students were irritated by Gertler's 'extreme fastidiousness, fussiness and conscientiousness', his nervous high-pitched way of speaking and his critical examination of their work. 'One did not go to his classes', one student wrote drily, 'in the spirit of an amateur wanting a little encouragement.'[21] However, the same student believed that Gertler's attitude also encouraged 'a true professionalism' in his pupils, and others believed that (with the possible exception of Matthew Smith) Gertler was 'the finest painter among the experimental artists of his generation and the one most likely to give a future lead'.[22]

Gertler's style was now as recognizable as his signature, and many students attempted to copy it. Photographs of student exhibitions at the Westminster show a proliferation of Gertleresque nudes, and more than one student recalls consciously working in Gertler's manner. When correcting a student's picture, Gertler would paint over it using the largest available brush, stroking on the paint thickly, gradually and laboriously, until his own familiar rounded forms began to emerge. He was, as Aldous Huxley would write, one of those artists who 'achieve the best of which they are capable only after much effort and repeated experiment'.[23] Indeed, one of his students observed that Gertler worked 'everything out on the canvas and painted every part of every picture three times', and he advised his students to do the same.[24]

When drawing, Gertler would begin at the top of a page and work down, his 'small, white-skinned hands, very fine-boned' moving loosely and irregularly over the paper, using a 2B pencil to build up tone.[25] The painter Diana Gardner remembered that when she joined the Westminster from the Regent Street Polytechnic, she had been taught

> to build up tone and form by using strong pencil lines from one direction, into which could be introduced other lines wherever the form needed emphasizing or modelling. Gertler at once changed this way of shading, saying that work must be more flexible and flowing. By the end of the week we were all working in Gertler's manner! The limbs of the female models, as then drawn by the class, became large and rounded and fully shaped![26]

Adrian Hill commented that Gertler 'didn't seem to mind how many little Gertlers he produced by this method.'[27]

Perhaps the most important relationship in Gertler's final decade was his friendship with the collector and publisher Thomas Balston, the last and most faithful of his father figures. Balston's difficult relationship with his own father, a prosperous but quarrelsome man, reluctant to spend money on his children's education, had made him independent at an early age. He won scholarships to both Eton and New College, Oxford, where he read classics, and afterwards supported himself by tutoring and 'literary hack work'.[28] A spell in the army during the First World War had given him a certain military precision: his tall, spare frame was always correctly and immaculately attired, and his rebellious black hair flattened into respectability. In the early 1920s Balston invested a small legacy in a junior partnership at the Duckworth publishing house, apparently 'on the strict understanding' that its 'shadowy' third partner, George Milsted – a sporting gentleman who wore a brown bowler, loud check tweeds and occasionally arrived driving a horse-drawn carriage – would be 'dead in six months'.[29] Although Milsted failed to fulfil this promise, Balston devoted all his energy over the next twelve years to building up a strong modern list, attracting such authors as Edith Sitwell, Rose Macaulay and Evelyn Waugh, which brought him into constant conflict with the more conservative senior partner, Gerald Duckworth.

Balston's sexuality was ambiguous and, according to his young friend the writer Anthony Powell, 'apparently non-existent in physical form'.[30] But to Gertler's friends it was clear from the start that, like Eddie Marsh and Monty Shearman before him, Tom 'adored' Gertler.[31] V. S. Pritchett paid mischievous yet affectionate tribute to their close relationship in his short story *The Skeleton*, written some twenty-five years after Gertler's death, and based on the character of an elderly bachelor, George Clark, and his love for the artist Jack Flitestone, 'a crude young genius from the slums',[32] who is always chasing women 'like a maniac and painting them with little heads and large bottoms, like pairs of enormous pink poppies'.[33] Flitestone is 'jealously loved' by the wealthy Clark, who is motivated by a mix of paternalism and passion. Clark never tires of Flitestone, to whom he can listen uninterruptedly 'for hours and hours'. 'For eleven years', Pritchett wrote, 'George had the sensation that he had married late in life someone who, fortunately, did not exist, and that Flitestone, was their fantastic, blindly-invented son.'[34]

Tom Balston was 'a man quite peculiarly prone to fear of scandal . . . suffering an obsession that he would be blackmailed', and often complaining of being accosted in the park, 'a form of nervousness', Antony Powell observes in his memoirs, 'that suggested a deep-rooted fear of sex'[35] – or perhaps of discovery. Gertler offered only companionship, but it was companionship of a rare order, and his vulnerability aroused in Balston a protectiveness that his own father had never offered him. Over the thirteen years of their friendship Balston became Gertler's most devoted patron and a discriminating collector.

Gertler's reliance on Balston began just as the two central female figures of his early life were about to depart from it. When, on 22 February 1932, after three years of pain and illness, Golda finally died, Gertler (and perhaps Marjorie) realized that despite years of searching for surrogates, he would never find anyone to replace her. Without Golda to hold them all together, Gertler's bond with the rest of his family was also considerably weakened.

Less than three weeks later Gertler also heard the shocking news of Carrington's death, which followed only weeks after that of Strachey, from stomach cancer, in January 1932. After learning of Lytton's death, Gertler had immediately written sympathetically to Carrington, recognizing what an 'enormous blow' it must have been, yet urging her to 'muster up all the strength and courage that is necessary to make one go on and rebuild some purpose in life'.[36] After an unsuccessful suicide attempt on the eve of Strachey's death, Carrington had spent the solitary weeks that followed writing long letters to Strachey in her diary, and parcelling up his possessions to send out to friends. She also sent the Gertlers a belated wedding present (a china ornament that she knew Gertler would admire), an appeal perhaps for Gertler's attention at this bleak spot in her life. In an accompanying letter Carrington also mentioned that she had been re-reading Gertler's old love letters. He replied that by coincidence only a few months previously he had been alone in the flat one day nursing a bad cold, when an old letter from Carrington had fluttered out of a bundle in the drawer where he was looking for a book. 'It certainly made most moving reading', he wrote in what must have seemed a coldly formal tone. Now he could look back on that 'most extraordinary and painful time' with the conviction that they had both been 'very young and probably unsuited. And it is over now and nobody's fault.'[37] It was a sober assessment of their now long distant affair that Carrington, in her emotionally precarious state, cannot have wished to hear.

On the morning of 11 March 1932 Carrington went up to her bedroom and dressed herself in Strachey's yellow silk dressing gown. After first arranging the room to make it look like an accident, she took up a gun she had borrowed on the pretext of shooting rabbits, and shot herself. Slipping on the rug, she misfired and missed her heart, but was fatally injured. It took almost six hours for her to die, but when she did so, with Ralph and Frances Partridge and David Garnett at her side, Garnett noticed the very 'proud' expression on her face.[38] In her diary was a final entry taken from a poem by Sir Henry Wotton:

> He first deceased, she for a little tried
> To live without him, liked it NOT, and died.[39]

'Nothing, I do believe', Frances Partridge later wrote, 'would have shaken her determination.'[40] Gertler's only recorded reaction to Carrington's death came in a letter to Brett five weeks later, where he merely admitted that the news had been a 'terrible shock'.[41] Immediately afterwards Balston whisked him off to Paris in style.

On the voyage out they held 'a salon' on the boat, with the Beddington-Behrenses – wealthy patrons of Stanley Spencer, who commissioned Gertler to paint Mrs Beddington-Behrens's portrait – and a 'French billionaire' among their companions. Paris was as 'hectic and stimulating' as ever.[42] They saw good works by Picasso and Braque and at the Deux Magots café Gertler bumped into the sculptor Ossip Zadkine, who invited him back for tea at his studio in the Rue d'Arras.

Meanwhile Marjorie, staying at Cookham Dean in Berkshire in the early months of a difficult pregnancy, was dismayed to find that she could no longer bear being alone. 'I used not to mind, used rather to like it, but persistent town life must have changed me', she wrote to Kot.[43] Gertler told her cheerfully from Paris that he was living 'in great luxury – taxis everywhere and [the] best food',[44] while Marjorie, miserable in her shabby rooms, survived off bread and cheese and felt increasingly isolated. She looked forward to Gertler's joining her in Berkshire after he returned from Paris and to moving into a decent hotel. However, 'in spite of my longing to see you again', he explained in his letter, 'I feel very torn between the two – work and you'.[45] Inspired by his trip, he was desperate to begin painting again and returned to Hampstead, leaving Marjorie to come back alone. In July she retired to the country for the last few months of her pregnancy, and stayed with an aunt at Hurstpierpoint in Sussex, where she admitted to feeling 'a bit dreary without Mark'.[46] He soon joined her for a few days, bringing Balston, now his inseparable companion. From then on he worked in Hampstead during the week and visited Marjorie in the country at weekends.

In Hampstead that same month Gertler finally met up with the sculptor Henry Moore and his wife, Irina, through the efforts of their mutual friend Bernard Adeney. Gertler took to the Moores immediately and when the Saturdays were restarted they were among the regulars. He was impressed by the Adeneys' huge garden, which was large enough to house a separate studio, and began to hope that he might one day have something along similar lines. However, Gertler had never seriously considered giving up Penn Studio, where he had been working (and sometimes living) for the past seventeen years, and it came as a terrible shock when he learned that the owner wished to sell and he was to be immediately turned out. As always, any sort of displacement threw him into acute depression and anxiety, which he struggled unsuccessfully to overcome when visiting Marjorie. She began to fear that he had become bored with her, and he had to reassure her that he had 'enjoyed both my weekends with you immensely. Only the fact is, I cannot get over the "tragedy" of leaving the studio. It comes over me suddenly', he explained, 'and I feel very very wretched.'[47]

He found working at home presented all sorts of problems: 'one gets in one's own light – casts shadows on the model – or one has to pop one's head round the corner of one's canvas to see the model at all', he wrote to Marjorie. He tried out various rooms in the house, even Marjorie's bedroom, and since he was concentrating on nude studies of one of his most striking young models, Jean Kemp Hogh, Marjorie was probably relieved to hear that this experiment had not been successful. More often he used the drawing room, but it was awkward for storing his elaborate still life arrangements, which sat about with little scraps of paper on them reading 'Do not touch' and made receiving visitors virtually impossible. Unused to working at home, he admitted to being 'a little hysterical as yet'.[48]

In mid-August Marjorie entered King's College Hospital for her 'lying-in'. On 16 August, after an exhausting labour, during which it was constantly feared that both she and the baby might die, she gave premature birth to a tiny boy, weighing only 3½ pounds. The baby was immediately wrapped in cotton wool and placed in an incubator, where his life hung in the balance for several days. Marjorie, still very weak after the birth, feared that he might die 'any minute', before she had even been allowed to see him. However, Gertler had seen him, she scrawled on a postcard to Balston. 'He says it's like him, which is [what] I wanted most.'[49] By the end of the month Gertler was able to report with relief that all seemed well with 'M and child'.[50] However, the traumatic birth had taken a toll on his own health, and nerves. He later told a friend that Marjorie had nearly died, the baby had nearly died and so had he. It was not an experience he wished to repeat.

In September Arthur Bliss's wife, Trudy, drove Gertler to the hospital to pick up Marjorie and the baby – now called Luke – and transfer them to a Highgate nursing home, where they remained convalescing until the end of the month. Gertler recorded the event in a quick thumbnail sketch in a letter to a friend, the only portrait he ever made of his small son.[51] Towards the end of the month Marjorie was allowed out for two hours in the evening, and able to visit Gertler for dinner, and he began to look forward to her return.

He soon found a new and 'charming' studio at 1 Well Walk, near the Heath and only £8 dearer than Penn Studio, and he and Marjorie decided to recommence the Saturday parties, albeit 'in a feeble sort of way'.[52] Gertler still had doubts about becoming a 'family' man, and secretly confessed to Ottoline that the thought of this new responsibility sometimes terrified him.[53] His relationship with the head at the Westminster, Walter Bayes, had not improved, but although he felt like 'chucking the 2½d. job back at him', Gertler wrote to Marjorie, little as the money was, it was now essential, and he forced himself to return to the college.[54]

In October he was to share an exhibition at the Leicester Galleries with Clara Kinghoffer. Despite an early and extensive 'puff' in *Studio*, which devoted several pages to an appreciative review of his career, Gertler was anxious about the exhibition's reception.[55] It included the recent portraits of Arthur Bliss, Thomas Balston and Mrs Beddington-Behrens, but otherwise concentrated on the familiar female nudes and still lifes, though he also included (possibly following his recent discussions with Henry Moore), his 1917 sculpture *The Acrobats*.

The Times picked out *The Acrobats* for special praise,[56] but *Apollo* described the show as 'frankly a disappointment', and wished that Gertler would return to his early style 'when the ideals of old masters like Chardin were still looked up to, and Post-Impressionism was unknown'.[57] More damaging still were Anthony Blunt's harsh allegations in *The Spectator*. At the age of twenty-five Blunt was already a rising star in the art world. He was particularly vitriolic about work he considered to be merely imitative, and under the headline 'Plagiarism and Vulgarity' falsely accused Gertler of displaying 'a fundamental lack of originality', singling out 'copies' of De Chirico, Derain, Matisse and even Gauguin, in Gertler's work, to support his claims.[58] By the 1930s Gertler's work did indeed reflect many of the influences that Blunt had identified. Increasingly, he made greater use of the dark, heavy outlines reminiscent of much of Gauguin's work and suggestive of the stained-glass techniques Gertler had been trained in in his youth, a fact to which Blunt referred with some derision.

Gertler does not seem to have made any response to Blunt's review. He remained generally dismissive of all reviewers (except Roger Fry) and did not expect to be widely appreciated. 'I do not think that isolation matters', he had told *The Studio* back in September. 'An artist cannot look for a wide circle of appreciation, for, as with music and poetry, the number of people who are developed in response is naturally limited.'[59] Nor did Blunt's review appear to affect sales. By the end of the show about a third of the pictures had sold, and Gertler called it 'a great financial success'.[60] It was, however, to be his last commercially successful show, for the tide of criticism had turned against him, and his old admirers were being replaced by a younger generation, to whom his work seemed merely imitative and repetitive.

22

The Pennies Stopped

'The little boy ran after the showering pennies as they bounced in the air, and rolled, span, and settled. He danced from penny to penny and . . . silver was thrown among the pennies to keep him dancing, but at last he was exhausted, . . . and the men hurried on.'

Gilbert Cannan, *Mendel*, 1916

GERTLER AND MARJORIE both had flu in the new year. Terrified that Luke, who was not a strong baby, would catch it, they employed a nurse to tend to all of them. 'But miraculously enough', Gertler scrawled on a note to Balston, the baby remained 'hail and hearty . . . Luke is marvellous', wrote his proud father. 'Happy and chirpy – The nurse says – she's never seen such a "good" baby.'[1]

Once recovered, the Gertlers took up their busy social life. Many acquaintances now came from the London Group and by March 1933 Gertler was telling Balston that he thought the Henry Moores 'a valuable asset' to their regular circle.[2] Moore was one of the few Gertler thought 'worthwhile', but their relationship, though intriguing, remains elusive. Gertler refers often to meetings, dinners and letters passing between them, but none of their correspondence has yet come to light, and there is no way of judging what the friendship meant to the rising young sculptor. Over thirty years later, when Gertler's letters were being prepared for publication, Marjorie wrote to Moore to ask if he could suggest someone suitable to write an introduction, and his only reply was that he could not.

It was perhaps through Moore that Gertler also met the poet and critic Herbert Read, whose influential book *Art Now* was published in December 1933, and Reginald Wilenski, a promoter of the modern movement in art, who also held very entertaining parties. Another new acquaintance in this period was the critic Arnold L. Haskell, a regular patron of the Leicester Galleries, who included one of Gertler's more recent drawings, *Woman with Mandoline* (a study of his dark-haired model Celia Dennis), and a paragraph on his 'noble use of drawing' in *Black on White: An Arbitrary Anthology of Fine Drawing*. And when Haskell purchased one of Gertler's works in 1933, he also gave him a free Maillol drawing, a gesture that both delighted and embarrassed Gertler.

Since Golda's death Gertler's ties with his family had slackened, but in early April he gave up an invitation to Balston's to spend Passover with them and he continued to try and help Jack. He also became involved in two specifically Jewish projects in 1933. On Tuesday 2 May he attended a reception in London to present his painting *The Coster Family on Hampstead Heath* (which had remained unsold) to the mayor of Tel Aviv for the new Museum of Palestine. He also produced a cover design, unique among his work, for *The Friday Night Book*, an anthology of Jewish literature, religion, music and cookery published by the Soncino Press. It shows a characteristically solid, simplified female figure standing in prayer before a menorah. Her massive arms and overall bulk recall the strength of his pre-war Jewish portraits but also anticipate the series of neo-classical studies that Gertler created over the forthcoming years, centred on one of his most striking female models, Jean Kemp Hogh.

Gertler and Marjorie's father continued to regard each other with distrust; 'Mr H. is a queer fish', Gertler told Balston.[3] However, the Gertlers' financial situation had improved a little after the success of the last show and since Balston and Philip Morrell had become joint trustees of Marjorie's investments. Now the Gertlers began to negotiate for the purchase of a house a few streets away in Haverstock Hill (for the grand sum of £200). It is not clear how much Edmund Hodgkinson contributed to this purchase, but certainly his assistance was vital. From now on Balston in particular would be an intermediary between Gertler and 'Mr. H.' whenever the contentious issue of money arose.

The Gertlers moved to 53 Haverstock Hill on 19 May. It was their first house and they were proud of it. Gertler described the drawing room in one of his letters to the poet Ralph Hodgson, a former Hampstead neighbour and 'Thursday' now living and working in Japan, as 'really a splendid affair',[4] and they were able to recoup some of their expenses by letting a furnished room in the basement and by letting out the garage.

Later in May Kot's household at Acacia Road was devastated by the sudden death of his landlord and close friend Michael Farbman, whose widow was left virtually penniless. Kot, who had practically adopted the Farbman family as his own, immediately sank into one of his 'black moods', which Gertler, despite offering sympathy and support, was unable to penetrate. Kot soon resumed his place at the 'Thursdays' but, 'nervously overwrought' with grief and worry, remained on the verge of breakdown.[5]

Although Kot's friendship was still important to Gertler, his paternal role was increasingly usurped by Tom Balston. By 1933 Balston had his own weekly supper date at the Gertlers' and often took Gertler to dine at the Café Royal. Marjorie was sometimes included on their nights out, but usually met friends of her own, particularly Greville when she was in England. In any case, Balston clearly preferred to see Gertler alone, and by 1934 the two men had become inseparable. When Balston went away Gertler missed him very much, and it was now Tom, rather than Kot – or even Marjorie – to whom Gertler wrote that there were very few people with whom he felt 'any real contact'.[6]

In mid-July Marjorie left for a month's holiday in Tossa de Mar, on the Costa Brava, with her Aunt Ethel, Greville Texidor and her family. The Texidors' marriage was already in difficulties, and among the new arrivals in Tossa that summer was a German refugee called Werner Droescher, who eventually became Greville's third husband. Gertler, meanwhile, remained in Hampstead with nine-month-old Luke for a fortnight (before he was sent to stay with friends), and in a letter to Marjorie wrote a wonderfully tender description of him:

> This morning I walked into his room, just as he was falling asleep. It was a fascinating sight. His eyes were already closed, but his little white arms were still waving about gently in the air, not yet having found, as it were, a place for themselves. At last they slowly descended to rest. He must have been awake only a moment before. He is looking wonderfully well; both his lower teeth are now out and the two upper starting. But he seems to get no more pain.[7]

He also admitted tellingly that while Albert (their maid Elsie's husband) was 'good technically' with Luke, Elsie was 'better humanely, because she talks to him, and that is what he loves and needs. I'm afraid I am not good at it myself.'[8]

In late July Gertler set off for Scarborough to stay with the poet and scholar Lord Derwent, who had commissioned Gertler to paint his portrait after seeing those of Bliss and Balston at the Leicester Galleries.[9] The Derwent estate, Hackness Hall, was a beautiful eighteenth-century mansion house full of 'efficient, well-behaved old-masterish portraits' and 'very special' furniture. Even the surrounding land, Gertler wrote to Kot, looked as if it had been 'designed by God expressly for a lord!' Gertler took an immediate liking to Derwent, whom he described as a 'genuine and a very decent young man' who was also a great admirer of D. H. Lawrence.[10] But his letters home were soon peppered with complaints: about commissions ('dreadful and degrading work'[11]) and the suffocating effect of his tasteful surroundings ('I should die of tedium if I had to live here six months'). Pencil and pastel sketches show that he did not skimp on the preliminaries, but the final oil was completed at top speed in under a week. Good manners dictated that Gertler stay on at Hackness Hall for the weekend, but after enduring a dull lunch with people who had discussed members of the royal family, he told Balston, 'as you or I might . . . Mavro or Christine,' he preferred to 'skip off'.[12] He was longing simply to immerse himself in work, but both he and Marjorie were worried about Luke, who had not put on any weight for three months, and he agreed to join them both for a week's holiday before returning to his studio.

Although he had no exhibition at the Leicester Galleries in 1933, Gertler's work was once again on show there in September, when, somewhat bizarrely, he was one of a dozen well-known British artists (the others included Nevinson, Edmund Dulac, Laura Knight, Philip Connard and George Sherringham) who entered an open competition organized by Cadbury's to come up with a new chocolate box design.[13] Gertler's willingness even to enter shows his awareness of the fashionable move towards a joining of 'Art and Industry', the buzz phrase of the early 1930s, first used in *The Listener* by Paul Nash and Herbert Read, who was now a regular at the Gertlers' 'at homes'.

Towards the end of the year, however, the Gertlers decided to give up their 'Saturdays' since they had become too much work, and only the 'Thursdays' struggled on. Gertler took over an extra afternoon's teaching from his old companion Adrian Allinson in January 1934, and gradually the Westminster became a larger presence in his life.

One of his new pupils, Margaret Geddes, recorded in her diary that when Gertler took over he seemed 'nice but quite revolutionary',[14] but a week later she had already began to find him 'very odd – [he] throws colour about without much purpose it seems to me'.[15] This was the beginning of a tense working relationship between teacher and student that was never fully resolved.

Geddes's diaries also make clear the continuing antagonism between Gertler and Walter Bayes. Since both tended to paint on top of students' work, Geddes found herself and her painting literally caught in the middle, and soon she was writing: 'Bayes got going on [my picture] at last! and Gertler in the afternoon, so now it's a muddle.'[16] Clearly, however, Bayes won and two days later Geddes noted that the 'last traces of Gertler [had been] now removed (on Bayes' advice)'.[17] However, when Robert Kirkland Jamieson took over from Bayes as principal later that year, he asked Gertler to keep a personal eye on Geddes, believing her to be 'a student of some promise', and Gertler became a significant influence on her early work.[18]

Jamieson, though an unexceptional painter, was an excellent head, and a total contrast to Bayes. He typified the open, tolerant and encouraging attitude of the Westminster in the late 1930s, when teachers as well as students were encouraged to develop their own individual style. Everyone worked 'seriously and extremely hard', one of Gertler's colleagues, Ernest Fedarb, remembered. 'Art was changing rapidly. New ideas were in the air and we wanted to be up with these changing approaches but at the same time to prepare students for the more conventional and academic studies.'[19] Jamieson even initiated 'Advanced Art' classes to explore new movements in art, such as abstract painting.

Gertler's own painting in this period remained centred on the female nude, which – unlike his desultory involvement in 'Art and Industry' projects – remained at the creative and emotional heart of his work. In 1934 Jean Kemp Hogh, a young, red-haired schoolfriend of Gertler's former landlady's daughter, sat patiently for the fifty-seven one-hour sessions it took to complete *The Mandolinist*, one of Gertler's finest late neo-classical studies. He produced a series of preliminary drawings and paintings for the picture (many are complete in themselves), and Jean recalled that his methods were very precise. First, 'he would decide on the pose he wanted', then, having positioned her limbs, he began by roughing in a charcoal figure, before adding general colour and then returning to fill in particular portions, 'say an arm or a leg or face or hair – in detail all through'. He was 'considerate throughout', and made it clear which portion he was not working on, so that Jean could move those parts of her body which became stiff, sometimes loosely tying a limb to save her the effort of supporting it.[20] In the finished painting the reason for this method becomes obvious, as Jean's right leg cuts straight across the middle ground of the picture, effectively dividing it in two.

Gertler was beginning to simplify and intensify his original vision and his late works magnificently attain the 'monumentality' that had sometimes eluded him in the 1920s. In *The Mandolinist* this monumentality is achieved not only through the solid bulk of the figure, but also through the equally solid application of paint in thick layers, scraped and moulded with the palette knife. 'If the Post-Impressionists were the great liberating event' in Gertler's life, Clive Bell observed in 1941, 'the next important was the discovery of the palette knife.'[21] Quentin Bell saw a specific connection between this new technique and that which Gertler 'had so magnificently done in sculpture'.[22] Henry Moore may have been an influence, but there is also a conscious debt to Picasso.[23]

The Gertlers were looking forward to a carefree summer in Spain. The Texidors had found them accommodation in Castelltersol, a remote village in Catalonia, and their young Welsh nursemaid Nan was coming along to look after Luke. But these hopes seemed dashed when the couple discovered that Marjorie was pregnant again. 'The prospect of having a second child so soon and having to go through another possible bout of poisoning', Gertler confided to Balston, 'was very depressing.'[24] The couple endlessly discussed the possibility of an abortion, but Marjorie was understandably 'rather nervous and so am I', Gertler admitted. Even if they decided to go ahead, where would they find the money? Although they managed to persuade the doctor to halve his usual fee, the total sum required still came to £40. They already owed the doctor 9 guineas, had just paid out nearly £30 for the holiday, and their position at the bank was, as ever, 'deplorable'. A solution occurred to Gertler. 'I thought that while in Spain you might let me do that profile portrait of you which you know I've been wanting to do for some time', he wrote to Balston. 'If you could possibly afford £25 it would be a wonderful help.'[25] Tom mailed him a cheque by return of post.

Balston had troubles of his own, however. At Duckworth he and the main partner, Gerald Duckworth, were forever at loggerheads over the author list. Balston found Duckworth lazy and obstructive, while Duckworth resented Balston's preference for modern authors. In June 1934, at a directors' meeting to discuss finances, a furious row broke out between them, and in a surprising finale the shadowy third partner, George Milsted, put in an appearance and supported Duckworth. Balston was forced to resign and suffered a nervous breakdown as a result.

Gertler expressed a polite interest in Balston's troubles, but was wrapped up in his own domestic crisis. He and Marjorie discussed the 'baby problem' endlessly, unable to make up their minds until at last, the day before they were due to leave for Spain, Marjorie went off by herself and had an abortion. Gertler was immensely relieved: 'All is well – she seems to feel nothing at all (except hungry),' he told Balston, 'and looks radiant! So now we really ought to have a first class holiday.'[26] Yet Marjorie was too weak to travel and was forced to stay behind to recover, while on 7 July Gertler and Balston set off for 'the wilds of Spain'.[27]

They found it even wilder than they had imagined; their accommodation, the Casa Sala, was a primitive house in the middle of Castelltersol, which 'squirm[ed] with children, dogs and cocks', its narrow streets reverberating with the noise.[28] There was no electric light and very little water. Marjorie set out on the 12th, and arrived in Spain with Luke, his nanny, Aunt Ethel, Greville Texidor, her husband, Manolo, their daughter Cristina and Cristina's nanny. 'The whole show was very nearly wrecked by this large number of varied people', Gertler reported to Ottoline. 'At first everybody quarrelled and got on each others nerves', Marjorie had a relapse and retired to bed 'miserable and ill – and things for a while looked very black'. Eventually the Texidors decamped to another villa and at once everything settled down. Marjorie recovered, light and water miraculously appeared, and they all decided to eat at the Hôtel Prudence opposite, to save 'trouble with servants'.[29] Luke flourished, and Gertler was amazed to compare the 'very lively noisy excitable little chap with curly hair and Blue eyes (very much admired in these parts)' with the 'tiny shrimp wrapped in cotton wool' he had been presented with at King's College Hospital only two years previously. At the local fiesta Luke, who was a great favourite in the village, was the centre of attention and as he ran about laughing, 'the people threw confetti at him' which 'showered from his head like golden rain . . . [and] caused great excitement among the audience'.[30]

Every evening they went to the local café, where Gertler enjoyed the company of the local peasants, and everyone became 'lively for about 6d. . . . every night'.[31] On these occasions Gertler became instantly alive and full of the old vitality, juggling with tapas from the table, standing on his head on an impossibly small table, and bringing the café alive with dancing and laughter. 'The peace and simplicity of the life here attracts me very much', he explained.[32] The beauty of this place is that it is so genuine. As Frieda [Lawrence] would say the people are so Real here, and the Landscape is REAL.'[33] During the day Marjorie and her party took daytrips or went swimming, while Gertler spent the languid days making pastel studies of the landscape, glorying in the 'actual texture' of this new medium and comparing its effect to fresco. Balston, whom Gertler was teaching to paint, laboured at watercolours by his side, displaying a characteristic 'obstinacy of purpose'.

Gertler returned to Britain with at least four oils from the holiday – *Stormy Sea*, *The Tent*, *A Village in Spain* and *The Monastery, Castelltersol* – one watercolour of the cemetery and a few pastels. He also completed the tiny (8½ × 6 inches) commissioned profile portrait of Balston, in which he captured something of his friend's nervous animation in its uneven surface, scraped and layered with a palette knife. Gertler admitted to Kot that he was reluctant to return to London with 'all its complexity and servant problems, telephone calls and above all, my show, which I dread'.[34] Behind this dread lay the knowledge of his own declining reputation, coupled with the fear that his powers of originality were beginning to wane and that perhaps the younger critics who detected only repetition in his work were right.

In mid-September 1934 Gertler and Balston travelled through Spain, visiting Madrid and Toledo, where they saw 'numbers of beautiful things', before returning to Britain. In a copy of *The Times* he had brought in Barcelona, Gertler read with dismay of Roger Fry's death. 'What a loss!' he wrote to Mary Hutchinson, 'I daresay you feel it very much.' He was saddened also by the thought that his forthcoming exhibition would be 'the first show of mine not seen by Roger'.[35] That autumn as a tribute to Fry's influence he painted a still life entitled *Homage to Roger Fry*.

They reached London on 23rd September, and thought everything looked dirty in contrast to the warm colouring of Spain. Gertler's relaxed mood evaporated and was replaced by the familiar panic about his show. Marjorie meanwhile stayed at Castelltersol for another month, and then went on to Tossa, which by the summer of 1933 had already become a 'refuge point for those in opposition to Nazism'. It was also – like Sitges – a colony for artists, writers and intellectuals, and favoured by Marc Chagall (who called it 'Blue Paradise') and other painters, including Masson, Brignoni, Frances Hodgkins and George Kars. Kars asked Marjorie to pose for him, as did 'an enormous sculptress called Madam Mica Micou'.[36]

Since Gertler had been well and happy when he left Spain, Marjorie was rather surprised to receive his 'extremely reproachful' letters from London, but, as she wrote to Balston, 'one reviews the woes and worries of London rather philosophically from this distance'.[37] When Gertler did not hear from her in almost a week, he became acutely anxious, especially when he heard of an outbreak of political violence in Barcelona. 'Numbers of people, including your father', he wrote to Marjorie in alarm, 'have rung up to find out if you and Luke are still alive!'[38]

The real trouble of course was his show. Although Gertler told Sidney Bernstein that his latest pictures were 'the best lot I have so far produced',[39] when the show opened, they proved 'generally very unpopular'.[40] Hampstead in the 1930s was home to a new generation of Modernists, a 'nest of gentle artists', as Herbert Read famously described them, whose reputation began rapidly to overshadow Gertler's own.[41] In 1933 a group of eleven artists, architects and sculptors had united under the banner Unit One, and their first and only exhibition had received extensive press coverage.[42] The group's name had been chosen, their spokesman Herbert Read later explained, to reflect the idea that 'though as persons each artist is a *unit*, in the social structure, they must, to the extent of their common interests be *one*'.[43] From Castelltersol in 1934 Gertler had written to the poet Ralph Hodgson:

> Unfortunately there is nothing new about any of it – the artists of the 'group' are nearly over forty and have suddenly decided to become more 'advanced' than before and in order to achieve this revolution [have] adopted formulas that are already pretty stale on the continent – But the English Public, always so ignorant on this matter – Became very excited and imagined they were confronted with something quite momentous![44]

Unit One brought prestige, however, and though its influence as a movement was short-lived, its most talented members, among them Ben Nicholson, Barbara Hepworth and Henry Moore, went on to make international reputations. But Gertler was comparing them to the likes of Paul Klee, who 'has been going strong for years in Germany – He has not become "advanced" to order', and to the Spanish Surrealist Joan Miró:

> These people are trying to do something different to the 'purely Plastic' picture. It is inevitable for artists to act and react[,] they are trying to get something other into their work than 'pure forms'. But really apart from the stimulating effect these movements have on young painters these changes are of very little importance.[45]

Gertler's friendship with Herbert Read appears to have flourished in spite of his views on modern painting. 'I have met him recently and we have become friendly', he explained to Ralph Hodgson. 'I like him very much – I think he is a nice man, and very serious – only his instincts for Painting aren't very strong – the Result is, that he works a bit too much from the head and is generally too theoretic. All the same I read his writings with interest.'[46] However, Gilbert Spencer claimed in his memoirs that the change in Gertler's personality in his last years coincided with his friendship with Read and his move from Haverstock Hill: 'All was sadly changed. The drawing-room was cold and large, with heavy curtains and gold chairs, and instead of the old group of friends, there sat Herbert Read, whose book *Art Now* I found unreadable.' Spencer also felt that Gertler's talent had 'decreased as his affectations increased. and he began chasing false gods'. He even claimed that on one visit to Gertler's studio in the 1930s he had been shocked to find the artist 'rubbing grease over his pictures and flicking at them with a silk handkerchief . . . then standing back affectedly to look at the result. Poor Mark', he concluded. 'Unhappily his early gifts were not sustained and when he felt his fame was slipping, he grasped at the straws offered him by *Art Now*.'[47] Ironically, Gertler was no more acceptable to the old guard. During this period for the first time he allowed his name to be put forward for nomination as a Royal Academician, but he was never elected a member.[48]

The critical reaction to Gertler's 1934 show was largely negative. Anthony Blunt retracted some of his previous comments, concluding that Gertler was 'unpleasant but serious',[49] but Geoffrey Grigson, who became famous for what he called 'savage use of the billhook', did not scruple to use it on Gertler, accusing him, under the heading 'Art-Liberalismus' in *The Bookman*, of painting 'like the son of a Liberal

Rechabite M. P. who has devilishly discovered the taste of Australian wine. Ruddy boldness and nudity plump out from the walls, wicked belles partly of the Maillol family through Frank Dobson . . . the quality of Mr. Gertler's giantesses is a sub-vegetative or rubber quality . . . He achieves a kind of inflated, rather than inspired, vitality . . . It is an art talented, tasteless and provincial.'[50]

Gertler tried to stay buoyant, claiming that his show had ended 'fairly well',[51] but even his dealers had begun to lose confidence in his appeal and immediately proposed reducing their monthly payments from £35 to £20. To make up the shortfall he arranged to increase his teaching hours at the Westminster but by the end of the year was also forced to sacrifice his studio. Having finally realized that his monthly advances were no better than 'borrowing money at 33⅓%',[52] he cancelled his arrangement with the Leicester Galleries, and though he had no trouble persuading Duncan MacDonald, the manager of the Reid & Lefèvre Gallery, to put on his next biennial show (scheduled for 1937), in the meantime he was forced to struggle bravely on without the customary advance.

PART VIII

Two Creatures

'There are two creatures in me – the painter and the man.
It is the painter . . . that causes difficulties.'
Mark Gertler to Thomas Balston, 27 September 1938

23

A Sort of Madness

'The last few days I have been suffering from an attack of awful depression; . . . I get these fits – like a disease . . . It's a sort of madness.'

Mark Gertler to Carrington, 5 December 1918

GERTLER'S ADDRESS BOOKS and diaries from this period are filled with the names of 'useful contacts', which he now worked harder to establish and maintain. One of these was with Agnew & Sons, whose senior partner, Sir George Agnew, he had invited to dinner in April 1933 with the painter Keith Baynes and his companion Louis Hoare. In the early 1930s Agnews had usually included examples of Gertler's latest work at their annual exhibitions, but after this they offered him a dedicated space for a series of his latest drawings alongside their annual exhibition of drawings and watercolours in February 1935.[1]

Gertler's original selection was almost twice as large as the number eventually exhibited. Only when he arrived to inspect the hanging did he discover that 'some of the latest and best' of the drawings had been judged too 'shocking' by Agnews' elders. Gertler's confidence was shaken, and he even began to regret, he told Tom Balston, agreeing to show at Agnews at all.[2] In the end Balston managed to persuade the dealers to include a further four drawings, but since this happened just two weeks before the end of the show it made little difference to sales, which were slow.

By then, however, the Gertlers had other worries. Luke, despite his progress the previous summer, the excellent care of his new young Welsh nursemaid, Nan, and his generally sunny nature, was still underweight. After several medical consultations it was discovered that complications arising from his premature birth had left him with a urino-genital disorder, which needed surgery. Exhausted by the responsibilities of marriage and fatherhood and by worries over money and his work, Gertler began to grow 'rather nervous of a breakdown'.[3] On his first visit to the hospital after the operation he found Luke having his first dressing changed and was 'completely unnerved' by his screams. 'Don't get married and have children', he advised Balston. 'Life is quite hard enough without the two extra lots of worries and complexities that a wife and child provide – at the moment I feel I shall never paint in peace again.' He 'hate[d] like poison the least little pain Luke must suffer', and in the event the whole process was 'much more complicated and painful' than the Gertlers had originally been led to believe.[4] This was in fact only the first in a series of harrowing operations that dominated Luke's early childhood, and added a serious strain to his parents' marriage.

Perhaps anxious to recapture the spirit of their last holiday, the Gertlers began to look forward to a second summer in Spain. This time there would be no Aunt Ethel and no Manolo. The Texidors had now separated and Manolo was living in Palma de Mallorca, while Greville remained in Tossa with Cristina and Werner Droescher, the German refugee who would become her next husband. Gertler planned to travel alone some weeks after Marjorie, and Balston was to join them in July.

Marjorie arrived in Castelltersol in June with Luke, Nan, Greville and an artist friend called Eric Hiller, whom she described in a letter to Balston as 'quiet and likeable'.[5] They settled immediately in the Casa Pineda, a beautiful sixteenth-century villa with dramatic stone staircases and ancient courtyards. Although romantic, it was less immediately comfortable than the Casa Sala, where they had stayed the previous year. For the first week the electric light failed unaccountably, leaving them in pitch darkness at night, and there was continual trouble with the water supply and toilets. But the villa was 'bright and sunny as to bedrooms', Marjorie wrote to Tom, and 'cool and very easy to run'.[6] The weather and setting were beautiful, and she was able to relax and enjoy being with friends of her own.

Since Marjorie's departure Gertler's depression had deepened, and when he set out by himself on 2 July he was already in a state of acute anxiety. After the crossing to Calais, he quailed at the thought of sharing a carriage overnight with 'perspiring strangers', and bargained for a sleeper at the Quai d'Orsay, eventually securing a carriage to himself. 'Travelling is a matter of money', he observed to Balston. 'If you can afford to spend enough money on it, it becomes quite simple.'[7] He arrived next day in a nervous state, which was not relieved by the primitive conditions at the villa. He immediately sat down and wrote a 'very gloomy letter' to Balston. 'The worst part is my own mood', he explained, 'I am going through an awful time.' He felt 'fundamentally upset and unhappy' and hinted ominously, 'I don't know how it will all end.'[8] By contrast Marjorie and her friends seemed to be experiencing 'an extasy [*sic*] of happiness'. At night he had difficulty falling asleep, and awoke frequently, haunted by fears.[9] One night he woke Marjorie twice, fearing he was going mad.

During the day Gertler tried to paint from his bedroom window, but he preferred the landscape at sunset, which brought out 'the gold and the sculpture' of the setting. He conceded to Mavrogordato that 'one can't paint for ever from one's window',[10] but he seldom painted outdoors, as he disliked watercolours and found oils irksome to carry in the heat. He experimented again with pastels and from this time on was never without paper and a set of pastels by his bed. After the first week his moods and headaches receded and he began to feel well enough to join the others for cocktails in the evenings. In mid-July Balston arrived with his brother, who stayed for the first week, but although Gertler was pleased to see him, Tom almost inevitably rowed with the other guests and left after only a month. Gertler struggled to finish two further pictures, including a study of a local monastery, but he could not recover his spirits.

His relationship with Marjorie deteriorated rapidly. He developed an uncontrollable dislike for Hiller, who constantly hung around her and (Nan was convinced) sponged money off her. Hiller also sunbathed naked in the courtyard and 'whenever I have to say a word to Marjorie there, and catch sight of his large, swollen[,] oiled and purple private parts, I feel sick for hours!' Gertler wrote to Balston with distaste, referring to Hiller as the 'little homo'.[11] He became convinced that Marjorie had feelings for Hiller which had come between them, and after his experience with Carrington and Strachey the fact that Hiller was homosexual would have done nothing to reassure him.

Marjorie finally 'revolted', causing a lasting rift between herself and Balston, who clearly felt that it was her duty to support Gertler. A year later she wrote to Balston that she had thought that 'it was no good submitting beyond one's capacity for generosity, or one's nature would react with hatred and bitterness . . . it was better to insist on running one's life on a 50/50 business . . . [and] this would be for the good of both in the long run.'[12] Gertler was secretly counting the days until his departure; no doubt Marjorie was too, and he stayed in Castelltersol only to celebrate Luke's third birthday on 16 August. What Gertler described as merely 'a sort of mood – a storm',[13] seems to have been a growing realization on Marjorie's part of their basic incompatibility, and some sort of rebellion against the constrictions of her life with him.

Gertler had other 'woman troubles' outside his marriage. Despite his distant manner, his good looks had not gone unnoticed by his female pupils at the Westminster, and one colleague remembered having to bundle him down the backstairs when a certain girl who had a crush on him was seen to approach. Nan recalled girls following him home and hanging around outside the house until shooed away by herself or the cook.[14] As soon as Gertler returned home from Spain, one girl in particular, whom he called 'the mad girl' – 'she is literally madly in love', he explained to Mavrogordato – began to stalk him.[15] One afternoon she turned up at the house when he was alone and flung herself upon him, refusing to leave the house. Gertler lost his nerve and 'began to beat and kick her out, but she kept returning through some window! Just like a nightmare.' Finally, he called the police, who took the girl home, but she returned again at 1.30 in the morning. 'For a few days', Gertler wrote, 'life was hell, but ultimately I interviewed her mother, and for many days there has been no sign – phew!'[16]

When Marjorie returned matters did not improve between them and Gertler admitted that his nerves were often 'at snapping point'.[17] They were both at a loss how to resolve the situation. 'Our lives are really very much involved and mixed up together', he told Balston, 'and an immediate parting is really very difficult – so there is nothing to do but to struggle on and hope for some changes to happen.'[18] Luke was about to undergo a second operation, and their anxiety about him added to the strain. Fortunately, the second operation proved less traumatic. By mid-November Luke was making good progress and Marjorie took him to the country for a fortnight to recuperate. But as winter set in Gertler's general health was so poor that he was forced to consult a lung specialist. The lung was pronounced clear, but he continued to suffer from strained nerves and headaches, and at Christmas retired to Taylor's at St Leonards on Sea, relieved to escape 'all the complexities of London life'.[19] Sometimes he fantasized about establishing a new life on the south coast near Taylor, with just a studio and 'a pleasant companion'.[20] Clearly, he no longer felt he had such a companion at home.

Gertler stayed on at St Leonards into early January, before returning to finish a pastel portrait of Maire Lynd, which he planned as a pair with a portrait of the Herberts' daughter Jocelyn. It was not exactly a commission, but he did hope that the Lynds might buy it. Marjorie made an effort at reconciliation, but Gertler remained unsure of her real feelings, and by tacit agreement they just 'let things drift for the time being'.[21] He was also drifting in his work, distracted by the need 'to make tea parties etc in order to sell pictures', and for the first nine months of the year he exhibited nothing.

In March 1936 the financial burden was unexpectedly eased by two windfalls. First, an admirer of D. H. Lawrence offered Gertler £60 for one of the writer's letters[22] – 'a godsend', he admitted to Ottoline – and second, the Gertlers were offered between £50 and £100 in compensation for swift removal from their house in Downshire Hill, which was due to be demolished in June. They had already begun house-hunting, he wrote to Ottoline. The upheaval was unsettling, but he tried to remain calm by cultivating 'the necessary detachment', which seemed to him 'the only way . . . not to be entirely overwhelmed by life'.[23] With Marjorie he was now on 'easier terms – It is true that if I had my choice I might have chosen a more accommodating wife', he told Ottoline, 'but one is in the hands of fate for so much – as a woman and friend I admire and love her very much and she returns the same kind of feelings'.[24]

The Gertlers' plans were dependent on the goodwill of Marjorie's father, who was to stump up the money, but he and Gertler continued to distrust one another, and there were tiresome squabbles over bills and surveyors. But at last the matter was settled. 'Mr H' paid the deposit on a house in Grove Terrace, Highgate, and Mark settled on a self-build studio, which was to be erected in the garden later. Balston, in addition to buying a nude for £45 in May,[25] obligingly sent him a cheque for the £20 deposit. By now the two men often preferred to meet tête-à-tête, since in Marjorie's presence Gertler no longer felt able to talk 'so freely'.[26]

A heatwave settled over London in June, making the air feel stifling and 'disgustingly still'. Gertler's 'old cough' resurfaced and, although he put much of his ill health down to his troubled relationship with Marjorie, nervous of another outbreak of TB he requested a prescription from Dr Morland. He and Marjorie had had further 'talks', he confided to Balston, but 'arrived nowhere as usual'. Marjorie swore that any change in their relationship had nothing to do with her feelings for Hiller, but Gertler, aware that her feelings had 'dulled' towards him, did not entirely believe her. Still, he told Balston, Marjorie insisted that 'there would be "no life" for her without me'.[27] They agreed to part for the summer in any case. Gertler was due to leave for France with Tom on 1 July, and Marjorie arranged to join Greville in Tossa later the same month. The separation would last for almost four months, 'a rest from each other', which Gertler admitted had become 'absolutely essential'.[28]

When Gertler returned to Dr Morland for a further check-up, Morland pronounced the lung 'suspicious', and urged him to forego his trip abroad in favour of six weeks at the Mundesley sanatorium. Gertler clearly found the diagnosis almost a relief. 'Life has been too much for me this past year', he admitted, 'and I felt that a crisis of some sort was inevitable – the strain was too great.'[29] He had become anxious to put the responsibility for himself into somebody else's hands.

Marjorie accompanied him to the sanatorium for the first night, and stayed in a hotel near by. On arrival Gertler suffered 'the usual fit of depression . . . But I soon got over it, and now feel thankful for the peace and rest, which I have not been able to enjoy for months and months.'[30] His room was large, modern and comfortable, and he immediately began to size up the landscape from his window, which he planned to paint as soon as he felt up to it. Meanwhile he was confined to bed for observation. Unusually, he agreed that Kot, Mackie (one of the regular 'Thursdays') and the Turners could visit him.[31]

For the next week he suffered 'excruitiating headaches' and his temperature ran at 104°. 'Life isn't worth living', he wrote to Balston in desperation, 'I don't know what will come of it all.'[32] Now he discouraged visitors, and when Marjorie offered to put off her holiday he refused to hear of it. 'I really don't want anyone here', he assured her. 'I think it is just a matter of patience.'[33] Taking him at his word, she set out for Tossa with Nan, Luke and Aunt Ethel.

At Mundesley, Gertler lay day after day with ice compresses clamped to his head. On Wednesday 15 July, a fortnight after he had been admitted, he finally lost all hope and cut first his throat, then a vein in his arm, before ringing for a nurse at the last moment. Profoundly shocked, the hospital sprang into action. A blood specialist in Cromer was traced within the hour, and carried out an 'agonizingly painful' transfusion – with, Gertler later maintained, 'inadequate apparatus' – but managed to saved his life.[34] Now, with both arms injured, unable to paint, write, eat or even wash himself, he dictated a letter to Balston to call off the holiday in France.

Meanwhile Dr Pearson had telegraphed to Marjorie in Spain that Gertler was dangerously ill. Leaving Luke in the care of Nan and Aunt Ethel, she hurried from Palma to Barcelona, tormented all the while by the thought that he was either dead or dying. She arrived at Mundesley on the Saturday afternoon to find him very weak but out of danger. The shock of the experience made her realize, she wrote to Tom two days later, 'that however difficult it was to live with Mark I couldn't live without him.'[35] Only hours after Marjorie's departure Spain erupted into civil war, with the uprising of a group of insurgent nationalists opposed to the socialist tendencies of the government. Luke, Nan and Aunt Ethel were stranded in Tossa, north-east of Barcelona, which remained in republican control. For the next ten days the Gertlers received no word of whether they had managed to reach safety.

A psychiatrist was called in to diagnose Gertler's mental condition and declared that, despite his assurances to the contrary, Gertler would probably attempt suicide again at the first opportunity and must not be left alone in any circumstances.[36] For the next few weeks he was watched day and night. On the first night the only person who could be found at such short notice was the night porter, who dutifully took his place at Gertler's bedside. Casting around for something to while away the hours and finding a book of Picasso reproductions on Gertler's table, he began slowly to leaf through the pages. Gertler, pretending to be asleep, watched as the porter turned the book first one way and then the other, then upside down and from side to side. At length, when he reached the end of the book, the porter began the performance all over again until gradually the long night passed into morning. Gertler claimed the man was never the same again.[37]

Marjorie, still in shock, was staggered to learn that the hospital wanted her to remove Gertler and hush up his attempted suicide. Any risk of scandal, the hospital explained, could ruin the sanatorium. After X-rays revealed no sign of either sinus infection or TB, and news finally arrived that Nan had managed to secure passage home for Luke, Aunt Ethel and herself, Gertler began to revive. Marjorie was finally able to convince the sanatorium that he was no longer suicidal and he was allowed to stay on.

For the first week Gertler was washed, fed and forced to perform 'all natural functions' in front of a nurse. A fortnight later he was still unable to write letters but could feed himself (with difficulty) and managed to walk fifty yards. Soon he hoped to be strong enough to go to the lavatory and take a bath by himself. 'So much for the practical part', he wrote to Kot (who had himself suffered a further 'nervous collapse' and was also confined to a nursing home). 'I have also to tackle the mental part. Can I take up life again as before, that is the question, – for the moment it seems hateful. I have suffered so much this last year. Married life with Marjorie is so difficult, so complicated – the accounts and bills etc. I feel I shall never have the strength to do it again – yet what can I do?'[38] The bill for the first month at the sanatorium, which included several specialists and extra nurses, was a staggering £72 and Marjorie's weekly hotel bill stood at £5 10*s.* a week.

Gertler was longing to see Luke again. He and Nan were already on their way to stay with the Morlands, who had offered to put them up, when news broke of an outbreak of whooping cough in England. The ever-resourceful Nan installed Luke safely with her family in Wales, where he celebrated his fourth birthday on 16 August without either of his parents. When they were eventually reunited with their fragile-looking son in October, they found that he spoke with such a strong Welsh accent they could hardly understand him.

As the news of his attempted suicide slowly filtered through, Gertler's shocked friends began to rally round, and Marjorie worked out a complicated rota of visiting times. One of the regular 'Thursdays', A. S. Fulton, was to come for the day on Wednesday 29 July, followed by Ottoline on the Thursday and the Turners at the weekend. Sidney Bernstein came the following weekend, and Balston arranged to come for a week from Tuesday 11 August. He also immediately sent a cheque for £55, and Sidney Bernstein generously offered to pay the sanatorium fees for the first two months.

Tom and Philip Morrell, as Gertler's financial advisers, recognized that he was unlikely to be able to earn any money for some time. Philip suggested they launch a general appeal drawing attention to Gertler's past achievements and the high hopes his friends and admirers still had for his future, but Balston argued that the current situation was 'not serious enough'. He suggested saving such an appeal for any future crisis, such as the failure of an exhibition, and proposed approaching a few chosen friends for specific sums instead. Morrell, however, argued that he could

> hardly imagine a worse time to make such an appeal than after the failure of an exhibition. People wd. then say: 'he is not after all a very interesting or important painter – why worry us about him?' and the response could be small and disappointing. But if the appeal were made now, – when the breakdown had been sudden and complete and he is actually confined in a sanatorium – Mark's friends and admirers wd. feel, as you and Bernstein have felt – that they must do all they can to help him to recover, and the success of the appeal I think wd. be in . . . drawing attention to the excellent work he has done (and the high hopes we still have of him) would contribute to the success of the exhibition.[39]

Morrell even thought that they might 'find ourselves with a larger amount than was immediately required', and he proposed holding it in a trust fund 'to be applied as and when it seemed desirable, and that in the event of Mark's becoming so successful that he wd. not require further help there cd. be a provision to enable the balance to be applied to other similar cases'. He felt that many people would want to contribute to a fund rather than respond to a personal appeal for charity, and hated the idea of 'Mark writing round his friends to ask for help'.[40]

Although both schemes must have seemed humiliating, Gertler was prepared to go along with either. In the end he and Balston decided to approach a few people themselves and ask for a specified amount from each. His friends' response was generous, and produced £270 in a matter of weeks. Balston, of course, had written one of the first cheques, for £55; Milne offered £25, Monty Shearman sent a cheque for £25, St John Hutchinson £10 and his daughter a further £40. Gertler was sure he could rely on Taylor to help, and hoped for a further £25 from Mavrogordato.

In the event, after writing three times, he received only £10 from Mavrogordato, and although Gertler assured him that he was not just grateful but 'particularly anxious not to cause strains on any resources' – being quite sure that 'we married ones have more money troubles than bachelors'[41] – to Balston he expressed surprise that 'a man in [Mavrogordato's] position should not be able to help a great friend to a greater extent than £10'.[42]

Gertler now began to relax and in the excellent Norfolk climate looked more tanned than he had done the previous summer at Castelltersol. Marjorie stayed with him until September, when she returned to London to prepare the new house in Highgate, and Gertler began to consider painting again. He was gradually putting on weight and beginning to take long walks again, but his blood tests remained 'unsatisfactory', and at moments he still felt 'extraordinarily weak'.[43] His legs were still so tremulous that he could only paint sitting down, but he knew that painting was vital to his mental health and began to size up the view from his windows. Gertler's room was now required though for a more 'ailing' patient and, despite protests that he was in the middle of a picture, he was asked to move to a bungalow for 'ambulant males'. 'It is an awful curse', he told Balston, 'this picture being my first effort after my illness is so important to me.'[44] In the event, he completed four colourful landscapes and at least one portrait during this last visit to Mundesley.[45]

In Highgate Marjorie battled valiantly with painters, builders and electricians. 'Apparently all sorts of hitches are cropping up', Mark wrote to Tom, and 'it wouldn't do for me to return to a state of chaos.'[46] By mid-September, though much better physically, he still felt 'incapable of facing the strain of life outside here. I feel that I need just a few more degrees of strength – and sometimes I feel that it is just those few degrees which is going to be difficult to acquire.'[47] All the same, he was determined to leave in mid-October, though he still felt 'bruised' and very apprehensive about returning to 'that all-in wrestling match we call "life"'.[48]

Both Gertler and Marjorie realized that it would not be easy to re-establish their former intimacy, and Marjorie acknowledged to Balston, though not apparently to Gertler, that their relationship was 'mutually destructive'; none the less, 'in such a relationship one has to be the destroyed, and I believe, generally speaking, that women as of less value than men [are] right to fulfil that role.'[49] Only Ottoline seemed to realize that Marjorie too needed support; she urged her to take a complete break from Gertler at least once or twice a year, although she avoided mentioning this in her carefully worded letters to him.

Towards the end of September, tired 'of having to ask people for money like a beggar', Gertler began to reconsider writing his autobiography.[50] 'The Book', which was to occupy him intermittently until his death, was, like teaching, something to fall back on when, owing to ill health or depression, he had temporarily to abandon painting. Friends who heard him speak of the project gained the idea that it was much further advanced than the short, vivid manuscript, 'First Memories', found after his death, and even suggested that it was finished only days before he died.[51] It is more likely that it was never completed, for Gertler soon became caught up in his own story and realized it would have to be done slowly, and 'not to any time limit or primarily for money'.[52] He told Ottoline the book was progressing slowly, 'as I only do it in my spare time – also – I get too tired and over excited if I write more than one hour at a stretch'.[53]

In mid-October Gertler was finally discharged from the sanatorium. Marjorie and Dr Morland took him home to 5 Grove Terrace in Highgate, which was still unfinished and which he consequently found 'bewildering'. A tall, elegant, end-of-terrace Georgian house with a basement and four storeys, it was in fact the grandest of all the Gertlers' residences. A spacious first-floor drawing room ran the whole width of the house, and the ground floor and basement were rented out to Greville's mother, Mrs Foster, who also looked after Cristina (Greville's daughter) whenever Greville was abroad. At the rear of the house, in the walled garden, pear trees blossomed in the spring, and Luke later remembered his father lifting him up to admire the blossoms and telling him that each of these would form a fruit: 'had he told me that potatoes turned into roses, I could not have been more surprised.'[54]

The garden also contained Gertler's last studio: a wooden one such as he had once admired in Bernard Adeney's garden. The studio was out of bounds to everyone. Ernest Fedarb recalled that it was 'always kept locked and it was an exceptional privilege for anyone to be allowed in'.[55] He and his wife, Daphne, were only invited to do so on one occasion. Luke never was; he had to wait almost forty years before setting foot inside it.[56]

Marjorie worked to mend the bridges between them, but Gertler knew that 'that something which has gone out of her feelings for me has not returned',[57] and sexual relations between them ceased. Marjorie did not seem to be able yet to admit, either to herself or him, that, although she still cared for him deeply, she was no longer in love with him. It was the beginning of the end of their marriage.

24

The Edge of Destruction

> 'I long nowadays to be alone – quite alone. I do enjoy painting so much when I am living alone. I have never been more full of new ideas than now, and how I long for a year of bachelorhood, to work them out.'
>
> Mark Gertler to Tom Balston, 11 August 1938

ONE OF THE first pictures Gertler painted in his new studio was the portrait of Dorothy Morland, which he completed in early 1937 and gave to the Morlands to thank them for their continued kindness and support. It was inspired by the sight of Dorothy wearing a high-backed Spanish comb in her hair (which in the picture is set off by a lace mantilla), and is one of the finest of Gertler's last years. During the six-eight week sittings Dorothy had to endure not only the icy temperature of the draughty wooden studio but also Gertler's equally icy silence, as he worked with ferocious concentration. At meal times, while she and Marjorie chatted amicably, Gertler seemed wrapped up in a world of his own, regarding them both as merely 'extraneous noise'.[1] Despite this, the serenity of the finished portrait is one of its most attractive qualities. When it was exhibited at the Lefèvre in April, Sidney Bernstein was keen to acquire it. Although the Morlands were willing to let Gertler have it back to sell – they suggested he do a sketch of Dorothy instead – he refused, telling them the portrait was a 'one-off'.[2]

There was scarcely a month in 1937 when some of Gertler's work was not on show. Three of his pictures were included in the Rosenberg & Helft exhibition of British contemporary art in January and February; one was in the London Group show in March; and from June to July three of his pictures (selected by Vanessa Bell and

Duncan Grant) were part of a mixed show at Agnews to celebrate the coronation of George VI. Gertler's first major show since October 1934 was also due to open at the Lefèvre Galleries in April. His arrangement with the Lefèvre meant that he could count any exhibition sales as profit, but until then he struggled financially with no monthly stipend, and Ottoline and Philip advanced him a small sum to tide him over. Gertler told Ottoline that if the show went badly, he would return to his autobiography.

The Lefèvre show opened with a total of twenty-nine pictures, including the Catalonia and Norfolk landscapes, the recent portraits of Tom Balston and Dorothy Morland and several nudes and still lifes; the catalogue introduction was written by Aldous Huxley. Gertler's elation at four sales on the first day dwindled in the 'absolute vacuum' that followed, and he admitted to Mavrogordato that he felt keenly the strain of 'having to make one's living for two years within a space of 3 weeks'.[3] His decline in popularity coincided with economic and political uncertainty throughout Europe and America. Gertler took no active interest in politics, but could hardly ignore what was happening around him. In April Dorothy Morland, who had been instrumental in setting up an organization to help Spanish refugee children fleeing the civil war, took Marjorie with her to Puigcerdá in northern Spain.

Marjorie was impressed by the Spanish children's 'thirst' for culture and knowledge, the dedication and enthusiasm of the teachers, the soldiers and their wives and families: 'a new country [is] being made with great struggles but an astounding vitality. I can't bear to think of their losing a freedom which they have been trying to achieve for hundreds of years', she wrote home. 'It would do Mark good', she concluded, 'to come and see what ordinary people can do if they are given a chance. One comes to rely on [the] innate goodness of everyone [in Spain], and not on a small aristocracy of talents and intellect.'[4]

Gertler had been aware of the rise of Fascism in Europe since the early 1930s. In July 1933 Kot had tried to persuade Sidney Bernstein to back a film produced by one of his Russian compatriots, S. Liberman, which was to provide a 'Jewish reply to Hitlerism', but nothing came of it since the British Board of Film Censors would not 'pass any film dealing with the Hitler regime . . . [which] show[ed] the Nazis in a bad light'.[5] In 1937, following the visit of a Nazi 'art ambassador' to the London Group's last exhibition (at which, Gertler, only recently released from Mundesley sanatorium, had not exhibited),

Gertler's old friend David Bomberg presented a 'radical set of proposals' to the annual general meeting to tackle the prejudice faced by Jewish artists.[6] 'But the London Group committee, determined to remain politically neutral, rejected all of his suggestions.

In the summer of 1937 Luke was facing yet another operation and, as Gertler reported grimly to Tom Balston, was 'absolutely beside himself with terror'.[7] The hospital staff proved unhelpful and aloof, and the operation itself was a failure: Luke's stitches reopened several times after surgery. Gertler was torn between a desire to protect his son and a feeling of helplessness, and when Marjorie took Luke to recuperate at the Morlands' country cottage in Henley, he made for his own 'retreat' with Balston at Holt End. Marjorie later set off on holiday, leaving Luke in the care of Dorothy Morland in Henley. Tom drove Gertler over from Holt End to visit him one day but, although his letters expressed his concern for his son, he spent most of the holiday wrapped up in his painting. He completed three landscapes, including *Through the Window*, which he finished in August, describing its vibrant colour scheme as 'somewhere between Sickert and Renoir'.[8]

Gertler's late still lifes demonstrate a final clarification of colour and design. Centred on familiar props – a Benin head, a lace mantilla, a guitar, a pair of stuffed fish, a Spanish fan – the same composition is often reworked, using a semi-cubist structure to balance complex combinations of curved and geometrical forms against the sheer ebullience of an ever more brilliant palette. In many of the pictures based around the Benin head and stuffed fish, for example, Gertler breaks all the rules of colour, placing 'shouting' combinations such as blue against orange, and yet ultimately reconciling the whole through the use of an internal frame or the careful positioning of a black line.[9]

One of Gertler's most accomplished late still lifes is *The Spanish Fan*, which exists in four different versions, the finest and most complete being the second one painted in 1938, and the only one of his paintings to be exhibited in Paris during his lifetime.[10] Gertler himself referred to *The Spanish Fan* as the 'most important picture' at his final exhibition at the Lefèvre in 1939.[11] In an interview in the *World of Art Illustrated* he explained, 'the background is divided into three areas. It is the placing of the dividing lines, the relative proportions, that go to making the picture. The picture is all planned out like that. It is architectural.'[12] His remarks recall the theory laid out in his essay 'The Architectural Element in Art' in 1923 that to achieve an 'integral whole' in a picture, the foundation must be 'built up as firmly and solidly as a well-built house', with each 'brick forming part of the final edifice'.[13] Despite their technical virtuosity, however, these late, highly structured compositions also suggest an imposition of order and design which Gertler continued to struggle hard to achieve in his private life.

During the short interlude at Holt End he had enjoyed a rare feeling of tranquillity, and for once returned to London feeling his holiday had been 'beneficial'. He looked forward to seeing Marjorie's 'beautiful and expressive face again,' and wrote tenderly of how he loved and missed her 'physical presence[,] your dear physical presence is always exciting[,] always comforting and stimulating'.[14] He wrote optimistically about their future and their relationship, assuring her 'I have never had serious doubts – really – only you have a way of becoming more attractive – more and more beautiful – at any rate – it seems so to me – and I can't help feeling that all my former loves were childs play in comparison.'[15]

In September they managed a week in Paris, having settled Luke at a local school in Hampstead. Gertler was keen to study the painting of his French contemporaries at the great Paris international exhibition 'Chefs d'Oeuvre de l'Art Français' at the Petit Palais, where, he wrote to Balston, 'all the important painters had from one to three rooms to themselves and the minor ones a wall or two'.[16] He was particularly impressed by the work of Georges Rouault, who like Gertler had himself been apprenticed to a stained-glass maker in his youth, an experience reflected in the vibrant colours and strong black outlines of Rouault's work. The increased use of emphatic outline in Gertler's own late paintings has suggested to some critics a similar correlation with Gertler's early apprenticeship to the stained-glass makers Clayton & Bell.[17] However, it was with Rouault in mind that Gertler turned back to his painting *The Jewish Bride* on his return from France, making notes in his pocket book about his use of a brush to create 'big contour[s]' in 'black or near to black' enamel and a white foundation to achieve thickness. He finally brought the picture to a finish with 'no wax no glazing except in dark broad contours' and the use of 'silver sand in abundance'.[18]

The new year, 1938, began badly. Mark, Marjorie and Luke all suffered bad colds, and a painful abscess in Luke's ear had to be lanced under chloroform. Gertler's endless headaches, colds and 'general debility' continued well into February, and he often missed his teaching, which led to a further dip in income. Nan was getting married and decided to move on and, although Gertler worried that Marjorie would not have the strength to shoulder the extra work, they were both keen to ease the 'financial burden' of keeping a nurse, so decided not to replace her. For the next year most of Marjorie's time was taken up looking after Luke. In the mornings alone it took her two hours just to take and fetch him from school.[19] Despite the saving, Marjorie's overdraft climbed to £229. They continued to keep separate bank accounts, with each paying exactly half of the bills, but Gertler forced himself to take their finances in hand and gradually began to reduce Marjorie's overdraft. Alongside the entries about his health in his pocket diary be began to chart its rise and fall as meticulously as a broker watching share prices.

By March Gertler appeared to revive and became quite convivial, taking tea with models, friends and patrons and socializing with his Westminster colleagues Blair Hughes-Stanton and Ernest Fedarb, with whom he sometimes 'did the wine-bars of the Strand'.[20] These teas were often thinly disguised sales pitches when prospective buyers would be invited to view his latest pictures. Gertler was disappointed when J. B. Priestley, who had indicated that he might buy a painting to present to the Hull Art Gallery, told him that he had a 'vast overdraft' and could no longer afford it. Later, Gertler read in the paper that Priestley had acquired an Augustus John instead. 'So his overdraft doesn't always bother him', he concluded.[21] However, Priestley later bought a painting purely because he felt sorry for Gertler and not because he liked it.[22] Another prospective buyer, a Mr Aprile, who had accepted several invitations to tea and taken three pictures away on approval, amazed Gertler by taking advantage of his absence over Easter to return all three 'without a word!'[23]

That March Brett too appeared on Gertler's doorstep on a rare visit from New Mexico. Her memoir of her intimacy with Lawrence (*Lawrence and Brett: A Friendship*, 1933) had so incensed Kot that even five years on he refused to meet her. So too did Ottoline, who, though identified only as 'X', came off as usual much the worst as a 'plucked hen' left with only one feather.[24] The youthful Gertler, however, had been described by Brett as 'a wild creature out of some Celtic myth',[25] and even in 1938 she apparently found him virtually unchanged.[26] But Gertler was astonished to find, in place of the spry, girlish figure of old, a decidedly grey-haired and elderly woman.[27]

Ottoline too had aged. Dogged by continuous ill health since 1935, she had suffered a serious stroke in 1937 and by the spring of 1938 was confined to a nursing home. Gertler's affection for her was undiminished. She was 'one of the very few people', he told her, who were part of his life, and who were 'always with me – whether we happen to meet – correspond – or not – In the way that my mother is – Marjorie or Kot.'[28] And as she lay dying, one of Ottoline's last acts was to write to comfort Gertler, telling him that Philip would continue to do what he could to try and sort out Marjorie's money.[29]

Although Julian had tried to warn Gertler of the seriousness of Ottoline's condition, the news of her death on 21 April came as a great shock to him. A few days later Gertler confessed to Philip that he still felt 'dazed and unable to do anything'[30] and a wave of loneliness swept over him, making him realize just how much he missed and valued Marjorie, who was back in Spain with Dorothy Morland. He immediately fired off a spontaneous letter to tell her that he loved her 'very very much – only so sad about Ottoline'.[31]

Ottoline's memorial service at St Martin-in-the-Fields on Tuesday 26 April was packed, and Virginia Woolf observed Gertler standing among the others mourners with 'tears in his eyes'.[32] His feelings for Ottoline had always been those of a son and at Garsington he had always preferred to be simply *en famille*. The writer and broadcaster Lance Sieveking had an enduring memory of seeing Ottoline and Gertler together at the theatre in the 1920s. To his amusement Ottoline had leaned over to straighten Gertler's fringe but, used to her motherly attentions, he had appeared not to notice.[33]

Ottoline's death coincided with the passing of an era. In March 1938 Churchill, speaking in the House of Commons, warned of the danger of the rise of Hitler, and at the end of April conscription was reintroduced. There was no question of Gertler being called up this time. His age (forty-six) and ill health disqualified him, but friends noted his violent reaction to the newspaper reports about Hitler.[34]

One of the most mysterious of Gertler's relationships at this period was with a gifted young Jewish pianist called Maria Donska. She had been born in Łódź, Poland, in 1912, and had begun to play the piano at the age of four. By seven she was giving professional recitals of Schubert and Schumann for British diplomats in Gdansk. In 1923 she made her début with an orchestra 'flawlessly carrying off a quick and complex piece by Weber', and a year later left school to study full-time at a conservatoire, before going on to Berlin at the age of fourteen to become a pupil under Artur Schnabel. She was notoriously determined and allegedly told her family that if they did not allow her to study with Schnabel she would run away.

Schnabel was invited to London in 1929 (when his friendship with Walter and Delphine Turner made Gertler jealous) to give a series of Mozart and Schubert recitals, and he took Maria with him. At a formal dinner she astonished the other guests by putting two fingers in her mouth and demonstrating how to whistle for a cab. Maria later lived in Berlin until 1933, when she returned to Poland. Horrified at the emergence of the Nazis and the rise of anti-Semitism, she left for good the following year, with only a ticket in her pocket, and travelled to London. There she set up house in St John's Wood with fellow musician Leonora Speyer (known as 'Baba'), found work with the BBC and later entrolled at the Royal College of Music, where she won several prestigious medals.

There is little evidence of her relationship with Gertler. One friend recalled that Maria used to talk 'often' of Gertler, another that she mentioned him 'occasionally'; to a third, however, she never mentioned him at all, and to a fourth she referred only to their 'tragic love affair'.[35] When Gertler's letters were published in 1965. Maria said that his letters to her had never been as passionate as those he wrote to Carrington.[36] Gertler's surviving letters and journals likewise make no mention of her, yet Baba appears as Mrs L. Speyer in his diaries from 1937 onwards, and Maria was certainly known to some of Gertler's friends, including Dorothy Morland, who noticed that she seemed proud of her attachment to such a famous painter.

The position of Jewish artists in Britain was also difficult. David Bomberg pointed out in a letter to fellow painter Jacob Kramer: 'The Jewish artists are starving, none of us can work, most of us receive one form of charity or another', but, he urged, 'we can make a market for ourselves if we organize'.[37] Bomberg's proposal was to reorganize the running of the Ben Uri (the gallery established in 1915 to celebrate the work of Jewish artists) by setting up a special artists' committee, in which, besides himself, he proposed to include Kramer, Harold Brodzky, Bernard Meninsky, Edward Wolfe, the German refugee artist Hans Feibusch and his old friend Gertler. But again Bomberg's plans seem to have been rejected, for nothing further was heard of it.

When Gertler returned to Highgate from his break at Holt End in Easter 1938, Marjorie's overdraft again stood at £229, as it had done in January, and with Luke due to undergo yet another operation further expenses were imminent. They were still struggling to settle their previous accounts with Doctors Ive and Mills, but, anxious to find a more 'humane' doctor for Luke, they had turned to the Harley Street surgeon Professor Kilner. The Gertlers had hoped to recoup some of their expenses through the rent they earned from Mrs Foster, but already found it only covered bills. By late May they were forced to give up their maid and, Gertler told Balston, had 'never lived so cheaply before'.[38] Even so, Gertler's wages from the Westminster would only last until the end of the summer and he had no idea how they would survive into the autumn, particularly with the threat of war. It had been one thing to face war as a poor but rising young prodigy on the British art scene, but it would be quite another to face it as an impecunious middle-aged husband and father, already forced to teach part-time to make ends meet. Finally, Gertler was forced to ask Balston to double his guarantee at the bank, though he insisted he would never do so again, and Balston as usual agreed, seemingly without reservation.

The Gertlers planned to spend the summer of 1938 in Cassis, near Marseille, where they reasoned that the cost of living was much cheaper, the warm air would be good for Luke (whose next surgery could be postponed until the autumn), and where the light was said to be marvellous for painting. Gertler's Westminster colleague Blair Hughes-Stanton and his wife, the poet Ida Graves, would be staying near by for the first month; Ernest and Daphne Fedarb would be close by, in Toulon; and Greville was due in August.

Before this, in early June the Gertlers accepted an invitation from Sidney Bernstein for a weekend at Long Barn and took Luke, now a lively and talkative five-year-old, with them. At mealtimes Luke was not at all intimidated to find himself seated opposite Charles Laughton, now a famous Hollywood star. On the contrary, Gertler reported, Laughton 'found it extremely difficult to keep up the "great man" stunt with Luke's extraordinary questions being shot at him all the time!'[39]

Marjorie and Luke set off for Cassis in mid-June, and Gertler settled down in Highgate for three weeks of concentrated work, though headaches and depression caused him to spend much of the time fretting about his weight. As the date for his departure drew nearer he became increasingly nervous. He was discouraged by Marjorie's descriptions of Cassis, which was packed with artists, critics and their hangers-on, and nicknamed 'Bloomsbury-by-Sea'. By this time Gertler had cut himself off completely from Bloomsbury. The deaths of Carrington, Roger Fry and Ottoline had distanced him still further, and he had neither reason nor desire to renew the acquaintance. None the less he left England on Saturday 9 July, and recorded his arrival with a terse diary entry on the 11th, which simply read 'Cassis'. On the Tuesday he recorded 'Very bad Depression' and 'XX' (his symbol for migraine[40]), both of which a month later had become 'more or less continuous'.[41] Troubled also by a persistent cough and sputum, he decided to give up smoking. He was deeply depressed throughout his stay, and avoided the Hughes-Stantons on the beach during the day and the 'crowd' for drinks in the evenings. Marjorie, whether out of concern or loyalty, stayed with him. His depression prevented him, at least initially, from painting. Certainly during the month the Hughes-Stantons spent in Cassis, Ida never once saw him with paints in his hands,[42] and when Gertler eventually returned to Highgate in September he took back only two landscapes. Yet Ida, who was fond of him and surprised by his 'moody' behaviour, later thought she had hit on the reason when she visited Marjorie and found that she had been secretly painting. It was clear to Ida that she wished to hide her canvases from Gertler.

From then on Ida noted that Gertler became 'particularly jealous' when Marjorie painted, and she sometimes helped by keeping watch at the window so that Marjorie could 'hide her canvases, clear the paint and open doors and windows to clear the smell of turps' before he came in.[43] V. S. Pritchett, who knew the Gertlers well in the last six years of Mark's life, also saw that, though the couple seemed 'charmed by each other and solicitous', Gertler 'could not bear it that his wife sometimes painted',[44] and Marjorie herself later cited this as one of the chief difficulties of their marriage: 'I had to give up all my own work, painting or what ever', she wrote, 'and it rankled terribly.'[45]

After the holiday, when he was alone again in his studio, Gertler regretted his behaviour, and wrote to her, 'do no think that you could help matters by not painting – It doesn't make the slightest difference whether you paint or not – on the contrary I used [to] feel bad in a worse way when you did not paint – I[t] goes deeper than that.'[46] But he never sent this letter and, though he tried to write again two days later, the second letter also remained unposted.[47] The letter he finally sent merely apologized for 'so many bad moods in Cassis'.[48]

Luke seems to have realized at a young age that he must compete for his parents' attention. He later recalled an incident with his father in Cassis:

> Since his treatment for tuberculosis he always took a rest in the afternoon. On that particular afternoon while he rested, my mother had gone out and I had wanted to go with her. She had told me, however, that I must stay at home. I retaliated in the way I knew best. I was very good at screaming and I began one of my supreme performances, standing outside the house. Now the studio on the ground floor had been let to a lady artist. Her window was open and music was coming from her wireless. Normally I love music which was something for being happy; I was doing my best to be miserable, also disliked the competition, so I howled even louder. This went on for some time, until my father could bear it no longer. Suddenly an agitated figure tore down the stairs, rushed out of the house, seized me and rushed back up into the bedroom, literally throwing me onto the bed. The shock of the whole manoeuvre, which lasted only a few seconds had the desired effect: I was silent. My mother has since told me that when she returned on that occasion she found us both exhausted and asleep in bed.[49]

After the Hughes-Stantons' departure from Cassis in mid-August Gertler settled down somewhat and found 'a lonely spot' where he could bathe unobserved in the mornings. In the afternoons he worked from two to six. Cassis continued to fill up with 'the "Bohemia" of London', whom he described to Tom Balston as 'futile men and prostitute-like women. Mostly semi-acquaintances of a sort one tries to avoid like poison in London.'[50] By implication at least, he appeared to include in this category several old friends: Greville, her sister Kate and boyfriend, Dick Carline and his girlfriend, and even his own niece Renée, honeymooning with her husband, Leslie Diamond. But this did not prevent him joining them in the evenings for dinner, and his friends decided that Gertler was simply in one of his 'very queer moods'.[51] To Balston, Gertler admitted that 'the whole place' seemed to him 'like a lunatic asylum. The only human being is Braque, a tall handsome man, but he keeps well out of the way and one only gets a glimpse of him occasionally.'[52]

Afterwards Gertler explained his behaviour to Marjorie as 'the stale old problem',[53] the irritation and depression caused by 'things that disturb my life as a painter – Family life . . . you know – you being a painter yourself . . . What grieves me also is – that my moods prevent me from expressing the fullness of my love for you – I don't believe you've ever realized How much I love you!' He aimed to 'adjust myself one of these days and then you'll see how happy we shall be – the most perfect couple!' She had been 'more than ever desirable and loveable [*sic*]' that summer but he regretted that their 'intellectual interests' were so similar. 'Most people', he admitted, 'would think this a good thing . . . [but] for us it is unfortunate – I have always made friends – instinctively with non-painters – for then only can I get that atmosphere of complete Isolation and detachment so necessary to my temperament as a painter.'[54]

Gertler's diary in Cassis, dominated by 'XX' signs (for migraine), agonized over how to achieve this desired isolation and detachment. His August diary entries are fragmented and show signs of desperation:

> Surely this must end – there must be some way out – surely the situation is exaggerated anyhow – spoiling such a good beautiful life! – To speak of it – cannot be satisfactory [–] to be apart – perhaps – but such upheaval – surely there must be an attitude of proximity and detachment at the same time – that would be the manliest and the easiest – easier because of no outward manifestation – but also for keeping so much that is good in the situation – this surely could be done by a controlled detachment – to treat proximity as if [it] were distant.[55]

On the 18th he wrote: 'a fearful night last night. How can this torture stop? It seems hopeless, getting near to open statement – yet what good can that do – perhaps wait till London? The close confinement may make things worse – or partial disclosement? Going to London to be alone', he concluded, 'give reasons', but the entry trails to a stop, ending with a question mark. Once back in London he simply wrote to Marjorie asking her to 'go on tolerating [his moods] as you have done up to now'.[56]

After Marjorie's return in the autumn they attempted some changes. The 'Thursdays' (now changed to 'Wednesdays' because of Gertler's teaching) were enlarged to include women, and occasionally new people. This was clearly a concession to Marjorie, and Gertler told Mavrogordato that they would be less tied to the old routine. However, both Gertler's depression and his wish to be 'undomesticated', which he admitted had now become 'a sort of obsession', only increased after his wife's and son's return, and after much discussion he and Marjorie agreed that if his mood continued 'some kind of separate life might be preferable. We both know that the trouble is not fundamental, and we do really love one another', he explained to Balston. 'But there are two creatures in me – the painter and the man. It is the painter in me that causes difficulties.'[57] They settled on a more 'detached' way of living, with Gertler lunching out just as he did when he was at home alone – 'That I know will greatly help', he told Balston, 'as I shall be alone with my thoughts all day'[58] – but it was not an arrangement likely to ease his depression.

In early October Gertler learned that in the event of war the Westminster would be closed instantly, with the immediate cessation of all salaries. 'From now till May, my teaching money was to be my only maintenance. So you can imagine what I felt like', he wrote to Balston in despair when the news broke.[59] Hitler's speeches on the radio horrified him. 'We may all be blown to bits any moment', he wrote. 'I heard the voice of the Brute pouring poison into the hearts of his countrymen last night on the wireless – it was awful – like Wild Beasts.'[60] In early winter Luke's rescheduled surgery took place, but the operation was a failure. Marjorie immediately took him off to recuperate at the Morlands in Henley, and he was soon as 'well and bright' as ever, but the knowledge that he would have to go through the whole procedure again distressed them both.

Even a visit from MacDonald of the Lefèvre Gallery, who seemed pleased and excited by Gertler's latest pictures – and anticipated another show even 'better than the last'[61] – could not lift Gertler's gloom. At Christmas he went first to Walter Taylor at St Leonards, then on to the Morlands in Henley, where he joined Marjorie and Luke, and in the new year he fled to Tom Balston's.

25

These Dark Glasses

'Julian was in one of his suicidal states. Holidays always seem to bring them on.'

Greville Texidor, *These Dark Glasses*

A FICTIONAL ACCOUNT of the summer of 1938 in Cassis appears in Greville Texidor's novella *These Dark Glasses*, which was published in New Zealand in 1949.[1] Her portrait of Gertler as the artist Julian also draws on the Castelltersol holidays of 1934–5.[2] Julian cannot bear to bathe with the others, and has to go to 'his own special rock . . . miles away'. In the afternoons he works in his studio and complains of the heat. 'It's unbelievable there in that studio', his wife comments, 'and of course he can only paint in the afternoon just when it's worst.'[3] His wife, Jane, is 'having a trying time. Julian is in one of his suicidal states. Holidays always seem to bring them on. Having to see all these bogus artists and having to work in this infernal heat because of course he won't paint out of doors. You'll never know how awful it is being married to a genius.'[4] Like Marjorie, Jane is an artist and keeps all her sketches, 'even the bad ones', which she can never show 'because of Julian but I go on making notes. One day, I tell myself, I shall know perhaps why I've been doing these things.'[5]

Both Julian and the narrator, Ruth (Greville), are preoccupied with suicide. Indeed Ruth regards Julian's inability to 'get to the point of departure' as yet another of his weaknesses. (Greville eventually committed suicide in 1964.) She cannot bear the 'lighted cabaret of the beach' any more than Julian, and attempts to disguise herself behind books and dark glasses. It is a savage portrait of one suicide contemplating another.

Christmas 1938 was the last holiday that the Gertler family spent together, for at some point over the holiday Gertler and Marjorie finally agreed that they would part, at least on a temporary basis, and as soon as she returned to Highgate Marjorie began to make the arrangements. Luke, who was still not 'a strong child and far too thin',[6] was to be settled (on Dr Morland's advice) in a sanatorium in Davos, Switzerland, while Marjorie planned to move to Paris, perhaps in an effort to recapture the freedom of her youth.

Gertler returned in time to see Marjorie off on 16th January, and marked the event with a double entry in his diary. 'M[arjorie]'s O[verdraft] and abroad [£]197. 4. 10'.[7] (This reveals how inextricably his feelings for Marjorie had become linked to his deep concerns about money; even the drinks they had before saying goodbye were carefully jotted down as expenses.) Many years later, when Gertler's letters were published, Marjorie was astonished to learn of this preoccupation, particularly since it was he who had always insisted on their comfortable lifestyle, including servants, whom Marjorie would far rather have done without. She always believed that if Gertler could have brought himself to live 'very simply' in a studio (like Henry and Irina Moore) they could have managed even on her meagre income.[8]

Gertler's diary for 1939 was almost exclusively concerned with his weight, which rarely went up or down by more than a couple of pounds, and with Marjorie's finances. A note on Sunday 1 January 1939 recorded her income for 1938 as £338 14*s.* 1*d.*, while another on Tuesday 10 January showed that her overdraft for 1939 already stood at £198, nearly two-thirds of her annual income. Meanwhile, the income from her investments was dwindling, and Gertler asked Tom Balston to contact Marjorie's father to see what might be done. At the same time, however, he was remarkably selfless about sharing Balston's patronage, and arranged meetings with his Westminster colleagues Elmslie Owen and Blair Hughes-Stanton, actively encouraging Balston to buy their pictures.

Gertler laboured away unenthusiastically at a flower piece in order to complete the requisite number of paintings for his next show at the Lefèvre in May. He wrote few letters and saw few friends, and the sparse personal comments in his diary steadily became more anguished:

> Thursday 9 February: 'Very bad day. Chester/Doctor not paid. Also wrote to M[arjorie?] about difficulty in living together XX – over[draft] – £201. What will come of it? Next year?'

Friday 17 March: 'Dreadful day. Fear equal of M. not wanting to return and/to return –'

Shortly after this he became ill with flu and, unable to work or teach, barely managed to 'crawl downstairs' to take supper with Greville's mother in the evenings.

Marjorie wrote that Luke was making good progress at Davos and that she had decided to leave him there until June. She had settled quickly in Paris and was enjoying the social and artistic life there, reunited with friends such as the American musician Virgil Thomson, who gave lavish parties. At last she was able to re-establish a studio of her own. Nevertheless, Gertler told Tom, she seemed 'very anxious' for him to join her at Easter and this may have encouraged him to go on thinking that the separation was only temporary.

In the last week of March Gertler also unexpectedly received an invitation – formally addressed to 'Mr Gertler' – to dine with Virginia Woolf.[9] At work on her biography of Roger Fry, Virginia wished to ask Gertler how Fry had struck the 'younger painters' of his generation. But Gertler was still housebound with flu, and the dinner was moved to the middle of May instead. The flu and its debilitating aftereffects persisted until the end of the month, and he cancelled his proposed trip to Paris in favour of recuperation at Holt End. It was vital that he regain his health in time for the summer term at the Westminster, since his teaching income was now absolutely essential and he already feared the strain of his next show in May.

At Balston's Gertler rallied a little, but on his return to Highgate his diary entries became desperate once more: (Tuesday 11 April) 'Tom's. M's O £198. 5. Awful day. Letter suggesting Luke's periodic return to Davos – and I think might be working up to one man show?'; (Wednesday 12 April) 'Rather better'; (Thursday 13 April) 'Worse again – thoughts that occur make me think complete Parting coming? The thing is can I stand alone?'[10] His concern about expenses, and who owed what between Marjorie and himself, became an obsession and detailed calculations occupied pages of his diary. The prospect of his show and uncertainty about the approaching war added to his anxiety.

Although Gertler had told Balston, soon after Marjorie's departure, that he would be leading 'a bachelor life . . . probably'[11] until Easter, he had quickly discovered that a 'bachelor life' was no more to his liking than a family one had been. It is not clear how often he saw

Maria Donska at this time, but Dorothy Morland believed that the couple were planning to live together, and there was even talk of them taking on Augustus John's old studio in Charlotte Street.[12] But Gertler seems no longer to have been able to lose himself fully in personal relationships, and the bonds between himself and Maria were not strong enough. Maria continued to live with her devoted companion Baba for the rest of her life, and passed up several invitations of marriage. Gertler also had a friendship with one of his models, Celia Dennis. Many letters passed between them in the 1930s and Gertler was clearly fond of her. An unfinished portrait of Celia was found in his studio after his death. She herself later wrote to Tom Balston that 'the affection' she had known while Gertler was alive was 'the only real thing that ever happened' to her.

Whatever his relationships, Gertler must have found the large, empty, echoing house unbearably lonely. When he ran into Betty Battiscombe, one of his students from the Westminster, with whom he had previously exchanged scarcely more than a few words, he bought her a meal and, after telling her that Marjorie was away and that he missed Luke terribly, he asked her to come and live with him.[13] Sensing that it was a cry of loneliness rather than a sexual invitation, Betty was touched rather than shocked, but she regretfully turned him down, having just moved in with one of the other teachers, John Howard, and his wife. When she arrived home and told the Howards of Gertler's invitation they laughed at her naïvety, but she was convinced that it was a cry for help. A few days later in a café near the school, as she and her friends sat chatting after classes, she glimpsed Gertler sitting alone in a corner but was too shy to go up and speak to him.[14]

In May 1939 Gertler's final exhibition opened at the Lefèvre Galleries in St James'. More than a third of the twenty-nine paintings were still lifes, and there were an equal number of landscapes and portraits, including the recent Holt End pictures, two studies of Cassis and Gertler's final self-portrait. There were very few nudes but to many of his students these generously proportioned females were so striking that they eclipsed all the other exhibits, and were so intense and uncompromising that some of them were shocked. One, Diana Gardner – who described her own full figure as 'somewhat along Maillol lines' – remembered how Gertler had once asked her to sit to him and was glad she had refused.[15] Apart from his students and close friends, including Tom Balston and Sidney Bernstein, there were few visitors to the exhibition and still fewer buyers. By the end of the first week Gertler had sold only one painting; a large flower piece (*Venus and Flowers*) and a tiny landscape (*The Heather Field*), both marked as sold, had already been purchased more than a year before.

John Rothenstein, by now director of the Tate Gallery, remembered a conversation he had after the show with Gertler's former patron Eddie Marsh. 'I saw Mark last night', Marsh told him. 'He was terribly depressed. He thinks you don't like his work. I told him you did, but it was no good.'[16] But while Rothenstein admitted that (until 1940) the Tate's only acquisition from Gertler's remarkably varied oeuvre was one of his early, and inferior, John-influenced portraits, he thought Gertler was being over-sensitive. Gertler was disappointed that the Tate had not acquired one of his 'more recent and larger' paintings, and when Marsh explained honestly that Gertler's recent pictures were unattractive to his former buyers, Gertler replied generously that as an old friend Marsh had the right to say exactly what he thought.[17] But he was heart-broken by Marsh's criticism.[18]

From Paris, Marjorie reassured him that 'the real mischief in England' was that buyers never had any 'personal tastes', though she naturally singled out Tom Balston as an exception. 'Even if people don't understand painting as well as Tom', she wrote, 'they can at least have the courage to buy independently and not what all their friends tell them.'[19] Gertler was consoled by this and quoted it in a letter to Balston. Other friends, such as Mavrogordato, V. S. Pritchett and G. U. Ellis (a minor novelist and 'discovery' of Tom's at Duckworth's), sent letters of support. Ellis called the exhibition 'easily the finest' Gertler had given to date. 'I came away', he wrote afterwards, 'with a sense of being a little breathless . . . like coming out of a dark room into perfect sunshine – and of having come . . . sharply into contact, with a tremendous show of vitality.'[20]

Virginia Woolf later wrote in her diary that Duncan Grant and Vanessa Bell had also considered Gertler's last show 'a great advance & very remarkable',[21] although they probably never told him so. There were perhaps fewer press notices than usual, but Geoffrey Robinson, in the *World of Art Illustrated*, devoted two and a half pages to an overview of Gertler's career, observing that at '46 [*sic*] years of age' Gertler still retained 'the clear vision of youth . . . [and] remain[ed] artistically the uncompromising rebel'.[22]

However, by the end of the show Gertler had made only three

sales. The monolithic *Red Shawl* and a nude, which he described dismissively as a 'tiny dot' (probably because it fetched only 12 guineas), together brought in just £50. His final self-portrait (now lost) was sold for £15 to Sidney Bernstein. In total, the exhibition realized only 75 guineas.[23]

Desperately worried about money, Gertler contacted Kirkland Jamieson at the Westminster and arranged to do the maximum amount of teaching for his post, two days and three evenings a week. War and health permitting, the salary would be enough for him to subsist on, though, as he pointed out to Balston, it would not cover the everyday expenses of painting materials, models and frames.[24] He was due only one more salary payment before the end of the summer term, after which he could expect nothing further until October. Meanwhile Marjorie, who had continued to send good reports of herself and Luke, was still pressing him to go over to Paris, and although he finally agreed to visit over Whitsun, he wrote to Balston that he instantly regretted it, concerned that he 'ought to save every penny for the summer'.[25]

On 14 May, the day after this letter, Gertler went to supper as arranged with the Woolfs; Virginia marked in her diary a laconic 'Gertler tonight'.[26] Despite his own private disillusionment, at this last meeting Virginia found him as strident and forceful as ever, and over dinner he 'denounced the vulgarity, the inferiority of what he called "literature"; compared with the integrity of painting. For literature', he explained, 'always dealt with "Mr and Mrs Brown . . . with the personal, the trivial."' For Virginia this criticism had a 'sting and chill, like the May sky', and forced her to concede privately that only an artist would be able to give an accurate 'sense' of the personality of a subject such as her own mother, something, she concluded, that 'it would be as difficult to do . . . as it should be done, as to paint a Cézanne'.[27] Later, they also discussed Gertler's previous (presumably 1936) suicide attempt, which he attributed to 'some hitch in his work'. He told the Woolfs he had 'completely recovered' and 'got through into a new stage as a painter'.[28]

Following this meeting Gertler hunted out his abandoned fragment of autobiography and asked his friend the poet Sylvia Lynd for her opinion. Her enthusiasm encouraged him to press on, and she also offered to act as his editor and agent, promising to contact the publishers Victor Gollancz to try and secure him an advance of £200, though Gertler, as he told Tom Balston, would have been satisfied with £100.[29] He worked intermittently on his manuscript, and was befriended by a stray cat which moved in with him. But when he ran out of milk and the cat refused to stop mewing, he kicked out at it violently. The next day a man came with a basket and took the cat away. 'Goodbye, cat', he added unsentimentally to his manuscript. Reconciling himself to writing full-time was difficult, for it seemed tantamount to admitting that his career as a painter was at an end. He found that the actual experience of writing (like painting) was 'rather moving and over-emotional' and, though he hoped that this would 'pass with habit', he also admitted to becoming 'almost feverish' when he wrote.[30]

He set off to Paris on 27 May, and put up there at an unfamiliar hotel in the Impasse du Rouet. The following day he met up with a thin and strained-looking Marjorie, who told him that she would not be returning either to Britain or to their marriage. Some twenty-five years later, in a letter to Beatrice Campbell (who, from her scribbled comments, clearly never forgave her for 'abandoning' Gertler), she tried to explain. During her five months in Paris she had already begun to establish a new life for herself and after meeting an Austrian refugee named Franz Kostenz at a party she had at once fallen 'terribly in love'. Franz was on the run – in and out of prison, never spending two nights in the same place – and to Marjorie his need seemed overwhelming. With war looming, she was terrified that if she left Paris she would never see him again. However, Marjorie said nothing of the affair to Gertler, although Beatrice Campbell's comments indicate that he already knew all about it from mutual friends. This perhaps explains why he told Marjorie that he was conducting 'several' affairs, and left her with the impression that he was 'contented'. 'We decided', she later wrote, 'that he was happier without me.'[31] Undoubtedly this was bravado.

Later the same week the painter and illustrator John Minton saw Gertler sitting alone in the Dôme café 'looking rather silly', unaware, writes Minton's biographer Frances Spalding, that what he saw was 'a state of mind similar to that which he [himself] would later experience'.[32] (Minton, plagued in his final years by doubts about his declining reputation, committed suicide in 1957.) In a letter to John Mavrogordato, Gertler underplayed the seriousness of the break-up, saying that Marjorie liked the life in Paris so much that they would 'not in future live together, much'. But he admitted that the situation was not very 'happy-making', that it was 'difficult to know what to arrange about Luke', and that things between Marjorie and himself had been strained for a long time.[33]

Following this, Gertler seems to have sunk into a state of intense depression. He wrote no further letters and remained in Paris only long enough to see Luke, who was due to arrive the following Monday.[34] However, in a postscript to his letter to Mavrogordato he also wrote that he would be meeting Picasso the same day. Given the many chances Gertler had passed up to meet Picasso in previous years, it seems unlikely that, even had Picasso agreed to meet him, Gertler could really have gone through with the meeting at such a time. Perhaps this postscript, like his 'contentment', was simply a display of bravado.

On Tuesday 6 June Gertler travelled home on the boat-train via Dieppe. Three days later he noted in a final diary entry that he had received a letter from the Jewish Education Aid Society reminding him that some twenty-seven years after they had withdrawn their help, his outstanding debt still stood at £80.[35] He could hardly have received a more cruel reminder of his early success and current failure. The following day he made a last entry in his expenses notebook of the costs of Luke's home in Davos, but did not send any payment to the JEAS.

The following Wednesday Gertler sent a telegram to Tom Balston at Holt End: 'Meet Stewart's [tearoom] Friday [16th June] 4.30. Important. Mark.'[36] Tom later pencilled a note on this which read: 'I had tea with Mark at Stewart's on Friday June 16th. He said that at Whitsuntide when he went to Paris with Marjorie, she told [him] she was never going to return. Depressed by this and the failure of his Exhibition that May at the Lefèvre Gallery, he made [an]other attempt to kill himself but Dr. Morland got him well in 2 days.'[37] He had taken 45 grains of Medinal and turned on the gas, before turning it off again and calling Morland.[38]

Dorothy Morland recalled that this attempt was triggered by a trivial incident when, on receiving instructions about some clothes of Luke's that were to be forwarded to Davos, Gertler attempted to tie up the parcel and was suddenly overwhelmed by the feeling that the task was too complicated for him to manage.[39] Once he was well again, the Morlands telephoned Marjorie in Paris, and she offered to come home, but Gertler assured her that he could manage and had plans for the future.

After this he seems to have rallied a little. On the evening of the 21st Gertler and Maria Donska had dinner with the Fedarbs at Chez

Victor in Soho. Gertler 'seemed to be happy with the world and quite buoyant', having apparently taken the manuscript of his autobiography to Sylvia Lynd for vetting that afternoon.[40] She had approved of it and Gertler was apparently 'delighted'. As the two couples left the restaurant Gertler noticed a large Rolls-Royce parked outside and told them, 'when I have made a lot of money from my autobiography I shall buy one like that and take you all to the South of France'.[41] But the night before, Blair Hughes-Stanton's wife, Ida Graves, had observed Gertler at the Westminster's end-of-term dance, standing uneasily by himself, lost in a cloud of depression. When Ida whirled by with her dancing partner he asked her to come back to the house with him, but caught up in the atmosphere of the dance she refused. Later she, like many others, would blame herself for not recognizing the depths of Gertler's despair.[42]

Meanwhile, following the separation, Marjorie's father arranged to send an agent to value the house on Friday 23 June. 'The worst part almost', Gertler admitted to Balston, 'is being so unsettled as to where and how to live.'[43] He would have to face all over again the 'tragedy' of leaving the studio, and his mood became very distracted. The following day Gertler showed the estate agent over the house, but repeatedly ignored his requests to see the studio. Afterwards Celia Dennis came to sit for her portrait as usual, and promised to return later. After she left, Gertler went back to the house and removed a mattress from one of the beds. Dragging it behind him, he returned to the studio, and after making sure the windows were tightly closed, stuffed it against the door. Then he turned on both gas ring and stove, and lay down to await death.

Towards evening Maria came to the house to meet Gertler by arrangement and, on getting no answer at the door, went down to the studio, where she found the door locked and immediately rang Andrew Morland. The Morlands, who were dressing for a party, left for Grove Terrace at once, and arrived, still in their party clothes, with their chauffeur, who broke down the studio door.[44] As Maria and Dorothy waited in the garden, Celia returned, just in time to see Gertler's body being carried out.[45] She later told the press that Gertler was still alive but unconscious[46]; but according to other reports he had been dead for some hours. Accounts also disagree as to whether Maria, Celia or even Kot – who was apparently expecting Gertler later for tea – found the body, and raise the question of whether this last attempt, like all the others, was simply a cry for help. Perhaps it was

Kot who best summed up the grief and amazement of Gertler's friends, who despite glimpsing his moments of profound depression had always retained a strong sense of the ardent spirit beneath. 'Gertler, who loved life', Kot said afterwards, 'how could he have killed himself?'[47]

Gertler appears to have left no suicide note and he certainly left no will. This and the manner and confusion of his death account for the haphazard parcelling out of his belongings afterwards. It was probably the Morlands who telephoned Marjorie in Paris, and she immediately arranged to return to London, leaving Luke in the care of the school in Davos. She also telephoned Gertler's family and told them to go to the studio and take what they liked, and in this way many of Gertler's unsold paintings passed back into his family. Among the pile of paintings and drawings still stacked with their faces against the wall was a copy of his unfinished manuscript 'First Memories', which Gertler's niece Renée found and gave to John Mavrogordato at Oxford for safekeeping. Marjorie later said that when she arrived a few days later, she found the studio virtually empty. She destroyed all her own letters to Gertler but kept his to her, and gave them to Luke many years later as a memento of his father.

'Talk at Nessa's last night. Much about Gertler's suicide', Virginia Woolf noted in her diary three days later. 'Why did he turn on the gas, when his model left him?'[48] they all wondered, and were still wondering the next day when Virginia recorded further 'talk of Gertler at Clive's'.[49] Virginia concluded that he had been 'perhaps too rigid, too self-centred, too honest and too narrow . . . to be content or happy'. But she remained perplexed that despite 'his intellect and interest . . . the personal life [had] become too painful'. She took her own life less than two years later.

The post-mortem confirmed only that Gertler had died from coal-gas poisoning,[50] and at the inquest on the morning of Tuesday 27 June the coroner, W. B. Purchase, brought in a verdict of suicide 'whilst of unsound mind'.[51] The first reports of Gertler's death appeared in the press on Sunday 25 June, and friends who had not yet heard the news read them in stunned silence. In the following week respectful obituaries appeared in most papers, including *The Times* and the *Daily Telegraph*, while Maria Donska and Dr Morland gave a brief, factual description of the finding of the body to the *Islington Gazette*.[52] Celia gave interviews to the tabloids, which splashed lurid headlines across the story: 'Artist died beside Unfinished Picture – his Finest: Girl who inspired him tells of tragedy' (*News of the World*); 'Death Robs Art Girl: 'I shall never forget' (*Sunday Mirror*); and 'Died Beside Dream Picture'.[53]

Luke, still at school in Davos, was told of his father's death by the head, who was known as 'Mother' – 'a most unmotherly person', he recalled – who called him into her office. Thinking he had done something wrong and fearing he would be punished, Luke hardly took in what she had to tell him: his father had died accidentally by turning on the gas fire and forgetting to light the gas. 'My father's dead', he told the other children, apparently 'quite cheerfully'. It was only later that night when he was in bed that the news began to sink in: 'Being dead meant that life was over; I would never see my father again. The full realization of the tragedy dawned on me and I began to cry. The boy in the next bed asked "What's the matter?" I answered "My father's dead". But this time it was said with real grief.'[54] It was more than a decade before he learned the truth about his father's suicide, when by chance he read the reviews of the 1949 memorial exhibition at the Whitechapel Art Gallery.

Gertler's family organized a Jewish funeral, which took place at Willesden Cemetery (where Golda had been buried) on the afternoon of Tuesday 27 June. Since he was a suicide the rabbi kept the service short and the family were not allowed to sit shiva. It was a beautiful, hot afternoon, and Mark's brothers, Harry and Jack, headed the procession of oddly assorted mourners, their black clothes strangely out of place against the bright blue sky. All of Gertler's family were present, as well as some (unidentified) East End neighbours; Marjorie, wearing a jaunty little hat with feathers, stood shaking with tears as she bent over the grave, supported by Andrew and Dorothy Morland. Duncan Grant was the only representative of Bloomsbury, and among the other painters present were Gertler's old friends Bernard Meninsky, clearly grieving, and Dick Carline. Many of his teaching colleagues were there, including Ernest and Daphne Fedarb, Robert Kirkland Jamieson and his wife, Dorothy, and so were faithful old friends such as Tom Balston, Monty Shearman and Julian Goodman, accompanied by her father, Philip Morrell, who wore full mourning clothes. The rabbi spoke briefly in Hebrew and then in English, and Harry and Jack threw earth onto the coffin in silence, as it was lowered into an unmarked grave.

Much later the family were finally allowed to erect a memorial stone to mark Gertler's grave, which reads simply:

In
Memory of
Mark Gertler
Died 23rd June 1939
Aged 46
Mourned By His Wife, Son,
Brothers, Sisters,
Relatives and Friends.

There was no mention of his profession.

Epilogue

GERTLER'S DEATH WAS soon forgotten in the greater tragedy of the outbreak of the Second World War in September 1939. The Westminster closed instantly, never to be reopened as an art school (though the building now houses Westminster College). Marjorie returned to France soon after the funeral and was reunited with Franz Kostenz, whom she later married. In the early years of the war they led a dangerous and difficult existence, fleeing first to Montpellier, where Franz (who had been a medical student) hoped to continue his studies. However, worried by the threat of his possible identification and arrest, they settled instead with Luke in the remote village of Cabrière d'Avignon, in Vaucluse in southern France. There, they survived the war in conditions of extreme poverty, eking out Marjorie's meagre income and sleeping on straw until the munificent Aunt Ethel sent them a packing case of proper bedding. Luke's half-brother Michael was born in 1942.

After the war the family returned to Britain and Marjorie later studied embroidery with Constance Howard at Goldsmith's College, producing a series of bold, colourful designs, which were later exhibited at Foyle's (for the Embroiderers' Guild) and at the Minories in Colchester. Franz, despite becoming a travel agent, rarely travelled again, but Marjorie returned every summer to Cabrière d'Avignon with Luke, and Provence continued to be the main source of her artistic inspiration. In later years the Kostenzes settled in Ealing, but their home and many of their possessions were later completely destroyed by fire. Franz died in 1976 and Marjorie in 1979, at the age of seventy-six. She is buried in Godstone, beside the grave of her mother, in a double plot with Franz. After the closure of the Westminster, Bernard Meninsky taught at the Oxford School of Art from 1940 to 1945, later becoming Instructor in Drawing at the Central School of Art. He committed suicide in 1950.

At the outbreak of war Maria Donska remained at the Royal College of Music, separated from her family (who later perished in Nazi concentration camps) and from Baba (who was interned in Holloway Prison for a year, on account of her father's German nationality, and her own brief marriage to a German). The following year Maria's own health collapsed, but by 1943 she had recovered sufficiently to play a memorable part in the National Gallery's lunchtime concerts for the rest of the war. She joined the Bryanston Summer School in 1948, and played annually until 1951, when the summer school was transferred to Dartington Hall, where she remained throughout the 1950s (and where she later met Luke Gertler as a young student). In 1955 Maria's Beethoven recitals inspired Epstein to produce a remarkable sculpture of her, and also led to a lifelong friendship between them. She continued to give concerts until the 1970s, playing at the Wigmore Hall, recording for the BBC and teaching at the Royal College of Music for many years. Baba Speyer died in 1987, and Maria's professional career ended in 1989 after she suffered a stroke. She died in Kent in 1996, aged eighty-four, and a memorial concert was later held for her at St Martin-in-the-Fields.

Some weeks after Gertler's death his former model Celia Dennis turned up on Ida Graves's doorstep, where she collapsed weeping, blaming herself for his death (since she had failed to take his story of a former attempt seriously). 'I know you to have been very devoted to him', William Rothenstein wrote to Celia on first hearing of Gertler's death, 'and his end must have been a grief to you.' In September 1939 Celia wrote to Tom Balston, that 'with Mark gone, and now with the war, the world seem[ed] a different place. Circumstances', she added, forced her to 'seek occupation apart from art', and she asked Balston to take her on as a domestic. He appears to have turned her down, and she eventually emigrated to America.

A small number of Gertler's friends (Tom, Kot and Beatrice Glenavy among them) never forgave Marjorie for 'deserting' Gertler, although many of them made a special effort to stay in touch with Luke. Some years after the family's return to Britain Marjorie once dialled Kot's number by mistake, but slammed down the receiver in alarm the minute she heard his stern voice on the other end. Kot remained 'rooted' at Acacia Road for the rest of his life, consoled in his last years by his friendship with the writer H. G. Wells and his family. Always on the verge of poverty, when asked by friends how he would manage Kot would simply shrug and say, 'I will sell some old trousers'. Despite fragile health, he retained his fierce independence until the end. Upon his death in 1955 he bequeathed his invaluable correspondence with Gertler, Katherine Mansfield, D. H. Lawrence and Wells to the British Library.

At the outbreak of war Thomas Balston returned briefly to army life as a staff officer and (nearly suffered another nervous breakdown in consequence). After his release from service he organized a Gertler retrospective at the Whitechapel in 1949 and contributed the first entry on him to the *Dictionary of National Biography*. In his last years he became an assiduous collector of book illustrations and a garrulous figure at the Garrick, relating stories of his Duckworth days. After his death in 1967 his large collection of Gertler paintings was bequeathed to the nation through the National Art Collections Fund. In 1939 Werner Droescher and Greville Texidor were both interned as German nationals: Droescher in a camp in Devon and Texidor in Holloway. After influential friends lobbied for their release they eventually emigrated to Auckland, New Zealand, in May 1940, and Greville began to write. She continued to see Marjorie for several years until the publication of *These Dark Glasses* in 1949 caused a rift. Greville's second daughter, Rosamund, was born in 1945, and the family continued its peripatetic existence by moving first to Brisbane, Australia (where Mrs Foster died in 1953), then returning in 1954 to Tossa, Spain (where Greville later purchased the artist George Kars's old house), and ending up in Sydney in 1962 after Greville's separation from Werner Droescher. Their final move was to Hazelbrook in the Blue Mountains, Australia, two years later. In 1964 Greville walked out into the bush and never returned.

Gilbert Cannan spent the rest of his life in The Priory, Roehampton, outliving most of the Cholesbury circle. He died there in 1955. Brett remained in Taos for the rest of her life, painting large canvases based on the life and ceremonies of the Pueblo Indians, and much sought after by Lawrence scholars. Retrospectives of her work were held in New York (1950) and the Taos Gallery of Contemporary Art (1980). She died in Taos in 1977, shortly before her ninety-fourth birthday.

Notes

CHAPTER 1: THE EMIGRANTS

1. Gertler's family always believed the date to be 1892. This is the date referred to in all records during Gertler's lifetime, and all age references given by Gertler himself. I follow the correct 1891 dating for all references to Gertler's age throughout. As a result, there is sometimes a discrepancy between his actual age and the age Gertler and his contemporaries believed him to be.
2. M. Gertler, 'First Memories', an autobiographical fragment published in edited form in Noel Carrington's *Mark Gertler: Selected Letters* [*MGSL*], pp. 15–27.
3. N. Davies, *God's Playground: A History of Poland*, vol. 2, *1795 to the Present*, p. 142.
4. Jack's date of birth is given as 19 June 1886 in his naturalization papers (Public Record Office [PRO], Kew HO 144/1246/232602–3).
5. R. Porter, *London: A Social History*, pp. 300–02.
6. Census for 1891 (London Metropolitan Archives).
7. W. J. Fishman, *East End Jewish Radicals: 1875–1914*, p. 215.
8. Some records of the Jewish Board of Guardians do survive but they show no trace of the Gertler family. However, Gertler related this information himself in 'First Memories', *MGSL*, p. 16.
9. Ibid.
10. Davies, *God's Playground*, vol. 2, p. 142.
11. Gertler, 'First Memories', *MGSL*, p. 18.
12. J. Woodeson: *Mark Gertler: Biography of a Painter*, p. 6.
13. Ibid., p. 19.
14. T. Balston, 'Mark Gertler 1891–1939'.
15. Contemporary reports as to the length of the journeys vary. Gertler gives the journey as 'weeks' in his 'First Memories', *MGSL*. p. 20.
16. Rose Robins, cited in Fishman, *East End Jewish Radicals*, p. 38.
17. Gertler, 'First Memories', *MGSL*, p. 20.
18. G. Cannan, *Mendel: A Story of Youth*, p. 12.
19. Newspapers such as the *Daily Graphic* carried news reports and warnings of this practice. A marvellous account of this appears in W. G. Sebald's semi-autobiographical novel *The Emigrants*. Erected in 1885, the Statue of Liberty remained a very potent symbol for generations of sea-travelling immigrants.
20. Gertler, 'First Memories', *MGSL*, p. 20.
21. Ibid., p. 21.

CHAPTER 2: THE IMMIGRANTS

1. Gertler, 'First Memories', *MGSL*, p. 20.
2. Ibid.

3. A. McGill, *Evening Standard* (20 August 1986).
4. Gertler, 'First Memories', *MGSL*, p. 21.
5. Ibid., p. 22.
6. Ibid.
7. S. Lynd, 'Time & Tide', *MGSL*, pp. 250–1.
8. The 'poverty line' was estimated by Charles Booth in 1897 to be about £1 10*s.* a week. At the time a loaf of bread cost between 10*d.* and a shilling (see Fishman, *East End Jewish Radicals*).
9. A map dated 1894 shows Union Row with Sion Square to the north, clearly marked. By 1899, however, in the official map of Jewish east London, the area to the north of Union Row is simply marked 'Square', and this is perpetuated in a map of 1903. Today Union Street has been renamed Adler Street (after Rabbi Adler) and Mulberry Street, which used to run south from Sion Square, has replaced Union Row. The name Sion Square has disappeared altogether.
10. Possibly Wolff Levy, bootmaker, although one of the witnesses at Deby's wedding ceremony was Solomon Levy.
11. Not to be confused with 'boarding' schools, these were local day schools run by school boards comprising fifty-five men and women, who were elected every three years. The schools were paid for by local rates.
12. Gertler, following the family dates, always gave the gap as seven years, but Jack's naturalization papers show he could not have been more than five when Mark was born.
13. In 'First Memories' Gertler mistakenly gives the name of his first school as Deal Street, but his school records (PRO, Northampton Road, London) show that he attended Settles Street School from 20 October 1897 to 1 July 1899, then Deal Street School from 12 March 1900 to 8 January 1906.
14. He is, none the less, listed on all his school records as 'Marks'.
15. Lord Rothschild declared in 1906, 'Our first business is to humanise our Jewish immigrants, and then to Anglicise them' (quoted in A. Davies: 'The Jewish Community in the East End', *The East End Nobody Knows: A History, A Guide, An Explanation*, p. 84).
16. Gertler, 'First Memories', *MGSL*, p. 25.
17. Mark Gertler to Ottoline Morrell, 23 April 1927, University of Texas, Austin.
18. J. Rothenstein, 'Mark Gertler', *Modern English Painters*, vol. 2, *Nash to Bawden*, p. 131.
19. N. Solomon, *Judaism: A Very Short Introduction*, p. 83.
20. Gertler, 'First Memories', *MGSL*, p. 25.
21. Marriage certificate of Deby Gertler and Abraham Attleson, 20 June 1899.
22. V. D. Lipman, *Jewish Chronicle* (5 February 1982).
23. A. Davin, *Growing Up Poor: Home, School and Street in London, 1870–1914* (London: Rivers Oram Press, 1996), p. 115.
24. Mark Gertler, cited in *Jewish Chronicle* (9 February 1912).
25. Ibid.
26. T. Balston, 'Mark Gertler, 1891–1939'.
27. *Jewish Chronicle* (9 February 1912).
28. Woodeson, Gertler, p. 33. This story is also told in Gilbert Cannan's *Mendel*, p. 26.
29. Woodeson, *Gertler*, p. 36.
30. *Jewish Chronicle* (9 February 1912).
31. Built in 1743 as a Huguenot church, the building was also used as a missionary centre and Methodist chapel before its conversion to a synagogue in 1898. It was converted into a mosque in 1975.
32. E. J. Fedarb, 'Reminiscences of Mark Gertler' (unpublished), from a letter to the author, 7 January 1998.
33. The Goldwaters are listed at 56 Leman Street in *Kelly's Commercial Directory* for 1905. The first listing for Louis Gertler's business appears in 1909, under the listing 'Gerty Gertler', which becomes 'Mrs Gerty Gertler' in 1910–11. Possibly this was deliberate (changing the name under which a business was listed was a common way of avoiding bankruptcy), but

it seems more likely that it was simply a further corruption of Louis's and/or Golda's name for in 1912, when the business is listed under Harry's name, it appears in the anglicized form as 'Henry'. Nineteen fifteen was the only year in which the business was listed under Louis's name, and that too was anglicized to 'Lewis Gertler'. After Louis's death in 1917, the listing included both brothers and for several years Jack's name was anglicized to John.

34. Cited in Woodeson, *Gertler*, p. 46.
35. M. Gertler, 'Fragment on the Death of John Currie' (*c.* 1916), Luke Gertler Collection.
36. Gertler to Mr Hayward, 14 May 1924, Manchester City Art Gallery Archives.
37. Entry headed 20 November 1929, recorded in 1927 diary, Luke Gertler Collection.

CHAPTER 3: MENDEL

1. V. S. Pritchett, 'Conservative Gipsy', *New Statesman* (15 December 1972).
2. 'Mark Gertler: The Man and his Art', *Studio*, 104 (September 1932), p. 158.
3. He would have been fifteen in December, but having given his date of birth as 1892, Gaskell could not have thought him more than fourteen. (The statutory minimum age for entry to the Polytechnic was fifteen.)
4. R. Floud and S. Glynn, eds., *London Higher: The Establishment of Higher Education in London*, p. 265.
5. Ibid.
6. Regent Street Polytechnic prospectus 1908, University of Westminster archive, London. Although the prospectus did not specify its achievements for 1908, during the previous eleven sessions (1897–1908) students had obtained the following medals (in addition to the usual school medals): 4 gold medals, 18 silver medals, 39 bronze medals and 90 national book prizes in national art competition; 26 king's prizes and 30 other national prizes; over 3,500 Board of Education certificates, 1 royal exhibition; 1 'Princess of Wales' Scholarship; 39 LCC scholarships; 15 students admitted to the Royal Academy Schools; and 88 works exhibited at the Royal Academy by students in the school at the time.
7. Floud and Glynn, *London Higher*, p. 201.
8. Ibid., p. 178.
9. Ibid., pp. 102–3.
10. After a visit by the City Parochial Charities (CPC) representative Cunnynghame, the CPC Act of 1883 made available £50,000 a year for the development of further education in London. By 1910 over 850 pupils were attending the Polytechnic day schools.
11. F. Spalding, *Dictionary of British Art*, vol. 6, *20th Century Painters and Sculptors* (Suffolk: Antique Collectors' Club, 1990), p. 13.
12. At least eight of them were RA exhibitors.
13. Cannan, *Mendel*, p. 52.
14. Traditionally vocational courses such as design attracted slightly more male pupils, while still life painting attracted slightly more women (1906–9 prospectuses, Regent Street Polytechnic, University of Westminster, London).
15. Headmaster: G. Percival Gaskell; evening life class: E. W. Appleby; modelling: F. Callcott; design: H. G. Theaker; antique, still life painting, elementary subjects and general assistance: W. R. Cope, H. S. Joyner, H. Watson, H. T. Wood, C. W. Norton, W. Matthews, Miss M. A. Merrick, Miss W. L. Stamp and Miss M. Spencer. Appleby, a 'Victorian' painter, had immortalized the Polytechnic's founder, Quintin Hogg, in a portrait executed in 1892.
16. Design stage 1, 1907: of the eighteen pupils on the course, five (including Gertler) failed, five achieved firsts and eight achieved second-class passes.
17. Fantin-Latour's *A Plate of Apples* (1861) was bequeathed to the National Gallery in1907, transferred to the Tate Gallery *c.* 1920 and has been on loan from the Tate since 1997.
18. It remains in the collection of the artist's family.
19. Regent Street Polytechnic records, University of Westminster archive, London.

20. *Sea Shells* (1907), Fitzwilliam Museum, Cambridge; *Fruit and Flask* (1907), formerly in Harrogate Art Gallery, now in Lloyd's boardroom; *Still Life with Coffee Pot* (1907), Tatham Art Gallery, Pietermaritzburg; and *Still Life with Bottle of Benedictine* (1908), on permanent loan to the Ben Uri Art Gallery.
21. Cannan, *Mendel*, p. 52.
22. Ibid.
23. Gertler, 'A Triumph of Education Aid', *Jewish Chronicle* (9 September 1912).
24. Mark Gertler to William Rothenstein, not dated [*c.* May–June 1910], *MGSL*, p. 33.
25. A 20 per cent reduction on the fee was offered for students and teachers from the Polytechnic (1908 prospectus, University of Westminster, London).
26. Balston, 'Mark Gertler'.
27. 'Mark Gertler: The Man and his Art', pp. 158–63.
28. Gertler's painting relates closely to the painting *Still Life with Bottle, Glass and Loaf* in the National Gallery, inscribed 'Chardin. 1754' but now recognized as a nineteenth-century imitation.
29. Cannan, *Mendel*, pp. 54–5.
30. The dates of birth of all the other students are not known, but of those others who went on to become professionals (roughly 10 per cent), all were between five and ten years older than Gertler.
31. These were Jack Betlem, Alice Braine, Gustave Barnes (later curator of the Adelaide Art Gallery), Olive Horsford and Katharine Frances Clausen (Mrs O'Brien). In all, there were nine firsts, six seconds and five fails.
32. Matthews, Hartley, Tresilian and Hounsell became teachers or pupil-teachers; Tresilian also went on to the RCA and became an illustrator.
33. Cannan, *Mendel*, p. 53.
34. Ibid., p. 67.
35. J. A. R. Pimlott (preface), *Toynbee Hall: Fifty Years of Social Progress, 1884–1934*.
36. The records themselves, however, were damaged by fire and Second World War bombs and are therefore incomplete.
37. Ernest Lesser (secretary) to Mark Gertler [1908], Luke Gertler Collection.
38. Cannan suggests that Tufness/Harvey used his influence with the Bishop of Stepney.
39. Quoted in P. Reyntiens, *The Beauty of Stained Glass* (London: Herbert Press, 1990), p. 123.
40. Messrs Clayton & Bell to Mark Gertler, *c.* 1908, Luke Gertler Collection.
41. Cannan, *Mendel*, pp. 64–5.
42. Ibid.
43. Mark Gertler to Carrington, 24 September 1912, *MGSL*, pp. 46–7.
44. N. Carrington, *MGSL*, p. 28.
45. Isaac Rosenberg to Miss Winifreda Seaton, *c.* 1910, S. Sassoon and I. Parsons, eds., *The Collected Works of Isaac Rosenberg*, p. 180.
46. Signed and dated 1908, oil on canvas 17 × 21½ inches. The painting was previously thought to date from 1906. However, Gertler did not begin drawing from casts until at least 1907, so it is likely that the date is in fact 1908. The current whereabouts are unknown.
47. There were 13,787 candidates from 236 schools of art and branch schools. A further 970 candidates were entered from 114 art evening schools and day classes. The following prizes were achieved overall: 12 gold medals; 79 silver medals; 269 bronze medals; 360 prizes of books and 1,008 commendations. The Regent Street Polytechnic achieved 1 gold medal, 3 silver medals, 9 bronze medals, 5 national book prizes and 19 commendations.
48. Hartley Library, Special Collections, University of Southampton: MS 135/AJ 35.1.
49. Minute Books of the General Committee, 21 October 1907 to 29 June 1910. Anglo-Jewish Archives, Hartley Library, Special Collections, University of Southampton, MS 135/AJ 35, p. 100.
50. Rothenstein, *Modern English Painters*, vol. 2, p. 130.
51. Cannan, *Mendel*, p. 76.

52. William Rothenstein to Louis Gertler, 3 October 1908, Luke Gertler Collection.
53. Others included W. H. Hudson, Eric Gill, Stanley Spencer and Augustus John.
54. Rothenstein, *Modern English Painters*, vol. 2, p. 130.

CHAPTER 4: THE SLADE

1. Slade died in 1868, leaving an endowment of £45,000 to found two lecturing professorships at Oxford and Cambridge and one or more at University College, London. £5,000 was voted by UCL to fund the faculty together with £10,000 for six scholarships for students under the age of nineteen.
2. P. Nash, *Outline*, p. 89.
3. B. Laughton, 'The Slade 1871–1971', introduction, *Centenary Exhibition Catalogue* (London: Royal Academy, 1971).
4. The South Kensington School became the National Art Training School in 1864 and the Royal College of Art in 1896.
5. M. Hutchinson, introduction to J. Hone, *The Life of Henry Tonks*.
6. Ibid.
7. Nash, *Outline*, p. 89.
8. Laughton, 'The Slade, 1871–1971'.
9. Cannan, *Mendel*, p. 83.
10. Walter Russell (1867–1949), painter, illustrator and etcher, was painting and drawing teacher at the Slade, 1895–1927. He was knighted in 1930.
11. A. Allinson, 'A Painter's Pilgrimage', MS, McFarlin Library, University of Tulsa, Oklahoma, p. 16.
12. R. Carline, *Stanley Spencer at War*, p. 25.
13. Mark Gertler to William Rothenstein, [October] 1908, *MGSL*, p. 29.
14. Cannan, *Mendel*, p. 83.
15. The episode is replicated in *Mendel*.
16. Hone, *Henry Tonks*, p. 74.
17. Stephen Chaplin, the Slade archivist, has pointed out that the Slade beadle, for example, would not have been able to afford to send his children there – the annual fee being one fifth of his wages.
18. Of the eight applicants for art training in 1907–8 only an (unnamed) 'female modeller nearing the end of her training' and Gertler were assisted. Five others were rejected out of hand and the remaining one was 'still awaiting consideration' at the close of the year.
19. It is not known where or when this term originated, but it came to be applied to the group of gifted Whitechapel youths which included artists Gertler and Bomberg, the poet and painter Isaac Rosenberg and the writers Joseph Leftwich, John Rodker and Samuel Winsten. See I. Parsons, ed., *The Collected Works of Isaac Rosenberg* (London: Chatto & Windus, 1984), n. 194.
20. Mark Weiner (later changed to Wayner), who attended the Slade 1909–10 with the support of the JEAS, later had his payments stopped when the JEAS accused him of poor attendance. Wayner, who was even poorer than Gertler and gave part of his JEAS money to his parents, was forced to leave the Slade as a result. (Information from Ruth Silver [Mark Wayner's daughter], 5 May 2001.)
21 Quoted in S. Hignett, *Brett: From Bloomsbury to New Mexico: A Biography*, p. 38. Bomberg's fees were actually paid by the JEAS (1911–13), after Bomberg met John Singer Sargent in 1907, and through him Solomon J. Solomon, who in this case made up his mind immediately and recommended Bomberg to the JEAS.
22 J. R. Taylor, *Bernard Meninsky*, p. 12.
23 This sort of support was still rare. The committee turned down Isaac Rosenberg on 11 June 1911.
24 Of the £5 expenses, 10*s.* per term was to go on season tickets and 2*s.* a week on materials (JEAS minutes, 17 November 1908, University of Southampton).

25 However, Tonks's critical faculty was not infallible. Duncan Grant later recalled how he had felt rather guilty at the ease with which he adapted himself to Slade requirements in order to earn Tonks's approval, by executing a drawing 'perfectly in the manner of Tonks'. When it was subsequently held up as an example of what good drawing should be, he felt 'rather mean and also disillusioned' (quoted in F. Spalding, *Duncan Grant*, p. 57).
26 JEAS minutes, 31 October 1908, MS 135/AJ 35, University of Southampton.
27 No such person is registered at this address in the Post Office Directory for 1909.
28 When they were broke the friends repaired to the home of Wayner's aunt Barbara in Wentworth Street, who would feed them as they sat outlining their ambitious plans for the future. (Information from Mrs Barbara Strauss and Ruth Silver, 5 May 2001.)
29 Cannan, *Mendel*, p. 59.
30 Ibid., p. 61.
31 JEAS report, 10 March 1909, University of Southampton.
32 Ibid.
33 Rothenstein, *Modern English Painters*, vol. 1, *Sickert to Lowry*, p. 49.
34 David Sassoon, cited in M. Reynolds, 'The Slade: The Story of an Art School, 1871–1971', MS, London, Watson Library, Slade School of Art, pp. 191–2.
35 William Rothenstein to Mark Gertler [12 May 1909], *MGSL*, p. 30.
36 Ibid.
37 Gertler, 'A Triumph of Education Aid'.
38 M. Lilly, *Sickert: The Painter and his Circle*, p. 124.
39 JEAS annual report, 1909, Art Section, p. 6, MS 135/AJ 35.33, University of Southampton.
40 Mark Gertler to William Rothenstein [12 May 1909], *MGSL*, p. 30.
41 University College calendar, session 1908–9, Slade Archive.
42 Carline, *Stanley Spencer at War*, p. 26.
43 William Rothenstein to Mrs Golda Gertler, 22 May 1909, *MGSL*, p. 29.
44 William Rothenstein to Mark Gertler, 12 May 1909, ibid., p. 30.
45 Mark Gertler to William Rothenstein, [August] 1909, ibid., p. 31.
46 Ibid.
47 Mark Gertler to William Rothenstein, [August] 1909, ibid., pp. 31–2.
48 Mark Gertler to William Rothenstein, [August] 1909, ibid., p. 31.
49 Dorothy Brett to Luke Gertler, 16 April 1968, Luke Gertler Collection.
50 Mark Gertler to William Rothenstein, [August] 1909, *MGSL*, p. 31.
51 Signed and dated, 'Myself. Age 17/M. Gertler 14 Aug. '09'.
52 David Burleigh remembered photographing it, but sadly this photograph does not appear to have survived (David Burleigh to John Woodeson, cited in Woodeson: *Gertler*, p. 74).

CHAPTER 5: THE QUINTET

1. Balston, 'Mark Gertler 1891–1939'.
2. C. R. W. Nevinson, *Paint and Prejudice*, p. 25.
3. Ibid., p. 30.
4. G. Gerzina, *Carrington: A Life of Dora Carrington, 1893–1932*, p. 22.
5. Allinson, 'A Painter's Pilgrimage', p. 17.
6. Ibid.
7. Ibid.
8. In *Mendel*, p. 121, the young hero quickly becomes 'much more like the others, affected their speech, grew his hair long, wore corduroys, a black shirt, and a red sash, and talked blatantly and with a slight contempt of great painters'.
9. Mark Gertler to William Rothenstein [c. May–June 1910], *MGSL*, p. 33.
10. Ibid., p. 14.
11. Ibid.
12. Allinson, 'A Painter's Pilgrimage', p. 18.
13. Nevinson, *Paint and Prejudice*, p. 23.

14. Allinson, 'A Painter's Pilgrimage', pp. 59–60.
15. Ibid.
16. B. Wadsworth, *Edward Wadsworth: A Painter's Life*, p. 27.
17. Allinson claimed in his memoirs to have fooled the Slade professors into awarding Stanley Spencer a prize for a work he himself had done in imitation of Spencer.
18. Allinson, 'A Painter's Pilgrimage', p. 18.
19. Mark Gertler to William Rothenstein [*c.* May–June 1910], *MGSL*, p. 33.
20. Nevinson, *Paint and Prejudice*, p. 16.
21. Ibid., p. 27.
22. Allinson, 'A Painter's Pilgrimage', p. 18.
23. Nash, *Outline*, p. 91.
24. See L. Tickner, *Modern Life and Modern Subjects: British Life in the Early Twentieth Century*, p. 280. Isaac Rosenberg, 'whose parents were pacifists, was mercilessly assaulted' by fellow student Alvaro Guevara 'until [Jacob] Kramer and Bomberg came to his aid'. After Bomberg (whose brothers were boxers) had blackened Guevara's eye, 'the Jewish students were left in peace.'
25. Darsie Japp to John Woodeson, cited in Woodeson: *Gertler*, p. 51.
26. Ibid., p. 69.
27. Allinson, 'A Painter's Pilgrimage', p. 51.
28. Cannan, *Mendel*, p. 89.
29. Allinson, 'A Painter's Pilgrimage', p. 18.
30. Nash, *Outline*, p. 90.
31. Reynolds, *The Slade*, p. 178.
32. Ibid.
33. Ibid.
34. F. Spalding, 'Gertler's Early Work', *Mark Gertler: The Early and the Late Years*, p. 6.
35. Ibid.
36. Nevinson recalled a second trip in May when the city was 'all smiles and warmth', but Sassoon and Allinson's accounts both agree that it was Easter and 'bitterly cold', so Nevinson may have been mixing this up with his later visit to Paris with Gertler and his mother in 1911.
37. Nevinson, *Paint and Prejudice*, p. 33.
38. Ibid.
39. Ibid., p. 26.
40. Laughton, introduction, 'The Slade, 1871–1971'.
41. David Sassoon, quoted in Reynolds, *The Slade*, p. 179. The visit is confirmed by Allinson's account, which stresses that they learned that 'our own Slade was considered quite as good a training ground as this famous Parisian Art School' (Allinson, 'A Painter's Pilgrimage', pp. 81–2.)
42. Ibid.
43. JEAS minutes, 4 May 1910, University of Southampton, MS 135/AJ 35.
44. Mark Gertler to William Rothenstein [*c.* May–June 1910] *MGSL*, p. 33.
45. Ibid.
46. Ibid.
47. Vanessa Bell to Clive Bell, Thursday [23 June 1910], Tate Gallery, Archive, 8010. 2. 32.
48. R. Shone, 'The Friday Club, 1905–1922', *Burlington Magazine*, (May 1975); repr. as a catalogue to an exhibition by the Michael Parkin Gallery (London, 1996), pp. 279–84. All quotations are from the latter edition.
49. The influence of Puvis de Chavannes is apparent in Duncan Grant's *Lemon Gatherers* of 1910 and Gertler's *Fruit Sorters* of 1914, which also owes a debt to Grant's picture.
50. Lees was on the hanging committee 1912–14, but did not contribute to exhibitions.
51. Shone, 'The Friday Club'.
52. Nevison joined in 1912 and served on the selecting jury from 1916; he continued to exhibit there until 1922.

53. Exceptionally, he did not exhibit in 1920 and 1921.
54. Mark Gertler to William Rothenstein [10 May 1910], *MGSL*, p. 32.
55. M. G. Lightfoot to Mark Gertler, 20 July 1910, Luke Gertler Collection.
56. JEAS minutes, 29 June 1910, University of Southampton, MS 135/AJ 35.
57. He did not officially leave until 1912, but his attendance was probably very limited from now on.
58. Workshop of Bellini, *c.* 1500, presented to the National Gallery by the Earl of Carlisle, 1895.
59. Gertler, *Jewish Chronicle* (9 February 1912).
60. The grey-haired man is one of the Gertler's most recognizable models of the period; but the dark-haired younger man was also the model for Rothenstein's *Reading the Scroll of Esther* (1907), which had been on display in May 1910. See Tickner, *Modern Life and Modern Subjects*, p. 293, n. 114.
61. JEAS minutes, 29 June 1910, University of Southampton.
62. Neither of these prizes is analogous with the Slade annual prizes awarded in the following categories: prize for the best painting from the life; prize for the best drawing from the life; prize for the best drawing from an antique figure; prize for the best composition from a given subject; and a prize for success in an examination in anatomy held by the professor of anatomy at the end of his course.
63. Allinson, 'A Painter's Pilgrimage', p. 20. According to Allinson, the competitions were monthly.
64. JEAS minutes, 29 June 1910, University of Southampton. In November, however (JEAS minutes, 9 November 1910), a further 5*s.* a week was voted for six months.
65. JEAS minutes, MS 135/AJ 35.2. Minute book (General Committee) 21 October 1907 to 29 June 1910: Gertler, M: 29 June 1910, p. 454.
66. Nash, *Outline*, p. 91.
67. H. Ginsbury, 'Two Students Recollect', *Mark Gertler: The Early and the Late Years*, p. 18.
68. Ibid.
69. Mark Gertler to William Rothenstein [*c.* December 1910], *MGSL*, p. 32.
70. Although Frances Spalding (introduction to *Jacob Kramer Reassessed*, p. 3) notes that when the JEAS put up the money to send Jacob Kramer to the Slade in 1912, they 'warned him of the need for greater seriousness and assiduity'.

CHAPTER 6: FOREIGNERS IN ENGLAND

1. Roger Fry to Sir Edward Fry, 24 November 1910, cited in A. Gruetzner Robins, *Modern Art in Britain, 1910–1914*, p. 15.
2. Spalding, *Duncan Grant*, p. 98.
3. Gruetzner Robins, *Modern Art in Britain*, p. 15.
4. Ibid.
5. Ibid., p. 21.
6. Spalding, *Duncan Grant*, p. 101.
7. Gruetzner Robins, *Modern Art in Britain*, p. 35.
8. Ibid., p. 182.
9. F. Spalding, *Vanessa Bell*, p. 92.
10. Cited in M. Holroyd, *Augustus John: The New Biography*, p. 327.
11. Cited in B. Ford, *The Cambridge Guide to the Arts in Britain*, vol. 8, *The Edwardian Age and the Inter-War Years* (Cambridge: Cambridge University Press), p. 202.
12. Nash, *Outline*, p. 93.
13. Ibid.
14. He is listed in the prospectus as lecturing on the history of art in the first and second terms of 1909–10, 1910–1911 and 1911–12, although after the first Post-Impressionist exhibition in 1910, Tonks developed a vehement and unquenchable personal antipathy to Fry. Frances Spalding (*Duncan Grant*, p.109) asserts that Fry gave 'a series of lectures at the Slade every autumn and spring term between September 1909 and December 1913'.

15. Gruetzner Robins, *Modern Art in Britain*, p. 46.
16. Allinson, 'A Painter's Pilgrimage', p. 22.
17. Cannan, *Mendel*, pp. 90–1.
18. James Bone, cited in Holroyd, *Augustus John*, p. 329.
19. Holroyd, *Augustus John*, p. 335.
20. Ibid.
21. Velázquez's painting was bequeathed to the National Gallery in 1892. The painter Dorothy Brett later recalled that one of Gertler's favourite paintings was 'Velazquez's painting of some eggs in the National Gallery' (letter to Luke Gertler, 11 July 1968).
22. Letter to the author from Rose Landau's daughter Phyllis Kutcher Martin, 11 November 1999.
23. JEAS minutes, 22 February 1911, p. 39.
24. Marriage certificate of Harry Gertler and Annie Hyman, 27 December 1910, Family Records Centre, London. Adrian Allinson ('A Painter's Pilgrimage', p. 18) remembered the wedding as 'a swagger affair' with 200 guests, where he caused 'general hilarity' by being demonstrably unable to eat his peas with his knife like the rest of the company.
25. The Rev. John Henry Cardwell MA (1842–1921), prependary of St Paul's since 1911; incumbent, St Andrew's, Fulham, 1868–91; rector, St Anne's Soho, 1891–1914. The painting was probably commissioned by his parishioners in preparation for Cardwell's forthcoming retirement in 1914. Although there is no evidence to this effect in extant church records, some records may have been lost during the bombing of the church during the Second World War. Recently restored, the portrait survived the bombing. Despite his Anglican appointment, Cardwell was ecumenical and progressive in municipal politics: he converted St Anne's churchyard into a public garden and appointed both a Catholic priest and a rabbi to assist him with his mixed parish. It would have been, apparently, quite in character for him to agree to sit for the painting in order to further a young artist's career. (I am grateful to Mr Bryan Burrough CBE for information about Cardwell's character.)
26. B. Arnold, *Orpen: Mirror to an Age*.
27. S. Olson, *John Singer Sargent: His Portrait*, p. 209.
28. John Russell, cited in Olson, *Sargent*, p. 208: 'One of Sargent's greatest charms, for Edwardian Society, was his ability to give new money a good opinion of itself . . . quicker than the Home Office, he naturalised those who would otherwise have lingered in the between-world where class, nationality, money, and money's provenance, were matters not to be raised without a qualm. For the reassurance-collector there was no other painter in the country.'
29. After the Second World War Conway Wertheimer changed his name, somewhat confusingly, to Conway Conway.
30. JEAS minutes, 18 January 1911.
31. Following the publication of *Mendel* in 1916, Gertler's friend the barrister Montague Shearman wrote to him about his mixed reactions to Cannan's novel, telling Gertler he had recognized and 'thoroughly enjoyed' the 'cutting picture of Conway'. When a short time later Shearman offered to make Gertler an allowance, he also stressed that 'there must be no feeling of patronage or obligation whatever.' He did not want to be another 'Conway'. Both Shearman and Conway were barristers who had been called to the Inner Temple, and the two men certainly knew each other. Shearman told Gertler he had dined with Conway (just after the publication of *Mendel*) in November 1916.
32. JEAS minutes, 29 March 1911.
33. Joseph Leftwich, diary entry for 17 May 1911, Tower Hamlets Local History Library, cited in Tickner, *Modern Life and Modern Subjects*, p. 294, n. 123.
34. Henry Nevinson to Michael Sadler, 9 May 1911, Tate Gallery Archive, 8212.2.120.
35. The evidence for a meeting at this time is not conclusive, but a letter from J. Woodrow to Noel Carrington, 12 August 1964 (Tate Gallery Archive 9217. 107), refers to the painter Philip Naviasky's recollection of meeting Gertler when on a visit to see Frank Rutter, then director of Leeds City Art Gallery. As Rutter did not take up this appointment until the following year, Naviasky may have been referring to a visit by Gertler to Leeds in 1912.

36. By 16 February 1916, however, Augustus John was complaining that Gertler's work had 'gone to buggery and I can't stand it. Not that he hasn't ability of a sort and all the cheek of a Yid, but the spirit of the work is false and affected' (quoted in Holroyd, *Augustus John*, p. 660, n. 41). The drawing bought by Quinn is so similar in pose and expression to the oil purchased by Sadler, it could well be taken as a preliminary drawing for the oil, were it not for the earlier dating on the drawing of 'December'.
37. Stanley Spencer in a letter to Sydney Spencer, 1 July 1911, referred to 'a prize divided between Gertler, Carline, Camilla Doyle and myself – £2. 5. 0. each', quoted in Carline, *Stanley Spencer at War*, p. 2.
38. JEAS minutes, 8 June 1911.
39. The exact date of Gertler's leaving is impossible to verify as the Slade register is missing for the years 1911–14, but he is included in the 'class of 1912' school photograph.
40. Mark Gertler to Carrington, 1 January 1914, *MGSL*, p. 61.
41. Gertler, 'A Triumph of Education Aid'.
42. Johnson and Gruetzner, *Dictionary of British Art*, vol. 5, p. 8.
43. A. Gwynne-Jones, *Portrait Painters: European Portraits to the End of the Nineteenth Century and English Twentieth-Century Portraits* (London: Phoenix House, 1950), p. 37.
44. Q. Bell, introduction to *MGSL*, p. 9.
45. Ibid.
46. Gruetzner Robins, *Modern Art in Britain*, p. 53.
47. B. Glenavy, *Today We Will Only Gossip*, p. 75.
48. H. Ginsbury, in *Mark Gertler: The Early and the Late Years*, p. 18.
49. Cannan, *Mendel*, pp. 125–6.
50. Ibid., p. 128.
51. Mark Gertler to Carrington, 1 January 1914, *MGSL*, p. 61.
52. Cannan, *Mendel*, p. 124.
53. Mark Gertler to Dorothy Brett, July 1913, *MGSL*, p. 54.
54. JEAS minutes, 15 November 1916, MS 135, AJ/35.4. Minutes: 29 January 1916–22 February 1916, p. 29.
55. JEAS minutes, 18 December 1912, ibid.
56. JEAS minutes, 20 December 1911, p. 78, ibid.
57. In April 1913 Wertheimer resigned from the JEAS, despite efforts to dissuade him.
58. Gertler gave his address to Carrington (*c.* August 1912, *MGSL*, p. 44) as 'c/o Waley Cohen, Courtlands, East Grinstead, Sussex'. Sir Robert Waley-Cohen (1877–1952) was chairman of the JEAS. A further letter from c/o Mrs Zeppard, Iyes Cross, East Grinstead, followed in January 1913 (University of Texas, Austin), suggesting that Gertler may have kept up a connection.

CHAPTER 7: THE IMPORTANCE OF BEING EARNEST

1. Gertler, 'A Triumph of Education Aid'.
2. It is impossible to be sure whether Gertler attended Roger Fry's Slade lectures on these painters. Although Jane Hill (*Carrington*, pp. 18–19) writes that these weekly lectures with lantern slides 'helped create the mood of the moment among students for the Italians' and that Carrington certainly attended them. Many of Gertler's own enthusiasms – Giotto, Fra Angelico, Piero della Francesca – match Fry's, but his letters make no mention of the lectures and many of these painters were represented in the National Gallery. Moreover, Fry himself complained that very few students attended the lectures, and that of these few only a handful were men.
3. Gertler, 'A Triumph of Education Aid'.
4. Harvey was MP for Leeds West from 1910 to 1918, during which time he also held the post of parliamentary private secretary to Ellis Griffith (1912–13), and afterwards to C. F. G. Masterman (1913–14). He later became MP for Dewsbury (1923–4).

5. Alice Harvey was dressed in Quaker costume for her portrait. Marcia Allentuck ('Mark Gertler: A Study of his Life', *Apollo*, October 1974, p. 336), states that 'the portraits of the Harveys are . . . legally under a dual [ownership], an important point not merely for the art historian, but for the social historian as well, as the Harveys were of great importance in the social history of Quakerism.'
6. Alice Harvey's portrait is signed and (indistinctly) dated 1912. Harvey's portrait is not dated but Gertler made a further trip to Yorkshire in 1914, probably to complete his portrait. More contemporary than Alice's portrait, it is closer in style to his portrait of Professor Michael Sadler painted in 1915.
7. Nevinson would also use the term 'Neo Primitives' in his autobiography (p. 33), and in Cannan's novel *Mendel* (p. 119) Gertler's *alter ego* is convinced that he and Mitchell (Nevinson) will give the world 'such art as it had never seen since the primitives'.
8. It is unlikely that Gertler and Nevinson revisited the Primitive room on their second trip to Paris. Gertler very much wished to visit it again on the proposed trip to Paris with Carrington in January 1913, which did not materialize.
9. *Daily Telegraph* (27 May 1914). Later commentators such as Andrew Forge drew similar comparisons. See 'The Slade, part 2' in 'Motif 5', quoted in S. Griffiths: *John Currie: Paintings and Drawings, 1905–14*.
10. *The Star* [December 1912], quoted in Woodeson, *Gertler*, p. 361.
11. John Woodeson suggests (*Gertler*, p. 79) that the introduction may have been made by William Rothenstein, who was friendly with Darwin's brother, but Darwin may also have seen Gertler's work at the Slade, where his own daughter Gwen was also a pupil.
12. Lady Darwin did not consider it a good likeness, preferring a drawing on canvas by her daughter Gwen (also given to the National Portrait Gallery in 1925), but thought well enough of it to offer it to the NPG some ten years later in 1923. Lady Darwin also indicated that the portrait was one of two executed on the same trip, although the second portrait has not come to light.
13. Nevinson, *Paint and Prejudice*, p. 25.
14. Mark Gertler to Carrington, 6 May 1912, *MGSL*.
15. The house, now listed, has been restored and is the only one of Gertler's surviving homes to bear a blue plaque.
16. The accommodation may have also have been shared with the Landau family: Mrs Fanny Landau, her two daughters Sarah (known as Sally) and Rose, Uncle Jack and Aunt Eva. Jack Landau was in the wholesale fruit and vegetable business in Spitalfields Market. The Landaus lived for many years at this address, sharing the accommodation with another family – though there is no proof that it was the Gertlers – and probably occupying the basement and ground floor. Rose Landau's beautiful long red hair caught Gertler's eye, and he is believed to have painted her more than once. *The Girl with Red Hair* (oil), exhibited at the Friday Club (129) in 1911 (current whereabouts unknown), is probably a portrait of Rose Landau (letters to the author from Phyllis Kutcher Martin [Rose Landau's daughter], dated 11 November 1999 and 22 February 2000). The name of Sam Kutcher (Rose Landau's uncle and a well-known concert violinist) also appears in one of Gertler's address books in the 1930s.
17. Woodeson, *Gertler*, p. 82.
18. Mark Gertler to Carrington, Thursday midnight [*c.* December 1912], *MGSL*, p. 48.
19. Gertler later claimed, however, to have loved her for exactly ten years to the day on which she married another man, 21 May 1921, which would put their first meeting around May 1911. His first dated letter to her is April 1912, but there are other undated letters which may predate this one. However, their first significant meeting seems to have been when Nevinson brought Carrington to Elder Street (as Gertler himself pointed out in his letter to Nevinson *c.* July 1912), which could not have been before April 1912.
20. Nash, *Outline*, p. 104.
21. Mark Gertler to Carrington, undated [*c.* 27–30 September 1912], University of Texas, Austin.
22. The quotation itself has not been traced.

23. J. Hill, *The Art of Dora Carrington*, p. 15.
24. Ibid., p. 11.
25. N. Carrington, *Carrington: Paintings, Drawings and Decorations*, p. 21.
26. Ibid.
27. Mark Gertler to Carrington, 13 November [1917], University of Texas, Austin.
28. Mark Gertler to Carrington, 10 April 1912, ibid.
29. Mark Gertler to Carrington, not dated [*c.* May 1912, written on the back of a crayon drawing], ibid.
30. Ibid.
31. Mark Gertler to C. R. W. Nevinson, not dated [July 1912], *MGSL*, p. 38.
32. Mark Gertler to Carrington, 1 July 1915, ibid., p. 98.
33. Mark Gertler to Carrington, July 1912, ibid., p. 43.
34. Mark Gertler to Carrington, not dated [*c.* July 1912], University of Texas, Austin.
35. Mark Gertler to Carrington, 25 July 1912, ibid.
36. Mark Gertler to Carrington, 29 July 1912, ibid.
37. Quoted in Hill, *Art of Dora Carrington*, p. 92.
38. M. A. Caws, *Women of Bloomsbury*, p. 119.
39. Quoted in Holroyd, *Lytton Strachey*, p. 352.
40. Nevinson to Carrington, 8 April 1912, quoted in Gerzina: *Carrington*, p. 32.
41. Mark Gertler to Nevinson, *c.* July 1912, *MGSL*, pp. 38–9.
42. Mark Gertler to Carrington, 19 June 1912, ibid., p. 36.
43. Gerzina, *Carrington*, p. 31.
44. Hill, *Art of Dora Carrington*, p. 20.
45. Gerzina, *Carrington*, p. 31.
46. Carrington to Mark Gertler, not dated [*c.* 1917], *MGSL*, p. 144.
47. Mark Gertler to Carrington, *c.* June 1912, ibid., p. 36.
48. Noel Carrington, ibid., p. 131.
49. Mark Gertler to Nevinson [July 1912], ibid., p. 38.
50. Nevinson to Carrington, not dated [*c.* July 1912], ibid., pp. 39–40.
51. M. Sadleir, *Michael Ernest Sadler, 1861–1943: A Memoir*, p. 253.
52. Ibid.
53. Allinson, 'A Painter's Pilgrimage', p. 21.
54. Sadleir, *Sadler*, p. 253.
55. Allinson, 'A Painter's Pilgrimage', p . 21.
56. Ibid.
57. The title probably alludes, however, to a subject seen at the theatre. See *John Currie: Paintings and Drawings, 1905–14*, n. 31.
58. Mark Gertler to Carrington [July 1912], *MGSL*, p. 43.
59. Not identified.
60. Gertler gives the name as 'the Society of Portrait Painters' but there is no mention of him in the papers of either the Royal Society of Portrait Painters or the National Portrait Society – begun by John Lavery, William Orpen and Ambrose McEvoy in 1911 – despite Gertler's claim in a letter to Carrington (13 July 1912, University of Texas, Austin) that he had been 'elected a member'.
61. Mark Gertler to Carrington, 13 July 1912, *MGSL*, p. 41.
62. Mark Gertler to Carrington, 16 July 1912, University of Texas, Austin.
63. Mark Gertler to Carrington, July 1912, *MGSL*, p. 43.
64. Ibid.
65. The painting features only head and shoulders and, despite its title, shows no musical instrument.
66. Mark Gertler to Carrington, *c.* August 1912, *MGSL*, pp. 43–4.
67. Holroyd, *Augustus John*, vol. 2, p. 35.
68. Fry himself had exhibited an 'erractic development' in promoting a revival of interest in mural painting (see Spalding, *Duncan Grant*, pp. 124–5).

69. The term 'tempera' actually refers to any kind of binding medium, but in the context of the early Renaissance painters it meant egg tempera, which was thinned with water and mixed with powder colour to produce a quick-drying film. Gouache is an opaque water-colour paint (also known as bodycolour or poster paint).
70. Mark Gertler to Carrington, 2 September 1912, *MGSL*, p. 44.
71. Mark Gertler to Carrington, 24 September 1912, *MGSL*, p. 46–7.
72. Quoted in F. Spalding, *Roger Fry: Art and Life*, p. 144.
73. Spalding, *Duncan Grant*, p. 123.
74. This was in an interview in the 1930s (*Studio*, 104, 1932, p . 163), by which time Gertler's exact memory of the show may have been affected, since there were no Gauguins in the second Post-Impressionist show. By this time, however, Gertler would certainly have been familiar with Gauguin from Sadler's collection. And Sadler also noted that when he visited Currie's flat in 1912 there were reproductions of Gauguin and Cézanne all over the walls.
75. Quoted in Woodeson, *Gertler*, p. 337.
76. Holroyd, *Augustus John*, p. 138.
77. Woodeson, *Gertler*, pp. 100–01, cites the *Daily Chronicle*, *The Observer* and *The Star*. *The Coster Woman and Child* is probably the painting also referred to by Gertler as *The Coster Family*, the 'Coster picture' and *Coster Mother and Child*.

CHAPTER 8: IN THE CLOTHES OF A GENTLEMAN

1. Mark Gertler to Carrington, [*c.* December 1912], *MGSL*, pp. 48–9.
2. Gerzina, *Carrington*, p. 45.
3. Mark Gertler to Brett, *c.* 1912, University of Texas, Austin.
4. Mark Gertler to Brett, not dated [*c.* 1913], ibid.
5. N. Hamnett, *Laughing Torso*, p. 36.
6. It must have been Currie who introduced Bennett to Gertler. Gertler completed a fine sanguine drawing of Bennett, *c.* 1912, but there is no evidence of any friendship between them, although they would occasionally mix in the same circles in the 1920s, when Gertler also knew Bennett's (estranged) wife, Marguerite.
7. Mark Gertler to Carrington, March 1913, *MGSL*, pp. 50–1.
8. Nevinson, *Paint and Prejudice*, p. 41.
9. Allinson, 'A Painter's Pilgrimage', p. 21.
10. Sadleir, *Sadler*, p. 256.
11. Mark Gertler to Brett, September 1913, *MGSL*, p. 55.
12. Ibid.
13. According to Balston (pencilled note, 6 July 1949, University of Texas, Austin), 'a friend of Mrs. Venn's [formerly Dora Plaskowsky] said that her husband was at school with Mark, about 1902, at the Central Foundation School in Spital Square.'
14. Mark Gertler to Carrington, March 1913, *MGSL*, p. 50.
15. Mrs Dora Venn (*née* Plaskowsky), cited Thomas Balston, pencilled note, 6 July 1949, University of Texas, Austin.
16. Quoted in Woodeson, *Gertler*, p. 338.
17. Mark Gertler to Carrington, 2 April 1913, *MGSL*, p. 51.
18. Ibid.
19. Ibid.
20. Mark Gertler to Brett, not dated [*c.* 1912–13], University of Texas, Austin.
21. Noel Carrington, quoted in Hignett, *Brett*, p. 40.
22. Hignett, *Brett*, p. 39.
23. D. H. Lawrence to Lady Ottoline Morrell, 12 December 1915, cited in J. T. Boulton, ed., *The Selected Letters of D. H. Lawrence*, p. 111.
24. C. Tomalin, *Katherine Mansfield*, p. 53.
25. Brett to Luke Gertler, 11 July 1968, Luke Gertler Collection.
26. Ibid.

27. B. May, *Tiger Woman: My Story* (London: First Impressions, 1993), p. 73.
28. Quoted in D. Hooker, *Nina Hamnett: Queen of Bohemia*, p. 72.
29. Allinson, 'A Painter's Pilgrimage', p. 40.
30. H. David, *The Fitzrovians: A Portrait of Bohemian Society, 1900–1955* (London: Sceptre, 1989), p. 114.
31. Gertler related this story to his friend and colleague at the Westminster Institute, Ernest Fedarb (Fedarb, 'Reminiscences of Mark Gertler').
32. T. Balston, 'Mark Gertler 1891–1939', introduction to Whitechapel Art Gallery Exhibition, 1949.
33. The hat was probably a fedora rather than a sombrero, but it seems to have been a regular part of Gertler's dress at this stage. He is wearing it (or a similar hat) in the portrait by John Currie (1913) and again in a photograph of Currie and himself taken in this period.
34. D. Wilcox, *The London Group 1913–1939: The Artists and their Works*, p. 2.
35. Marsh's collection had begun over a decade earlier under the watchful eye of his friend Neville Lytton, whose traditional taste had favoured the early English watercolourists, such as Girtin, Cotman and J. R. Cozens – a taste emphatically not shared by Gertler. But with the acquisition of Duncan Grant's *Parrot Tulips* in 1911 (which Lytton considered 'a disgrace'), Marsh had turned his own 'perceptive eye' towards modern art and, dispensing with Lytton's help, began to forge his own authority as a collector. Although he rarely spent more than £200 a year on his purchases, by 1938 Marsh had established a truly remarkable collection of contemporary British art consisting of 'about 150 pictures' by '86 different hands'.
36. Mark Gertler to Dorothy Brett, June 1913, *MGSL*, pp. 53–4.
37. Edward Marsh to Rupert Brooke, 26 August 1913, quoted in C. Hassall, *A Biography of Edward Marsh*, p. 244.
38. Edward Marsh to Michael Sadleir, quoted in Hassall, *Marsh*, p. 256.
39. Gertler may have seen two studies from the 'blue period' in 1912 at a show of Picasso's drawings at the Stafford Gallery in April. A further twelve Picassos were on show at Fry's second Post-Impressionist show in October 1912.
40. Mark Gertler to Brett, dated only 1913, University of Texas, Austin.
41. Quoted in Woodeson, *Gertler*, p. 362.
42. John Currie to Edward Marsh, 21 October 1913, Berg Collection, New York Public Library.
43. Mark Gertler to Brett, not dated [*c.* June 1913], University of Texas, Austin, partly reproduced in *MGSL*, pp. 53–4.
44. The painting may have been influenced by Cézanne's *La Vieille Chapelet*, which was exhibited at the second Post-Impressionist exhibition.
45. Mark Gertler to Carrington, Sunday [December 1913], *MGSL*, pp. 59–60.
46. Mark Gertler to Edward Marsh, *c.* 13 November 1913, Berg Collection, New York Public Library.
47. Mark Gertler to Brett, August 1913, University of Texas, Austin.
48. Mark Gertler to Brett, July 1913, *MGSL*, p. 53.
49. Gertler excepted from this Jim, or James, Strachey Barnes, one of Marsh's particular friends, who was the brother of Gertler's future friend Mary Hutchinson and a cousin of the Stracheys. Barnes's memoirs were later reviewed with 'amused detachment' by Vanessa Bell in her only review for the *New Statesman and Nation* in summer 1923, where she noted that he boasted of friendships with T. S. Eliot, Sacheverell Sitwell and Gertler, among others, but managed to spell all of their names incorrectly.
50. Mark Gertler to Edward Marsh, October 1913, *MGSL*, p. 57.
51. Mark Gertler to Brett, September 1913, ibid., p. 55.
52. Mark Gertler to Carrington, Sunday, December 1913, ibid., p. 59.
53. Ibid.
54. Mark Gertler to Carrington, Christmas 1913, ibid., pp. 58–9.

CHAPTER 9: THE WIDENING CIRCLE

1. Mark Gertler to Carrington, Christmas 1913, *MGSL*, pp. 58–9.
2. Mark Gertler to Brett, undated [January 1914], University of Texas, Austin.
3. Mark Gertler to Brett, undated [January 1914], ibid.
4. Mark Gertler to Carrington, January 1914, *MGSL*, pp. 61–3.
5. Mark Gertler to Carrington, 1 January 1914, ibid., pp. 60–1.
6. Ibid.
7. Mark Gertler to Brett, [early] January 1914, *MGSL*, p p. 63–4.
8. The magazine was founded and edited by John Middleton Murry (still an Oxford undergraduate at the time) and first appeared in the summer of 1911. Katherine Mansfield became assistant editor in April 1912. Murry's inexperience led him to overestimate demand, and the financing of the magazine was taken over by Charles Granville ('Stephen Swift') in June 1912, at which stage it also became a monthly, with Mansfield as co-editor. Swift went bankrupt later in 1912 and fled the country, upon which Eddie Marsh guaranteed Murry's overdraft and the editors continued without pay. Martin Secker took over publication from November 1912 and the magazine's final three issues (May–July 1913) appeared under the name the *Blue Review*. See V. O'Sullivan and M. Scott, eds., *The Collected Letters of Katherine Mansfield*, vol. 1, *1903–1917* (Oxford: Clarendon Press, 1984), pp. 109–10.
9. Quoted in D. Farr, *Gilbert Cannan: A Georgian Prodigy*, p. 100.
10. Ibid., p . 102.
11. Mark Gertler to Brett, [early] January 1914, *MGSL*, pp. 63–4.
12. Mark Gertler to Carrington, [January] 1914, University of Texas, Austin.
13. Gilbert Cannan to Ottoline Morrell, 20 May 1914, ibid.
14. Edward Marsh to Mark Gertler, quoted in Hassall: *Marsh*, p. 265.
15. A draft plan emerged from the evening for a book called *Georgian Drawings*, which was to consist of about fifty drawings by some twenty artists, including – apart from those present – Nevinson, Eliot Seabrooke, Rupert Ihlee and the brothers John and Paul Nash. Marsh managed to engage the interest of two prominent collectors, Gertler's old friend Professor Michael Sadler and Lord Henry Bentinck, the brother of Lady Ottoline Morrell. Marsh decided that the book would be best financed by subscription, and planned to go ahead once 400 promises of half a guinea had been collected, but in the event the necessary subscriptions failed to materialize, and the project finally petered out in the autumn.
16. Gilbert Cannan to Ottoline Morrell, 20 May 1914, University of Texas, Austin.
17. Farr, *Cannan*, p. 111.
18. Ibid.
19. Mark Gertler to Carrington, Sunday night [*c.* 12] April 1914, *MGSL*, pp. 67–8.
20. Mark Gertler to Carrington, 9 April 1914, *MGSL*, pp. 66–7.
21. Mark Gertler to Carrington, 1 April 1914, ibid., p. 64.
22. Gilbert Cannan to Ottoline Morrell, 1914, University of Texas, Austin.
23. Quoted in Seymour, *Ottoline Morrell*, p. 74.
24. M. Seymour, *Ottoline Morrell: Life on the Grand Scale*, p. 3.
25. R. Gathorne-Hardy, ed., *The Early Memoirs of Lady Ottoline Morrell*, p. 253.
26. Ibid.
27. Gilbert Cannan to Lady Ottoline Morrell, 28 April 1914, University of Texas, Austin.
28. Seymour, *Ottoline Morrell*, p. 191.
29. Gathorne-Hardy, *Early Memoirs*, p. 253.
30. Mark Gertler to Ottoline Morrell, not dated [*c.* May 1914], University of Texas, Austin.
31. W. Sickert, *New Age* (June 1914), quoted in Woodeson, *Gertler*, p. 141.
32. Gilbert Cannan to Ottoline Morrell, *c.* April 1914, University of Texas, Austin.
33. Introduction, 'Twentieth Century Art: A Review of Modern Movements', quoted in Gruetzner Robins, *Modern Art in Britain, 1910–1914*, p. 140.
34. These were *Jewish Family* (1913), *The Artist's Mother* (1913) and *Mother and Babe* (1913), all three of which ended up in the collection of Eddie Marsh.

35. 'Jewish Art at Whitechapel: Twentieth Century Exhibition', *Jewish Chronicle* (15 May 1914), quoted in Gruetzner Robins, *Modern Art in Britain, 1910–1914*, p. 140.
36. J. Byrne, *A Genius for Living: A Biography of Frieda Lawrence*, p. 165.
37. Mark Gertler to Carrington, July 1914, *MGSL*, pp. 70–1.
38. Mark Gertler to Brett, [*c.* 18] July 1914, University of Texas, Austin.
39. Mark Gertler to Carrington, July 1914, *MGSL*, pp. 70–1.
40. Mark Gertler to Carrington, Sunday, July 1914, ibid., pp. 72–4.
41. Mark Gertler to Carrington, July 1914, ibid., pp. 70–1.
42. Mark Gertler to Carrington, August 1914, ibid., pp. 74–5.
43. Gilbert Cannan to Ottoline Morrell [August 1914], University of Texas, Austin.
44. Mark Gertler to Carrington, August 1914, *MGSL*, pp. 74–5.
45. Mark Gertler to Brett, 20 August 1914, University of Texas, Austin.
46. Ibid.
47. Reginald, 2nd Viscount Esher to Brett, 1914, quoted in Hignett: *Brett*, p. 58.
48. Mark Gertler to Brett, 16 September 1914, University of Texas, Austin.
49. Gilbert Cannan to Ottoline Morrell, not dated [*c.* August 1914], ibid.
50. Mark Gertler to Brett, 16 September 1914, ibid.
51. Mark Gertler to Carrington, not dated [*c.* autumn 1914], ibid.
52. Mark Gertler to Brett, [*c.* autumn] 1914, ibid.
53. Ibid.
54. See M. Gertler, 'Fragment on the Death of John Currie' [*c.* October 1914], 6 loose pages in black notebook, Luke Gertler Collection. The portrait was probably abandoned.
55. Clive Bell, quoted in Q. Bell, *Bloomsbury*, p. 42.
56. Holroyd, *Strachey*, p. 359.
57. Mark Gertler to Carrington, April 1915, *MGSL*, p. 89.
58. See S. Sillars, '"Terrible and Dreadful": Lawrence, Gertler and the Visual Imagination', *D. H. Lawrence in Italy and England*, ed. G. Donaldson, (London: Macmillan, 1998), pp. 193–209.
59. L. Woolf, *Beginning Again: An Autobiography of the Years 1911–1918* (New York: Harcourt Brace Jovanovich, Inc., 1972), p . 248.
60. B. Glenavy, *Today We Will Only Gossip*, p. 59.
61. Ibid., p. 75.
62. F. Lawrence, quoted in R. Jackson, *Frieda Lawrence*, p. 142.
63. Mark Gertler to Carrington, January 1915, *MGSL*, pp. 78–9.
64. Gilbert Cannan to Ottoline Morrell [*c.* 26 December 1914], quoted in Farr, *Cannan*, p. 115.
65. Mark Gertler to Lytton Strachey, 1 January 1915, *MGSL*, p. 77.
66. C. Tomalin, *Katherine Mansfield*, p. 133.
67. Completed in 1918, the story was later published as part of the collection *Bliss and Other Stories* in 1920.

CHAPTER 10: RARE TIMES

1. Mark Gertler to Lytton Strachey, 1 January 1915, *MGSL*, p. 77.
2. Ibid.
3. Mark Gertler to Brett, [January 1915], ibid, p. 78.
4. Mark Gertler to Carrington, January 1915, ibid., p. 81.
5. Mark Gertler to Lytton Strachey, 27 January 1915, Luke Gertler Collection.
6. Mark Gertler to Carrington, January 1915, *MGSL*, p. 81.
7. Marsh was one of the heirs of the former prime minister Spencer Perceval, who was shot in the House of Commons in 1812. Perceval's widow was awarded £1,000 a year for life and £50,000 was held in trust for the Perceval children and their descendants. Marsh spent his allowance entirely on art, and always referred to it as 'the murder money'. This was the origin of Gertler's subsidy.
8. Mark Gertler to Edward Marsh, *MGSL*, p. 75.

9. Mark Gertler to Carrington, 20 January 1915, ibid., p. 80.
10. Mark Gertler to Carrington, Sunday, [28] February 1915, ibid., pp. 84–5.
11. Mark Gertler to Carrington, January 1915, ibid., pp. 80–1.
12. Carrington to Mark Gertler, [Friday] 29 January 1915, University of Texas, Austin.
13. Mark Gertler to Carrington, February 1915, *MGSL*, pp. 82–3.
14. Mark Gertler to Lytton Strachey, Thursday, 14 January 1915, Luke Gertler Collection.
15. Mark Gertler to Carrington, 20 January 1915, *MGSL*, p. 80.
16. Mark Gertler to Carrington, February 1915, ibid., pp. 82–3.
17. This was Christine Kühlenthal, a Slade contemporary of Carrington's, who later married John Nash.
18. Mark Gertler to Carrington, February 1915, *MGSL*, pp. 82–3.
19. Carrington to Mark Gertler, not dated [*c.* March 1915], University of Texas, Austin.
20. Mark Gertler to Carrington, February 1915, *MGSL*, pp. 82–3.
21. Carrington to Mark Gertler, not dated [early January 1915], University of Texas, Austin.
22. Mark Gertler to Carrington, Friday, [*c.* 5] February 1915, *MGSL*, pp. 83–4.
23. Mark Gertler to Carrington, Sunday, February 1915, ibid., pp. 84–5.
24. Mark Gertler to Carrington, Sunday, [28] February 1915, ibid., pp. 84–5.
25. Mark Gertler to Carrington, [Tuesday, 2] February 1915, ibid., pp. 82–3.
26. *The Observer* [*c.* April 1915], quoted in Woodeson, *Gertler*, p. 170.
27. Mark Gertler to Carrington, [5 April] 1915, *MGSL*, p. 88.
28. Mark Gertler to Carrington, Sunday [28] February 1915, ibid., pp. 84–5.
29. Mark Gertler to Carrington, [5 April] 1915, ibid., p. 88.
30. Carrington to Mark Gertler [2 April 1915], University of Texas, Austin.
31. Mark Gertler to Carrington, 1 July 1915, *MGSL*, pp. 97–8.
32. D. Garnett, ed., *Carrington: Letters and Extracts from her Diaries*, p. 17.
33. Ibid.
34. Mark Gertler to Carrington, *c.* July 1915, University of Texas, Austin.
35. Mark Gertler to Carrington, [5 April] 1915, *MGSL*, p. 88.
36. Lytton Strachey to Mark Gertler, 3 February 1915, Luke Gertler Collection.
37. Ibid.
38. Mark Gertler to Lytton Strachey, [Sunday] 23 May 1915, *MGSL*, pp. 91–2.
39. Mark Gertler to Carrington [*c.* June 1915], ibid., pp. 95–6.
40. Mark Gertler to Carrington, not dated [*c.* May 1916], University of Texas, Austin.
41. Quoted in Hassall, *Marsh*, p. 344.
42. Ibid.
43. The post has been described by Churchill's biographer Martin Gilbert as 'a non-departmental post of an entirely ornamental nature', although Churchill retained his seat on the war council. When Lloyd George replaced Asquith in 1917 he recalled Churchill to office as Minister of Munitions.
44. Mark Gertler to Lytton Strachey, 23 May 1915, *MGSL*, pp. 91–2.
45. Ibid.
46. Mark Gertler to Carrington [June 1915], ibid., pp. 95–6.
47. Mark Gertler to Carrington, 1 July 1915, ibid., pp. 96–7.
48. Ibid.
49. Rothenstein, *Modern English Painters*, p. 134.
50. Mark Gertler to Edward Marsh, 15 August 1915, *MGSL*, pp. 99–100.
51. Ibid.
52. Mark Gertler to Carrington, not dated [May 1915], University of Texas, Austin.
53. Mark Gertler to Edward Marsh, 17 August 1915, *MGSL*, pp. 100–01.
54. Ibid.
55. Edward Marsh to Mark Gertler, 8 August 1915, *MGSL*, p. 101. The concurrent fates of Keats and Haydon may also have served as a warning. Gertler identified strongly with Keats on a personal level, particularly over his unrequited love for his beloved Fanny Brawne, and – in his more self-pitying moments – Keats's early death before his genius

had been recognized. On the other hand, there must also have been a fear of turning into the ambitious historical painter Benjamin Haydon, who despite great aspirations, had steadily declined in both power and fortune, and eventually committed suicide in 1846 after a disastrous exhibition of his paintings.

56. They had purchased the estate in 1913 but did not move in until 1915, owing to a sitting tenant.
57. The phrase is Juliette Huxley's, quoted in Seymour, *Ottoline Morrell*, p. 234.
58. L. A. G. Strong, quoted in Seymour, *Ottoline Morrell*, p. 223.
59. Seymour, *Ottoline Morrell*, p. 233.
60. Mark Gertler to Ottoline Morrell, not dated [July 1922], University of Texas, Austin.
61. J. Vinogradoff in *Mark Gertler: The Early and the Late Years*, p. 13.
62. Ottoline Morrell to Mark Gertler, not dated [*c.* 1916], Goodman family papers.
63. Ottoline Morrell to Mark Gertler, not dated [*c.* 19 October 1917], ibid.
64. The paintings included *Garden Statues and Pool, Garsington* (*c.* 1916), *Trees at Garsington* (*c.* 1918), *The Pool, Garsington* (1918), *Landscape at Garsington/Horse in an Orchard* (1919), *The Bathers at Garsington* (1919), The *Pigeon House, Garsington* (1919), three studies; 1920; *The Manor House, Garsington* (1921), *The Pond, Garsington* (1916, *c.* 1917, 1919, 1923), *The Statue* (*c.* 1920) and *The Garden, Garsington* (1923).
65. Noel Carrington, *MGSL*, p. 76.
66. Ibid.
67. J. Huxley, *The Leaves of the Tulip Tree*, p. 47.
68. Quoted in Farr, *Cannan*, p. 124.
69. Quoted in Seymour, *Ottoline Morrell*, p. 246.
70. D. H. Lawrence to Ottoline Morrell, 20 June 1915, quoted in Holroyd, *Lytton Strachey*, p. 325.
71. Quoted in K. Sagar, *D. H. Lawrence: Life into Art*, p. 163.
72. Murry claimed, however, not to have recognized the portraits of himself and Katherine until they were pointed out to him by Frieda Lawrence.
73. Mark Gertler to Edward Marsh [*c.* September 1915], *MGSL*, pp. 101–2.
74. These views were both recorded and parodied by Compton Mackenzie in his novel *The South Wind of Love*, which featured ficionalized portraits of both Cannan and Lawrence. See Farr, *Cannan*, pp. 120–22.
75. Mark Gertler to Edward Marsh, 19 October 1915, *MGSL*, p. 102.
76. Ibid.
77. Ottoline Morrell to Mark Gertler, 17 August 1918, Goodman family papers.
78. Mark Gertler to Brett, [October 1915], University of Texas, Austin.
79. Mark Gertler to Carrington, 14 November 1915, *MGSL*, pp. 102–3.
80. Mark Gertler to Carrington, 21 November 1915, ibid., p. 103.
81. D. Farr, *English Art*, p. 198.
82. Quoted in Woodeson, *Gertler*, p. 99.
83. Wilcox, *The London Group*, p. 4.
84. Ibid., p. 6.
85. *New Statesman* (18 December 1915), quoted in Wilcox, *The London Group*, p. 10.
86. Mark Gertler to Carrington, November 1915, *MGSL*, pp. 104–5.
87. Carrington to Mark Gertler, Wednesday, 1915, quoted in Garnett, *Carrington*, p. 20.
88. Both letters are quoted in *MGSL*, p. 106.
89. Mark Gertler to Carrington, Sunday, December 1915, *MGSL*, pp. 106–8.
90. Ibid.
91. *Daily Telegraph* (13 June 1916).
92. Quoted in Woodeson, *Gertler*, p. 185.
93. St John Hutchinson to Mark Gertler [*c.* November 1916], *MGSL*, p. 128.
94. Walter Sickert, quoted in Woodeson, *Gertler*, p. 185.
95. Mark Gertler to Carrington, December 1915, *MGSL*, pp. 106–8.
96. Carrington to Mark Gertler, Monday, December 1915, quoted in Garnett, *Carrington*, p. 23.

97. Mark Gertler to Edward Marsh, April 1916, New York Public Library.
98. Mark Gertler to Carrington, [*c.* 5] December 1915, *MGSL*, p. 106.
99. Carrington to Mark Gertler [*c.* 6 December 1915], Garnett, *Carrington*, p. 23.
100. Carrington to Mark Gertler, December 1916, ibid., p. 51.
101. Carrington to Mark Gertler, Friday, December 1915, ibid., p. 21.
102. Ibid.
103. Carrington to Mark Gertler, Friday, December 1915, ibid., p. 21.
104. Mark Gertler to Carrington, Sunday, December 1915, *MGSL*, pp. 106–7.
105. Carrington to Mark Gertler [*c.* 6 December 1915], ibid., p. 23.
106. Carrington to Mark Gertler, Friday [January] 1919, ibid., pp. 124–5.

CHAPTER 11: ARTICULATE EXTREMITIES

1. Mark Gertler to S. S. Koteliansky, 3 February 1916, *MGSL*, p. 108.
2. D. H. Lawrence to Mark Gertler, 10 February 1916, J. Zytaruk and J. T. Boulton, eds., *The Letters of D. H. Lawrence*, vol. 2, *June 1913–October 1916*, pp. 530–1.
3. It was followed in June by the Second Military Service Act, which was extended to cover married men and widowers. Under this, Lawrence was forced to undergo further medical examination.
4. Mark Gertler to Brett, 10 February 1916, University of Texas, Austin.
5. Mark Gertler to Lytton Strachey, [*c.* 11] May 1916, *MGSL*, pp. 110–11.
6. Mark Gertler to Richard Carline, 3 May 1916, Tate Gallery Archive 9217.60. (This letter is partially quoted in *MGSL*, p. 112.)
7. Mark Gertler to S. S. Koteliansky, 13 September 1916, British Library.
8. Holroyd, *Lytton Strachey*, p. 349.
9. Gilbert Cannan to Edward Marsh, 15 August 1916, Berg Collection, New York Public Library.
10. Hassall, *Edward Marsh*, p. 406.
11. D. H. Lawrence to Mark Gertler [29 April 1916], *The Letters of D. H. Lawrence*, vol. 2, pp. 601–2.
12. The Lady Ridley who was interested must have been the Hon. Rosamond Guest, the wife of the 2nd Viscount Ridley, who died in 1916. The Hon. Sir Jasper (Nicholas) Ridley was the second son of the 1st Viscount. He served in the First World War and was married to Countess Nathalie Benckendorff, daughter of the Russian ambassador.
13. Mark Gertler to William Rothenstein, 4 April 1916, *MGSL*, pp. 109–10.
14. Vanessa Bell to Ottoline Morrell, 17 March 1916, R. Marler, ed., *Selected Letters of Vanessa Bell*, pp. 192–3.
15. Mark Gertler to Carrington [*c.* May 1916], University of Texas, Austin.
16. Ibid.
17. Carrington to Mark Gertler, 18 January 1916, ibid.
18. D. H. Lawrence to Mark Gertler, 20 January 1916, *The Letters of D. H. Lawrence*, vol. 2, pp. 508–9.
19. Mark Gertler to Carrington, Sunday, [*c.* 5] December 1915, *MGSL*, pp. 106–8.
20. Mark Gertler to Carrington, 27 February 1916, ibid., p. 108.
21. Ibid.
22. R. Gathorne-Hardy, ed., *Ottoline at Garsington: Memoirs of Lady Ottoline Morrell, 1915–1918*, pp. 256–7.
23. Quoted in Holroyd, *Lytton Strachey*, p. 362.
24. Carrington to Mark Gertler, April 1916, University of Texas, Austin.
25. Carrington to Mark Gertler, April 1916, Garnett, *Carrington*, p. 25.
26. Ibid.
27. Carrington to Lytton Strachey, [20 April 1916], ibid.
28. Mark Gertler to Carrington, 20 May 1916, *MGSL*, pp. 112–3.
29. Mark Gertler to Carrington, 30 May 1916, ibid., p. 114.

30. Carrington to Mark Gertler, 31 May 1916, ibid.
31. J. Carswell, *Lives and Letters: A. R. Orage, Beatrice Hastings, Katherine Mansfield, John Middleton Murry, S. S. Koteliansky, 1906–1957*, p. 88.
32. Huxley, *The Leaves of the Tulip Tree*, p. 146.
33. Mark Gertler to S. S. Koteliansky, 20 July 1916 [misdated 20 June], *MGSL*, pp. 114–5.
34. S. S. Koteliansky to Mark Gertler, not dated [July 1916], ibid., pp. 115–6.
35. Glenavy, *Today We Will Only Gossip*, p. 162.
36. Montague Shearman to Mark Gertler, Wednesday [*c.* 2 August 1916], Luke Gertler Collection.
37. Montague Shearman to Mark Gertler, not dated [*c.* June 1916], ibid.
38. Gertler in a letter to Kot mistakenly gives the date of 20 June instead of 20 July, but has been correctly redated by Mansfield's biographers (Claire Tomalin, p. 150, and Anthony Alpers, p. 439). See also Paul Delaney, *D. H. Lawrence's Nightmare* (1978). This appointment has given rise to some speculation among Mansfield's biographers that their planned meeting was for some sort of assignation, but given the intensity of Gertler's feelings for Carrington in this period, it seems unlikely.
39. Mark Gertler to S. S. Koteliansky [20 July 1916], *MGSL*, pp. 114–5.
40. Lytton Strachey to Barbara Hiles, 17 July 1916, quoted in Holroyd, *Lytton Strachey*, p. 370.
41. Lytton Strachey to Mary Hutchinson, 23 July 1916, ibid.
42. Carrington to Lytton Strachey, 30 July 1916, Garnett, *Carrington*, pp. 32–3.
43. Mark Gertler to Ottoline Morrell, 1 August 1916, University of Texas, Austin.
44. Ottoline Morrell to Mark Gertler, 8 August [1916], *MGSL*, p. 117.
45. Montague Shearman to Mark Gertler [probably 2 August 1916], Luke Gertler Collection.
46. Mark Gertler to Mary Hutchinson, 15 August 1916, University of Texas, Austin.
47. Carrington to Lytton Strachey [5 August 1916], Garnett, *Carrington*, pp. 34–5.
48. Mark Gertler to Carrington, 14 August 1916, *MGSL*, pp. 116–7.
49. Lytton Strachey to Carrington, quoted in Holroyd, *Lytton Strachey*, p. 371.
50. Mark Gertler to Carrington, 15 August 1916, *MGSL*, pp. 118–9.
51. Carrington to Mark Gertler, August 1916, Garnett, *Carrington*, p. 36–7.
52. Mark Gertler to Carrington, [Tuesday] 15 August 1916, *MGSL*, pp. 118–9.
53. Mark Gertler to William Rothenstein, 4 April 1916, ibid., pp. 109–10.
54. Mark Gertler to Mary Hutchinson, [Tuesday] 15 August 1916, University of Texas, Austin.
55. Mark Gertler to Carrington, [Tuesday] 15 August, 1916, *MGSL*, pp. 118–9.
56. Mark Gertler to Carrington, 20 August 1916, ibid., pp. 119–20.
57. Mark Gertler, 'Poem 1916 Aug', black leather notebook, pp. 3–5, Luke Gertler Collection. (There is also an undated copy of this poem at the University of Texas, Austin.)
58. A letter from Iris Tree, dated September 1917 (Luke Gertler Collection), also asks Gertler to send any poetry he might have written, although none but these fragments appears to have survived.
59. Mark Gertler to S. S. Koteliansky, 29 August 1916, *MGSL*, pp. 122–3.
60. Mark Gertler to Carrington, 20 August 1916, ibid., p. 119.
61. Mark Gertler to Carrington, 24 August 1916, ibid., pp. 120–2.
62. Carrington to Lytton Strachey, Tuesday morning [13 June 1916], Garnett, *Carrington*, pp. 28–9.
63. Mark Gertler to Carrington, 1 September 1916, *MGSL*, pp. 123–5.
64. Brett to Mark Gertler, Tuesday 29 August 1916, Luke Gertler Collection
65. Mark Gertler to Carrington, 14 August 1916, *MGSL*, pp. 116–7.
66. Farr, *Cannan*, p. 138.
67. Gerzina, *Carrington*, pp. 90–1.
68. Mark Gertler to Carrington, 29 August 1916, *MGSL*, p. 123.
69. Mark Gertler to Carrington, 1 September 1916, ibid., pp. 123–4.
70. Mark Gertler to S. S. Koteliansky, 29 August 1916, ibid., pp. 122–3.
71. One of the young Indian undergraduates, Huseyn Shaheed Suhrawardy, a Bengali Muslim from Bangladesh and a non-collegiate law student at Oxford, ran into Aldous Huxley the

next day and told him the story. Huxley immediately wrote and told Ottoline all about it. Suhrawardy had recognized Gertler from Garsington.

72. Mark Gertler to Mary Hutchinson, 2 September 1916, University of Texas, Austin.
73. Mark Gertler to Ottoline Morrell, 2 September 1916, ibid.
74. The drawings were a sepia wash on paper (1915, formerly in the collection of Montague Shearman) and a charcoal (*c.* 1916).
75. Mark Gertler to Carrington, 13 September 1916, *MGSL*, p. 127.
76. Mark Gertler to Carrington, 30 November 1916, ibid., pp. 132–3.
77. D. H. Lawrence to Mark Gertler, 9 October 1916, ibid., pp. 129–30.
78. For a fuller discussion of this, see S. Sillars, ' "Terrible and Dreadful" – Lawrence, Gertler and the visual imagination', in G. Donaldson and M. Kalnins, eds., *D. H. Lawrence in Italy and England* (London: Macmillan Press Ltd, 1998), pp. 193–210.
79. D. H. Lawrence to Mark Gertler, 9 October 1916, *The Letters of D. H. Lawrence*, vol. 2, pp. 660–1.
80. D. H. Lawrence to Mark Gertler, 5 December 1916, ibid., p. 133.
81. St John Hutchinson to Mark Gertler [*c.* November 1916], quoted ibid., pp. 128–9.
82. Montague Shearman to Mark Gertler, 12 September 1916, Luke Gertler Collection.
83. Montague Shearman to Mark Gertler [12 October 1916], *MGSL*, p. 126.
84. Mark Gertler to Lytton Strachey, [*c.* Thursday, 11] May 1916, ibid., pp. 110–11.
85. D. H. Lawrence to S. S. Koteliansky, 21 November 1916, Boulton and Robertson, *The Letters of D. H. Lawrence*, vol. 3, p. 35.
86. Carrington to Mark Gertler, 1 November 1916, quoted in *MGSL*, p. 254.
87. D. H. Lawrence to Barbara Low, 11 December 1916, Boulton and Robertson, *The Letters of D. H. Lawrence*, vol. 3, pp. 50–1.
88. Montague Shearman to Mark Gertler, Sunday night [*c.* November 1916], quoted in *MGSL*, p. 254.
89. William Rothenstein to Mark Gertler, 30 June 1918, quoted in *MGSL*, pp. 254–5.
90. Mark Gertler to William Rothenstein, 3 July 1918, ibid., p. 255.
91. Rothenstein, *Modern English Painters*, vol. 2, p. 136.
92. Mrs Kostenz (formerly Gertler) to Diana Farr, quoted in Farr, *Cannan*, p. 148.
93. Mark Gertler to Carrington, 2 November 1916, ibid., p. 132.
94. Carrington to Mark Gertler, September 1916, University of Texas, Austin.
95. Carrington to Mark Gertler, Saturday, December 1916, Garnett, *Carrington*, p. 50.
96. Mark Gertler to Carrington, December 1916, *MGSL*, p. 134.
97. Carrington to Mark Gertler, Thursday, December 1916, University of Texas, Austin.
98. Mark Gertler, black leather notebook, Luke Gertler Collection.

CHAPTER 12: FUGITIVE THINGS

1. Mark Gertler to Carrington, Tuesday [c. 16] January 1917, *MGSL*, pp. 136–7.
2. Ibid.
3. Mark Gertler to Richard Carline, 22 January 1917, ibid., p. 138.
4. Ibid.
5. Quoted in Woodeson, *Gertler*, p. 236.
6. In August 1916, when Gertler's sculptural conceptions were throwing him 'into chaos', Fry wrote an article on Gaudier-Brzeska for the *Burlington Magazine*, accompanied by an illustration of a tray featuring the *Wrestlers* design. There is no way of knowing whether Gertler saw this article, but he may have seen Gaudier-Brzeska's designs at the Omega. He certainly admired Gaudier's work, after seeing a posthumous exhibition of his work in London, but that was more than a year later, and he made no direct comment on any link in their work.
7. J. Epstein, *An Autobiography: The Modern Jewish Experience*, p. 227.
8. Quoted in Wilcox, *London Group*, p. 12.
9. *Sunday Times*, 29 April 1917.

10. Mark Gertler to Carrington, Monday morning, January 1917, *MGSL*, p. 136.
11. Ibid.
12. Carrington to Mark Gertler, 5 February 1917, University of Texas, Austin.
13. An abnormal constriction of the penis, requiring minor surgery.
14. Mark Gertler to S. S. Koteliansky, Friday, [9] February 1917, *MGSL*, p. 139.
15. Mark Gertler to Carrington, Saturday, [10] February 1917, ibid., p. 140.
16. Mark Gertler to Carrington, 8 February 1917, ibid., p. 139.
17. Mark Gertler to Carrington, Saturday, [10] February 1917, ibid., p. 140.
18. Ibid.
19. Mark Gertler to S. S. Koteliansky, Friday [6] April (Good Friday) 1917, British Library.
20. Montague Shearman to Mark Gertler, Thursday evening [1917], Luke Gertler Collection.
21. Montague Shearman to Mark Gertler, dated only Thursday night late [*c.* 1917], ibid.
22. Montague Shearman to Mark Gertler, Thursday [*c.* April 1917], ibid.
23. Michael Dickens in conversation with the author.
24. Brett to Luke Gertler, 2 July 1968, Luke Gertler Collection.
25. Montague Shearman to Mark Gertler, Monday night, 15 July 1917, ibid.
26. Ibid.
27. Mark Gertler to Carrington, Friday, April 1917, *MGSL*, p. 141.
28. Mark Gertler to Carrington, Monday, April 1917 [probably 9th, Easter Monday], ibid., pp. 141–2.
29. Carrington's diary, Monday 13 [actually 16] April 1917, Garnett, *Carrington*, pp. 63–5.
30. Ibid.
31. Ibid.
32. Ibid.
33. Ibid.
34. Carrington to Mark Gertler, Tuesday night, 14 [actually 17] April, 1917, University of Texas, Austin.
35. Mark Gertler to Carrington, 18 April 1917, *MGSL*, p. 142.
36. Ibid.
37. Clive Bell to Mary Hutchinson, 2 May 1917, University of Texas, Austin.
38. Garnett, *Carrington*, p. 67.
39. Clive Bell to Mary Hutchinson, Whitmonday [28 May] 1917, University of Texas, Austin.
40. Ibid.
41. Carrington to Mark Gertler, Saturday, [*c.* 12] May, 1917, ibid.
42. Mark Gertler to Carrington, 24 April 1917, *MGSL*, p. 143.
43. Ibid.
44. Carrington to Mark Gertler, Monday, [late] May 1917, University of Texas, Austin.
45. Fry had reviewed Vollard's *Cézanne* in the *Burlington* in 1917; see Spalding, *Roger Fry*, p. 190.
46. Mark Gertler to Carrington, Friday, April 1917, *MGSL*, p. 141.
47. Quoted in Spalding, *Duncan Grant*, p. 196.
48. I. Anscombe, *Omega and After: Bloomsbury and the Decorative Arts*, pp. 78–9.
49. Examples include *After Severini* (*c.* 1928), *The Virgin and St Anne* ('*After El Greco*'; 1931) and *After Giotto* (*c.* 1936).
50. S. Spender, 'The Life and Talent of Mark Gertler', *The Spectator* (2 December 1972).
51. Mark Gertler to Carrington, 15 May 1917, *MGSL*, pp. 145–6.
52. Clive Bell to Mary Hutchinson, 20 September 1917, University of Texas, Austin.
53. *Three Weeks* was a lurid and highly successful popular novel of the time; quoted in Hignett, *Brett*, pp. 90–1.
54. Clive Bell to Mary Hutchinson, 20 September 1917, University of Texas, Austin.
55. Hignett, *Brett*, p. 92.
56. A. Huxley, *Crome Yellow*, p. 22.
57. Clive Bell to Mary Hutchinson, Sunday, 1 April 1917, University of Texas, Austin.
58. Mark Gertler to Richard Carline, 2 September 1917, *MGSL*, p . 150.

59. Carrington to Mark Gertler, 21 September 1917, ibid., p. 152.
60. Mark Gertler to Carrington, 12 September 1917, ibid., pp. 150–2.
61. Mark Gertler to Richard Carline, 12 July 1917, ibid., p. 148.
62. Mark Gertler to S. S. Koteliansky, 29 August 1917, ibid., pp. 148–9.
63. Ibid.
64. Carrington to Mark Gertler, 21 September 1917, ibid., p. 152.
65. Mark Gertler to Carrington, 4 October 1917, ibid., p. 152.
66. Mark Gertler to Carrington, 1 November 1917, ibid., p. 153.
67. Mark Gertler to Ottoline Morrell, 2 October 1917, University of Texas, Austin.
68. Ottoline Morrell to Mark Gertler [*c.* 19 October 1917], Goodman Papers.
69. Mark Gertler to Brett, 3 October 1917, University of Texas, Austin.
70. Mark Gertler to S. S. Koteliansky, [Saturday] 20 October 1917, British Library.
71. D. H. Lawrence to S. S. Koteliansky, not dated [*c.* June 1917], British Library.
72. Mark Gertler to Ottoline Morrell, 10 November 1917, University of Texas, Austin.
73. Roger Fry to Vanessa Bell, 6 October 1917, D. Sutton, ed., *Letters of Roger Fry*, vol. 2, *1913–34*, p. 417.
74. Spalding, *Roger Fry*, p. 196.
75. Ibid.
76. Ibid.
77. Roger Fry to Vanessa Bell, 23 October 1917, Sutton, *Letters of Roger Fry*, vol. 2, p. 417.
78. A. O. Bell, ed., *The Diary of Virginia Woolf*, vol. 1, *1915–1919*, p. 72.
79. The group comprised Oliver Strachey, Maynard Keynes, Harry Norton and Saxon Sydney-Turner.
80. Mark Gertler to S. S. Koteliansky, 26 December 1917, *MGSL*, p. 154.

CHAPTER 13: A COMPLEX BEING

1. Mark Gertler to S. S. Koteliansky, 19 July 1918, British Library, Add. MS 48,969. This letter is partly reproduced in *MGSL*, pp. 161–2.
2. Mark Gertler to Ottoline Morrell, 3 January 1918, University of Texas, Austin.
3. Ibid.
4. Mark Gertler to Carrington, [Saturday] 19 January 1918, ibid.
5. Mark Gertler to Ottoline Morrell, Friday, February 1918, ibid.
6. Ibid.
7. Mark Gertler to Carrington, Sunday evening, 10 February 1918, *MGSL*, p. 155.
8. Hamnett, *Laughing Torso*, pp. 102–3.
9. Carrington to Mark Gertler, Sunday, February 1918, *MGSL*, p. 156.
10. Mark Gertler to Carrington, 20 February 1918, ibid., p. 155.
11. Ibid.
12. Lytton Strachey to Clive Bell, 18 February 1918, quoted in *MGSL*, p. 156.
13. Carrington to Mark Gertler [Friday, 15 February 1918], Garnett, *Carrington*, p. 96.
14. Mark Gertler to S. S. Koteliansky, Monday, 18 [but probably misdated, and actually 25] February 1918, British Library partially quoted in *MGSL*, p. 157.
15. Mark Gertler to Carrington, 24 February 1918, *MGSL*, p. 158.
16. Carrington to Mark Gertler, [28 February 1918], Garnett, *Carrington*, p. 97.
17. Mark Gertler to Carrington, 2 March 1918, *MGSL*, p. 158.
18. Mark Gertler to Ottoline Morrell, dated 29 February 1918 [actually 1 March 1918], University of Texas, Austin.
19. Mary Hutchinson to Mark Gertler, 28 February 1918, Luke Gertler Collection
20. Mark Gertler to Carrington, [Thursday] 7 March 1918, University of Texas, Austin.
21. Mark Gertler to Carrington, 2 March 1918, *MGSL*, p. 158.
22. Mark Gertler to P. G. Konody, 23 March 1918, Art Department, Imperial War Museum, London.

23. Mark Gertler to S. S. Koteliansky, Monday 18 [but probably misdated and actually written on 25] February 1918, British Library, Add. MS 48,969, only partially reproduced in *MGSL*, p. 157.
24. Mark Gertler to Brett, 2 March 1918, University of Texas, Austin.
25. Mark Gertler to Brett, 4 May 1918, ibid.
26. Mark Gertler to P. G. Konody, 23 March 1918, Art Department, Imperial War Museum, London.
27. Mark Gertler to Ottoline Morrell, 24 April 1918, University of Texas, Austin.
28. P. G. Konody [letter not signed] to Mark Gertler, 31 May 1918, Art Department, Imperial War Museum, London.
29. Mark Gertler to Ottoline Morrell, 24 April 1918, University of Texas, Austin.
30. Ibid.
31. Mark Gertler to Ottoline Morrell, June 1918, ibid.
32. David Bomberg's experiences show that this was not entirely without foundation. Bomberg was devastated by Konody's rejection of his commissioned painting of Canadian sappers, although he later submitted a second, accepted version of the picture.
33. Mark Gertler to Mary Hutchinson, 18 July 1918, University of Texas, Austin.
34. Perhaps ironically, the subject of shelterers in the underground was eventually carried out by the artist Walter Bayes (*The Underworld*, 1918), with whom Gertler came into open conflict in the early 1930s, when he was employed under Bayes as a teacher at the Westminster School of Art.
35. Carrington took tea with Virginia Woolf on 6 June 1918 and the latter noted that Carrington had 'taken over the Strachey valuation of people and art', A. O. Bell, *The Diary of Virginia Woolf*, vol. 1, p. 153.
36. Mark Gertler to Ottoline Morrell, May 1918, University of Texas, Austin. The tubercular poet Keats had suffered similar 'periods of profound exhaustion, malaise, depression and insane jealousy, alternating and sometimes overlapping with sublime poetic inspiration' in the year leading up to his own tubercular collapse, possibly owing to the 'slowly advancing' onset of the disease. In Gertler these symptoms were further complicated by his history of depression; see T. Dormandy, *The White Death: A History of Tuberculosis*, p. 14. Dormandy also draws attention to the disproportionate number of sufferers among artists, musicians and writers.
37. Mark Gertler to Ottoline Morrell, May 1918, University of Texas, Austin.
38. Mark Gertler to Mary Hutchinson, 8 July 1918, ibid.
39. Mark Gertler to Mary Hutchinson, 23 June 1918, ibid.
40. In Virginia's version Gertler had suddenly asked himself to dinner. 'God knows why,' she wrote to her sister Vanessa (18 June 1918, Nicolson, *The Question of Things Happening*, pp. 251–2), but a diary entry a week earlier (Monday, 17 June 1918, A. O. Bell, *The Diary of Virginia Woolf*, vol. 1, p. 154) suggests that she had already extended a general invitation to Gertler and Kot and that they were 'waiting to be fitted in'.
41. Mary Hutchinson to Mark Gertler, 11 July 1918, Luke Gertler Collection.
42. Mark Gertler to Mary Hutchinson, 23 June 1918, University of Texas, Austin.
43. Virginia Woolf to Vanessa Bell, 25 June 1918, Nicolson, *The Question of Things Happening*, p. 255.
44. Diary entry, 10 September 1918, A. O. Bell, *The Diary of Virginia Woolf*, vol. 1, pp. 158–9.
45. Carrington to Lytton Strachey, *c.* 8 November 1918, British Library.
46. Clive Bell to Mary Hutchinson, Monday, 12 August 1918, University of Texas, Austin.
47. Virginia Woolf, Monday, 29 July 1918, A. O. Bell, *The Diary of Virginia Woolf*, vol. 1, pp. 173–6.
48. H. Lee, *Virginia Woolf*, p. 375.
49. Mark Gertler to Mary Hutchinson, [31] July 1918, University of Texas, Austin.
50. Mark Gertler to S. S. Koteliansky, 25 July 1918, *MGSL*, p. 162.
51. Clive Bell to Mary Hutchinson, 12 July 1918, University of Texas, Austin.
52. Mark Gertler to Brett, 28 August 1918, ibid.

53. Brett to Mark Gertler, 29 August 1918, Luke Gertler Collection.
54. Quoted in S. J. Darroch, *Ottoline: The Life of Lady Ottoline Morrell*, p. 224.
55. Mark Gertler to Brett, 27 December 1918, University of Texas, Austin.
56. Mark Gertler to Lady Ottoline Morrell, 13 August 1918, ibid.
57. Leonard Woolf to Lytton Strachey, 22 September 1918, F. Spotts, ed., *Letters of Leonard Woolf*, p. 278.
58. A. O. Bell, *The Diary of Virginia Woolf*, vol. 1, p. 198.
59. Virginia Woolf to Vanessa Bell, 27 October 1918, Nicolson, *The Question of Things Happening*, vol. 2, pp. 286–7.
60. Virginia Woolf to Vanessa Bell, 19 November 1918, ibid., p. 296.
61. Mark Gertler to S. S. Koteliansky [Monday, June 1919], *MGSL*, pp. 171–2.
62. Virginia Woolf to Vanessa Bell, 1 May 1920, Nicolson, *The Question of Things Happening*, vol. 2, p. 431.
63. Aldous Huxley to Juliette Baillot, 14 September 1918, quoted in Hignett, *Brett*, p. 94.
64. Quoted in Hignett, *Brett*, p. 94.
65. Glenavy, *Today We Will Only Gossip*, p. 79.
66. Mark Gertler to Brett, November 1918, University of Texas, Austin.
67. Glenavy, *Today We Will Only Gossip*, pp. 102–3.
68. Mark Gertler to Carrington, 15 December 1918, *MGSL*, pp. 165–6.
69. Tancred Borenius was a Finnish art historian who lectured at the Slade.
70. Carrington to Mark Gertler, 22 December 1918, *MGSL*, p. 166.
71. Mark Gertler to Carrington, 31 December 1918, ibid., pp. 167–8.
72. Ibid.
73. Mark Gertler to Carrington, 22 December 1918, ibid., pp. 166–7.

CHAPTER 14: A PERMANENT TRACE

1. C. Harrison, *English Art and Modernism, 1900–1939*, p. 145.
2. A. Johnson and A. Gruetzner, *Dictionary of British Art*, vol. 5, *British Artists, 1880–1940*, p. 11.
3. Ibid.
4. Mark Gertler to Carrington, 31 December 1918, *MGSL*, p. 168.
5. Wilcox, *The London Group*, p. 14.
6. C. Bell, 'The London Group', *The Athenaeum* (25 April 1919), pp. 241–2.
7. With the exception of 1921, 1923 and 1926.
8. Mark Gertler to Ottoline Morrell, 18 March 1920, University of Texas, Austin.
9. Harrison, *English Art and Modernism*, p. 148.
10. R. Carline, introduction, 'Hampstead One, *c.* 1915–*c.* 1925', Gallery Edward Harvane, February 1973.
11. Mark Gertler to Carrington, 5 January 1919, *MGSL*, pp. 168–9.
12. Carrington to David Garnett, no date, quoted in Gerzina, *Carrington*, p. 139.
13. Virginia Woolf, diary, Thursday 6 June 1918, A. O. Bell, *The Diary of Virginia Woolf*, vol. 1, p. 153. Ottoline also subscribed to this view. Defying Gertler's feelings to go and stay with Strachey and Carrington at Tidmarsh in 1918, she found to her dismay that Carrington had become 'a mere snobbish echo of the Bloomsburyites, always thinking of who is important'. She left convinced that Strachey's recent fame had gone to both their heads (Seymour, *Ottoline Morrell*, p. 308).
14. Carrington to Lytton Strachey, 25 February 1919, British Library, Add. MS 62,889.
15. Carrington to Lytton Strachey, 26 February, ibid., Add. MS 62,890.
16. Carrington to Lytton Strachey, [Thursday] 27 February 1919, ibid.
17. Carrington to Lytton Strachey, 16 May 1919, ibid.
18. Carrington to Lytton Strachey, 29 August 1919, Garnett, *Carrington*, p. 143.
19. N. Carrington, foreword, *MGSL*, p. 13.
20. Mark Gertler to Carrington, February 1919, University of Texas, Austin.
21. Seymour, *Ottoline Morrell*, p. 306.

22. E. M. Forster to Alice Cara Foster, 4 June 1922, M. Lago and P. N. Furbank, *The Selected Letters of E. M. Forster*, vol. 2, *1921–70*, pp. 28–9.
23. Lilly, *Sickert*, p. 78.
24. Ibid., p. 79.
25. Mark Gertler to Carrington, February 1919, University of Texas, Austin.
26. Carrington to Gerald Brenan, 11 June 1922, quoted in Gerzina, *Carrington*, p. 191.
27. Mark Gertler to Carrington, Sunday, June 1919, *MGSL*, pp. 172–3.
28. One of the portraits was purchased by the Contemporary Art Society in 1920 and later presented to the Auckland Gallery, New Zealand. Commenting on it in 1922, Mrs Gordon-Stables, critic of the *International Studio*, identified it as having been painted under the spell of 'the French movement'.
29. Mark Gertler to S. S. Koteliansky, 13 August 1919, *MGSL*, pp. 174–5.
30. Julian Morrell to Mark Gertler, dated 3 June [probably 3 July] 1919, Goodman Papers.
31. A. Causey, 'A Certain Gipsy Gaudiness: Gertler after the First World War', *Mark Gertler: Paintings and Drawings*, pp. 29–30.
32. S. S. Koteliansky to Mark Gertler, Wednesday [*c.* 16 July 1919[, Luke Gertler Collection.
33. Mark Gertler to Ottoline Morrell, 29 May 1919, University of Texas, Austin.
34. Ibid.
35. Mark Gertler to Ottoline Morrell, 16 June 1919, ibid.
36. Ibid.
37. Ibid.
38. A total of 39 artists were represented by a total of 177 paintings and sculptures and 141 drawings. The exhibitors included Picasso, Matisse, Derain, Dufy, Soutine, Léger, Vlaminck, Othon Friesz and the sculptors Alexander Archipenko and Ossip Zadkine, but the works of Modigliani and Utrillo had the biggest impact. A corresponding show in Paris of English Vorticist paintings had been planned, but this scheme had to be abandoned because of lack of time.
39. Mark Gertler to S. S. Koteliansky, August 1919, *MGSL*, pp. 175–6.
40. Mark Gertler to S. S. Koteliansky, 31 August 1919, ibid., p. 176.
41. Carrington to Lytton Strachey, 29 August 1919, Garnett, *Carrington*, pp. 141–3.
42. Mark Gertler to Brett, June 1919, University of Texas, Austin.
43. Gathorne-Hardy, *Ottoline at Garsington*, p. 120.
44. Brett to Lord Esher, April 1919, quoted in Hignett, *Brett*, p. 98.
45. Mark Gertler to Carrington, 3 September 1919, University of Texas, Austin.
46. Mark Gertler to Ottoline Morrell, 17 October 1919, ibid.
47. Mark Gertler to Mary Hutchinson, 8 November 1919, ibid.
48. Mark Gertler to Ottoline Morrell, 8 September 1919, ibid.
49. Mark Gertler to Carrington, December 1919, *MGSL*, pp. 176–7.
50. Ibid.
51. Quoted in N. Carrington, *Carrington*, pp. 25–6.
52. Mark Gertler to Carrington, 14 December, *MGSL*, p. 177.
53. John Middleton Murry to Katherine Mansfield, 5 December [1919], C. A. Hankin, ed., *The Letters of John Middleton Murry to Katherine Mansfield*, pp. 235–6.
54. Valentine Dobrée to Mark Gertler, dated only 'Thursday' [*c.* summer 1919], Luke Gertler Collection.
55. Mark Gertler to Carrington, 2 January 1920, University of Texas, Austin.
56. Mark Gertler to Valentine Dobrée, 18 March 1921, Brotherton Collection, Leeds.
57. Mark Gertler to Carrington, [Friday] 2 January 1920, *MGSL*, p. 178.
58. Mark Gertler to Ottoline Morrell, 9 March 1920, University of Texas, Austin.
59. Mark Gertler to Ottoline Morrell, 18 March 1920, ibid.
60. Ibid.
61. Mark Gertler to Ottoline Morrell, 25 March 1920, ibid.
62. Mark Gertler to Ottoline Morrell, 2 April 1920, ibid.
63. Mark Gertler to Carrington, 9 April 1920, *MGSL*, pp. 178–9.

64. Ibid.
65. Ibid.
66. Mark Gertler to Brett, 24 March 1920, University of Texas, Austin.
67. Mark Gertler to Ottoline Morrell, 25 March 1920, ibid.
68. Ibid.
69. Mark Gertler to Brett, 29 March 1920, ibid.
70. Mark Gertler to Carrington, 9 April 1920, *MGSL*, pp. 178–9.
71. Mark Gertler to Ottoline Morrell, 15 April 1920, University of Texas, Austin.
72. Mark Gertler to Carrington, 9 April 1920, *MGSL*, pp. 178–9.
73. Mark Gertler to Ottoline Morrell, 15 April 1920, University of Texas, Austin.
74. Ibid.
75. Mark Gertler to Ottoline Morrell, 20 April 1920, ibid.
76. Mark Gertler to Carrington, 17 May 1920, *MGSL*, pp. 179–80.
77. Mark Gertler to S. S. Koteliansky, 5 January 1921, ibid., pp. 194–5.
78. Mark Gertler to Carrington, 17 May 1920, ibid., pp. 179–80.
79. Mark Gertler to Carrington, 1 July 1920, ibid., pp. 181–2.
80. Carrington to Lytton Strachey, 24 July 1920, British Library, Add. MS 62,890.
81. Mark Gertler to Carrington, 22 July 1920, *MGSL*, p. 182.
82. Mark Gertler to Mary Hutchinson, 24 August 1920, University of Texas, Austin.
83. Mark Gertler to Brett, 4 September 1920, University of Texas, Austin.
84. Mark Gertler to Carrington, 12 September 1920, *MGSL*, p. 184.
85. Mark Gertler to Brett, [Friday] 10 September 1920, University of Texas, Austin.
86. Ibid.
87. Carrington to Lytton Strachey, 12 October 1920, British Library, Add. MS 62,892.
88. Mark Gertler to Ottoline Morrell, 23 September 1920, University of Texas, Austin.
89. Carrington to Lytton Strachey, 18 November 1920, British Library, Add. MS 62,893.
90. Carrington to Alix Strachey, 2 October 1920, British Library, Add. MS 65,158.
91. Mark Gertler to Ottoline Morrell, 23 October 1920, University of Texas, Austin.
92. Mark Gertler to Carrington, 22 July 1920, *MGSL*, p. 182.
93. Carrington to Lytton Strachey, 21 October 1920, British Library, Add. MS 62,892.
94. Ibid.

CHAPTER 15: EXILE

1. Mark Gertler to Mary Hutchinson, 14 November 1920, University of Texas, Austin.
2. Mark Gertler to Carrington, 19 November 1920, *MGSL*, pp. 185–6.
3. Mark Gertler to Brett, November 1920, University of Texas, Austin.
4. The building was bought by Rest Hotels and converted into Glen O'Dee, a luxury hotel, in 1934, but requisitioned by the army for billets during the Second World War. In 1945 the Scottish branch of the British Red Cross Society purchased the building to treat tubercular ex-servicemen and -women, and it was reconverted to a sanatorium in 1948 (officially opened in 1949). It later became a National Health hospital and the main building is now no longer in use. [I am very grateful to Miss F. R. Watson, Archivist for Northern Health Services Archives for providing this information.]
5. *Celebrating a Century at Nordrach on Dee: The History of Glen O'Dee* [privately printed, n.d.] pp. 2–9.
6. Mark Gertler to Brett, 21 December 1920, University of Texas, Austin.
7. Mark Gertler to Mary Hutchinson, Christmas 1920, ibid.
8. Mark Gertler to Carrington, 17 December 1920, *MGSL*, pp. 190–2.
9. Mark Gertler to S. S. Koteliansky, 19 November 1920, ibid., p. 186.
10. Mark Gertler to Carrington, 26 November 1920, ibid., pp. 187–8.
11. Mark Gertler to Montague Shearman, 11 January 1921, University of Texas, Austin. A second portrait executed the same month (current whereabouts unknown) is less harsh, but may be compared to the 1920 studio self-portrait with the shadows of illness already apparent.

12. Mark Gertler to S. S. Koteliansky, 12 December 1920, *MGSL*, p. 190.
13. Mark Gertler to S. S. Koteliansky, 28 November 1920, ibid., pp. 188–9.
14. Mark Gertler to Carrington, 17 December 1920, ibid., pp. 190–2.
15. Mark Gertler to Carrington, 7 December 1920, University of Texas, Austin.
16. Mark Gertler to Mary Hutchinson, 14 November 1920, ibid.
17. Mark Gertler to S. S. Koteliansky, 22 November 1920, British Library.
18. Mark Gertler to Brett, 1 March 1921, University of Texas, Austin.
19. Mark Gertler to Brett, December 1920, ibid.
20. Mark Gertler to S. S. Koteliansky, 5 January 1921, British Library, Add. MS 48,969.
21. Mark Gertler to Brett, 1 February 1921, University of Texas, Austin.
22. Mark Gertler to S. S. Koteliansky, 5 January 1921, *MGSL*, pp. 194–5.
23. Mark Gertler to Valentine Dobrée, 18 December 1920, Brotherton Collection, Leeds.
24. E. S., *Nation & Athenaeum* (18 February 1922), p. 772.
25. Set up in 1906, the Goupil Gallery's autumn show was one of the chief events of the season until stopped by the advent of war in 1914. It resumed in 1919 and the tenth show (autumn 1920) re-established its prestige. It was also a showcase for the NEAC and the London Group.
26. Mark Gertler to Carrington, 18 February 1921, *MGSL*, p. 198.
27. Carrington to Alix Strachey, not dated [c. February 1921], British Library, Add. MS 65,158.
28. Mark Gertler to S. S. Koteliansky, 28 February 1921, British Library, Add. MS 48,969.
29. Mark Gertler to Brett, 15 February 1921, University of Texas, Austin.
30. Mark Gertler to St John Hutchinson, 21 January 1921, ibid.
31. Gertler himself gave this figure in a letter to Carrington (14 March 1921, *MGSL*, pp. 199–200). Few brochures for the sanatorium have survived, but the weekly fee some ten years earlier (in 1910) was 5 guineas a week. Gertler's letter implies that this cost had doubled over the last decade to nearer £11 a week in 1920.
32. Mark Gertler to Carrington, 18 February 1921, *MGSL*, p. 198.
33. Mark Gertler to Brett, 8 April 1921, University of Texas, Austin.
34. Mark Gertler to Carrington, 18 February 1921, *MGSL*, p. 198.
35. Mark Gertler to S. S. Koteliansky, 11 April 1921, ibid., p. 201.
36. Mark Gertler to Brett, 1 March 1921, University of Texas, Austin.
37. Carrington sent Gertler a magazine of Renoir reproductions at the sanatorium in March 1921.
38. Mark Gertler to Carrington, 14 March 1921, *MGSL*, pp. 199–200.
39. Mark Gertler to Carrington, 21 March 1921, ibid., pp. 200–01.
40. Q. Bell, *Virginia Woolf: A Biography*, book 2, p. 78.
41. Mark Gertler to Carrington, 21 March 1921, *MGSL*, pp. 200–01.
42. Mark Gertler to Carrington, 26 April 1921, ibid., pp. 202–3.
43. Mark Gertler to Carrington, 17 May 1921, ibid., pp. 203–4.
44. Ibid.
45. Carrington to Lytton Strachey, [14 May 1921], Garnett, *Carrington*, pp. 175–8.
46. Glenavy, *Today We Will Only Gossip*, p. 164.
47. Mark Gertler to Ottoline Morrell, 1 June 1921, University of Texas, Austin.
48. Mark Gertler to Carrington, 14 July 1921, *MGSL*, p. 207.
49. Quoted in Caws, *Women of Bloomsbury*, p. 121.
50. Mark Gertler to Carrington, [21 December 1921], *MGSL*, p. 209.
51. Mark Gertler to Brett, 18 June 1921, University of Texas, Austin.
52. Mark Gertler to S. S. Koteliansky, 25 June 1921, British Library, Add. MS 48,969.
53. Mark Gertler to S. S. Koteliansky, [September] 1921, *MGSL*, p. 208.
54. Mark Gertler to Ottoline Morrell, 6 September 1921, University of Texas, Austin.
55. Mark Gertler to Valentine Dobrée, 11 November 1921, Brotherton Collection, Leeds.
56. Quoted in S. Bedford, *Aldous Huxley: A Biography*, p. 128.
57. Quoted by N. Carrington, *MGSL*, p. 185.

58. Apart from Gertler the main members of the 'Thursdays' were: Kot, John Middleton Murry (until 1924), the scientist and journalist J. W. N. Sullivan, the music critic and writer W. J. Turner, the poet James Stephens, the Greek scholar John Mavrogordato, the classical scholar Herbert J. Milne, and A. S. Fulton, Keeper of the Department of Oriental Books and Languages at the British Museum. D. H. Lawrence, the poet Ralph Hodgson and the diplomat Sydney Waterlow were regulars whenever they were in London.
59. Virginia Woolf, diary, [Sunday, 18 December 1921], *The Diary of Virginia Woolf*, vol. 2, p. 149.
60. Virginia Woolf to Vanessa Bell, 22 December 1922, Nicolson, *The Question of Things Happening*, p. 595.
61. Mark Gertler to Ottoline Morrell, 8 November 1921, University of Texas, Austin.
62. Mark Gertler to Ottoline Morrell, Saturday, December 1921, ibid.
63. Mark Gertler to Valentine Dobrée, 26 November 1921, Brotherton Collection, Leeds.

CHAPTER 16: NEW DEPARTURES

1. Carrington to Gerald Brenan, 21 September 1921, quoted in Gerzina, *Carrington*, p. 179.
2. J. Gathorne-Hardy, *The Interior Castle: A Life of Gerald Brenan*, p. 175.
3. Quoted in Holroyd, *Lytton Strachey*, pp. 506–8.
4. According to Gathorne-Hardy, Ralph Partridge broke off the affair with Valentine in September, but she was in any case abroad between mid-June and the end of September.
5. Garnett, *Carrington*, p. 216.
6. Collioure, south of Perpignan, a few miles from the Spanish frontier, was a favourite resort of Matisse and Derain, while Braque and Picasso had favoured Céret, about twenty miles inland.
7. R. R. T[atlock], 'Gertler', *Burlington Magazine*, 40 (1922), p. 151.
8. R. Fry, 'ART: The Goupil Gallery', *New Statesman* (18 February 1922), p. 561.
9. Carrington to Lytton Strachey, 15 February 1922, Garnett, *Carrington*, p. 204.
10. Sophie Bowness and Clive Phillpot, *Britain at the Venice Biennale, 1895–1995* (London: British Council, 1995), pp. 24–7.
11. Hignett, *Brett*, p. 124.
12. Katherine Mansfield to S. S. Koteliansky, 2 August 1922, quoted in Hignett, *Brett*, p. 128.
13. Mark Gertler to Ottoline Morrell, 10 May 1922, University of Texas, Austin.
14. Mark Gertler to Valentine Dobrée, 8 May 1922, Brotherton Collection, Leeds.
15. Carrington to Gerald Brenan, 1922, quoted in N. Carrington, *Carrington*, p. 26.
16. Holroyd, *Lytton Strachey*, p. 515.
17. Valentine appears to have written several letters to Ralph Partridge from Paris. Carrington makes particular reference to a letter written from there on 27 June 1922. See Garnett, *Carrington*, p. 230.
18. Mark Gertler to Ottoline Morrell [July 1922], University of Texas, Austin.
19. Brett also recalled how as students they used to visit the 'low' bars of Limehouse where the 'tarts' were all consistently kind to her (Brett to Luke Gertler, 2 July 1968, Luke Gertler Collection).
20. However, Brett, when told that her London maid had given notice, wrote to Kot that she wondered whether Gertler and Valentine 'had been indiscrete [sic]' (quoted in Hignett, *Brett*, p. 127).
21. These pictures are dated only '1922', but it seems likely that *Adolescence* pre-dates this trip, although Gertler may well have passed through Paris on his journey to Villefranche-sur-Mer in January. Classical titles are rare in Gertler's work, and it is possible that *Pomona* may have been inspired by Poussin's famous statue of the same name in the garden of Versailles.
22. Mark Gertler to Mary Hutchinson, not dated [*c.* July 1922], University of Texas, Austin.
23. Ibid.
24. Mark Gertler to Ottoline Morrell, *c.* July 1922, ibid.

25. Ibid.
26. Mark Gertler to Ottoline Morrell, Saturday, December 1922, ibid.
27. Ibid.
28. Mark Gertler to Ottoline Morrell, 22 August 1922, University of Texas, Austin.
29. Ibid.
30. Mark Gertler to Ottoline Morrell, 30 September 1922, ibid.
31. Mark Gertler to Mary Hutchinson, 5 September 1922, University of Texas, Austin.
32. Virginia Woolf to Vanessa Bell, 22 December 1922, Nicolson, *The Question of Things Happening*, vol. 2, p. 595.
33. Brett to Luke Gertler, 2 July 1968, Luke Gertler Collection.
34. Mark Gertler to Ottoline Morrell, 30 September 1922, University of Texas, Austin.
35. Mark Gertler to Ottoline Morrell, 28 September 1922, ibid.
36. Seymour, *Ottoline Morrell*, pp. 330–31.
37. Quoted in Furbank, *E. M. Forster*, p. 110.
38. Mark Gertler to Ottoline Morrell, 16 December 1922, University of Texas, Austin.
39. From an address by Mrs Julian Goodman (*née* Morrell) at the opening of the exhibition of the works of Mark Gertler at the Ben Uri Gallery, London, 16 November 1944.
40. Mark Gertler to Ottoline Morrell, 28 October 1922, University of Texas, Austin.
41. Carrington to Lytton Strachey, Friday, 23 June 1922, British Library.
42. Rises in temperature, loss of weight, overwhelming tiredness, exuberant high spirits and persistent anaemia were all recognized symptoms of tuberculosis (see Dormandy, *The White Death*, p. 220).
43. There is however, one recurring cipher: 'C' is a term used frequently but inconclusively. It may refer to copulation, in connection with managing his stricture, but there seems no way of being sure of this, especially since any women with whom he was having a relationship (whether emotional or sexual) are designated only by their initials – a practice that becomes particularly difficult to decipher in the entries for his later years).
44. The reason for Prewett's 'faded Hamlet' routine became apparent in the new year, when Sassoon forwarded a postcard to Philip Morrell which revealed that the poet-turned-cheesemaker, who had been running the dairy at Garsington for almost a year, had 'swindled Philip beyond the dreams of avarice', apparently on the grounds that Philip (whose extra-marital affairs had become public knowledge) did not deserve such an admirable wife as Ottoline (Seymour, *Ottoline Morrell*, p. 328).
45. Mark Gertler to W. J. Turner, 4 January 1923, *MGSL*, p. 209.

CHAPTER 17: A CONSISTENT AND INEVITABLE SELF

1. 'Augustus John and Mark Gertler', *The Spectator*, 130 (17 February 1923), p. 288.
2. Mark Gertler to Ottoline Morrell, February 1923, University of Texas, Austin.
3. The most important are: *Studies of Alice Edwards* (1923), *Young Girlhood* (1923), *After Bathing* (1924), *Young Girlhood II* (1925), *Girl with a Musical Instrument* (1926) and *Reclining Nude* (1928).
4. Several of them were exhibited at the Goupil Gallery in 1924.
5. There are two nudes by Titian in the Ufizzi collection: *Venus and Cupid* and the *Venus of Urbino*. Gertler may also have been referring to *Flora*, who is golden-haired, but draped rather than nude.
6. M. Gertler, 'A Note on Michel Angelo', *The Adelphi*, vol. 1, no. 2 (July 1923), pp. 154–5.
7. M. Gertler, 'The Architectural Element in Painting', *The Adelphi*, vol. 1, no. 3 (August 1923), p. 247.
8. Gertler's black notebook, p. 5: 'From letter to V[alentine]. D[obrée]. Aug: 1923', Luke Gertler Collection.
9. Mark Gertler to Walter Turner, 28 September 1923, partly quoted in *MGSL*, p. 210; original in University of Neuchâtel, Switzerland.
10. Mark Gertler to S. S. Koteliansky, 22 July 1924, *MGSL*, p. 211.
11. Siegfried Sassoon, diary entry, 24 October 1923, *Sassoon Diaries, 1923–25*, p. 59.

12. Mark Gertler to W. J. Turner, 28 September 1923, partially quoted in *MGSL*, p. 210; original in University of Neuchâtel, Switzerland.
13. Mark Gertler to Mr Hayward (curator of Manchester Art Gallery), 14 May 1924, Manchester Art Gallery files.
14. Although the picture is popularly believed to be a portrait of Gertler's eldest sister Deborah, the identity of the model is not certain. Gertler's niece Mrs Minnie Jacques (unidentified paper, *c.* 1965, Tate Gallery Archive 9217. 119) certainly believed that the picture was a portrait of her mother. However, in a letter to Walter Turner (28 September 1923, University of Neuchâtel, Switzerland) Gertler simply refers to the sitter as 'the model', implying she was a professional model.
15. Mark Gertler to Valentine Dobrée, 20 October 1923, Brotherton Collection, Leeds.
16. Quoted in Hignett, *Brett*, p. 142.
17. Quoted in Carswell, *Lives and Letters*, pp. 201–2.
18. Mark Gertler to Ottoline Morrell, 24 January 1924, University of Texas, Austin.
19. Ibid.
20. Mark Gertler to Ottoline Morrell, 16 November 1924, ibid.
21. Mark Gertler to Ottoline Morrell, 8 April 1924, ibid.
22. Mark Gertler to Ottoline Morrell, 21 April 1924, ibid.
23. Mark Gertler to Valentine Dobrée, 6 April 1924, Brotherton Collection, Leeds, partially reproduced in *MGSL*, pp. 210–11.
24. Ibid.
25. Mark Gertler to Ottoline Morrell, 16 November 1924, University of Texas, Austin.
26. Mark Gertler to S. S. Koteliansky, 22 July 1924, *MGSL*, pp. 211–12.
27. Quoted in V. Glendinning, *Edith Sitwell: A Unicorn among Lions*, p. 147.
28. O. Sitwell, 'Triple Fugue', *Triple Fugue*, pp. 235–6.
29. There may also be a trace of Gertler in the poet Jacques Rosenheimer: 'short, dark and thick-set, he was curly-haired and curly-nostrilled.'
30. Lilly, *Sickert*, p. 158.
31. Mark Gertler to S. S. Koteliansky, 22 July 1924, *MGSL*, pp. 211–12.
32. Wadsworth, *Edward Wadsworth*, p. 96.
33. Woodeson, *Gertler* (p. 294), writes that she was 'related to one of his brothers-in-law'.
34. Quoted in Woodeson, *Gertler*, p. 293.
35. Mark Gertler to Valentine Dobrée, 24 November 1925, Brotherton Collection, Leeds.
36. Mark Gertler, notebook entry, 9 October 1924, Luke Gertler Collection.
37. Mark Gertler to S. S. Koteliansky, 30 December 1924, *MGSL*, p. 212.
38. Mark Gertler to Valentine Dobrée, 29 December 1924, Brotherton Collection, Leeds.
39. Mark Gertler to S. S. Koteliansky, [10 February] 1925, *MGSL*, p. 213.

CHAPTER 18: A LIFE WITHOUT COMPROMISE

1. Mark Gertler to Valentine Dobrée, 12 February 1925, Brotherton Collection, Leeds.
2. Mark Gertler to Ottoline Morrell, 5 March 1925, University of Texas, Austin.
3. Ibid.
4. Ibid.
5. Mark Gertler to Valentine Dobrée, 12 February 1925, Brotherton Collection, Leeds.
6. Mark Gertler to John Mavrogordato, 3 August 1925, Bodleian Library, uncatalogued papers.
7. Mark Gertler to S. S. Koteliansky, 29 July 1925, *MGSL*, pp. 215–6.
8. Mark Gertler to S. S. Koteliansky, 18 July 1925, British Library.
9. Mark Gertler to S. S. Koteliansky [22 August 1925], British Library. Part of this letter is reproduced in *MGSL*, pp. 214–5.
10. Mark Gertler, diary entry [*c.* 29 August–9 September 1925], green notebook, Luke Gertler Collection.
11. Ibid.
12. Mark Gertler to Ottoline Morrell, 4 September 1925, University of Texas, Austin.

13. Carswell, *Lives and Letters*, p. 264.
14. Dormandy, *The White Death*, p. 172.
15. Mark Gertler to Ottoline Morrell, 8 September 1925, University of Texas, Austin.
16. According to the prospectus, 90 per cent of the vegetables consumed on the premises were provided by the 10 acre kitchen gardens, milk was supplied from a neighbouring farm where 'a carefully inspected herd of cows' was kept for exclusive sanatorium use, eggs and poultry were supplied by the sanatorium poultry farm half a mile away, and all meals were 'carefully planned in conjunction with the Chef and his staff so as to combine body-building nourishment with a variety of choice to suit all tastes'.
17. Mark Gertler to S. S. Koteliansky, 11 September 1925, *MGSL*, p. 216.
18. Ibid.
19. Mark Gertler to J. Mavrogordato, 15 September 1925, Bodleian Library (uncatalogued correspondence).
20. Mark Gertler to Ottoline Morrell, 20 September 1925, University of Texas, Austin.
21. Mark Gertler to Carrington, 1 October 1925, *MGSL*, pp. 217–8.
22. Ibid.
23. Carrington to Mark Gertler, 7 October 1925, ibid.
24. Mark Gertler to S. S. Koteliansky, 20 November 1925, British Library.
25. Mark Gertler to Ottoline Morrell, 9 December 1925, University of Texas, Austin.
26. Mark Gertler to S. S. Koteliansky, [28 January] 1925, *MGSL*, p. 213.
27. Mark Gertler to Ottoline Morrell, 6 January 1926, University of Texas, Austin.
28. Mark Gertler to Ottoline Morrell, 6 March 1926, ibid.
29. Ibid.
30. Mark Gertler to Mary Hutchinson, 5 September 1920, ibid.
31. Seymour, *Ottoline Morrell*, p. 349.
32. J. Vinogradoff, *Mark Gertler: The Early and the Late Years*, p. 13.
33. Nevinson, *Paint and Prejudice*, p. 183.
34. JEAS minutes, Wednesday, 14 July 1926, University of Southampton.
35. Mark Gertler to Valentine Dobrée, 3 August 1926, Brotherton Collection, Leeds.
36. W. J. Turner to Ottoline Morrell, 10 August 1926, University of Texas, Austin.
37. Mark Gertler to S. S. Koteliansky, 19 August 1926, *MGSL*, p. 220.
38. Mark Gertler to Ottoline Morrell, 28 September 1925, University of Texas, Austin.
39. Mark Gertler to S. S. Koteliansky, 19 August 1926, British Library.
40. Mark Gertler to Christine Mavrogordato, 19 August 1926, Bodleian Library, uncatalogued papers.
41. Mark Gertler to Marjorie Hodgkinson, 25 September 1926, Luke Gertler Collection.

CHAPTER 19: BUILDING BRIDGES

1. R. Carline, obituary of Marjorie Kostenz, *Hampstead & Highgate Express* (2 November 1979).
2. Marjorie Kostenz to Diana Farr, 13 March [1976] and 30 April 1976, Cambridge University Library.
3. Luke Gertler, introduction to 'Marjorie Kostenz, Embroideries and Other Works', Gunnersbury Park Museum, 6 December 1981–10 January 1982, Tate Gallery Archive, 9217.117.
4. Marjorie Gertler to Thomas Balston, 22 July 1936, University of Texas, Austin.
5. Mark Gertler to S. S. Koteliansky, 25 August 1928, British Library, Add. MS 48,969.
6. Mark Gertler to Marjorie Hodgkinson, 20 September 1927, Luke Gertler Collection.
7. Taylor, *Bernard Meninsky*, p. 60.
8. Mark Gertler to Marjorie Hodgkinson, 25 September 1926, *MGSL*, p. 221.
9. Mark Gertler to Marjorie Hodgkinson, 10 October 1926, Luke Gertler Collection.
10. Mark Gertler to Marjorie Hodgkinson, dated only 'Tuesday night' [*c.* 30 November 1926], ibid.

11. Mark Gertler to Ottoline Morrell, 2 November 1926, University of Texas, Austin.
12. Mark Gertler to Mrs Mavrogordato, 7 November 1926, Bodleian Library, uncatalogued papers.
13. Mark Gertler to Marjorie Hodgkinson, 9 November 1926, *MGSL*, p. 222.
14. Mark Gertler to Ottoline Morrell, 2 November 1926, University of Texas, Austin.
15. The others were Samuel Courtauld and Hindley Smith.
16. Spalding, *Duncan Grant* (p. 270), comments that 'it must have seemed a rather blatant piece of favouritism, as the seven artists were all in some way connected with Bloomsbury: Duncan, Vanessa, Keith Baynes, Frank Dobson – the sculptor much admired by Fry and Clive Bell – and Frederick Porter, whose presidency of the London Group had reflected his sympathy with Roger Fry's ideas, as did the work of Bernard Adeney, who also joined.'
17. Mark Gertler to Ottoline Morrell, 8 November 1926, University of Texas, Austin.
18. Mark Gertler to Valentine Dobrée, 24 June 1924, Brotherton Collection, Leeds.
19. Mark Gertler to Ottoline Morrell, 8 November 1926, University of Texas, Austin.
20. Mark Gertler to Ottoline Morrell, 17 November 1926, ibid.
21. Mark Gertler to Ottoline Morrell, 21 November 1926, ibid.
22. Carrington to Lytton Strachey, Sunday evening 26 December 1926, British Library, vol. 62,894.
23. Mark Gertler, 8 January 1927, green notebook, Luke Gertler Collection.
24. Mark Gertler, 5 February 1927, ibid.
25. Mark Gertler to Valentine Dobrée, 10 April 1927, Brotherton Collection, Leeds.
26. Mark Gertler to Marjorie Hodgkinson, 18 January 1927, Luke Gertler Collection.
27. Mark Gertler to Valentine Dobrée, 10 April 1927, Brotherton Collection, Leeds.
28. Mark Gertler to Ottoline Morrell, 23 April 1927, University of Texas, Austin.
29. Seymour, *Ottoline Morrell*, p. 353.
30. Mark Gertler to S. S. Koteliansky, 29 April 1927, partly reproduced in *MGSL*, pp. 222–3; original in British Library.
31. Mark Gertler to S. S. Koteliansky, 4 May 1927, British Library.
32. Mark Gertler to Ottoline Morrell, 30 April 1927, University of Texas, Austin.
33. Ibid.
34. Mark Gertler to Valentine Dobrée, 24 May 1927, Brotherton Collection, Leeds.
35. Mark Gertler to Marjorie Hodgkinson, 7 August 1927, Luke Gertler Collection.
36. Mark Gertler to S. S. Koteliansky, 5 August 1927, British Library.
37. Mark Gertler to S. S. Koteliansky, 9 August 1927, *MGSL*, pp. 223–4.
38. Mark Gertler to Marjorie Hodgkinson [20 September 1927], ibid., pp. 224–5.
39. Mark Gertler to Marjorie Hodgkinson, 13 August 1927, Luke Gertler Collection.
40. Her name and address are listed in one of Gertler's (undated) address books, however, alongside contacts from the Westminster, which suggests there was still contact between them in the 1930s.
41. 'D. C. Partride [*sic*]: Her Book', 1 January 1928, British Library.
42. Ibid., Tuesday, 10 January 1928.
43. Ibid.
44. Gerald Brenan later acknowledged that Carrington was 'attracted to those who are less attracted to you, and Repelled by Reciprocity' (undated and not sent, quoted in Caws, *Women of Bloomsbury*, p. 121.) Gertler later confessed to Dorothy Morland that once during this period Carrington had 'offered herself' to him. He had refused her, horrified that she could offer herself so cheaply after their long and tortuous history (Dorothy Morland in interview with the author, April 1996). Towards the end of 1928 Carrington did find some happiness in a final affair with the sailor Beakus Penrose, which ended in 1930.
45. Mark Gertler to Marjorie Hodgkinson, 4 February 1928, *MGSL*, pp. 225–6.
46. Mark Gertler to Marjorie Hodgkinson, 10 February 1928, partially quoted in *MGSL*, p. 226; original in Luke Gertler Collection.
47. Mark Gertler to John Mavrogordato [*c.* 28 June 1927], Bodleian Library, uncatalogued papers.

48. Mark Gertler to Marjorie Hodgkinson, 20 September 1927, Luke Gertler Collection.
49. Mark Gertler to Marjorie Hodgkinson, 29 February 1928, ibid.
50. Mark Gertler to Marjorie Hodgkinson, 15 March 1928, MGSL, p. 227.
51. W. Egerton Powell, *Artwork*, 4 (summer 1928).
52. 'Mark Gertler and Laura Knight at Leicester Galleries', *The Times* (12 March 1928).
53. R. Fry, 'Mr Gertler at the Leicester Galleries', *Nation & Athenaeum* (24 March 1928), p. 935.
54. Mark Gertler to Roger Fry, [March 1928], Sutton, *The Letters of Roger Fry*, vol. 2, p. 84.
55. Mark Gertler to Marjorie Hodgkinson, 1 February 1928, Luke Gertler Collection.
56. Mark Gertler to Brett, 1 June 1928, University of Texas, Austin.
57. Marjorie Kostenz to Beatrice Campbell, 10 December 1965, private collection.
58. Mark Gertler to Marjorie Hodgkinson, 15 March 1928, partially quoted in *MGSL*, p. 227; original in Luke Gertler Collection.

CHAPTER 20: A LITTLE DEATH

1. Quoted in Woodeson, *Gertler*, p. 293.
2. Ibid.
3. Mark Gertler to S. S. Koteliansky, 11 April 1929, *MGSL*, p. 228.
4. Mark Gertler to Thomas Balston, 2 July 1929, University of Texas, Austin.
5. Mark Gertler to S. S. Koteliansky, 15 July 1929, *MGSL*, p. 230.
6. Ibid.
7. Mark Gertler to Ottoline Morrell, 31 July 1929, University of Texas, Austin.
8. Mark Gertler to Ottoline Morrell, 21 July 1929, ibid.
9. Mark Gertler to Ottoline Morrell, 27 July 1929, ibid.
10. Mark Gertler to Ottoline Morrell, 31 July 1929, ibid.
11. Ibid.
12. JEAS minutes, Wednesday, 18 September 1929, MS 135, AJ 35.5. Minutes dated from 20/3/1928 to 27/2/1939: Gertler, Mark: 60, 266, p. 60, University of Southampton.
13. Mark Gertler, 20 November 1929 [in 1927 diary], Luke Gertler Collection.
14. Glenavy, *Today We Will Only Gossip*, p. 81.
15. R. Church, 'Travellers in Depth', *Country Life* (30 December 1965).
16. Mark Gertler to Marjorie Hodgkinson, 3 March 1920, Luke Gertler Collection.
17. Marjorie Kostenz (formery Gertler) to Beatrice Campbell, 10 December 1965, private collection.
18. Mark Gertler to Ottoline Morrell, 1 April 1930, University of Texas, Austin.
19. Marjorie Kostenz to Beatrice Campbell, 10 December 1965, private collection.
20. Marjorie Hodgkinson to Ottoline Morrell, 1 April 1930, University of Texas, Austin.
21. Mark Gertler to John Mavrogordato, 24 March 1920, Bodleian Library.
22. Carrington to Lytton Strachey, Wednesday, April 1930, British Library, Add. MS 62,897, f. 228.
23. Mark Gertler to John Mavrogordato, 24 March 1930, Bodleian Library.
24. Mark Gertler to Ottoline Morrell, 29 April 1930, University of Texas, Austin.
25. Ibid.
26. Mark Gertler to S. S. Koteliansky, 22 April 1930, British Library.
27. Mark Gertler to S. S. Koteliansky, 2 May 1930, British Library.
28. Mark Gertler, green notebook, August 1930, Luke Gertler Collection.
29. R. Carline, 'The Tragedy after Too Early a Triumph', *Express & News* (17 November 1972).
30. Mark Gertler, green notebook, October [1930], Luke Gertler Collection.
31. Mark Gertler to Thomas Balston, 21 October 1930, University of Texas, Austin.
32. Ibid., 3 November 1930.
33. T. W. Earp, 'Mark Gertler', *The Studio*, 100 (November 1930) pp. 352–7.

CHAPTER 21: SEPARATE BEINGS

1. Mark Gertler to S. S. Koteliansky, not dated [January 1931], British Library, Add. MS 48,969.

2. Mark Gertler to Marjorie Gertler, 15 May 1931, Luke Gertler Collection.
3. A. Bliss, *As I Remember*, p. 108.
4. Gertler's only known portrait of Marjorie is the pastel *Marjorie Gertler/The Artist's Wife* (1933; Abbot Hall Art Gallery, Kendal).
5. Mark Gertler to S. S. Koteliansky, 15 August 1931, British Library, Add. MS 48,969.
6. Marjorie Gertler to S. S. Koteliansky, *c.* 15 August 1931; ibid.
7. Ibid.
8. C. Moorehead, *Sidney Bernstein*, p. 75.
9. Seymour, *Ottoline Morrell*, pp. 378–9.
10. Mark Gertler to Marjorie Gertler, 30 August 1931, Luke Gertler Collection.
11. Marjorie Kostenz to Beatrice Campbell, 10 December 1965, private collection.
12. These included selling electric bulbs and stockings, but after both these ventures failed Gertler wrote later the same year to Sidney Bernstein to ask if he could find work for Jack as a commissionaire in one of his theatres. Later, Taylor, Bernstein and Balston became the backers for Jack's loan from the Jewish Board of Guardians to start a shop, which also failed.
13. D. J. Wilcox, *Margaret Geddes*, p. 12.
14. Joan Day (*née* Lowenthal), interview with the author (Monday, 11 August 1997).
15. Wilcox, *Margaret Geddes*, p. 11.
16. Mark Gertler to Marjorie Gertler, 'Monday', September 1932, Luke Gertler Collection.
17. Dunbar Marshall-Malagola to Professor Marcia Allentuck, 6 November 1970, quoted in M. Allentuck, 'Mark Gertler: A Study of his Life', *Apollo* (October 1974), pp. 334–6.
18. Adrian Hill to Professor Marcia Allentuck, 7 November 1970, quoted in Allentuck, 'Mark Gertler', pp. 334–5.
19. Diana Gardner, 'Mark Gertler at the Westminster, Part One', unpublished MS, 1977.
20. Adrian Hill, quoted in Allentuck, 'Mark Gertler'.
21. Dunbar Marshall-Malagola, quoted in Allentuck, 'Mark Gertler', p. 335.
22. F. Gore, 'The Resilient Figure: Mark Gertler and Matthew Smith', *British Art in the 20th Century*, p. 172.
23. A. Huxley, introduction, 'Recent Paintings by Mark Gertler', Lefèvre Gallery, April 1937.
24. Frederick Gore, in interview with the author, 29 December 1997.
25. Gardner, 'Mark Gertler at the Westminster, Part One'.
26. Ibid.
27. Adrian Hill, quoted in Allentuck, 'Mark Gertler', pp. 334–5.
28. A. Powell, *To Keep the Ball Rolling: Memoirs*, vol. 1, *Infants of the Spring*, p. 60.
29. A. Powell, *To Keep the Ball Rolling: Memoirs*, vol. 2, *Messengers of the Day*, p. 8.
30. Ibid.
31. Dorothy Morland, in interview with the author, April 1996.
32. V. S. Pritchett, 'The Skeleton', *The Complete Short Stories*. p. 721.
33. Ibid., p. 721.
34. Ibid., p. 722.
35. Powell, *Infants of the Spring*, p. 94.
36. Mark Gertler to Carrington, 20 February 1932, *MGSL*, p. 234.
37. Mark Gertler to Carrington, 1 March 1932, ibid., p. 235.
38. David Garnett, quoted in Gerzina, *Carrington*, p. xxiv.
39. Quoted in Holroyd, *Lytton Strachey*, p. 690.
40. Frances Partridge to Rosamond Lehmann, ibid., p. 693.
41. Mark Gertler to Brett, 19 April 1932, University of Texas, Austin.
42. Mark Gertler to Marjorie Gertler, 24 March 1932, Luke Gertler Collection.
43. Marjorie Gertler to S. S. Koteliansky, 8 April 1932, British Library, Add. MS 48,969.
44. Mark Gertler to Marjorie Gertler, 'Tuesday after Easter' [*c.* March 1932], Luke Gertler Collection.
45. Ibid.
46. Marjorie Gertler to Thomas Balston, 13 July 1932, University of Texas, Austin.

47. Mark Gertler to Marjorie Gertler, 9 July 1932, Luke Gertler Collection (misdated as 6 July 1932 in *MGSL*, p. 235).
48. Ibid.
49. Marjorie Gertler to Thomas Balston, postmarked 19 August 1932, University of Texas, Austin.
50. Mark Gertler to Thomas Balston, 29 August 1932, ibid.
51. Mark Gertler to Mrs Christine Mavrogordato, 8 September 1932, Bodleian Library.
52. Mark Gertler to Thomas Balston, 21 September 1932, University of Texas, Austin.
53. Mark Gertler to Ottoline Morrell, 24 September 1932, ibid.
54. Mark Gertler to Marjorie Gertler, 'Monday', September 1932, Luke Gertler Collection.
55. 'Mark Gertler: The Man and his Art', *Studio*, 104 (September 1932), pp. 158–63.
56. *The Times* (11 October 1932), 12c.
57. 'Mr Mark Gertler's Paintings at the Leicester Galleries', *Apollo*, 16 (October–November 1932), pp. 258–9.
58. A. Blunt, 'Art – Plagiarism and Vulgarity', *The Spectator* (15 October 1932).
59. 'Mark Gertler: The Man and his Art', *Studio*, 104, pp. 158–63.
60. Mark Gertler to Ralph Hodgson, 16 December 1932, uncatalogued, vault 263, Beinecke Rare Book and Manuscript Library, Yale University.

CHAPTER 22: THE PENNIES STOPPED

1. Mark Gertler to Thomas Balston, Tuesday, [24] January 1933, University of Texas, Austin.
2. Mark Gertler to Thomas Balston, 28 March 1933, ibid.
3. Mark Gertler to Thomas Balston, 31 March 1933, ibid.
4. Mark Gertler to Ralph Hodgson, 8 December 1933, Beinecke Rare Book and Manuscript Library, Yale University.
5. Ibid.
6. Mark Gertler to Thomas Balston, 8 July 1933, University of Texas, Austin.
7. Mark Gertler to Marjorie Gertler [July 1933], *MGSL*, pp. 237–8.
8. Ibid.
9. George Harcourt Vanden-Bempde Johnstone, 3rd Baron Derwent (1899–1949), was a poet and scholar, whose writings included books on Goya (1930) and Rossini (1934) and a memoir, *Return Ticket* (1940).
10. Mark Gertler to S. S. Koteliansky, Thursday, 24 August 1933, British Library.
11. Mark Gertler to S. S. Koteliansky, 21 August 1933, University of Texas, Austin.
12. Mark Gertler to Thomas Balston, 24 August 1933, *MGSL*, p. 238.
13. Gertler's design was made up into a model box, but was never used commercially.
14. Margaret Geddes, diary, 9 January 1934, quoted in Wilcox, *Margaret Geddes*, p. 13.
15. Margaret Geddes, diary, 16 January 1934, ibid.
16. Margaret Geddes, diary, 23 January 1934, ibid.
17. Margaret Geddes, diary, 25 January 1934, ibid., pp. 15–16.
18. Ibid., p. 15.
19. Fedarb, 'Reminiscences of Mark Gertler'.
20. Jean Kemp Hogh to Marcia Allentuck, 23 November 1970, quoted in Allentuck, 'Mark Gertler: A Study of his Life', pp. 334–6.
21. C. Bell, *New Statesman* (24 May 1941).
22. Q. Bell, introduction, *MGSL*, p. 12.
23. The form of the figure is very close to the neo-classical *Three Women at the Fountain* (1921), and the arrangement of the limbs is strikingly similar to Picasso's *Seated Woman in a Chemise* (1923), but as the critic of *The Spectator* noted, 'the borrowings have been developed into something original'.
24. Mark Gertler to Thomas Balston, 6 July 1934, University of Texas, Austin.
25. Mark Gertler to Thomas Balston, 24 June 1934, ibid.
26. Mark Gertler to Thomas Balston, 6 July 1934, ibid.

27. Mark Gertler to Ralph Hodgson, 28 August 1934, Beinecke Rare Book and Manuscript Library, Yale University.
28. Mark Gertler to S. S. Koteliansky, 7 August 1934, British Library.
29. Mark Gertler to Ottoline Morrell, 1 August 1934, University of Texas, Austin.
30. Mark Gertler to S. S. Koteliansky, 29 August 1934, *MGSL*, p. 238.
31. Mark Gertler to S. S. Koteliansky, only partially cited in *MGSL*, p. 238; original in British Library.
32. Mark Gertler to Ralph Hodgson, 28 August 1934, Beinecke Rare Book and Manuscript Library, Yale University.
33. Mark Gertler to S. S. Koteliansky, 7 August 1934, British Library.
34. Mark Gertler to S. S. Koteliansky, 29 August 1934, *MGSL*, p. 238.
35. Mark Gertler to Mary Hutchinson, 4 October 1934, University of Texas, Austin.
36. I have not been able to trace either of these works.
37. Marjorie Gertler to Thomas Balston, 1 October 1934, University of Texas, Austin.
38. Mark Gertler to Marjorie Gertler, 11 October 1934, partially quoted in *MGSL*, p. 239; original in Luke Gertler Collection.
39. Quoted in Woodeson, *Gertler*, pp. 297–8.
40. Mark Gertler to Marjorie Gertler, 11 October 1934, *MGSL*, p. 239.
41. H. Read, 'A Nest of Gentle Artists', *Apollo*, 86 (September 1962), pp. 536–8.
42. The group included the painters Paul Nash, John Armstrong, John Bigge, Edward Burra, Tristram Hillier, Ben Nicholson and Edward Wadsworth, the sculptors Barbara Hepworth and Henry Moore, and architects Wells Coates and Colin Lucas.
43. Read, 'A Nest of Gentle Artists', pp. 536–8.
44. Mark Gertler to Ralph Hodgson, 28 August 1934, Beinecke Rare Book and Manuscript Library, Yale University.
45. Ibid.
46. Ibid.
47. G. Spencer, *Memoirs of a Painter*, pp. 98–100.
48. There has been some suggestion that this was due to anti-Semitism at the RA, but there were some prominent Jewish Academicians such as Jacob Epstein, and no trace of anti-Semitism has been found in the RA election minutes. Gertler's name was included in the nominations for Associateship, 1932–54 (E/24/717a). See also general election minutes 1931–62 (c/22/403/c).
49. A. Blunt, 'Art, English Painting', *Apollo* (July–December 1934), p. 227.
50. G. Grigson, 'Art-Liberalismus', *The Bookman* (November 1934).
51. Mark Gertler to Ottoline Morrell, not dated, [*c*. December 1934], University of Texas, Austin.
52. Ibid.

CHAPTER 23: A SORT OF MADNESS

1. The original catalogue for this exhibition, 'Drawings by Mark Gertler' (Thomas Agnew & Sons, 26 February–30 March 1935), does not appear to have survived.
2. Mark Gertler to Thomas Balston, 24 February 1935, University of Texas, Austin.
3. Mark Gertler to Thomas Balston, 17 February 1935, ibid.
4. Mark Gertler to Thomas Balston, Tuesday, 26 March 1935, ibid.
5. Marjorie Gertler to Thomas Balston, dated 6 June [1935], but note in pencil reads 'July' [i.e., Saturday, 6 July 1935], University of Texas, Austin.
6. Ibid.
7. Mark Gertler to Thomas Balston, 3 July 1935, *MGSL*, p. 239.
8. Ibid.
9. Gertler was displaying the classic symptoms of the 'agitated depressive': 'difficulty in falling asleep, frequent awakening during the night, waking early in the morning without being able to resume sleeping, or all of the above. The wakeful nights of agitated depressives are often haunted by anguished thoughts and ruminations about real or imagined misdeeds in

their past, or by frightening, discouraging apprehensions about the future' (D. Jablow Hershman and J. Lieb, *The Key to Genius: Manic Depression and the Creative Life*, p. 30).

10. Mark Gertler to John Mavrogordato, 10 July 1935, Bodleian Library.
11. Mark Gertler to Thomas Balston, 17 August 1935, University of Texas, Austin.
12. Marjorie Gertler to Thomas Balston, 22 July 1936, ibid.
13. Mark Gertler to John Mavrogordato, Sunday, 1 September 1935, Bodleian Library.
14. Nan Evans (*née* Marley), in conversation with the author.
15. Mark Gertler to John Mavrogordato, Sunday, 1 September 1935, Bodleian Library.
16. Mark Gertler to Thomas Balston, 3 September 1935, *MGSL*, p. 240.
17. Mark Gertler to Thomas Balston, 1 October 1935, University of Texas, Austin.
18. Ibid.
19. Mark Gertler to Thomas Balston, 30 December 1935, University of Texas, Austin.
20. Ibid.
21. Mark Gertler to Thomas Balston, 3 January 1936, ibid.
22. Probably the *Merry-Go-Round* letter of 9 October 1916 (University of Texas, Austin), as this was found copied out in Gertler's own hand among his papers after his death.
23. Mark Gertler to Ottoline Morrell, 20 March 1936, University of Texas, Austin.
24. Ibid.
25. Possibly *Nude with Mandolin* (black chalk, *c.* 1934; Fitzwilliam Museum, Cambridge).
26. Mark Gertler to Thomas Balston, 23 May 1936, University of Texas, Austin.
27. Mark Gertler to Thomas Balston, 7 June 1936, ibid.
28. Mark Gertler to Thomas Balston, 2 July 1936, ibid.
29. Mark Gertler to Thomas Balston, 23 June 1936, *MGSL*, pp. 240–1.
30. Mark Gertler to Thomas Balston, 2 July 1936, ibid., p. 241.
31. Dr Stuart Mackie was an ophthalmologist at Moorfields Hospital.
32. Mark Gertler to Thomas Balston, 10 July 1936, University of Texas, Austin.
33. Mark Gertler to Marjorie Gertler, 11 July 1936, ibid.
34. Mark Gertler to Thomas Balston, 27 July 1936, *MGSL*, p. 242.
35. Marjorie Gertler to Thomas Balston, 20 July 1936, University of Texas, Austin.
36. Dorothy Morland in interview with the author, April 1996.
37. This incident is recounted in Glenavy, *Today We Will Only Gossip*, p. 163, although Lady Glenavy confuses the occasion with his first visit to Banchory sanatorium in 1920.
38. Mark Gertler to S. S. Koteliansky, 2 August 1936, *MGSL*, pp. 242–3.
39. Philip Morrell to Thomas Balston, 19 August 1936, University of Texas, Austin.
40. Ibid.
41. Mark Gertler to John Mavrogordato, 5 October 1936, Bodleian Library.
42. Mark Gertler to Thomas Balston, 6 October 1936, University of Texas, Austin.
43. Mark Gertler to Thomas Balston, 1 September 1936, ibid.
44. Mark Gertler to Thomas Balston, 9 September 1936, ibid.
45. These include *Hautbois, Norfolk* (1936), *The Sanatorium Garden, Norfolk* (1936) and *The Heather Field* (1936).
46. Mark Gertler to Thomas Balston, 9 September 1936, University of Texas, Austin.
47. Mark Gertler to S. S. Koteliansky, 14 September 1936, British Library.
48. Mark Gertler to Ottoline Morrell, 15 September 1936, University of Texas, Austin.
49. Marjorie Gertler to Thomas Balston, 22 July 1936, ibid.
50. Mark Gertler to Thomas Balston, 21 September 1936, ibid.
51. Fedarb, 'Reminiscences'.
52. Mark Gertler to S. S. Koteliansky, 30 October 1934, British Library.
53. Mark Gertler to Ottoline Morrell, not dated [*c.* December 1934], University of Texas, Austin.
54. L. Gertler, 'Memories of my Father', *Mark Gertler: The Early and the Late Years*, p. 10.
55. Fedarb, 'Reminiscences'.
56. L. Gertler, 'Memories of my Father', *Mark Gertler: The Early and the Late Years*, p. 10.
57. Mark Gertler to Thomas Balston, 23 October 1936, University of Texas, Austin.

CHAPTER 24: THE EDGE OF DESTRUCTION

1. Dorothy Morland in interview with the author, April 1996.
2. Ibid.
3. Mark Gertler to John Mavrogordato, 15 April 1937, uncatalogued papers, Bodleian Library, Oxford.
4. Marjorie Gertler to Ottoline Morrell, April [1937], University of Texas, Austin.
5. C. Moorehead, *Sidney Bernstein*, pp. 86–7.
6. See 'The Shadow of the Right', in Wilcox, *The London Group*, pp. 24–9.
7. Mark Gertler to Thomas Balston, 11 July 1937, University of Texas, Austin.
8. Gertler private journal, 6 August 1937, Luke Gertler Collection. The other landscapes were *Cypresses* (1937) and *The Terrace Garden* (1937).
9. One of Gertler's students, who acquired two of these late compositions in the early 1940s, and herself became an art teacher, believes she is still learning lessons about colour from these pictures today. Diana Gurney in interview with the author, 24 May 1999.
10. 1938, New English Art Club, Georges Petit Gallery, Paris (35), *L'éventail espagnol.*
11. Geoffrey Robinson, 'Mark Gertler Explains Why He Is Not Content with Naturalism', *The World of Art Illustrated* (17 May 1939), pp. 10–12.
12. Ibid.
13. Mark Gertler, 'The Architectural Element in Art', *The Adelphi*, vol. 1, no. 3 (August 1923), p. 247.
14. Mark Gertler to Marjorie Gertler, 13 August 1937, Luke Gertler Collection.
15. Mark Gertler to Marjorie Gertler, 23 August 1937, ibid.
16. Mark Gertler to Thomas Balston, 27 September 1937, University of Texas, Austin.
17. R. Shone, *Mark Gertler: The Early and the Late Years*, p. 16.
18. Diary entries, 20 September 1937 and mid-October 1937, Luke Gertler Collection.
19. Mark Gertler to Thomas Balston, 12 January 1938, University of Texas, Austin.
20. Fedarb, 'Reminiscences'.
21. Mark Gertler to Thomas Balston, 27 May 1938, University of Texas, Austin.
22. Woodeson, *Gertler*, p. 405, n. 165.
23. Mark Gertler to Thomas Balston, 25 April 1938, ibid.
24. D. Brett, *Lawrence and Brett: A Friendship*, pp. 16–17.
25. Ibid., p. 16.
26. Brett to Luke Gertler, 16 April 1968, Luke Gertler Collection.
27. Mark Gertler to Thomas Balston, 6 March 1938, University of Texas, Austin.
28. Mark Gertler to Ottoline Morrell, 14 March 1938, ibid.
29. Ottoline Morrell to Mark Gertler, 30 March [1938], ibid.
30. Mark Gertler to Philip Morrell, not dated [*c.* 22 April 1938], Goodman papers.
31. Mark Gertler to Marjorie Hodgkinson, Sunday evening, 8 o'clock [24 April 1938], Luke Gertler Collection.
32. Virginia Woolf, diary entry [*c.* Wednesday 27 April 1938], *The Diary of Virginia Woolf*, vol. 5, *1936–41*, p. 134.
33. L. Sieveking, *Eye of the Beholder.*
34. Fedarb, 'Reminiscences', and Ida Graves in interview with the author, January 1998.
35. To friends in later years she 'occasionally spoke of M. G.' (Wynne Godley); 'often used to talk about Mark Gertler' (Alan Rowlands); 'never mentioned him' (John Penry); and 'had a tragic love affair' with him (Stephen Gardiner).
36. Alan Rowlands in interview with the author (2 December 1998).
37. David Bomberg to Jacob Kramer, quoted in *Jacob Kramer Reassessed*, p. 18.
38. Mark Gertler to Thomas Balston, 27 May 1938, University of Texas, Austin.
39. Mark Gertler to Thomas Balston, 16 June 1938, *MGSL*, pp. 244–5.
40. Woodeson, *Gertler*, p. 322.
41. Diary, 14 August 1938, Luke Gertler Collection.
42. Ida Graves, interview with the author, January 1998.
43. Ida Graves, quoted in P. Hughes-Stanton, *The Wood Engravings of Blair Hughes-Stanton*, p. 45.

44. V. S. Pritchett, 'Conservative Gipsy', *New Statesman* (15 September 1972).
45. Marjorie Kostenz to Beatrice Campbell, 10 December 1965, private collection.
46. Mark Gertler to Marjorie Gertler, 3 September 1938, fragment of letter, unposted, Luke Gertler Collection.
47. Mark Gertler, diary entry, Friday 9 September 1938: 'wrote but retained letter'.
48. Mark Gertler to Marjorie Gertler, 10 September 1938, *MGSL*, p. 246.
49. L. Gertler, 'Memories of My Father', *Mark Gertler: The Early and the Late Years*, p. 11.
50. Mark Gertler to Thomas Balston, 11 August 1938, *MGSL*, pp. 245–6.
51. Richard Carline to Noel Carrington, 3 December 1965, Luke Gertler Collection.
52. Mark Gertler to Thomas Balston, 11 August 1938, *MGSL*, pp. 245–6.
53. Mark Gertler to Marjorie Gertler, 3 September 1938, Luke Gertler Collection.
54. Ibid.
55. Mark Gertler, diary entry, 14 August [1938], Luke Gertler Collection.
56. Mark Gertler to Marjorie Gertler, 10 September 1938, *MGSL*, p. 246.
57. Mark Gertler to Thomas Balston, 27 September 1938, *MGSL*, p. 247.
58. Ibid.
59. Mark Gertler to Thomas Balston, 10 October 1938, ibid., p. 247.
60. Mark Gertler to Thomas Balston, 27 September 1938, partly quoted in *MGSL*, p. 247; original in University of Texas, Austin.
61. Mark Gertler to Thomas Balston, 20 November 1938, University of Texas, Austin.

CHAPTER 25: THESE DARK GLASSES

1. G. Texidor, *These Dark Glasses* (Christchurch: The Claxton Press, 1949), republished in G. Texidor, *In Fifteen Minutes You Can Say a Lot: Selected Fiction*. All page references are to this edition.
2. Originally the character of Julian was called Julius, which Kendrick Smithyman (introduction, p. 17) believes Texidor changed to diminish 'the likelihood of him being identified as Jewish'.
3. Texidor, *These Dark Glasses*, p. 34.
4. Ibid., p. 28.
5. Ibid., p. 44.
6. L. Gertler, 'Memories of my Father', *Mark Gertler: The Early and the Late Years*, p. 11.
7. Diary entry, Monday 16 January [1939], Luke Gertler Collection.
8. Marjorie Kostenz to Noel Carrington, 7 November 1964, ibid.
9. Virginia Woolf to Mark Gertler, Tuesday [21 March 1939], *Virginia Woolf: Collected Letters*, vol. 6, *1936–41: Leave the Letters Till We're Dead*, p. 324.
10. All entries from diaries in the Luke Gertler Collection.
11. Mark Gertler to Thomas Balston, [*c.* 17] January 1939, University of Texas, Austin.
12. Dorothy Morland, in conversation with the author, April 1996.
13. Betty Battiscombe, in conversation with the author, June 1999.
14. Ibid.
15. Diana Gardner, in conversation with the author, 16 July 1997.
16. Rothenstein, *Modern English Painters*, vol. 2, p. 142.
17. Mark Gertler to Edward Marsh [11 May 1939], *MGSL*, p. 248.
18. Dorothy Morland, in conversation with the author, April 1996.
19. Quoted in Mark Gertler to Thomas Balston, 13 May 1939, *MGSL*, pp. 248–9.
20. G. U. Ellis to Mark Gertler, 5 May 1939, Luke Gertler Collection. Marcia Allentuck ('Mark Gertler: A Study of his Life', p. 336) records that Gertler 'made an unsuccessful suicide attempt' at the Ellises' home in the 1930s.
21. Virginia Woolf, Monday 26 June 1939, A. O. Bell, *The Diary of Virginia Woolf*, vol. 5, *1936–41*, p. 221.
22. G. Robinson, 'Mr Gertler Explains Why He is Not Content with Naturalism', *The World of Art Illustrated* (17 May 1939), pp. 10–12.

23. Mark Gertler to Thomas Balston [26 May 1939], *MGSL*, p. 249. 'I'm afraid I've not sold anything more to speak of. Just my self-portrait for £15. That's all 75 guineas – 12 guineas and £15 is the lot and I get that minus 33 1/3 per cent!'
24. Mark Gertler to Thomas Balston, 13 May 1939, *MGSL*, pp. 248–9.
25. Ibid.
26. Virginia Woolf, Sunday 14 May 1939, A. O. Bell, *The Diary of Virginia Woolf*, vol. 5, p. 219.
27. V. Woolf, *Moments of Being*, p. 95.
28. Virginia Woolf, Sunday 14 May 1939, A. O. Bell, *The Diary of Virginia Woolf*, vol. 5, p. 221.
29. Mark Gertler to Thomas Balston, 26 May 1939, *MGSL*, p. 249.
30. Ibid.
31. Marjorie Kostenz to Beatrice Campbell, 10 December 1965, private collection.
32. F. Spalding, *Dance Till the Stars Come Down: A Life of John Minton*, p. 33.
33. Mark Gertler to John Mavrogordato, 2 June 1939, Bodleian Library.
34. In fact, Luke never did arrive, and remained in Davos until after Gertler's death.
35. Diary entry, Friday 9 June 1939, Luke Gertler Collection.
36. Mark Gertler to Thomas Balston, Friday [16 June] 1939, University of Texas, Austin.
37. Ibid.
38. Woodeson, *Gertler*, p. 330.
39. Dorothy Morland, in interview with the author, April 1996.
40. Fedarb, 'Reminiscences'.
41. Ibid.
42. Ida Graves, in conversation with the author, January 1998. 'No one', Marjorie later wrote to Mary Hutchinson after Gertler's death, 'really believed he was determined to die' (16 July 1939, University of Texas, Austin).
43. Mark Gertler to Thomas Balston, 22 June 1939, University of Texas, Austin.
44. In some reports it was the Morlands' butler.
45. Many stories abound as to who was expecting to meet Gertler and who found the body, and how. In another version it was Kot who, expecting Gertler to tea at Acacia Road, went to seek him out and found him dead in the studio 'beside the gas fire with his head on a pillow' (Carswell, *Lives and Letters*, p. 266).
46. This was the version that Virginia Woolf heard (Monday, 26 June 1939, *The Diary of Virginia Woolf*, vol. 5, p. 221).
47. Quoted in Carswell, *Lives and Letters*, p. 266.
48. Monday 26 June [1939], *The Diary of Virginia Woolf*, vol. 5, p. 221.
49. Tuesday 27 June [1939], ibid.
50. Owing to a ruling that only 10 per cent of inquest papers be kept, Gertler's papers have not survived. However, Gertler's first biographer, John Woodeson, states that the post-mortem revealed that 'the old tuberculosis had healed completely' (Woodeson, *Gertler*. p. 330).
51. Death certificate.
52. *Islington Gazette* (Wednesday, 28 June 1939). Maria Donska also later told her friend the writer and architect Stephen Gardiner that Gertler had made a previous suicide attempt by putting his head in the gas oven, and that she had come round and pulled him out. She also spoke of finding the body when he actually committed suicide (Stephen Gardiner in interview with the author, 6 May 1999). She told a similar story about Gertler's previous attempt to gas himself to the pianist Alan Rowlands (interview with the author, 2 December 1998).
53. *News of the World*, *Sunday Mirror* and unidentified paper (all 25 June 1939). A copy of the unidentified article is in the Tate Gallery Archive.
54. L. Gertler, 'Memories of my Father', *Mark Gertler: The Early and the Late Years*, p. 11.

Bibliography

GERTLER'S WRITINGS

N. Carrington, ed., *Mark Gertler: Selected Letters* (London: Rupert Hart-Davis, 1965) [*MGSL*]

M. Gertler, 'A Note on Michel Angelo', *The Adelphi*, vol. 1, no. 2 (July 1923), pp. 154–5

——'The Architectural Element in Painting', *The Adelphi*, vol. 1, no. 3 (August 1923), p. 247

——'A Triumph of Education Aid' [interview], *Jewish Chronicle* (9 February 1912)

GERTLER'S BACKGROUND

Clayton & Bell: A Brief History [from a handsheet to accompany an exhibition by Angela Farrar Bell]

A. Davies, *The East End Nobody Knows: A History, a Guide, an Explanation* (London: Macmillan, 1990)

N. Davies, *God's Playground: A History of Poland*, vol. 2, *1795 to the Present* (Oxford: Oxford University Press, 1981)

T. Dormandy, *The White Death: A History of Tuberculosis* (London: The Hambledon Press, 1999)

W. J. Fishman, *East End Jewish Radicals, 1875–1914* (London: Duckworth, 1975)

R. Floud and S. Glynn, eds., *London Higher: The Establishment of Higher Education in London* (London: The Athlone Press, 1998)

A. Kershen, 'The Jewish Community in London', *The Peopling of London: Fifteen Thousand Years of Settlement from Overseas*, ed. N. Merriman, foreword by C. Holmes (London: Museum of London, 1993)

P. Larkworthy, *Clayton and Bell, Stained Glass Artists and Decorators* (London: The Ecclesiological Society, 1984)

A. Palmer, *The East End: Four Centuries of London Life* (London: John Murray, 1989; repr. 2000)

J. A. R. Pimlott (preface), *Toynbee Hall: Fifty Years of Social Progress, 1884–1934*, (London: Dent, 1935)

R. Porter, *London: A Social History* (London: Hamish Hamilton, 1994)

N. Solomon, *Judaism: A Very Short Introduction* (Oxford: Oxford University Press, 1996)

GERTLER'S LIFE AND WORK

M. Allentuck, 'Mark Gertler: A Study of his Life', *Apollo* (October 1974)

——*The University of Toronto Quarterly*, 45 (summer 1975)

——'Greville Texidor's *These Dark Glasses*: Bloomsbury in New Zealand', *World Literature Written in English*, vol. 19, no. 2 (autumn 1980)

I. Anscombe, *Omega and After: Bloomsbury and the Decorative Arts* (London: Thames & Hudson, 1989)

T. Balston, 'Mark Gertler 1891–1939', introduction to Whitechapel Art Gallery Exhibition (1949)

British Artists of Today, no. 1, *Mark Gertler* (London: The Fleuron, 1925)

R. Carline, 'Richard Carline and his Circle', *Hampstead in the Thirties: A Committed Decade*, ed. Michael Collins (London: Camden Arts Centre, 1974)

S. Compton, ed., *British Art in the 20th Century: The Modern Movement* (Munich: Prestel-Verlag, and London: Royal Academy of Arts, 1986)

D. Farr, *English Art, 1870–1940* (Oxford: Oxford University Press, 1978)

J. Ferguson, *The Arts in Britain and in World War I* (Southampton: The Camelot Press, 1980)

A. Gruetzner Robins, *Modern Art in Britain, 1910–1914* (London: Merrell Publishers, 1997)

M. Harries and S. Harries, *The War Artists: British Official War Art of the Twentieth Century* (London: Michael Joseph, in association with the Imperial War Museum and the Tate Gallery, 1983)

C. Harrison, *English Art and Modernism, 1900–1939* (New Haven: Yale University Press, 1994)

D. Jablow Hershman and J. Lieb, *The Key to Genius: Manic Depression and the Creative Life* (New York: Prometheus Books, 1988)

A. Johnson and A. Gruetzner, *Dictionary of British Art*, vol. 5, *British Artists, 1880–1940* (Woodbridge: Antique Collectors' Club, 1994)

B. Laughton, intro., *The Slade 1871–1971: Centenary Exhibition Catalogue* (London: Royal Academy, 1971)

Mark Gertler: Paintings & Drawings (London: Camden Arts Centre, 1992)

'Mark Gertler: The Man and his Art', *Studio*, 104 (September 1932), p. 158

'Mr Mark Gertler: An Artist of Great Integrity', *Jewish Chronicle* (30 June 1939), p. 16

V. S. Pritchett, 'Conservative Gipsy', *New Statesman* (15 December 1972)

J. Rothenstein, 'Mark Gertler': *Modern English Painters*, vol. 2, *Nash to Bawden* (London & Sydney: MacDonald & Co., 1952).

R. Shone, 'The Friday Club, 1905–1922', *Burlington Magazine* (May 1975), pp. 279–84 [repr. as a catalogue to an exhibition by the Michael Parkin Gallery, London, 1996. All quotations are from the latter edition.]

——'Mark Gertler: The Late Years', *Mark Gertler: The Early and the Late Years* (London: Ben Uri Art Gallery, 1982)

——*Bloomsbury Portraits* (London: Phaidon Press, 1993)

F. Spalding, 'Gertler's Early Work', *Mark Gertler: The Early and the Late Years* (London: Ben Uri Art Gallery, 1982)

L. Tickner, *Modern Life and Modern Subjects: British Life in the Early Twentieth Century* (New Haven and London: Yale University Press, 2000)

D. Wilcox, *The London Group, 1913–1939: The Artists and their Works* (Aldershot: Scolar Press, 1995; repr. 1997)

J. Woodeson, *Mark Gertler: Biography of a Painter, 1891–1939* (London: Sidgwick & Jackson, 1972)

J. Wolff, 'The Failure of a Hard Sponge: Class, Ethnicity and the Art of Mark Gertler', *New Formations*, 28 (spring 1996), pp. 46–64 [issue on 'Conservative Modernity']

GERTLER'S CONTEMPORARIES

A. Alpers, *The Life of Katherine Mansfield* (London: Jonathan Cape, 1980)

B. Arnold, *Orpen: Mirror to an Age* (London: Jonathan Cape, 1981)

S. Bedford, *Aldous Huxley* (London: Macmillan, 1993)

A. O. Bell, ed., *The Diary of Virginia Woolf*, vol. 1, *1915–19* (London: Penguin, 1979)

——*The Diary of Virginia Woolf*, vol. 2, *1920–24* (London: Penguin, 1981)

——*The Diary of Virginia Woolf*, vol. 3, *1925–30* (London: Penguin, 1982)

——*The Diary of Virginia Woolf*, vol. 5, *1936–41* (London: Penguin, 1985)

C. Bell, *Potboilers* (London: Chatto & Windus, 1918)

Q. Bell, *Bloomsbury*, London: Weidenfeld & Nicolson, 1990)

——*Virginia Woolf: A Biography* (New York: Harcourt Brace Jovanovich, 1972)

A. Bliss, *As I Remember* (London: Faber & Faber, 1970)

R. Blythe, *First Friends* (London: Viking, 1999)

J. T. Boulton, ed., *The Selected Letters of D. H. Lawrence* (Cambridge: Cambridge University Press, 1997)

J. T. Boulton and A. Robertson, eds., *The Letters of D. H. Lawrence*, vol. 3, *October 1916–June 1921* (Cambridge: Cambridge University Press, 1984)

D. Brett, *Lawrence and Brett: A Friendship* (London: M. Secker, 1933)

J. Byrne, *A Genius for Living: A Biography of Frieda Lawrence* (London: Bloomsbury, 1995)

R. Carline, *Stanley Spencer at War* (London: Faber and Faber, 1978)

N. Carrington, *Carrington: Paintings, Drawings and Decorations* (London: Thames & Hudson, 1978)

J. Carswell, *Lives and Letters: A. R. Orage, Beatrice Hastings, Katherine Mansfield, John Middleton Murry, S. S. Koteliansky: 1906–57* (London: Faber and Faber, 1978)

M. A. Caws, *Women of Bloomsbury: Virginia, Vanessa and Carrington* (New York & London: Routledge, 1990)

S. J. Darroch, *Ottoline: The Life of Lady Ottoline Morrell* (London: Chatto & Windus, 1976)

H. David, *The Fitzrovians: A Portrait of Bohemian Society 1900–55* (London: Sceptre, 1989)

G. Donaldson, ed., *D. H. Lawrence in Italy and England* (London: Macmillan, 1998)

J. Epstein, *An Autobiography: The Modern Jewish Experience* (New York: E. P. Dutton & Company, Inc., 1955)

D. Farr, *Gilbert Cannan: A Georgian Prodigy* (London: Chatto & Windus, 1978)

P. N. Furbank, *E. M. Forster: A Life* (London: Abacus, 1994)

D. Garnett, ed., *Carrington: Letters and Extracts from her Diaries* (Oxford: Oxford University Press, 1990)

J. Gathorne-Hardy, *The Interior Castle: A Life of Gerald Brenan* (London: Sinclair-Stevenson, 1992)

R. Gathorne-Hardy, ed., *The Early Memoirs of Lady Ottoline Morrell* (London: Faber & Faber, 1963)

——, ed., *Ottoline at Garsington: Memoirs of Lady Ottoline Morrell, 1915–18* (New York: Alfred A. Knopf, 1975)

G. Gerzina, *Carrington: A Life of Dora Carrington, 1893–1932* (London: John Murray, 1989)

B. Glenavy, *Today We Will Only Gossip* (London: Constable, 1964)

V. Glendinning, *Edith Sitwell: A Unicorn among Lions* (Oxford: Oxford University Press, 1986)

S. Griffiths, *John Currie: Paintings and Drawings, 1905–14* (Stoke-on-Trent: City Museum & Art Gallery, 1980)

N. Hamnett, *Laughing Torso* (London: Virago, 1984)

C. A. Hankin, ed., *The Letters of John Middleton Murry to Katherine Mansfield* (London: Constable, 1983)

C. Hassall, *A Biography of Edward Marsh* (New York: Harcourt, Brace & Company, 1959)

S. Hignett, *Brett: From Bloomsbury to New Mexico: A Biography* (New York: Franklin Watts, 1983)

J. Hill, *The Art of Dora Carrington* (London: The Herbert Press, 1994)

M. Holroyd, *Lytton Strachey: The New Biography* (London: Chatto & Windus, 1994)

——*Augustus John: The New Biography* (London: Chatto & Windus, 1996)

——*Augustus John*, vol. 2, *The Years of Experience* (Chatham: Book Club Associates by arrangement with William Heinemann Ltd, 1974)

J. Hone, *The Life of Henry Tonks* (London: William Heinemann Ltd, 1939)

D. Hooker, *Nina Hamnett: Queen of Bohemia* (London: Constable, 1986)

J. Huxley, *The Leaves of the Tulip Tree* (London: John Murray, 1986)

R. Jackson, *Frieda Lawrence; Including 'Not I, but the Wind' and Other Autobiographical Writings* (London: Pandora, 1994)

A. John, *Chiaroscuro: Fragments of Autobiography* (London: Grey Arrow Books, 1962)

M. Lago and P. N. Furbank, eds., *The Selected Letters of E. M. Forster*, vol. 2, *1921–70* (London: Collins, 1985)

H. Lee, *Virginia Woolf* (London: Vintage, 1997)

M. Lilly, *Sickert: The Painter and his Circle* (London: Elek Books Ltd, 1971)

R. Marler, ed., *Selected Letters of Vanessa Bell* (London: Bloomsbury, 1993)
E. Marsh, *A Number of People* (London: Heinemann, 1939)
C. Moorehead, *Sidney Bernstein: A Biography* (London: Jonathan Cape, 1984)
P. Nash, *Outline* (London: Columbus Books Limited, 1988)
C. R. W. Nevinson, *Paint and Prejudice* (London: Methuen, 1937)
N. Nicolson, ed., *The Question of Things Happening: Virginia Woolf Collected Letters*, vol. 2, *1912–22* (London: Hogarth Press, 1994)
——*Leave the Letters Till We're Dead: Virginia Woolf Collected Letters*, vol. 6, *1936–41* (London: Hogarth Press, 1994)
S. Olson, *John Singer Sargent: His Portrait* (London: Barrie & Jenkins, 1989)
V. O'Sullivan and M. Scott, eds., *The Collected Letters of Katherine Mansfield*, vol. 1, *1903–1917* (Oxford: Clarendon Press, 1984)
A. Powell, *To Keep the Ball Rolling: Memoirs*, vol. 1, *Infants of the Spring* (London, William Heinemann Ltd, 1976)
M. Reynolds, 'The Slade: The Story of an Art School, 1871–1971', unpublished MS (London: Watson Library, University College, London)
W. Rothenstein, *Men and Memories* (London: Faber & Faber, 1932)
M. Sadleir, *Michael Ernest Sadler, 1861–1943: A Memoir* (London: Constable, 1949)
K. Sagar, *D. H. Lawrence: Life into Art* (London: Penguin, 1985)
S. Sassoon, *Diaries, 1923–25* (London: Faber & Faber, 1985)
S. Sassoon and I. Parsons, eds., *The Collected Works of Isaac Rosenberg* (London: Chatto & Windus, 1984)
M. Seymour, *Ottoline Morrell: Life on the Grand Scale* (London: Hodder & Stoughton, 1992)
L. Sieveking, *Eye of the Beholder* (London: Hulton Press, 1957)
O. Sitwell, *Laughter in the Next Room* (London: Macmillan, 1949)
F. Spalding, *Duncan Grant* (London: Chatto & Windus, 1997)
——, *Vanessa Bell* (London: Macmillan, 1987)
——, *Roger Fry: Art and Life* (Norfolk: Black Dog Books, 1999)
——, *Dance till the Stars Come Down: A Biography of John Minton* (London: Hodder & Stoughton, 1991)
——, intro., *Jacob Kramer Reassessed* (London: Ben Uri Art Gallery, 1984)
G. Spencer, *Memoirs of a Painter* (London: Chatto & Windus, 1974)
F. Spotts, *Letters of Leonard Woolf* (London: Bloomsbury, 1992)
D. Sutton, ed., *Letters of Roger Fry*, vol. 2, *1913–34* (London: Chatto & Windus, 1972)
J. R. Taylor, *Bernard Meninsky* (Bristol: Redcliffe Press, 1990)
C. Tomalin, *Katherine Mansfield: A Secret Life* (London: Viking, 1987)
B. Wadsworth, *Edward Wadsworth: A Painter's Life* (Wiltshire: Michael Russell, 1989)
D. J. Wilcox, *Margaret Geddes* (London: Woodlands Art Gallery, 1998)
V. Woolf, *Moments of Being*, ed. J. Schulkind (London: Grafton, 1989)
Word and Image, 6, *Isaac Rosenberg 1890–1918* (London: The National Book League, 1975)
J. Zytaruk and J. T. Boulton, eds., *The Letters of D. H. Lawrence*, vol. 2, *June 1913–October 1916* (Cambridge: Cambridge University Press, 1981)

LITERARY PORTRAITS

G. Cannan, *Mendel: A Story of Youth* (London: Fisher & Unwin, 1916)
A. Huxley, *Crome Yellow* (London: Chatto & Windus, 1921; repr. 1929)
D. H. Lawrence, *The Rainbow* (Harmondsworth: Penguin Classics, 1987)
——, *Women in Love* (Harmondsworth: Penguin Books, 1981)
K. Mansfield, 'Brave Love', *Landfall*, vol. 26, no. 1 (March 1972), pp. 3–30
——, 'Je ne parle pas français', *Bliss and Other Stories* (London: Marshall Cavendish, 1988)
V. S. Pritchett: 'The Skeleton', *The Complete Short Stories* (London: Chatto & Windus, 1990) [All page references are to this edition]

O. Sitwell, 'Triple Fugue', *Triple Fugue* (London: Grant Richard Limited, 1924)
G. Texidor, *In Fifteen Minutes You Can Say a Lot* (Wellington: Victoria University Press, 1987)
W. J. Turner, *The Aesthetes* (London: Wishart & Company, 1927)
——, *The Duchess of Popocatapetl* (London: Dent, 1939)
V. Woolf, 'Solid Objects', *A Haunted House and Other Stories* (London: Hogarth Press, 1944)

Index

Note: G refers to Mark Gertler throughout